# You
# Must
# Remember
# This

The
Johns Hopkins
University Press

Baltimore and London

# You Must Remember This

An Oral History of
Manhattan from the 1890s
to World War II

Jeff
Kisseloff

Originally published in hardcover by Harcourt Brace Jovanovich, Publishers, 1989
Published by arrangement with Harcourt, Inc.
Johns Hopkins Paperbacks edition, 1999
2 4 6 8 9 7 5 3 1

The Johns Hopkins University Press
2715 North Charles Street
Baltimore, Maryland 21218-4363
www.press.jhu.edu

Grateful acknowledgment is made for the following:
"I'm a Little Blackbird Looking for a Bluebird,"
copyright 1952 Fisher Music Corp. (renewed), used by permission;
the quotation from *A Ministry to Man: The Life of John Lovejoy Elliot*
by Tay Hohoff, used by permission of Harper & Row, Publishers, Inc;
"If We Must Die" by Claude McKay, from *The Selected Poems of Claude McKay,*
used by permission of Harcourt Brace Jovanovich, Inc;
the lines from "The Hotel Chelsea" by Edgar Lee Masters
used by permission of Ellen C. Masters;
the quotation from *The Fortunate Pilgrim* by Mario Puzo used by permission
of Candida Donadio & Associates, copyright © 1964 by Mario Puzo;
"Forty-Second Street" by Harry Warren and Al Dubin, 1932,
Warner Bros., Inc (renewed). All rights reserved, used by permission.
The author acknowledges that "You must remember this" is a
portion of the lyric from the song "As Time Goes By," copyright 1931
Warner Bros., Inc. All rights reserved. Used by permission.

Library in Congress Cataloging-in-Publication Data will be found at the end of this book.

A catalog record for this book is available from the British Library.

ISBN 0-8018-6306-6

*To the memory of my friend Gene Rachlis
and my grandmother Sonia Kisseloff.
They made listening a treat.*

*I know that Perugino's name was Pietro Vanucci,*
*that the Louvre began as a hunting lodge (la louve is a wolf),*
*that Dante, a ladies' man, Boccaccio says,*
*often wrote only three lines a day,*
*that King Arthur was small (there's the armor),*
*that crocodiles on the ancient Nile*
*had their forefeet circled with gold,*
*and Shakespeare learned his colloquial French*
*     (see Henry the Fifth)*
*from a wigmaker settled in London.*

*Forgive me if I don't remember the dates of the Thirty Years'*
*     War,*
*or whether it's -ible or -able*
*and how to dig out a square root.*

*Be careful of me*
*for I'm an endangered species beset by computers and cubbyholed*
*     brains.*
*The fare I provide*
*is not a roast with potatoes*
*but just hors d'oeuvres with dozens of dabs.*
*I offer a whiff, a taste, a tune*
*you can do well without,*
*but sometimes—perhaps—*
*you'll think of my ends and odds,*
*that the world is the plaything of gods*
*and that it was I*
*who showed you Orion, large and clear,*
*at the heart of the autumn sky.*

—OLGA MARX

# Contents

# Preface, 1999

TEN YEARS ago, Harcourt Brace Jovanovich published my book about a group of small towns on an island flanked by the Hudson and East Rivers. Anybody who lived in New York's neighborhoods before World War II knows what I'm talking about. Instead of Mayberry and Moose Creek, the towns on Manhattan island were Greenwich Village, Harlem, and Washington Heights, among others. Maybe it's a stretch to call the Lower East Side, which was then more crowded than Calcutta, a small town, but even in that stewpot of humanity, relations among neighbors across the air shaft of a tenement were as familiar as the relations of those who shared a backyard fence or veranda in the Midwest.

That small town quality still touched those readers who wrote me wonderfully detailed letters about their own lives in New York, seventy and eighty years ago. These were the kinds of letters I had dreamed of getting when I was still cobbling the book together: I read about apple orchards on 125th Street, weekend trolley excursions to Van Cortlandt Park, catching blue-claw crabs in the Hudson, playing "Jimmies" on the curb with cut-out cheese boxes, and kindly firemen who would close off a city block and put up a fire-hydrant shower for the kids.

I heard from the widow of Norman Matson, who shared a flat in Greenwich Village with the great journalist John Reed. She told me about the day Reed and Matson had decided to install a tub in their tiny Village apartment. They found an old one on the street and managed to haul it up the stairs before remembering that they inhabited a cold-water flat. Reed thought about it for a moment before coming up with what seemed to be the perfect solution: He placed several candles under the tub to warm the water—it never occurred to him until he sat down and promptly toasted his buttocks that the candles would also heat the iron tub itself.

I received wonderful letters from long-lost neighbors and teachers of mine. There were even suggestions for other books. One came from a fellow who was certain a proper sequel to *You Must Remember This* would be "a comprehensive biography about the most beautiful and fascinating woman who ever lived—Hedy Lamarr."

I also heard from many of the book's "witnesses," some of whom pointed out errors (which have been corrected in this edition). All the living witnesses were invited to a publication party HBJ threw at the New-York Historical Society; about fifty were able to attend. They had a grand time. The other guests treated them like royalty. They drank Stanley Auster's magic egg creams (he made the formula for the first time in forty years) and greeted each other heartily as if they were members of an elite club (as well they were). They signed each other's books and found mutual connections beyond its pages.

Sadly, this group has been winnowed drastically since then, as most of the witnesses have died. For years, it seemed as if I was attending a funeral every month. Fortunately, when I feel blue about my lost friends, I can still visit Stanley, and he mixes up a batch of syrup and shares a few more great stories. And every so often I dip into my tape box and listen to Olga Marx sing an off-color ditty from the 1890s or Lenny Del Genio strum his guitar while singing "Paper Doll" in a duet with a screeching oral historian.

I recently came across a memorial book I put together for Emily Strunsky Paley before she died in 1990. Emily, whose sister married Ira Gershwin, was simply the loveliest woman I have ever met. I wasn't alone in that opinion. When I assembled the book, I went through the hundreds of letters she had saved over the years from her many friends, who included the Gershwins and other admirers such as Edgar G. Robinson, John Huston, and S. N. Behrman. They were all captivated by Emily's otherworldly beauty, warmth, and generosity.

In one of the letters, George Gershwin wrote, "A warm day in June could take lessons from you." Ira scribbled one July 4, "Patriotic and personal greetings to you who even if I had 963 other sisters-in-law, would always be my favorite."

My favorite letter came from Zero Mostel—Emily was godmother to his two sons. It was two lines: "Dearest Emily, I have nothing to write to you in a letter, but my secretary has nothing to do, so I am writing to you. Love, Zero."

She was, in so many ways, truly the daughter of Albert Strunsky, the most (and maybe the only) beloved landlord in New York history. Whenever I am asked to speak about New York, I always tell the story of the landlord who couldn't bring himself to take rent from his struggling tenants, many of whom went on to have brilliant careers thanks to his extraordinary generosity.

The story is even more poignant when one remembers that for a long time New York was a haven for those who were struggling to carve out artistic careers, and this is what made the city so special. In Papa Strunsky's day, there were plenty of cheap apartments, which meant that young artists could paint, dancers could dance, actors could act, and writers could write without starving. Their subsequent success drew others to Manhattan and helped make New York the Big Apple.

Such places still existed when I moved to the city in 1978. I settled on the Upper West Side, which was noted for its quirky population of writers, artists, and political activists. I wrote *You Must Remember This* in a studio apartment atop a brownstone where the rent was $298 a month. This low rent allowed me to live and circulate among the people I interviewed, and the book was so much better for it. The rent for that same apartment is now over $1,400 a month. There is simply no way I could afford to write this book if I were living in New York today.

My introduction to the original edition noted the rapid disappearance of the individual nature of each Manhattan neighborhood, and I'm afraid my concern proved to be correct. Only the

wealthy can now afford to live on my old block. The residents shop
in the same stores that can be found on the East Side as well as in
malls across America. As the joke goes, "I'm so old, I remember
when Columbus Avenue was on the West Side."

It's the same story with Route 66 and the long-gone Lincoln
Highway, "Main Street to America." In many ways, this book wasn't
written so much about a city as it was about the flickering lamp of a
generation. That bulb is just about extinguished, but I hope the new
edition of *You Must Remember This* will allow it to burn a bit longer—
this generation still has much to teach us.

# Introduction

MY FRIEND Olga Marx believed that jokes and anecdotes could reveal a lot about the times from which they originated. One of her favorite stories from the turn of the century concerns a college professor who boards a trolley car in New York and asks a woman sitting next to him for directions to a certain downtown location. "Oh, if you took a different trolley, you would have saved yourself fifteen minutes," she says.

He looks at her quizzically. "But what would I do with the fifteen minutes?"

This is a book about Manhattanites who remember those simpler, quieter days when you could live in one of the world's great metropolises and still have a farmer for a next-door neighbor. Sometimes it's hard to believe there is a whole generation of New Yorkers still alive who at one time had never heard of radio, television, airplanes, refrigerators or electricity. This was a time when the only people applauding the exploits of Babe Ruth or Lou Gehrig were their respective parents.

Even after the Babe's retirement in 1935, Manhattan was still an island of small towns with disparate milieus, from Washington Heights down to Hell's Kitchen. Back then, neighbors knew each others' lives intimately. They endured the hard times and celebrated the good times together. When a mother had her new baby (usually at home), the other children were dropped off with a neighbor for the day. When a family was hungry, a neighbor's pot was always filled with warm soup.

The local grocer let you buy on credit and ladled out fresh milk from a tin can. For many poor families, the local political leader was the most important man in the neighborhood. He was the one who doled out the jobs, gave away food baskets on Thanksgiving, and smiled benignly at the Election Day bonfires. All he asked in return was a straight-ticket vote for Tammany Hall.

Then again, the neighbor might have been a drinker who fought with her husband in the wee hours and was a bit too nosy for your taste; the kindly old grocer might have been watering the milk; and the warmhearted political leader might have had your shop windows broken if you dared vote Republican. So much for nostalgia.

The Greenwich Village character Joe Gould once remarked, "What people say is history." Though Gould was not always the most reliable historian, in this case he had a point. Of course, to some extent what people say is their own version of history. Therein lies its charm, its value, and its danger. For instance, over the course of nearly three years of research, several claims were made to me time and again:

1. Nobody ever locked their doors.
2. All mothers were saints.
3. All mothers were the best cooks in the neighborhood.
4. You always respected the neighborhood girls. This was especially true in East Harlem, where everybody respected Joe the Heat's sister.

For the record, while I found numbers one and four to be somewhat doubtful, I can say from personal experience that two and three are the absolute truth.

Despite the risks, neighborhood tales are wonderfully suitable for oral history. Every New Yorker has a good story. Some even have great ones, especially when the narrator turns the clock back eighty or ninety years.

This book began as a supplement to a neighborhood weekly called the *Chelsea Clinton News.* I had been assigned to do a neighborhood history for the paper's forty-fifth anniversary. Several other histories had been done, but while sifting through the material, I thought they were all interesting but dry. It occurred to me that the story of the neighborhood from a third-person perspective had been told over and over again, but nobody had ever told the story through the voices of the residents themselves. It seemed to me that an authentic neighborhood history would be the sum of their stories.

When the supplement appeared, we found that people loved reading the interviews. And why not? The old-timers told wonderful tales of turn-of-the-century New York that could have come out of any Mark Twain novel. What was surprising was that the tone of the two bordering neighborhoods—Chelsea and Hell's Kitchen—could not have been more different. Instead of just being on opposite sides of 34th Street, they seemed to be at different ends of the state. I wondered at that point if the same would hold true for the rest of Manhattan. Would each of the neighborhoods take on its own rhythm and feel if its story was told?

The more research I did, the more I found that to be true. Each neighborhood had its own life force, its own values and heroes. These things were sometimes determined by the area's geographical features—for example, the islandlike nature of Marble Hill or the remoteness of Washington Heights—at other times by the kind of people who lived in the area and took responsibility for it—such as Dr. John Elliott of Chelsea's Hudson Guild—and at other times by twists of fate, the best example being the tragic *General Slocum* steamboat fire, which nearly emptied the Lower East Side of its German population in 1904.

The idea of a book on Manhattan took on added urgency when I realized how much of that individuality has eroded over the years. High rents have driven out many small businesses and lower-income residents. The old tenements and low-rise apartments have been replaced by scores of assembly-line high rises, plugged into holes in the ground like tubes on a circuit board, with little thought given to their impact on the surrounding neighborhood. The old neighborhoods and the neighbors themselves have become endangered species.

An oral history of Manhattan could easily fill ten volumes instead of one. I realized early on that I could not possibly include every aspect of every neighborhood over the fifty years or so covered in this book. Instead, after considerable research, I sought a cross section of those living in the residential neighborhoods back then.

I also looked for people who could discuss specific events or who had been important to an area. On the Lower East Side, for instance, I hoped to find a survivor of the Triangle Shirtwaist fire; in Harlem I looked for people who remembered the great Fats Waller, a much beloved figure in the neighborhood. I found a survivor of the fire, and I was also fortunate in meeting Waller's sister Naomi, who is the spitting image of her brother and remembers him with great fondness more than forty years after his death.

Other times I wasn't so lucky. I had the name of the last shepherd in Central Park's sheep meadow, but despite a valiant try by the city's Parks Department, I was never able to find him. And after considerable effort, I located a man who was in the London Chemists on West 23rd Street when Vincent "Mad Dog" Coll stepped inside to answer a phone call. Moments later Coll was cut down by a hail of machine-gun bullets, one of the most famous murders in gangland history. I was thrilled to hear from the fellow's son that it was a story his father loved to tell. Unfortunately, when I called his father, he refused to talk about it, and despite repeated pleading, he refuses to this day.

Most of the participants were found through nursing homes, local senior citizen programs, newspaper articles, friends, family, and my own network of contacts around the city. I also received valuable tips from local shopkeepers, pedestrians, and bench sitters during my walks around Manhattan. For the most part, I avoided interviewing people who were well known. I was more interested in the recollections of ordinary New Yorkers, and I thought their remarks would be less self-conscious as well. Anyway, it was soon apparent that there was no correlation between fame and quality of storytelling.

I sought those who were known to be open and reliable, but I was amazed at how candid people were with a perfect stranger. The usual comment was, "Why are you talking to me? I have nothing interesting to tell you." They would then proceed to tell one fascinating story after another.

Few actually believed they had led interesting lives. I spent months tracking down one of the Tenth Avenue Cowboys, the great romantic figures of Chelsea and Hell's Kitchen who rode their horses down the avenue to warn against arriving freight trains. Even hardened old-timers became wistful as they recalled seeing the men gallop down the cobblestone street on their stallions. When I finally located one of the last surviving cowboys, he was incredulous that I'd want to see him at all. "It was just a job like anything else," he protested.

Then there was Louise Barlow, who, as a speakeasy chanteuse, was duty-bound to dance with the better-heeled clients. Most of those guys were gangsters, who were always well armed. This petite ninety-year-old woman with holes in her stockings nonchalantly related how she could feel Legs Diamond's gun against her hip when she danced with him. Didn't it make her nervous?

"Nah, they all had 'em," she replied.

I couldn't use all the information I obtained, even though some of the people who don't appear in the book offered priceless stories. For instance, Aimee Myers told me how her grandfather had once bought the area around Columbus Circle for two coops of geese. Down in Florida, I met Ralph Taylor, who was then 107 years old. He had gone up San Juan Hill with Teddy Roosevelt, and his stories of the Spanish-American War were eerily vivid. Finally, there was Dorothy Sexton, whom I interviewed for the Upper East Side chapter. She grew up in the Depression and had been poor all her life, but she was a warmhearted person and she never uttered a word of self-pity. Two weeks later, I went back to visit her, and I was told she had just won five million dollars in the New York State lottery and was last seen packing her bags for Florida.

Once the interviewing process for each chapter was finished, I sat down in front of my computer and imagined a warm summer night on a city side street before the war. A bunch of the neighbors have gathered on the stoop for some post-dinner visiting. In my mind, they are old-timers reminiscing about days past. They agree with each other; they disagree. They listen and they interrupt. At times the conversation is hilarious. At other times it's deadly serious. Over the course of the evening, as each one unfurls his story, a picture of the neighborhood is gradually drawn and completed.

Their stories are told in loosely chronological fashion, ending with the Depression and World War II. The war broke up the old gangs and brought so many changes to Manhattan it seemed to be the logical place to stop. The chapters close with a round-robin exchange to give the more prominent participants a chance to reflect on their lives and/or careers.

As I edited the chapters, the stories were weighed for their importance to the larger picture. For example, in Chelsea, there is a lot of conversation among the old seamen and longshoremen about life along the waterfront, simply because they were the most dominant force in the neighborhood. On the Lower East Side, socialism was always a hot topic, especially among garment workers before World War I. This is reflected in the chapter, along with an in-depth portrait of life in and around the candy stores, where many East Siders enjoyed schmoozing with their friends.

Most of the neighborhoods had one or two dominant figures who made a real impact on the residents' lives. Some, like Vito Marcantonio in East Harlem, West Harlem's Adam Clayton Powell, and Dr. Elliott in Chelsea, were champions of community causes and real-life heroes to those who remember them. There were also people like Joe Ryan in Chelsea, who had a powerful but nefarious influence on the neighborhood. Others made their presence felt in different ways, as did Fats Waller in Harlem and the saintly Papa Strunsky in Greenwich Village. What they all have in common is that they still conjure up vivid feelings of fear, love, respect, and even awe. They are given extra attention in their chapters, and deservedly so.

The chapters vary in length, because some neighborhoods are larger and more complex than others. I have also tried to keep repetition to a minimum, so some chapters skip over small details that appear in others. The introductions that precede each chapter are intended to act as extended notes, to fill in gaps in information when necessary. They are not interpretative essays about the neighborhoods. That kind of information is outside the scope of this effort. However, there are a number of wonderful books about Manhattan and its neighborhoods, and I've listed in the back of this book some of those that were helpful in my research.

This is also a book about listening. Senior citizens are largely shunted off to the side in our country. Yet they often have active minds, and in many ways can still be valuable contributors to society. They are of a generation that has survived two world wars and a nasty depression. They are our last links to a world that is rapidly disappearing, a world from which we have much to learn and gain. They are survivors, and their stories are worthy of our attention.

Finally, just as one doesn't have to be Jewish to enjoy Levy's Rye, it isn't necessary to know the difference between the IRT and the DMZ (contrary to some news reports, the IRT *is* safer) to enjoy the reminiscences in this book. Who couldn't be fascinated by a bootlegger's tales of Prohibition; an insider's view of a smoky Harlem nightclub with Art Tatum or Fats Waller at the piano and Lester Young on sax; a woman's tale of terror of being locked inside the Triangle Shirtwaist Company factory as the sweatshop went up in flames?

The everyday memories of those years are no less intriguing: growing up in the stifling atmosphere of a Victorian household; the blossoming of young men and women into adulthood; the wonder of hearing the first squawks from a phonograph or radio. These are the stories not only of New Yorkers, but also of all Americans, as this country entered the modern world. As the man says, "There are a million stories in the naked city." Here are a few of them.

# Lower East Side

DOPEY BENNY FEIN may have been a thief, a racketeer, an extortionist, and a murderer, but at least he had principles.

For years, Dopey Benny and his thugs manned picket lines for striking garment workers on the Lower East Side. Called on for such extracurricular duty as simple intimidation or a well-placed bone fracture, Benny was only too glad to oblige. But when he was approached by management to work the other side of the line, he became irate. Dopey Benny Fein broke only management legs.

"He put fifteen thousand-dollar bills in front of me," he said later, "and I said to him, 'No, sir, I won't take it . . . I won't double-cross my friends.' "

Fein got his nickname because an adenoidal condition made him appear sleepy, but he was no dope. He just had an odd set of scruples. Benny wasn't unusual in that regard, either. Tillie Taub was a Jewish prostitute who regularly worked Allen Street, except on the High Holidays. "It makes no difference whatever I do," she told a reporter. "On Yom Kippur and Rosh Hashanah, I go to *shul.*"

In their strange ways, Fein and Taub illustrate an important point about life in a neighborhood where gangsters were former *yeshiva buchers* and nice little ladies made great *kreplach* and fenced a little stolen property on the side. Amid the rubble of abject poverty, traditional Jewish culture and thought and the dreams of immigrants for the most part survived. They would educate their children, escape the ghetto, and become "Americanized." It was a large task against stiff odds, but by and large, with determination (and a little humor), they succeeded.

The Lower East Side, generally bounded by East Houston on the north, Broadway to the west, and Worth and Catherine streets on the south, was actually an exclusive neighborhood on the northern outskirts of the city when it was first settled in the 1700s. With the area's decline, it has housed an amalgam of mostly impoverished ethnic groups. In the 1820s, there were the poor Irish and freed slaves, followed by Italians, American Indians, Scandinavians, Chinese, then the great waves of Jewish immigrants, who dominated the area from the 1880s until World War II.

Long before then, George Washington had set up housekeeping at 1 Cherry Street when the city was the nation's capital. John Hancock lived at Number 5, and Captain Samuel Chester Reid, a hero of the War of 1812, lived there as well, in a home that was the first in America to be gaslit.

Bullbaiting was a popular sport among the wealthy people living in the neighborhood. This involved placing a dog in front of a tethered bull and watching the gory results. The sport became so popular that an arena was built on a spot named Bunker Hill (now Grand Street and Mulberry), so that several thousand sports fans could enjoy what was presumably major-league bullbaiting.

Before the Revolution, what would become the most notorious slum in America, the Five Points section (now Chatham Square), was a lake called the Collect. The spot was a favorite of fishermen and local farmers, who brought their cows to the Collect for watering. A small island in the center of the lake had a more sinister history. It was used for executions and punishments. Scores of black slaves were hanged and buried on the island in 1741 after they revolted and attempted to burn down the city.

The winter of 1807–08 meant the end for the Collect. Weather was so disastrous that businesses in the city virtually shut down. Angry workers marched through the streets demanding bread and money. In what would be a forerunner of Franklin Roosevelt's WPA, the city created a public-works program to drain the Collect and use the land for housing and businesses.

By the 1840s, the mansions were replaced by tenements with evocative names like Brick Bat Mansion and Gates of Hell, but these were luxury hotels in comparison with the Old Brewery. The building, which was right in the heart of the Five Points section, had one wing affectionately called Murderers' Alley and another known as the Den of Thieves. Police estimated an average of one murder occurred there every night for fifteen years.

For decades, Five Points was ruled by a string of street gangs, among them the Chichesters, the Plug Uglies (for their plug hats, not their looks), the Dead Rabbits, the Bowery Boys, and the Whyos. A fearsome character named Monk Eastman brought gangdom into the twentieth century. He was one of the first to venture into the profitable field of labor racketeering. At his peak, Eastman commanded an army of 1,200 young thugs. He was also one of the earliest Jewish gang leaders, and, like Benny Fein, he saw himself as a moral man. It was said that Eastman would never hit a lady with a club. No, at most he would blacken her eyes with his fist.

During Eastman's heyday, Jewish immigration sharply escalated, especially after the assassination of the supposedly liberal tsar, Alexander II, in 1881. News of America traveled quickly around the European shtetls. Word was that even if the streets of the "Golden Land" weren't paved with gold, at least a Jew had a chance. Remaining behind meant poverty and possible death at the hands of the tsar's soldiers. Leaving also meant poverty, but maybe not forever, and in America you would have religious freedom, educate your children, and maybe earn enough money for your old age.

Except for the poverty, the new world couldn't have been more different from the old one. At 700 people per acre, the Lower East Side was more crowded than Bombay. The streets were crammed with shoppers, kids, horsecarts, and pushcarts, which sold anything from pickles and damaged eggs to suspenders and hernia trusses. For those used to the wide-open spaces of the Russian countryside, life in a neighborhood with hardly a tree took some adjustment.

"No grass is found in this petrified city," says the protagonist in Michael Gold's novel *Jews Without Money*, "no big living trees, no flowers, no bird but the drab lecherous sparrow, no soil, loam earth; fresh earth to smell, earth to walk on, to roll on, and love like a woman. . . .

"Once Jake Gottlieb and I discovered grass struggling between the sidewalk cracks near the livery stable. We were amazed by this miracle. We guarded this treasure, allowed no one to step on it. Every hour the gang studied 'our' grass, to try to catch it growing.

It died, of course, after a few days; only children are hardy enough to grow on the East Side."

Nobody better symbolized the plight of the first generation than the desperate peddler, his pack heavy on his back, hopelessly pleading for a customer. His aching cries—"I cash clothes. I cash clothes"—reverberated off the tenement walls before he moved on to the next block, always searching, always hopeful that the next block would mean salvation.

Yet, even in the depths of poverty, the Jews struggled to maintain a sense of dignity, if it only meant a pretty cloth covering a rickety table. They rarely forgot why they came. Immigrants burning with the desire to learn jammed the Seward Park Library. Education was their food, their hope, and their key to the ghetto's gates.

Overworked East Siders found time to read the short stories in the *Jewish Daily Forward*. They attended lectures by Meyer London or Morris Hillquit at the Educational Alliance and stood in Rutgers Square to hear the political speeches of Baruch Vladeck, Joseph Barondess and Rose Schneiderman.

Those who could afford it frequented the theaters on Second Avenue, where Shakespeare and Ibsen were performed by leading Yiddish actors. If that was too highbrow, there was always vaudeville and the bawdy burlesque comedians at Minsky's.

Settlement houses, such as Lillian Wald's Henry Street Settlement and the Educational Alliance, played an integral role in the "Americanization" of the immigrants, teaching them everything from the importance of brushing their teeth to the theories of Karl Marx. The Jews themselves developed a unique network of quasi settlement houses, quasi social clubs called *landsmanshaften*. These were societies of immigrants from the same hometowns in Europe. The *landsmanshaften* had their own shuls. They also provided burial services and gave badly needed funds to members who were down on their luck.

Many Jews saw their salvation in the Socialist Party. Under Abraham Cahan's influence, the *Forward* (*Forvitz* in Yiddish) made no secret of its Socialist politics, and Cahan, Eugene Debs, Meyer London, and Morris Hillquit were real heroes on the East Side. The paper promoted trade unionism and backed Socialist candidates in local and national elections. With the *Forward*'s help, Socialists were elected to the state assembly, and the Socialist Meyer London was twice elected to Congress.

Politics and unions were hot topics among workers, who suffered terribly at the hands of penurious sweatshop owners—many of them German Jews. When they were lucky enough to get steady work, men and women worked side by side in airless rooms, six or seven days a week, for a weekly salary as little as four dollars. There was no use in complaining. So many were desperate for work, company owners had no problem finding replacements for malcontents, and loss of a job could mean disaster for a family.

Yet in 1908, 20,000 shirtwaist makers, most of them girls, courageously walked off their jobs. The strikers won only mild concessions, but, for the first time, workers realized their potential strength. The shirtwaist strike was soon followed by a long walkout of cloakmakers. When the historic Protocol of Peace was signed in September 1910, it provided for a shorter workweek, wage increases, and what was in effect the first recognition of the International Ladies' Garment Workers' Union.

It was a great victory for the union, but any doubt that dangerous shop conditions continued was erased on March 25, 1911, when a fire broke out on the eighth floor of the Asch Building on Washington Place. Within a few minutes, 146 employees of the Triangle Shirtwaist Company were dead. The East Side seethed with anger over the fire and the subsequent acquittal of the shop's owners for negligence. More walkouts followed, often vicious affairs with violence from both sides of the picket line. These were busy days for Dopey Benny Fein and his gang.

"Violence," wrote Louis Adamic, "was often all that could save unions in the face of the brutality of many employers, with their gunmen, their police, militia, and anti-labor unions."

So Dopey Benny played a key role in the unionization of the garment industry. He even armed female strikers with sharpened hairpins and lead umbrellas to work on the distaff scabs. His services came with a price. According to Jenna Weissman Joselit in her book *Our Gang*, Fein had standard fees for shooting a scab in the leg ($60), wrecking a union shop ($150 to $200, depending on its size), all the way up to murder ($500).

Not all Lower East Side criminals were as interested in social justice as Benny, though they sometimes demonstrated an unusual flair for their work. One group that was particularly feared was the Yiddish Gomorra, the Jewish Black Hands, who might be called, in garment-center terms, a knockoff of the notorious Sicilian Black Hands. The Yiddish Gomorra specialized in poisoning the horses of merchants and peddlers who refused to pay protection money. The group's leader was a dark-skinned fellow named Joseph Toblinsky, aka Yushke Nigger, who allegedly poisoned more than 200 horses during his career.

Oddly, most of the crimes committed were crimes against property as opposed to murder or rape, which apparently broke one commandment too many. But pickpocketing was popular. Dopey Benny was so adept at it that he ran a Fagin-like school for aspiring pickpockets. Arson was another common crime, so much so that it was nicknamed "Jewish Lightning." The East Side's leading fence was Fredericka "Marm" Mandelbaum, who, according to a source quoted by Joselit, was "as adept in her business as the best stockbroker on Wall Street was in his."

The phenomenon of Jewish criminals was largely a single-generation one. As families recovered from the jarring experience of resettlement, and parents were able to reassert traditional values, antisocial behavior decreased. With time, the community itself matured. An array of social services became available, and youngsters found other avenues open to them than the streets. While Jewish criminals like Arnold Rothstein, Waxy Gordon, and Meyer Lansky would continue to be prominent, the East Side soon earned a reputation for producing doctors, not bootleg gin.

Gang wars were a continuing problem in Chinatown, which, due to restrictive immigration laws, was a small enclave of three East Side blocks: Pell, Mott, and Doyers. Fierce battles were often fought there among fraternal organizations called "Tongs." These groups, such as the Hip Sings and On Leongs, controlled gambling, opium, and prostitution in the area.

Most Chinese were not involved in the Tong wars. For years, Chinatown was one of the safest places in the city. Immigration restrictions eased after World War II and were cut back even further by the Immigration Act of 1965, which reunited families and made Chinatown the fastest-growing neighborhood in Manhattan.

After years of lobbying by organized labor and anti-Semitic groups, Jewish immigration was sharply curtailed in 1923. Until then, nearly two million Jews had come to America, with the majority settling on the East Side. By the 1920s, shop conditions had improved dramatically, allowing thousands of eighteen-year-olds to attend college instead of looking for full-time work. Families had already succeeded in moving up the economic ladder and out to enjoy the suburban pleasures of the Bronx and Brooklyn. Even for those left behind, there were some marked improvements. Many tenements had been torn down and replaced by modern apartment houses.

Success allowed more time for leisure pursuits. Debating always seemed to be a favorite sport among Jews. In the old days, it was socialism versus anarchism, and the heroes were Abe Cahan and Meyer London. Now, the heroes were Barney Ross and Benny Leonard, David Dubinsky and Alex Rose. Street-corner arguments erupted over not only the merits of the New Deal but also whether Guss or Hollander had the tangier pickles, and the purveyor of the best egg cream in the neighborhood.

The origin of the egg cream (a misnomer, since it has neither egg nor cream) is still debated today. One legend has it that the great Yiddish actor Boris Thomashefsky sampled a delightful drink called *chocolat et crème* while sitting at a Paris café. He carried the recipe home to an East Side candy store, where the counterman successfully reproduced the concoction, presumably stamping his East Side accent to the *et*.

True? Who knows? Stanley Auster, scion of the great East Side candy-store dynasty, makes a good case for his grandfather as the drink's sole creator. Either way, many old-timers remember Auster's drink as the Lafite-Rothschild of egg creams.

Aside from supplying the egg creams, Mell-O-Rolls and Hooton's Bars, the candy stores were like local *landsmanshaften*. Whole societies formed around the soda fountains, where men gathered to kibitz for hours at a time. If they took a moment to reflect on how far they had come from the shtetls of Europe, perhaps they even hoisted an egg cream in memory of their ancestors.

# The Witnesses

STANLEY AUSTER (1928–) is the grandson of Louis Auster, the patriarch of the Lower East Side's first family of egg creams. After working in the family business and then for the city, he is now retired.

BETTY CHEN (1908–) is a pseudonym. She was born and raised in Chinatown and is a retired schoolteacher.

MARTY COHEN (1897–) was born and raised on the Lower East Side. He is a boxing manager and is also vice president of the World Boxing Council.

MARTHA DOLINKO (1898–) immigrated to the United States from Russia when she was a little girl. Her family settled on the Lower East Side, where she worked in the garment industry for many years. She lives in the Workmen's Circle nursing home in the Bronx.

JOHN W. ENG (1924–) is a longtime Chinatown resident. He works in the New York City school system as a teacher's aide.

SAM FLEISCHER (1914–) lives only a few blocks from where he was born on the Lower East Side. He is a very busy unpaid community activist.

NAT FORMAN (1907?–77) was a widely respected boxing manager. Before he died, he wrote a series of letters to his nephew about his youth on the Lower East Side. Those letters are excerpted here with permission.

HENRIETTA GILBERT (1907–) is a graduate of New York University. She worked in the advertising field for many years and also taught high school English.

ROSE HALPERN (1917–) is a retired Hebrew-school teacher. She is the author's cousin. Her husband, MURRAY, also participated in this interview.

SELMA HANNISH (1920–) is a pseudonym. She lives a few blocks from where she was born on the Lower East Side. She writes poetry and works with local schoolchildren.

ABRAHAM HYMAN (1896–1988), a combat veteran of World War I, and MOLLIE HYMAN (1898–) both worked in the garment industry for many years before they operated candy stores in Manhattan and the Bronx. Mrs. Mollie Hyman lives in the Workmen's Circle nursing home.

SOL KAPLAN (1911–) is the man behind the pickle barrels at Guss/Hollander Pickles on Essex Street on the Lower East Side.

SAMUEL KISSELOFF (1927–) is, as Red Smith once wrote, the "coauthor of the author." He practices law in Manhattan.

BLANCHE LASKY (1923–) is a lifelong Lower East Side resident. She works at the Educational Alliance.

DR. ROBERT LESLIE (1885–1987) was educated at City College and Johns Hopkins Medical School. In deference to his wife's professional interests and their marriage, he left medicine to become a printer. He was an active president of the Typophiles, a group he helped found in the 1930s, until he died at the age of 102.

PAULINE CUOIO PEPE (1891–) was a machine operator for the Triangle Shirtwaist Company. She lives in a nursing home on Long Island.

SIDNEY PITTER (1917–) is the author's uncle. He runs a wholesale dry-goods business in Manhattan.

SAMUEL POGENSKY (1895–) was raised on the Lower East Side. He is a former musician, trolley-car conductor, bootlegger, and construction contractor. He now owns a paint and hardware store on Second Avenue.

LARRY SCHNEIDER (1922–) is a World War II veteran. He is retired after spending thirty years as an inspector with the New York City Board of Health.

ABRAHAM HYMAN: America was the Golden Land. That was the way we were talking. We came from a very small town in Russia. There was no future in it. First, my father came to America. He wrote letters. We heard that he was working hard, but that there was a future and you are free, not like in Russia. There is no anti-Semitism like in Russia. You are in the big wide world, and we are in a little town with no industry, no life, except a religious life.

MOLLIE HYMAN: We went through everything over there. In 1904, Russia lost the Russo-Japanese War. The soldiers were coming back home. Before they passed through our little town, there was always a messenger from the little town before that let the Jews know that the soldiers are coming. If you had any girls, hide them. They used to rape them and kill them.

ROSE HALPERN: When the soldiers came to the town on the big horses with their swords dangling, everybody would run for shelter. But many times they wouldn't let my mother into the cellars, because I was an infant, and they were afraid I would cry. She had to run and hide with me wherever she could. When she came out, many people would be laying on the ground, shot and tortured. I was born in Russia in 1917. Your great-grandmother, who was my grandmother, Bubbe Mary, was considered really wealthy in Russia. They had a dry-goods store in a town called Yarmolimnitz. Your grandfather, Max Kisseloff, worked for them. That's how he met your grandmother.

I couldn't go to school in Russia because I was Jewish, and my mother, your aunt, was adamant about leaving the country so I could get an education. We came over in 1923 with my mother and my grandmother. My grandmother's family lived in Pittsburgh. They were well-to-do, and they brought us across on the *Paris*, second-class.

SAMUEL POGENSKY: My father was a shoemaker. He was the only Jew that ever reenlisted in the tsar's army, because he wanted to be a musician, and they were gonna train 'im. But the first time he got there they didn't train 'im. Somehow he figured the second time it was gonna be different. But they hollered out, "We need shoemakers! Who is a shoemaker?"

My father kept his mouth shut, but somebody hollered out, "Pogensky is a shoemaker!" That was the end of his music career.

JOHN W. ENG: My grandfather came in the 1880s as a coolie. There was a company that came to Hong Kong and recruited them. They said they would get fifty cents a day. You know, to a Chinese person that's a lot of money.

Have you ever heard the phrase "a Chinaman's chance"? Well, things were so bad over there, they could barely exist. This was when they were living under the Manchu Dynasty and all the men were forced to wear their hair in ponytails as a symbol of their being under domination. There was nothing for them, so they came here.

BETTY CHEN: They referred to the United States as the "Golden Mountain."

JOHN ENG: I think my grandfather worked on the railroads out west for five years. He didn't get all his pay. The bosses were very cruel, but if they said something, "accidents" happened—guns. They disappeared. It was very rough. They couldn't do anything about it, because by law Chinese people couldn't testify. They couldn't go to the police; they weren't allowed to do any of that.

He survived, and he brought my father over here. After a while, my father went back and got married. He was here fifteen years when he was able to get my mother a merchant's wife visa. When I got off the boat, this man was there, and my mother said, "This is your father."

My father? I never knew I had a father, but he was it.

BETTY CHEN: My mother also came as a merchant's wife. Otherwise she couldn't come. That was because of the Chinese exclusion laws. People always said to me, "Why are there so many men and no women in those days?" Then, the women were not allowed in because there was a great commotion about the immigration of the yellow race. The main word was "they cannot be assimilated to the American way of life."

HENRIETTA GILBERT: My father came alone even though he was married, with a child. It took two years for him to earn enough money to send my mother a *shifskart* [a steamship ticket]. But she refused to come. He went back to get her, but she still refused, mostly because when he went back, he was clean-shaven. She would not even walk in the street with him, because he looked like a goy.

However, they still conceived another child. She was religious. There was a tradition of Fridays. An orthodox woman who is not menstruating prepares herself for the coming of the Sabbath by going to the *mikvah*, and then, that night, having intercourse is a religious duty, even if you hate the man!

He left without her, but she promised to come. He worked again for her passage, sent her the money, and again she said absolutely not. He made enough money to come back a third time. This time, he kidnapped his oldest son, who was then eleven, because he knew she would follow him because he was about to be bar mitzvah. My brother was not a good student, and he was thrilled with the whole idea of not having to go to school anymore. He thought coming to America was a great adventure. Subsequently, my mother followed, and I was born here in 1907.

ABRAHAM HYMAN: I came here alone in March 1911, when I was fifteen. My mother and three sisters were left in Russia. At first, I couldn't get a passport because I hadn't served the tsar. They had agents in Russia. They took people similar to my situation, and they make up a passport or something. In my case, the agent got a family to sell their passport. The man had a daughter and two sons. I was to be one of the sons.

The boat was about fifteen, sixteen days. It was bad. You wouldn't want to put pigs in it. In steerage, there were four rows of beds, like bunks, one on top of the other. The lucky one was on top, because they used to throw up. The smell was bad, worse than a stable. I threw up down there if I couldn't hold it. Otherwise I went up to the deck and leaned over the railing to feed it to the fish.

MARTHA DOLINKO: When we passed the Statue of Liberty, the way she stands up with her hand outside and everything, you think it's so heavy it's going to sink. It's a wonderful thing, a human being right in the middle of the ocean with her hand up. It's the freedom of the world. After I grew up, my husband and I went up to the arm of the statue. It's the most marvelous thing to see. I was still worried that I'll go down with that thing all together, but it's so solid you don't sink.

DR. ROBERT LESLIE: Before I graduated medical school in 1910, I read about the millions of people who were coming to Ellis Island. I went down on my own to check. Tammany Hall sent slews of men there. They were supposed to be guides, but some of them were there to hire strikebreakers. They'd get a dollar for every one they brought in. They would also ask the immigrants for money and scare them to death by saying, "We're gonna send you back."

They would say, "Doctor, I cannot go back. I am a revolutionary. They are gonna kill me."

"Well, give me a couple dollars."

Ellis Island was called the Island of Fears. I called it the Island of Tears. There were too many doctors there wearing uniforms. I asked for a white coat because I didn't want to identify myself with the guys in uniform. The immigrants were afraid of police or badges and afraid of uniforms. My white coat saved the situation. They put me up on the mezzanine, and cases that they couldn't handle they sent to me. They called me neurologist even though I knew nothing about neurology. In those days the biggest problems were trachoma and erysipelas, and of course venereal disease.

Rose Halpern: At Ellis Island, they were very anti-Semitic. I was a beautiful child with long platinum hair, but the one who examined me insisted I had nits. Another doctor said I had nothing. My mother begged and cried, but she insisted, and they shaved my hair off completely. When I came into New York, I wore a kerchief because I had no hair at all.

Robert Leslie: While I was there, I remembered how my own mother had suffered. She was an orphan. Her and her brother were the only two left of a family of twelve. She lived in Vilna, which was an educational center and also a hotbed for nihilists. Because she worked in a bakery, she was inducted into the nihilist group. Her job was to put pamphlets in the bread. Well, they finally caught her, and she was arrested. My mother used to say, "Ruvela, don't be proud of your mother. I'm an ex-convict." *[He laughs.]*

She went to jail. At the end of thirty days, the *procurata,* who was like a district attorney, called her in and said, "You have served your thirty days. If you promise you're not going to do this anymore, we'll give you a choice: Siberia or out." So she said, "Out." Her brother was here in 1880, a couple of years before she came. He sent her a *shifskart.* In those days, it cost twenty-three dollars, three weeks on a ship in steerage. She became seriously ill. She didn't know what to do, but this sailor said, "Strong tea three times a day." She told this woman, "This man saved my life. I will marry him if he jumps ship."

My brother found out he was a goy from Aberdeen, Scotland. "He's not Jewish. You can't marry him. He's got to be circumcised." So at twenty-two he was circumcised, but he couldn't adjust himself to conditions, so he took to the bottle. That's one way out.

I was born in poverty on the East Side on December 18, 1885. I was delivered by what they call in German a *heybom,* a midwife.

I was the *bekhor*, the first born in the family. My mother had twelve children, but four died in infancy of malnutrition. They had then the Broome Street Doctors, a corps of medical students who did all the deliveries on the East Side. They were the first group of doctors with any social feeling. But, in those days, Bellevue Hospital's ambulances had horses, and it took them hours to appear for any kind of emergency. They tried very hard, but it was too late.

ABRAHAM HYMAN: My father picked me up and brought me to a shop on Chrystie Street, up three flights. It was a little shop of men's vests. We lived there because he had to send money home to Mother and he couldn't pay the rent of about four or five dollars a month to live together in a bedroom with three or four other people. There was a small gas stove where he could cook some hot water. He slept on a folding bed, and he had a cutting table in the shop. I slept on the cutting table.

MARTHA DOLINKO: My father took us to Rutgers Street and East Broadway. He had an apartment for us—what an apartment! The toilet was in the yard. The sink was a black sink in the hall. Everybody was washing there. There was only cold water running. There were three rooms. If it wasn't enough, we slept on the roof. Why not? Or I slept on the fire escape. Somebody else slept on the roof. If they wanted to urinate, they urinated on me.

ABRAHAM HYMAN: My first day, I was disappointed in the appearance. I see old buildings crumbling and the darkness. On East Broadway, the square was full of newspapers flying in the wind. I was happy to be here, but I was wondering, where is the Golden Land, the land where the streets are paved with gold?

Actually, we didn't believe they were paved with gold, but in Russia we saw that people lived a better life in America. People used to come back to visit with good shoes, good clothes, pressed pants. But that first evening, we ate our supper in a restaurant on Madison Street. I was amazed, it looked so plentiful. White bread in my family was only on Saturday nights. Here, you eat as much as you wanted.

BETTY CHEN: I was born in Chinatown in 1908. In Chinatown, the immigrants looked down upon the American-born Chinese.

There was an expression for people born here, that you're like a "hollow bamboo," that they don't know any of the customs or the language. That's how they referred to the *jip sing*. They in turn called the foreign-born Chinese *jum kah*, meaning they were thick inside, and they cannot see what is happening.

In those days, Chinatown was Mott, Pell, and Doyers. That was it. I didn't know there were other streets. My world was very small. I just went from home to school and back. I had a Jewish friend, Eva, who was the first person who took me out of the neighborhood—to Henry Street, and I thought I was in another part of the world.

To go anywhere, I had to get my father's dispensation. They had a Hearn's on 14th Street—if I wanted to go there, I had to tell him. Then there was a library that I went to on East Broadway. I told my mother, "I'm going there to borrow books, and I don't have to pay. I get them for two weeks."

"What kind of place is that that would lend you books to hold for two weeks?"

My father had to go with me to see what the place was like. Then I told him that I was gonna study with Eva in the library, and he went over to see if we were there. You just didn't walk out of the house.

ROSE HALPERN: When we were brought to Pittsburgh, we only stayed there nine months, because during the time we stayed there, my relatives, who had a dry-goods store, made my mother become a customer peddler. She would go house to house with these big bundles, not knowing the language and trying to sell the material. It was a very difficult time for her.

She went by herself to New York because she had *landslayt* there. They got her a job in one of the factories, and then she sent for us. The first place we came to was Ludlow Street. The apartment was right across the street from a funeral home. Every Sunday, there was a funeral. I don't have to tell you the screaming and the yelling that went on. I used to sit there and watch. It was a regular show for me.

ROBERT LESLIE: I had a miserable life as a boy. I would follow the trucks that would have the cannel coal. All the streets were cobblestone. When the coal fell off, I'd have a bag to put the stuff in. When I came home, I was as black as a black man. My mother would wash me and say, "You mustn't do that no more," but we needed the coal.

The flat was on Allen Street. It had five or six rooms for twelve dollars a month. Allen Street had a railroad, the Second Avenue El. The locomotive engineer was Red Mike Hylan, who later became our mayor. We had to keep our windows closed because the cinders from the train would come in the house. The middle rooms were dark. Only the back room and front room were light. It was so hot in the summer, you couldn't breathe. We slept on the fire escape or in the yard where the toilets were.

Orchard and Ludlow were tenements one on top of the other with back houses. Tammany Hall permitted them to build all of that stuff. There were no parks at the time. Seward Park wasn't even built yet. The only recreation was to go down to the East River where the barges were. The people would swim in it, but they also moved their bowels there.

Monk Eastman's gang was in that area. At one time, they thought they were Robin Hoods. They said they were stealing from people who had it to give it to the others. They never gave it to the poor, but the police were afraid of them. They were protected by Tammany Hall.

You never knew where your next meal was gonna be, and we dreaded the installment man, who came for fifty cents every week. They'd sell you phony things. My mother had a bunch of stuff on the mantelpiece which the peddlers left. It was terrible. They came for life. They never seemed to collect enough money.

My mother as a baker would bring bread and rolls home. She made those big *hollies*, and she'd dip a feather into the yolk of an egg and make cherubs. She supported the whole family. Even though my father didn't help out, my mother loved him, so he'd fill her full of semen and disappear—especially when babies were born. He didn't want to have anything to do with it.

He once had a job. We had a blizzard in New York in 1888, and he had to do snow shoveling. He had to wrap his shoes with burlap because there were no rubbers in those days. Well, after one day of snow shoveling he came back with a bottle. "I can't do that kind of work."

Samuel Pogensky: My mother's name was Ida, but my father used to call her Tillie. They weren't in love, but he never talked bad about her, except to say, "Oy, dat *frooma* Tillie," that religious Tillie. They were matched together in Russia. His father and mother died of a plague, and he was an orphan, so they went to my mother and said, "Oh, you're almost twenty-five and you gotta get married, you know? You'll get old and nobody will marry you, and we got a nice man for you. He's a good boy and he's got a house." Of course he never finished that house. It needed a couple of more boards, but she married him anyway.

She had a guy before, and my father used to throw it up to her. My mother said, "The most he ever done was try to touch me."

He said, "Oh, I don't believe that."

She used to smile. You know, she had that woman in her yet. You know what I mean? "So he did like me, so who the hell are you?"

My father came over here with his son. He left his wife in Russia. He had left her before. My mother used to say, "He comes, makes a baby, and runs away."

She wanted to be with her man, not that she ever liked him, but she believed in God, that's all. Her friends there told her, "You know in America, your husband, he goes with all kinds of women."

"Ooh, is that so? I'll go after him." So she sold the house, and that gave her enough money to come to America.

If they weren't in love, that's how the world spinned that time. You don't need that. The Jewish religion says you gotta get married. You gotta be faithful. My mother and father got along, except she didn't talk to him and he didn't talk to her.

She was a religious woman. She slapped me in the mouth if I didn't say the Jewish prayers. I used to wear *tsitsis* and the *tefillin* on the hands. She demanded that. My father was more radical. My father said the day he died, "Do you believe in God?"

I said, "Sure, I believe in God," although I was never a believer in God.

He said, "I swear to God, Sam, I don't believe in him, but if I served him, what the hell did I lose?" He never worked Saturday, you know? He was buried by the people who never worked Saturday, you understand. He was one of those guys who could go up there and read the Torah. He never believed in it, but five o'clock he would throw the hammer down on Friday night and go to *shul.*

Before he died, I remember my mother sayin', "Yussel Chaim, are you afraid?"

He said, "I swear to God I'm not afraid."

My father died when he was seventy-four. The day before, he asked my mother to give him a piece, so she said, "Go away from me, you old bastard, you"—in Jewish. The next day he died, and she cried all her life why she didn't give it to him.

SELMA HANNISH: My great-grandfather lived in this neighborhood over a hundred years ago. He used to tell us that the area where the Williamsburg Bridge is was all farmland. He came over here to make a living, but he couldn't succeed and he went back home. He kept coming and going. The very last time he came was just before World War I started.

What didn't he do: peddler, painter, floor scrubber. The main thing was the sweatshop. He was a magnificent figure, that great-grandfather of mine. They all were. He was fun. His beard smelled so nice. He told stories. His love just poured out. I used to think he was a magician. Saturday night they made *kiddush.* As part of the ritual, he used to put a drop of brandy on the table and he lit it briefly. This little blue flame would spring up, and he put it out. I used to call him a *kintzen macher*, a magic maker or a wizard.

But with my own parents, I never saw anything but fighting. A boy once told me that a mother and father had a baby when they kissed. My mother and father had five babies, which meant they kissed five times. I would walk around and say to my mother in German, "You!"

My mother said to my father, "Hershel, I think that kid is *mishugah.*"

I was horrified. My mother? I used to watch to make sure they wouldn't kiss. Maybe there would be another baby. Once, I found something to play with in the house. "Hey, Ma, here's half a ball." She grabbed it out of my hands. It was a diaphragm. I didn't know. I was angry because she took away my half a ball.

BETTY CHEN: My mother was of the old order. She had bound feet—real bound feet. She was a farmer's girl—on her bound feet.

She had them bound when she was very young, but not as young as some people. I think she was ten or twelve.

They crushed her toes underneath, and they kept binding them with cloth. She said it was very painful. She cried and fought it, but they said, "A man will never marry you if you have big feet."

I think they mutilated her to keep her at home and to keep her pregnant. To her dying day, she always said, "If I knew the emperor, I'd shoot him."

My mother was the last generation of women who had their feet bound. After Sun Yat-sen established the republic in 1912, nobody in their right mind allowed it. She couldn't do her house-work. She always sat on the high chair. When she walked, she walked on her toes all the time—she tottered. Later, they tried to unbend her toes by putting cloth in between, but it didn't work. She always complained how they hurt, but when we were young, we weren't that sympathetic. I used to tell her to take an aspirin, as if that would wipe away all her pain.

She wouldn't dare leave the house alone. One of us would have to take her. Even if they weren't bound, women didn't appear on streets. That's called "bold and brazen." I never jumped rope. I never played marbles or jacks on the sidewalk, because it was un-ladylike. My father bought us the twenty-volume set of the *Book of Knowledge,* and we sat home and read. We also learned to knit, sew, and crochet, things like that.

My parents didn't talk about birthdays or children that they had lost. I really never knew just what they did in China. Certain things were left unsaid. I never knew my mother's name. She never told us. I never knew when her birthday was. And you couldn't just ask, because she'd say, "What do you wanna know for?"

•   •   •

ROBERT LESLIE: People's salaries were so small, working con-ditions were so hard. People were getting pneumonia and tu-berculosis. They called it consumption. I would say that nearly one-third of the population had consumption. When a man or a woman began to cough, they said, "This is the end."

SAMUEL POGENSKY: The reason they were gettin' consump-tion, they're not lettin' air in for the lungs. Yeah, they had maybe a little window in each bedroom. We lived in the cellar of a buildin' on 3rd Street and Avenue D. It was more of a modern buildin' because it had more windows. Later, I owned a buildin' at 343 East 24th Street. It got a medal because it had a window in every room.

We had no apartment. It was just a cellar with a wood floor and plenty of rats. My mother always tried. One of the babies— she was so tired, instead of givin' her a little sugar, she gave her salt and the baby died. She had a baby when she was forty-eight. One day she had a toothache, and he was playin' in the cellar, and he got 'amonia and died. At that time, everybody was dyin' with 'amonia. In those days, people walked up to you and said, "Where's John?"

"He died of 'amonia."

When my brother died, they had no place to bury him, so they went to *heshes sclemmer*. It meant that they'll pay for the funeral. I think they gave you one carriage, but they'll only bury you with a little stone. I went once to the grave with my father. He cried. When he died, my father said, "As long as I live, I'll never go to a *shul*."

ROBERT LESLIE: I would say most of the people suffered from anxiety. When the Spanish-American War came, they were all scared to death. People were asked to be recruited. "Why do we have to fight the Spanish? Why do we want the Philippines?" So they explained these lands will give people more work. It's all done because capitalism had to create more jobs. One of the things it does is make war.

My mother, she respected religion, but she wasn't religious. How could she? She worked Saturdays and she worked Sundays. I was never bar mitzvah. I didn't know about that. I never celebrated Jewish holidays. I knew when Purim was or Passover, but I had no one to celebrate with. I went to maybe one or two sessions of a *cheder* where a guy would drop a penny and pinch my behind.

SAMUEL POGENSKY: I went five years to *cheder*. It was in the man's house. He had a red beard. I paid him a dollar a month or so. I went every day after school. He generally had six or seven students. He'd take out the book, and he'd call you a couple of times a *dummkopf*—"You can't learn nothin'."

He was a mean bastard. He'd always have a stick in his hand, and he'd whack you if you didn't pay attention. Then the father would come and say, "Give him another whack."

Betty Chen: I went to Chinese school every day from 3:30 to 7:00, including Saturdays, to learn Chinese. It was hard when you're speaking English all the time. You have to hold your pen straight up and down to write. They speak a very refined Chinese dialect, and we speak the provincial Toysan dialect.

In those days, the people used to say, "Oh, the Chinese children are wonderful. They're not delinquents." That was why. We were stuck in Chinese school. Then we'd go home and eat and do our homework. So how could you be a delinquent?

Robert Leslie: When I was twelve, I went to work for a printer who wore pince-nez glasses. The man's name was Max Lebron. He couldn't afford to pay me, but he said he would teach me printing. Lebron was an intellectual; he introduced me to Tolstoy, to Gorki, to all the Russian authors. I got a marvelous education from him.

The print shop was a storefront. He had two presses there. To set a page of type, depending on the size of the type, it would take anywhere from two to three hours. Now, you do it in fifteen minutes on the machine. We had to lock it up in forms and put it on the press. It was a long job, but I fell in love with printing.

Printing is called the basic art of all arts. It was printing that gave us education. It was printing which fought the church, because the Catholic church wanted to control all education, and it was the early printers who had to jump from city to city to save their printing presses. It was finally called "the preservative of all arts." It seemed to carry out my ideals.

I was also a lamplighter when I was fourteen years old. The Welsbach Lighting Company advertised for lighters, $2.50 a week, seven days a week, in every kind of weather. There was no electric in New York. They gave me thirty streetlights on Rivington and Stanton streets. They gave me a long stick with an end that turned the gas on. At five o'clock in the morning I would put it out. At five o'clock at night I would put it on.

When I was fourteen or fifteen, I met a remarkable man—Jacob Riis. They named a park after him. He wrote a book, *How the Other Half Lives.* He used to go from house to house. He saw me in the backyard after I sat on the pot. I came out. I had knickers and he liked my face. He said, "Boy, you come with me."

He became my father image, a wonderful man. He was from Denmark. I even knew a few words of Danish, so we got along fine. He would take me on his rounds to see the poverty. When I saw how the other people lived, we were rich. We saw a lot of prostitution—women giving themselves for fifty cents. Right next door to the synagogue on Allen Street was a whorehouse, and the guy who was the *shammes* of the synagogue was the manager of the house. That was a big scandal.

A lot of girls from poor families became prostitutes. They had no other ways of making a living. You would hear, "Psst," from the prostitutes, "mister, psst, *kumt arein.*" Nice Jewish girls, yeah, they had to make a living. There was no money, and they couldn't find a trade. The woman in the house would say, "Give it to a man, it won't cost you anything. We'll split it fifty-fifty and you can use my apartment."

We also saw people who wanted to be religious but they couldn't afford it. We saw people wearing rags. We went to the Five Points, which was infested with criminals, pickpockets, *shikers* [drunks]. He always had a gun in his belt. One day he took me to the police station to meet the commissioner. He was a blustering man.

"Hello! Who's this little fella?"

"He's my friend."

So we shook hands. It was Teddy Roosevelt.

SAMUEL POGENSKY: I think every fuckin' house in New York had a whorehouse. They were all over on Allen Street.

They had what they called chains of whores. That meant somebody had about twenty-five whores, and every week he'd change 'em for ya.

Sometimes if I wanted to screw a lady, a guy would say, "All right, go to my friend here. It's a dollar." In the colored neighborhoods like 99th Street, there the lady would give you two fucks for a dollar. And I noticed that the best fuck was a colored woman, 'cause she was like, "Did you enjoy yourself?" A Puerto Rican was very nasty and a Jew wanted to only marry ya.

I went to a Jew once, and I go to lay her, and I see she got a big belly. *[He imitates her Yiddish accent.]* "You wanna marry? I marry you and I make money. I make money."

Some married them, made money, and gave it to them. I wouldn't marry her if she had all the money in the world, but I thought, Keep your mouth shut and fuck her. What the hell, do you want to upset the cart?

Anyhow, the man came out and he slugged her in the mouth. "When he comes in to fuck you, you fuck him. Don't tell no stories to that young fellow about marryin'. You son of a bitch, you lousy whore, you."

He wanted to keep the whore. Anyway, we got through and she said, "You're my friend." I said, "I am your friend, and here's a dollar for it."


BETTY CHEN: Chinatown was called a "bachelor society" because there were very few women, but most of the men were married. They were the ones who left their families to come here and prove themselves. The men who didn't have their wives were lonely. Their wives were all home. They all lived alone. They had to take care of themselves.

Every few years they would make a trip back to China. That trip was so long. It took twenty-three days, eighteen by boat and five days on a train. So they had to take up to two months to travel and then time to see the family. People didn't have that kind of money to leave work for so long. My father never saw his mother again after he left. I asked him why didn't he go back. He said, "You go back and you have a good cry, so what's the use?"

People who were born here don't know how sad it was to have the families separated like that. All they could do was send money home to China to keep them going. Despite the sadness, they accepted. They earned money and sent it back periodically. Except those who gambled had nothing to send back, and that's even sadder for the woman at the other end, who doesn't know if he's living or dead.

·   ·   ·

HENRIETTA GILBERT: When I was growing up, I never knew about the poverty in the neighborhood. I never saw poor kids. We had a three-room apartment on Bayard Street, where we were five people and a servant. My father rented a store right around the corner at 68 Division Street, which means he had entered the prosperous fashion world. They were modest stores, but it was the shopping center for the whole East Side.

My father made cloaks and suits, and he prospered greatly. He was able to buy a building at 25 Division Street. On Division Street, they were not just retailers. The clothes were made there and they were superior, like Saville Row in London. The buildings even looked like those in a London street shop.

My father was a cultivated man, very proper. He wore very fine clothes. He even had his shoes made. He didn't go to a shoe store. He wore a suit and fedora to work. He wore a separate collar that was fastened with studs. My mother was always dressed formal and proper. I never saw her undressed. My mother was the saleswoman in the store. The only day she took off was Friday, when she baked *holley* and made herring, *rugelach* and noodles.

We went to *shul* on the High Holidays, but my parents worked in the store on Saturdays. My mother had no difficulty in reconciling the changes in her outlook. She said God always forgave you if you had to do that for *parnussa,* which meant income.

ABRAHAM HYMAN: The families we knew couldn't make a living on their own, so they had to take in boarders. The average family had three boarders. We had four.

ROSE HALPERN: We had a boarder who waited for me when I got home and tried to kiss me. Who could throw him out of the house? We needed the three dollars a week. Then we had one Polish boarder. When she moved out, my grandmother's jewelry went with her.

ABRAHAM HYMAN: You used to hear a lot of stories about the boarders and the wives. The youngsters would stand on the corner and sing these immoral songs about the boarders. These things happened, a young boarder and a young wife.

SAMUEL KISSELOFF: Later on there was a song about the boarders and the wives. It was to the tune of "Down Mexico Way":

*That louse of a boarder, who else could it be?*
*While I was out to work, I think that jerk stood in for me.*
*What did he do with my Esther? How far did he stray?*
*South of the border, down my Esther's way.*

*I told that boarder, "You're ruining my life.*
*When I gave you that price, it did not include my wife."*
*I cut out his bolero. No more will he stray*
*South of the border, down my Esther's way.*

ABRAHAM HYMAN: The *Forward* had a column called *Farsh-vundener Mennen*, "Disappeared Men." That was a service. It was a problem. After thirty years the wives were old *kvetches*. He finds a younger one and they run away. The spirit was freer here. You did things that you were not supposed to do in the old country.

MOLLIE HYMAN: Abe and I are *landslayts*. We are also cousins. Our mothers are sisters. When we came here, we went to his apartment, but it was so crowded, we couldn't stay there too long. His mother had four boarders, plus his family, and then my family. There were five rooms. There were three boarders in each room. The living room looked like a ward in a hospital.

MARTHA DOLINKO: In my apartment, I waited a long time for a special couch just for me. I was the only girl among four boys, and my mother says, "You're not going to sleep in this room with that one. You're gonna have a bed of your own."

The bed came, and the next day she rented it to a boarder.

If you had an apartment, you had two weeks free. So after two weeks you moved away to another place. They kept moving. When I used to come from school or work, sometimes I didn't know where we lived. The neighbors had to tell me.

ROSE HALPERN: After a while, we moved to Stanton Street. At that time, your grandmother and grandfather came with your father's sister, Jeanie. We all shared a four-room flat. They had the room with the windows in front of the house, and my grandmother, my mother, and I stayed in one tiny bedroom. We were so closed in in that little tiny room with no windows, I used to have these terrible dreams as a child. I dreamed that everything all of a sudden began to close in. It would get closer and closer until I started to become stifled. Then I would wake up.

Grandma was spotless. They'd wash the floor and then put all the newspapers on the floor. Jewish people did that. I don't know why, because the print would run all over the floor. Even though she was so clean, we always had rats. I remember looking outside to watch these two pussycats fighting, but they turned out to be two big rats. Once, I was washing my hands in the sink and a rat dropped right into my hands. Or they would be marching across the stove while I was eating, and I was horrified of rats. It was terrible.

BLANCHE LASKY: When we lived on Cherry Street, we had plenty of rats runnin' around. I'd be in bed, and I'd feel somethin' heavy on me, and there it was, a rat. I had a neighbor who had a big dog. She sicced the dog at me. I was afraid of dogs. I was runnin' and screamin'. I got even with her the next day. I saw a big dead rat almost the size of a cat layin' in the street. I picked it up by the tail, and I started chasin' her, swingin' it. That taught her a lesson.

We lived on Cherry between Rutgers and Jefferson. I was born in 1923. Even at that time, we didn't have electricity. We had the gaslight. We had no Frigidaire. We had iceboxes, coal stoves, turlets in the hall. In fact, the outhouse they used to use was still in the yard.

There was a stable right next to me. I used to play on the dead horses. They'd just leave 'em layin' on the street, and then we'd play king of the hill on there. After a while, the smell didn't bother us.

When I had the whoopin' cough, that was funny. The old wives' tale was the stable was very good for whoopin' cough, so I used to sit in the stable and get the smell. There were goats there too. Then at night, we'd sit out on the pier by the water, 'cause you couldn't sleep.

MARTY COHEN: We had about ten horses for our ice-and-coal business. The stable was at 9 Hester Street. When the horse would die, they would have to lie on the street until the SPCA came by with this big hearse. They had a crank. They put this thing around the horse's neck and crank it up and get him in the hearse. Before they came, the horse would be lying there for a few days, and to the kids, what the hell, if they played around a dead horse or a live horse, it didn't make any difference.

The major place to buy horses was Fiss, Doerr & Carroll on 24th Street between Third and Lexington Avenue. They held sales twice a week. These were big dray horses, work horses. You'd buy 'em or take others there to sell. We also bought 'em from West Point. They would ship 'em on the Erie. Then we would ship 'em across on the ferry and, like the circus walks the animals through the street, we used to walk the horses down from Chambers to Park Row into East Broadway over to Hester Street.

We had horses for ten years. The biggest problem was everything was cobblestone. They used to pour tar in the streets, and the damn tar used to melt in the summertime and the wheels would get caught. Then they started to do away with the cobblestones, but the asphalt was worse.

On the Williamsburg Bridge, if you get a runaway horse, the only way to stop him, they would notify the guy in the middle of the bridge, and he would put a barrier across. Now and then a horse would break a leg and you would have to put the horse away. We'd call the police or the SPCA and they'd treat the horse. We had a policeman named Fred Well. Fred was a hell of a guy. In those years, the cops had stationary posts. The policemen didn't have much to do, so they used to hang out in the back of the coal yard. There was a big potbellied stove. One of the cops was a good cook. They used to go into every pushcart and every store. They'd glom this and that—never paid for anything.

Anyway, once while he was back there, somebody was screaming out across the street that he was robbed. The burglar was running away. Fred told the guy to stop. When the guy kept running, Fred took his gun out and shot him. He shot him right square in the asshole. After that they called him Dead-Eye Dick.

Now this horse had to be shot, so Fred is elected to shoot the horse. Instead of putting the gun to the horse's head, Fred said no, he's Dead-Eye Dick. He went back about twenty paces and shot. Hit the horse in the ear. He unloaded the goddamn gun, but he didn't hit the son of a bitch squarely once. Finally, one of the other cops had to come over and put the horse away.

Horse poisoning was a big problem. They were called the Jewish Black Hands. They were a bad bunch of people. They wanted tribute, a dollar a month for your horse. If you had ten horses, they wanted ten dollars a month or they poisoned your horses.

My father was a rough old guy. He had a horse poisoned. He knew who did it. The guy was on Ludlow Street. We went over there. He found the guy, and he said, "This horse cost me $17.50. If you don't pay me the $17.50, I'll kill you."

With that the guy took out a gun. My father said, "If you don't put that gun away, I'll stick that gun right up your ass."

The guy threatened him. The old man walked right up to him, took the gun away from him, and did exactly what he said. He stuck the gun up his ass and threw the guy down a flight of cellar stairs. They never bothered us again after that.

I was born in 1897. We were living on Clinton then. The toilets were in the back. The toilet in the hallway came later, and it was a luxury. When it was out in the back, either it was too cold or it was too hot. Every apartment had chamber pots. You used to crap in the pot instead of going downstairs. A lot of times, people would just crap on the floor of the apartment. There was a guy in the toilet, you couldn't get in, bang! They used to throw the stuff out of the windows. You'd get nailed with it. That was very common.

R OSE  H ALPERN : We used the orange wrappers or the newspaper in the toilet.

S AMUEL  P OGENSKY : I think we used the *World,* and the *American.* They were the mornin' papers.

M URRAY  H ALPERN : People used to fight for the pear wrappers from the pushcarts, and if you were a good customer, he would give them to ya. We were lucky. We had a neighbor who was an insurance broker, and he had a telephone. So whenever he got a new phone book, we were the first ones to get the old one. We would cut it in half, hang it on the wall with a nail, and use that for toilet paper.

M ARTY  C OHEN : My father delivered ice. We got our ice from the Knickerbocker Ice Company. Everybody did. Our area took in Clinton Street, Suffolk Street, Grand Street, Hester Street, Division Street. We would ride around on a wagon, and my father would yell, "Iiice!" We were the most aggressive and popular in our little section.

People would come to the wagon and buy it. We would chop it in cakes, a piece for a cent, a bigger piece for two cents. In some cases we got an extra penny if we had to carry it up to the fourth floor or the fifth floor.

In those days, there was a beer saloon on every corner. It was all draft beer then, and they had to keep the coils cold for the beer. We sold them ice, twenty-five cents a pail, which were butter tubs that we got from the original Breakstone. They were the Breakstone Brothers. One was on Division Street, and the other was on Suffolk Street.

Samuel Pogensky: My father was the best shoemaker, but for nuttin'. He was an honest shoemaker. He never made enough to eat fish Saturday. He used to hock his brush—had a beautiful brush. He used to go to the pawnshop, hock it, and they used to give him back a dollar somethin', and he used to buy fish. Instead of usin' the brush, he used somethin' else. When he got a dollar somethin', he went back to the hockshop and got his brush back. Trustin', trustin' and trustin'. But he was honest and a good man, and he used to always pay for my lessons, a dollar.

Abraham Hyman: I got a job immediately after I came. The boss offered me a job to carry bundles of vests to the clothing stores on Canal Street. I was paid three or four dollars a week, but my father said there was no future. "Let him learn to be a businessman."

He read the want ads in the *Jewish Evening Journal,* and he sees an ad for a boy to work in a grocery on Prince Street. He practically sells me for four dollars a month. I got food and board—lodging, they used to call it. There was one condition, that I should be allowed to go to school between eight and ten o'clock at the Seward Park Evening School.

When I went to school, I used to doze off. The teacher had to wake me, and the students were making fun, so I stopped going to school, but from the store I got to Seward Park, sat down on the bench, and dozed off for two hours. After a month, the work was so hard, I lost weight, I lost the color in my face, and my father says, "It's not for him," so I quit.

BETTY CHEN: My mother was, in today's language, "functionally illiterate." She did not know Chinese, she did not know English. She just spoke a local dialect. Only the boys were educated then, no girls. My father was ahead of his time. He educated six girls through college and a boy. This was when boys didn't go to college, let alone girls.

People used to criticize him. "What are you educating the girls for? They're gonna get married."

The laws said the Chinese couldn't work in many professions. That was another reason why they didn't bother to send their children to college. They said, "What's the reason to send them to college? They'll come out and they'll work in a laundry or work in a restaurant," and my father said, "Look, give them an education first, and we'll let the future take care of itself." If my father hadn't taken that stand, I'd be without a college education now.

MARTHA DOLINKO: My father was a cabinetmaker. He used to make drawers for the drugstores. One day as he was fixing it up, a brick came down and hurt his hand, and he took sick. That's the time they shipped me to work. I wasn't fourteen years.

I don't blame my parents. Life is not a bowl of cherries. In Europe I didn't go to school at all. When I came here I went to night school until my father got hurt. I saw a sign, "Examiner wanted." I couldn't read English. A man passed, a Jewish man with a beard. I said in Jewish, "Mister, what does that sign say?"

"It says an examiner."

So I knocked at the door and said, "So you need an examiner?" I worked as an examiner on Third Avenue. I examined police coats. I used to take a police coat on my lap. The coat was heavier than me.

I worked sixty hours a week. We had to be there before seven. We went home at eight o'clock. Lunch was whatever Mother gave along. You had fifteen minutes to eat. Years ago, they didn't give you a chance to breathe. The windows were shut. People were standing and working all sorts of hours. And you couldn't go up to the shop in an elevator. The elevator was for baggage and other things. We used to walk up and down.

They had inspectors for child labor, but sometimes the man who ran the elevator got a few dollars to say that children weren't working in the shop. When an inspector came up, I used to hide under the cutter's table. When I saw a mouse go by, I screamed.

I was across the street from the Triangle fire. I'll never forget that. My God, the people couldn't get out. The windows were shut, so some of them with the feet broke the windows and they jumped. Oh, I'll never forget. I close my eyes and zip! goes a girl. A lot of them got hurt.

They didn't have any real burial—greenhorns working. People didn't take care of the working people like they do now. You can go to Montefiore Cemetery where the Workingman's [sic] Circle buried them all.

PAULINE CUOIO PEPE: I came here when I was five years old with my mother, my brother, and my sister in 1896. We lived on Broome Street. My father was a tailor in Siegal-Cooper. We never went out much, except to go to school and to church.

I went to work when I was nineteen. My first job was at the Triangle Shirtwaist Company. I went to work because a woman in the building said to me, "C'mon, we have a lot of fun. What ya doing at home?"

She introduced me to the boss, Mr. Blanck. They hired me as a sewing-machine operator for twelve dollars a week. It was easy work. You just sat there and the machine would run the tucking. I was there almost two years before the fire. We loved it. We used to sing while the machine was going. It was all nice young Jewish girls who were engaged to be married. You should see the diamonds and everything. Those were the ones who threw themselves from the window.

I got in at half past eight, and we got out at four o'clock. When we left, we never went out the front door. We always went one by one out the back. There was a man there searching, because the people were afraid we would take something, so that door was always locked.

We were just leaving that Saturday. I was fixing my hair at my machine. The cutters were right there. They generally lit a cigarette when they go out. The man was right there. His match lit the scraps under the table. Suddenly, another cutter said, "C'mon, let's run."

I said, "Ooh, my God, a fire." I ran and I left everything—pocketbook. I was running and the people were all at the door. I saw the people throwing themselves out the window. I wouldn't dare. I didn't have the courage. "I'm not going out, I'd rather die here," that's what I said.

The door was locked. We were about a hundred people. We were hollering and crying. "Open the door!" Banging and banging quite a long time. We saw quite a lot of people throwing themselves out.

We waited a long time. We didn't feel any of the flames, but it was getting warm. The fires went to the windows. I thought about my mother and father. What would they do if I died?

Then all of a sudden we all fell over. Somebody opened the door. "Thank God!" We were all crying and yelling. The noise was terrible. When I got down, the three flights were blazing. The firemen came up and helped us, but we were tumbling down terrible. We were shivering and crying and holding on. It was terrible.

When we got down the stairs the firemen told us to wait because those young people were still jumping down. When we got out, we saw the ladder was pointing up to the sixth floor. It couldn't go up to the eighth. We saw those people jumping down. And the people in the hotel were yelling, "Don't jump down. Get in!" But they wouldn't listen to us. They had made up their mind. They went right through the glass in the pavement, some of them. There was a big hole there.

They didn't have to throw themselves. Something would have happened. That's too bad all those women died—young girls. Their families must have found some diamonds. You should see the diamonds on those Jewish girls.

I had a lot of friends who were killed. Then I had one friend—when we got down, I was looking for her. Sure enough, she was there. She was looking for me. Oh, my God, we hugged each other, and this man saw us crying. He said, "Oh, don't worry, we'll take you home." We told him where we lived, and they were very nice to take us home.

We were all torn to pieces. My hair was a mess. My coat was torn. I had no pocketbook or nothing. When my mother saw me, she thought somebody got ahold of me and was killing me. I told them about the fire, and they started hollering terribly.

The Red Cross sent us for two weeks' vacation. They treated us wonderful. Don't you think there was a fire a block away? A house was burning. That's all we had to see. We didn't sleep right, always afraid. We would get up again and talk.

We were also angry. "What the hell did they close the door for? What did they think we're going out with? What are we gonna do, steal a shirtwaist? Who the heck wanted a shirtwaist?"

SELMA HANNISH: My grandfather worked in the sweatshop for eighty hours for three dollars a week. Then he joined a union, and he said, boy, did he break scabs' heads. He said, "Now these young sprouts, they take a union for granted. Little do they know the blood we shed to get those unions going."

MARTHA DOLINKO: I didn't know about strikes. Then I saw a man walking with a sign, and I said to him in Jewish, "Mister, what's that?"

He said, "We're picketing. You shouldn't work." So he put the damn board on me, and I walked up and down. The police arrested me. The union took me out. The policeman told me to walk in the gutter, not on the sidewalk. I said, "Pardon me, horses walk in the gutter."

He said, "You're like a horse."

I said, "If I'm like a horse, you're worse than I am." So he arrested me.

My God, the company used to hire strikebreakers. All right, so they wouldn't let us up the elevators, so we used to walk up the stairs and holler, "Hey, scabs!" There were fights, hitting one another everywhere. But I raised my mouth. I never raised my hands. Hands, I could be punished. My mouth, they couldn't punish.

MOLLIE HYMAN: Oh, I beat up a lot of scabs. I worked in my brother's millinery shop, and I organized for the union in our shop. Being that I was assistant forelady, I was the one that gave out the work and took away the work from the girls. In other words, I could talk to them. I told them to come down to a meeting.

Even though I was the assistant forelady, I got them together, and we went out on strike. We didn't want it for ourselves. We had it in mind to make it better for the men, that they should be able to make a living to support you, that you could stay home.

My shop happened to be the biggest millinery shop in New York. They figured if the big one was organized, the others would follow. I was on the picket line for three months. And how, was there violence! We knew what station the scabs came out of, so we used to watch, and when they came out of the subway, we used to beat them up. We'd hit them with our umbrellas, our pocketbooks, pull their hair. We never really hit them so they would get sick. We tried to chase them away, stop them so they shouldn't go up to the elevator. Eventually, they would go up anyway. One girl would say, "I'm sorry, we are not from Russia. We are Americans. We don't believe in unions."

PAULINE PEPE: The union used to come around. I liked the union organizers, but I didn't join the union. We were young girls. We never wanted to bother with the union. We were here today, but we might get married tomorrow. We told them that and they used to laugh.

ABRAHAM HYMAN: At that time, the East Side was beginning to unionize. They were all beginning to blossom up because of the speakers mostly on East Broadway near the *Forward* building. The whole year, you saw speakers on every corner around there. I listened to Hillquit or Judge Panken, Joseph Barondess, Vladeck who was a marvelous speaker, with a glib tongue and a little fire in his soul.

Everybody was talking about unionism. The politicians used to come fishing on the East Side, because they had a raw crowd— a crowd that was not polished yet. They could make them into a frenzy. They would talk about capitalism, and socialism, and sweatshops. The problems were always there, Tammany Hall was always on your tongue.

ROBERT LESLIE: Tammany Hall was both the lifesavers and the disturbers. When I graduated City College, I was given my diploma. There was no Board of Education at that time. So I was sent to the office of the Arthur Ahearn Association, which was Tammany Hall. I showed the fellow my certificate.

"So you want to be a teacher, huh?"

I said, "Yes, sir." I was always very polite. "Yes, sir." They never heard the word *sir*.

"Where do you live?"

"I live on Madison Street. There is a school on Henry Street where I graduated."

"We can send you there."

They wrote a note to Birnbaum, the principal, "Hire this fellow." And that's how I got to teach at PS Number 2.

The Socialist Party gave me the idea that the world is unequal, and that socialism is the answer for all the workmen. That's why my mother called me Lincoln. She said, "He freed the black slaves. You free the wage slaves." So I was actually in a family that wanted freedom for workers.

I started speaking for the Socialists when I was fourteen, in 1899. That's how I met Abe Cahan of the *Jewish Daily Forward*. The Socialists called me "the Boy Orator." I got up on a soapbox, and I would say [*loudly, as if he was making the speech again*], "Comrades, you have been slaves long enough. You have to strike out for your own freedom, and the way to do that is to educate yourselves and join the Socialist Party. If you join the Socialist Party, you will forget your poverty. We will divide everything for you. It won't cost you anything, maybe a dollar a month, but you'll get an education."

When Debs came to New York, I booked him in Webster Hall. He was six feet two, and he'd bend over and say [*again, in a loud voice*], "Comrades, if you steal a loaf of bread you go to jail, but if you steal a railroad you go to the Senate." I loved that man.

I started out as a member of the Honest Ballot Association, with my celluloid collar. I was on Cherry Street, and I saw these fakers took names of all the people and put it on their cuffs. Then they'd go and vote. And I, as a member of the Honest Ballot Association, began to object. I was a little fella. They grabbed me by the back of the pants and threw me out. That was my experience as an Honest Balloter.

I worked with Emma Goldman. I met her on Ludlow Street. She spoke at Terrace Lyceum about birth control, and I schlepped along. She was an excellent speaker. She was with Alexander Berkman then. She believed in free love, but she thought I was too young for her.

People on the East Side loved her. She gave a speech at the Terrace Lyceum that if you have sex, go to the bathroom and wash yourself out, so a Jewish woman in front of me said, "She's smart, but you can't go eight times a night."

She was short, a little stocky, with frizzly hair, and she never stopped talking—always talking. She learned I had an interest in printing, and so she said she wanted to get out a magazine, and could I help her. I said of course I will. I was then working for a printer and I knew all the work.

The magazine was called *Mother Earth*. There was a Jewish newspaper called *Freie Arbeiter Shtime*, which was an anarchist paper. It was on East Broadway, and she told me to meet her there to look at the proofs. An anarchist fellow named Hippolyte Havel and I would make corrections. Actually, I would make them and Havel would cross them out. He didn't like my corrections.

Havel was quite a schnorrer. He was more like Greenwich Village. He was a fancy guy, always looking for a handout. He was an editor of *Mother Earth*, but you could never find him. He was always in back of a saloon. In those days, saloons would give you a free lunch with a beer. His hands were always full of pockmarks, because he would hold his hands out for money, and the people would stab him with their forks to push him away.

She was generous. When I'd come there after school, she'd say to me, "Take half my sandwich. I didn't finish it." She knew I was always hungry. I never weighed more than 114 pounds.

I was working with Barondess in the labor movement. He was also a favorite of Morris Hillquit and Meyer London and Abe Cahan. Emma Goldman called us watered-down proletariat. I left her after I started *Mother Earth*. I didn't agree with anarchism. Later, she was deported. A guy like John Reed was never bothered. He was considered American. Emma Goldman was considered a Russian, so they got rid of her.

ROSE HALPERN: I once went on strike—against your grandfather. When I was eight years old, I already started to work. Your grandfather would make me stand in front of the store and sell Eskimo Pies. I didn't want to do it, but I couldn't say no because I had to do it. He would pay me to stand from eight o'clock in the morning to twelve o'clock at night.

I wanted him to give me a raise, twenty-five cents, and he wouldn't do it, so I went on strike. I didn't work for two Saturdays. That meant I lost a dollar. Finally, he came to the house, and he agreed to give me the extra twenty-five cents.

We had a very, very rough time at home. My mother at first was working with Christmas lamps. They used to make these lamps in the shape of little animals, and she would test them. All those that didn't light up she would bring home to me, and I would have like a menagerie. They were my only toys.

Your grandfather also brought work home for my mother and grandmother. After they worked in the shop until nine, they would do the homework until after midnight. They didn't really do this so I would have a better life, they did it to exist.

Could you imagine, for dinner there would be a quarter of a little chicken for three of us? Since I was the child, naturally they gave me the most out of that quarter. They gave me the drumstick, and they had the rest for themselves. And that was a special dinner—for Friday nights.

When I came home for lunch, I had a bowl of chocolate pudding and bread. I never knew what a vegetable was. I didn't even know they existed. I was very anemic. They had to send me to the Loeb Home, which was a special camp in the country sponsored by very wealthy Jewish people. They had to keep me there an extra week because I was so undernourished.


NAT FORMAN: Life was quite rough around my house. We were seven children. I was not even brung up, I was dragged up. When we were hungry on a Saturday night, five or six of us would go to a hall in the neighborhood that had a Jewish wedding. In front would be a guy with a badge painted gold to see who goes in is a member of the family. I would say my mother is upstairs and that I had to go home to take away the *shissel* of water from the icebox. In I'd go. In ten minutes, all of us were in.

As soon as the kazatsky dance was over, we would slide on the polished dance floor like Krazy Kids. Time and again, the women would ask in Jewish, "Whose kids are they?" Then in another ten minutes, the boys from the bride and groom would also be sliding on the polished floor.

Around 11:30, we would one by one sneak down to the dining room. We would load up on the food, no hot stuff, because that would be served when the guests went down at 12:00. Until then, we would devour whatever our stomachs could hold. We drank seltzer and spritzed it all over the dining room. Then, as soon as we heard them get ready, we would fill up our blouses with oranges and apples and out we would sneak.

◆　◆　◆

MOLLIE HYMAN: Almost every family had the *pushkas*, little boxes on the walls. Come Friday night, you'd throw in a penny for your favorite charity. There were separate boxes for each charity, for Israel, yeshiva, poor people.

BLANCHE LASKY: Schmaltz is chicken fat. My mother used to render the fat from the chicken. We'd get this corn bread and toast it on top of the coal stove, and we'd rub it with garlic, put chicken fat on it. That was a meal. She also made her own pickled herring and pickles, and we'd eat that with bread and butter. It was delicious. There was always potatoes, potatoes, potatoes. To this day I love potatoes. I have potatoes with everything.

SAM KISSELOFF [*sings*]:

> *Zuntag, bulbeh*
> *Muntag, bulbeh*
> *Dienstag und Mitvach, bulbeh*
> *Donnershtag und Freitag, bulbeh*
> *Shabbos delebt min a bulbeh, kugel,*
> *Und Zuntag veiter bulbeh.*

The English translation is:

> *Sunday, potatoes*
> *Monday, potatoes*
> *Tuesday and Wednesday, potatoes*
> *Thursday and Friday, potatoes*
> *Saturday we live to see a potato pudding,*
> *And Sunday we have potatoes again.*

SELMA HANNISH: No matter what it was, my mother used to make a soup, just plain potato and onion—if she was lucky, a carrot, and if she was extra, extra lucky, some dill. She would cut those onions and boil them with the carrot and the dill. That and a piece of black bread with garlic and butter and a cup of cocoa, let me tell you, no gourmet could have eaten anything better, 'cause my mom cooked with love. She said, "If you can't cook with love, you do not cook at all."

"What's love, Ma?"

"Well, I love you. I love your sisters. I love your brother. I love my house. I love making this stuff. That's what you call cooking with love."

She had five children. She never hit any one of us ever. She said, "I'm not a murderess."

BLANCHE LASKY: We also ate a lot of herring from the barrels on Hester Street. That was a very big shopping street with the bakeries, fish stores, herring and smoked stuff.

MOLLIE HYMAN: I had herring every day, once herring, once tomato herring, once sardines. Every grocery sold herring. You came in and you asked for a little herring. It would be three cents. He would give you a little herring. If you asked for a large herring, he would charge you six cents, but it was the same little herring.

SAM KISSELOFF: A couple of doors down from Pop's store on Orchard Street was Herzog—appetizers. He had an open-front store. In front of the store were maybe four or five huge vats filled with schmaltz herring. Each vat supposedly had a different size. What the difference was between the herrings nobody knew except Herzog. People said he made a fortune shifting the forty-nine-cent herrings into the fifty-nine-cent barrels, and the thirty-nine-cent herrings into the forty-nine-cent barrels, because all you ever saw of Herzog was his ass and his feet sticking out of the barrel.

Since he dealt mostly in silver, whenever we needed change, we went to him. We always knew his change because the coins and the register stunk of herring for days on end.

SOL KAPLAN: That time, every corner had a pickle store. People ate. It was European people. Americans don't eat that stuff much. When I came to America in '21, my father had a place over here, right here on Essex Street—pickle business. Then he sold his place to Lebowitz, which is now United. Then I had a chance to buy. Rothman has a place, he wants to retire on Orchard Street, so I bought it. I bought it in 1930 and I stood there until 1973. I had my own place, pickles, yeah, on Orchard and Rivington—forty-three years.

SIDNEY PITTER: Guss and Hollander were high-class pickle stores. We bought ours from the lady on the pushcart. She had them out on barrels and on slabs of wood. When she was finished, she brought them down to the rat-infested basement and left them there for the next day. Then she went down to the rat-infested basement and brought up the barrels. Those that had rat bites, she threw away.

SOL KAPLAN: There was business for everybody. They did it the same way they're doin' it now. You pickle 'em, you sell 'em right away green, or if you want for the winter to age 'em, you put them in storage in refrigeration.

Cucumbers used to come from Long Island—all the pickles. There's no Long Island no more. There's no farms. From Jersey they used to come. Now it comes from the South—North Carolina, South Carolina, Virginia.

When you're buying wholesale, you look for the quality. If it's a fresh pickle, that's good. It's gotta be hard, nice, crisp. If it's soft or wrinkled, it means it was travelin' long. Years ago you didn't have to watch, it was all near farms, but now it's a problem. It travels six or seven days on the train. What do you know if the guy doesn't put ice on the way?

After he buys 'em, then he'd throw 'em into barrels, make brine up, put in garlic and spice, water 'em and cover 'em up, press 'em down, that's all. The brine is made from salt and water. Then you put the spice in.

Rothman used to mix their spices specially. They didn't use mixed spices like we do now. They used to buy mostly cloves, the *nagelach*, and they bought hot peppers, and they use all kinds of coriander. It takes longer, but if you wanna make something good, you gotta do a lot of work. That's what the people came for.

Then you gotta age 'em. You age 'em as much as you want. Some people like 'em green, some like 'em a few weeks old. Some like 'em old like a few months old, so you gotta age it for them. Then they get brown. They get half sour, then sour, and then even more sour.

I also made my own sauerkraut during the war, 'cause I couldn't get enough sauerkraut. They were shipping a lot of it to Russia, so I got a machine and I cut it myself, and I cursed the man that gave it to me—the machine. It's hard work. Now it's made in tanks. It's a big factory—500 barrels in a tank. A man goes inside can get drownded. He goes in with boots. You should see how they do it. It takes a few weeks to pickle sauerkraut, but some people like it fresh. Like I like it fresh, but most people like it sour.

The Jews ate anything. They had appetites like horses. Now, they're fancy. That's why there are no stands. They don't eat it. It's a dyin' industry. Soon you'll only get pickles in the supermarkets made by manufacturers. The homemade pickles have a different taste. They have no preservatives, but Americans don't care. That's all they use—preservatives, and vegetables in cans.

◆ ◆ ◆

ROBERT LESLIE: Most of the good Jewish boys in my group went to Townsend Harris. There were never any dropouts. Our groups supplied doctors, dentists, lawyers, accountants, all eager to make a living. My mother said to me, "America is a land of gold. There is no gold in the streets. The gold is in your head. When you are educated, you obtain the gold," and she inspired me.

I loved going to school. I used to work hard. I wore a celluloid collar. You could wipe it off, and it was fresh every day. When I came to the school after I graduated City College '04, I asked the principal if he remembered me, and he said, "Sure. You're the boy with the collar."

City College was free. I got the first Jewish boy Phi Beta Kappa in chemistry. That's how I got the scholarship to Johns Hopkins University. I had no idea where Baltimore was, because I never traveled. The Kehillah was a group of Germans who took care of the Russian Jews. They said to me, "Young boy, we will send you to Baltimore, but we have to raise the money."

It took 'em four years to raise the money. Of course, there were other things they had to take care of. One year I was a school-teacher. For the next two years I was in social service at the Henry Street Settlement. The third year I was an active Socialist. I made speeches.

I lived in the Village then, on Waverly Place. I was a boarder in people's houses without pay. Today, they would call me a freeloader. At the *Masses* [a radical magazine of the period], they felt I had business experience, so they said, "We'll make you business manager." I knew Max Eastman and Floyd Dell. I knew John Reed and his girlfriend, Louise Bryant. She was beautiful. They took me to their home on Patchin Place. He was a wonderful man. He would take me along with him when I didn't have a penny to spend.

ABRAHAM HYMAN: When I saw the houses on Fifth Avenue, I couldn't dream that I would ever have a home with a bathtub, with a shower, with electric, with steam heat.

MOLLIE HYMAN: When we moved to a nicer apartment, we still didn't have a bath. We had a toilet in the house, but no bath. There was a bathhouse on Monroe Street. We'd pay two cents. They give you a towel and a piece of soap. There was a timer, and after five minutes was up, if you were under the shower with soap on you, you were stuck. You had to rush, unless you paid another two cents.

LARRY SCHNEIDER: We had to go to the Rivington Street baths. There were maybe a hundred kids lined up to take a bath. They'd slap each other on the fanny. They would fight with each other. One guy would say, "Look, he's not Jewish."

NAT FORMAN: As a youngster, I used to see quite a lot of bearded men go each Friday afternoon to Schmoolkie's Palm Garden. That was a *mikvah* owned by Schmoolkie Schmulowitz. They used to carry a small bag with them. They'd go in for a *tush*—a shower, in English—and take a dip in a two-by-four pool of water that looked like the muddy Mississippi.

One Friday, I got me three cents together, and in the afternoon I went to Schmoolkie's for a *tush* and a dip in the muddy waters of the pool. What do I see there? These old whiskered men, they take out of their packages a hammer and a chisel and they start to hack off the clay from their feet. They did not want to dirty up Schmoolkie's beach near the pool.

Schmoolkie's cost twenty-five cents to sleep in the joint. There were about fifty beds in the dormitory. The better-class places charged a half a dollar, and the swell places like the Forsyth Street baths and the Second Avenue baths and Lafayette Street baths cost one dollar. Many a night I would put a sign up in Schmoolkie's, "You can play with the cockroaches, but you cannot take them home."

MOLLIE HYMAN: Nobody had a telephone. If you had to get somebody or you wanted to get somebody a message, you had to call the drugstore, and the druggist usually had a kid to run up and tell us that there was a call and to come down. You had to tip that kid.

LARRY SCHNEIDER: The telephone would ring in the drugstore. "Telephone for Mrs. Bloom!" She lived on the fifth floor. The druggist would say, "Sonny, go upstairs. Call Mrs. Bloom. Tell her it's the telephone."

I ran up five flights, come down. If she didn't give me a penny, I'd curse her. I swore everything on her. "You shouldn't live to see another day," 'cause I needed that penny. That penny bought me a piece of khaki—water taffy. This water taffy would last you all day. Then you had a two-cent sucker—a big lollipop. You'd suck on the lollipop for an hour, put it in your pocket, even without paper, and an hour or two later, you'd start lickin' it again. You called it an all-day sucker.

We also spent our money on movies. The Cannon Movies on Cannon Street was two for a nickel. You'd come to the movie in the summer like 8:30 in the mornin' and you'd see about 200 kids in the street, minglin' around. Nobody got three cents. They had the three cents but they wanted the penny for candy. Whoever argued the most got in for two cents.

"C'mon, I sprung last week. I got two cents."

"No ya didn't. Ya liar."

We'd cuss each other and everything. Eventually you hadda give up, so you went for three cents. I used to give up most of the time.

You'd go in and about twelve, one o'clock it'd go on again, and the guy would come around, "C'mon, late check. Show us your late check. How long ya here?"

"I just came in."

"Whaddya mean? You're here four hours."

SAM KISSELOFF: I saw *King Kong* four times in one day. Grandma wasn't too happy about it. All of a sudden, I saw her walking up the aisle, screaming, "Seymour, Seymour!"

"What ya want, Ma?"

Whop!

MARTY COHEN: There was a firehouse on Clinton Street which they turned into a movie. That was the silent movies. Not only did they have the man playing the piano, but because people couldn't read, they had a man and woman with megaphones who would read the titles. When the actor spoke, the man read to the audience. When the actress spoke, then the woman would read.

MOLLIE HYMAN: I happened to see a movie before in Warsaw. We came here, his mother says she is gonna take me and my brother to a movie. To go to a movie in Europe, you have to get dressed if you go someplace, so she dressed up. The best jewelry she had years ago was a watch with a chain. When you had this on, you were all dressed. We go down. She paid a nickel each. It used to be a stable, and inside the smell was still there, and that was the movie, but still she dressed up to go.

In the shtetl, nobody ever heard any music. The only music we knew were the *klezmer*. They were only when there were weddings and bar mitzvahs. But we had a druggist. He used to go away for a vacation. One day he came back with a phonograph and records. Every Friday night, he would put the phonograph in the window and play the records. The whole little town would stand there at his window for two or three hours.

ABRAHAM HYMAN: Her brother bought a phonograph. With the phonograph, he bought about three or four records. We had Caruso, and Caruso records were ten-inch Red Label Victor, one side, cost three dollars. We listened to those records over and over again. We would put the records with the speaker to the yard and let the neighbors enjoy it.

MOLLIE HYMAN: Over here, when my brother was going to college, he used to come home and he used to work on this little thing—a radio. Nobody ever heard of radio. The whole neighborhood, the doctor, everybody came to listen. A few women wouldn't try it. They were afraid to put the headphones on. He was always working at it. The neighbors used to look out of the window and see him, and they used to say, "Gee, a very intelligent boy. He goes to college and everything, but he's deaf. He always has earphones."

ABRAHAM HYMAN: You had music on the High Holy Days. Every little *landsman's shul* and the big synagogues, for weeks, months, before the High Holidays, they would call *chazanim*, the cantors. The *chazanim* had agents. They would get them to audition before the board of trustees. Everybody was an expert.

LARRY SCHNEIDER: There were also thousands of voices out there. Singers were a dime a dozen. Tickets for the High Holy Days were a dollar a ticket. People all knew the cantors' voices, so if they liked the one up the block, so you went to him for the holidays. It wasn't right if you prayed in the other one the whole year, but they did it. There were a lot of fights over that, because they would compete with each other.

"Why are you stealin' my congregant? He belongs in this synagogue."

"What ya mean? He came here for High Holy Days."

"Yeah, but he's been prayin' with me all year."

SELMA HANNISH: Saturday nights were really great. All the cronies would gather at my grandmother's to celebrate *Shabbas*. The women would be there just to serve them. They'd get together and have the *kiddush*. Then they'd have their little brandy, and then the philosophies that were expounded, the world situation, the spiritual situations that were *pinkled*, where one asks a question and the other asks a question back.

The holidays were sheer joy. You never questioned God. He was always with you. It was like living in a sea of golden honey. Even going to *shul* was great. You felt the joy of the *Shabbas*. You were literally in a glow because it was a day closer to the Messiah.

One Yom Kippur, a group of non-Jewish fellas who we never encountered before went looking for trouble. They started with the nastiness, "You lousy stinking Jew bastards." That's all. They said the two magic words, but they didn't know that little Jewish boys

and girls away from their mommies didn't turn the other cheek.
Pow! And they got it. The Jewish fellas and girls beat the living
Jesus out of them. I remember slapping one girl in the mouth and
the blood started to drip, and I almost felt sorry. Then she went to
swing on me, and I grabbed her hair and I hit her. They never
bothered the Jewish kids again.

BETTY CHEN: When I went to elementary school it was all Italians, and then when I got to high school it was all Jewish. We
didn't know the difference and we didn't know we were different.
Once, some girls asked me if I had furniture in my house, because
they thought I was Japanese.

Sometimes, out in the street there were problems. In those
days, if a Chinese woman went out, she wore the Chinese loose
pants and blouse. It looked like pajamas.

"Oh, look at the Chinks."

They follow you, and there's nothing you can do because there's
a whole gang of them. We never went to Columbus Park at night
in the dark, because they would rob you. Then there were some
Chinese men who knew karate and put them down and it was
quiet for a while.

JOHN ENG: I went to school down here, I had lot of trouble, and
I was expelled. The problem was the Irish and Italian kids. You
know, "Hey, Chinky, go back to Chinatown!" You think Mulberry
Street was Chinatown then? It was all Italian.

I fought back. I had to. If you didn't, they would get you, but
my father didn't like it. He said I should just accept it and keep
quiet, but I refused and I was the one who got expelled.

• • •

LARRY SCHNEIDER: My whole bar mitzvah cost eight dollars.
A bottle of whiskey, two or three pounds of cake, a dollar or two
for the synagogue, and if you had a rabbi, say a dollar for the
rabbi. He hadda make a livin' too, and that was the whole bar
mitzvah.

Holidays at home were strictly observed. We had somethin' to
eat, but I wouldn't call it a big meal. We had the traditional wine,
plus the little bagels. Passover was a very strict tradition. We started
cleanin' up the house two months in advance. There were separate
dishes that you put away in a special place. They would lay there

all year long. You couldn't take 'em out until the day before. You were afraid they would mix 'em up. My mother feared that the older boys, who weren't religious, that they shouldn't take one of them dishes and make some food and then put it back in the same place. They were wild kids.

NAT FORMAN: The first time I got drunk was in 1912. School was over for eight days because it was the first eve of Passover.

My friend Bummy Gutterman and I went over to Goreck Street to get a gallon of wine from the wine cellar where his grandfather worked. Down in the cellar, I see the old man blow on a red tube that was in the barrel. Then he put the tube from his mouth into the gallon jug. I went to the side where he didn't see me and I blew into another tube. The wine comes up. I have no jug, so I drink and keep drinking. Then Bummy yells, "Let's go home, Natie." Goreck Street is all cobblestones. As we were walkin' home, I kept saying, "Bummy, what's the matter with these cobblestones? Are they slipping out?"

"Naw," he says, "they're in tight."

I said they were loose, but he said they never get loose. When we got to my house, I was holding on to the banister five floors up into the bedroom onto the bed. I flopped onto the bed dead drunk. Seder time came. My mother tried to wake me, but I couldn't get up. I had a headache.

SAM KISSELOFF: On Passover, we would go to Streit's on Rivington Street to get matzohs. You'd stand on a long line, and you could see the hot matzohs coming off the assembly line. We'd buy a five-pound box, and they would pack it right there and give it to you. Then we went further down Rivington to the next street to buy Shapiro's kosher wine. They had the wine in big casks. You went with the guy, and he would show you the Málaga, the Concord, extra heavy Málaga. You could take a taste from all of them, and by the time you bought the wine you were dead drunk.

BETTY CHEN: For the Chinese New Year, which is a Buddhist holiday, Mother made *har gow*, which was like dim sum with the dough and a filling of pork and shrimp. We were one of only two Christian families in Chinatown then, so I didn't particularly look forward to the New Year. All the girls stayed home, but I went to school because we didn't celebrate it. The parade wasn't much then either.

In her heart, my mother was still a Buddhist. She celebrated the New Year by putting new flowers in the house, a red tablecloth and all those proverbs hanging around, like "God bless our home" or "Good health to you."

In the Buddhist home, they worshiped their ancestors. There was a wooden platform, and they had incense burning and their ancestors' pictures, like the mother-in-law and father-in-law, not her own mother and father. *[She laughs.]* They burned the incense and bowed three times before the pictures. They did this on the first and fifteenth of the Chinese calendar.

JOHN ENG: Twice a year, on New Year's and Easter, my mother made a ceremony for the spirits. She put out three cups of wine and three chopsticks on a table for the God in Heaven, Earth, and the human spirit, so they could eat. Then we went to the cemetery and she put out the cup and chopsticks on the grave.

BETTY CHEN: All Chinese people believe in ghosts. They say if a person dies, his spirit or ghost comes back and haunts the house. This was Buddhist thinking. When the Chinese have a funeral, they have the cortege go in front of their home or the store where he worked. Then they have a person sit in the house and keep all the lights on in case the spirit wants to come back and visit the house.

ABRAHAM HYMAN: The *landslayt shul* was just like a storefront. Inside is benches, the east wall with the *orem kodesh*, the ark. Some of the richer congregations could afford better ornaments, and some were just simple. Some would have 100 people. Some could have 200 people.

There were about 200 people in our *landsmanschaft*. Sometimes, in time of need, you went to the *landsmanschaft*, or *landslayt* would find out that a fellow is starving or the wife is sick or a child is very sick, and it would go through the community, and they would make a little money for them. The *landsmanschaften* and the Workmen's Circle also had a medical service.

MOLLIE HYMAN: And you would get a lot of news from Europe about this one or that one.

ABRAHAM HYMAN: That was very important. You still had a feeling for the old country. And when you died, you were entitled to a burial plot in a *landsmanschaft* cemetery. Later on, they disappeared, the *landsmanschaften*, because the second generation didn't need them anymore.

MOLLIE HYMAN: Every *landsmanschaft*, if they wanted to raise a little money for the destitute member or the organization, they would buy tickets in blocks and sell them to the members.

We'd go to all the operas and concerts. You never had enough money to get a seat. You go standing for a quarter or fifty cents. You had to come early because they let in only so many standees. You'd end up spending two hours standing on the line to get in. Then you wait an hour until the show starts. Still, you wanted to be there.

You had all those Jewish shows on Second Avenue, the Thalia on the Bowery, the Jacob Adler, and there were a few more smaller theaters. These theaters uplifted the quality of life in the neighborhood.

ROBERT LESLIE: You couldn't keep me away from the Russian Theater. Thomashefsky, Jacob Grodin, *God, Man and the Devil*, Paul Muni. I went to all of the plays. I was a reporter for the *Call*, so I had a ticket. We saw translations of Shakespeare. The people who saw them were uneducated. After one of the plays, the audience shouted, "Author, author!" They wanted Shakespeare to come out. My wife, Dr. Sarah, was a great lover of the theater. Once, we were sitting there and the woman in back was eating grapes and spitting the pits in back of our neck. She turned around and said, "Spit down, not up."

They didn't have what we call "politeness," or bourgeois reactions. They paid a ticket $2.50, and they were the bosses.

MOLLIE HYMAN: I saw Chaliapin in *Boris Godunov*, that I'll never forget. I heard Caruso two days before he died. One day, I stood in line and was very close to see Galli-Curci in the Chicago Opera. I was freezing, and I didn't have a ticket, and just when I was in front, they closed the window. I was so cold and aggravated, I started to cry, and you know, they let me in, one more.

•  •  •

HENRIETTA GILBERT: When my parents went to meet my brother's in-laws, they were, let's say, lower class, because her parents were butchers. They lived on Orchard Street, where they had a store. We got all dressed up, and we went to visit her parents, who lived in back of the store. My father was extremely uncomfortable. He held my hand and my brother's hand so that he didn't have to talk. He was "taking care of the children."

SAM KISSELOFF: Pop started the store on 157 Orchard Street in 1930 with a man named Wallach. Eventually, he took it over. He sold domestic items. He worked from ten o'clock in the morning until past midnight. When I was a kid, I never saw him vertical, except Yom Kippur, Rosh Hashanah, and Passover. Later, when things got better, we would see him Sundays during July and August.

You stayed open late because you never knew if somebody would wander in. He didn't have any help until later on. He sat in front of the store on an orange crate waiting for someone to walk in.

On Orchard Street between Rivington and Houston, there were seventeen stores just like his. The merchandise was exactly the same. The competition was fierce, but they were all friendly except Kaplan and Goldberg, who had the stores next door to him. As long as one would open, the other one wouldn't close. At one time, some of them came around with a petition, "Let's all close on Sunday." If one of them wouldn't sign, they all stayed open. If Kaplan signed, my father wouldn't sign. If Kaplan didn't, my father would.

Pop and Kaplan were mortal enemies. There was a stand outside the store. You laid all your stuff on that stand. In order to block off Kaplan, my father would pile up blankets and beach towels so you couldn't see Kaplan's store when you came up the street. Of course Kaplan piled up his stuff on the other side. If my father put out towels four for a dollar, Kaplan put out towels five for a dollar. My father would put them out six for a dollar, Kaplan would put his out seven. It got to a point where it was crazy. Of course, if you tried to buy the seven towels for a dollar, you had very little chance of getting them.

"They have holes in them." "They're not the right color for you."

It was a bait-and-switch type of thing. They had to do it. They couldn't sell them for below cost.

ABRAHAM HYMAN: We would go to Canal Street. Almost every men's clothing store there had a puller. Otherwise, how would you have customers? They would stand at the door—men with a derby. He would say, "C'mon, *guten* suit." If you resisted, they would pull you. They would almost pull your sleeves off.

He would promise you a bargain. He'd say, "Your son is in rags. C'mon in."

"But I'm not on Canal Street for a suit."

"That's no answer," and sometimes they pulled you in and sold you a suit.

They would bargain. My brother once bought a suit with a lot of small price labels on it. When he came home, he found under every label was a hole.

SAM KISSELOFF: Orchard Street was absolutely jammed with pushcarts that lined both sides of the street, corner to corner. They were out there every day from ten in the morning until midnight. In the middle of winter, they kept themselves warm with kerosene stoves.

They sold food off the pushcarts. They even sold eyeglasses. They gave you a newspaper, and you just tried on one pair after another until you found a pair that you liked. They probably did a better job that way than going to an optician.

LARRY SCHNEIDER: My father peddled bananas and sometimes potatoes. He was one in a million peddlers. He'd push the pushcart to Greenpoint in Brooklyn. It took him over an hour to get where he had customers. He'd get up at 5:30, go get his pushcart from the pushcart stable on Sheriff Street, where he rented it for about a quarter a day. Then he'd wheel it over to the wholesaler on Attorney Street. Then he'd take it over to the ferry to Greenpoint. He'd make about $2.00 or $2.50 a day, six days. That's all, them years. He'd help feed a family of seven on that.

Eventually, my father got a little old. He couldn't push it so far, so he wound up with a pushcart on Rivington Street, which was called Pushcart Alley. They had pushcarts lined up from the river all the way up to First Avenue, but there was practically no profit. He'd buy a banana say eight for a dime, ten for a dime and sell them for two cents apiece.

SIDNEY PITTER: When the horse-drawn wagons used to pass by up the street, the pushcarts used to team up for a joke. As the wagons passed by, the peddler would say out of the side of his mouth, "Halt!" The horse would stop. Every pushcart. They did that up the whole block. The driver would curse like crazy, because it would take him an hour to get up one street.

SAM KISSELOFF: My father used to attract all the characters. There was Abie, who was a very sweet dark-haired man, but he liked to put heavy talcum powder on his face. He was one of these Boris Thomashefsky types right out of Cafe Royale. He would mince around, but he used to brag how tough he was. He would hold up his elbow and ask my father to feel the bone. "Touch it, see how hard it is."

NAT FORMAN: In those years, lots of leaden dimes, quarters, and half-dollars were in circulation. Housewives and storekeepers were always getting stuck with them. The candy-store lady across the street from me once showed me a leaden quarter that somebody had stuck her with. She felt like crying.

My father was a peddler, and time and again he would end up with them. He would put it in his back teeth and see if he could bend it. If he couldn't, then he knew it was lead. Then he would take a "hommer," slam it down and straighten it out.

He would take a potato, cut it in half and put in the leaden coin. The next night he would take out the coin and it would be all shined up. Then he would instruct me to go to Itzak Goldberg, who was blind as a bat and who owned a large liquor-and-wine store on West Houston and Pitt Street. I would buy a bottle of brandy for my father. I put the coin on the counter. He takes it, gives me the bottle and out I go. That's how we got rid of the leaden coins. • • •

SAMUEL POGENSKY: My parents pushed me to be a musician. I loved it, but I didn't have it in me. I played the violin for many years. I used to play with a band in the tough neighborhoods in, say, 1915. We had a piano, cornet, drum, and fiddle. I got seventy-five cents a night, and Saturday afternoon $1.25 and Saturday night $1.75. I played quadrilles and a lot of waltzes and two-steps.

All the people they came from Europe, they went to the dances on Eldridge Street and Rivington Street, toughest neighborhoods in the world. They liked the way I used to play the "Weddin' March." They used to holler out, "Pogensky, play the 'Weddin' March'!"

I played job after job. I played a show called *George M. Cohan's Stock Company: It Pays to Advertise*. After school, I'd be playin' the fiddle in my father's shop, and he'd say, "Go on there, you bastard, I have to fix a pair of shoes." He didn't like me in there scratchin' all day.

LARRY SCHNEIDER: I went to religious school, and there was no money around, so I used to steal from the pushcarts. Not that I wanted to steal, I was just hungry. If somebody stole from my father and I seen it, there would be a big battle. The yeshiva kids used to steal. They were rough kids, too. One day, when I was eleven years old, the rabbi pulled my ear, and he spit at me, so I said, "What'd ya do that fer?"

He said, "You're a bad boy."

I hauled off and hit him a shot and knocked him flat. I kayoed the rabbi. They called up my mother and father and said, "Your son's a gangster."

"Eleven years old and a gangster?"

"Yes, take him out."

They threw me out of parochial school.

We had fights galore, the Italians and the Jews. They called us kikes and we called them wops. The Italians lived on one side of the bridge, and the Jews lived on the other side. There were terrific battles with stones and bottles, and broken heads. There were gangs that were bad, kids with knives. I never joined gangs like that, because I came from parochial school. Still, Lepke Buchalter was on the honor roll at the Jacob Joseph Yeshiva, one of the greatest yeshivas in the city of New York. It was filled with learned people. Louis Buchalter—how could a man like that become the top gangster in Murder Incorporated?

SAMUEL POGENSKY: It was very tough around Avenue D. You couldn't walk through there. That's where they had, at that time, Black Hands. They were Italians. They'd show you a knife. "Give me your money or I'll kill you."

The Jews were thieves of the smaller class or the biggest class. We had a little club in the cellar. One day, I said to one of the fellas we needed some cups. He brought little cups, a thousand of them. He stole them all. One day, we said we wanted pearl knives. He came back with so many pearl knives I was ashamed to look at 'em.

They were all thieves. But they were decent thieves. I hung out with a nicer crowd. They weren't pickpockets—they would steal a whole store. They were well dressed. Their mothers bought them nice clothes. They would go in the store. One of them would distract the guy, and the other one would steal.

We used to talk about stealin'. Any store I walked in, I took away somethin'. Look, you didn't have ten cents in your pocket. They also used to steal from one another. The junkies [junkmen] they bought all the stuff you stole. He'd buy it just as quick as he could get it. He didn't ask so many questions, neither, but he knew it was no good to be caught.

My brother was not a pickpocket, but wherever he would go, he brought back a lot of stuff. That was different. My father used to holler at him, "I sent you for a pound of butter, you brought back four pounds. I send you for a package of fish, you bring back nine." But we ate 'em. What the hell.

SAM FLEISCHER: I was born in 1914 on 92 Cannon Street. That was the area where either Murder Incorporated or good decent families would live. Meyer Lansky, Bugsy Siegel, every single one of the major crime people in those years were more or less meeting on the corner of Cannon and Stanton. It was called Auster's Candy Store. It was a very famous egg-cream place. It was the first egg cream in the country, if not the world. Everybody knew Auster's. One of them was killed as a gangster. He looked like the softest, quietest guy. The other Auster ran the store after coming out of jail, and he was a tough little bastard.

LARRY SCHNEIDER: Auster's was also at 3rd Street and Avenue D. He had the most famous egg cream in the United States.

He never told anybody how he made it. They also took numbers. They had a numbers business, and they were probably sellin' illegal liquor, too.

STANLEY AUSTER: We had bookmakers in our stores. They had a lot of customers who would come in and place their bets and have an egg cream. Bookmaking was not considered undesirable among the people. It was the same thing with numbers.
"Who you marrying?"
"Oh, I'm marrying Jakey."
"What does Jakey do for a living?"
"He runs numbers."
"Oh, that's nice."
Sometimes, the bulls would come in and they would pinch everybody in the store, but most specifically they wanted to catch the bookmaker. Nobody was frightened or scared. It was fun. The police station was only three blocks away from the store, so sometimes they didn't bother calling a truck, they just walked them through the street. All they needed was one or two detectives to take in forty people.

There were a couple of bookmakers who used to write the numbers in a hallway on the marble wall. They would have their hands against the wall all the time. If the detective ran in, they would just wipe it clean with their fingers. Once, the detectives took a whole marble slate off the wall as evidence.

It was all really amusing to everyone, because they hardly ever went to jail. Sometimes they went for a couple of days. The most I ever remember a bookmaker going away for was thirty days.

There was a lot of crime at that time, because people were very, very poor and there were a lot of little mob groups. Sometimes they used to shake down businesses for protection money, but there was very little brutality. It was almost like a business. I knew many of these people. Most of the activities were in the numbers game, bookmaking, petty theft and burglary, occasionally armed robbery. They didn't want violence. It wasn't a happy profession, but this was how they made their living. Some of these guys were burglars, but they would only burgle certain places that they felt could afford it. They had a certain ethic about it.

My family was quite well known and comparatively prominent, in the sense that people in that time did not make very much money. There were a lot of small businesses, but they just managed to eke out a living. My family had a number of candy stores. They were very busy and successful stores, and really owed it in part to the very famous egg-cream formula, which my grandfather, Louis Auster, originated.

He was a very dapper-looking man. He was very short, and he was always known as the old man as far back as I remember him. He was an exceptionally good dresser. He wore a diamond stickpin in his tie. He had white-on-white shirts, and almost always with a suit and jacket, even behind the counter.

He came here around 1890. He really didn't have any particular trade or profession. They were just looking for something better. He opened his first candy store on Stanton and Cannon. We sold cigarettes and cigars and everything else that a candy store would have, but our business was ninety-eight percent egg creams.

My grandfather was such a popular character that instead of being like the mayor of the East Side, he was more the pope of the East Side. People would come, and they were delighted not only to get the drink, but to get some kind of acknowledgment from him. He would smile and chuckle. If a pretty girl walked by, give her a little pinch. It was his form of papal benediction.

He was also a sponsor and a patron of the arts, without knowing very much about art or music, poetry, literature, but he knew about the great names: Paul Muni was his idol. There were eight or ten people he gave financial support to. He helped one or two of them come from Europe and supported them until they got started.

He had six sons after the first store got started. He thought he'd have a candy store for each of his children. None of them had much of an education. People say that Jewish people are supposed to be very educated. Well, there were groups of Jewish people who were intellectually oriented and who were scholars, but, for the most part, the original generation were not the scholars. They were the hard-working people who were trying to make a living. They made the money so their children could go to school.

He opened up his most famous store in the late '20s on 3rd Street and Avenue D. The biggest store the family had was at Second Avenue and 7th Street. It had an ice-cream parlor in the back with 125 seats. We had about eight people working there, including my grandfather, who worked there until his eighties.

Second Avenue was like first class—uptown. The swells were there. At that time, it had a lot of Jewish theaters. We were next door to Loew's Commodore. A lot of the actors and actresses came in for egg creams. We were like Sardi's.

He really was an ingenious person. It all started because he wasn't happy with the soda he was selling. He was fooling around, and he started mixing water and cocoa and sugar and so on, and somehow or other, eureka, he hit on something which seemed to be just perfect for him. It is a secret formula. We never reveal it to anybody. People tried to find out how we did it. We had to seal off the back part of the store where we made the syrup. We also painted the windows brown so that no one could watch us. People tried to scrape the paint off the windows so they could look in. They used to study our deliveries to figure out what ingredients we used. I'm the only one alive who knows the formula. I'll probably carry it into my grave.

The formula was delightful. It was more than just a soda, it was like a reason for coming down to mix socially. People came from miles and miles. It seemed preposterous that people would travel so far for a drink, but the egg cream was tantalizing. It was like marijuana. They needed it.

We had fellas that would drink ten drinks while standing in front of the store. There was a group. In order to get into the group, you had to drink ten egg creams in thirty minutes. Most people could drink three easily, but when it came to the seventh and the eighth, you had to be a champ. I remember seeing one fellow on his eighth drink. As he was drinking the egg cream, his feet were swelling up like a balloon. When he drank the ninth drink, the shoelaces popped right off the shoe. It was astonishing.

People would talk for hours about whether or not the egg cream was as good today as it was yesterday. Almost every day, the major topic of conversation in front of my store was who made the egg cream that day. Was it me? Was it my father? One said it was better yesterday. Another said I was stingy. All kinds of things were suggested. There was a group that used to consider themselves experts. They would have heated debates. Sometimes they would engage my grandfather in this kind of dispute. Sometimes I would be questioned. Then they had theories that I didn't make it as good as my father. Or that the egg cream on Second Avenue was better than the egg cream on Avenue D. We of course made the same drink.

The name egg cream was really a misnomer. People thought there was cream in it, and they would like to think there was egg in it because egg meant something that was really good and expensive. There was never any egg, and there was never any cream. There were milk products, but not cream, although it looked and tasted creamy, because we also made a delicious chocolate syrup, which was the base drink.

We had unique cocoa that we used, and a certain substitute type of dairy product. The other syrups have a preservative that makes them flow like glue. Our syrup poured like the water of a lake. We put no preservative in it. We had to sell our supply of egg creams within three days. Otherwise it would start to spoil, even though we had it iced up. So we used to make egg-cream syrup every day, sometimes twice a day. I would make fifty-two quarts a day in the summertime, sometimes more, and that was just my store. Now we didn't serve the syrup we made on Monday that day. It didn't have the same body, and it had sort of an aftertaste. It was too fresh. It had to be cured. We served it on Tuesday.

It was a combination of little things, almost imperceptible, that made the drink extraordinary. We sold the egg cream in glasses — absolutely no paper cup. Very important. It tastes entirely different in a paper cup. Not only did we sell it in glasses, but we had special glasses that had a certain rim, like a bite, and that little edge on the glass somehow or other made the drink seem more satisfying.

It was the bittersweet chocolate. It was the creaminess. It was that it had a lot of foam. It was the chilling of it. It had to be very, very cold. The syrup was chilled, and the seltzer — we had an elaborate system to make the seltzer. We had the most delicious seltzer in the world. Most of the other stores bought canned seltzer. We used two seltzer-making machines. They're called carbonators. We made the seltzer so alive that if you put down the glass, you could watch it from the side and see the bubbles bouncing up in the air like a little geyser for five or ten minutes.

We used chopped ice to cool it. Somehow, with refrigeration it didn't have the same flavor. We used a ten-ounce glass, about three ounces of syrup and seven ounces of seltzer. We didn't use U-Bet and milk and seltzer, like they do today. I can't even drink that.

We sold on the average warm day about 3,000 egg creams. That was Avenue D. Second Avenue was more than double, maybe triple. We worked very fast. My uncle Mendy was like a whirlwind. I used to dish out three glasses at a time, but I couldn't keep up with him.

My uncles were very interesting individuals. Uncle Mendy, for instance, played the violin and the piano simultaneously by playing the piano with his toes. He liked music, especially Rimsky-Korsakov. When he would hear something he thought was beautiful, he would cry, and he was a tough guy.

His friend Louis Cohen was a good whistler. He used to ask Louis to whistle "Scheherazade," and while he was whistling, Mendy would cry. Heaven forbid anybody would say to him, "A man like you crying?" because Mendy would have to show he was a man. Once, a man accused him of having weak tear ducts, and he was last seen running for his life with Mendy in hot pursuit.

My father's name was Julius. He always smoked a lot of cigars. Typically, you would see him behind the counter with his foot up on a low shelf, puffing away, completely satisfied. He was always completely free of worry. Honestly, he never seemed to be preoccupied with anything. I was just the opposite. I was always worried about everything. One day when I was about ten, I asked him about it.

"Daddy, why don't you ever worry?"

He thought for a moment, and then he said, "If I tell you, do you promise not to tell anybody?"

"Yeah."

"I have someone who worries for me."

"What do you mean?"

He had a friend, Little Ike. They both loved cigars and they were inseparable. They didn't talk much, but they liked being together. Ikey was out of work most of the time, but somehow he could afford these cigars.

My father explained it to me. "Little Ike and I have an understanding. Anytime something bothers me, I tell it to Little Ike, and he says he will worry about it. I tell him these things, and the moment I tell him, it's over. I wipe it out of my mind, and Ike takes care of it."

He was serious. He then suggested that when I get older I should find someone. "It's worth it. I pay him for it."

He actually paid Little Ike to worry for him, and that was how Ike could afford his cigars. It was what you call a symbiotic relationship.

My mother was jealous of their relationship, because my father never expressed his worries to my mother. She would ask him sometimes, "What do you worry about?"

"Nothing, I have nothing to worry about."

When they married, immediately after the ceremony they went down to the car to start their honeymoon, and Little Ike was inside ready to go along. My mother blew her stack. Ike shrugged his shoulders, and he just drove them to the station, then got out.

My father later died of a heart attack when he was a relatively young man. I couldn't reconcile that, because he was never sick, and he never worried.

I was about thirteen years old when my father got an attack of what was called a rupture then. Today it is called a hernia. The doctors who came to drink egg creams would warn him about it, but he never wanted to have it operated on because he was afraid. One day, a Dr. Korn came in, and he said, "Julius, you think you have a rupture? Look at this." He took down his pants and showed my father his. I never saw anything so big. He was also scared to have it operated on.

But my father got an attack, and it became an emergency. He was out of commission for almost the whole summer. What to do? He told his brother to make the syrup. When Milton showed up, he said, "Stanley, come into the back room. I'm gonna show you how to make the egg cream."

I came of age suddenly that summer. Like my bar mitzvah: today I am a man. In one afternoon, he showed me how to make the chocolate syrup and then the egg cream. Then he came back the next day to watch me do it. He was satisfied that I did it perfectly. I cooked the syrup and managed the store with my mother and two hired people the whole summer. I'm still very proud of that.

I worked in the store from when I was five years old right through college. I worked there after school until ten or eleven at night, when I went to bed. I had a very limited social life outside the store, but it was a tremendous social life in the store. Every candy store had people hanging around who were out of work. My store had an average of fifty or sixty men—kibitzers. They would have two, three, or four egg creams a night while they were standing there talking.

They were fun and folksy. The candy store was sort of like a stock exchange. Everyone had some little things going on in their lives, and they would sit around and kibitz all day. There was Tiger, who was always laughing. Then there was Pussil, who was called Pussil because his last name was Katz. He had an unusually loud voice. If you needed a public-address system, you would say, "Pussil, the store is too crowded. Ask everybody to leave." He would bellow out in English and Yiddish, and immediately the whole store would be empty.

There was Shamo, a derivative of Sam, who looked like Ichabod Crane, and Shamee, who was a midget. He became very famous for a while because he was one of the Philip Morris Johnnies. He was so small that when I was eight and he was twenty, I was bigger and heavier than him. They tried to get him and me into a prizefight, but it never came off.

There was another fellow named Yanke Pollack. He was a very tall, but very pleasant man. He and Shamee had a little routine. They would walk along a corner and wait for some people to walk by who didn't know them, and they would get into a fight. At one point, Yanke would pick him up by the scruff of his neck and toss him a few feet, and Shamee would kick him in the shins. These people would gather and they'd be all aghast at what this monster is doing to this little fellow. Then, just when it seemed that the anger would boil over, Yanke would pick up Shamee like a little child, and they would walk away hugging each other. They did that every two weeks.

BLANCHE LASKY: At that time, everybody had nicknames. Take my old gang. There was Moose. He looked like a moose. Bagels, Shy, Tippi, and me they called Legs, 'cause I had a nice pair of legs. My brother who was very skinny was called Schmaltz, which means fat in Yiddish. My other brother, who was never in a hurry, they called him Jeep. My kid brother, they called him Gangy. He used to talk like a tough guy. If somebody came around and asked for Joe or Pete or Willy, we'd say, "Who?"

STANLEY AUSTER: At our store, there was also Shpuggie, Swindler, and Bumblenose, who had a very large nose, Stuart Meshugenah and Hots, who wanted to be a singer and would break out into a song at the drop of a hat. The only way to stop him was for my father to take a wet rag and throw it smack in his face. There was Ali Baba, who headed a gang of thirteen, fourteen, fifteen-year-old kids. There was Beany, Belly, Boots, Beenchy, Bones, Chatchkiss, Barrelass, Duddy, the Head. The Head was a very mischievous person. He would just sit there and think about some mischief he would do to people. There was Chickie. That was the word you used when the police were coming, "Chickie, the cops!" I think he was a bookie. There was also Chicken, who looked like one.

Then there was Fatstuff, Bigboy, Red Peppers, Pickles, Trigger, and Spikey. Trigger had a broken nose, and he looked like an ex-prize fighter, but he was not. He was a very good-natured guy. Spikey was a war hero. He fought in the African campaign and was listed as missing in action. We thought he was dead. Then one day, I'm sitting at the door. I look up and Spikey walks in. I got a chill up my spine that I can still feel today. Everyone rushed over and hugged him and congratulated him. He didn't talk much about it, but he had been separated from his group. Seeing him was one of the great experiences, to see someone come back from the dead.

There was a guy we called Pipick—Yiddish for navel. He was lost in the war. Everybody liked him. He was very quiet. When people talked to him, he was always looking down—at his *pipick*, I suppose. "What are you looking at your *pipick* for?" That's how nicknames are formed. So you had to be careful where you looked, otherwise that's what you would be called.

LARRY SCHNEIDER: There was a guy named Pretty Amberg [*pronounced AM-boig*]. He was a gangster. He was ugly as could be. He hung out in a delicatessen on Cannon Street. If you were to sit down at a table near him and stare at him because he wasn't so pretty lookin', he would go over and throw all your delicatessen off the table. Him, they killed. They bombed his car. He blew up— you know, a loaded car.

STANLEY AUSTER: Pretty Amberg got his nickname after he was shot in the cheek. He was a very sick and violent man. You heard stories about him getting a shoeshine from a kid, and when the kid was finished shining the shoes, he would kick him in the face—real senseless cruelty.

One day I was visiting my grandfather at Second Avenue and 7th Street. Suddenly, my uncle said to me, "We're gonna be visited by someone who is very well known." It was Bugsy Siegel.

A few minutes later an unusually wide automobile drove up and six men came out of the car. Each of them were like wrestlers. They were big, big men. Three of them came in and looked around the store and waved to my grandfather and slapped him on the back.

"Hello, Louis, how are you, Pop?"

My grandfather was delighted to see them. They looked over the store like Secret Service men. The other three were standing outside. When they got the signal that all was clear inside the store, the three went out and stopped all the pedestrian traffic on Second Avenue and 7th Street in order to open up an aisle for one person, who came in another car. He got out of the car with two men.

I was more impressed with the six men working with him than him. They had that look like you don't mess with these people. So he came in, and they cleared all the customers out. He ordered a whole box of cigars, and he brought presents for my grandfather, a couple of shirts and Sulka shorts and ties, which were enormously expensive.

They were there for about fifteen or twenty minutes. The egg creams flowed. Then he peeled off some bills from a roll of money, but my grandfather said, oh no, it was on him. They went back and forth about it, and then they left with lots of regards for each other.

"Any time you need anything, Pop, let me know." It was just like a visiting dignitary.

Jews were not supposed to be very good fighters, but we had some who were very tough. There was one guy there, Lefty Louis. He never fought with one person. He was too good. He would seldom even fight with two people. He would only fight with three or four at the same time. No one was a match for him. He was a very nice man, but he was like steel.

Bigboy was a very powerful person. I once saw him pick up the back of a car and move it. Bigboy once knocked out a horse that suddenly panicked. It started running away with its wagon and knocked over a baby carriage. Bigboy ran after it. He grabbed the reins but the horse kept going. He jumped down, ran ahead of the horse, and he punched the horse in the head. The horse dropped in his tracks. It was a complete knockout, and Bigboy was the hero of the day.

There was another tough guy, who had just come out of jail. He always liked me. He had been in jail most of his life, and he always spoke very, very softly, as convicts were supposed to speak.

He expressed his friendship by asking me about my schoolwork. [*He whispers:*] "Hi, Stanley, how are you today?" He was always full of smiles and warmth and fondness. He would have his egg cream, pay for his drink and out he would go. Then I found out things about this guy, that he was a cold-blooded murderer. He was his own Murder Incorporated. When he would come by, even the tough guys would stay away from him.

He was severely psychopathic, and later he was machine-gunned in the street. But before that, his wife's brother came into the store when I was in charge. I was maybe thirteen. He started fooling around with the girls in the store. He was pestering them, and he started using some dirty words. You didn't do that around girls then. They'd say, "Hey, there are girls here." Of course, the minute a girl walked out you heard all kinds of things.

Anyway, I said to him he was going to have to leave. He said a dirty word to me. I had to do something. Years ago, the proprietor had a great deal of authority. If he said, "Get the hell out," no matter who he said that to had to leave. My uncle Mendy once threw Rocky Graziano out of the store.

I wasn't a fighter, but I had to do something. I put my arm around his arm, and tried to get him out. We pushed each other, but I made a maximum effort and I pushed him out. Then I realized: What did I do? I just pushed out the kid brother-in-law of this killer. I was really worried—really worried.

Two days later, he comes into the store. I was all alone. I said to myself, "Oh, my God, I'm dead."

He walked very quietly. I was trying to see if he had a gun on him. He comes over, the same sweet smile. [*He says in a faint voice:*] "Hello, Stanley, can I see you in the back for a moment?"

I give him his egg cream. He takes it and walks to the back, and I say to myself, "Now I'm gonna get it."

The only thing that made me happy was that he was holding an egg cream, and I said to myself, "I don't think anybody has ever been shot by someone who had an egg cream in his hand."

He says, "I heard you had some trouble with my kid brother-in-law."

"No, it was nothing, really nothing."

"No, I heard he misbehaved and spoke out of turn and you and him had a little shoving match."

"It really wasn't anything. Don't think of it."

I tried to talk to him about my schoolwork, but he didn't want to hear it. Then he says, "Well, I want you to know. You won't have any trouble with him again."

Years ago, when they said that, it meant the guy was dead. He said he saw him the day before and beat the hell out of him. "I gave him such a beating I broke one of his arms. I think he's still in the hospital. He'll never bother you again." And he never did.

Larry Schneider: The gangsters used to be practical jokers. Everyone thought they were serious. They would take a man. They'd lay him out on the sidewalk, and they put a white sheet over him, and they'd start prayin'. I seen it. They were saying *Yisgidal, yisgidash*, the chant for the dead. People would stare, and they wouldn't laugh. They didn't dare.

Charlie Workman killed Dutch Schultz. He did twenty-six years in jail for it. You looked at this man, and you wonder how he could be that vicious. He looked like a dapper little college man. He was short, well dressed. He hung out on the corner with Pretty Amberg. They didn't see eye to eye. So one time, they were gamblin' with each other, and Charlie Workman won everything from Pretty Amberg, but Pretty Amberg said, "Look, I still wanna play."

"What ya got for collateral?"

"My false teeth."

"Gimme the teeth."

And he gave him money for the teeth. Now Charles Workman won the teeth, too, and he refused to give 'em back.

There was one guy, Moe Sedway. His mother lived on Pitt Street. In later years, he was a big shot in Las Vegas. His mother never knew that he was a racketeer. He used to come down and give his mother a thousand dollars at a time. This fellow never killed nobody. It was rackets.

He said, "Ma, I got such a job in California, I'm rollin' in money."

She never knew. She would take these thousands and put it in the bank. The police were lookin' for him. One day he wrote her a letter, "Dear Ma, I'm comin' in next Tuesday." She said around the neighborhood, "My Moe is comin' in." The police heard, and they were waitin' for him. She was the one who gave him away.

S A M  F L E I S C H E R : I remember Charles Workman's father passing by our grocery, and he said to a friend of his, "My son, he hangs out with those bums—those gangsters." And here his son was one of the biggest. He killed Dutch Schultz.

S T A N L E Y  A U S T E R : There was a time that a card game was running in back of the store on a Friday night. The game began at 1:30 in the morning. There were four players and about fifteen kibitzers. I was in the front, taking care of a few customers. They would make some noise, arguing, shouting. A complaint was made to the police about the noise. Two detectives came into the store. They came rushing behind the counter to the back.

Now we had a toilet. It was the most uncivilized toilet you could ever imagine. It really stunk. There was no ventilation. You had to have an awful bellyache to want to use the toilet. I think I used it twice in all the years I was in the store—then, for no more than twenty-five seconds, which was as long as I could hold my breath. Well, the cops came in. Shamo ran into the toilet and closed the door. When the detectives came in, one of them slid a bar over the door to make sure nobody would try to escape by running to the toilet. He didn't know Shamo was in there.

The cops said they had to take everybody in. It was all good-natured when these things happened. They didn't usually arrest them, but just took their names and let them go after a couple of hours. They sent them all outside and told them to walk down to the station.

My father asked the detective if he could lock up, take me home, and then go to the station. The detective said okay, so he and I went home. Then my father figured they wouldn't miss him, so he went to bed. Suddenly, he started laughing hysterically as he realized Shamo was still in the toilet. My mother was worried that he would be asphyxiated. "You can't survive more than a couple of minutes in there."

A few minutes later, the doorbell rang. It was the two detectives, looking for my father. On the way to the station he asked them if he could go back to the store to let Shamo out. "I hope he's still alive."

"You're not gonna fool us this time," the cop said. He wouldn't let him go.

Poor Shamo. My mother went down and got him. She said he was on the floor of the toilet breathing air through the crack. She said he was screaming. He had completely taken leave of his senses. For weeks people talked about him being stuck in the toilet. We gave him free egg creams for a week in order to make it up to him.

NAT FORMAN: Around the corner from my house was a small street, Manhattan Street. It was about ten feet wide, and it ran from East Houston north to East 3rd Street. As kids we used to play on the street. Sunday the big guys used to have crap games. In front of 3 Manhattan was a lamppost about ten or twelve feet high with a mantle inside. The outside was a glass round dome. Every evening a man would come with two poles and light the lamp. Next morning he would come around and put the lamp out.

Goo Goo Bishop was one of the big guys. Time and again when the crap game would start, he would climb up the lamppost, put his glass eye somewheres on the lamp and say, "You watch for a cop."

STANLEY AUSTER: We used to close our store at one o'clock in the morning, but people didn't go home. They just hung out in the street. One of the guys was Babe Cannella. He had a huge appetite and was enormously heavy. One night, Babe happened to say he could eat ten pounds of hot dogs at one time. Immediately, two or three carloads of people drove off to Coney Island on a bet that he couldn't do it.

On the way, we had to figure out how many hot dogs would be in ten pounds. We decided around sixty-two. Then there was some dispute whether you had to eat the roll with it or not—mustard, and so on. How much you could drink in between? Should you drink in between?

Babe started eating. He was up to thirty, thirty-five, approaching forty, and at three o'clock in the morning people were coming from all over to watch. The boardwalk became deserted as everybody crowded into Nathan's. He finished 'em. But part of the bet was that he had to drive back home. He got into his car and he collapsed behind the wheel. They needed eight men to take him out, and they took him to the hospital nearby and they pumped his stomach. The next day he was back at the store having his egg creams.

LARRY SCHNEIDER: Most of these guys around us were rum-runnin'. On the East River they had a rum boat, and maybe two or three in the mornin' they'd unload this illegal liquor. In fact, we had an Orthodox Jew we called the Rabbi sellin' illegal liquor. He got locked up quite a few times. He got put in jail with the beard, with the *tefillin,* and with his siddur—an orthodox Jew. He used to sell hootch, almost wood alcohol, to the Bowery bums, and he'd make a livin' from that. He sold it out of his apartment on Ridge Street. They gave him ten days in jail, and in jail he did all his *davenin'* [praying].

STANLEY AUSTER: There were two guys who used to hang out in the store. They were bootleggers. One day, as they were in the store, a car pulled up outside, and two detectives got out and started running into the store. One of the guys inside pulled out two bundles of money and thrust them into my pocket and told me to go outside and play.

I walked across the street to my friend Jackie, whose father was a dentist. I showed him all the money. He said, "Good, we can play Monopoly."

He took out his Monopoly set, and instead of using the paper money, we started using the real thing. At some point his father came in and did a double take. He screamed, "My God, Jackie, where did you get all that money?"

"Stanley gave it to me."

He called my father. My father came up and took the money and gave it back. Forever after that, those guys loved me.

• • •

LARRY SCHNEIDER: The Depression was terrible. People were livin' in cardboard boxes under the Williamsburg Bridge. I seen people on the street beggin' for pennies, sellin' whatever they could find—apples, a fountain pen, somethin' they picked up or stole—to get a coupla pennies. People that didn't wanna steal had to steal. Basically, they were honest people, but they stole to survive. They'd steal clothin' off a rack on Orchard Street, pants, shirt, shoes.

SAMUEL POGENSKY: Oh, you don't know what a depression means. I punched the wall and I hollered, "Enough is enough. I don't wanna go through no more."

Mostly, I was a contractor. They used to say, "If Sam Pogensky don't do the job, the job is no good."

I had five men workin' for me. I used to take a job for nothin' in order to keep them goin'. I needed the men, you know? I took a job for $800. He says, "Why do you take it for so cheap?"

I say, "I have men not workin'. I might get a good job." He might have another guy to take it for $800. I probably pay out $900 to my men. I went to loan sharks tryin' to cover. I always had friends. With loan sharks you'd pay one for five. My friends would charge me one for ten. They always gave me a break.

It was no good, that's all, and you suffer like a fuck. Every month I lost money to the loan sharks. Sometimes you didn't pay, and he'd come over here, "You got a couple of saws here?" The saw cost me eight or ten dollars, I said they cost me thirty dollars. I gave them to him, and I made a little money that way. If I had a drill that sold for $150, I let it go for eighty, but that drill only cost me sixty.

SELMA HANNISH: My dad left us. He loved us all in his way, but his way was a very peculiar way. In my family the father figures are very vague. They're there to make babies, to beat up on you, and to make trouble. They're not there for anything else.

Things were so bad for us but the landlord would still beg her, "Please, don't move. You're such a nice clean lady, I'll write it down."

When things got better, my mother kept a record, and she paid what she owed him. He couldn't believe it. "I should have a medal made up for you."

What did we pay, seven dollars a month? When he was there, my father didn't make seven dollars a month to pay the rent. Oh, things were so bad. You borrowed from everybody. When you didn't borrow, you didn't have, but you didn't go on charity. One winter it was so bad my mother had to cut up the dining-room furniture piece by piece and feed it to the stove. They talk about poor today!

The streets were paved with wooden blocks. They set the wooden blocks with tar, and when they ripped up the streets to replace them with asphalt, all the women in the neighborhood ran, because it was a source of firewood—wooden tar-impregnated blocks. My mom was walking up with a sack on her back and one in her hand. I was walking behind her to steady her sack, and she said, "Oh, my God," and she doubled over. She ruptured herself. It didn't stop her. She was like a beaver. We loaded the storage room up with enough wooden blocks that she didn't have to buy coal.

ROSE HALPERN: The Depression hit us very badly. My mother lost her job. Finally, our neighbors started to plead with her to go on welfare. Grandma thought, how could she do that to me? To us it was a terrible thing.

Finally, they were about to put us out, and she agreed. We applied for it, and they asked us a million questions. I had to go for my mother, to be the interpreter. They asked you if you worked, how much money you had. You had to be poor all the time. They paid your rent and a little more, but you couldn't exist on that little money, so my mother finally got herself a part-time job. She didn't report it. Whenever the investigator came to the house, my mother wasn't there, so we told her that she went to the welfare office.

After I graduated high school, an agency used to send me on one interview after another. They said to me, "If you didn't say you were Jewish, I could get you so many positions."

The agency then sent me to Blue Cross in Brooklyn. As soon as the man looked at my application he said, "This job has already been filled."

I said, "You know that job isn't filled. You saw I was Jewish."

He was astounded that I talked to him like that. He said he used to go through the damn thing because he was Catholic. Then he said that one day I would have a job there. In the meantime I got a job doing accounting for a laundry in Brooklyn. Two weeks later, the man from Brooklyn left a message at your grandfather's store that he had an opening.

I went to work for Blue Cross. On sixteen dollars, I supported the whole family. I paid the rent, food, everything. My mother wasn't well, and she never went back to work, not because she didn't want to work, but because she couldn't. She was worn out.

We had a fire one night. Everything went down. Three buildings. Two people died. There were bars on the windows, and they couldn't get out. It was winter. We got out in our nightgowns, and I had one shoe of my grandmother's and one shoe of my own. That was it. We had nothing.

We stayed outside, and we watched the building, and then some neighbors took us in and gave us something to drink. In the morning, my mother borrowed some clothes and took the trolley car to Williamsburg and there got some more.

At Blue Cross, they got together and they made a collection for me. With that I was able to buy some things to wear. After that we moved to Blake Avenue in Brooklyn.

MOLLIE HYMAN: We went into business with a candy store or a luncheonette. We had a store where the World Trade Center is now. Abe calls it a tomb over our store. The *Journal* was in that building. All the newspapers were in that area. Hearst, Jr. used to send down somebody to buy cigars from us. He still owes us a few dollars.

ROBERT LESLIE: At Ellis Island, I had too much empathy with the immigrants. I found out after five hours a day I was exhausted. I was reassigned to the Public Health Department. They made me a cholera expert. I was soon sent to Africa and the Philippines. Then I met my wife, Dr. Sarah. We got married, but I was away too often, so I gave up medicine and I became a printer.

My mother died when she was eighty-two. With all his drinking, my father actually outlived her by two years. Don't laugh when I tell you this. I had an autopsy done on him. I wanted to see what his liver looked like. Cirrhosis of the liver makes a liver look like it is corrugated. His liver was smooth, and Dr. Hyman said to me, "Your father drank to preserve his liver." I couldn't believe it.

LARRY SCHNEIDER: All durin' the Depression, I couldn't take out no girl. You sat there by the stoop, talkin' with her and everything. Then she went up to the house and you went up to the house. You couldn't take her no place. You had no money. You went to Pitt Street Park or Jackson Street Park and fooled around with a girl for free. Some went a little further than others. Babies were born, and some families moved out because they were shamed.

I didn't take out a girl until just before I went into the service. I put in about three and a half years, almost four years in the South Pacific. I came out of the service, and they owed me four years of schoolin'. I never took it. I thought, "Why waste it?" Schoolin' was a fraud. You'd go to school, sign your name and go home. I didn't wanna waste it.

I had a good singin' voice. I sang with some of the biggest cantors in New York. I bummed around from 1945 to 1947. Then I worked in the post office until 1949. I worked thirty years as an inspector for the Board of Health.

HENRIETTA GILBERT: My father went bankrupt in 1931. Division Street had been deteriorating. Businesses were moving to other areas. He had wanted to move the business to Saratoga, but my mother refused to move because my mother was obsessed with my oldest brother, and she thought we'd be leaving him behind. My parents stopped talking to each other. The business went bankrupt. In 1932, my father had a stroke and he died a week later.

MARTHA DOLINKO: When I wasn't working, I went to the *Forvitz* building to hear speakers. I also went to Socialist meetings. I am still a Socialist.

I met my husband at a meeting. I knew him in Europe. Then I bumped into him in a delicatessen. He said he was going to a meeting, so we went to a meeting. I must have been thirteen. My mother hollered at me I'm not fourteen, why did I keep company with a boy? I got married when I was sixteen. My mother made a wedding in a small hall near East Broadway. There was a small band and dinner. It was very simple.

My husband worked in shops. He worked in a capmaker's shop for many years. He was a plain person and we loved each other. He worked during the day and studied in the evening. We studied English and we studied socialism.

Sometimes, the Workingman's [sic] Circle, God bless them, had a place where they used to take us on weekends. Everybody went to Coney Island to put their feet in the water. Sometimes, the Henry Street Settlement used to take us on the bus, and we would ride all the way up Fifth Avenue. We would see where all the German Jews lived with the goyim. And I would ask the question, "Why do they show me all those beautiful buildings and on the East Side there are so many dumps? That's a capitalistic system? I don't like it."

SELMA HANNISH: I met my husband in a social club. He was a neighborhood kid. He was in the Navy. It was a very quick courtship. I think it was because my mother had four girls. I was the oldest. She said, "Nobody is making me a first." The idea was if I made a first, the others would get married, too.

We got married right here. I still remember the rabbi saying, "I now give you permission to engage in marital cohabitation." I had no idea what it was. I was the oldest sister. Nobody spoke about those things. I never even discussed it with my daughter. Oh God, it was the most horrible function that the human body can perform. If you're not taught, you don't know what to expect. It's not a very pleasurable thing.

SAM KISSELOFF: Pop loved to go to the beach on Sundays. He was a great swimmer. He could swim on his back all day. After World War II, things got a little better, and he got Saturdays off, too. Then he liked to stay in the bathroom. He'd go in there Saturday morning and come out nearly Saturday afternoon. He took a shower, a shave, and whatever else he did in there nobody knows. That time was a luxury to him, and he enjoyed it.

SOL KAPLAN: I knew Kisseloff, sure I knew Kisseloff. He was a powerful man, a smart man, too. I used to have fun with him. He was well-to-do, he told me. He told me he's got a car, so I says, "A car, well, where is it?"

"It's in the garage."

So I asked, "Does your wife got a fur coat?"

"Sure!"

"Where is it?"

"It's in storage."

I asked, "Does she got jewelry?"

"Sure."

"Where is it?"

"It's in the box."

"Do you got money?"

"Sure."

"Where is it?"

"It's in the bank."

"You got nothing! If anybody's got nothing, he can also say the same thing. You can't use it. You can't display it."

I remember when he got sick. I walked him home. It was on a Sunday. I was coming home from my work and I saw him standing. I said, "Mr. Kissel, what are you doin' here?"

He says, "I don't feel good." So I took him up the house, and his wife let him in. I never saw him after that.

Me? I made money during the Depression. If I was in the desert, I'd make money, because I'm willing to work. Sure. I don't eat many pickles. The doctor tells me not to eat salt, so I only eat a raw pickle a little bit. I used to miss it. No more. I don't eat herrings, too. They stopped me. But some of them are soaked out, so once in a blue moon I cheat a little. And that's what it is.

ROSE HALPERN: My mother had a terrible life. She never had any social life. Her social life was getting together with the neighbors or family. In some ways she had a better life in Russia. She didn't have to work. She was dressed beautifully. There was no such thing as hunger. They were middle class.

They thought there was gold in the streets over here. Whoever thought she would have to work like this or do such dirty work? Imagine coming to a land she knows nothing about, not knowing the language and going door to door trying to peddle things.

Now, all of a sudden they actually became servants. My mother went up to the Catskill Mountains as a chambermaid. What could be worse? You have servants in Europe, and then you became a servant. She had to wait to see what they would leave her as tips. In that way, for her, it was a much more difficult time, because she knew the better times.

Then again, we didn't fear for our lives, and the beauty of it is if you look at it, you say, "My God, these people really didn't give up against such terrible odds."

BETTY CHEN: I never thought of rebelling against my parents. I would have liked a little more freedom, but I would never have thought of asking them. In high school, the others were in the same boat. I never had a date until I was in college. I didn't know anybody who went to dances. Even in college it was hard to get out of the house.

When I was at NYU, someone said to me, "Why don't you ask your father if you could go out of town?"

I said, "Oh, my heaven. I would be scared to death even to suggest it." But I wouldn't even want to go. I would be scared. What would I do in an apartment alone? We were so sheltered. Even NYU seemed far away, and the people there seemed very sophisticated. These wealthy Jewish girls had been to Europe, and the men had been all over the United States. I was in awe. We were really small-town girls.

In my last year in college, someone brought my husband to the house. My mother didn't object. She realized you couldn't meet a young man by sitting in the house. We went out a normal year. I was married in a church on Second Avenue in October 1930.

He worked in a laundry with his father. His father had three sons and everybody left him. He expected the first son to stay with him, but he was going to college and he taught school. My husband was the second son. His father said, "Are you going to leave me, too?" So he stayed with him even though he went to college. The third son got a Ph.D. His father said, "Are you going to leave me, too?" He did. He went to California. They weren't going to stay and work in a laundry, but my husband's conscience bothered him.

Finally, in 1946, his father's daughter said to him, "It's about time you went to see your family." His wife had been in China and he hadn't seen her since 1923, so he went back home and he stayed there until he died.

STANLEY AUSTER: In those years, Schrafft's was best known for their ice cream. They had terrific ice cream but terrible sodas. They contacted my grandfather and told him they wanted to buy the formula. But he felt that if he were to lose the egg-cream formula, what would the family do? He was very reluctant, but big numbers kept flying, thousands of dollars, so he said, "At least I'll go and talk."

There was something like $20,000 involved. They wanted the exclusive use, but my grandfather said no, because then we would have to close the candy stores. Then they said the family could continue to use the formula. Now Schrafft's had a reputation that time of being anti-Semitic. When they were about to come to some terms, someone said something to my grandfather like, "You Jews ought to be happy with the money we're giving you." My grandfather got up and told them what they could do with the deal, and that was it.

We left the Avenue D store just after the war because the area was condemned to build the Jacob Riis and Lillian Wald projects. All of the businesses were given very small amounts of money in settlement. I think we were given $400 for one of the busiest candy stores in the city.

My grandfather died around 1955. He was ninety-seven. Very few people came to the funeral. He left the store when he was eighty-five. He became quite feeble in his early nineties. A lot of people had moved away. The Jewish theaters started closing down. People weren't so interested in egg creams anymore. The Jewishness left the area. It just became an ordinary candy store after a while. That's why my uncle closed up the store on Second Avenue.

The last batch of syrup was made by my uncle Mendy about 1974. Someone did me a favor where I was working. When I asked him how I could pay him back, he asked me if he could have some egg-cream syrup. I asked my uncle Mendy. It was difficult. He had to use a substitute cocoa and one other substitute. He made around eight quarts, and he gave me two. It was delicious, but not exactly the way it was. The soda didn't have enough pressure.

But there was something else. The egg cream is not only a great drink, but it's associated with a certain camaraderie or folksiness among people. Just having an egg cream alone today is not the full flavor of it. It's having an egg cream with a group of people. It's having an egg cream with a pretzel. It's having an egg cream while talking about various things. Nobody ever sat down to have an egg cream. People usually drank it while standing and kibitzing, and those days were long gone.

SELMA HANNISH: I didn't know how to speak English. I used to go home and cry to my mother, "What are they talking?" My poor little mother went to night school, paid my aunt a quarter a week to stay with us so she could learn how to read and write and speak English so she could teach us. My mother deserved any diploma we got.

She insisted we go to school. My mother said, "I gave up my lunches in Europe to learn how to read and write, and I'm giving you the chance to go to school. It's free here. You can go to school here and be anything you want to be. I'm not killing myself so you wouldn't go to school."

We lived in Edgies—the Educational Alliance—or the Seward Park Library. What didn't we do at Edgies? Anything that was beautiful, anything I learned in the way of culture or aspiring for better things, I learned at Edgies. They showed us all the lovely things about art, how to keep clean. If you don't have a bathtub, you heat some water up and you wash yourself, and you have to eat nicely, and you have to brush your teeth. I learned Ping-Pong. I learned how to embroider. I learned how to sing. You name it, Edgies was a home away from home.

ROSE HALPERN: I spent my best years in the Rivington Street Library. There were a lot of kids there. I loved to read fiction. You always like to read about things you don't have. Friday night started the weekend. You used to put your feet in the stove to keep 'em warm, and you would sit and read. That was the best time. We had no movies or radio, so reading meant everything. There was a tremendous desire to learn. I went to the library every free moment I had.

ABRAHAM HYMAN: You have to consider the spirit of the East Side. Like Adam Clayton Powell said, "Don't burn, learn." And that was the spirit. You saw more *landslayt shuls* than saloons. There were educational clubs. Everyone was reading newspapers and reading books. The spirit itself was electric—ambition to get out of this poverty.

You saw kids hanging around the candy stores, but generally it was a drive for education, to get out of this someday. I spent a lot of time at the Educational Alliance Library and the library on East Broadway. It took a little time, but after a little while you could see it flourish. You could see the Jews from the East Side spreading to Brownsville, to Harlem and the Bronx, and each one became an isle of activity, idealistic. The feeling was such that you could feel it with your hand. Your feeling is that a better time is coming, if not for yourself, for your families, for your children.

# Upper East Side

THE GAY '90s found New York society in a restless mood. The elite were bored with million-dollar costume balls and lavish Waldorf dinners. The "right" people needed something new and exciting to stimulate their blue blood cells. Enter Harry Lehr, impresario to the rich. It was his idea to invite a hundred of society's leading canines for a special dinner of pâté and chicken. The master of one unpedigreed guest even purchased a $15,000 diamond-studded collar just for the occasion. Then there was the party for toy dolls, who were seated at a sumptuous dining table while their otherwise adult owners chatted amiably in baby talk.

No wonder Mrs. O. H. P. Belmont threw up her hands in frustration one day and declared, "I know of no profession, art or trade that women are working in today, as taxing on mental resources as being a leader of society."

And who qualified for aristocratic status? In the mid-1800s, Nathaniel P. Willis, editor of *The Home Journal*, defined the select crowd as those who "keep carriages, live above Bleecker, are subscribers to the opera, go to Grace Church, have a town house and country house, give balls and parties."

Maybe Mrs. Belmont was right. Take those arduous nights at the opera, where all ladies of society were required to display their husbands' wealth creatively, and a late and disruptive entrance was *de rigueur.* One night, while the other ladies arrived in their usual sparkling regalia, Mrs. Frederick Vanderbilt appeared dangling a large ruby from a rope of pearls that hung around her waist. She then kicked the jewel all the way to her seat, arriving just in time, one imagines, for the end of the first act.

Mrs. Belmont may also have been responding in part to the rigors of managing a house staff who at times were even haughtier than their employers. Once, Mrs. Stuyvesant Fish invited more guests to a luncheon than her butler, Morton, chose to serve. "I suppose that because you happen to be Mrs. Stuyvesant Fish, you think you can drive up and down the Avenue inviting whom you like to the house," he admonished her. "Well, let me tell you, you can't. Sixteen is my limit, and if you ask any more, they go hungry!"

To be sure, Morton was looking for work the next day, but not before he took his revenge by dumping 300 pieces of gold dinner service onto the dining-room floor.

At least some of society's denizens showed a social conscience. When Mrs. Bradley Martin read newspaper accounts of the Panic of 1893, she decided to help alleviate the suffering by holding a costume ball. After all, she reasoned, if her guests spent thousands of dollars on new outfits, think of all the people who would be employed making them.

From the mid-1800s to World War I, New York society was its own neighborhood, and Fifth Avenue its main artery and showplace. Like any Horatio Alger story, the avenue had a humble beginning, as a dirt path, snaking its way through the hills and forests of Manhattan. It was called the Middle Road until designated Fifth Avenue on the Commissioners' Plan of 1811. By 1824, the newly widened street set out on its cobblestoned way northward from Washington Square, carrying society along with it, like a remora on a whale.

Fifth Avenue extended to 42nd Street in 1837. Where the public library now stands between 40th and 42nd, the Murray Hill Reservoir opened in 1842, to the relief of Manhattanites who were uneasy at drinking water discolored by soot from the city's rooftops. The first World's Fair was held in 1853 just west of the reservoir. It featured a replica of London's famed Crystal Palace. The American version was built of "fireproof" iron and glass. It lasted five years before it burned to the ground in a spectacular fire in 1858.

Following the completion of Central Park in 1876, Fifth Avenue entered its golden age, as some of the country's wealthiest men built their palaces on the street. Eleven mansions were occupied by one or another of the prolific Vanderbilts. Andrew Carnegie, Ogden Mills Reid, and John Jacob Astor owned castlelike homes there as well. Maybe the most spectacular (or vulgar, depending on one's point of view) belonged to Senator William A. King, a copper magnate from Montana. His 130-room white granite mansion at 79th and Fifth inspired this poetic ode:

*Senator Copper of Tonapah Ditch*
 *Made a clean billion in minin' and sich*
*Hiked fer Noo York, where his money he blew*
 *Buildin' a palace on Fift' Avenoo*
*"How," sez the Senator, "can I look proudest?*
 *Build me a house that'll holler the loudest."*

One woman who owned a home on the avenue but was certainly not society material was Madame Restell, abortionist to the rich. From the income of nearly forty years as a "female physician," Madame Restell built an expensively decorated four-story house on the corner of 52nd Street in 1870. She operated openly, daring anybody to shut her down and risk exposing her list of well-connected clients.

Finally, Anthony Comstock, a one-man vice squad in those years, took her on. In February 1878, he placed her under citizen's arrest. Soon after, he supposedly received a huge cash offer to forget the whole thing. When he refused, she went home and slit her throat in the bathtub. Her list was never exposed, but an artist at the humor magazine *Puck* enjoyed a good laugh at her and society's expense a few years later with a lithograph called "Fifth Avenue Four Years After the Death of Madame Restell." It depicted a multitude of society men and women jamming Fifth Avenue with their baby carriages.

To New York society, which certainly didn't mind accepting a robber baron or two, Madame Restell's profession was probably less reprehensible than the fact that she was "new money." Had her family been successfully conducting abortions among the *Mayflower* Pilgrims, her acceptance would have been guaranteed.

Even the spectacularly wealthy Cornelius Vanderbilt had a tough time breaking the barrier. Everybody knew the Vanderbilts were new money. The Commodore, as he liked to call himself, made his fortune as a Staten Island ferryman. It wasn't until he had *so* much money that his family received grudging acceptance. The Vanderbilts were lucky though. They could have been Jewish.

The Queen of Society was Catherine Schermerhorn Astor. According to Fifth Avenue historian Theodore James, Mrs. Astor, aka *The* Mrs. Astor, boasted neither brains nor beauty (she wore a wig to hide a nearly bald pate), but she did have a rather large fortune, owing to a fortuitous marriage and a tireless promoter, her social secretary, Ward McAllister. It was McAllister who insured that the annual Astor ball was the most exclusive of all by limiting the invitations, so that only those who demonstrated proper "fitness" were welcomed. McAllister termed the cream of society "The Four Hundred," noting that 400 was the maximum number who could be accommodated in the Astor ballroom.

*The* Mrs. Astor's presence at her annual affair was a sight to behold, glittering, as she did, like the Milky Way in her diamond tiara, diamond necklace, and diamond-studded corsage. Unfortunately for the guests, there wasn't much sparkle to the conversation. Perhaps due to Mrs. Astor's own intellectual torpor, discussion was limited to what the writer Lloyd Morris called "matters of genuine import. The approved topics were sufficiently absorbing," he wrote. "Thoughtful discussion of food, wines, horses, yachts, cotillions, marriages, villas at Newport and the solecisms of ineligibles would exclude the dangerous attraction of ideas."

One highly visible pair was the hefty "Diamond Jim" Brady and Lillian Russell. Though past her prime, Miss Russell was still considered the most beautiful woman in the world. The two were a common sight parading down the Waldorf-Astoria's famed Peacock Alley or riding their gold-plated bicycles in Central Park.

At 250 pounds, Brady was a fairly obvious symbol of the Age of Consumption. Morris quotes the restaurateur George Rector as saying that Brady was the best twenty-five customers he had. Diamond Jim reveled in his own girth and liked nothing more than four dozen oysters before dinner, just to get his digestive system moving.

"I always make it a point to leave just four inches between my stomach and the edge of the table," he said once. "And then when I can feel 'em rubbin' together pretty hard, I know I've had enough."

Then there were the ubiquitous Vanderbilts. One could hardly walk ten steps on Fifth Avenue below Central Park without bumping into a Vanderbilt mansion. The most talked-about of the eleven were the twin palaces that took up the whole block between 51st and 52nd streets. One block to the north was a huge château built for William K. Vanderbilt, while the Cornelius Vanderbilt house, staffed by thirty servants, sat between 57th and 58th streets.

It seemed to be a rule among merchant princes of the era that money was meant to be earned, spent, and displayed. In an article for *American Heritage*, Henry Hope Reid recalled Fifth Avenue during those years:

> The dominant note on Fifth Avenue in 1911 was opulence: opulence in the mansions filled with gilded Louis Seize furniture, opulence in the hotels with their marble oyster bars and rococo dining rooms, opulence in the shops selling rosepoint lace and crêpe de Chine, opulence in the Brewster-built carriages and in the newfangled motorcars with names such as Simplex and Pierce-Arrow. And there was opulence in dress, too: women in high-waisted flaring skirts of silk, with flowered and feathered hats; men in gray toppers and Prince Alberts and spats; servants in brass-buttoned, multi-colored liveries.

The upper stretches of Fifth Avenue, however, remained undeveloped even past the turn of the century. Andrew Carnegie displaced a shanty when he built his home on 90th Street in 1901. A herd of wild goats had to find a new home in 1908 when Felix Warburg put up his mansion on their lot at 92nd Street. Warburg was one of many wealthy German Jews who settled in the area and established a society of their own, known as "Our Crowd."

Next to the Warburg house was the home of beer baron Jacob Ruppert, who, along with another brewer, George Ehret, employed hundreds of workers in their Yorkville breweries. The smell from the two breweries hung over Third Avenue in the low 90s like a fog, but to at least one youngster, the men were true heroes. That

boy's name was Adolph Marx, later known as Harpo. In his engag-
ing memoir, *Harpo Speaks*, Marx wrote of visiting the Ruppert
mansion—uninvited, of course—to sample the delicious peach trees
in the yard. He also recalled the excitement of seeing Ehret's carriage race past the Marxes' tenement building on 93rd Street:

> Thunder and lightning. Pomp and circumstance. Glory and
> Magnificence. I wonder how a poor kid who never watched a
> brewer ride to his brewery, who never shivered with goose
> bumps when the coachman rose to start the downhill gallop,
> could ever know there was another kind of life, the Good Life.
>     Thanks for the show, Mr. Ehret. Thanks for the peaches,
> Mr. Ruppert. Sorry, I never liked beer.

The Marxes lived on a block inhabited mostly by Jewish families around the turn of the century. The surrounding neighborhood was mostly Irish. The number of German residents increased
dramatically following one of the worst marine disasters in this
country's history, on June 15, 1904.

That bright spring morning, nearly 1,500 people from the Little Germany area of the Lower East Side boarded the steamboat
*General Slocum* for a day's excursion up the East River. The trip
was organized by St. Mark's Lutheran Church. It was a workday
for the men, so most of the revelers were women and children.

No one knows precisely when the fire broke out in the second
cabin, and arguments still rage over whether the captain fatally
erred by not beaching the ship when he first learned that fire was
raging inside. However, there is no argument that within a few
hours a whole neighborhood was decimated by over a thousand
deaths. Many survivors and relatives of those who were lost packed
their belongings and left Little Germany for good. There was too
much sadness around the neighborhood: they picked up and moved
uptown to join the other established German community, in Yorkville.

Yorkville was settled in the 1790s in the area now bounded
by 83rd and 89th streets. Like other outposts on the island, it was a
small isolated community surrounded by wealthy country estates.
Yorkville was finally linked to the city in 1834, when the New York
and Harlem Railroad extended its line through the area. New

housing was constructed and soon occupied, a process that accelerated after the *Slocum* disaster.

The newcomers transformed the area around 86th Street into another Little Germany. German was soon heard more often than English on the streets. They patronized the *konditereien*, the German pastry shops, made sauerbraten and weiner schnitzel from meat bought at the German butchers', watched German films and entertainment at the Yorkville Casino, and drank in the beer halls or local pubs, where Ruppert and Ehret kept the taps flowing.

The German domination of the 86th Street area has left the mistaken impression that all of Yorkville was German. In fact, there was a large Irish population—James Cagney's father owned a bar in the neighborhood—as well as large communities of Hungarians, Poles, Italians, and, in the Little Bohemia area of the mid-70s, Czechs and Slovaks.

The error can be attributed in part to the period before World War II, when Fritz Kuhn's German-American Bund made Yorkville its home, and pro-Hitler Brownshirts swaggered around the neighborhood. Not all Germans supported the Bund, of course, but enough did to insure a regular audience at their outdoor rallies on 86th Street.

While the Bundists paraded around Third Avenue, Fifth Avenue was going through upheavals of its own. Those changes were part of a process that had been set in motion when the first federal income tax was levied during the Wilson administration. Suddenly, owning a Fifth Avenue château was no longer practical. Fortunately, the new tax nearly coincided with a decision to move the New York and Harlem Railroad tracks underground on Park Avenue. Development proceeded apace, and the wealthy set found that they could maintain their large staffs in a fifteen- or twenty-room apartment on Park Avenue and survive just fine.

The stock market was less kind. After the crash in 1929, people who had never even visited their kitchens suddenly found themselves wearing aprons. The flappers in their cloche hats and rolled stockings, and the cake eaters, with their hip flasks and raccoon coats, suddenly toned down their acts. They had no choice. Besides, it didn't look right anymore. When their spiritual leader, Mayor Jimmy Walker, got caught with his hand in a little tin box and suddenly decided it was a nice time to see Europe, that hurt, too.

Of course, not everybody suffered from the crash. Generally, the superrich became, well, merely rich. The tea dances continued at the Plaza, and dinner at the Colony was still elegantly served. But the coming-out parties were less lavish, and the color line between blue and red blood faded a bit. *The* Mrs. Astor and her world became a distant memory, and for some former society matrons, being a leader was an easier job than finding one.

# The Witnesses

FRANK DITRAPANI (1916–) was born in Sicily and immigrated to America with his family in 1921. He is a World War II veteran. After the war, he opened his own television and radio repair shop and also taught in a vocational high school.

EDNA DOERING (1898–) is a retired schoolteacher. She lives in New Jersey.

TINA DONALDSON (1893–) is a longtime Upper East Side resident, born in Brooklyn.

FREDERICK VANDERBILT FIELD (1905–) was raised in a Fifth Avenue mansion. He is a graduate of Harvard University and was a staffer for the Institute of Pacific Relations. His work there caused him to be a target of witch-hunting committees during the McCarthy period. He fled to Mexico, where he became an archaeologist. He and his wife now split their time between Mexico and the United States.

MARTIN HARRIS (1895–) is a pseudonym. He went from a private home on 92nd Street and Fifth Avenue to the trenches in Europe during World War I. He later became a successful investment banker and also saw combat in World War II, where he flew several missions over the dreaded "Hump."

JOE HENRY (1912–) is a pseudonym. He is a World War II veteran. He worked until his retirement for Sunshine Biscuits, the makers of Hydrox and Lorna Doons.

JOE HINZMAN (1910–) was born in New York and raised in Austria-Hungary, where he was trained as a chef. He spent many years working in Ruppert's Brewery in Yorkville.

LUDWIG KOTTL (1916–) was, for a time, a staffer for the *Hobo News*. He was later a machine operator in a print shop and now does volunteer work at the Stanley Isaacs Senior Center on the Upper East Side.

MIKE LEWIS (1916–) is a retired interior decorator. He lives in New Jersey, where he devotes much of his time to painting.

FRANCES LEHMAN LOEB (1906–) is the granddaughter of Adolph Lewisohn and Mayer Lehman, two of the leading patriarchs of the New York German-Jewish society popularly known as "Our Crowd."

JOSEPH LOVITZ (1917–) is a lifelong Upper East Side resident. He is a retired home instruction teacher.

CLAUDIA HATCH STEARNS (1907–) is a direct descendant of Priscilla Alden. She is a graduate of Vassar College and worked for many years as an editor and writer. She is the author of several books for young adults.

HELEN WAGNER worked in a knitting store until her retirement. She is a lifelong Upper East Side Resident. She chose not to reveal her age for this project.

CLAUDIA HATCH STEARNS [*very much amused*]: Who were the Astors anyway—fur traders? The Astors were pretty nouveau, and the worst thing you could be was nouveau riche. We would receive them and see them, but my grandparents would not be impressed with Mrs. Astor.

In those days, breeding counted much more than it does now, and money didn't matter as much as a pedigree. The Hatches go back to the *Mayflower*, to Priscilla Alden. My great-grandfather Alfrederick Smith Hatch came to New York around the early 1800s from Massachusetts. He dealt in money. He was president of the stock exchange. His sister married Lincoln's Secretary of the Treasury, so he floated all the bonds for the Civil War.

The Hatch family came up from 13th Street as New York went crawling uptown. Then they went to 37 Park Avenue, but they couldn't stay on the East Side because the people on the West Side kept their horses in stables on the East Side. They didn't want to live next to a stable, so they moved to the West Side.

The truth of why my grandparents moved back to the East Side was because the "immigrants," the Jews, came in and took over, and they couldn't very well live with them, so they moved. After that there was no place to go except the river. It was too bad, because the East Side wasn't half as nice.

FRANCES LEHMAN LOEB: I remember my father saying his address, 10 East 62nd Street, was not very chic, because the word *East* was in it, and Park Avenue had the trains and the smoke. He used to walk a few steps to Fifth Avenue and look uptown, up the hill where there was a meadow and a farm with some goats grazing on it. That was about where the Frick house is today.

My father was born in the family home at 10 East 62nd Street in 1873. He went to Dr. Sachs' school and then to Harvard. His brother, Herbert, who later served as senator and governor of New York, went to Williams.

My mother was born in 1882. She was the daughter of Adele and Adolph Lewisohn. My mother went to a stylish school called Miss Annie Brown's. She also went to Barnard for a year, before she left to be married in 1901.

Were we snobby! Only German Jews were even permitted in our circle. For instance, at the Century Country Club, when Harold Lehman put up a young man called Paul Mazur, there was terrible excitement around our dinner table because they let a Russian Jew in there.

CLAUDIA STEARNS: There isn't a single Jewish name in the first edition of the Social Register. People were much more anti-Semitic then than they are now. We would never be rude to anybody of that race, and they were wonderful people, but they weren't acceptable in society unless they were terribly rich. Somebody told me the Belmonts were Jewish, so he was probably the first one to crash what I call the "wall of silence."

FREDERICK VANDERBILT FIELD: I think the anti-Semitism was traditional. I have to assume it existed widely in the high-society circles in which my parents moved. Whatever my father said about Jews would be derogatory. Even the wealthy Jews were of course not in his class—they were on the periphery of social life. Because they were so damn rich, they were tolerated on the outskirts.

My mother's name was Lila Vanderbilt Sloane. The original Commodore Vanderbilt was my great-great-grandfather. My father was William B. Osgood Field. We were, of course, all in the Social Register from way back. I was in it as far back as childhood. It was also supposed to be quite disgraceful to be in it and then be thrown out of it—which I was. It was really a terribly snotty organization. It was one of the first things I remember as being socially ridiculous—to give a damn whether you were in that book or not.

CLAUDIA STEARNS: The Social Register was considered very special if you were not in it, but if you were in, you realized there was nothing to it. The Hatches were in the first issue of the Social Register, but my mother-in-law, Mrs. Stearns, wouldn't be in it because, she said, "I have my own visiting list."

I'll tell you something my grandmother said: "Everybody in this world is divided into two classes, snobs and slobs. For my part, I'd rather be a snob."

Actually, I don't think she was that much of a snob. They were always going broke. My mother-in-law was more of a snob, but she came from Philadelphia. The Stearnses were much more stylish than the Hatches. They had a brownstone next to Bergdorf Goodman's, and before that they lived near St. George's Church around Gramercy Park. You can still see the Stearns name all over the ceiling of the cathedral.

They entertained more. John Noble Stearns founded a very popular silk business. He brought the silk from China on a clipper ship. There were relatives of the Hatches who were in trade, which was looked down upon. My uncle Ed's brother founded Lord & Taylor. That's why I say the Hatches were not quite as stylish as the Stearnses, because the Stearnses manufactured their silk.

My great-grandparents had eleven children. My great-grandfather paid Eastman Johnson to do a family portrait for $1,000 a head. When the baby, Emily, was born on the yacht in Newport, my great-grandfather sent Eastman Johnson a telegram that he had another $1,000 coming. He couldn't put the baby in until she was born. They painted the whole picture before then and left a place for her in Aunt Flora's lap.

Uncle Fred had the painting for years. He was the richest, and he had the best wallpaper to hang it on. He knew he was going to die soon, and he loved the painting and thought it was very important, so he persuaded the Metropolitan Museum to accept it. I don't think they paid for it. Then, the museum was very snobbish and didn't think it was great art, so they put it in the cellar. It didn't come out of the cellar until a good many years later.

Nobody is really sure when it was painted. The baby, Emily, was born in 1870, but she didn't want anybody to know it, and she was a painter. So the night before the painting was to go to the Metropolitan, she went with her paint box and changed the date.

The young man on the left, going out the door, was my grand-father John Ruggles Hatch. He drank, and he died when he was forty-five. My father said he was not really a nice man. The young man in front of him, writing on the pad, is Uncle Will. He was a genius with the stock market. He died when he was in his forties.

The fellow in the back with the beard was Dr. John Ruggles Hatch, my great-grandfather's father. Dr. Hatch lived in Vermont until his son got rich and he came down and lived with him. The woman doing the sewing is Grandma Rose, my great-grandma's mother. She and Dr. Hatch would argue over who got to read the newspaper in the morning. Sometimes, she would sit on it so he couldn't get it. You can see them there. She's reading over his shoulder. She's not letting him get away with it completely.

My great-grandfather's wife, Theodosia, is standing on the right. The eleven children in the picture are all hers. The oldest is Aunt Mary, in the blue. My sister later went to work for her. The Hatch women were very enterprising. Aunt Mary made wonderful chicken broth that she sold to sick people. She also started an agency for nurses and cooks and all kinds of domestic help.

My father hoped that when my sister finished Vassar she would go to work for Aunt Mary. She did, but she didn't like Aunt Mary. Nobody liked Aunt Mary. She was married to a man named Mr. Willard. Mr. Willard disappeared. Nobody ever knew what became of him. I asked my father, "Why do you think he did that?"

My father said, "Because nobody could stand that Mary."

Of the two children in front of my mother, the one facing out is Uncle Fred, the only Hatch not in the Social Register. Maybe his wife had her visiting list, too. Next to him is his sister, my aunt Jane. The girl with the red hair holding the baby was Aunt Dora. She drank. The two in the front right are Uncle Horace and Uncle Ed, but I don't know which is which.

Our family was always being rich and being poor. They were all on the Street at first, because my great-grandfather bought them each a seat on the exchange. They went broke in the Panic of '76. After that, my uncle Ed taught dancing. The only ones who kept their seats were Uncle Will, who was a snob, so he *had* to be rich, and Uncle Fred, who kept his seat till he died.

After the panic, most of the family moved up to my great-grandfather's house in Greenwich. The horses he had were all gone, and there were so many kids, the housekeeper put curtains up over stalls and put a child in every one. Every day, more and more children would come, and my great-grandfather would look at one and say, "Whose are you?"

• • •

MARTIN HARRIS: I was born in a brownstone at Number 9 East 92nd Street in 1895. There is an interesting story about the block. My father had a great friend called Judge Blanchard. My father sold him on the idea of living on 92nd Street. The judge found a house he wanted to buy. Everything went fine except that the house number was thirteen, and Mrs. Blanchard was very superstitious.

My father was not to be daunted. Ninety-second Street between Fifth and Madison was a block where everybody knew everybody else, so my father went to the people who lived from thirteen down to one and asked them if they would mind changing their numbers, and everybody agreed. So I was born in Number 9, but I lived in Number 7.

The Blanchards did have to pay for our new stationery, the visiting cards that my mother had. "Mrs. George L. Harris, 9 East 92nd" became "7 East 92nd." Down at the bottom was "Even Tuesdays." That was her day at home.

Carnegie had his house on 90th Street. They called it Carnegie Hill. I always remember when I used to go down to the park and I would see Carnegie's daughter in her pram with her nanny and a detective. That was very impressive.

On our corner of Fifth Avenue was this big empty lot with wild goats. That's where we would play baseball. Later on, that became Felix Warburg's house, which is now the Jewish Museum. It would have been 1 East 92nd, but that number was already taken, so he had to take the Fifth Avenue number, 1109. The Warburg mansion had a ballroom, and we went to dances there. It was lovely, but somehow or other we weren't impressed. We were accustomed to good living, and of course it took away our playground.

Warburg's house abutted Mr. Jacob Ruppert's house and garden, which was on the corner of 93rd Street and Fifth Avenue. He was a nice man. He used to give us passes for the Yankee games in Highland Park. Next to him on 93rd Street was where my aunt lived. My mother and my aunt were very close, and our gardens abutted. We built a stile over the gardens so the ladies could visit each other, to say nothing of the private telephone of their own so they could talk.

We had the ninth telephone in the district. The district was called 79th Street. To reach us, you would crank up your telephone and tell the operator, "Nine 79th Street." That was our phone number.

In those days, the horse-drawn streetcars only went as far up as 86th Street and Madison Avenue. You had to walk home from there. That was the depot where they overhauled the cars. From there on, there were farms. To the east, 96th Street was the end of the tunnel. North of that was all shanties, like the end of Fifth Avenue at 110th Street, which was shacks and small wooden buildings, dirt and hills.

The stagecoaches that ran on the avenue were like opera buses. They were pulled by two horses. You got in the back and sat along the side on leather seats. There was a coachman, who sat up front. You paid ten cents. If you gave a quarter, it was sent up to the coachman through a window and you got your change back in an envelope. Inside, they sat maybe twelve or fourteen people. You would tell the driver how far you were going and he would pull over at your stop.

Of course, we also had horses and carriages. We had a surrey and a high cart. The surrey was a square four-poster with a cover on top and a curtain, and the high cart was a formal cart just for two people to drive, a very dressy-type thing. The surrey was great fun. We used to drive around the park and up to Riverside Drive. People checked out each other's surreys and horses. You had to have a good carriage maker.

There were no traffic lights at 92nd and Fifth. There was nothing, so there were lots of horse-and-carriage accidents. Horses shied and the carriages knocked up against one another. The traffic in carriages up and down Fifth Avenue was enormous. Sometimes it would take you a half an hour to get down to 42nd Street.

We lived in a very German neighborhood, because all the brewers lived there, the Ehrets, the Rupperts, all those people. We went to school with the Piel boys, and I also went to school with Emil Schaefer.

JOE HINZMAN: There was quite a few breweries in the neighborhood. The biggest one that stayed in business was Ruppert. They started by goin' house to house with their beer. Finally, they became such a big success that Ruppert built the Yankee Stadium, and he sold his beer in the Yankee Stadium.

Ruppert built bars for the people. It cost them nothin'. "We'll put a beautiful wood bar in there. We'll pay for everything. All you sell is our beer." They became a success with it. All you had, practically all over Yorkville, was Ruppert's beer.

I am born here in 1910. My mother was a sick woman, and she had most of her sisters in Europe, and that's where she wanted to die. So when I was a year old, we went to Austria-Hungary. I didn't come back until 1930. A few years later, I went to work in Ruppert's.

HELEN WAGNER: I drank beer from little up. Anything my father had at the table for supper, we could have. He always had his beer, so we all had our little glass of beer. Ruppert's, Ehret's, it's all the same, and you could smell those places for miles.

JOE HINZMAN: Holy Christ, the smell was so bad, some people walked out and they got drunk out in the street. Them days, the stuff was just malts and hops. That made it so strong, because there was nothin' in the beer that was chemical. The fumes alone would kill ya. We had two guys goin' in to clean the tanks after they were empty. They made a mistake by goin' in without masks. One dropped right there and suffocated. The other guy they rescued. He died later. That's how much odor was in there.

JOSEPH LOVITZ: People think that Yorkville was strictly a German area. While there was a big concentration of Germans around 86th Street, the most popular ethnic group on the East Side was Irish. You also had a lot of Hungarians and Czechs and then Italians just north of the bridge.

My father came to America in 1887 from a province in Latvia called Courland. He lived on 87th between Lexington and Park Avenue. He had a tailor shop in the front and he lived in the back. From the time I was twelve, I lived on 88th Street. In the back of our building, there was somebody who was always asking, "Whatsa matter, Mama? How do ya feel?"

My mother would say, "What a wonderful daughter, thinking of her mother like that." When we kept hearing it, we finally found out that it was a parrot that was trained to say that.

HELEN WAGNER: Eighty-sixth Street was Little Germany. You had all the German restaurants, like the Lorelei, the Switzerland, the Bauhaus. We always spoke German. I spoke it, I read it, and I could write it. When you walked around the neighborhood, you heard mostly German. I was born on 84th between Second and Third. Most of the people on our block were German.

We lived in a little three-family house. The house was three stories with a store downstairs. We had five rooms up on the top floor. My father was a cigar maker. He came from Europe in 1881. He said when he came over here, you had the squatters and farms on Lexington Avenue. You had the cows walking around the neighborhood.

JOSEPH LOVITZ: Many Germans moved up here from the Lower East Side after the *General Slocum* disaster in 1904. There was too much sadness down there. It was a terrible tragedy. It burned right up here in the East River. My father said he saw the smoke from his building on 87th Street and Lexington.

TINA DONALDSON: I was born in 1893 in Brooklyn, but my mother didn't like it, so she moved to the area where the other German people were—the Lower East Side. Then in 1904 all those people died on the *Slocum*. It was mostly women and children. I remember watching the funerals and seeing a man coming down the church steps crying because he had lost his wife and children.

HELEN WAGNER: My sisters and brothers were supposed to go on the *General Slocum*, but my youngest brother misbehaved, and my father wouldn't permit any of them to go. If he hadn't acted up, they might have all died.

EDNA DOERING: The German community was more around 8th Street. That's where St. Mark's Lutheran Church was. My father was a Lutheran minister. He was director of an immigrant house in that neighborhood.

In 1904, my brother was nine and my sister eleven. I was only six. That day, we were going on a Sunday-school picnic on Brother's Island. That's where we were headed for. Of course, we never got there.

I remember the excitement going to the ship. We got seats with my mother right near the railing. She brought a nice big shiny tin box for our lunch. In the initial excitement, when they called "Fire," she threw it overboard and I felt so bad that our lunch was being thrown over.

My mother tried to get life preservers but they were rotten. I remember some of the cork actually falling down over her. Then my mother had my hand and she tried to go to the upper deck. But it was so hot that she turned around. At that point we got separated. When the people heard "Fire!" they rushed toward the railing and broke it off. The next thing I knew I was standing at the opening. There was a woman at the other end sitting, and she came over and threw me overboard. I don't know who she was, and I never saw her again, but I owe my life to her.

I don't remember ever being afraid, and I don't remember falling. I remember the feeling of being in the water, and there were so many bodies I just kept pushing. I guess that's what kept me alive. I was floating on the bodies.

Then, my mother, who had already been taken in a rowboat, spotted me, and she asked the man please to get me, so I got in the same rowboat with my mother. The next thing I remember I was on a barge, and a man had me in his arms and put a blanket around me.

At first I was put with the dead, and a doctor came along and he saw there was life. I was put in an ambulance and taken to a hospital. There was a man there who worked in the immigrant house. He came to the hospital where I was and he saw me. He asked me where my mother was. I said I didn't know. A short time later he came back with her. She was in the same hospital.

My mother lived six days after the accident. She was badly burned and she had pneumonia. My brother was found the next day. Of course he drowned. My sister wasn't found until six days later. By that time, she was decomposed and it was hard to identify her. An uncle of mine went out every day looking for her. They laid the dead in rows. Another woman was claiming the body at the same time, but my uncle came home and asked where different articles of clothing were bought, because they found some markers. The big store in those days was Siegel-Cooper. My mother said the shoes were bought there, and that's the only way they identified my sister.

My mother was very sick. My father didn't want her to know that the other two children were dead. That's all she did for six days—call to her children. I remember one day there was a lot of commotion, and somebody told me my brother was being buried that day, the same day they found my sister. They didn't even bring her to the house. She was buried from another immigrant house.

My father never once spoke of it after that. I never asked him about it. It was too much for him. My father remarried in two years. We were never allowed to go to the seashore. My father just wouldn't take us. I don't know how to swim, and I've never been on a boat for pleasure.

You could imagine the poor little church. It had over a thousand people in the Sunday school, and after that it dwindled down to almost nothing. The poor minister—I can't imagine what his thoughts or life was like. He lost his whole family, his whole congregation. They lost 1,500 people on the *Titanic*. We were 1,030, and when you think of 1,030 people—especially from one neighborhood—it's hard to picture that.

They say time heals everything and it's true. When I look back now, I see how fortunate I was. It's still hard to think of those days, but it's not as bad as it was.

$$\bullet \quad \bullet \quad \bullet$$

MARTIN HARRIS: Before the First War, Fifth Avenue down to below 57th Street was all private homes. The sidewalks were quite narrow, because people built their houses out close to the street. Some of them had lawns in front. Of course, the sidewalks were less crowded because there were no stores.

The streets were cleaned by sweeps. I always remember the story about the street cleaner who died. They were having a wake and were talking about him. "He was a fine man and a fine street cleaner, but he was a little weak around the lampposts."

My father was a self-made man. He supported his family before he was married. He educated himself and went to law school while taking jobs in the theater as an usher. It wasn't until quite a bit later on that he made a start at his success. He eventually became a partner in a very fine law firm.

My father knew how to live well. The men on the block had a barber who went around in the morning and would shave the gentlemen in bed. Each man had his soap box with his name on it, and the barber would come in and shave Father while he was resting. Then he would go over to Mr. Burden and shave him.

When cars came in, they were very exciting, but when I was about nine or ten, I went out to Mineola, and I had my first plane ride, in an open plane between my father's legs. The flier was Sopwith himself. We sat right on the wings, which were made of cloth. The pilot sat on one side and my father and I sat next to him. It was not a very sturdy vehicle. There was no runway. We just took off from an open field.

FRED FIELD: On the east side of Fifth Avenue at 51st Street, a block down from us, between the Union Club and St. Patrick's was a fire station. One of the great excitements was when you heard the sirens and you saw the black-and-white dogs running ahead of the engines toward the fire. Whichever floor we were on, we would rush to the Fifth Avenue end of the house and look out of the windows and watch this thing.

HELEN WAGNER: The grandest sight was to see the white fire horses coming down the block. You'd be surprised how they knew that bell, and they'd be all ready to be harnessed up. The dalmatian was the first one on the engine, sitting there as proud as you could imagine.

FRED FIELD: We split the year between our estate in Massachusetts and our house on Fifth Avenue. Our section of Fifth Avenue, in the 50s, was nearly all private houses. Our house, where I was born in 1905, was between 51st and 52nd.

When we were little, we didn't use the sidewalk very much. We were taken places by coach. I can certainly remember when I was a little boy more or less on my own on the sidewalk, because I remember Jess Willard [the former heavyweight champion] walking by. He carried a very heavy iron walking stick. Much later, I remember Woodrow Wilson just walking by with a couple of people protecting him, nothing more, no fancy business.

In our house, the men's servants' quarters were in the basement. They were only lit by a light that showed through from the sidewalk. They were very dreary rooms, with nothing to them at all, maybe a bureau and a chair. It was a lousy way to live, especially in contrast with the way we lived upstairs.

Still, they were doing pretty well. The butler and the number-one chauffeur were paid a flat $100 a month plus room and board. That was a very good salary. After our second man married a very attractive young German woman, they established a little ski place in the Adirondacks. My grandmother's butler, a man named Stride, was a very dignified English fellow. When my grandmother died, he bought a house in Newport and lived the rest of his life there. I imagine he would have been unhappy in any other type of environment.

We had either three or four servants. They had different duties. There was a butler, who was quite superior to the other man. When there was any kind of a formal dinner, which was not infrequent, the butler always stood behind my mother, and he would serve the important dish, the roast beef or whatever the hell it was. The other men would come along with the spuds and the vegetables. But he was posted behind my mother, and the point was, when my mother was finished eating, he would give the signal to the others when it was time to start clearing the dishes and so on.

The lowest-ranking man took care of the garbage and the furnace, all the worst aspects of keeping that kind of a house going. You never saw him upstairs. The other two men were the men who waited on tables, cleaned the silver, and washed the dishes. One of them would be also my father's valet, taking care of his clothes, laying out his pajamas, all the goddamned things you could think of.

J O S E P H  L O V I T Z : As a tailor, it was good for my father to make friends with the service people. They might be asked to recommend a tailor, and if he gave them a *schmeer,* they might recommend him.

Sometimes, the elevator operators or the doormen would stop in and make deals. If the butler got to be a friend, he took you in preference to another tailor for less *schmeer,* because he liked you. Of course, the butler might divide it among a number of tailors if there was enough work.

F R A N C E S  L O E B : The butler we had for a long time was called François. He was really a very difficult, horrid man. If he didn't approve of the things we ate, he simply didn't serve them. He would also scold us if we were late. He was so difficult, but my father liked him 'cause he was a very good valet, and he did everything he liked. He did set the table well. He did serve beautifully, and he polished the silver well. I'm sure he was very useful, but Mother couldn't stand him, and as soon as my father died she let him go. Ten years later, we were at some reception, and there he was, serving drinks. I went up and said hello, and he started to be cross all over again.

F R E D  F I E L D : There was a very wide hall in our basement that led right through the house to the back, where a very large kitchen was. The hallway was large enough to play softball. We used to do just that, much to the annoyance of the servants.

My relationship with them was very important to me. I saw them a great deal. They were more than nice in the way of courtesy to us. I used to tease them endlessly. They wore very fancy uniforms. Part of that was the old boilerplate shirt—the very stiff shirt. When I was a little guy, I remember, I used to creep up and give the shirt a whack with my little fists. They kidded me along too, so we had good relations.

In the early days, we would go to the park with the coachman, who later became our chauffeur. I never went to the stable, but it was a block or two west. In the city we used two coaches. One was a brougham. That was a contraption where the driver sat in front, and there was a seat sticking out from the back of it, in the caboose, where the footman would sit. All he did was jump off his seat and open the door after we stopped and remove the lap robe from the passenger. Then he would do the reverse when we set forth on an expedition.

MARTIN HARRIS: The maids had uniforms, black dresses with aprons. They were more or less standard. My mother got them from Bloomingdale's or wherever. Actually, she couldn't get anything from Bloomingdale's except kitchenware or that kind of thing. It was a cheap little store.

We had a cook and a maid. Then, you could get people in. The maid would go down to the boats at Ellis Island. If someone would be congenial to her, she would bring them back. They were very glad to get a place to live. You kept your people quite a long time then.

Ours was a four-story house with no elevator. It had a bathroom on each floor, except the floor where the maids lived. They had to bathe down in washtubs in the basement laundry. There was a toilet there for them, too. They would be up in their rooms, and every time the doorbell rang they would have to run down four flights.

FRANCES LOEB: You never had any thought if you rang bells or called that they wouldn't answer. Me, answer the door? We had a butler, a second man, and a waitress. They would think we were crazy if we answered the door.

FRED FIELD: Our house was entered through a large double front door. It opened on five or six marble stairs that you took up to the actual door that entered into the house.

There was a silver tray on the table in the large marble entranceway. On it would be cards from people who left them there every day. There was some deal about whether you turned the corner down. It may have meant that you came to really make a visit or it was a courtesy. I used to carry a little leather thing with my own cards in it. They were part of the formality.

MARTIN HARRIS: When you turned the corner down, that meant you were there in person. Otherwise, you might have been invited to a party, and you didn't go, but you might have the footman go inside and drop off a card.

My mother's day at home was even Tuesdays. After you paid a visit, you left your card at the entrance just to show that you had been there, and people wanted to remember who had come on their day at home. My mother had cards that said, "Mr. and Mrs. George L. Harris." The cards were printed by Tiffany. As a matter of fact, Tiffany's biggest business in those days was stationery.

FRED FIELD: As you went down a very large hall, on the left was the elevator for the family, the men's pantry, and then the servants' elevator. In the back, the whole width of the house was the dining room. It was a very large room with two tables, one a long oblong table for when there was a party and then a family table that held maybe six people. It was a noticeably somber room. The curtains were very dark. The back windows were stained glass, so you couldn't see a damned thing through them anyway.

That whole bottom floor was very, very gloomy. It was a very scary entrance. The circular marble staircase was two stories high. It was very poorly lighted. On the corners, they had these armored creatures my father collected, with helmets and something stuffed inside. I still have shivers thinking about it. When I used the stairway, I went just as fast as I possibly could.

The second floor just had two rooms. In the back was a formal ballroom. It ran the whole width of the house, the same size of the dining room under it. It was hardly ever used. The front was a very beautiful room, which was my father's library. He had a very fine collection of books. This room I remember very much because it fronted on Fifth Avenue and gave way to a balcony that stretched also the full width of the house. My brother and I would watch all the parades on Fifth Avenue from the balcony. I remember all the World War I preparedness parades that passed by.

There was another very gloomy, but carpeted, stairway, that led up to the third floor, where my parents lived. My mother had a very large bedroom and a marble bath on the Fifth Avenue side. Also facing Fifth Avenue was her boudoir, which was very French-style, very formal, with a fireplace and uncomfortable chairs. She had a desk there where she kept her records. Then there was a large room where the dumbwaiter was next to the boudoir. She always had her breakfast there. I often had it there, too.

On the other side of the hallway was a huge closet where all my mother's clothes were kept. It had one conspicuous feature, a very large safe, in which she kept a great deal of the jewelry that she used. What she didn't use was, of course, in the bank. She always kept a lot of cash in it. The combination was such a secret that when she opened the safe, I was never allowed to watch her doing it.

They had separate bedrooms. The traditions in those days were sexually very formal, at least in my family. In all our houses they had separate bedrooms. My father's whole setup was in the back of the house, where he had a bedroom and a bathroom and what was called a den.

The fourth floor was the children's floor. My brother and I had the front of the house. The other room in the front, which was a large room, was our nursery, and the bathroom, which took off from the nursery. The nursery was a rather pleasant room where we did our homework. We were in the nursery when, exactly five o'clock every afternoon, my mother came up and spent exactly one hour with us. She'd leave at six to dress for dinner or to dress for the opera—whatever was going on that evening. I didn't object when she left—there had simply never been anything else.

We were served supper up in the nursery while she was there, and she would also watch us do our homework. Friends of hers would often come in and visit her and see the kids up there. My mother would form close friendships with women who were totally different from her, both in their traditions and in their worldliness. My mother was not at all a worldly person. She was very simple and straitlaced.

The Gerry Flappers were quite a thing in those days. Geraldine Farrar was a friend of hers and she would visit us in the nursery. She was a very, very glamorous celebrity. To me, she was a most unusual person because there was a tremendous amount of gossip about her around the dining-room table. She was sought after a great deal by the glamorous young men around, and she had been the Kaiser's mistress. That's what got her started. To a little kid, these things were so outside his world.

TINA DONALDSON: Among our people, wives of men were very industrious. If your husband had to get up early and go to work, the wives had to get up first and light up the coal stove. It was a tough life for them. One day, one of the embers fell out and ignited my mother's nightgown. She flew down the stairs, her hair aflame and everything. A milkman threw his cloak over her. She was in the hospital fifteen months. Then, when she was forty-one, she told the druggist she wanted to kill a cat and kittens. They gave her chloroform. When my father came home from work, she was lying in bed with the chloroform over her head. I didn't know she was in such pain. She never complained.

FRANCES LOEB: My mother was a suffragette, and she went to college, and she was interested in crippled children, but her independence ended with all that. She didn't take a strong stand at the dinner table. She had a few close friends, but most of them were wives of my father's friends. My father had a delicious roving eye, which I don't think was useful to Mother, but that was typical with the men of that generation, and she never said "boo."

FRED FIELD: I don't remember much conversation between my mother and father except about real trivial things, like organizing the chauffeur for whether or not you were going to play golf or tennis or whatever the hell they did.

When we had guests, then my father would talk a great deal about the war or whatever was on his mind. That's when I really began to know him at all. He talked a lot about it, and he talked very well about books, and with all the war business, he was very, very definitely pro-German until we got into the war. My mother would not participate very much. She talked about people and friends, but not about ideas.

I had a wonderful relationship with my mother. I don't remember her crawling around the floor, and I don't remember much physical relationship, hugging and kissing and sitting on laps. I don't think that happened. It was a formal relationship, but it worked with me. All through my young life, I always enjoyed being with her.

FRANCES LOEB: I was a big disappointment to the family. After two daughters, they wanted a son. First Dorothy was born, and everybody was happy. A year and a half later, Helen was born, another little girl. That was fair—not so happy. After that, my parents wanted to wait a while before adding to the family.

Mother also didn't want to get pregnant again because she got very fat. She was a very good athlete. Women wore corsets then, except when they were in "delicate condition," and since she couldn't go out without hers, she had to stay indoors for almost six months of her pregnancy, which she found very difficult.

She told me she burst into tears when she was first told she was pregnant. However, it would have been all right if I was a boy. Well, I wasn't. When my grandmother was told it was a girl, her response was, "Oh, isn't that too bad."

My mother was so depressed, for about two months I was called "It." My nurse was named Frances Harkness, and as she was leaving, she said, "You *have* to name this child."

They said, "We don't care that we don't have a name for it, we cannot think of it."

"Well, I've been with your family a long time. Why don't you call it after me?"

That's why they named me Frances.

• • •

MARTIN HARRIS: When my parents gave a party, it took about three or four days to get ready, because every glass had to be washed, and every plate and all the silver had to be washed. It was quite a deal. The table was set with four or five glasses. You would have your sherry, your red wine, your white wine, your champagne and water glasses. When the guests came they had cocktails. Then they had an appetizer like oysters, then soup, another dish, then an entrée, chicken or squab. Then they had sherbet, then the red meat. All of this was with vegetables and salad. After that was dessert, like ice cream, which I used to be able to grind up, and then coffee.

FRANCES LOEB: For dinner, my parents would have lobster Newburg, then they'd have soup, then some roast, a vegetable and potatoes, then a salad with foie gras, then a rich dessert. That's six courses. That was often after a very good lunch. That's part of the reason why they all died young—all that fat.

MARTIN HARRIS: The guests would come, I suppose, at 7:00 or 7:30 and it would be over by 11:00 or 11:30. They would spend most of their time eating. In back of our staircase was the gentlemen's coatroom. It had a toilet and washbasin and a place to hang clothes. At the end of the dinner party, while the ladies went upstairs, the gentlemen smoked cigars and drank brandy and used that room for themselves.

When there weren't guests, we always had dinner with the family. We always dressed for dinner in a suit and tie. Maybe when I was younger I didn't wear a tie, but we always had to wash behind the ears. I was the youngest, so I was on my father's right. He liked martinis. I learned to mix him one before dinner. Then at dinner he had Irish whiskey and soda at the table. Of course, they served wine, and we were able to have anything we wanted to drink, so we became accustomed to wine very early on. We had a wine cellar in the basement, and every few years, my father had a man come up to turn the bottles so they wouldn't get corky.

HELEN WAGNER: If my father came home on a very cold winter night and he was having a glass of liquor, we all had it. We always ate German food, a lot of beef, sauerbeef and meat loaf. At night we had a full-course supper, and rest assured you better eat it. It was soup and potatoes and vegetables and meat and some kind of a cooked dessert.

We were permitted to talk to one another until it was time to eat. Then we had to keep quiet and eat. My dad always said you couldn't do two things right at one time. If we wanted to ask my father something, that was permitted, but we couldn't converse with one another at the table.

FRANCES LOEB: In the evenings, Helen and I ate separately, and the food was very poor, except for Saturday night, when we had squab, which was marvelous. We had stewed fruit for dessert. I grew up hating stewed fruit because the cook made it so badly. Still, we were devoted to her. She let us clean the pan when she made chocolate. We had midnight feasts. I love sardines and pickles, and she always had them for me.

We always knew what was going to be served, because Mother
made seven menus, and unless it was company, big company, it
was always the same. On Monday we had chicken. On Tuesday we
had steaks. On Wednesday we had lamb. Thursday we had fricas-
seed chicken. Friday was fish and Sunday was roast beef.

We were brought home from the park to meet a fixed sched-
ule. On Tuesday, a Miss Vietrich came in to wash our hair. On
Wednesday we had our Bible lessons. Thursday was French, and I
think Friday was music lessons. All this gave me a nice sense of
security. No matter what went on in the world, there was always
our well-managed cocoon of a house where we ate the same food,
where people went out at the same time in the morning and came
in at the same time in the evening.

Every Friday evening, Mother and Father went to Grandma
Lehman's for a family dinner. That was a command performance.
Everybody had to be there. That was common then among German Jews, except, with Grandma Lehman, each one of her children also had to visit her every single day. I loved her though.

We ate with the family only for Sunday lunch. Even in the
country there was a children's dining room. If we had any company we had our supper early. When I think of it, it doesn't sound
like much fun, but on the other hand, if this was the way everybody else was living, you didn't think of it as bad. Neither of us
felt neglected or unloved.

Then again, we were given no understanding. Nobody ever
thought to say, "How do you feel?" or "Do you really like your
school?" or "Were you sorry you weren't invited to that party?" or
"Is that a very good book you're reading?" or "I have something
wonderful to show you that will tell you about animals." Nobody
ever thought of that.

Fred Field: We were not an affectionate family. I don't think
I ever saw affectionate relations among other kids and their families, although I know now that more informal relationships did take
place. My mother would have been affectionate, but she was brought
up otherwise. I had an Uncle Fred, who once took me out to the
country to look at the moon. That was the only thing that approached intimacy during those years.

There were just accepted taboos and there were lots of them.
You just didn't cross the line until you broke free. I was not al-

lowed to look at my father when he was in the bathtub. I remember when we went camping together, he walked way upstream from where we camped before taking off his clothes.

MARTIN HARRIS: I was spoiled. My father loved living, and he was very happy and very generous. Life was so pleasant and easy around him. We always kissed our father. He didn't knock you out with his affection, but his affection was what he did for you. Our relationship was warm but not sloppy. There wasn't anything he didn't do to be helpful. We could always confide in him.

He was a great guy. I grew up with him as he grew up. When I came around he had nothing, he was a typically self-made man. He was very successful, very charming. He liked people. He was very outgoing, and he liked having us with him.

HELEN WAGNER: Sundays was my father's treat to take me to Central Park with a bag of peanuts and something for the pigeons, and we'd walk all the way down to 59th Street and all the way back home again. We would stop across the street, and I would be treated to two Cel-Ray tonics and my dad would have two glasses of beer. My brother would meet him and we'd go up with the growler [a bucket of beer], and that was our Sunday relaxation.

FRANCES LOEB: In those days, mothers did not do things with their children. It's interesting what women did in those days, because we had women come to wash our hair, so Mother's hair was washed at home. I know she had a woman come to do her nails. I know she had a deep interest in the Crippled Children's East Side Free School, which was down on Rivington Street. She was also very athletic. In the wintertime, it seemed like the 59th Street lake was always frozen, and I think she went every afternoon. Now she didn't go with us very often because it was more boring to go with us. She went with her friends, and she waltzed and did all sorts of wonderful things on the ice.

I suppose she did a certain amount of visiting, because my father had a number of sisters who were considerably older than my mother, and so she would have tea with them or they would come to her for tea. She spent quite a lot of time in Palm Beach during the summer, because her father, Adolph Lewisohn, spent his winters in Palm Beach. I wasn't allowed to go. We never went.

How she truly occupied herself all day, I don't know, but she did seem busy. Of course, she ran an establishment, because she had a cook and a kitchen maid, a butler, her own maid, a waitress and a chambermaid. That was quite a staff.

I don't think Mother expressed frustration. She was bored talking to her children, but she was not at all bored with life. I don't think it crossed her mind to have a little flirtation, although it crossed almost everyone else's mind.

FRED FIELD: I was taken to the opera quite often. We didn't have a box. My grandmother and that generation had one. We had two seats. They were perfectly awful seats. I think they were maybe the second or fourth row from the stage, so we got a distorted view. For some, it was important to come into the box during intermissions so everyone would look up at you. It was a disgracefully showy kind of thing. That was done very often. We were not part of that scheme, even though that was all that we saw. My mother was extremely punctual, and she wasn't interested in making a late appearance.

My aunt Lulu had the box. She was considerably older than my uncle Fred, and she had a real problem about being accepted by the rest of the family. At one point, it was noted that she was beginning to bulge a bit. Then she and Uncle Fred went to Europe. Whenever the proper time was, the family got a cable saying that she had a child and it had died. But it was all a fake. She had been stuffing her dress with pillows. I got the impression that the stunt was very successful, not because anybody believed that she had been pregnant, but, by doing this, she had showed her concern about what the family thought.

• • •

MARTIN HARRIS: A great many of our clothes were made at home. My mother also shopped at Lord & Taylor, Lichtenstein, DePinna, Best. I used to get a wholesale suit from Sam Peck. When I grew up and went to school, the great suit was dark blue serge at Brooks Brothers for twenty-five dollars. The pants shone after a while and they were finished, but that was the suit that every boy in school wore.

B. Altman was down on 34th Street. My mother did a lot of buying there. The woman from Altman's would call us up and she would say, "Mrs. Harris, we are having a sale on linen that I think you might be interested in." It was all very personal.

FRANCES LOEB: We did our shopping at Macy's—of course the Strauses and the Lehmans knew each other. In those days, you left an account there, and you had numbers. I think Mother's number was eleven.

I was also taken to DePinna for clothes. We would walk there. We were allowed to walk and we were allowed to take buses. We were not allowed to take trolley cars, and we never took a taxi. My mother had a car, a Minerva. It had a very small motor in front. Of course the chauffeur sat outside where there was no cover. It was a landaulet, so it opened in the back like a baby carriage. Traffic or parking wasn't a problem. Policemen were stationed in the intersections, and you got to know those in your neighborhood. At Christmas, mother would be driven to the various corners, and with a rather quiet smile she would give five or ten dollars to the men on the beat.

HELEN WAGNER: We didn't have much to do with the police. We never knew what it was like to be assaulted or mugged. There was just mischief. On the Fourth of July, they would take a manhole cover off, put gunpowder in there, put the cover back down again, and turn around and put a match to it. It would explode and the manhole cover would go flying.

On their way to school, my brothers would go by the grocery stores with the cans all built up. One of them would come along and pull out the bottom can and they'd fall down.

They stole all the doors of all the buildings to build the bonfires. We had a stable on the block where they had the funeral coaches, and they even stole those for their fire.

FRED FIELD: We were never in a position to meet any other kinds of kids. In the area where we lived, there weren't such people. There was no stickball on the street or anything like that. There were two extracurricular activities in my life: One was the Knickerbocker Greys, where we learned military drilling, and the other was Dodsworth Dancing School.

The Knickerbocker Greys was a little-gentlemen thing. We went once a week, and it must have been a Social Register selection. We had our military uniforms on, with the epaulets and medals. I dressed at home, and I had to walk through the streets in my uniform, which was a little bit embarrassing.

We learned very formal drills, how to turn left, how to turn right. We all carried guns, and we spent hours on the manual of arms. I did work very hard at it, and I was a finalist at it one year and got a medal of some sort. I don't remember we learned anything of any possible use, but we certainly learned how to drill.

One time, I was walking on Fifth with my uniform when I saw a crowd on the steps of the library. An ex-soldier was urging them to enlist. That went on all the time. The heroes from Europe came over and stood on a soapbox and gathered people around. He spotted me standing there with my rifle and put his hand on my shoulder and said something about "this little fellow who is preparing himself for the war, while you people are standing there with your hands in your pockets." Walking home, I felt like a million dollars. I thought I was changing things in our favor.

HELEN WAGNER: Those war years were really pathetic. You couldn't walk the street with a German paper under your arm. You'd be abused from one end of the block to the other. They went so far they abused the poor little German dogs that walked the street. That's the hatred that was. We kept speaking German at home, but we avoided it on the street. We had cousins and uncles over there. Lord knows how many of them were nearly killed by my brothers.

FRED FIELD: Dodsworth was a dance school. My brother and I went once a week after school. It was a little ways down the avenue, around 48th Street. All the sons of the Four Hundred went there. We had to get all dressed up in Eton suits before we went.

Those suits were a horrible, terrible business. I still shiver when I think of that suit. It had a starched Buster Brown collar, a short jacket, a vest with lapels, a gold watch and chain that was double looped into one of the pockets, a black tie and stickpin in the shape of a flying duck, long pants and patent-leather shoes with a large black bow on the toes. I also wore white gloves. I walked down the avenue alone to class. The obvious reason I was allowed to do that was there were no hoodlums on Fifth Avenue, so I was safe in my Eton suit.

FRANCES LOEB: There were two Jewish dancing classes. Our dancing class took place at my grandfather's house in his ballroom. I suppose it was, like, every Friday afternoon. There were about a dozen little boys and about the same amount of little girls, all from families that you knew. I was a wallflower. I was very tall, and I didn't even dance very well, so nobody wanted to dance with me.

Grandfather's house was an enormous brownstone mansion on Fifth Avenue between 69th and 70th streets. It was fifty feet wide and six stories high. It had supposedly one of the largest private ballrooms in the city. Overlooking it was a musicians' balcony that was quite decorative but rarely used. When I was eighteen, Helen and I had our coming-out party there. It was a wonderful affair with about 200 or 300 people. John and I also married in that room.

The house also had a very large dining room that was separated from the ballroom by a conservatory, which had a fountain in its center. All the rooms in the house were large, with high ceilings. He [Grandfather] had an outstanding art collection, including pieces by Gauguin and Van Gogh. There was also a Monet over the staircase that led to the basement and a Renoir, which hung over the mantel in the library.

My grandfather Lewisohn made a lot of money in the mining business. There was very little left when he died. He was a great philanthropist, and he also spent his money on things he liked. When his son told him to be more careful about his spending, my grandfather said, "I have this money, and I'm going to enjoy it," and he did.

FRED FIELD: I remember my grandmother's house quite well. It was a very cold formal place. There was an enormous marble entrance hall. On the walls were alternate marble slabs and European tapestries. I never saw the second floor. We could never do what you would imagine children do, ring the bell and tear down the hall to see Grandpa or Grandma. The butler would announce you. "You will find Madam in the living room." It was done very carefully by rules.

As life went on between the adults, we'd be pretty totally ignored as we sat somewheres nearby. There was no running around or playing with anything. There were no toys there.

Actually, it was a horrible relationship to look back on. It was so utterly meaningless and formal. Everybody was very nice. You were never scolded. We behaved extremely well. We knew the rules inside out without knowing the rules.

I always got very nervous at my grandfather's house. As you ate, a manservant wearing an operetta uniform and gloves stood behind your chair. I couldn't get through the food fast enough before they began scooping it up.

My grandmother sat stiffly in a straight-backed chair, and our conversation consisted of "Good morning, Nanan" and "Good-bye, Nanan." That was it. We went out of duty, not because we were going to have fun or were fond of them or they of us. I had no sense that they were my loving grandparents. There was absolutely no hugging. We'd give them a smack on the cheek. You never put your arms around them or they around you in this particular case. They showed their damn Pekinese dogs, who had their own satin pillows, a lot more consideration.

On Sundays we went to St. Bartholomew's. My father was a vestryman and my mother was a regular churchgoer. They were serious about it—more socially than religiously. We had our own pew, which was very conspicuous. You were expected to show up there. You knew all the people who were in the adjoining pews. My mother, in any case, was an unquestioning believer. Still, it was not very different from an opera box, and I don't think it was terribly important, although I think her belief in religion came to her rescue when she was dying from cancer.

For a person in her position, my mother was a remarkably tolerant person. The word *democratic* was used in describing her. I think it simply meant that she was decent to people, let's say, beneath her. She was nice to servants. She was very thoughtful about their families.

My father was quite the opposite. He didn't work. He just had his stocks and bonds and his hobbies. He was very well read. He read the *Nation* and the *New Republic*, strangely enough, although I don't see they had the slightest influence. I often wondered what he got out of them. He was anti-Catholic because Catholic meant Tammany and the Irish poor, the radicals. There were social people who were, occasionally, Catholic who would come into the house, and there would be some comment made that in spite of their Catholicism, they were okay.

We did have one Jewish friend who had come up to Lenox for a week or so. He got thrown out because my father found a pill that was used to cure gonorrhea in his medicine cabinet.

FRANCES LOEB: There was also a lot of feeling that we were outcasts, that Jews were different from other people, not in a good sense. I imagine there was also a certain amount of envy. I'm pretty sure that my family never spoke to or entertained or went with anybody but Jews until later on. Still, our circle was so closed that when my son was a young man, he said to me once, "It always surprises me that there is anybody else in the world but Jews."

On the other hand, it was the era of assimilation, meaning of fading into the background, not bringing out the Jewishness. I think that's partly why we behaved so badly during the whole Hitler thing. We were wonderful to the people that we brought over, but I had the feeling that nobody had any real need to help these people because they were part of us.

MARTIN HARRIS: In some ways, those years before World War I were very good times. We went away for a month every summer to Thousand Islands. The kitchen and front door and windows on the first floor were completely boarded up. You would send down to Grand Central Station or Pennsylvania Station and they would send a carriage to pick up our big heavy Innovation trunks.

I went on my first trip to Europe in 1910. It took ten days, and the ship had beds, not berths. In 1912, when I started to go out, that was probably one of the most extravagant eras as far as parties were concerned. The Guggenheims would take over the whole orchestra of the theater for a debut party. Then you'd go back to the Ritz for a supper party. The parties in the Waldorf, they were very dressy—black tie and tails.

People who were *très chic* paraded through Peacock Alley there. You could sit there and watch them go by. I saw "Diamond Jim" Brady and Lillian Russell go by together. She was quite beautiful, very heavy, big-breasted, milk-fed. She was well along then. Actually, both of them were pretty big.

For two weeks at Christmastime, the parties went on night after night, luncheons, skating parties in the park. Nothing was ever done second-rate. We went to Sherry's, Delmonico's, the Plaza, St. Regis, or in the homes, where you had beautiful dinner parties

for twelve, fourteen people. After dinner, they'd have some vaudeville star for entertainment and then breakfast.

For the tea dances at the Plaza or the Waldorf, the girls would
meet their dates under the Biltmore clock, and they would be
chaperoned by their maids. In my case, when I came in from
Princeton, my girl didn't need her maid. She was allowed to use
their chauffeur. He would drive us to parties and then call for us
at two o'clock in the morning. I would say to him, "You can come
tomorrow night at eight o'clock," for the next party.

Often, Irene and Vernon Castle appeared at the parties. They
were absolutely magnificent. She was so attractive, and everybody
tried to imitate the way they danced and the way they dressed,
especially her hair. When she bobbed her hair, all the women followed.

◆   ◆   ◆

FRED FIELD: I went to a school called Alan Stevenson, which
was a boys' day school. It was up on the East Side around 56th
Street. The students were from wealthy families. I didn't know what
the term *prominent* meant. You don't learn that until you go to
prep school. Then you learn whether a Ford or a Chrysler is in
your class.

I remember as a little boy I used to be kidded by my brother
about having Vanderbilt in my name. I didn't become conscious of
the fact that I was a Vanderbilt for a long time. I don't think I gave
it much of a thought until I began to have ideas that ran counter
to the tradition, which would mean the last couple of years at college—really pretty late, and then shortly afterward, when I began
to take an interest in socialist ideas.

FRANCES LOEB: At Horace Mann, I was completely on my own
for the first time, and I loved it there. The classes were nice and
big. I was fairly popular, and there were a lot of extracurricular
activities.

We took the bus, but every now and then Mother would send
us in the car, and we would always tell the chauffeur to stay a
couple of blocks away, because that big Pierce-Arrow looked so
ostentatious, although I'm not sure I even knew the word *ostentatious* in those days.

CLAUDIA STEARNS: The right man went to a rich school and a rich college. It was much more important to go to a rich school than a rich college. My husband went to a rich school, Pomfret, so he was socially impeccable. When a friend of ours came up for membership at the Rockaway Hunt Club, they asked him where he went to school. He said the University of Virginia. He didn't know at the Rockaway Hunt Club a school was a school and a college was a college.

FRED FIELD: When I was thirteen, I went to Hotchkiss, where there were a rather large number of scholarship boys. I made great friends there with a boy who came from Montclair, New Jersey. I remember being conscious of that. What the hell was Montclair, New Jersey? It's not Fifth Avenue. It was something very different from me. I brought him home, and my parents didn't mind. It was such a mild difference, and they didn't even know that anybody went to the school that came from such a strange place as Montclair, New Jersey.

Hotchkiss was awfully good for me. It certainly ranks among the fancy prep schools in the East, but it was the first time I really ran into a large variety of people my own age. Hotchkiss was really a short drive from Lenox. Occasionally, we would have rather surprise holidays. I'd call home and the chauffeur would come and pick me up and I'd bring a couple of friends with me. The scholarship boys happened to be the best companions I had found there. They were better-formed, better-disciplined guys than the ones who had no responsibility.

MARTIN HARRIS: In 1914, we moved, because my mother was ill and she wasn't able to climb stairs. So we moved to this apartment hotel called the Hotel Essex, on 56th Street and Madison Avenue. We had a lovely apartment. The china and the glassware were absolutely beautiful, and in the bathroom they even had an icebox that made ice water.

The hotel had a restaurant, and we had all our meals served up from there. We never cooked. We didn't need any servants. In a way, it was sort of a step up. We could have dinner parties in a private room in the restaurant, or we could have our dinner served upstairs.

We soon saw the war coming along. In '16, General Wood brought a group of us up to Plattsburgh for a month at our own expense for officers' training. Later, I was assigned to the Liberty Division, the 77th, at Camp Upton.

I made a good friend on the train to Yaphank. His business was service to breweries, and he knew all the Rupperts and the Ehrets. He was a very amusing, funny guy. His real claim to fame was that he was Mae Murray's first husband.

Bill was a great guy. He introduced me to Broadway and all the nightlife around there. Soldiers lived well then. There was a lot going on. On a Saturday night at the Biltmore Hotel were great doings. Then we went overseas, where a rat would crawl over you while you slept in the trenches. It was a long way from Broadway.

FRANCES LOEB: It was very expensive to take a girl out. First, you had to send her an orchid or a gardenia. That would be whatever, five dollars. If somebody asked me on a date, they might ask me to a place like the Colony, which was the city's most elite restaurant. You got there in a taxi. Then you had two tickets for the theater, which were eight or ten dollars apiece. Then he takes you dancing. So we figured seventy-five dollars, almost a hundred, before the evening was over. We thought that was terribly expensive, and the only thing I could think of doing—I can't tell him not to send me an orchid, which I don't want anyway—I thought maybe we could go dutch on the dinner. My father thought that was a very good idea and gave me the money to do it.

I had a lot of boyfriends. I liked Adam Gimbel, who took me to the Colony. He introduced me to Sam Goldwyn and his wife and took me to Vassar in his Mercedes touring car. The two years before I got married were very exciting. Evidently, I got to be better looking, more used to my height, although you must remember, if you were a nice-looking Jewish girl from a good family with plenty of money, you could even be ugly and have fun.

LUDWIG KOTTL: The good old days—to us it was very bad. You never had an overcoat. You never had new shoes. You always had shoes that you stuffed with cardboard. I got a pair of shoes when I was fifteen years old. That was the only pair I ever got. My father would fix 'em. If a nail was stickin' up when you put them on, you don't say nothin'. You limped away and tried to get a stone to hit it down yourself, 'cause if you made a noise, he knocked the shit outta ya. He had worked so hard to fix shoes, you couldn't say a word.

I was born at 410 East 73rd Street in 1916. Oh my God, there were so many kids around there. Seventieth Street alone must have had 500 kids. It was wall-to-wall kids, the whole place. I think we must have had one of the smallest families. We had five. The rest all had nine, ten, fifteen.

When I was a little kid all the kids were dyin' of influenza. All the hospitals were loaded. My sister and I got sick with scarlet fever, so they grabbed my sister and they put her in the hospital, but they couldn't get me. I was under the bed kickin' and bitin'.

She died, but I lived, 'cause my mother took care of me. In the hospital they just threw you in bed and you just laid there. They didn't know nothin'. At home, your mother puts a cold thing on your head and pets you and takes care of you. Sure, I woulda died in the hospital. Kids were dyin' by the thousands.

FRANK DiTRAPANI: I was born in 1916 in Sicily. My father was the only electrician in this small town. Anybody who wanted lights had to come to him. He did very well, but he came here to save his life in 1921.

In those days, the Mafia was practically running the country. My father was a very hotheaded man. He got in a fight with his boss, who was Mafia. He threw a wrench at him and landed the boss in the hospital.

It was common knowledge that if you offended the Mafia you were dead, so he told my mother he couldn't stay. He decided to go to America a couple of years to let things cool off. My mother said if he went, she went too. They left quickly, and before he went, he had his brother walking behind him wherever he went.

He came here with the idea that maybe in five years he would return. After all, he had a house, land, but he never did go back, even though over here we were just ordinary people scraping a living.

The first apartment we had was on 59th Street, right next to the bridge. It wasn't noisy, because it was mostly horse and wagons with an occasional car going over the bridge. In those days, 62nd Street, 63rd, 64th, and 65th were practically ninety percent Italian. They used to have feasts like crazy. They would have kids dressed as angels hanging on a line across from one side of the street to another. They strung 'em up across the street, real live children. They'd tie them up with belts. It scared me to watch it.

LUDWIG KOTTL: My father was a chef. He was workin' here, workin' there. Bein' a chef, you worked twelve, fifteen hours a day, six or seven days a week, till you wind up with ten dollars, fifteen dollars at the end of the week. We were always very poor, but he never cared. He didn't bring nothin' home except some stale cake. Then when he wasn't workin', we got dispossessed from the apartment. All the furniture was on the sidewalk. When you can't pay the rent the marshal comes and out you go. You just sat there until some other landlord took you in.

We were all outside, the whole bunch of us. The mother and father they shrink, you know. It was a big shame. My mother cried. We sat out there on the furniture and everybody comes and stares at you. The neighbors didn't take a collection. Are you kiddin'? The neighbors would try to steal your furniture.

JOE HENRY: We called the area by the river on 62nd Street and 63rd Street the Dead End. Down there was just a bunch of big rocks and about three or four buildings. The rest of it was wide open. Those buildings had a lot of Irish people. They were mostly the so-called Dead End kids. They were the rough kids. If you went swimming in the river down there, you never knew when you would be assaulted by them. They would take a nickel from you or they would even take your pants. There were times when I had to go home in my underwear.

LUDWIG KOTTL: The water was clean at high tide, and when the ferry pulled out, we swam around there. The water rats were gigantic, but if we didn't bother them, they didn't us. People used to call *us* the water rats, 'cause we used to go down there any time of the day or night, midnight swimmin', you know. At high tide, it was beautiful.

FRANK DiTRAPANI: The 67th Street library was my second home. I would take two books home and come back the next day. The girl behind the desk couldn't believe it. When the kids at school would have an argument, they would say, "Why don't you ask Frank? He knows."

My parents never encouraged it. My mother would say, "You're like Archimedes with your nose in a book all day and you don't know what's going on." She knew about Archimedes because she had wanted to be a teacher, but her father didn't let her.

LUDWIG KOTTL: We'd play hooky, buy cigarettes and sneak into the Yorkville Casino by climbing the drainpipe into the toilet. If it was summertime, we'd go down to the dock and go swimmin'. We used to hang out by the dock, just sittin' there talkin', makin' up stories. There might be forty or fifty of us out till two, three o'clock in the mornin'. At home, sometimes we had twenty guys layin' all over the floor in the front room. They didn't wanna go home. We'd talk about anything and everything. Like guys hitchhiked down south. They put you on the chain gang. Some of our friends were on a chain gang for six months.

We didn't talk about girls. You never talked about cars. At that time, all you wanted was a job. Everybody wanted to work, but what were you gonna do? I had nothin' to do. I wanted to work and there was no work, but when I was ten, if I helped the driver, he would buy me coffee and a doughnut or a bowl of soup.

I worked in a laundry when I got bigger. They'd give me fifty cents to make deliveries. Once I got held up, up in Harlem. There were three or four guys in this hallway with ice picks. I gave 'em the money. I was only ten years old. I went outside and cried like hell.

When we had a few pennies, we rode the ferryboat to Astoria. It was like the country. There was a little house here, a little house there. It was all dirt roads and a little trolley car goin' out on Main Street.

FRANK DITRAPANI: I spent a lot of time at the Kip's Bay Club, mostly making model airplanes from balsa wood. I would cut them out and carve my own propellers. They had rubber-band motors inside. I built a Cecil Paoli. It was an unusual plane because it had a small front wing and a big wing in back and two propellers that were in the back.

There were two rubber bands. They were very heavy, and took a long time to wind. So we took an eggbeater with the two beaters, and we put two hooks on. With the eggbeater, we could wind it up real quick. That thing flew! Wow! It would fly two, three stories high and half a block.

I built a complete replica of the *Spirit of St. Louis*, including a moving joystick, the ailerons and rudder. It took months to build and it was a beautiful thing. It was so good. They had a show at the Armory, and they displayed it along with others.

LUDWIG KOTTL: Pechter's Bread used to be on 90th Street between Avenue A and First Avenue. They seen us stealin' so they made some extras for us. They knew you were hungry. They had the bread coolin' off when we were out at two o'clock in the mornin'. That hot bread took all the skin out of the inside of your mouth. You were so hungry, you're tryin' to eat it when it's red hot. Then one day somebody stole the bakers' lunches. After that we had some job tryin' to get bread. They would close the doors and bar them. We don't know who stole 'em. That was a bad thing to do. Those poor guys worked so hard.

JOE HENRY: I came here with my mother when I was sixteen, in 1928, from Perth Amboy, New Jersey. I had left high school and had to go to work because I had lost my father. We moved to 75th Street between First and Second. That time, there were four- and five-story buildings with railroad flats. There was no privacy, and in the summertime it was wicked. You could get a little air in the kitchen or in the front room, but then we had two or three bedrooms in the back, and you got no air in there because there were no windows. I spent a lot of nights sleepin' in Central Park.

Around 1930 I went to work in the wholesale flower market on 28th Street. I used to deliver flowers. That's how I got to know New York. That's how I got to know a lot of things. I found out that lots of men had mistresses, especially on Central Park West. They used to have apartments there where they kept their women. Then I knew the hotels. Like the Essex House was an old whorehouse. Absolutely. And some of the other hotels. I used to know the Sherry Netherland. Even the Waldorf-Astoria. Same thing.

I was pretty wise. Lots of time when you go in these hotels, the bellboys want to do the delivery, because they always figured there was a little tip. I wouldn't let 'em do it. I used to tell 'em, "If

I can't take it up, I'll take 'em back to the shop." Eventually, they let me up. Then I would see things. I rang the bell, a woman would come out and she would be in lingerie, and you could hear the guy in bed.

A lot of these guys had charge accounts. They bought the best flowers. We were a high-class florist. We had the best customers, the Park Avenue trade—the rich whore trade, that's what I called it. They had these nightclubs. I used to deliver flowers to N. T. G. [Nils T. Granlund]. He ran a big nightclub. I delivered the flowers for the show girls. Sometimes a rich bugger would order fifty orchids for the show girls. They would be about seven dollars apiece, and sometimes I got a five-dollar tip.

I delivered flowers to the gangsters' funerals, like Legs Diamond's. If they order a blanket, they might spend $200. Guys like Owney Madden and Dutch Schultz were our customers. When they sent flowers, they usually enclosed a little card. They wouldn't sign their full names. It might just say "From Owney." He would have Little Frenchie come into our store and order something special. There were two or three of 'em used to come in.

My boss always told me if Mrs. Madden walked by, call her in and give her a flower, and I used to do that. She was a lovely lady. I'd give her a nice rose or I'd tell her to pick one out. Sometimes she wanted to pay for it, but we never charged it. I just told her the boss said it was all right. I never mentioned Owney Madden to her, but she must have surmised.

The gangsters were good and bad tippers. It all depended. Most of the time, no, because if I delivered a piece to Campbell's, either I would give it to some guy in Campbell's or he would send it right back to the body. I walk in the room. There's the body laid out and that would be it. He certainly wouldn't tip me.

FRANCES LOEB: This was the Roaring '20s. Your skirts were up to your knee. Your stockings were rolled up, and your cloche hats were pulled down. There was a lot of drinking, unfortunately. Mostly kids did it, and they mostly did it at football games. Of course, they wore raccoon coats, but I think we were just past the age of Stutz Bearcats.

MARTIN HARRIS: I didn't have a raccoon coat. I borrowed one from a friend. We would drive down to Princeton or even take a train to New Haven and hang onto the trolley cars. When I was married, I always had a hip flask. I insisted my wife drink only that whiskey, because it was stuff a group of us would get off a truck we hired from Canada with Canadian whiskey all sealed and everything. Once he came over the border, he drove over to somebody in the country and then we divided it up. About four of us had the truck. There were about twenty cases. It wasn't too expensive—about $120 a case, but it was good.

FRED FIELD: Those were fun times. We were young guys from Harvard with money to spend and we strutted around and enjoyed it in that sense. The guys I went out with turned out to be a very interesting bunch. We weren't a bunch of playboys, but we were a pretty fancy bunch of guys. We went out with society girls. They got all dressed up. We got all dressed up in top hats, tails, and white ties, went to decent expensive places and talked our heads off.

I lived on an expense account. There was no need to think about working while in college. It would be the furthest thought from my mind. There would be no point in doing it. Nobody in my crowd was working.

MIKE LEWIS: I grew up in speakeasy times. From 48th to 56th from Fifth Avenue to Sixth Avenue was total brownstones. Years and years ago, King's College—Columbia University—had owned all that property. All the elegant people lived there a long time. Then it became a run-down area, and by Prohibition they were rows of speakeasies and rooming houses.

Frequently, before dinner, myself or one of my brothers would be sent out to search one of the local speakeasies for one of our parents. I'd knock on the door, "Joe sent me." That was a big joke. Anyone could go in.

My mother had a favorite one on 49th Street. I'd look around, and usually my mother would be with some guy, and I'd say, "C'mon home, it's dinnertime."

My father and mother went their own way most of my life. My mother ran a studio that designed silk scarves and hatbands for straw hats that they sold to Dobbs Hatters, one of the Fifth Avenue shops. My father was a lawyer. He had two practices. He was a real estate lawyer with clients like Schulte Cigar Stores, which hired him on a yearly retainer. Then he was in politics. In 1928, he managed Al Smith's presidential campaign in New York.

In the early '30s, we were living on 48th between Madison and Park Avenue. We were right near the Chatham Hotel and Pierre's and the Park Lane, which were all very fashionable. Our building belonged to the King of England. Every year we got a Christmas card from England. It was engraved and signed "The Crown."

We didn't live on Park Avenue because below 79th Street no Jews lived on Park Avenue. It was totally out of the question. But who the hell cared? There were plenty of rich Jews. We didn't care about the Vanderbilts or the Astors. We had our own society—the families that are big today, like the Tishmans, whose children went to Ethical in chauffeured limousines. There was no shortage of monied people.

Even in Depression times, our neighborhood was very elegant. There was Maillard's and in front of Sherry's would be cabriolets like Hispano-Suizas, which was a very big foreign car, or an Isotto-Fraschini, which was very big, Brewsters, which were American-made Rolls-Royces, and the Minerva, another Spanish car. It was all "veddy" fashionable.

After we went shopping, we would go to Pierre's restaurant for a bite. It always made the shopping trip worthwhile. There was a barbershop across the street, Charles DiZembler. He had been in some hotel in Cairo. You went there and had a shampoo and a haircut and the whole works. It was also very elegant.

The Sunday procedure was to walk up Park Avenue, maybe to 79th Street and back, and tip your hat to this one and that one and to all the important people. My father was a politician and all the way up and down the street, people tipped their hats to him. He never wore a hat, so he didn't have one to tip, but he went through the motion. He wore gray pin-striped trousers and a black morning coat with a swallow tail and a stiff wing-tipped collar. My mother had mostly made-to-order clothes by Natasha Rambova, who was the wife of Rudolph Valentino and was also a very fashionable dressmaker.

I wore gray flannel short-pants from DePinna or Best & Co. We never wore clothes that came from anyplace else. Except, my grandmother was a great sewer and we would go to Best or De-

Pinna and buy pongee shirts and bathrobes, and they would be sent to her house. She would copy the clothes and send them back after she was done.

I had coats and tails from Lord & Taylor. For years, there was a man, Mr. Anderson, there who outfitted every fashionable young Jewish boy, and we never went to anybody else. At one point, he left there and went to Wanamaker's, so we went to Wanamaker's. Wherever he was, you went.

Ludwig Kottl: We never had an overcoat, so I used to deliver coal or wood and then get warm by the stove in the ice cellar. We never got nothin' no matter how many deliveries we made. I got a nickel tip once for deliverin' laundry up in Harlem. This colored lady had about six or seven kids all over the place and she gave me a nickel. It was the first nickel I ever made, but I gave it back to her. I said, "Gee you have so many kids, spend it on them."

I wore dungarees with patches. In the winter we wore whatever rags we had. We used to find a lot of old overcoats—old rags— and pile them on our beds, because we only had a little blanket to keep us warm. It was so cold in our rooms that ice would form inside on the windowsill.

We hated winter because we was always cold. We didn't have clothes. It took you an hour before you stopped shiverin', 'cause the bed was like a piece of ice. The only time I ever enjoyed the winter was when we used to pour water in the middle of the gutter and make ice on half the block. Then we'd run like a son of a bitch and we'd slide, "Heyyyyyyyyyyyy!"

Frank DiTrapani: After school, kids would play baseball in the street, and they would choose sides, but they never chose me. I was pushed away. Nobody wanted me. I couldn't throw a ball. I couldn't catch. I was small. I was terrible. I was just not one of the crowd. There were times when I felt very sad about it, and I used to go to church every day and pray like crazy that I would get bigger, but my prayers never got answered. Instead, I would go home and play piano for hours. My mother would say, "Please, please, stop!"

Claudia Stearns: My father didn't like New York, so when he inherited money, he bought farms and grew hops in Waterville.

He never milked a cow, never did anything except supervise it. He was in for a big fortune because nobody could make beer without hops, and he sold his hops to all the big New York brewers. So we were brought up on the farm. I didn't come to New York to stay until I got married, which was 1929, when I was twenty-two.

I did visit when I was in Vassar. I'd go to a tea dance or something. They were wonderful if you had a date. See, if you had a date for the movies, all you did was sit and hold hands. That was considered very racy. The tea dances were just great, because it was more fun to dance *and* hold hands.

MIKE LEWIS: You'd get Paul Whiteman and Ramona, all the top-notch talent at the tea dances. You'd have them at 4:30 and they'd last an hour and a half or so. The Pennsylvania Hotel was very elegant for a tea dance, and so was the Biltmore and the Roosevelt. The help at the Ritz Carlton were all dressed in Louis XVI costumes, very elegant, you know. And in those days, homes on Park Avenue were fourteen and fifteen rooms with big salons, so it wasn't unusual to have coming-out parties in the homes. There would be dinner parties with twenty kids and two or three servants.

CLAUDIA STEARNS: I wrote something for my class reunion, and one of the lines was, "We were the last of the flappers. We were the last of the virgins." We just didn't do that sort of thing. Externally, the flappers were wild, but they were all virgins. At Vassar, we had to be back by ten o'clock Sunday night. There was one girl who didn't come home one night from a weekend, and she was fired.

Maybe others did, but my friends didn't. I found out about what to expect on my wedding night by reading Freud. My mother never told me anything. We had a girl at Vassar who didn't know how babies were born until her roommate enlightened her. She was horrified when she found out.

JOE HENRY: I screwed nice girls. They were not tramps. They were just regular people. I never liked the idea of shackin' up with a prostitute. I could get a girl if I wanted one, anyway.

I knew the park like the back of my hand. Many a time I spent all night there. I was young, and I used to go there with girls. The hell they *didn't* do those things then—I got news for ya—all that stuff went on. Only today everything's out in the open. I screwed plenty girls in Central Park. I had a favorite spot—in a little shelter near the 79th Street transverse. We never felt any danger, and I never forced a girl or anything like that. Girls were willin' most of the time. If they weren't, I didn't bother with 'em.

Sometimes we used birth control. I knocked up a couple girls, but I helped 'em get an abortion, 'cause I figured I was responsible. I went to some friend I knew and he recommended a woman doctor in the 70s. I think she charged $100 or $150. That was a lot of money durin' the Depression. It was a problem gettin' it, but I managed. I used to gamble a bit, and I had a few friends.

Actually, the woman doctor didn't perform the abortion. She sent us up to a well-to-do physician up in the Bronx. He owned a whole apartment house. He had *some* office. He must have done ten or twenty a day.

MIKE LEWIS: We went to the park with the Toltec Club. Everybody who was anybody in Jewish society belonged to the club. You were picked up by a car every afternoon and taken to Central Park to play baseball and basketball. There was competition between teams.

Although we had nannies, I always roamed freely around the neighborhood. From early childhood, I had a little bicycle, and I could go anywhere I wanted. I'd be wearing my gray flannel shorts and shirt, and I'd go to the Ogden Mills Reid house on Park Avenue. It was much bigger than the Vanderbilt mansions, and it was a great place to skate.

FRANK DiTRAPANI: Union Hardware skates. Everybody had them but me, so I wanted them. They were $1.98. My mother told me to save for them. I saved pennies and she'd give me a few a week. I finally had thirty-five cents, and came Christmas I had a pair of skates. I think I was the happiest boy in the world.

MIKE LEWIS: I went to elementary school at a boarding school in Croton-on-Hudson, and then I went to Walden. I think my parents wanted to get me out of the house. I didn't know anybody who went to public school. We used to live across the street from a public school, and it was fascinating to watch all the little children who went there. The concept of going to public school was completely foreign to me.

LUDWIG KOTTL: I went to a lotta schools. I went to continuation school. It was like a work school. You were supposed to learn a profession like carpentry or plumbin'. It was just that you were supposed to go to school till you were sixteen. I went because my two brothers got beat up and they were demoted from school because they came in late, so my father went over there and started to argue. They said they would throw them out of school if he didn't like it, and then they said about me, "Take him, too."

I also went to the Catholic school. This Brother Austin was a nut. Oh, God. He used to beat the shit outta me every single day of the week. He'd call me a Polack. He didn't like Polacks. I wasn't even Polish, but to him I looked like a Polack. He'd come into class. If you missed one word of catechism, you held your hand out and he hit it with a stick.

My little brother was six years younger than me. He had welts all over his body from him, so he went home and hid in the cellar. He wouldn't go to school. That Brother Austin—if you was Irish, you was all right, but if you was somethin' else, he just hit you. He died in the crazy house, 'cause he beat so many people up.

They finally sent me to truant school, PS 37, on 88th Street between Lexington and Park. That was a tough place. Some fellas were nice, but the other guys were always takin' money off you. Everybody had to give money or they want to beat you up all the time. These were big guys. They were nineteen, twenty. They were out of reform school. They ruled that school. I used to get shellacked there all the time by the teachers, too. If somebody was smokin', they grab the whole bunch. You hold your hands out and they got whips. If you duck or pull your hand away, you get it across your face.

The schoolteachers were all war veterans. They all had plates in their heads, and all they wanted to do was hit you. There was one guy, he always had a grin on his face. I laughed back at him. He said, "Come up here, you. Lemme see your hand."

Wham! He had a cane. I'm tellin' you, I had no hand left.

"That'll teach you to laugh."

Hell, the guy looked like he was laughin' all the time. I didn't know what the hell to make out of these people. These teachers were so confusin'.

There was no such thing as homework in that school. It was survival, that was it. What could you do? There was screwballs in that school. There was murderers. You should see the knives they collected from them. They had guns.


JOE HENRY: You had all kinds of thugs playin' craps in our neighborhood. They were holdup guys, reformatory graduates, you name it. I got to know these guys. They would be drivin' around in a stolen car, and they would invite me to go for a ride. If they were hard up, some of them would go around muggin' people. They used to mostly mug the drunks or guys they knew they could get away with. The hell there wasn't muggin' in those days. In certain neighborhoods there were. You name it, any of those blocks, 74th, 75th, 76th, right up to 79th Street, there were muggin's all the time. A lot of these guys would get caught stickin' up a laundry or stickin' up a chicken market and they would end up in Sing Sing.

We were mostly workin' people, poor people. The first time I went into a house on Fifth Avenue and I saw a ceiling about two stories high, I couldn't believe it. And they had chandeliers and stuff like that and butlers and maids.


CLAUDIA STEARNS: After I graduated, my husband and I were married in Paris in 1929. We couldn't afford to be married in New York, because my father lost his shirt during Prohibition, so we figured we would get married in Paris, where I was working anyway, running the shopping service for the Holland America line. My husband was very stylish, and people would have thought it too queer if we hadn't had a big wedding. Paris sounded just right. We knew we could get away with it, and everybody would think we were wonderful.

After we were married, we couldn't live on the West Side. People didn't. Our crowd was on the East Side. I never thought about it, and my husband never thought about it. We first took an apartment at 320 East 53rd. The next year we got one on Washington Square. We stayed there a year, and then the next year I was expecting, so we had to be up here right near the doctor and we moved back here to 89th Street between Madison and Park.

The crash hit my husband very hard. He still stayed in the insurance business, but he lost his zest for it. Even though we didn't have much money, we always had servants. We had enough for that. My mother was a debutante from way back, and she said to me once, "The So-and-So's have a car, and they haven't even got a maid." So you always had to have a maid instead of a car. All my friends had maids. Even people with no children would have a maid, just because they were used to it, I suppose.

We were both Socialists then. One year, we went to vote at the Rockaway Hunt Club, in Cedarhurst. We voted on bits of paper for Norman Thomas. When we went to our car, this little old lady came running toward us holding a piece of paper. She said, "You can't vote for Norman Thomas at the Rockaway Hunt Club!"

MIKE LEWIS: My mother did all kinds of charitable work. She was head of a day nursery, and she worked for the Hudson Guild. Sunday nights my brothers went to a dance at the Guild, where they danced with poorer people.

CLAUDIA STEARNS: I used to speak on street corners for the Common Man when Roosevelt was running for governor. He was as close to socialism as we could get. We were recruited out of Vassar. On Sunday, I used to leave the Common Man and go up to Hyde Park and have lunch, with the footman behind my chair. Nobody saw the joke except for Eleanor, who had this sardonic smile. Roosevelt's mother reminded me of my mother-in-law. They were so haughty, and we thought we were great democrats. Maybe other people thought we were haughty.

I took a job teaching at one of the settlement houses. There I was conscious of the different races. I had Jews and Italians and so forth. But before I had my first class, my mother-in-law called on me, and she said, "Your job is to take care of my son," so I was scared into giving up the job. If a woman worked in those days, it made the headlines.

Women were supposed to talk about servants and about shopping. One night, we had an old friend of my husband's for dinner and his wife. The men were talking after dinner in the living room about Russia, and I tried to get into the conversation, because I was interested in Russia, but Sylvia didn't know what Russia was! How was I supposed to talk to her?

• • •

Mike Lewis: Of course we were aware of the Depression, but it didn't have any impact on my life. But obviously you had to be aware of it, because on every corner in the area we lived in there were apple sellers. They would polish them and pile them up, and they were a nickel or a dime. We saw plenty of that.

Joe Henry: When things got real bad, they had soup lines. They didn't feed 'em much, but they fed 'em a bowl of soup and a piece of bread. I saw the Hoovervilles in Central Park. A lot of these men, they weren't only the bums. I'm talkin' about people that lost their jobs—decent people. They had to move to Central Park. They lived in paper crates and wooden crates and tents and you name it. There must have been a few hundred.

I talked to a few of the guys. They considered things hopeless, but some of 'em told me they were still lookin' for work, and then some of 'em told me they were sellin' apples or fruit or bananas. Most of 'em were workin' people. Some of 'em had families, but the families broke up. They went back to their families. In the Hoovervilles were mostly men. Some of 'em were pretty ragged. If you gave 'em a shirt or a piece of clothing, they would appreciate it. It was sad. Hoover got most of the blame. When he became president he said there was gonna be a chicken in every pot, but the chickens were all missin'.

Frank DiTrapani: Everybody was poor, but I didn't see anybody suffering. After the crash, my father didn't work for three years, but we were never on welfare for the reason that my father was a skinflint. During good times, he just socked it away.

My mother said to me, "You're the oldest, I want you to go out and make some money." So I went out and sold different kinds of cards. I didn't make any money. I tried to sell subscriptions. I tried to sell vacuum cleaners. I went up and down steps like crazy with Eurekas and Premiers. I sold maybe two or three of them.

What sustained me was I was able to play piano. I played in back of bars. I'd get three dollars for six hours. That money would last me all week. I could hardly play, but musicians were in great demand, especially for three dollars. Every bar had a place in the back for Saturday nights. There was no TV. People didn't have cars, so that meant they went to bars or social clubs.

MIKE LEWIS: There were still balls at the Waldorf-Astoria and the Plaza, benefits for charities where the tickets were twenty-five dollars. If you were smart, you got the girl's father to buy the tickets. I liked to roller-skate to my dates. I'd leave my skates with the doorman, but I hoped the girl's family had a family car and chauffeur.

There were two things that you did after any big party. One was to go to Childs, which was between 56th and 57th Street on Fifth Avenue, where they made pancakes in the window. Or you went to Reuben's, which was the famous delicatessen of its day. But you didn't go for the food, you went to be with your friends.

Around that time, I went to high school with a young man whose family was totally loaded with money. My father used to give me four or five dollars a week spending money, and this boy got $350 a week.

We would take a cab and go to the Stork Club for lunch. We would go to El Morocco. If you handed the headwaiter five bucks when you walked in, he cared less how old we were.

I was more or less a caretaker for this boy, because he could neither handle his liquor or his money, and he usually handed me his money to take care of his things. We had no problem spending it.

He happened to be fantastically wealthy and fantastically handsome, and he had no problem with women. There was a girl he liked. I arranged for an evening with her and another one. I had naively asked my father, if he was taking a girl out where would he take her. He said, "Oh, I'd take her to the Surf Club," so we went there. I wore evening clothes, and the girls wore evening dresses. We handed the headwaiter ten bucks, and they had a table for us where the stairway went up to the third floor. Lights were low, and they had a woman singing, a chanteuse. When the lights went up, the chanteuse walked over to a ringside table and sat down with my father! I decided never to ask him for advice again.

CLAUDIA STEARNS: I became a Socialist after Vassar. It was purely intellectual. It had nothing to do with sympathy with the poor. If they asked us to sympathize with the poor, we would have. I don't think I was aware of the poverty of the '30s. Our ideas came from our heads. We talked a good line.

The crash upset the social structure. All of a sudden, people stopped giving these big parties, and they never came back. Once they had thrown off the harness of convention, they didn't return. People would suddenly find themselves without servants because they couldn't afford them. The servants became harder and harder to get. They got too expensive.

We got them from Father Divine. He trained them so they were a pleasure to have around the house. He gave them all crazy names. We had a wonderful cook called Everlasting Life. We just called her Ever.

'Twenty-nine was really the end of the stylish life. There were probably lots of people who kept it up, but my friends found themselves without maids. Then they got themselves washing machines, and everybody had a new kitchen. They'd do over their downstairs so the kitchen was part of the dining room, and they'd cook while they were entertaining. My grandmother said, "If you never learn to cook, you'll never have to." Still, I became a good cook.

FRANCES LOEB: I had an Aunt Settie, who was living at what was then the Savoy Hotel at Fifth Avenue and 59th Street. There were a lot of apple sellers on the street then, and for a while Aunt Settie would leave her apartment at noon every day and go to Madison Avenue. She would then send the apple seller at that corner off to lunch with a dollar while Settie tended her stand.

MIKE LEWIS: My father died then, and both my brothers had left home. My mother and myself were living in this huge apartment, and she said to the landlord, "We're going to move. We can't afford the space."

He said, "Well, I'll reduce your rent to $150 a month." So she said all right and we stayed another year. Then she said, "We've got to move. This is just ridiculous, two people in a four-bedroom apartment."

He said, "Well, I'll reduce the rent to $100."

She said, "I don't care what you reduce it to, we're moving!"

LUDWIG KOTTL: When I turned sixteen, I didn't go back to school no more. I didn't get no work for quite a while. When I was twenty years old we grabbed a ship to Africa. I was an ordinary seaman. We got the job 'cause of the strike. I know we were scabs, but what the hell did I know? I didn't know anything. There were no pickets.

My father started to do a little better then. When his boss wouldn't give him a raise, he opened up a store across the street. At first, he worked on a shoestring 'cause he had no money. Little by little he did well.

JOE HINZMAN: When I went to the Army, they said, "You're from Germany. If you go to the United States Army, what would you do? Would you shoot our lines or the Germans?"

I said, "You stupid bastard, they would shoot me before I had a chance to shoot back. Who the hell you kiddin'? I'm born here, you fuckin' Jew, fuckin' cocksucker. You have this nerve to ask me this kind of questions? Who the fuck you think you're talkin' to?" and I nearly knocked him on his fuckin' ass.

JOSEPH LOVITZ: In the '30s, they had the street-corner meetings on 86th Street between Lexington and Third Avenue. They'd sometimes have as much as eight meetings in one night. The meetings were loud. They ranged from everything imaginable, but they were mostly political, with talk about cures for our Depression troubles.

There were Communists. There were Socialists. There were guys who just had pet ideas they were selling. One fellow had a hang-up on John Hanson, who he said was really the first president of the United States. He spoke with a bad lisp. "It'sh John Hanshon, not George Washington. It'sh a big fake!"

Of course, many years later I found out that John Hanson was a president under the Articles of Confederation, but he wasn't the first one.

A fair amount of the speakers were youngish college students, Communists and Socialists. The Communists had a nasty habit of breaking up the meetings of the other leftist parties. Being totalitarians, they couldn't see that the other guy had a right. "Get down, you enemy of the working class!"

They'd heckle and scream. The cops, who enjoyed this, would conveniently go around the corner, as long as it didn't get too violent.

Later on, the Nazis began to get active. They began to appear wearing uniforms. They would have brown shirts with swastikas. Then the Communists, who in some ways were not too smart, got the idea that if they wore uniforms of the Red Army, this would show people that they were anti-Nazi. One night they hired a truck, put on Red Army uniforms, and were singing the "Internationale"—a very silly thing to do.

Joe Henry: We had the Bundists right here in Yorkville. Back in the '30s and '40s, 86th Street was part of Germantown. I first saw 'em around 1931 and '32, and then I saw 'em in the late '30s. They conducted meetings around 86th and York, which was called Avenue A then. Most of the time they wore their brown-shirt uniforms. A guy would get up on a platform, and they would make speeches just like Adolf Hitler used to do. They would talk about why we had the Depression, about the Jewish bankers. If the Bund was running things, things would be better.

There were certain cliques in Yorkville that gave 'em sanctuary. People tolerated 'em up here. If they tried to go somewhere else, they would be in trouble. But what would happen was they would hold the meetings and the Jewish guys would get together and go over there and they would have a fight. [He laughs.]

Joe Hinzman: We had guys that belonged to the Brownshirts. It was a lot of bullshit. To me it was only to show that "I'm a German."

They were popular, but that didn't mean a damned thing. I remember listenin' to Hitler raise hell. I liked to listen to the bullshit. A lot of times, that man only had one thing in mind—to organize Europe into a United Europe, that was his scheme. You know, all political guys, he had no use for, other organizations, and not only were the Jews thrown in concentration camps, also them people. It wasn't only the Jews. The Catholics and Christians were also killed because they did not believe his bullshit. That's a lot of horseshit if you think it was just Jews.

For your information, I went to Austria one time. I said to my cousin, "Good lord, wherever you look, there's a Jew in business.

Hester Street, from the corner of Clinton, ca. 1890 *(Photo by Jacob A. Riis; Courtesy of the Museum of the City of New York)*

Abraham Hyman *(second from right)* with his family in Russia, 1898

Sonia and Max Kisseloff at the Allen Street entrance to his dry-goods store, ca. 1951

Mollie and Abraham Hyman in 1919, just after his return from World War I combat duty

Nat Forman, amateur champ, ca. 1922

Julius and Stanley Auster behind the counter of Auster's Candy Store, Third Street and Avenue D, 1942

The twin Vanderbilt residences on Fifth Avenue between 52nd and 53rd streets in 1894; Frederick Vanderbilt Field's grandparents occupied the mansion on the left *(Courtesy of the Museum of the City of New York)*

Helen, Dorothy, and Frances Lehman, 1910

Frances Lehman, 1923
*(Photo by Edward Steichen)*

Skating on Central Park Lake, ca. 1890; the Dakota in the background
*(Courtesy of the New York Public Library)*

Olga Marx, Barnard College,
Class of 1914

"Bullets" Bressan on an Upper West
Side rooftop, ca. 1917

"Isaac Gellis, 100 Years of Delicious Memories," sign at the corner of Delancy and Essex streets *(Photo by William Goidell)*

Princess Naomi and her grandchildren in Inwood Hill Park, ca. 1930 *(Courtesy of the New York Historical Society, New York City)*

Stanley Marx, P.S. 132, Class of 1932

Nora and Ernest Mair on their wedding day, 1925

McGill University Medical School, Class of 1920; Harold Ellis third row, fifth from left

Isabel Washington in her Cotton Club days, ca. 1935

Did the cocksuckers all come out of their graves and open the business up?" That's what it looked to me like.

It wasn't only the Jews that suffered. [*He raises his voice and pounds on table.*] Millions of Christians had to die because they didn't like his attitude. Why make one issue and the others they didn't mention? Were they the only human bein's suffered? There were more Christians in the concentration camps than Jews. No, I never heard of the Nuremberg laws. I never heard of shit like that. Let me tell you, we dropped bombs that burned everything to a crisp. Women and children were jumpin' into lakes, burnin'. You never heard a fuckin' thing about that, did you? Only a Jew? Where the fuck is my cousins what they burned up there? What, they're not human? Only a Jew was human?

JOSEPH LOVITZ: In the evenings on 86th Street, you saw them in their brown shirts fairly frequently. Does that mean most of the people wore them? No. But it was not unusual. Most people—many of whom were unemployed—enjoyed the meetings. For a while, it was a great show. They liked arguing. It was the days before television.

There was a fellow named Joseph E. McWilliams who ran for Congress. He liked to say, "Howdy, howdy, folks. I'm from Oklahoma." He got in with a group known as the Christian Mobilizers, who were an offshoot of Father Coughlin's group. They were more for street corners than the Nazis. Later, they became the American Destiny Party. Whenever they had a meeting, there would be somebody who would ride around in a covered wagon pulled by a horse. They brought in people from around the city. They entered the Republican primary, but he was swamped and he disappeared for a few years. Later, he turned up in Chicago and was working in, of all places, the garment industry, where practically everybody was Jewish.

JOE HINZMAN: After the war started, Ruppert's started makin' beer for the boys in the Army. It was considered an essential job. It was called Army beer, but there was no difference between Army beer and the other beer—it was just a federal-government contract.

The brewery produced 1,400 cases a day. By then they needed people, so I was mostly workin' strappin' the boxes so nobody could break 'em open. It was a nice job. We were singin' practically on the job. It was there for nothin', so they boozed themselves up so they didn't know what their name was. If you done your work, they didn't care if you were boozed up. There was not one brewery worker that wasn't soused.

I was thirty years in the brewery and I never came home sober. I wonder how I put my day in. For thirty years drunk. When I walked to 86th Street I took the whole sidewalk. All the cops from 86th to 94th Street knew me.

"Where you goin', Joe?"

"Ah, go fuck yourself. I'm goin' home."

I spent a lot of time in the bathroom, with all that beer. Sometimes I couldn't make it up to the bathroom and I stunk like a skunk. I drank all day long. And then I wasn't satisfied. I went to the bar yet. When I woke up and had the hangover, I used to go to the bars in the middle of the night. In other words, I became a regular booze hound, because it was there for nothin'. Eventually, it burned out my stomach, and I had to stop.

I buried about a half a dozen brewery workers with cirrhosis of the liver right here in this neighborhood. I got away with it because I ate like a horse. That saved me from bein' six foot under.

# Upper West Side

EDWARD CLARK had to be crazy. Nobody in his right mind would want to live in a luxury apartment house twenty blocks from the fringes of New York society. His new building was so far uptown, his detractors sniffed, it might as well have been in the Dakota Territories.

Clark liked that one so much, he named his building at the corner of 72nd Street and Eighth Avenue the Dakota. To almost everyone's surprise, it was an immediate success. Soon, a host of luxury apartment houses sprang up in the area. They even imitated the Western motif, with names like the Montana, the Nevada, and the Yosemite. The newcomers were mostly upper-middle-class businessmen. They represented new money who thumbed their collective noses at established society. Who needed Mrs. Astor anyway? They created their own society, and in the process set a nonconforming tradition on the West Side that continued for many years.

Only a few years before Clark built the Dakota, most of the area on the West Side between 59th and 110th streets was covered by farmland. The region was originally part of what the Dutch settlers called Bloemendael (Vale of Flowers), later Bloomingdale. In his *A History of New York by Diedrich Knickerbocker*, Washington Irving rhapsodized over Bloemendael, "a sweet rural valley, beautiful with many a bright flower, refreshed by many a pure stream-let, and enlivened here and there by a delectable Dutch cottage, sheltered under some sloping hill, and almost buried in some em-bowering trees."

Through most of the eighteenth century, it remained a bucolic haven of small farms and country estates. Only the Battle of Harlem Heights in 1776 broke that tranquillity. In one of General Washington's few Manhattan successes, the rebel army forced a British retreat to a buckwheat field where Barnard College now stands. His men pushed farther south, to 105th Street, before Red-coat General Howe appeared with fresh troops to halt the rout.

Real change set in when the Hudson River Railroad tracks were laid down in 1851, opening up the area for commercial de-velopment. Then, in 1868, the Central Park Commission drew up the first plans for the West Side street lines. When the Western Boulevard (now Broadway) was opened along the path of the old Bloemendael Road in 1869, the West Side's first land boom was on.

Speculators with bold ideas for development bought up huge parcels of land. The proposed mansions for Eighth Avenue (Central Park West) were to be the most splendid in the city. West End Avenue, then an amalgam of squatters' farms, odd buildings, and empty lots, would be an exclusive shopping area serving the elegant manor homes on Riverside Drive. But land values plunged after the Panic of 1876, and most of the grandiose plans were shelved. Few buildings were erected, and the squatters and farmers, who still occupied much of the land, for the most part went about their business as they had done for generations.

However, work continued on the first wing of the Museum of Natural History. The building was completed in 1877 on the site of a small lake at 77th Street that had been a popular fishing hole. That same year, Edward Clark purchased his two acres of land at 72nd Street and Eighth Avenue from August Belmont and set about finding an architect for his new project.

Clark died before the Dakota was completed. Certainly, if he had lived, he would have had the last laugh. The Dakota was fully rented when it opened its doors in 1884. And if the names of its tenants weren't Astor, Van Rensselaer or Whitney, they were Schirmer and Steinway, people of wealth and taste, who saw no reason to mourn their exile from a society that had always treated them as outcasts anyway.

The Schirmers, the leading music publishers of the day, were active hosts. Their parties were often stimulating affairs, in sharp contrast to the Astor dinners. Evenings with the Schirmers were attended by some of the city's leading literary lights, including Mark Twain, William Dean Howells, and Stephen Crane.

In the course of a party, Gustav Schirmer enjoyed escorting his guests to the roof so they could marvel at the sumptuous view of Central Park. At least one guest was less than thrilled by the sight. When the Russian composer Peter Ilich Tchaikovsky was shown to the roof, his flawed English prompted a misunderstanding. "No wonder we composers are so poor," he wrote in his diary. "The American publisher, Mr. Schirmer, is rich beyond dreams. He lives in a palace bigger than the Czar's! In front of it is his own private park!"

The Ninth Avenue Elevated train also brought new settlers, and developers quickly capitalized on the heightened demand for housing in the area. Soon, rows of brownstones, tenements, and luxury apartment houses sprang up throughout the neighborhood.

A spirit of individuality pervaded the building boom. The new buildings seemed to incorporate nearly every architectural ornament and style ever known and then some. Perhaps the most visually striking of all the West Side residences was the Ansonia Hotel, at Broadway and 73rd Street. Its interior walls were designed to be thick enough to allow an artistic clientele to follow their whims without fear of disturbing their neighbors. However, it is the building's exterior, a veritable explosion of rococo design, that has made it and the Dakota the West Side's most visible landmarks. And true to the neighborhood's penchant for individuality was the Ansonia's owner, W. E. A. Stokes, who kept a rooftop menagerie that included a bear, goats, ducks, and chickens whose eggs he sold to his tenants at half price.

Though Riverside Drive never attained the level of splendor developers had hoped for, it did boast two of the city's most opulent homes. The grounds of the seventy-five-room Schwab House took up an entire block between Riverside Drive and West End Avenue from 73rd to 74th streets, and the mansion belonging to Mrs. Alfred Corning Clark showed an unexpected sporting touch with its colonnaded bowling alley. Riverside Drive was also the home of William Randolph Hearst and his family. The Hearsts lived in an enormous apartment that took up the top three floors of the Clarendon apartment house on 86th Street and the Drive. Their home contained, among other things, a two-story ballroom, the publisher's huge collection of medieval armor, a rooftop dining room, and a huge bathtub formerly used in the White House to immerse the 300-plus-pound bulk of William Howard Taft.

For sheer extravagance, few could top the Babylonian Gardens that Edward "Daddy" Browning built on the rooftop of his 81st Street apartment. "I wanted to do something different," Browning explained after his "country estate" was built. According to Stanley Walker, in his book *Mrs. Astor's Horse*, the apartment included a lake deep enough to float a rowboat. Browning was often found gliding around his living room, inspecting the more than 10,000 houseplants that lined the shores of his pond.

Browning was divorced in 1923 when he accused his wife of running off with her dentist. "A dentist of all people!" he exclaimed. "How can any sensible woman fall in love with a dentist, particularly with the dentist who has done her work?"

For her part, his ex-wife accused him of preferring young girls. Apparently, she was on the right track. In 1925, he advertised in the New York *Herald Tribune* for a young girl of about fourteen who might like to be "adopted" by a wealthy family. The girl he selected turned out to be twenty-one. Although she insisted he was well aware of her age, he filed to invalidate the adoption.

Daddy Browning was not to be deterred, and the next year he announced he'd found true love with a sixteen-year-old high school student named Frances "Peaches" Heenan. He had met her at a sorority dance, for a sorority he had organized himself. "Why shouldn't I help young girls?" he asked.

The two were married in April and separated in October. She went on to a vaudeville career. He received 40,000 proposals of marriage. Presumably, he read through them all before his death in 1934, but he never married again.

Another fashionable Upper West Side address was the Hotel des Artistes on West 67th Street, where the cafe is decorated with frescoes of nudes by Howard Chandler Christy. With its two-story living rooms and airy studio space, the hotel has been the home of a number of artists and celebrities over the years. Among them were the popular-fiction writer Fannie Hurst, Noël Coward, the explorer William Beebe, Isadora Duncan, Mae Murray, Charlie Chaplin, and Rudolph Valentino.

Valentino's two-day stay around the corner, at Campbell's Funeral Home in 1926, was one of those momentous events that old-timers don't forget. More than 100,000 mourners and curiosity seekers stood on line for two days, not always patiently (at one point they crashed through the funeral home's plate-glass windows), for a last good-bye to Hollywood's most exotic leading man.

Despite its glamour, Des Artistes' immediate surroundings were decidedly less so. Most of the homes in and around the southern portion of Columbus Avenue were working-class. To the south and west was an even poorer neighborhood, of mostly Irish and Italian immigrants, known as Lincoln Square. Most of those tenements have since been replaced by the Lincoln Center complex.

Another area that has largely disappeared is the San Juan Hill district, which covered 59th to 64th streets from the river to Amsterdam Avenue. San Juan Hill was a poor black community. Its name was both a tribute to the black soldiers who had fought in the Spanish-American War and a rueful reminder of the racial strife between the blacks and the Irish that erupted on its streets.

Although most San Juan Hill residents lived in tenement apartments, after the turn of the century some fine model housing was built in the neighborhood. The most notable were the Phipps Houses, which still stand. They were the first apartments for working-class black families built in this country.

Several factors contributed to the neighborhood's decline. Perhaps foremost were the race riots of 1900 and 1905, which caused many black families to flee. Fortunately, a vast and improved housing market had suddenly opened to them uptown. In 1900, plans were set to extend the IRT subway line through Harlem, which was then a quiet middle-class community. Hundreds of new apartments were erected, seemingly overnight, but when the anticipated influx of newcomers failed to materialize, desperate landlords offered their empty apartments to blacks. The population of San Juan Hill declined steadily over the next few years as many blacks took advantage of the modern housing that was virtually handed over to them.

As the uptown black population increased, Harlem's Jewish residents began to flee their old neighborhood. Many settled in the

Bronx and on the Upper West Side. By 1930, fully one-third of the population between 79th and 110th streets was Jewish. In their wake, a host of kosher delis and butchers and cafeterias set up shop on the avenues as parts of the Upper West Side took on a distinctly European flavor.

The wealthier newcomers found an abundance of private schools ready to educate their children properly, among them the progressive School for Ethical Culture and other prestigious academies, including Columbia Grammar, Walden, Collegiate, and Trinity. The Upper West Side also stuck its foot in the door of the Ivy League when Columbia University uprooted itself from Midtown and, along with Barnard College, hunkered down on Morningside Heights, north of 110th Street.

The Upper West Side's reputation as a home to some of the country's leading writers can be traced back to the 1840s, when Edgar Allan Poe spent his afternoons searching for inspiration on the rocky banks of the Hudson. Poe was living in a farmhouse on West 84th Street when he wrote "The Raven" in 1844. Much later, the area was home to J. D. Salinger, F. Scott Fitzgerald, Carl Van Vechten, Isaac Bashevis Singer, and a host of other literary notables.

Up at Columbia, the sibling English professors Carl and Mark Van Doren influenced two generations of writers during their combined tenure from 1911 to 1959. Mark, a Pulitzer Prize–winning poet, gave a portentous A to one of his Shakespeare students in the 1940s. The grade helped convince Jack Kerouac to quit the football team and spend more time on his writing. His books sparked a major literary movement, the Beat Generation, whose anti-establishment attitude arguably helped pave the way for the upheavals of the '60s. Much of that activity centered around the Columbia campus, where rebellion continued what was, at least on the Upper West Side, a long-established tradition.

# The Witnesses

FRANK AMERUSO (1909–) is a pseudonym. He was born on West 69th Street and has spent most of his working life as a gambler and bookmaker.

SELMA BLICK (1913–) is a retired office administrator. She has lived her entire life within a ten-block radius of her Upper West Side birthplace.

GUIDO ''BULLETS'' BRESSAN (1907–) is also a lifelong Upper West Sider. He is a veteran and has held a variety of jobs in the neighborhood during his working life.

EDWARD O. D. DOWNES (1910–) is a musicologist and professor of music at The Juilliard School of Music in New York. He has also written several books on classical music, and his commentary is heard on WQXR, a classical-music station in New York City. He has lived in the Dakota, a West Side landmark, since 1928.

ABE GELLIS (1903–) is the grandson of Isaac Gellis, the former Hot Dog King of New York City. He operated the family business until his retirement.

Moe Greengrass (1926–) is the son of Barney Greengrass, the "Sturgeon King." He owns a store by that name, which has been on the Upper West Side since 1929.

Dorothy Greenwald (1917–) is a free-lance researcher and editor. She was born in Harlem and raised on the Upper West Side.

William Randolph Hearst, Jr. (1908–) was the second son of the publishing baron. He is currently editor in chief of Hearst Newspapers.

Olga Marx (1894–1988) was born on West 77th Street. She was a graduate of Barnard and earned a Ph.D. in literature from Bryn Mawr. She published a volume of her own poetry, newspaper and magazine articles, including several mysteries for *Ellery Queen's Mystery Magazine*, and translated several books into English, among them Martin Buber's *Tales of the Hasidim* and the works of German poet Stefan George.

William Quinlan (1928–) is an attorney who practices in New York. He was raised in the Dakota and lived there until 1960.

Lee Silver (1921–) is a former reporter for the New York *Daily News*. He is now director of public relations and vice president for community relations for the Shubert Organization.

Rosanna Weston (1918–) is a widow and has one child. She is a lifelong resident of the Phipps Houses, on West 64th Street.

Olga Marx: The residential district when my parents got married was 34th Street. It was considered brave of them to move so far uptown, to 77th Street and Columbus Avenue. When my parents built our house around 1870, on the other side was sort of wild terrain, and people used to ask, "If you come home late at night, aren't you concerned that there might be robbers lurking among the boulders?"

I was born there in 1894. In those days, women didn't go to a hospital to have their babies. They had their babies at home. I had one sister, almost six years older. My mother lost one child from scarlet fever and one from pneumonia, and that was the norm, that you lost half your children.

The house was four stories, like all the houses on the street. Actually, if you count the basement, you had five. When the house was built, my mother, who liked to be different, had it built of cream-colored brick. People lived in brownstone houses, but she could tell everybody, "One hundred and eight is cream-colored." So it sort of stood out. There were all one-family houses in our neighborhood. There was no such thing as more than one family living in a house.

The streets were mostly empty and quiet. The loudest noises were the sounds of the horses' feet clip-clopping on the cobblestones as the hansom cabs and open carriages drove down the street. I would hear that, along with the rumbling of the El and the newsboys shouting "Extra!" when I was lying in bed at night.

The clip-clopping started in the morning with the milkman. He was followed by the baker's truck. The bakery man would deliver a loaf of rye bread and a twist. He came every morning, and sometimes we would save lumps of sugar, and we would give them to his horse. I still can feel the soft lips of the horse taking the sugar from my hand.

There would also be deliveries from department stores like Altman's, Best's, Stern's, and McCreery's. Because there were no telephones, my mother would write a penny postcard to please call for such and such a thing that was sent on approval. All the deliveries were made through the areaway of our house. They were never done through the main entrance.

Vendors came around selling sweets, and there was a special man who sold freshly roasted peanuts. A ragman also came around. We always gave things to him. He would call out:

> *Rags to give, old rags to give,*
> *Rags to give, old rags to give,*
> *Any old clothes, any old clothes.*

That was his call. Then there was a man who said, "Knives to sharpen, scissors to grind."

The only person on our block who owned an automobile was Dr. Weiner, our neighbor across the street. The first ride I ever had was in Dr. Weiner's car. It was such an event when he sent his little girl over to get us. He'd say, "I have a little time this morning. How would you children like to ride two or three blocks before I start on my rounds?" In the houses down the street people were watching nervously. "Are the children going to be all right? Is something terrible about to happen?" Yes, the neighborhood street urchins really did yell, "Get a horse."

GUIDO ''BULLETS'' BRESSAN: The peddlers in the horse and wagon also came around to our block on 69th. Some of 'em had a kid. You holler out what you want, and the kid would bring it up. We got most of our fruits and vegetables from the peddlers. One guy came around with potatoes. Another guy came around with fruit. You'd also get the knife man and the umbrella man to fix the umbrellas.

OLGA MARX: Then there was the lamplighter. That was wonderful, to see him coming down the street to turn on the streetlamps. He had this long contraption with a hook on it to turn on the gas. We had the same contraption for our home, because there was no electricity.

When the lamplighter came in the summer, that usually meant it was bedtime. I loved to wait for him on the stoop. On mild evenings, you'd bring down a chair and sit out there, although my mother thought it a little vulgar to visit back and forth between neighbors.

One mild evening, she said to me, "Instead of just sitting on the stoop a little before you go to bed, I want to show you something." She told me to look up, and there was a sky full of stars. It was the first time I had consciously seen just a lot of wonderful stars.

A lot of people sat out there. It was like sitting in a café and watching the world go by. You'd see mostly children coming home from the park or the women coming home in their long skirts. A woman would hold up her skirt with her little finger sticking out— that was stylish.

People who'd been to the theater would come home. Many of the men wore high hats that were collapsible. They were wonderful. You could just push against it, and, without hurting it, it would just come down and be flat. The reason was, if you went to the opera or anything like that, it was very inconvenient to leave your hat in the garderobe. Then you had to wait when you got ready to go home. So what you did was, you wore your high hat, and just before you entered the opera you pressed it and you carried it under your arm. That was called a chapeau claque.

BULLETS BRESSAN: I was born on 69th Street in 1907. Our flat was four rooms. It was between West End and the river. There were six kids, three boys and three girls. That was the average. We were all born in our homes. A couple thousand kids around here were delivered by the same midwife.

My father was a tile setter. He learned his trade over in Italy. He worked around the Vatican as an apprentice. Then he came over here, but in them days they didn't make much at all. He did some work at the Ansonia and the Central Savings Bank across the street. That's a landmark. He was a skilled worker, but bein' he was Italian, there was mostly Irish and German doin' that work, and there was what you call bias against him. He got work, but not too much. When they had that boom in the 1920s there was work, but he was too old then.

DOROTHY GREENWALD: I was born in 1917 up in Harlem, at 118th Street and Lenox Avenue. When I was about five years old, we moved down to 93rd Street between Columbus Avenue and Central Park West. The reason the Jews moved out of Harlem was because the blacks moved in. We moved because my grandfather's synagogue moved from Harlem to 93rd off Amsterdam. He was like an assistant rabbi there.

My father died when I was eighteen months old. He had been a theater manager. His whole family was in the theater. My mother's family was in tennis courts. We owned all the tennis courts in Manhattan at the time. On the West Side, they ran from 94th to 96th on West End. They were outdoors, and in the winter we flooded them for ice skating.

We were seven people living together. The furthest down we moved was 92nd, the furthest north was 99th. Beyond that was the pale of black, and all that Irish and Italian. There were a lot of tenements there because it was closer to Harlem. Ninety-ninth and 100th around Columbus were like a no-man's-land. I knew girls who lived in those tenements over there, and their families were the butchers—you know, the lower class of service business. They didn't speak much English.

We lived at 310 West 95th Street, so my grandmother was able to look out her window and see her wonderful son's tennis courts. We also moved there because at one point we liked to change apartments. We were upwardly mobile. If you could do a little better, you got a bigger apartment with maybe a bigger kitchen.

Our neighborhood was constant and secure in the sense that we were all the same. We were living in the "Gilded Ghetto," which was the expression. Living on West End Avenue was the equivalent of Park Avenue. We were not allowed to leave the neighborhood. Not until I was much older did I venture downtown. You were not encouraged to leave the neighborhood, because then you would meet people who were not commensurate with your background.

EDWARD O. D. DOWNES: Between 72nd and 73rd and West End and Riverside Drive was a one-house place. That was the Schwab Mansion. It was startling to see the house in the middle of this great big yard with big trees and a great lawn. It was all surrounded by a fence with high iron bars. So indeed there were remnants, at least along the river, of the time when the West Side was a home for the wealthier set. Certainly, when we moved here, Central Park West wasn't very exclusive.

Some of the houses on Riverside Drive were very beautiful, and it had the added attraction that on the other side it was not built up. It was just a forestlike area. It was a beautiful view in the fall, when the colors were out. The drawback, though, was that there were open railroad tracks. The park came in later.

There were enough middle-class families that lived all up and down the West Side. It was just that the fashionable part of town was the East Side. Mostly, if you were wealthy enough to have your own house, larger than a brownstone, then it was probably on the East Side. The division was sharper then than it is now.

In the '20s, I used to go to coming-out parties, as they called them. I don't remember a single one being on the West Side. Although I was living on the West Side, the only social disadvantage I was aware of was not having as much money as the others. I remember when I took a girl to a dance, afterward I would take her home in a taxi, and then take the taxi a couple of blocks away, and then get out and walk home. In those days, when you went to those dances, you didn't wear a black tie, you wore a white tie and an opera hat. There I was, walking across the park at one, two, or three A.M. with an opera hat and white tie.

OLGA MARX: Everybody had a cook. Everybody had an upstairs girl. Everybody had a laundress coming in three days a week, and everybody had a cleaning woman. There were lots of personnel, and the basement was used for the personnel to have meals.

When it was a rainy day and we couldn't go out, we'd roller-skate around the long round table in the basement. There was also a big beautiful kitchen with an icebox. You put different colored signs in the kitchen window which told the iceman how many pounds you wanted. Our cook and the iceman had a relationship, and my mother, who was very prudish, would have frowned on it had there not been very great advantages. Sometimes, ice ran short for some people, but it never happened in our house, so mother patronized this relationship with the iceman.

If you wanted ice for drinks or something, you had an ice pick. We also had a big black coal stove in the kitchen. The flame was covered with a flat black cover that had a little notch in it so you could pick it up with a little instrument. One of the favorite ways of warming a bed was to take the cover and wrap it up and warm the bed with it.

The house was heated by a coal furnace. In every room was a square vent that you could open and close. On the side of the house where the areaway was, there was an opening onto a slide. I can still hear the rumble of the coal going down to the cellar.

BULLETS BRESSAN: We used to steal the coal. We'd hit all the private brownstones. The coal was right there. We'd send a guy down the shute to load the bags, and then we'd pull it up. A couple of times, the furnace guy would come, and we'd run, forget about our buddy down there. We got caught a couple of times, but they never did nothin'.

OLGA MARX: It was filthy. Everybody had two furnace men, one who tended it in the day, and one who tended it the last thing in the evening, around ten o'clock. They would fix the coal so it wouldn't flare up, so it would smolder for a longer period of time. Houses were not very warm in winter. Children wore to bed little one-piece flannel affairs that buttoned. We had feather beds that were very cozy. The only place you were really warm was the bed. When we moved from room to room even, we had little warm capes to put on over our long wool dresses.

LEE SILVER: I was generally cold in the wintertime. I had a light sweater. Once I got a suede jacket and a muffler from some-where. I put on the jacket and muffler because I had seen some actor in a movie wearing this jacket and a muffler and he was protected. So I put this on and went out in the midwinter, and I froze my ass off. I kept jumping up and down, saying, "There must be something wrong."

I lived on 100th Street between Columbus and Amsterdam Avenue. We were dirt poor. Our rent was around thirty dollars a month, and it was a hardship. We went from month to month without saving anything. I don't think my father saved anything in his lifetime. I'm the youngest of three children. I was born in 1921. It was a distasteful time, not happy-go-lucky. My father had a gro-cery at 158 West 100th, and we lived in 160, on the second floor.

All of this later helped me in the Army, because I learned how to get dressed putting on my socks and shoes first on the cold floor. Congoleum, which I learned later was not a bad word for floor covering, to me was one of the worst words for poor people. If you had Congoleum floors, that was terrible. There were no rugs. I didn't have any slippers, so I would immediately get my socks on if I could. If it was warm, maybe I'd walk a little bit, but it never felt right. To this day I don't like to walk barefoot except on my own rug at home. When I went to the stove to heat up my stock-ings, I would walk on my heels. Because the kitchen was warm, I'd do my homework there or in the back of the store.

OLGA MARX: I hated winter underwear. We wore union suits tucked into the tops of the stockings, so that no flesh showed. It was all covered up. It was so itchy, I hated it. It was horrible. I was always so glad when I saw the thermometer outside my parents' bedroom and it showed seventy degrees. Then we could shed our winter underwear.

We were well wrapped up then. Over our underwear, we wore a thing called the bodice. That was just white cotton. Onto the bodice was buttoned white panties, usually edged with hand-crocheted lace. You had a lot of unbuttoning to do if you had to go to the toilet. You wore long stockings, and you had to tuck the underwear into the long stockings so that there wouldn't be any cracks.

Then you wore a petticoat. We'd wear a flannel one and then a white one in the winter. They were buttoned onto the bodice. On top of the two petticoats, you wore your dress. Usually it was a plaid wool dress. Then we wore button shoes or laced shoes.

Six layers. It wasn't very comfortable, and we were terribly excited when it was warm enough that we could go into socks. That was glorious. In the summer, we wore low shoes and socks. We wore lovely white straw hats, very soft. Around the crown was a colored ribbon band. Underneath our clothes we just had the little bodice with the white panties buttoned onto it, and then a white petticoat and then the dress. We only wore four layers.

When a woman went swimming, she also wore several layers. Over a bathing corset and substantial bra came what looked like a dark union suit. It was topped by a dress reaching only to the knees. But your legs weren't exposed. There were also long stockings and bathing shoes. You never wore a plain cap. The cap had like a scarf that drew up in front and tied, and it had two pert little wings in front. You couldn't really swim in an outfit like that. The best you could do was to hold onto a line that was strung out into the water and bob up and down.

Girls had clean-shaven legs, but only actresses, dancers, and whores shaved under their arms. Those three were lumped together generically as stemming from "the gutter."

When you were asked, "What do you want to be when you grow up?" I know a number of girls who said they wanted to be actresses, because they were the only people who could use cosmetics with impunity. It was a saying that only actresses and whores used makeup. You couldn't, for instance, use lipstick. As good bourgeois girls, when we began to be interested in boys, we used to bite our lips, because that made them red.

My mother's one concession was that she wore her hair in a pompadour. She combed it down in front, and then put something in it to make it stand up. Her hair was lovely. We had a woman come by every other week to wash the family hair. We never washed it ourselves. The first thing she did before she washed it was break an egg over our hair. I still feel the little thud and that gooey feeling, and then she would massage the egg into the scalp, and then she would wash the hair, not with these shampoos that we have nowadays, but with a reddish-brown soap that was supposed to be very good.

WILLIAM RANDOLPH HEARST, JR.: I was about two when we moved uptown in 1910. Riverside Drive was considered very hot stuff then. Schwab had a house on 73rd Street, and there were mostly private houses all the way up. It was mostly Jewish for a while, and it was considered to be a plush neighborhood.

I almost didn't live right after I was born. There was something stuck in my windpipe or something, and the doctors just about gave up. Then somebody on the paper, I think it was the editor of the *American Weekly*, put Pop onto a Christian Science reader. Mom was a Catholic, and Pop's family was Church of England, but there seemed to be no hope, so they figured they would try it.

This man came and stayed up all night with me. I was too little to understand a word he was saying, but the next morning the damn little valve opened up. Well, the two of them became great fans of Mary Baker Eddy, who was alive at the time, so I was raised in that church, and I went to kindergarten in the Christian Science church on Central Park West. Still, my parents didn't go to church, and they didn't go to extremes. They just knew that this appeared to help save my life, and they were naturally beholden to the idea of mind over matter.

OLGA MARX: If there was the slightest thing wrong with us, my mother called the doctor. If our stomachs were upset or when we had the usual children's diseases, like the measles or chicken pox, Dr. Weber came. He used to call my mother a quack doctor because, for instance, if she thought I wasn't having enough of a movement, she would give me an enema, and the doctor told her that was all wrong. I remember how enormously impressed I was that the doctor had the nerve to tell my mother she was wrong!

When I had an ordinary cold, he said, "Keep the child at even temperature. Don't take the child from a cool room to a warm one." He also suggested she put a little flannel cape around me. For a sore throat we had a wet poultice, and over the wet poultice I can still see sort of a pale yellow rubber. Plastic wasn't invented yet. It was very thin rubber and darn uncomfortable. There were no zippers, so it was fastened with safety pins.

When my sister Lucy looked a little pale, Dr. Weber decreed that she needed a tonic of iron. Just to be on the safe side, she made me take it, too. She also gave us Hoff's Malt Extract, which was guaranteed to turn adolescent skinniness to lovely curves. I had it in my cocoa, and those extracts really rounded me out.

WILLIAM RANDOLPH HEARST, JR.: Our family was well off even then. As a matter of fact, Pop owned the building where we lived on 86th Street. Our apartment was on the top three floors. He built that extension on top. That was a banquet hall. It was reserved for special parties or fancy balls. The ground floor was a dining room and a big-domed living room. I think there were two apartments to a floor, but they were not together on every floor. We lived downstairs with our cousins, a mother and father and two boys and a girl. My grandfather, my mother's father, also lived downstairs with us. We didn't have much immediate family supervision.

There was a ballroom of sorts connecting the bottom floors. It was two floors high with a balcony at each end on the level of the eleventh floor. Pop liked suits of armor. There were about half a dozen of them up there, and he had a couple of horses on the balconies, one on each side and several single soldiers' uniforms. We thought they were great as kids.

Mom and Pop entertained a lot. Mom had been on the stage herself. She and her sister and their father, Grandpa Wilson, were billed as "George Wilson and the Wilson Twins." This was in vaudeville. That's where they met. Pop had always been sort of a Stage Door Johnny. He and Mom married in 1903. As we grew up, they used to have the local vaudeville stars as after-dinner entertainment at some of their parties, like Ed Wynn. I remember when Bergen and that little midget first came along.

Because he was naturally sympathetic to the arts, Pop also gave a lot of publicity in his newspapers to the stage. They would have benefits, and we could hang out in the wings. There were the Duncan Sisters and the Dolly Sisters. We met a lot of them.

OLGA MARX: My mother was a pianist, with four years at the conservatory in Europe, and my uncle was an accomplished violinist. They had lots of musical friends. On the first floor of our house was the parlor where my mother kept the piano. We had lots of musical evenings in the parlor.

In the backyard, we would get the German oompah bands two or three times a week. They were very famous in New York. They'd play patriotic songs and popular songs that German children had learned at home, and we sang along lustily. Very often they had a little monkey that collected the coins, and we just loved the little monkey. I would ask my mother to give me some coins, and the little monkey would take the coins and put them in the pocket of its little coat. The band would play until they got some money and usually something good to eat, and then they would go on to the next house.

Another thing that was very popular was the organ-grinders. They'd wheel it in front of a house and see what they could get that way. We would dance in front of him, and sometimes follow him from house to house. He also had a monkey.

BULLETS BRESSAN: Sometimes there'd be guys who'd come around and make speeches. There was a communist group that came to 69th and West End one night. They'd take out the box and an American flag. The guys from the neighborhood went up to the rooftops, and they threw so much stuff on 'em, they didn't last five minutes.

We used to hang out on the roof with pigeons, flyin' the birds. That was the style. Every roof had 'em, West Side, East Side, all over. We used to catch their pigeons. You see a stray one flyin' around, and you'd get him into our coop. There were bird stores all over. They had some good racin' pigeons. Throw 'em up in Florida and Cleveland, and see which one gets back first. Everybody had 'em. Owney Madden had a big coop on the roof of the Belnord, and that was a high-class buildin'.

We spent a lot of time up on the roof, mostly just to kill time. The tar on the roof, we chewed that. We'd take it right off the roof and stick it in our pockets. Naturally, if it was too hot, it would melt. If we were chewin' it in school, the teacher would pull us up front. "Take out what you got in your mouth." It was a wad of tar. It didn't taste bad, especially in the summertime, when it was nice and soft. Our teeth were better than the rich kids we went to school with. They all had braces.

We were also smokin' when we were seven, eight years old. You go to the candy store, some guys would give you two for a penny. Sometimes you just pick 'em off the street. All the kids smoked—Beechnuts, Sweet Caporal, Piedmonts, Home Runs. In the streets you'd pick up a lot of Turkish cigarettes. You'd pick up a Murad, but it was strong. You'd take one puff and throw it away. The Italian old guys used to smoke what we called Guinea Stinkers, cigars. They were strong.

• • •

OLGA MARX: Our parlor had several rather fragile chairs with gilded seats, and when we had fat visitors, my mother always engineered them past those chairs, because she was afraid they were going to break them down.

There were plenty of fat people then. People didn't know anything about counting calories, and once a woman had made it— and to make it was to get a good husband—she let herself go as she pleased. A slender woman was something unusual. The heavy ladies used to take saltwater baths. They thought it would reduce their bottoms.

Of course, all the women wore corsets then. When my mother had her corset on, it was out of the question that she could bend down and button her shoes. I remember when I was four years old, I had just learned to button shoes, so I came in very handy, and very often I helped her dress. When it came to the corset, I laced her into it, and she would say, "Tighter, dear, tighter." I remember that very well. I had to pull on that lace with all my strength to get the corset on her. When I was done, we were both exhausted.

Anyway, the parlor led to the dining room, and after a musical evening, the doors would be slid back, and there would be refreshments ready in the dining room. Off the dining room was the butler's pantry. That had a cupboard for dishes and a sink where the dishes were washed. The dumbwaiter was also there. It went down to the kitchen, and when you had meals, the cook would put whatever she was serving on the dumbwaiter.

The dumbwaiter was a big part of my life, because my mother invented a brand-new birthday story for me. The legend was that one day she was sitting in the dining room and the dumbwaiter bell rang. She pulled it up, and there was a basket lined with blue with me in it. I was always very fond of the color blue, and my mother said, "No wonder. The basket you were brought to me in was lined with blue silk."

On the next floor in the front was my parents' bedroom. In the back was my mother's living room. In between were two window-less rooms with washbasins and closets for clothes. Every week, my mother would sit at her desk and write her mother in Europe and her sister in Germany and one sister who lived in Poland. She would write "per" on the envelope and then write the name of one of the fastest steamers. Later, she sent one that said, "Per *Titanic*," and that letter went down with the ship.

Every other Thursday was my mother's day at home. Then, you couldn't phone people and say you would be at home, so everybody in her circle of friends had a definite day at home, usu-ally once every two weeks. With all her friends, about four days a week were occupied with visiting friends that she was sure were going to be home. The preliminaries for that day were wonderful. I loved helping my mother with the baking, which took up most of the day before.

Sometimes I would open the door for the guests. I was very aware that I was an awkward little girl. Once, when the ladies came in, one of them looked at me and said to her friend, "Not very p-r-e-t-t-y."

I just looked at her and I said quietly, "Not very p-r-e-t-t-y but s-m-a-r-t." She didn't know what to say.

When the women came, they would just sit and talk. They would complain about the servants. One friend would say, "You know, I have to pay my upstairs girl twenty-two dollars a month now." Or they would talk about the high price of stamps. "Five cents to Europe now!"

Usually, the children were called in for a quick *knicks*, which was a curtsy. Some polite questions were asked, and then we were sent back upstairs. Upstairs was our floor. The front room was our playroom. Again, there were two windowless rooms, and in the back room was where my sister and I slept. My mother kept a chamber pot there so we didn't have to go all the way to the bathroom if we needed to. I remember a little poem about that:

*Who took me from my warm, warm cot*
*And put me on a cold, cold pot?*
*My mother!*

Behind our room was a bathroom with the toilet and bathtub. You didn't take a bath every day. That was unheard of. In the bathroom was a stove with a round top. If you wanted a bath, you had to heat the water in advance. There was hot water in the sinks, but there was never enough for the baths without heating the water. When I was four, our grandmother came to visit us from Germany, and I remember she was very unimpressed with our bathrooms. "A lady," she said, "can keep clean with a finger bowl."

I think our fräulein undressed in our room. She always undressed under a nightgown. A lot of people did that. I heard about one woman who covered her parrot cage before she undressed. Nightgowns were sturdily opaque, long-sleeved, and up to the chin. I remember there was a shocking joke: "She wears a fur-bordered nightie because she likes to keep her neck warm."

Upstairs, the maid slept, and the cook had a room. Then there was the sewing room. That was where Mrs. Doke, the seamstress, worked. I think she came every other week to do the mending. Twice a year, she came for three weeks at a time to make some of our clothes.

Every room had a spittoon. That was a sine qua non—a spittoon in every room. It matched the interior decoration. Men spat, and they need someplace to do it. Still, my mother was so shocked at this whole thing. One time, before you had signs up in the streetcar that spitting wasn't allowed, she drew the conductor's attention to the fact that a man on the streetcar was spitting on the floor, and the conductor said to my mother, "Lady, this is a free country. Here a man can spit wherever he feels like."

My best friend across the street had a little brother, and she came to see me with him. While they were visiting, he had to go to the toilet, and she said to him, "Why don't you just use the spittoon." That was the first time I realized the male anatomy was different from the female anatomy. My mother was dreadfully shocked at what he had done. She said the little boy must never come to see me again.

You know the prudery was incredible in those days. When I

asked my mother where babies came from, she didn't want to tell me. She just told me that story about the dumbwaiter. Then she told me where babies come from in a very sentimental way. She said, "You see So-and-So, and you see how big she is, and that's because she has a little baby forming inside of her."

Then I said, "But how does it get started?"

She said, "When the time comes, then your husband will explain that to you."

I went on a trip to Europe when I was about eleven. There were dances every night, and this boy who was about three years older than me, but about a dozen years wiser, took a fancy to me and asked my mother whether he could take me dancing. My mother was very standoffish and said no.

But we sat outside on a coil of rope, and he sang me a song that the fellows at prep school made up. It had a jolly tune:

*Paddy went awalking one fine day,*
*Lost his britches on the way.*
*Two little girls came walking by,*
*And they saw the scenery fly.*

"What scenery?" I asked. When he realized how retarded I was, he anticipated what my husband was supposed to tell me. Then, all these things I noticed about dogs and pigeons getting on each other's backs began to clear up.

He told me not to sing the song or mention it to my mother. But there were a number of things that I still wanted to know. There was nobody to ask. I couldn't ask my sister Lucy, or Fräulein.

When I was taking a Latin course at Barnard, I remember Professor Knapp asked us after one class if we had any questions. I raised my hand, and I said, "This is a love poem, and it's written to a boy." And Dr. Knapp hemmed and hawed, and he said, "Go home and ask your mother, dear, and she won't tell you."

BULLETS BRESSAN: When we were eight or nine years old, we were playin' craps. We all shot craps, on Sunday mostly. There'd be fifteen or twenty of us. We played for pennies, nickels, and dimes. If there was a pretty big game, they'd go on the roof or in the backyards, so the cops wouldn't see 'em. We were poor kids, and when the cops would come and break up the games on the streets, and everybody would run away, we'd go pick up the change.

FRANK AMERUSO: It was wonderful. There was always somebody out. I lived on the same block as Bullets. I could look out my window at night, and you either got card games or crap games goin' on under the lamppost—all that kind of stuff. We played on the steps of the Presbyterian church on 69th Street. Sometimes we switched into the backyard so the cops wouldn't see us. But mostly we played in the streets. The cop on the beat used to know how to throw that stick. It would go right between your legs. They were good at it.

OLGA MARX: We went to Adolph Newberger's dancing school every Saturday. I loved aesthetic dancing. It was better than dancing with the boys, because I wasn't very brilliant at dancing. In aesthetic dancing, you could do whatever you wanted. You could adjust yourself to whatever music there was. [*She sings:*]

> *Every little movement has a meaning of its own.*
> *Every thought or feeling by some gesture can be shown.*
> *Every love thought that comes astealing o'er your being*
> *Will be revealing all your sweetness in some appealing little*
> *gesture all its own.*

We also learned the two-step, which was very easy. Then we learned the waltz. We learned a barn dance—one, two, three, hop. At the end of the lesson, he would say, "And now we will end with the waltz, gentlemen's choice." And I was always so afraid nobody was going to choose me. I remember sitting and looking down at my shoes in an agony to see whether anybody was coming to choose me, and I was so happy when my cousin Carlton approached. Nobody else really liked to dance with me, because I stepped on their feet.

BULLETS BRESSAN: We also played a lot of stickball, three games on a Sunday. A guy like Howard Cook, who was a big gambler, he'd buy the balls, and he'd watch. They all went for that. Sometimes they'd bet cash on the games. They might play for a barrel of beer.

There were bookies all over the place. These were like the runners. They'd be on the corners, in a bar or speakeasy or a hallway. All the horse men gave you the same odds. Say the horse paid a hundred dollars, they had a limit of seventy-five dollars. You wouldn't get no more than that. All of 'em were the same.

We also went out stealin.' Four or five of us, maybe more. We'd go in a drugstore, say 74th, walk in—you'd grab and run. You get those big grocery stores on West End and Broadway, they'd throw the cases of food on the sidewalk, and we'd grab a case or a bag of potatoes, throw it over your shoulder and go.

You'd go down to the pork store, get some knockwurst, bologna. Put it in some Italian bread. Sometimes you go over to the park, and on the way over to Central Park, you'd hit a grocery store. One kid would steal the beans, you'd steal the bread. That time the American bread wasn't sliced, so we'd pull the insides out, throw the beans in, and make a beans sandwich.

Later on, a few guys went for bigger things. One guy went around on certain days—we never knew how he found out—but he'd go to a certain apartment house, ring the bell, "Tailor." They'd give him suits, dresses, coats, then he'd go down and hock 'em.

Some of 'em, not too many, went big time, stealin', stickin' up. There was no organized-crime stuff, not like in Hell's Kitchen. *They* were killers.

◆ ◆ ◆

OLGA MARX: We were less than a block from the Columbus Avenue El, which I adored riding. I'd kneel on the seats and look out the window to catch glimpses of windows with flowerpots inside and clotheslines in the yards. The El rumble was audible to our house, but there was something somnolent and steady about it. Nobody seemed to mind the noise of the El.

There was a nickelodeon on Columbus Avenue, not far from us. It was a small store with rows of these little machines that you look into for a nickel. On the side was a crank that you could turn. I think the whole thing was about ten minutes at the most. My mother was not for it at all, because she was afraid I might see something improper. Our Fräulein would take us, and they were very harmless little stories. For instance, there was one where a child fell into the water, and a dog jumped after it, and as the child held on, the dog swam ashore.

We didn't have anything like television. You couldn't even imagine something like that in those days, but we had what we called a magic lantern. That was wonderful. There were sliding doors that separated our parlor from the dining room. For the children's parties, they would put up a sheet, and they would throw pictures on the sheet. These stationary pictures, one after another, were fascinating.

I saw my first moving picture after we moved uptown in 1901. Of course, the movies were black and white and they were silent. But somebody sat at a piano in the pit and adapted the music to what was happening on the screen. That was considered a very desirable job.

Of course, the movies then were chiefly things with fast-riding horses and the sheriff coming in at the end. The cliché gestures were always fascinating. You expressed anger in a certain way, and the girl used to stand on her toes to reach around and embrace her man.

Movie stars like Charlie Chaplin didn't come until much later. But Mary Pickford was a favorite. So were the Gish sisters and Douglas Fairbanks. My uncle Igel also liked the movies. He used to put himself to sleep reading. But when the movies came in, he said, "This has it all over a book. When you go to a movie, you get so exhausted that when you get home you fall asleep like a breeze." So he used the movies like a soporific.

We read the *St. Nicholas Magazine* when I was young. It had stories, puzzles, and riddles. You could contribute to the magazine. I think I had some little verse printed in it. That was my first published piece. Then I had an elaborate poem published in a magazine called *Moods* when I was twelve.

> . . . *And the murmur of the water,*
> *Melancholy weird mysterious,*
> *Filled my heart with endless longing,*
> *Turned my mind to dreams delirious.*

The magazine then got out an anthology called *The Younger Choir*. It was great to have my poem published in book form.

The family always had breakfast together, along with our fräulein. Even when I was very small, my father wanted me sitting at the breakfast table, so he had a high chair made that fitted nicely to the table. People did not drink orange juice in those days. You cut an orange in half. Then you had a certain kind of knife to loosen the segments, and when the segments were loosened we would eat each segment. It was considered vulgar to squeeze an orange, so after you had eaten out the segments, that was it. Then we got oatmeal or something like that, then an egg, except for Wednesdays and Sundays, and then instead of an egg we had little pancakes filled with jelly. They were delicious. I still relish the thought of them. If I didn't want to eat my egg, my father would say, "Just think how happy some poor Russian children would be to have your egg." I was too well brought up to say, "Let 'em have it."

We ate at 8:00, and we had to be punctual. If you were late, you were just told that this was extremely impolite and it must never happen again. To be punctual for breakfast was almost a religion, but the most awful thing was if you were late for supper.

The one restaurant that German people enjoyed going to was Luchow. We'd take a hansom cab down there. There were also some Chinese restaurants in the neighborhood. When I was in college, my cousin Herbert wanted to take me to one, and my mother said, "Herbert, use my bathroom before you go. I don't want you to leave Olga alone for a minute in a Chinese restaurant. They might snatch her and give her dope, and she might end up in an opium den for the rest of her life." She was serious.

LEE SILVER: As a family, we were always considering survival. We were teetering on the brink of survival because we didn't have resources. We didn't know where to get jobs or how to get jobs. We didn't know where to get income. There wasn't anybody who was going to give you anything. We weren't clothed too well, and there wasn't anybody to give you a sweater from outside. But we were unique in the sense that we had the grocery store and my uncle had the butcher store, and so we could get meat or chicken from there at a good price. Then my mother would put the big pot on the stove and throw everything in it and cook it for two days. She was a very bad cook. My mother could make a lamb chop taste like a hot dog. She'd cook the food 'til it fell off the bone. I used to tell people I didn't know what good food was 'til I went into the Army.

OLGA MARX: The tradition at the Ethical Culture Day School was that every paying child paid for herself and a poor child to go to that school. That was how for the first time in my life I was able to hobnob with unprosperous children and find out that at their homes a lot of things were not like they were at mine.

If I made a friend of an unprosperous child and asked her home to my house, there was always trouble, because my mother would say she had bad table manners or didn't dress neatly enough, something like that. There was a lot of petty bickering over that.

The greatest surprise was when we compared Christmas gifts. They mostly got for a great Christmas gift a new dress or something. In my circle, it was a matter of course that you got new dresses during the year. You got luxury things for presents. You got a fur piece with a muff to match. I was always surprised that they thought it was wonderful if they got a new pair of shoes.

I wasn't allowed to go their homes. My mother was afraid that they were unsanitary, that they weren't careful about colds the way we were. I felt very bad. I felt I was being a snob without it being my fault.

BULLETS BRESSAN: We never bothered with any of the rich kids above 69th Street. They went to mostly private schools like that Collegiate on 77th Street. We used to go to Riverside Park, and we'd see them with their nice fancy coats and their gloves and their skates. They were ours. We used to steal 'em. A bike was a rarity in this neighborhood. You'd steal it, then sell it for a couple dollars.

LEE SILVER: I was jealous of the wealthier kids. Why them and not me? They had rugs. We never saw rugs. They were very impressive.

There were class differences that were very prevalent. You didn't have homogenization with clothing. You knew poor clothing, and you knew good clothing. I had knickers with holes. You wore the same pair of shoes every day for a year or more, and they had holes in the soles. The only time they got changed was when they broke a hole in the surface. You had maybe two pairs of socks to wear the whole year around. The rich person had the argyle-look sweater, and he had a coat that went over that. He had high shoes. He changed to long pants before I did.

WILLIAM RANDOLPH HEARST, JR.: We used to play down in Riverside Park. It was a tough neighborhood down at the bottom of it, and these tough kids used to come up if they caught any of us alone with any equipment like a ball or a bat or a glove. They'd kind of surround you and say, "Let's have a look at that," and you'd have to give it over, and that was the last you'd see of it.

BULLETS BRESSAN: We never hit the kids for it. You wouldn't go out and mug an old woman like these guys do today. We'd steal, burglarize a house and stuff, but we wouldn't hit nobody. I remember that Hearst. I delivered orders in there. If you see him again, say you seen one of the guys that stole the glove.

OLGA MARX: It was a special treat to be able to go out driving in the park and then stopping somewhere to have refreshments. That was always special. Sometimes we'd go up Riverside Drive to Grant's Tomb. Driving was very popular, but I didn't know anybody who had his own horse and carriage. They hired, but very often, because they did it every Saturday or Sunday, they hired the same coachman, the same carriage. It was also a little bit of social rivalry. People would see if you were very well dressed in the carriage. There was always the element of social competition.

Some very rich people had their own carriages. To get a cab, you went to a place where they lined up. I think there was a stand at 78th Street. You could hire a hansom cab, where the coachman sat way up in back. The people he was driving were inside, and there was a contraption, like a tube, they could talk up to give the man directions.

The horses made the streets dirty. There was a sanitation cart that came along and the man swept up the street. He had a pole with a big net at the bottom, and he would scoop the dirt up and dump it in. But the streets were quite dirty. New York is much cleaner now than it was then. There was also a blacksmith on our corner. We loved to go watch him.

BULLETS BRESSAN: When I was sixteen, I started deliverin'. I'd work for Sheffield Farms or a butcher shop, tailor shops, anything. Sheffield was at 91st and Broadway. I drove a horse and wagon for them. Their stable was at 56th and Eleventh Avenue. I'd go in there every morning, harness the horse and bring him down. Them days, it was a kick, you know. They had their own blacksmith. The stable was just for their horses, and they had hundreds of these big truck horses, Clydesdales.

Sometimes, they had eight or ten pullin' a cart. I only had one. Back then, they had waterin' stops for the horses along the road. On 66th Street there was one. On 71st, they had a sink there with a regular faucet. We used to drink from there when we were goin' to school. When there was ice on the road, they put something on the horse's foot with little spikes on them. Still, if you were goin' down a hill, you said your prayers. The fire engines were at 77th Street, and down 69th Street was a hill, and they had those iron picket railin's over the tracks. One day, the fire wagon was going down, and the horses couldn't stop. Two horses went over that railin'. Right after that they put the wall up.

LEE SILVER: Our store was right next door to a livery stable. I spent a lot of time as a kid in that stable. It was my escape. It was called Krilov & Chasen's. They would rent out horses and wagons to grocers, including my father, when he needed it. I hung around there at night, helping the night man feed the horses, putting pails of oats out and watering them. The night watchman was such a wonderful old-type Scotsman with a corncob pipe. He'd talk quietly in the office when the work was done at nine or ten o'clock. I loved listening to him, and my mother always knew she could find me there at night.

OLGA MARX: When I was younger, all the trolley cars were horse-drawn. They were the norm until the cable car was introduced. The cable car was regarded with such suspicion by the older generation that they had a song:

> *Twinkle, twinkle, little star,*
> *Rising on a cable car.*
> *Cable car went off the track,*
> *Wish I had my nickel back.*

The trolleys were drawn by two horses. I was crazy about anything to do with driving, and sometimes the coachman let me sit up beside him. Once he gave me the reins to hold. Still, I wasn't sorry when the horses were replaced. I thought the cable cars were very exciting, to think that the cars were going along by something that was attached in the air. I thought that was wonderful. That's one thing about children. They don't feel regretful that something old is passing, and I didn't.

I loved to go marketing with my mother in the stores on Columbus Avenue. There weren't supermarkets, of course. You went to the butcher to get meat. To get fruits and vegetables, there was a man who had just that. And then there was a place you called the dry grocer's. That's where you bought rice or sugar, coffee and tea. The stores had noted down the coffee blends of their customers, and they would give you that blend. It would be ground at home.

BULLETS BRESSAN: Sheffield Farms had those forty-four-gallon milk cans. I used to clip the wires holdin' the top on, and I'd get the dipper and enjoy that cream at the top. In the wintertime, a bottle of milk left outside a door, you could see the cream pop out. You had to shake the milk in them days. People would come in with their milk cans, and they'd buy a pint or a quart. You also brought an empty pail to the bars, where they would fill it with beer. That was called rushin' the growler. Sometimes, your pop would grease the bottom of the can, so when the beer goes in, the head melts, and you'd get more beer in the can.

Later, when I was workin' a newsstand at 66th Street and Columbus, I'd do that for an Irishwoman on the other corner. She would call this guy, who would then call me. She was fat, she didn't wanna walk down the stairs. So I'd go across the street, and she'd send the can down on a piece of cord. I'd get the can and go to this bar on Columbus, bring it back and tie it to the string, and she'd bring it up. I made sure to take a big slug before I gave it to her. She'd holler down, "Don't drink it all."

LEE SILVER: In the back of the store, my father had alcohol in a barrel, pickle-barrel size. He was making his own liquor. He'd give me a bottle and say, "Take this down to the newsstand at 96th Street" or "to the newsstand at 100th Street." I'd take my skateboard, which was made of skates on a board and a box on top of that with some handles. That was what I used to deliver the bootleg booze.

When I dropped it off, the guy would take the brown paper bag and tell me to say hello to my father and that he'd pay him on Thursday or whatever. I didn't really know what I was doing, but it was fun because I was given a responsibility.

We didn't have cash, but we had food. We didn't have enough money to pay the landlord for the apartment, but we always managed to be able to get some food into the store, and the turnover created an income enough to be able to get our everyday needs. Sometimes, we had food when others around us didn't. I could open a tin of sardines when a friend of mine might be hungry or I could take an apple from the stand.

The neighborhood wasn't too wealthy, so people would come in even if they didn't always have the money. My brother used to argue with my father when he gave credit to somebody who couldn't pay him the week before. For that period, my father was a well-schooled guy. He was more philosophical than most, which was one of the reasons my brother said people took advantage of him. He was the man everybody came to for guidance. He had this wonderfully schooled mind, and he deserved more than a grocery store. He was also too lenient for a grocery store, too amenable to people. He was the good guy who wouldn't press a debtor. He was the guy anybody could come to and borrow some money out of the cash register.

BULLETS BRESSAN: I made deliveries for a couple of years. Then I used to ride a bike for the kosher butcher at 75th and Amsterdam, deliverin' beef. He wanted to make me a plucker. That was a real trade. Those guys would pluck chickens all day, fast, and they wouldn't ruin that skin. The first time I did it, I didn't know how to do it, and I ripped the skin right off the chicken. You're not supposed to do that, 'cause people wouldn't like that, so I didn't bother with that no more. I didn't like it anyway. Imagine that guy, he had a whole room full of chickens. When a guy goes home at night, he used to pull his pants cuffs out, and all the chicken pieces would fall out.

We had the chicken market right up here on the corner of 64th and Amsterdam. He supplied all these little kosher butchers in the neighborhood. Also, the Italian people used to come down and buy a live chicken, have it killed there and then bring it home.

For the kosher chickens, they'd have the rabbi there, and they'd have it over the barrel and they'd kill it. I never looked at that. The regular Christians, when they bought a chicken, the guy would throw it in a barrel of hot water and hold it underneath by the head. I didn't like to look at that stuff either.

I used to deliver to the Ansonia. That was really high class. A lot of opera singers and actors up there. You'd hear 'em singin'. Every floor had a big, thick red rug. Then they had the pantries. We used to steal silverware from there. You'd take two or three spoons from the pantries. We used to steal the linen, put it in the basket goin' out. We were stealin' from off the hotel. The people inside didn't have nothin' to do with it. I'd take it home. My mother didn't ask no questions. I got stuff from the Hotel Majestic. [He goes to a kitchen drawer and pulls out several tarnished pieces of silver. The words Hotel Majestic are imprinted on the back.] I also have stuff from the Westover, which was on 72nd. Those were high-class hotels.

OLGA MARX: When my mother bought a hen at the Washington Market, they were sold alive with their legs tied together. I didn't like to see it being carried by the feet with its head hanging down. Then there was the great question, who was going to kill the hen? First she would take it to the kitchen, and the cook gave her dictum on whether she thought it was a good buy or not. Generally, what happened was that the cook, who, as I said, had a flirtation with the iceman, would get him to kill the hen. Then she would pluck it, which really was an awful job, and with the hens, she would keep the feathers to fill pillows with them.

For Thanksgiving, the Germans favored roast goose. My mother got that from the Washington Market as well. Goose quills were popular, because we used them for drawing and writing. And everybody liked the neck of the goose, which was usually stuffed with its liver.

BULLETS BRESSAN: Thanksgivin', the kids in the neighborhood used to dress up in those raggedy clothes. Then we'd go to the Dakota and sing into those high-class houses. We didn't get dressed up on Halloween. Halloween, we'd go around with a stockin' full of flour, jacket turned inside out, and when some guy would come along, you'd nail 'im with the stockin'. It was a lot of fun.

• • •

EDWARD DOWNES: We came from Boston. My father was the music critic on the Boston paper. Then he came to the *Times*. We first lived on Central Park West, because Fifth Avenue and all that over there was just far too expensive for a journalist and his family, but Central Park West was not. We were first on the corner of 83rd Street and Central Park West and then on the corner of 81st Street, and then we came here to the Dakota. That was 1928. I was seventeen. Actually, my first memory of this building is coming to school from 81st Street and going past this forbidding-looking place. I thought it was probably either a prison or an insane asylum.

Musicians used to live here. The Schirmers, the music publishers, and the Steinways used to live here, too. When the building went co-op, I was coming down in an elevator from the top floor when this was happening, and there was a porter with an armful of these very old-fashioned letter files. He said they were burning them. I asked if he would give me what I could carry, so I brought in about four or five of these things and went through them. One of the letters was from the superintendent of the building to the manager. It was a list of complaints of Mrs. Steinway. One of them was about Dan, one of the porters, who was drunk too much and who smelled, and she didn't think that was nice. But her chief complaint was that the doormen were being much more attentive to the people arriving in these newfangled automobiles, and they weren't paying enough attention to people who stayed in carriages. That really put her off.

WILLIAM QUINLAN: In the 1920s, my father was in the real estate business on the West Side. I think we moved into the Dakota when I was one, which was 1929. My first memories of anything were in the Dakota. I thought it was a fabulous building, and I assumed everybody else lived in the same kind of place.

After my father died in 1933, we moved down to the third floor from the sixth, and the people in the house were very helpful. Without our asking, they said to my mother, "You need someplace where you can keep your papers," and they had a carpenter come up, and for nothing they built something for her in the closet where she could store her papers. Then they suggested a rent for the apartment, and my mother said it was too high. She offered a lower rent, and they said, "Of course." That was the entire negotiation. It's amazing, but the thought of profit didn't cross their minds. I don't think the Dakota broke even or paid expenses. There were a lot of empty apartments and the rents were low.

EDWARD DOWNES: It was kind of like a medieval setup. We had our own restaurant and our own dry cleaning, our own laundry. We used the laundry and the dry cleaning. We never used the restaurant except when one of my sisters got married, and for that we got them to empty a great big room right on the corner of 72nd and Central Park West. They cleared out the whole thing and made a kind of little chapel out of it. The real function of that restaurant was for families when it was cook's night out. Then they could go down there, and you could have friends. It was not open to the public, but it was a fine restaurant.

WILLIAM QUINLAN: I think there were some spinster ladies on the second floor who ate there every night. Once in a while we ate there. They would also send things upstairs with a big tray. Afterward, somebody would come up and take it away. The restaurant was never very crowded. It had to be a loss.

EDWARD DOWNES: Our apartment was the first Dakota apartment that was ever cut up. It was on the third floor. The original apartments were ten, twelve rooms. Our apartment was cut in three, and we were a family of five, and we were in one of the thirds. It did seem a little small, so we took a second third. We had plenty of room then.

We had four bedrooms, a living room, and everybody had a dining room in those days, and a very sizable kitchen. The walls are very thick. At first, when I practiced piano, I was concerned that I might be disturbing our neighbors, but they assured me that they couldn't hear my playing at all.

Our apartment looked out over a lot, which had a sort of tar-paper roof with the heating system under it. The rest of it was grass. My mother looked out on this empty lot, and she said, "Why don't they have a tennis court out there?"

She asked the desk, and they said, "Well, Mrs. Downes, there aren't many people here who would play tennis." When we moved in, we were the only youngsters in the place. Everyone seemed to me to be a hundred years old. But my mother called up all her ancient friends and asked them to request a tennis court, and by golly we got a tennis court there. I used it for years and years, until the building went co-op.

WILLIAM QUINLAN: Underground was a whole little city. They had the power plants down there, and it was fun to run around down there. The building had DC current, which made it tough to get a transformer for the electric trains.

We also liked to run around and explore some of the empty apartments. Another great thing was that there was a woman on the ground floor named Mrs. Leo. She kept a stuffed horse in the apartment which you could see through the window. That apartment was so dark, it was like Dracula's castle. She also collected coats of armor in there.

EDWARD DOWNES: I don't know whether I was aware that there were floors up here where I am now. I'm pretty certain the apartments here were all for servants. Some of the apartments had a maid's room, but some of the people had, you know, a dozen servants. I remember a friend of my mother's who lived here. She had fifteen or sixteen rooms. They would go to concerts together, and then they would go to each other's apartments for a cup of tea. So Mrs. Thomas came one day to my mother for tea. It was a winter day, and there was a fire going, and Mrs. Thomas said, "Mary, I don't know how you manage to keep a clean apartment. I can't use my fireplaces when I only have three in-help."

If they couldn't accommodate all those servants in their apartments, they rented rooms on the top floor. Most of them just had a washbasin and used the toilet in the hallway. The corner apartments, like the one I'm in now, were for the elite staff, like a butler or something like that.

WILLIAM RANDOLPH HEARST, JR.: Our house staff would be considered bigger today than it was in those days. There was a cook, naturally, and an assistant cook, probably, a couple of parlormaids, and a waiter. Pop always had a valet, and Mom had a maid. And there might have been sort of furniture-dusting people. We had a driver, Chris MacGregor, who came and drove us to school on 76th Street. He was sort of our caretaker.

Pop had a garage in the back on 85th Street, and he had several cars. He was always a car buff. They had a town car and their own chauffeur. Chris took us around in a Big Six Studebaker. Sometimes he took us up to the Polo Grounds or Yankee Stadium. We used to go in the press box, and we'd meet Damon Runyon, Bill Slocum, and Sid Mercer. In certain respects, we led quite a different life. We did things that not every kid does, but we also did things that every kid does do, and we were always treated the same except for this press angle. It didn't mean anything to us, because my father was in the newspaper business, that's all. If their father was the head of Macy's, they'd probably be able to go anywhere they wanted to in the store.

WILLIAM QUINLAN: My whole life was centered around the area of the Dakota. It was basically a small town. Everything was there. The main thing about Columbus Avenue was the El, which put it in a perpetual shadow. Alongside were, basically, stores that people would want to use, drugstores, grocery stores, delicatessens, and saloons, real honest-to-God saloons. There were a lot of tenements on the avenue. Amsterdam was more or less like Columbus, except there wasn't any El. Lincoln Square, which was in the low 60s, was pretty run-down. It wasn't far from Hell's Kitchen, and it was pretty depressed. I didn't go there much.

EDWARD DOWNES: Columbus Avenue was dark and dirty and noisy. That's the chief way I thought of it. I didn't think of it as a place where people lived. Probably they did, and I was just unaware, but there were mostly shops underneath, and the Elevated went nearly building to building. I don't think we even went shopping very much there. I don't remember where our groceries came from. My mother did our shopping. They probably did come from there. Otherwise, we went downtown to Macy's or other department stores. There was an old question that allegedly used to be asked of girls without visible means of support: "Are you married or do you live on 72nd Street?"

SELMA BLICK: I've heard people say that Columbus Avenue was a slum. It wasn't. Columbus Avenue was working-class. There were policemen who lived in the neighborhood, butchers, bakers, and candlestick makers. On the side streets, the brownstones were private homes. A lot of them were my father's customers. My father was a tailor. He had a shop on Columbus Avenue between 67th and 68th Streets.

I was born in 1913 on Columbus between 70th and 71st on the east side of the street. We moved around, but we lived at 68th Street and Columbus for many years. We were right above the El, but it got so that I never heard any noise.

Business was good for my father. He had a big store. Originally, it was two stores. My mother ran the cleaning department, and my father ran the tailor shop. Most customers didn't know that they were man and wife. My father sometimes had a very grumpy disposition, and if he didn't like a customer, he'd say, "Yaaah." He didn't say "Get outta here," but it was the equivalent. And they'd say to my mother, "That man next door is just terrible."

A lot of well-known people lived on 67th Street. Fannie Hurst, who was a customer of my father's, lived with her housekeeper in a ground-floor apartment at 27 West 67th. Her windows were filthy. She never washed them. She had little dogs that she used to keep up the sleeves of her mink coat. Then she moved to Des Artistes at 1 West 67th. I don't know if she was any cleaner there or not. She always wore black, because she was a heavy woman and she thought black made her look a little thinner, I guess. My father used to say, "She wears her black dresses until they turn green."

We used to see her meeting her husband on the south side of 67th Street three days a week, Monday, Wednesday, and Friday. He was a lawyer. They had what was called a companionate marriage. Apparently, in order to keep the marriage going, they'd meet three days a week at nine o'clock in the morning, and the marriage lasted a long time that way. It went on for years.

There were lots of movie stars that lived in Des Artistes. There was Charlie Chaplin. I used to watch him go down the street with a cane, but he didn't have that funny walk. Robert Z. Leonard, who was married to Mae Murray, lived there with her. She was a customer of my father's. My father used to take me to the movies. He would sleep through it, while I was enthralled. One morning after we went, this petite little blond with high heels came in and threw a sequined dress on the counter and said she wanted it cleaned. I stood there gaping at her. My father handed her a slip so that she could pick up the dress.

When she went out, I said, "Papa, do you know who that is?"

He said, "Yeah, Number 401 in Number One." He couldn't have cared less. For me, that I touched her dress, this was excitement.

We used to go to lunch at Des Artistes. The thing that always thrilled me was that the Howard Chandler Christy gals who are pictured on the walls were often there in the dining room with him. Every few weeks there was a different girl. Mrs. Christy lived in Des Artistes like he did but on a different floor.

My father used to go to a barber between 66th and 67th on the west side of the street Saturday nights. He'd come back and he'd say, "He was there again with another girl. Why do they always call him Daddy?"

Rudolph Valentino lived in that block, at Number 50. When I knew him on 67th Street, he was married to Natasha Rambova. She was weird-looking, with a lot of money. You didn't know whether he had money or not, but he was always around. He was handsome, Latin handsome, but I didn't like that kind of looks. I'm more Paul Newman. I think Valentino had a gallon of grease on his hair all the time.

My father knew the guy that ran Campbell's, and when Valentino died, my father said, "If you wanna go and see him, I know the manager and he'll get you in." But I didn't want to see him. The lines were many times around the block. Most of the people on line were just curious.

BULLETS BRESSAN: I was there those two nights. There was a line of all women for about five or ten blocks along Broadway, screamin', hollerin'. Then the mob got so great, they knocked in two plate-glass windows in front of the funeral home. Valentino was a few feet from the sidewalk, layin' there in his coffin. We just wanted to take a look. What a mob! Fat ones, skinny ones, screamin', with roses in their hands.

OLGA MARX: I remember we used to go to Columbus Avenue, and because we had a German fräulein and we spoke German, the street urchins would follow behind and taunt us, saying, "Dutchy,

Dutchy." We also loved to go to Central Park and breathe the fresh air, but the park was not approved of by everybody. Some said that, with its shrubbery and boulders, it offered an excellent milieu for all sorts of immoral activities. So there was some frowning on it, but we practically considered it a home. In the wintertime, we brought our sleds. I remember some girls did the belly flop, but our mother thought that was déclassé, so we would sit on the sled with our legs out on the sides for brakes.

Of course, we saw sheep in the sheep meadow. I don't know who they belonged to. We went up to the sheep and ran our fingers through that curly fleece. They were very tame. There was a whole flock of them, with only one ram, with very curly horns.

There was also a meadow where the peacocks promenaded. They would strut right up to us and let us touch them. If the peacock man was friendly to us, he would let us take home a peacock feather. That was a great thing. Each meadow had its own attendant. There was also a duck man, who took care of the ducks on the lake.

Some of the homeless children slept in the park. There were certain shelters there, like the place where food was kept to feed the ducks. Wherever there was a little shelter like that, if a kid could sneak in without being detected, then he had a place to sleep at night. There were a lot of homeless street urchins. They were really quite harmless on the whole. Their clothes were all torn and tattered-looking, and in the summer they were barefoot.

BULLETS BRESSAN: In the summertime, we never wore shoes. Most times we went barefoot. We'd be jumpin' around the rocks near the river in bare feet. When there wasn't any work, so many kids just hung around the corners or in the park, or we went swimmin' off the dock at 75th Street, Bare-Ass Beach.

OLGA MARX: We also loved to play on the meteors which were then out in front of the Museum of Natural History. I remember saying to my fräulein, "Look, I'm standing on a star."

But she was so prissy, and she said, "Get down immediately. I can see your panties."

Before the museum was built, there used to be a lake there, and my mother told me that she used to see the men go fishing there on Sunday mornings.

We also liked to promenade down Broadway on Saturday. It was very leisurely. Everybody would be sauntering down the street. We'd stop and look at the window displays, and just put on our pretty clothes to show them off. My mother enjoyed it, too. She was always proud of the way she dressed me.

Dorothy Greenwald: It was the same when I was young. We'd get dressed up and put on a nice dress and shoes. Boys were not in the picture then. It was just like a social thing to do with your friends. Like girls going to Bloomingdale's today. You'd shop, talk about things. You'd want to see what the other girls were wearing, how good they were, and how smart they were. There wasn't much else to do. You didn't get on the El and go downtown.

Olga Marx: It reminds me of a summer song I liked:

> On a summer afternoon in the merry month of June,
> take a trip up the Hudson and down the bay,
> a trolley to Coney or Rockaway.
> On a Sunday afternoon you can see the lovers spoon.
> There's Monday and Tuesday but no day like Sunday
> on a Sunday afternoon.

I went to fourteen different schools. My mother kept listening to her friends, and they'd say this is such a wonderful school, or that one is such a wonderful school. When I had to fill out my application for Barnard, they asked me to list all the schools I attended, and I ran out of space on the application and had to ask for another piece of paper.

Miss Hayman's kindergarten was my first school. My sister went to Dr. Sachs' School for Girls. I went there in second grade. It was a school for rich children. My mother thought we were terribly spoiled there. For instance, we never had to sharpen a pencil of our own. If you had a dull pencil, you dropped it into a box, and the school had a sort of boy-of-all-work called Max, and Max sharpened the pencils. We didn't do anything for ourselves.

A friend of my mother's said it was so expensive and the children were so spoiled, and she told her about an excellent public school nearby. I was put in public school, and I didn't like it very much. So then I went to an excellent private school called Miss

Jacobi's School for Girls. There, I had a wonderful teacher named Miss Cahn. One day, she told us that one reason a dog has such a keen sense of smell was that a dog's nose is always moist. And so I came home and I moistened my nose, and I went along the rugs on my hands and knees smelling. My mother got furious at me. She said, "My place always smells fresh and clean."

When I went to the Ethical Culture Sunday School, they wanted to demote me. They thought I was too immature. My mother asked them why, and they said I cried when I sang "My Old Kentucky Home." Well, I did cry. My old Kentucky home was so far away, and it was so sad.

My first experience with a boy-girl setup was at Ethical Culture. On my first day there, I realized what fun boys could be. The director told us a Greek myth that might have had some double meaning, and when the boys snorted mischievously, the teacher said, "If any boy here has dirty thoughts, let him leave the room." And all the boys got up and walked out!

I didn't like boys at that time. In any case, boys were always being presented by parents as potential dangers. The sex education was dreadful in those days. When we had a summer cottage, and the boy living next door wanted to play with me, my mother said, "I don't want you to play with Eddie." Then she said to my father, "She won't learn anything but naughtiness from him." Anything to do with potential sex was absolutely taboo.

Goodness, I never knew a divorced woman, and to be an actress was also a very questionable thing. We had a friend who was an actress, and we adored her. My mother's friends said, "Don't leave the children alone with her too long. She might put notions in their heads."

A woman was supposed to be tolerant of her husband's infidelity. It was considered to be the norm, but a wife, that was a different story. A wife was supposed to be adoring and admiring of her husband. My mother treated my father that way.

It wasn't so easy to have an affair. First of all, it was expensive. Your wife was usually undemanding, but an affair would expect to be taken to a fine restaurant. Another problem was being found out, and finding a place where you could go. You had to go out of your neighborhood to some restaurant that nobody you knew patronized. Besides, there was always the dreadful danger of pregnancy, because contraceptives and all these things were not as advanced as they are today. There were abortions, but they were considered pretty dangerous. Not every doctor would consent to perform one, and it all had to be very secret and very elusive.

I knew all this because we used to hear this from the fräuleins when they got together and sat on a park bench and gossiped while we were supposed to be playing.

I wasn't allowed to go to my friend Edith Weiner's house because her sister Belle was known to be having an affair with a married man. She [Mother] thought that seeing her might contaminate my childish innocence. Being divorced was nearly as bad. There was a professor at Columbia who was asked to resign because he had been divorced. He was suspected of going after his students. People who were divorced were suspect. You were supposed to be a good bourgeois to be a professor.

Lesbians were also suspect. The woman who was the head of Barnard, they wouldn't give her her Ph.D. because they suspected her of being a lesbian. She had to go and get it in Europe. Then a friend said to me once, "If you want to graduate with honors and Phi Beta Kappa, you have to be very careful, because there is an upperclassman who is being very affectionate and protective to you, and if you get a reputation of being a lesbian you'll never make Phi Beta Kappa." I knew it was wrong, but what was I to do? That's the way it was in those days.

I wanted to get into Brander Matthews' English class at Columbia, and I told him, "I will not disturb you with any questions or anything." But he said, "That isn't the reason I don't want you in my class. The only way I can lecture comfortably is tilting back my chair and putting my feet on the desk in front of me, and they tell me that is too impolite to do when you have women in the class."

Still, my years at Barnard were so wonderful because the school opened up areas of knowledge that I had never been introduced to before. For instance, a required course was Psychology A. That was extremely interesting to me. Later, one of the first books that I translated and sold was Freud's *Introduction to Psychoanalysis.*

I also learned so much about myself. I had a big crush on Charles Sears Baldwin, an English professor. I took every course that he offered. When we had a Chaucer course, there was a girl who knew how to pronounce Chaucer perfectly. I said to Dr. Baldwin, "Oh, I wish I could read Chaucer the way she does."

And Dr. Baldwin leaned over to me and said, "She can read Chaucer, but you have something entirely different. You're a poet born, or I know nothing of English literature."

Even now, I have a cold shiver of delight running down my back when I hear those words.

LEE SILVER: My mother couldn't write. I would bring home a report card, and I could hardly get her to sign her name on it. Nobody ever looked at it. Once in a while my father would look at it and give it back to me. Nobody ever asked me how I was doing in school. I was an exception, perhaps, to the rule of Jews wanting their kids to be scholars. That didn't occur in my life at all. My mother wanted me to stay out of trouble and later work for Papa in the store. The pressure was constant to stay in the store. The reason for that was ignorance, her ignorance, not knowing what else was out there.

I'd go out and walk over to 102nd Street, where I went to school at PS 179. There was a lot of subtle anti-Semitism around, and there was a lot of overt anti-Semitism around. The words *Jew, kike, sheeny* were prevalent. On my block, there were Jews, Italians, and some Irish, and some Hungarians, who were generally janitors. The Irish were laborers, and the Italians came and went with whatever they could get. To the Irish, the Italians were guineas and the Jews were kikes, and they were antagonistic and aggressive, so the Italians and the Jewish kids would coalesce against the Irish when the Irish would come to attack or to break up a stickball game or ring-a-leevio games.

At the school, there were fights and arguments, but there were no knives, and the blood was incidental and accidental. If a guy called you a kike and you punched him, you weren't afraid that somebody would take a knife out. There was none of that. The kids mixed pretty well. There were a few blacks. They were called Negroes, and the Irish called them niggers. We didn't, and I don't remember the Italians calling them niggers too much. They lived on 99th Street between Columbus Avenue and Central Park West. They were also on the other side of Columbus and down to Central Park on the side of the El, mostly between Columbus Avenue and Manhattan Avenue, and then spilling over between Manhattan and Central Park West.

There wasn't a problem between the blacks and the whites. There was an uneasiness. There was never any clash, but they never played against each other or played together. They were entirely segregated. I walked up that block, and I never had any problem. The only problem I had was as a Jew, not as a white.

BULLETS BRESSAN: We used to fight the niggers down on San Juan Hill. It was all black down there. We were up on 69th or 68th, then we come down, beat 'em, threw rocks, plenty of that. They never come up there, we usually went down there. One guy might say that some colored guy hit this guy, and we'd all go down, and they'd be on the corners here. We'd throw rocks, cans, everything. We didn't care if they were ready or not, if they were black, we'd go after 'em. We had some pretty good fighters. Some of 'em went in the ring. Some of those guys were always lookin' for fights.

ROSANNA WESTON: My parents said they called this neighborhood San Juan Hill because there was so much fightin' goin' on. They said on this side lived all the black people, and on that side lived all the Irish. That was forbidden territory. You weren't supposed to go over there. They used to come over on this side and they would fight.

The boys used to fight with the Irish. They used to go out on Tenth Avenue with bats and things. The Irish would call 'em bad names, niggers and everything like that, and they'd be out there fightin'.

My mother told me about a big meeting at one of the churches after a terrible riot, and the minister said to the people, "We've taken enough. The police won't help you. The only way to stop it is to fight back. The next time they come, you arm yourself with whatever you got." Well, the next time they crossed that avenue, some had legs of chairs or tables, whatever they could find, hatchets. They took them down to the cellars, and my mother said the blood was flowin'. That was the last time they came across.

My parents were from the West Indies. My mother came here as a kid. My father left the West Indies when he was twelve. At that time, they used to take the young boys aboard ships, and my father went out on a ship when he was twelve years old, and he never returned.

My mother was fifteen when she met my father. They got married in a church on 69th called St. Stephen's Church. The minister there agreed to marry them, but they were told they couldn't bring their children to join the Sunday school. They didn't allow black children there.

She was livin' in a tenement on 62nd Street. Then, these houses, the Phipps Houses, were built. They were the first houses for workin'-class blacks. My mother used to walk around the streets pushin' a carriage, and she was goin' to have me. She saw these houses, and they looked so nice.

So she came here the next day, and the lady told her the rent is six dollars a week. Well, my mother was payin' six dollars a month. Then the lady told her she would have to bring references. The man she was workin' for, Carl Fisher, his wife came, and she said to her, "You give the family that apartment. They're very nice people." On her recommendation, they got the apartment.

The management was the most strictest people. They had armed guards in the hallway, and you couldn't hang on the stoop. Our apartment then was three rooms and a kitchen for eight of us. My mother had a divan that slept two children. We had a couch in the kitchen. There were two beds in the bedroom, and then she had one in her bedroom. She'd complain that there wasn't enough room, but my father would say, "One day you'll have the whole house to yourself. You'll miss it." He was right.

Because they couldn't join St. Stephen's, my parents used to go to a storefront place called the Mission on 62nd Street. She liked them, but it wasn't organized. Then one day my brother met this little friend, and the friend belonged to St. Cyprian's Church, which was Episcopal. He took my brother to Sunday school, and when my brother came home, he said, "Mother, I joined a choir."

"What choir?"

"You must come to church." There was my mother following these two little boys up the street to this church. We all became members, and my parents were buried through the church. We all went to Sunday school, and we went to service at eight o'clock on Sunday night. She'd line us all up. There were eight of us, and we'd take up a whole church bench. One brother became a minister in the Episcopal church. We all went to high school. Two graduated from college. My brother was one of the first blacks to graduate from City College, in 1935. My sister graduated from Morgan State, and then she got a master's from Yeshiva.

FRANK AMERUSO: I went on the newspapers—deliverin' papers. I got a job here on the *New York Journal.* Then I worked for the *Telegraph,* the *World, Graphic.* I worked for the *New York Sun,* and I had a Harlem route, 135th to 145th.

I had a lotta fun with them colored people. The number used to come through the *Sun.* It came from the stock exchange. When I used to go up my route, "Hey, Tony"—that's me—"what ya hear?" They're crazy about numbers up there. In them days you got along with the colored people on the block real good. On 69th Street, Number 304 were colored people, and 323, 325, all colored, but you always got along. If a colored guy walks through that street, and nobody knew him, we questioned him. "Where you goin'?" They stood in their place then. It's different today. Today, you can't do a thing. You can't even call 'em nigger.

ROSANNA WESTON: We'd walk up to the wealthier neighborhoods or we'd walk up to Riverside Park, and people would stop us. "What you lookin' for?" They would do it more to the males. "What you lookin' here for?" And the person wasn't doin' anything.

My mother told me how she went into an A&P, and there were a lot of white people in the store. As soon as she came in, the man ran right to her. "What do you want?" He wanted to get her right out of the store.

At that time, they had to climb up high on the shelves to get things down, and she decided that she would let him work a little bit. She asked him to get her something from the top of the shelf. He brought one thing to her, and he said, "Anything else?"

She said, "Yes." She had him climb up there again and again. Finally, he brought all the things down, and when he put them on the counter, she said to him, "I guess you can put them all back, because this money wasn't given to me. I had to work hard to get it, so I'll spend it where I'm not gonna be mistreated."

My first school was right here in the middle of the block. It was called the Henrietta School, and it was run by one of the charities. It was a segregated school, all black children. The teachers were all white. Then I went down to PS 141 to go to the fifth grade. That school was integrated, but I didn't have any problems. They had Irish children and Jewish children. See, if you leave children alone, then the prejudice will disappear. It's the grown-ups that tell the children to stay away or to call the children names.

FRANK AMERUSO: I started takin' bets up in Harlem. I used to take ten cents a bet on the horses, no numbers. I had three colored guys workin' for me. I loved to have a good time. I used to play cards a lot. After I got through work, I used to play in a club. I got fired because I was playin' cards instead of workin'. When I lost out, I met a friend on 69th Street. His name was Mu Kow. He had a little store there with nothin' in it, no merchandise, just maybe a counter where guys come in and bet with him. He says, "You can stay in here. Start a game. Whatever you want to do. Run me the bets."

From there I went to work for a guy named Georgie. Georgie was bookin' in a poolroom right off a bar. You could get results off the telephone with a scratch sheet, and I was gettin' three dollars a day to get 'em so he could run it back and read it to the customers. I soon met my wife, and she said, "Three dollars a day, what are you goin' to do with three dollars a day?" So I started bookin' 'em up myself. Then I made money. I had a nice flat on 70th Street for five dollars a week, beautiful place. I got another apartment in the same building. I used to run card games, and I used to cut a lot of money. People knew I had a game, and they came down to it. I had one big table, a place to sleep, a bathroom, and a little kitchen. I'd buy them cigarettes, some liquor, and I cut five percent. The first night I made over $500. I made money. I'm still livin' on the interest.

BULLETS BRESSAN: At 84th, Billy Cook had a regular horse room. That was high class. They had results comin' in and the prices. That was a real bookie's room. He also had a speakeasy there that was high-class. Judges, racketeers, Capone, they all went up there. He had it fixed nice. They had pictures of the old fighters, the old baseball players, that fancy mahogany bar—boy, what a high-class place.

FRANK AMERUSO: Around the neighborhood, the cops weren't a problem. The cops in them days were so much better than the cops today. You could pay them off on anything, five dollars, two dollars. They were all good, the cops in them days. You could buy 'em a drink. The cop on the beat used to bet with me. You'd give him a two-dollar double for nothin'. Today, they're all scared of everything.

BULLETS BRESSAN: Charlie Cook had the bar right on the corner of 69th. There used to be a cop on the corner of 68th Street. They had the boxes, you know, and the cop would call up, "Madden's beer truck is comin' up." He'd come up, the truck would stop, give the cop five or ten, whatever it was, and then go on. If they didn't have the five or ten, they'd stop that truck.

There were all kinds of small speakeasies in the neighborhood. In each neighborhood so many had 'em—home-brew places, whiskey places. Home brew was the big thing. We'd go to, like, the German woman on 69th. She used to make gin in the bathtub and would give you a drink free if you took a bottle out. There was an Italian fellow at 66th and West End. He just made wine and sold it. He'd give you a glass or two and you bought a bottle. It was good business around the neighborhood, especially Saturday night. There was always an Italian girl gettin' married on a Saturday night—free food, you know, and drink. We'd get dressed up Saturday night, Sunday, and some guys would hock the suit on Monday for five dollars.

We used to go to Loew's Lincoln and pay fifteen cents to sit in the orchestra for vaudeville. Then we had Keith's Colonial at 62nd. That was also vaudeville. The Arcade on 65th was the Dumps. There, you'd see the guy comin' around with the roach spray. At the Loew's, if we didn't have enough money, we'd give the ticket taker a nickel and he'd let us in. So the manager comes in, and he looks over the audience. "Oh, quite a few people here." But when he'd go down to the ticket office, there was no money in there. The ticket guy took it all. Then we used to go up to the pits, way up. Up there, you could smoke if you wanted to.

LEE SILVER: I went to a movie house on 102nd Street between Amsterdam and Columbus called the Rose. I'd go in at ten o'clock in the morning and stay there until four or five in the afternoon. They knew if I wasn't in the horse stable, I'd be watching a cowboy movie. There were some serials and some feature-length films. The prevalence was Buck Jones, either in serial or feature length, and Hoot Gibson, and then it would repeat. The theater was loaded with kids on Saturday afternoons. They had giveaways to get the kids in there, like a small statue of George Washington or a dime-store soldier.

A couple of blocks away, at 100th Street and Broadway, was an Isaac Gellis Delicatessen. Isaac Gellis was the Hot Dog King, kosher Hot Dog King, the only really savory hot dog that anybody could have had in his whole life. I'm not just reminiscing, saying it was better in the old days. It was better than Hebrew National, much better than Nathan's. I picked up on that post–World War II, hanging around with some of the guys after work. Somebody would say, "I got a car. Let's go out to Nathan's Coney Island and have a hot dog." It would always come to mind, This is no Isaac Gellis.

ABE GELLIS: We had the Isaac Gellis stores for years, going back to World War I. They were all over the West Side. The store on 100th Street, that was Rosenbloom, but they all used the name Isaac Gellis. Everything we put into our product was quality, and the quality kept up. That's why we had the slogan "A House of Quality."

My grandfather, the original Isaac Gellis, came over here in the early 1800s. He had been in the meat and cattle business in Germany, so when he came here, naturally, he went into the butcher business. He sold beef to the Union Army. Then he had a butcher store on Essex Street. He met Mrs. Gellis on the boat coming over, and he married her. She was quite a gal. She could pick up a 400-pound forequarter, throw it on the bench, and break it apart.

In our day, the cuts were prime, choice, good, and utility, which is scrawny beef. Some people, if they had the good or choice beef, they would take the cow beef and mix it in, but what we used was bull beef, which was the leanest beef around, and we took the kosher end of it.

The bull beef is lean. You've got to get bull beef that is not watery. If you get watery bull beef, it doesn't blend in with the trimmings, and it falls apart. It usually tends to turn your product green, even if you smoke it too well.

Now [Hebrew] National just moved out west. Lovely boys, nice boys. I knew his father when he was in business. But by moving out west, he wasn't sure of his water. Now, when he shipped a load in here, most of the stuff turned green. The water has a great deal to do with the manufacture of sausage. You can't make sausage all over the country. Half of our water in the United States is bad. It has a lot of lead in it. They have to put additives into the water when they make it out in California. Vegas has good water, but who the hell wants to open up a sausage factory in Vegas? All the people out there are just gambling. New York water is excellent. We have all rainwater coming in from the reservoirs, and the impurities haven't come into our water.

The most important thing for the taste, I think, is the spices, because they give the hot dogs their flavor. We used Griffith for our spices. Their laboratories would take the spices and shoot 'em up to a six- or seven-story bin, and they blow it around and get rid of the impurities. Then the spices would come down, and they would do it again. After doing that five or six times, that would purify the spices. They were the first ones who did it. We took their spices as soon as they came on the market.

Nathan never made his own product. He bought it from another manufacturer. He got a good formula and a good frankfurter. I can't knock it, because as a kid I used to go out to Coney Island and eat 'em. I think we made a better frankfurter, but he got away with murder because he had a hot griddle, and he used to throw it on it and get it hot. If it was cold outside, they'd heat the frankfurter and roll. People would burn their lips, and they would think it was good because it was cold outside.

Another thing, Hebrew National uses hydrolyzed plant protein, which is an additive and to me not kosher. If the product is good, you get the taste from the beef itself and the spices that we use. They add the hydrolyzed plant protein to enhance it. We don't add anything.

You also have to be careful who you're dealing with, because if you don't have a good rabbi, you don't deal with him. What's stopping him from taking a nonkosher bundle and putting it in for kosher? The most important thing for the rabbi to do is to watch the koshering of the meat. He is on the butcher floor all day long. He watches the koshering, the salting.

We made a good frankfurter. We strived for quality. At the store we had 'em griddled, but I put 'em into boiling water for five minutes. If it's frozen, it's about six or seven minutes. Take 'em out, a portion of beans, sweet red pepper, pickle, coleslaw, whatever you like, and you've got no problems. I like 'em boiled, but of course you can't knock the griddled frankfurter. If you bite into a frankfurter that's fresh, you can't beat it.

ROSANNA WESTON: My mother wasn't a great cook, but she knew how to manipulate with food. Like we used to eat all kinds of stew. We had so much stew, I can't eat it anymore. She made corn bread, biscuits, apple pie. We didn't get much meat, because it was expensive, but she used to cook chicken on Sundays. That was a special meal.

She used to make meat loaf for dinner. She'd cook greens, and she would cook neck bones, which was part of the pig, smoked neck bones, they call them. They boil them into the collard greens.

We bought most of our food from white people, but there were a couple of colored merchants on our block who sold West Indian things. West Indian people use a lot of cornmeal and codfish, and they had them. She'd boil the cornmeal and put it in a bowl, and then she'd roll it into a ball. They'd call that *fungie*. Then she'd cut it up and put it with the codfish, along with chopped onions, green peppers, and pieces of pork. You'd sauté it all together. I wasn't crazy about it, but we ate plenty of it.

LEE SILVER: I never had sturgeon until I was an adult. We didn't have the up-class fish in our store. We had whitefish and lox, jarred herrings. I'd take some herring and roll, make a sandwich, and that was my lunch.

OLGA MARX: There was a song about sturgeon I liked [to the tune of "Reuben, Reuben"]:

> *Caviar is a virgin sturgeon.*
> *Sturgeon is a very fine fish.*
> *Very few sturgeon are ever virgin.*
> *That's why caviar is my dish.*

That's a good song on sturgeon, isn't it?

> Barney Greengrass may not have ruled any kingdoms or written any great symphonies, but he did a monumental job with sturgeon.
>
> —Groucho Marx

MOE GREENGRASS: Groucho Marx used to come in all the time. He had a young wife, maybe eighteen or nineteen years old. George Burns, Eddie Cantor, we'd call up every morning. Cantor had a big household on Central Park West, and we would send an order down to them every day. Every week we got ten to twelve tickets to his broadcasts, which in them days was really a big thing. Everyone you could mention in the theatrical field. Marilyn Monroe used to come in with Arthur Miller. Joe DiMaggio used to come in.

As a kid my father, Barney Greengrass, worked down on Ludlow Street for a man named Morris Cohen. It was a typical herring-and-appetizer store. Herring was very popular. It was very cheap. Jews always seemed to like salty foods. They used to wash off the herring, take out the bones, and eat it. They'd have a little piece of herring for lunch. It stimulated your appetite.

Anyway, my father came up to Harlem, and he opened his first store at 1403 Fifth Avenue around 1903. From there he moved to 57 St. Nicholas Avenue on 113th Street. In 1929, he opened up down here. This was just about the nicest area of New York in them days. West End, Riverside Drive, and Central Park West were all very nice neighborhoods.

In the early days, people went for *schmaltz* herring, but as the years went by, they wanted pickled herring because the pickled herring didn't have that much salt. In that case, the herring is soaked out, then put in vinegar, and in that way most of the salt is out of it. It had a delicious flavor. Today, we get very, very little call for *schmaltz* herring. You can't believe how much pickled herring we sell, which we prepare right here in the store. For the next couple of weeks for Yom Kippur and Rosh Hashanah, there's no telling how much we sell.

Years ago, when I was a kid, everybody used to order lox. It was salty. Today, we sell like eight-to-one poundage of Nova over lox. They're getting away from lox. The sturgeon we sell is strictly domestic, which years ago used to come from the Great Lakes. Then they became polluted, and now we sell sturgeon that only comes from Canadian waters.

There's lake sturgeon, river sturgeon. Some sturgeon comes from Russia. It's called ocetrima. There's a beluga sturgeon and a sevruga sturgeon. The beluga sturgeon, they catch that in the Caspian Sea. Some say it's Russian. Some say it's Iranian. It's like New York and Jersey. It's from in between. The Hudson River runs in between. There, Iran runs on one side and Russia is on the other.

The Russian sturgeon weighs anywhere from 200 to 2,000 pounds, and it's like horse meat. They sell it on Broadway and some of the stores. It makes big beautiful slices, you know, because it's a big fish. Lake sturgeon might weigh anywheres from ten pounds—forty pounds is a tremendous lake sturgeon. And it's sweet as sugar. Compared to the other, it's day and night. But we don't go in for that. We sell a lot right now of Nova Scotia salmon. Some comes from Canadian waters, from the Gasbe Peninsula. A lot of it comes from Norwegian waters. Then there's some other waters called the Faroe Islands, and that gives off some beautiful salmon. You can't believe how good it is. Then of course there's what they call a western salmon, a western Nova Scotia. It comes from Alaska, and it's treated like a Nova, and it's not as expensive. I guess primarily because it's like a western item, you know?

Sturgeon isn't too fatty. It's very tasty. A good sturgeon ain't too salty. I like Nova Scotia. I love sturgeon. When it comes in good, there's nothing better than a sturgeon—Nova Scotia—combination sandwich.

But lake sturgeon is becoming extinct, really so. They just are getting dried out, the waters, and you just can't get too much. There's a shortage every so often. We can't order as much as we want because they don't fill your order, and they tell us in a few years sturgeon will be out altogether. What can I tell you. There goes our reputation. We'll have to be the Salmon King.

And people's tastes for sturgeon aren't as strong, chiefly because the prices are getting out of hand. It's now *thirty-eight dollars a pound.* I remember selling it for $1.80 a pound, going back forty, fifty years. When my father started buying sturgeon, he paid under a dollar.

Pop started billing himself as the Sturgeon King back in 1920. There was a Senator Frawley, a customer of ours up in Harlem, and he gave my father that name, and it stuck with us ever since. When we were on 113th Street and St. Nicholas, two buildings away lived Judge Samuel Rosenman. That was President Roosevelt's right-hand man, his adviser. He used to write his speeches, and he was my father's friend. Through him we got an order to ship around ten pounds to the White House. We got a reorder, too. Later on we shipped to Eisenhower. We used to sell to all of

Hollywood. Al Jolson used to come in here every weekend. He was a Yankee fan, and he used to go up there every week. Once, he made a bet on a game with my father and he won. My father wanted to pay him, but he insisted that we send him sturgeon for the next three months on the house.

I've been in the store since I was a baby. I used to take cash when I was a kid eight, nine years old. Someone is waiting to be waited on, so little by little I started cutting. With a knife, cut salmon, cut sturgeon, it ain't easy. You have to watch and you have to listen. I would say my son here is the best cutter in the country, honest to God. You can't believe how nice, evenly thin or thick, however you want it, he can cut a salmon. That's the God's honest truth. I'm really proud of him. It don't take long to learn, but you just have to get the feel how to hold a knife at a certain angle. You have to cut it on the bias, you know? It's an art.

•   •   •

ROSANNA WESTON: Thelonius Monk lived in our building. He went to school with me. He had a piano in his apartment. He could play it by feel. I was not a fan of his music. I didn't understand his type of jazz. I had a relative who played in Louis Armstrong's band. I could understand that kind of music.

You'd look in the window here, and you'd see Dizzy Gillespie, Max Roach, Benny Carter. You'd seen them all out there on the street. There were other people that played music here, too. Monk used to play until you put your head out the window. "Shut up. Turn it off." He'd play until two o'clock in the morning, and the neighbors were bangin' away. They didn't want to hear no more music. They wanted to sleep.

SELMA BLICK: Sixty-sixth Street seemed to be the poorest block because of St. Nick's Arena. The people that would go there didn't necessarily have the same values of other people, and that street was a little bit lower in class than the others. When they had the El station there, and I would go visit an aunt of mine, my father would know when I was coming home. He would then walk down to 66th Street and say to Big Bill, who hung around one of the newsstands, "My daughter's coming home in a few minutes. Watch out for her." So he would watch me come down the El steps and walk a block and a half to where I lived to make sure that none of the sailors nabbed me. It was full of sailors there. They would hang around the seafood restaurant on the corner called Mike's Ship Ahoy.

BULLETS BRESSAN: There were a lot of sailors there then. The fleet used to come up here, and you'd have sailors here for three or four weeks. Before they left the ship, they got orders, "Keep away from 67th Street." When they went down that block, Christ, they'd get beat up. The Irish crowd at 67th and Amsterdam used to rob 'em, beat 'em up, steal their pea coats. There was a speakeasy there in an empty storefront. You'd see about fifty, sixty sailors there, and Christ, they'd get beaten up all the time.

SELMA BLICK: Even though it was kind of scroungy, I liked to go to St. Nick's to see the heavyweights. I also had a crush on Benny Leonard, who had been the lightweight champion. He had a restaurant on 72nd Street. He was a handsome, beautiful man. If I had a date, I wanted to go there. I didn't care what they fed me, I just wanted to look at him. He was a nice man, too.

On the corner near my father was the famous Joe Da Palma, who had a very exclusive fruit-and-vegetable place and butcher shop for the rich customers between Columbus and Central Park West. At the time of Mussolini, he picked up himself and his wife and went back to Italy. Then he came back with his tail between his legs. It seemed he couldn't bring any of his money back with him, because Mussolini had adopted it. He decided then that the United States was a pretty good place after all.

Across the street was Healy's Golden Glade, which was a nightclub on Columbus between 66th and 67th. I could look out from my bedroom window, and I could remember very poshly dressed women and men arriving in horses and carriages, dressed in long evening dresses, very shiny, and the men in top hats. James Montgomery Flagg, who also lived on 67th Street, did a sketch of this particular place. I thought the place was fascinating. I would say to myself, "Someday, I'm going to have a long satin dress with a velvet cloak." I don't think I ever did.

There were also lots of rooming houses on the side streets with red lights on them. Beneath us was a woman with dyed red hair that always fascinated me. She had two daughters who were beautiful and who didn't live at home. They would drive up in chauf-

feur-driven limousines every once in a while. They were chorus
girls. I thought they were so elegant then, and it never occurred to
me that they may not have been making their money honestly. It
didn't bother anybody else.


BULLETS BRESSAN: Oh, we had whorehouses, especially in the
brownstones in the 70s and 80s. You'd go up to 80th Street, 79th,
81st, 82nd. Two dollars for a room. On 71st near the park was a
brownstone. All the millionaires went there, weirdos. They used to
get whipped. It was in the paper, havin' the beautiful girls whip
'em with no clothes. They had no clothes and the girls had no
clothes.

If you went into a real good house, with pretty girls, they wanted
ten or twenty dollars. We couldn't afford that. But one fella might
be deliverin', say, and he'd find out. She'd talk to him. "You know
any friends, send 'em up." I never caught anything. You always
used a condom. Although some guys got gonorrhea. They had to
go to Bellevue, and they got what they call the sound treatment.
They stick this thing up your penis, and it expands—ooh. This guy
was tellin' me once, he was out there waitin', and there was a big
colored guy, enormous like a giant, he said. He hears him in pain,
hollerin'. Boy, this guy just ran out the door.

When Mae West was in that play *Pleasure Man*, she had all
her fairy chorus boys in a big apartment on 71st Street. We were
teenagers, and we used to go up there. Naturally, they wanted young
boys, and I never went for that much, but a couple of guys did.
You know, they made a few dollars. You know, like I say, they get
sucked off and they get paid a few dollars. I didn't like that. We'd
just go up there and steal a silk shirt and stuff.

One night, me and this fella were up there, and these kids
liked to drink gin. They were only about nineteen—our own age.
They were gonna buy us a drink. They say, "Meet you tomorrow
on the corner at 8:30." Them two and us two. So we go up there
on the corner, and we don't see nobody, but there are two girls on
the other corner. They're teasin' us. It was the two gays we hadda
meet. They was dressed as girls, but we didn't know. Then one of
them started laughin', and she nudged the other one. They told us
then, and we went into the speakeasy. There were quite a few guys
in there we knew, and our girls looked better than theirs. They all

thought, "How did those two creeps get such nice pretty girls?" They couldn't believe it when we told 'em.

• • •

ROSANNA WESTON: We used to get toys on Christmas, and we always had a Christmas tree. In 1929, we didn't have hardly anything in the house that reminded you of Christmas. Christmas morning, my mother called us into the kitchen. She had some packages that were wrapped in green paper. She gave each one of us a package, and when we opened them, it was winter underwear, which may have cost about fifty cents. She must have spent between two or three dollars, which was a lot of money at that time.

She had nothing else to give us. I thought that she should have gave us something else, and I started to cry. Then my brother told me there was no such thing as Santa Claus, and that made it worse. He said, "There's no such thing. Santa Claus is your mother and your father, and if they don't have nothing to give you, you don't get nothing." I was heartbroken. In those days, I believed anything they told me.

He said, "Rosanna, how can you be so dumb." [*She laughs.*]

OLGA MARX: My mother didn't bring us up knowing we were Jewish. We had a Christmas tree. She wanted to do everything as American as possible, and Christmas was very American to her.

New Year's was also special. On New Year's Day, all the women stayed at home to receive callers, and the men went visiting. The men would wear heavy overcoats, a high hat and cane, which was a very important part of the outfit. When a man would call, it was a sign of gentility to leave an engraved visiting card in an urn at the door. Then my mother would use them to compare with friends. Of course, it was very important to have more cards than anybody else.

The men wouldn't stay long, just enough for a chat and a drink, and then they would be on to the next call. The depressive ones would say, "I wonder if there is going to be another war this year" or "The price of help is getting very dear." While the cheerful ones would say things like "There are all kinds of new inventions. You can send a cablegram by wireless. It's just like magic!"

The biggest New Year's Eve was when we went from 1899 to 1900. My mother had a big party. I was dressed up as the New

Year. My sister was dressed up as Father Time. Somebody was dressed up as the old century. She was carried out, and I was carried in, and the guests made a big fuss over me.

There was a lot of talk about things being better in the new century. They were saying that with so many new inventions, like the steamer which went faster than any other steamers, and who knows the time may come when we will be able to fly across the ocean.

Around that time, my mother found getting around the house with all those stairs too strenuous. I remember when she came home once, and she said, "They're putting up houses with all the rooms on one floor," and that was the beginning of the end, because she was set on finding an apartment.

When we moved into the new flat in 1901, that was my first experience with electric lights. The new apartment was all electric. My mother was so enchanted by this that the minute it would get dark, she would prance from room to room, turning on all the lights. When my father got the bill, he was really surprised.

I was in Europe when my friend Edith Weiner wrote me saying, "We have a wonderful new thing called the telephone, and when you get back, I'm sure you'll have it, too. Then we can talk to each other in the evening when we're not allowed to go out anymore!"

That was around 1905, and we soon had one installed in our flat. My mother didn't like it at all, with that bell ringing all day. She also didn't like the phonograph. I thought it was wonderful, and I was always sorry we didn't have one.

I also remember hearing people talking about the Wright brothers, but it was just some more of that magic, the idea that something could fly up there. Of course, there was always, in a child's head, "Why doesn't that thing fall? What's keeping it up there?" But children don't puzzle unduly about those things.

•   •   •

LEE SILVER: The crash was something that we heard about on the radio or was in the newspaper, and was happening out there to those other people. We were always poor. We didn't have stock, so it didn't have any impact on us. The garage on the block still received the cars that came from the other side.

When Herbert Hoover was on a newsreel, I didn't understand a word he was saying, and I thought I was a fairly bright kid. I listened, and he was talking in political terms about the finances of government. There was nobody I knew who understood what he was talking about. It wasn't until Roosevelt came on, with his method of repeating what he had to say and speaking with mellifluous and deliberate cadences, that people began to understand what politicians were talking about. The only politicians they understood were Roosevelt and people like Jimmy Hines, who simply said, "We're gonna get those Republicans."

Jimmy Hines was the local political leader then. He was connected with the Jimmy Walker regime. Jimmy Hines had a great reputation for being a friend of the people. He'd come on the block from time to time to shake hands. He'd put his head in the door and say, "Hi, Dave" to my father. You heard his name so often, "Jimmy Hines" was like one word.

We had torchlight parades on Election Night with torches and sparklers and signs. People came down Amsterdam carrying the torches, and there were horses and wagons with people sitting on the tailgates. There was always the big star on the side of the wagon. It was the eagle for the Republicans and the star for the Democrats. And in that neighborhood it was always for the Democrats.

BULLETS BRESSAN: We used to have bonfires on Election Day. There'd be a big flame, five or six stories high. We'd use any wood we could find. I remember this guy, he unhooks the horse from a pushcart. He tied the horse on the lamppost and pushed the wagon right down the hill on 69th to the fire and put it in.

OLGA MARX: When I was a girl, around election time gold was Democratic and silver was Republican, and we would ask our classmates, "Are you gold or are you silver?" Then, we thought it was loyal to pal up with people who were gold. Election time was tense and important. My father was in the textile business, so he would always vote against people who were in favor of an import tax.

If I brought anybody new into the house, and politics came up at all, my father would ask my schoolmate, "Is your father for or against Dreyfus?" If she didn't know or if he was not particularly for, he did not approve of my having her for a friend anymore. People were very split on the Dreyfus case. It was a tremendous topic of discussion.

We were in Europe when McKinley was assassinated. That was very shocking. But that night, we were in a restaurant, and the waiters served us little cakes with small American flags stuck in them. It was their way of saying they were sorry, and it was very touching.

My oldest political memory is of the soldiers returning home from the Spanish-American War. I remember my mother sat me on the windowsill as the soldiers paraded by, and she said to me, "There'll never be another war."

I saw the women's suffrage parades, but I didn't think much about them. I wasn't thinking about such things. I was delighted to spend time with my books and my poetry. And my mother thought that it was so revolting for women to put themselves in the foreground this way. There was an old German slogan that men are the ones to participate in public life and for the women it was children, church, and kitchen. My mother thought that was fine.

• • •

SELMA BLICK: During the Depression, I got a job working for several doctors, and that was much more important than going on to college. I lied when I was fourteen and still in high school and said I was sixteen. I got a job for $28.75 a week, which was top pay.

My father's business was lousy then. The rich people on 67th Street never paid their bills. If they had, life would have been wonderful. But we ate. One of the reasons why was that my father had two friends who were in the fruit-and-vegetable business, and I think they bartered for his services in return for their food. One was a guy on 68th and Columbus—Joe Sabatini. He was a great big man. He ran the fruit-and-vegetable store during the day, and at night he was a wrestler, and my father was his second on a few occasions. It was very funny.

But the men on the corner selling apples always looked cold. Then the government decided to pay the bonuses to the veterans, and they were lined up from the armory where the State Theater is now, way up to our store. They didn't look too happy either.

BULLETS BRESSAN: They had the shantytowns up around 75th near the river. Oh, there was a lot of them. The veterans had them up there. Some of them had some pretty good things there, fixed it nice, pots and pans, clean, neat. Some were tin, cardboard. There were 200 or 300 up there. We used to go up there all the time.

There were two fellas in the neighborhood who were in the war. They had a shanty. It was like the Bonus March in Washington. They were like showin' their solidarity. Then they got their checks. Some guys got $2,000. When they got them, there were more drunks around. Two thousand dollars was a lot of money in them days.

During the Depression, three-quarters of the neighborhood was on relief, on welfare. I made a livin' at a newsstand at 66th and Columbus. There were four other guys on that corner, and we all made a livin.' I was right on the corner where St. Nick's was. We'd have fights there on Monday nights, and I'd sell a lot of papers. And the papers were only two cents. You sold a hundred papers, you paid a dollar forty and made a sixty-cent profit. Then I started takin' horse bets from the stand, and the papers didn't mean nothin' to me then. Sometimes, I made a couple hundred a week takin' bets, but I only did it for about a year and a half, that's all. Too many cops. One tells the other. Too many knew about it, and they all wanted to get paid. You only gave the cop on the beat five dollars. It was the detectives that was the problem. They wanted the big money.

LEE SILVER: In those days, we liked to hang out at Mike's Candy Store. He had a countertop with a couple of stools, but he didn't have sandwiches. He had chocolate seltzer, ice-cream soda, and Coke in a bottle. For three cents you could get an egg cream. Or there was the Two Cents Plain, which was an egg cream without the chocolate. It was just plain seltzer. I didn't like the milk, so I'd order the three-cent version with more chocolate. The long pretzel out of the jar was extra.

We played a lot of stickball. The rules were, anything you hit was good as long as it was in the baseline, which was usually the width of the two sidewalks. You could play fifteen or twenty minutes at a stretch before a car came along. There were hardly any parked on the streets.

Then there was kick-the-can. In kick-the-can, you loaded a can so that it got some weight. Then one guy was it. You would either hide and he would be walking around, and then while he was walking around, you ran out and kicked the can and disappeared before he could tag you. Or if you were very brave, you would come out and dance around and see if you could kick the can and run off someplace. If you got beyond a certain boundary, he couldn't tag you.

Another thing we liked to do was on Halloween. We'd get, like, a coffee can and put holes in the bottom, and put a fire in there. Then we'd get a sweet mickey in the can, whip it around, and roast the mickey. To us that was exciting.

OLGA MARX: When I was around twelve, a schoolteacher told us about another new invention that they were exhibiting downtown. She had a number of extra tickets they were giving to teachers, so they could talk about this new invention, which was the radio. I went with my mother. There was a show every half hour. A man told us we could sit in a room and hear a concert. We sat down, and he turned on the radio, and it was like magic. Still, my mother didn't altogether approve. She said, "If you want music, make it."

ROSANNA WESTON: I liked the mystery stories and "The Shadow" on Sunday afternoons, the soap operas and "Make Believe Ballroom." We'd dance and play it so loud, the neighbors would be pounding on the ceiling. "Turn that down!"

SELMA BLICK: I didn't like the soaps, but I used to run home like crazy from my job so I could listen to "Amos 'n' Andy" at seven o'clock. Edgar Bergen and Charlie McCarthy were on Sunday nights. I heard the "War of the Worlds," and I turned it off. They said something about the world falling apart, and I wasn't impressed. I just turned the station. And the Goldbergs. Also, I must have been quite sloppy, because Fibber McGee's closet sounded normal to me.

LEE SILVER: Thinking back, we weren't happy. There wasn't any laughter, not much of it. Maybe it was the poverty or maybe it was just my own father and mother. My mother told dirty jokes to customers. My father was able to give advice to any relative who came along but not to his kids. In order to gain a little survival for myself, I did what no other Jewish kid of the time did: I joined the Boy Scouts.

There was no settlement house. The survival was what each kid could find his own way. You were always looking for a few pennies and nickels. When I delivered orders, somebody would give me a tip for three cents. When I was carrying the booze around in my scooter, the newsstand dealer would give me a couple of pennies. I'd get a couple of pennies or a nickel after helping out in the stable.

I had a little tin box for the money, which was not something to spend but to hold onto for security. There was nothing very specific. I felt stronger because I had the money.

It was also the horse and wagons. A couple of doors down from us was a store in which delivery people got papers from the *News* and the *Mirror* and wrapped 'em, put 'em on the horse and wagons, then delivered them to the various newsstands. I helped wrap and load them. Once I asked where they came from. He said they came from a newspaper in a big building. "I bet I make more from this than your father makes in a whole week." And he did. I think that's what put the germ in my head about newspapers.

ROSANNA WESTON: A few years after I left high school, I got married, and I married a man that believed a woman's place is in the home. And I mean a adamant one. He worked, but he believed that. "You don't need no job, no place. Stay home." But he was a good husband. I was lucky I got a person as good as him. He was so kind.

I lived here after I was married. These buildings were nicer than the others. Most of the others were tenement houses, and there were wooden houses still up until the late 1940s. But we had some other nice houses. We had a good house on 62nd Street called the Tuskegee. Then we had the Hamilton House. I don't know why they tore those houses down. We protested, but a man came one day, and he said, "You don't need a lawyer, because you cannot win that case. The city has condemned the property, and they're gonna tear it down," and they did.

They were nicely kept. They were run just like this. It was one of the saddest things when they were loadin' those people's things onto the trucks to make 'em move out. Some of 'em broke down on the sidewalk and cried. They couldn't believe that it could have been done to 'em.

They put 'em in a house on 92nd Street. It was a white neighborhood, and they put these four or five tenants up there, and do you know those people rioted? La Guardia was mayor, and he sent the police, and they pelted them with garbage. This was right here in New York. This wasn't the Mason-Dixon line.

I never forgot. One of the fellows, he put on his Army uniform and came down in the street to be attacked by those people. He said, "Yes, I just came back from the Army, and this is what I'm comin' back to."

Now everybody's gone from here. The church is long gone. They kept these buildings up nice, but with the new landlord, the buildings went right down. There's a bunch of squirrels under the roof, and you can't get the landlord to do anything. When it rains, the water leaks down over everything. People sell drugs in the hallway. There's mostly empty apartments. I'm just about the last one from those days still in these houses, and they want me out of here, too, but I don't have any place to go.

LEE SILVER: For a kid, the hope was that you would be able to get work or improve your work. You aspired to get good work and to get good income, and for some it was to have enough work to get off the block. I wanted off the block. That was all I could think of. I didn't know where or which direction to go in. Nobody I knew ever used the word *career*. That was for middle class. You should find yourself a business or find yourself a trade. Find yourself a job. These were the references.

I know why I became a reporter, because, a poor Jewish kid, growing up in a cold-water flat, I was able to be a peer with the Rockefellers. I was the equal of anybody I encountered. For me that was what I lived to become.

Later, after the war, when it was impossible to find an apartment, we were looking for someplace to live. My friend Bill, who was working at the *Daily News* with me, had a railroad flat on 55th Street. He told me that another flat was going to be available in the building. But I told him, "I grew up in one of these things. I fought my fuckin' way out of it, and I just don't want to go back in it. I can't."

BULLETS BRESSAN: I never had a trade or nothin.' I think about it sometimes, but what can I do now? When I was sixteen and I got out of school, a guy wanted to give me a job with the telephone company. I was a jerk, and I didn't do it. I just didn't want to.

Most of the guys them days, I don't know, they didn't do nothin'. Some kids did good. I wasn't stupid like some kids, but my parents didn't push us. A lot of kids didn't even graduate, fifth grade, sixth grade, out. I went to trade school two terms and I quit when I was sixteen. I'm sorry now, but I was just one of those kids who didn't want to go.

I got my nickname because I got shot in the neighborhood in 1931. We had a few drinks and we got into a little argument. This guy thought I was foolin' around with his daughter. I chased him up the block, and he went up to his apartment. I see him come down the hall. I picked up a milk bottle. I'm tryin' to fight him with that and he's got a gun. He hit me in the stomach. A few fellas there put me in a cab. I was in the hospital three weeks. I never pressed charges. It was over with, that's all. I was half drunk anyway. It could have been my fault. Then, some guy come out of Sing Sing. He said he heard about me. "I'll give ya a name," he said. "Bullets." So the nickname stuck.

Sometime after that I was in a bar. A fella comes in with a friend of his. He introduces me to the other guy. "Hey, Bullets, meet Machine Gun. Then there was another guy, "Meet the Hatchet Man." There were three strangers there. They must have been sayin', "What are we doin' here?"


OLGA MARX: For me, my best memories fall into three periods of life. One was my early childhood in the house on 77th Street, and the second are my years at Barnard. My college years were my best years. The third period was working ten years with my friend E. M. on the Stefan George translations. We were extremely attuned to each other. It was just wonderful.

Perhaps when I was young there were less distractions, so that everything that happened to you was an experience. It had a chance to expand. There weren't so many things going on. The pace was slower, and it wasn't considered necessary to entertain children all the time with new toys or new inventions or devices for entertainment.

My mother was very strict in many ways, but I don't bear her a grudge at all. My pet name for her was "Mommychen." Sometimes, even now, if I feel sort of caught in a lurch, I say out loud, "Mommychen, *hilf mier.*" Mommy, help me.

And she always says, "*Nimmdich zusammen.*" Get yourself together. And then I try to pull myself together, and I usually find a solution.

I had a poem published in the Barnard magazine that I thought about recently:

> *I am free of friend and free of foe.*
> *My lover left me long ago,*
> *And the world is little and far.*
> *There's not a body cares or knows,*
> *I follow where the west wind blows,*
> *My eyes are on a star.*
> *And no one asks me why so late*
> *the like of me has never a mate,*
> *It's just the road and I.*
> *The touch of wind is swift and sweet*
> *I run on eager restless feet into the open sky.*

I guess I always felt lonely. I never felt that I had a friend with whom I really could share ideas and everything. And I didn't have a boyfriend of my own. My mother hedged me around so carefully. But there were two things I found out about poetry when I was quite young. One was that it was company, and the other was that it could make things that had passed, or that were far away, everlasting and with you. I found that out by myself, and that really made me happy.

# Northern
# Manhattan

✤

AN OLD HORSE lazily pulls a plow by a brick farmhouse through what will soon be a thriving cornfield. It is a typical rural American scene, except for the apartment houses whose shadows darken the horse's path.

The farm sits between 213th and 214th streets. The year is 1954, the final planting season for the last farm in Manhattan. Soon, the telephone company will take over the land and erect a modern office building on the site. Some 345 years after the Dutch first set eyes on the island, the urbanization of Manhattan will be complete.

Since the city's growth followed a northerly pattern, it isn't surprising that the neighborhoods above 155th Street—Washington Heights, Inwood, and Marble Hill—maintained a rural flavor so late into the twentieth century. Yet there is still something odd in hearing an old-timer recall his exploration of the pristine forests of Inwood, spotting an occasional fox in Fort Tryon Park or a snake slithering through the quiet neighborhood streets. After all, this *is* Manhattan. Today, New Yorkers grouse about the forty-minute subway trip to the area from Midtown. In pre-Revolution days, the journey through hostile Indian territory, treacherous swamps, and nearly impassable rocky terrain took two days.

When Henry Hudson's *Half Moon* first anchored off the northern tip of Manhattan in 1609, he was met by Delaware Munsee Indians, who occupied much of the surrounding land. The Indians lived among the cliffs and caves around Inwood Hill, subsisting on game and fish, especially fresh oysters. They also had easy access to the fields and hunting grounds of the mainland by way of Spuyten Duyvil Creek, then narrow and low enough to be forded on foot.

The Dutch established a farming community known as New Harlem on the northern end of the island in 1658. Because of Indian warfare, the farmers had to work the fields with weapons at the ready. Their muskets also came in handy in battling the wolves and bears that roamed the land until the settlers eliminated the last from the island in 1685. Three years later, they succeeded in driving most of the Indians from Manhattan as well.

Still, few settlers wandered that far north to stake their claim, and the Heights remained an area of unparalleled beauty on Manhattan. In his excellent book on the region, *Washington Heights Manhattan Its Eventful Past*, Reginald Pelham Bolton recounts how two Labadist monks marveled at their first view of the Heights in 1679: "As they reached the heights of Central Park, and saw the vista of valley and wooded hills open before them, they write of the 'ridges of very high rocks, displaying themselves very majestically and inviting all men to acknowledge in them the majesty, grandeur, power and glory of their Creator.' "

Nearly a hundred years later, the hills formed a natural line of defense for Washington's army during its retreat from the British in 1776. Their principal fortification was Fort Washington, built just west of the avenue that today bears its name, between 181st and 184th streets. Fort Tryon and Fort George were also erected in the area, to no avail. All of them fell quickly to the British that autumn—not, however, without some courageous fighting on the American side.

One of the defenders was twenty-five-year-old Margaret Corbin, the first woman injured while fighting for the rebels. Corbin joined the battle after her husband was shot and killed defending Fort Tryon. She calmly picked up his musket and fired it until a hail of grapeshot nearly tore off her arm. She was subsequently captured, treated, and released by the British.

Washington's headquarters in New York was the Morris mansion at 155th Street and Convent Avenue. The mansion was later bought by Stephen Jumel, who lived there with his wife, the comely former call girl Eliza Bowen. After Jumel died, Bowen married Aaron Burr. Ironically, not far from the Jumel mansion stands Hamilton Grange, the home of Alexander Hamilton, who was killed by Burr in a duel in 1804. In the period that he was out of government service, Hamilton did his own landscaping around the house. When asked about it one day, he is supposed to have said ruefully, "A garden, you know, is a very usual refuge for a disappointed politician."

In 1823 (or 1824; the date isn't definite), the Heights were the scene of one of the grandest hoaxes ever played in New York. A retired carpenter named Lozier declared that Manhattan was getting too heavy at the Battery. The solution, he said, was to saw the island off at Kingsbridge and then turn the island around. That apparently made sense to enough people that soon hundreds of volunteer workmen offered their services. Barracks were erected to accommodate the huge work force. The different aspects of the procedure were discussed in technical detail. But on the morning the project was to begin, there was no Lozier and no saw. He remained hidden for several weeks, until the threat of red-faced carpenters to "saw *him* off" receded into laughter.

About the same time, a small fishing village, Tubby Hook, later renamed Inwood, was established near what is now Dyckman Street and the Hudson River. The outlying area was mostly large estates. One of those was the Bussing farm, which extended north from 147th Street and what is now Eighth Avenue. The land later passed into the hands of James Coogan, Manhattan's first borough president. When Bobby Thomson hit his home run "heard 'round the world" at the Polo Grounds in 1951 to give the New York Giants the National League pennant, it was called "the Miracle of Coogan's Bluff." Coogan had had the salt meadows on the farm filled in for use as a field and polo grounds. The rocky hillside west of the grounds, known as Coogan's Bluff, was later a popular spot for watching the ball games below.

Another athletic facility in the area was Highland Park, the home turf of the New York Highlanders, later renamed the Yankees. When the park wasn't being used as a ball field, the evangelical preacher—and former major-league ballplayer—Billy Sunday erected a huge tent on the grounds for his traveling ministry. The site is now occupied by the Columbia Presbyterian Medical Center.

The artist and naturalist John James Audubon found the backwoods area near Riverside Park a perfect setting for a home in 1841. His house was so isolated that construction workers living in temporary huts had to survive on wild animals they trapped and killed in the surrounding forest. After the house was completed, Samuel F. B. Morse sent his first telegraph message from Audubon's laundry room.

Huge estates in the Inwood section were also maintained by James Gordon Bennett, the publisher of the New York *Herald*, the Isham family, and John D. Rockefeller, among others. Rockefeller later turned over a portion of his estate to be used for the Cloisters museum, which grew out of the immense collection of medieval art belonging to the sculptor George Grey Barnard.

Northern Manhattan also boasted one of the most popular amusement parks in the city, Paradise Park, on the site of the old Fort George. The upper crust had their own playground, at Harlem River Speedway. There, one could find various Vanderbilts or a Gould racing their sulkies. The Velodrome arena on 225th Street drew crowds to its bike races and prizefights. All three locations played a key role in the area's development, attracting not only visitors, but also future settlers.

Others came to work specifically at the Johnson foundry in Marble Hill. Their tiny community was later severed from Manhattan, not by Lozier's saw, but by the widening of Spuyten Duyvil Creek into the Harlem Ship Canal.

In the second half of the nineteenth century, the city began purchasing some of the estate properties, to be used as parkland. The largest tracts became Inwood Hill and Isham parks, at Manhattan's northern end. Inwood Hill was completed when Julia Isham Taylor turned over the last of her family property, at 212th Street and Broadway, to the city in 1915.

Well into the twentieth century, Indians still inhabited Inwood Hill Park. Every September, they held a powwow beside the park's legendary tulip tree, estimated to be some 350 years old when it was cut down in 1938. According to legend, the tree had shaded the first meeting between the Indians and Henry Hudson.

Before World War I, the neighborhood began attracting Irish emigrants who were working on the growing subway lines. As Harlem expanded northward after the war, the southern portion of the Heights was increasingly dominated by blacks. German Jewish refugees began arriving in large numbers in the 1930s. They came uptown to take advantage of the low rents. The neighborhood's hilly terrain and wide boulevards also gave it a sort of European ambience that reminded them of home.

The refugees broke an unwritten ban on Jewish tenants in many apartment buildings west of Broadway. For years, the Hudson View Gardens complex, one of the city's first cooperatives, had a notorious restrictive policy. Unfortunately, anti-Semitic incidents were not uncommon, particularly in the area around Dyckman Street, where a "Buy Christian" billboard stood for years.

The German Jews also faced a difficult economic adjustment, made harder by the Depression. Many came from middle- and upper-middle-class backgrounds, but could now find only menial jobs. Life in America was a jarring experience, but they coped, knowing that the alternative in Europe was surely worse.

Eventually, they prospered. The neighborhood grew, and though it remained startlingly rustic in comparison with the rest of the city, new construction brought dramatic changes to the Heights. The final curtain on rural Manhattan began its slow descent in 1934, when plans were drawn up to extend the Henry Hudson Parkway through Inwood Hill Park. Area residents prized their unspoiled parkland, and they fought the proposal, but to no avail. In 1938, the same year the park's tulip tree came down, the Automotive Age reached the last corner of Manhattan.

# The Witnesses

RICHARD ARNSTEIN (1904–) was born in Germany. He came to this country in 1938. He is a sales representative in the garment industry and lives in Washington Heights with his wife, CHAR-LOTTE, who also participated in this interview.

ADINA BERNSTEIN (1920–) is a retired school guidance counselor. She has lived in Washington Heights since 1936 and has three children and nine grandchildren.

JOSEPHINE BENEDETTO BILLANI (1928–) was raised on a farm in New York City. She now lives in Yonkers.

ANGELA CORRADO (1908–) was born in Harlem and lived there until her family moved to Washington Heights when she was a young girl. She is a retired clerk and receptionist. She works at the Star Senior Center in Washington Heights.

MARY DEVLIN (1900–) is a retired telephone operator. She was born in Harlem and moved to the Washington Heights–Inwood area after her marriage.

WILLIAM EXTON (1907–) is a city planner and author. His battle with Robert Moses detailed in this chapter was one of three occasions on which he took on the Parks Commissioner. He emerged victorious from the other two.

ROBERT LEHMAN (1927–) was born in Germany. He is rabbi at the Hebrew Tabernacle Synagogue in Washington Heights.

STANLEY MARX (1919–) was born and raised in Washington Heights. After a long career in the advertising business, he runs Bookmarx, an out-of-print and used-books store in Roslyn, New York.

DOROTHY MENKIN is an artist and interior decorator. She moved to Inwood from the Bronx in 1933. She chose not to reveal her age for this book.

LEWIS MICHELS (1902–) formerly manufactured handbags. He is the father of New York City Councilman Stanley Michels.

GLORIA MIGUEL is a Native American. She works at the American Indian Community House in New York City. She also chose not to reveal her age.

JULIA SLOCUM (1906–) was born and raised in Marble Hill. She worked for the New York State Unemployment Insurance Division for many years.

DOROTHY MENKIN: From the lowest road in Inwood Hill Park to the top was a field of daisies. They overlooked the Hudson. I used to lay among them and forget I was in New York. There were these rose-of-Sharon trees along the topmost road, and to the west a small but beautiful patch of violets. It was all so exhilarating. I remember one winter day I was walking along Seaman Avenue and Isham Park, and the snow was covering the park. A couple of kids were walking along. There was a little boy about nine years old. He turned to his friend and he said, "Isn't this the most beautiful thing you ever saw? Look how beautiful it is."

STANLEY MARX: If you live near a river, you have to be influenced by it. I sure was. It makes you more adventurous. There's just something about water that makes you want to cross it or be in it.

We came up here when I was six, in 1925. Even then, the neighborhood was wild. Everything from 181st Street up, except for Fort Washington Avenue, was wide open. It was a wonderful place to grow up in and explore. All around the house were open lots. The streets weren't very crowded. You might see one car every hour. We'd go ice-skating at the old Bennett castle, or we'd go hunting for snakes.

In Inwood Hill Park, you had foxes. You used to see a lot of traces of the Indians, because of the clamshells that you found all along the shore and in the park. There was even a farm up here— the last farm in Manhattan, on 213th Street.

JOSEPHINE BENEDETTO BILLANI: Our farm had very good soil. We had the best corn. They were small because there wasn't a lot of room, but they were round and delicious. We raised all different kinds of vegetables. We had tomatoes, corn, lettuce, and string beans. We had pear trees and peach trees, and we had chickens, rabbits, and a goat. We rented a horse when we had to do the plowing. My parents earned their living selling the eggs, vegetables, and fruit.

Chickens were nasty and dirty. I stayed away from them, for sure. My brothers did most of the farm work. I helped sell the vegetables from the farm stand. Everything was cheap. The eggs were fifteen cents a dozen. Corn was a dozen ears for a quarter. Tomatoes were five cents a pound. String beans five cents a pound— very cheap, but delicious.

It was just a farm. It wasn't a very big farm—only a city block, from 213th to 214th and from Tenth Avenue to Broadway. For me it was just a place to live. We moved there in 1924, when I was three. My father was an iceman until the Frigidaires came in and that went kaput. That's why they took the land.

Our house didn't have any electricity or gas or anything. We had to bring everything in. Our friends had to build a bathroom inside. The owner of the property didn't want to sell it. He just wanted to make sure the property was being taken care of. But when he passed on, the property was passed on to his niece, who was married to the party who sold it. Before that, when they started raising the rents too high, they cut down half of it and made a parking lot on one half. Then they sold it in 1954 and that was it.

MARY DEVLIN: We got all our fresh vegetables from the Benedetto farm. You got sweet potatoes, carrots, lettuce, string beans, and eggs. It was lovely.

My father came to America in 1895. He got work in Manchester, New Hampshire, in the mills up there. When the work slowed down, he learned about some openings in the copper mines in Butte City, Montana, so he took my mother out there with two small children. She became pregnant there with me, but she couldn't stand the climate, so she crossed the continent with the two children and went back to Ireland, steerage, in the old *Mauritania*. She wasn't there too long when I was born, at the beginning of the century, January 1, 1900, as the chapel bells were ringing in Kerry, Ireland. They always said I was hatched in Butte and born in Ireland.

I was ten months old when we came back. We were living in Harlem then, on 143rd and Lenox Avenue. My father was the district leader and he owned the property where the Cotton Club later was. In those days, you could buy property for peanuts. Around there was all filled-in land. All along the Harlem River there were streams and chicken farms. That's where we got our chickens and fresh eggs.

I loved Harlem. I swam in the Harlem River with the boys at the Daley Brothers Sand & Gravel pier. You had to be careful when you went in. My brothers would say, "We can't go in now, because the water is murky low." You had to wait till the tide came in.

The neighborhood was Irish and German and a lot of lovely Jewish people. We got along very well with the black people, but everybody fled because they were coming in. They were either going to Highbridge or Inwood. I was getting married, and my mother-in-law was living on Sherman Avenue, so they got the apartment

for me on Seaman Avenue, and in June of 1925 we moved there.
I've been in the same building ever since.

Ours was the corner house, and that whole block around us,
there was nothing there from 204th to 207th. On the other side,
down below on the water was the old Johnson Iron Works, in Marble Hill. They had lovely houses over there, and most of them worked
for the ironworks. We called that Polack Town.

JULIA SLOCUM: There used to be a lot of Polish people that
worked there. I think they called them Puddlers. The foundry was
along the water's edge. It was like something you'd see in a fron-
tier town, with a saloon and a few stores. A man and five sons, the
Johnson family, owned the foundry, and he built each one of them
his own white house in Spuyten Duyvil.

Everybody up there worked some time in their life in the
foundry. Our family came to Marble Hill from Brooklyn in 1905.
My father worked for the Johnson foundry as an accountant.

Marble Hill was either Irish-American or German-American.
It was an island. The water went all the way around it. We lived
right on the corner where the Harlem Ship Canal came through.
When my parents first came here, the canal was just a little stream
of water. I knew a couple of brothers who were born in Spuyten
Duyvil, and they said you could spit across the stream of water
which separated Manhattan and the Bronx before they widened
the canal.

The day liners came through there. We saw the boats all the
time from our window. It was really very nice. Marble Hill was like
a small town. There were a lot of big, wood-frame houses. Everybody went to the same butcher and the same grocer. You know
how those things are in a small place.

I was born there in 1906. As I said, there was a lot of water
around us. Right behind us was what the kids called "the crick."
We went skating on the crick. Some boys had a canoe club there,
and people went out sailing. It was clean. We went crabbing, sure.
My father was a fisherman. He fished there, and he'd hire a boat
and go fishing in the Hudson. He caught tomcods and a lot of
bass.

We went swimming in the crick, too. A girl wore shoes and
stockings when she went. You could swim from there out to the

ship canal. You just went under a little bridge called the Farmer's Bridge.

LEWIS MICHELS: I was born in 1902 between 146th Street and 147th at Eighth Avenue, which was the lower part of Washington Heights. There were vast open properties around us, and I vividly recall many of them were covered with beautiful daisies. We thought they were weeds. They didn't mean anything to us because they were in such abundance. They were in our way when we played ball.

We didn't really appreciate all the natural landscape. We just did these things. For instance, near the Polo Grounds, there were some wild-cherry trees. We would pick these cherries, and my father used to put them in some kind of alcohol and make whiskey out of them. It was quite good, too. But we didn't stand there by the hour and pick cherries because it was fun, we just did it for the whiskey.

We did like going to the farms in Macombs Park, right over the river. As a matter of fact, I used to say to myself, "I'm surprised that I'm living yet," because the farmers would milk the cow in front of us and then pour it into a glass and we'd drink it. It was hot milk, right from the cow, but we never got sick from it.

Around that time, tribes of Indians used to pitch their tents in Macombs Park. They were with Buffalo Bill's show. They were really Indians, and they used to live there in tents for the period of the show. We'd go over there and visit. They'd show us the beads and rugs that they made.

Colonial Park ran from 145th to 155th, where the Polo Grounds used to be. Before they turned it into a park, there was a moving-picture studio there called the Urbagraph Studio, at 146th and Seventh Avenue. A sister of mine worked there. She called me up one day to come running over fast, because they needed a little boy for the movie to dress up as a messenger boy to deliver a message. The message organization wasn't Western Union then. It was called MUT—the Mutual Union Telegraph. They gave me a hat with those letters on it. All I had to do was go through a door, tell them I was from the Mutual Union Telegraph and that I had a message for somebody. That was the extent of my acting career.

They had a lot of actors that used to show off. There was a saloon on the corner of Eighth Avenue and 145th Street. It was the regular old-time saloon with the swinging doors, the big bar, and a few tables. These cowboys used to come along on their horses and ride right into the saloon and have a drink while sitting on the horse.

I was very much in love with horses. We had some of the finest stables nearby, where they kept the racehorses that raced on the Speedway. That's the Harlem River Drive now. We loved to go in there and clean up and help with the horses, brush them. Every once in a while they would allow us to take them out and sit on them and maybe take them for a little exercise.

My father would rent a horse and buggy from the stable and go on picnics in Fort George Park. Usually it would be an open carriage with two rows of seats. I'd be in my best clothes, my knickerbockers and a white shirt. My father was always in a suit and a celluloid collar. My mother would have on a long dress with a ruffled shirtwaist and a hat. As we rode, we passed a lot of open space. You wouldn't see too many apartment buildings, but a lot of single-family houses of wood.

Up here was Paterno Castle. It was a real castle. We would marvel at it. We pictured it like the castles of royalty, where kings and queens used to live. It looked like that. It was huge. It went from 182nd to 186th Street, but it was surrounded by a fence, and there were gatekeepers, so we couldn't get in there, but people used to come from all over the world to look at it.

When we went to the Polo Grounds, we would sit out on Coogan's Bluff, which was a hill just to the west of the stadium. You couldn't get to see much of the game—maybe just the outfielders. But if you went down there and a ball was hit over the fence and you retrieved it, you could bring it to the gatekeeper, and in exchange for the ball he would allow you in. We also took jobs turning the turnstile. If you did that, they would permit you to see the game.

That was long before the Yankees came in. They used to play up on the hill here where Columbia Presbyterian is now. They called that Highland Park, and the Yankees were called the Highlanders. Highland Park wasn't a stadium. It was just a field with a lot of seats all around. We only went there once in a while. The Highlanders weren't baseball—the Giants were baseball in those days. Our heroes were Christy Mathewson, Rube Marquard, and Chief

Bender. Mathewson was very sweet to the boys. McGraw was a bit gruff—even when he was sober.

JULIA SLOCUM: Marble Hill didn't have any parks. It's only about six or eight streets, and they go around and around and around. There was a baseball field. You'd sit on the hill and watch the game, and then a guy would come around with a satchel and collect some money.

There was a great place to play down the road. It was called the Turtle Club. They had an open pavilion in the back. The kids played there all year round, except when the club had brunches and a dinner meeting in the summertime. For the meetings, someone delivered big turtles, and they made soup from them. Then they hung the turtle shells from the ceiling. The kids loved it, because as the day wore on, the men felt no pain, if you know what I mean, and they would throw money out to the kids who were outside. When the club wasn't being used, the kids would go into the place where they stored the horses and carriages, and they would jump out of the hayloft.

In the wintertime, everybody went tobogganing and sleighriding on the hill down to Riverdale. You walked up the hill so you could ride down again, but the rich people would go tobogganing, and their families would send carriages to take them back up the hill.

There was a very famous wealthy woman who lived in Riverdale. Her name was Julia Morosini. She had horses and sleighs, carriages and a tallyho. She raced them at the Speedway. She used to come down to Marble Hill every night to pick up her father on the train. While she was waiting, she'd take all the kids to the candy store. Every year, maybe the week before Christmas, she would come with her carriage and her flunkies, and every kid got a cap.

ANGELA CORRADO: Pop came to America in '98, and Mom followed him six years later. They left behind real poverty in Italy. When the Depression came, that was no poverty to them. It was much worse over there. They never talked about the old country, and they had no desire to go back. This was their country. They were thrilled to be here.

I was born in Harlem in 1908. We were living at 145th Street in Harlem. When the colored people started coming up, around 1923, we moved up here to Audubon Avenue and 178th Street.

My father was an iceman—ice, coal, and wood. He had his business on 145th Street near Broadway. There was an icehouse on 184th and Amsterdam Avenue. He got up at two o'clock in the morning every day to go there. He used to get my brothers up to go and help him, and they didn't like it. We did like going to the stable at 134th and Lenox. We loved to get on the wagon when he'd come home, and take a ride.

He would take the ice to a basement on 145th Street. There were several icemen who shared it. They would cook down there. It was the way of life for quite a few men who came from Italy at that time.

He was self-employed. He had to get his own customers. He delivered to rich people with steam heat and elevators around the neighborhood. But he also had poorer customers in walk-up apartments. My brother used to always complain: "He made me go to the top floor all the time. Why doesn't he go?"

My brothers were about seven or eight years old when they started going with him. Italian people believed in getting their children working early. It really wasn't work. The customers used to tip them, and they liked the idea of making a few cents each. It was a fun thing.

MARY DEVLIN: Before World War I, I started working for the phone company at 145th Street and Convent Avenue. Everything was manual then. The old system worked beautifully. It was very hard to think of a dial. I remember in the late teens or the early '20s, these men came out from Chicago, and they were then putting in some dials. We had a meeting, and I said, "It'll never work in New York. We have enough difficulty reaching people as it is."

In those days, when people picked up the receiver, the operator answered, "Number, please," and you gave her the number that you wanted. If it was local, she had jacks to plug in, or if it was, like, Queens, they had circuits to connect. Say you wanted Elmhurst or even Staten Island. You pressed the circuit, and the girl at that end answered, and you gave her the number you wanted, and she had the jacks to put them in. You had to have fast hands. And when you removed a plug, you had to be careful, because you could take down another plug and disconnect somebody's conversation.

When I was in high school, I was working there in the evenings from 6:00 to 9:30 because I lived right by. I worked in the Audubon exchange—AU. They were all on the board right in front of you. There was also Washington Heights, Bradhurst, Murray Hill, Academy, Endicott, Schuyler, Riverside, Spring, which was downtown. I trained in the Spring exchange.

ANGELA CORRADO: I was in Schuyler, on 89th Street and Columbus Avenue. I worked with the company from 1924 to 1932 and I made twenty-five dollars a week. That was big money. There was a light for every phone in Schuyler, and the board in our exchange of Schuyler numbers extended around the room. On my board were a certain amount of Schuyler telephones. As a matter of fact, we got presents from people who recognized our voices. They knew that I was their operator. I recognized their voices, too.

MARY DEVLIN: I was there a few years before her. I worked six and a half days a week, and I started at six dollars, but I loved working there, and I graduated from high school and everything. It was near home, and it was sort of a competitive thing. The woman would come along and say, "You did very well, you had ninety-five calls," and maybe down there she only had seventy-eight.

I was sent to Columbia to take a course in elocution, because the operators were speaking too fast, and they weren't pronouncing. Or they were rolling their numbers like thuh-ree or ni-yen. They had to do away with all of that.

You didn't really have to speak fast, but you had to work very fast. I remember when I first worked there in high school, these women said, "Watch out if there's a snowstorm or something, the place will blow up." I went home and I said to my mother and father, "I can't work there. They said the place might blow up." I didn't know they meant it was going to be so busy you couldn't handle it. That was the saying.

I also worked on the information board. The information center was at 109th Street and Manhattan Avenue. That was a very hard job. You had all these big books in front of you in a booth. We had books for all of New York City. And you weren't supposed to give the numbers out from memory. My exchange was mostly the theaters downtown and the hotels, so you got to know most of those numbers. But if you gave them out from memory, you had to be careful, because if you had a couple of wrong ones, you got in a lot of trouble. It's a funny thing: to this day I have a fantastic memory for numbers.

I was also evening chief operator. My job was to take the number of calls on each position. The girls had to have so many calls each. If she didn't come up to the number of calls, we'd say, "What happened?" She may have been tied up by one call. There was a lot of extra work that had to be done.

ANGELA CORRADO: That's why I left, because the pressure was too severe. They used to have observations of your work, and they would pick minute things and criticize. When they felt they had someone that was vulnerable to the criticism, you got it all the more, and I couldn't take it. Maybe they didn't like your tone of voice, the way you handled your cords, things that really weren't important. When the Depression came, it got worse. I think they decided they had to get rid of so many people from the company. By 1932, I had had it.

My father was long retired then. He spent most of his time playing boccie and talking with his friends in a park on Amsterdam Avenue. He also had a little patch of ground on Amsterdam near Yeshiva. They let people plant, and he used to grow little things. Everything homegrown was a treasure. He was a farmer back in Italy.

While we were living in Harlem, he had a lot in the Bronx. That was his big project. He had tomatoes, pepper, squash, celery, basil, parsley, all kinds of herbs, and eggplant. The lot was maybe thirty feet by thirty feet. We'd go up there on Sundays and have a picnic. We got a lot of our food from that lot—tomatoes especially, and Mama used to make tomato sauce out of them. She would boil them down, and in order to concentrate them into tomato paste, she would bring the mixture up to the roof and let the sun absorb the moisture. That was the real McCoy tomato sauce. She'd put basil leaves in it and then put it in jars.

STANLEY MARX: Sometimes, we got fish from the Hudson. Every seven years they had a run of bergalls, and my father would take us down there. This was before it was polluted, so you had a lot of fish. We'd bring them home, and my grandmother was a good cook. In the summertime, she'd make cold sweet-and-sour fish with raisins. We fished right by the Little Red Lighthouse underneath the bridge. The lighthouse was also sort of romantic. You'd sit there as it got dark.

MARY DEVLIN: Wakes were a great way to socialize. In those days, the people were waked in the homes for three days, and all the people would bring in food. The *Evening Journal* used to have big obituary columns, and my girlfriends would say, "Look up, see if you know anybody. It might be a good wake to go to." Instead of going to a party, we went to a wake. Half the time, the fellas would have the same idea, so you went there and you said your little prayer and paid your respects. Then you went to the dining room and had some refreshments. Nine times out of ten you'd meet somebody who'd say, "I'll walk you home." That was our social life.

ANGELA CORRADO: The Audubon Ballroom on 160th was our playground. It was beautiful. All the young people went there to do ballroom dancing. Dancing was the name of the game then. If you could dance, you were in. We did the Peabody. That was the ultra. Mostly we went Saturday and Sunday afternoon. You got dressed up to the hilt—long blue taffeta or satin dresses and high heels. The boys always wore jackets, ties, and bell bottoms. The wider they were, the more in style they were.

There were different morals then. If you got a peck on the cheek, that was a big thing. There were petting parties in the hall-way, but there was no "my place or your place." In the evenings, we went to ice-cream parlors. They had a lovely one on 184th Street and St. Nicholas Avenue. It had decorated mirrors all around. It was a German place, and it was there for many years. You went there in the evenings, and you knew boys and girls would be mill-ing around.

WILLIAM EXTON: I have pleasant memories of taking young ladies with me to Inwood Park and lying around in the sun and that sort of thing. Up there you could forget you were in the city. When I really felt a yen to get out into the country in a hurry, I would go up there. The first days of spring were my idea of the time to be there. Parts of that area were regarded as the last vestiges of what you might call a primeval forest, where nothing had ever been lumbered out of it.

Very early after I got out of Harvard, I became interested in parks and recreation, city planning and housing, all that sort of thing. Back in the late '20s or early '30s, Inwood Hill had not been developed as a park. It had been a choice residential section. There were vestiges of a road that only led to the summit of Inwood Hill, where there were foundations of a few very large houses. There were three or four of them with considerable grounds built up there. One of them belonged to the Lord of Lord & Taylor.

There was one enormous tulip tree there, and there was a tradition that Henry Hudson had stopped off there on the way up the Hudson River. They also found an enormous bed of shells—oyster shells, mussel shells—that had accumulated from the Indian meals.

DOROTHY MENKIN: I love nature even though I don't know anything about it, and Inwood Park was marvelous. For a while when I was younger, I was ill and I couldn't chase around. I just wandered in there with crayons in my pocket to draw.

I'll never forget the first time I was in the park. I wandered to the top of the hills, where I found some berries—huckleberries, blackberries, raspberries. I was doing some sewing, but I was so enchanted, I left the sewing right there, and I never went back for it.

There were also two peach trees at the very top overlooking Dyckman Street. The kids used to eat them, and of course they got sick. Then there was the famous tulip tree. It was almost dead then. They were propping it up with cement. The Indians would come in September and dance around that tree and sing their songs. Princess Naomi had her little gift shop next to the tree. She was some character. She was in costume all the time, but come Sunday she took the costume off and walked around 207th Street with high heels and everything.

There was also a pottery shack in the park run by the Voorhees sisters. They were squatters, and they weren't very friendly. They made pottery out of this little hut that was all tumbledown. It was put together any old way. But they had beautiful pottery. Every piece was from the sand in Inwood Park.

MARY DEVLIN: I used to take my children to Inwood Hill Park every day. There was a big spring right by Princess Naomi's shop. I would bring my empty milk bottles, fill them with the spring water, and bring them home. It was so fresh.

Princess Naomi was lovely. My children were crazy about her. She had a little museum with trinkets and things. On Labor Day weekend, they had powwows every year. The Indians came from all over, and they pitched their tents. Then the men would put up a platform, where they all did their dances, and they had Indian contests.

GLORIA MIGUEL: My mother's tribe was the Rappahanock of Virginia, part of the Algonquin. That tribe was one of the first to be wiped out, so she knew very little about them. My father's tribe is still going very strong. His was Cuna, from Central America. His Indian name was Eagle Eye. My name, translated, was Bright Moon.

We all participated in the powwows in Inwood Hill Park. They used to get a big crowd that came from miles around. I didn't like going up there for powwows. I was uncomfortable with anything we did for show. My father was a seaman, and then he worked as a longshoreman in Brooklyn. My parents retained their culture at home, but in order to make some money, they did things that I would not do now.

As a child I was always conscious of being different. We lived in an Italian neighborhood in Brooklyn. The kids would make fun of me all the time. When I went to school, any time I stood up to say anything, they would say, "Wooo Woooo Wooo." Or they would call me Injun Joe or pull my hair because I had long braids. It wasn't pleasant, and these were kids who just came from Italy.

When I went up to Inwood, it was like a big spotlight on me. I went along with my family because they took me, but I was very shy about it. I didn't want people to look at me or take photographs of me. It wasn't until later that I realized that my background was something to be very proud of and that those people were just ignorant.

We went up on the subway. The powwows were on Indian Day, on September 25. All the Native Americans living in New York City would come. I remember Crazy Bull, Sitting Bull's grandson, used to come around and participate.

The ceremonies weren't always authentic. It's according to who does it. They had one where they exchanged blood to make blood brothers, and they would have peace-pipe ceremonies. Now, you have to have a chief conduct the ceremonies. But, as I said, in those days it was more for show.

They also had a ceremony where all the men would get in canoes and paddle down the river. When they landed on shore, they would shake hands with people dressed like Peter Minuit. There was also an old mock ceremony that we used to have. We had an old friend who was a Frenchman, and he liked Indian people. He would let them hang him as a white man.

Each man had a solo dance. My father would do a hunter's dance. A man called Sharpshooter would do a spear dance. He was Hopi. He did a beautiful dance. Someone else would do a deer dance. His name was Little Moose. There were two brothers called Two Bear Earl and something else, and they were from the rodeo. They did tricks with ropes. A man named Swift Eagle did most of the singing.

I had a North American outfit that my mother made for me. It was a little dress made of cloth with some fringe on it. I had moccasins and a beaded headband. It was just a show outfit. It wasn't from the background of my people. Since my parents did this for show business, they dressed according to what the show was. They both had authentic costumes at home. I just sat in my costume and watched.

With the powwows, they were grasping onto the culture, trying to be proud, in their way. That moment was there for them before going back to welfare and their own neighborhood. It was their way of holding on.

◆   ◆   ◆

Stanley Marx: There was no real poverty up here when I was young. Today, it would be called lower middle class. My father was a cutter in a pants factory. He worked steadily, and he made about forty dollars a week. We lived pretty well. We had four rooms in an apartment on Wadsworth Avenue, and our rent was about forty dollars a month.

I had one brother, and there was my grandmother and my parents, so there were five of us. My grandmother, my brother, and I slept in one room. Later, we had five rooms, and my grandmother had her own room.

We played all the usual games, like ring-a-leevio and saluggi. Saluggi was a ball game. You played it against the steps. Stoopball was another name for it. Then you had another game called asses up. That was if you lost. You had to bend down, and the kids would throw the ball at you.

You played boxball on two concrete boxes, and you just hit the ball back and forth. You could cut it so it would spin, but you had to keep it in the box. It was like tennis without a net. Now 185th Street between Wadsworth and St. Nicholas was the big street to play stickball, because it was wide and flat. There were three sewers. If you could hit that block, you were pretty good.

We also liked going to the river at Dyckman Street, where there was a ferryboat that took you over to Alpine. There, you could walk all along the Palisades, and we'd make a fire and roast potatoes. It was marvelous.


DOROTHY MENKIN: We loved the ferry. Sometimes, we paid one fare and went back and forth on the ferry all night. Nobody minded. We danced. We had ukuleles, kazoos, and the men were singing. Sometimes we went to the Palisades and made a fire there and stayed all night. I got home at six o'clock one morning.

One night on the ferry, this German woman was astounded. "You make such a fuss about our Rhine. It's nothing compared to your Hudson." She was so excited, she couldn't talk.


STANLEY MARX: From over here, we could see over to Fort Lee, and there was a very famous nightclub over there that had a huge sign we could see, "Ben Marden's Riviera." It was a tremendous sign that was lit up at night.

The George Washington Bridge was completed in 1931. I was at the dedication, which Governor Roosevelt attended. I was a Boy Scout, and I couldn't afford a uniform, so that day I had to borrow one. The only one I could borrow had short pants. The bridge opened in October, but it was a very hot day. I was in my uniform, and I was the only comfortable one there. I remember Governor Roosevelt standing there and saying [*he talks as if making a speech*]: "In ten years this bridge will be paid for and it will be free for everybody." That's what he said, because the bridge cost ten million dollars, and they figured, at twenty-five cents apiece, in ten years they could make it up. Well, they're still trying to make it up. *[He laughs.]*

The best thing about the bridge for us was that you could walk over to Fort Lee and buy firecrackers, because they were legal in New Jersey. There used to be stands right across the bridge. We'd go over right before the Fourth of July and buy all that stuff. There was a gal who lived across the street from us who had a lot of money, and every Fourth of July she would put on a display right in front of the house, and every Fourth of July she got hurt. She was always burning herself.

Inwood Hill Park was a great place to hike. So was Fort Tryon Park, which was something of a lovers' lane. It was pretty wild. The Cloisters was just a wooden building—a one-story wooden building that smelled like medieval times. A lot of people were unhappy when the Cloisters building was put up, because so much concrete was being poured. The park was magnificent then. It was just an undeveloped piece of property the city owned.

Next to it was a studio of George Grey Barnard. He did heroic statues, and his studio was there for many years until he died. He's a rather obscure guy now, but he did statues which are in a lot of prominent places.

Once, when I was a young kid, I went in there when he was working on a figure of Christ. Everybody has a vision of Christ being a sort of thin, ascetic-looking person. His figure of Christ was muscular, heroic. So I said to him, "Why are you making him so muscular?"

He said, "Well, he survived a pretty long time on the cross, so he must have been a strong, muscular person. And he was a carpenter, and therefore he was not a weakling."

William Exton: I don't know about any statues of Jesus. The only thing I can tell you is about a photograph I have of a representation of Jesus that Barnard made. He did it by putting a heavier beard on Lincoln. He explained that, when he was a boy, his father and his father's friends remembered Lincoln, because they were his contemporaries. They said when Lincoln was told about the deaths in the war, people thought his facial expression was Christ-like. Therefore, Barnard just put a different beard on Lincoln. He said, "Nobody knows what Christ looks like, but what I've heard about Lincoln, this is probably as good as any."

When he was active, Barnard was regarded as the outstanding American sculptor of his time. He was an associate of the French Academy. Practically no American ever made that. And he had two beautiful daughters, Vivia and Barbara. He also had a son, Monroe, and a lovely wife, who came from a New England family.

I knew him very well. I don't know how many times I dined in his home. Of course, I was more interested in his daughters than I was in him. He talked a great deal. He would dominate the conversation at dinner, which was always excellent.

I can still remember him saying something which I think is a remarkable manifestation of a personal characteristic: that when he went from one studio to another or one class to another, he would not only walk as fast as he could, but he would also stick out his elbows to try to keep everyone else from getting ahead of him.

At any rate, there was an enormously wealthy man named Billings. I think Billings, Montana, was named after him. He made his money from copper. He came to New York, and he bought a helluva lot of property in Manhattan. The whole northern end of Tryon Hill was his, and he built a helluva mansion for himself.

If you go up Riverside Drive, there is a structure made out of granite with a lot of arches in it. That was the entrance to his house from Riverside. The upper part was a terrace where his guests and he could look at the Hudson. On the other side of Fort Washington Avenue from his house, he built tremendous stables. In those days, you were judged by your horseflesh, and his were the first steam-heated stables in the world.

Well, John D. Rockefeller, Jr., bought the whole setup. Barnard had commissions from Rockefeller to do a number of pieces of sculpture for Pocantico Hills. Since they were going to be quite large and his own studio wasn't large enough, he made arrangements with Rockefeller to use the Billings stables as a studio. They were steam-heated. They had plenty of room and no horses. He just holed up in that studio and knocked himself out doing his work.

Then, Rockefeller made a deal with the city to close a street on the East Side for his Rockefeller University and New York Hospital. In order to get the Board of Estimate to agree, he offered to give them this whole hilltop for a park. The city agreed and wanted to take down Barnard's stable, which meant he would be without a studio. Of course, he was hysterical.

A friend and I took on his defense. I'll never forget going down to the hearing before the Board of Estimate. My friend, Arthur, as a lawyer, was facing Raymond Fosdick, the Rockefeller family attorney, and I was facing Ivy Lee, the most famous public-relations son of a bitch that ever lived—the founder, practically, of public relations. We just stood there in front of the board and hassled the hell out of 'em. It was rather amusing. They couldn't imagine being faced by a couple of kids. I was in my early twenties. Arthur was probably about thirty. Anyway, we lost.

But there's more to Barnard's story. When he was a student in Paris, and later when he was out of being a student, he knew in the cathedral towns in France the dilapidation of the cathedrals was partly the result of the vandalism of the locals. He would get on a bicycle and ride out to the cathedral villages. He would go into the backyards of these cottages of the farmers, and he would see baptismal fonts being used to feed hogs. He would buy these things for practically nothing. As he progressed as a sculptor and had more money, he would buy more of them. Some of them he would sell at an enormous 10,000-percent profit. He got quite a bit of money together, which he used to buy these antiques with his special knowledge of where they could be found.

Because he was an associate of the French Academy, he was probably the only American that could get them out of France. So he had this incredible collection of medieval and early Renaissance art.

Now there was a house on Park Avenue that he always admired. He walked by it one day when they were tearing it down, and he bought the facade. He put the pieces in boxes, and he had them in storage. When he got enough money together, he bought this piece of land up on upper Washington Heights, south of where Billings was, and he erected this front wall of this Park Avenue house. He just put the house onto the wall.

That's where I had many and many a dinner. It was charming. In the back, he had a studio, which he had built, and there was a garden. In the back of it, he had the Cloisters, this huge collection of art and antiques, which are now in the Cloisters museum. I can't tell you how many times I had dinner there and went out to the Cloisters with Vivia Barnard in the moonlight. You saw the moon over the other part of Fort Washington, which made it look almost like old castles in the distance. It was very goddamn romantic.

He had a chance to sell the collection to two major galleries in New York for $1.5 million. We're talking 1929–31 dollars—a fabulous sum, but he wanted the collection kept together, so Rockefeller bought it from him for $700,000. Then Rockefeller wanted to do something with it. He decided to build a building to exhibit it in some relationship with the Metropolitan. His architect wanted to build a medieval castle sort of thing. Barnard was vehemently and violently against building what he called a phony medieval castle, but, as you know, he didn't prevail.

◆ ◆ ◆

ADINA BERNSTEIN: We moved to West 190th Street, off St. Nicholas, in 1936, when I was sixteen. The Depression was tough for us. My father manufactured expensive neckties and people weren't buying a lot of them. There was food on the table, but that was just about it. One of the reasons they moved to Washington Heights was my brother was going to Yeshiva here, and they couldn't afford the carfare.

We had to cut corners with clothes. I had a skirt and two blouses to wear to school, and two dresses for *Shabbas*, and that was it. I had a spring jacket and a winter coat. You didn't have *Shabbas* shoes. That was my job *Erev* [night of] *Shabbas*, to polish everybody's shoes. We polished them, because we didn't have another pair to wear.

MARY DEVLIN: My husband was a policeman, and in the '30s, the policemen, the firemen, and sanitation all took two big cuts in salary in order not to lose their jobs. Nobody did, but along the river they had tents set up for others, who had no place to go. We used to go around, and if you had leftover vegetables or leftover bread, you'd bring it down to them.

ADINA BERNSTEIN: Much of our life surrounded the Yeshiva. There were a thousand guys across the street at Yeshiva, so socially it was great. My mother also had open house on Friday nights, and the guys would come over. We'd see twenty or thirty at a time.

I'm sorry to say I don't think it was my sex appeal that brought them. It was my mother's cooking. During Passover, because we lived here, we had many kids for whom it was too far to go back home, so they would come to my mother. You never knew how many people would sit down.

My mother was a fantastic cook, but there, too, she had to be careful. In those days, she made her own noodles. She baked her own bread. She made her own challah, her own cake. We ate together every night. Even though we didn't have much money, dinner was always elaborate, with a tablecloth and cloth napkins. There was always an entrée, a fruit entrée, a hot entrée, soup, poultry or meat, two vegetables, dessert, and tea and cake. That was every night.

We'd eat things you see now in restaurants. My mother would roll out a piece of dough and have chopped liver rolled in it. When she served a Sacher torte, which had layers of whipped cream, or seven-layer cake or babka, it was the real thing, not the bakery stuff. She used two pounds of butter for them. Or she made blintzes or crepes or sweet-and-sour tongue. Things you had in restaurants, we had for meals.

She was ingenious about food, which meant we didn't suffer pangs of hunger, because she could buy a bunch of carrots and two potatoes and an onion, and we would have a vegetable soup. Then, she would take those soft vegetables, mash them up with an egg and fry them, and we would have vegetable cutlets.

On *Shabbas* you needed two meals, and we were four people. We'd have a half a chicken for each meal. She would boil four eggs. She would take that small chicken liver, broil it, brown some onions, and mash up that chicken liver with those eggs. That gave you an omelet.

For one meal, it was Southern fried chicken, dipped in egg and bread crumbs. It really looked like a lot. Soup she made out of the giblets, and the vegetables were added to the soup to give it strength and flavor. Then she would boil noodles to go with it.

Now you needed side dishes. She would buy a cabbage. That, with a drop of tomato sauce or ketchup, became one vegetable. Or she bought a noodle. That was a Hungarian dish—cabbage and noodles with a drop of ketchup for color. You browned the cabbage with onion before you added the noodle. Then, you sautéed it all together with a little ketchup or tomato sauce.

With the influx of the German Jews, a lot of stores up here were German. First there were grocers, then there were butcher shops, which sold both delicatessen as well as meat and poultry. Delicatessen was big with the Germans. After '33, you heard a lot of German in the neighborhood. You walked down St. Nicholas Avenue, and that was all you heard. I did go to the German synagogue. You'd see if there was somebody newly arrived. People would surround them and ask them about specific people. "What did you hear about So-and-So?" It was depressing. Those who didn't get answers walked away with their heads down. It was very hard.

ROBERT LEHMAN: I was born in Germany in 1927. We came over in March 1938. My father had been a banker and a prominent person in the community, but he was put in jail at the end of '37. It was still early enough that they had to let him go after a while because they couldn't find anything on him. Then we were able to get an affidavit to come here.

I was not able to go to school in our town. Kids were beating us up and were calling us names like Dirty Jew and Smelly Jew. I had been sent to Frankfurt for boarding school when my father was taken off to jail. Actually, I didn't even know about it until we were on the high seas.

Being eleven, I didn't have any concept of what it meant to go to America or be an American. I was reading the stories of Karl Meyer then, which were cowboys-and-Indians sort of things. I think I associated that with America. When we got here, we went to a rooming house in the 90s. We stayed there a week, until we got a flat on 145th Street between Broadway and Riverside Drive. We lived there until we moved to 157th Street. That area between 155th Street and 165th Street was almost exclusively German refugees. The dividing line was Amsterdam Avenue, with Broadway and Riverside Drive the main strips, especially in the summertime.

We went a lot to Fort Tryon Park, and in the summer we sat a lot on Riverside Drive. That's what drew a lot of these people. There was a great deal of European ambience in Washington Heights in those years. They sat on Broadway. On Riverside Drive you had the trees in full bloom. Of course, there was no air conditioning, so everybody was outside. It was a genteel kind of neighborhood for a long time.

Very few people would allow themselves a nickel to take a bus or a subway on weekends. A nickel was a lot, so they mostly stayed in their own neighborhoods to try to get a breeze off the Hudson. Or we sat in front of the house a lot. That was vacation. There was a lot of socializing in their homes Saturday or Sunday evenings. They sat and they talked. It was very congenial. And it was organized generally by towns of origin. It was almost a self-contained community. People spoke German in the streets. They spoke German in the stores. They had cafés where they could go for afternoon coffee and on the weekends. It was really a piece of Europe transplanted into America.

There were stores owned by Germans and which catered to Germans. Sometimes, if you wanted to go into a store to buy three pounds of potatoes, you would bring out your English laboriously, and they would answer you in German. They served German products, like potato salad without mayonnaise, like you got it over there, or coleslaw that wasn't creamy, but with vinegar and oil, and sauerbraten and sausage without pork. They served German chocolate, and they made German cakes as we were used to. They built up the cafes and the *Konditoreien*. Those were the pastry shops where you eat rather than just buy, the way they did on the other side. You would go in and buy coffee and a piece of cake and sit and talk for a couple of hours and then go about your business.

RICHARD ARNSTEIN: I came alone in September 1938. When I left Germany, I was allowed to take ten dollars. I came over on the *Manhattan*. I spent six dollars on tips and I arrived with four on a Friday. I got a job on Saturday. I started working on Monday. I sent an affidavit for my family on Tuesday. I was working as a shipping clerk for a textile firm. Then, the family in Brooklyn said, "As long as you didn't have a job, it's okay, but now that you have a job, you can go get a room." So they got a room for me up here on Wadsworth Terrace. I paid four dollars a week for the room. My income was twelve dollars a week, and it wasn't easy to live.

At that time they had a wonderful Horn & Hardart right here on 181st Street. Coffee was five cents. A roll was five cents. Vegetables were five cents each. You got four vegetables and a roll for a quarter. That's how I lived. There was another in Times Square, where I worked. It was really a blessing at that time.

When my family came in May 1939, I found another apartment on Wadsworth Terrace. We had two rooms and a kitchen and a bathroom, and we paid thirty-eight dollars a month. We could afford it because my wife started working right away cleaning houses. She didn't work in Germany, because we had been well off.

R O B E R T   L E H M A N : My mother got work first. She didn't work in Germany, where they were well off, but here she went into a household to take care of children and clean. After that, she spent many years in a hairnet factory doing piecework. My father worked as a dishwasher. He held that job for about a week. Then he went into a fountain-pen factory, and there he stayed for a while. Then, he made himself independent by working as a Fuller Brush man. He did well. Later, he left them and added merchandise that he sold on the installment plan. There, I would say he moderately prospered.

Though they had to struggle here, I don't think it was the end of the world for them. They didn't go off the deep end. All their friends were in the same boat. After a while, when they were able to enter into mainstream American life, they became citizens. Their self-esteem rose all the time. I'm sure they complained when they got together among themselves over potato salad and frankfurters, but they were smart enough to understand that the alternative was persecution for sure. Death, I don't know if they knew about at that stage of the game. What really was the issue was that they left people behind. That caused more hardship than anything else.

We became Americanized slowly but surely. I went to PS 138, on 138th Street and Amsterdam Avenue. Most of the students were Americans—Irish. There were some German-Jewish kids in the class. In the beginning, we were all in the same boat. We had no idea what was going on.

My problem was that I didn't speak English, and I knew when I got to school that I was different. We wore different clothing. We had different interests. We did different things. We didn't know how to play baseball. I didn't understand what a comic book was. I didn't think it was funny either. I spoke a different language from the comic books. I had no friends, and I knew that my parents both worked and I had to go to work early on.

ADINA BERNSTEIN: The Irish who lived up here were very anti-Semitic. Any Jew who walked on Dyckman Street on a Saturday night, you didn't come home with a whole head. It was a very, very ugly Father Coughlin area, and it lasted, I'm sorry to say, way into the early '40s.

I remember there was a movie I wanted to see at the Alpine. I was walking along Dyckman with one of the guys from Yeshiva. Two got on either side of him and shoved him from side to side, "The Jew Boy! The Christ Killer!" It was an ugly time. Kikes, sheenies, whatever. It was a constant problem. They fought back, but they were outnumbered, and they were ready for you. They had the rocks, the water. They were aching that someone should come down, so we just stayed away.

On Haven, Pinehurst, Cabrini, Jews were not allowed into those apartments. You couldn't get an apartment with a Jewish name until the Germans started to come. My mother wanted an apartment over there, but she couldn't get one. But because of the influx of Germans, when two families and sometimes three took one apartment, and they could charge an inflated rental, they were allowed in.

I didn't see ads saying, "Jews need not apply." It wasn't as overt as that. Sometimes you'd see, "Near churches," that kind of thing. It was subtle. Look, when my husband was sent to Boca Raton for training, you had huge signs, "No Jews. No Dogs. No Niggers."


ROBERT LEHMAN: There were some problems with the non-Jewish kids. I don't know if it was so much anti-Semitic, but rather that we were different. In gym, for example, we wore different undershirts, with holes in them. They were perforated. In those years, no self-respecting macho teenager would wear such a sissy shirt. Also, we had different interests. We had to take a part-time job. We could not spend so much time playing in the street. We were told to do our homework. The Irish or Italian kids were as our kids are today—"if it's not done now, it will be done tomorrow."

We were not concerned with gentiles. We were concerned with being citizens. "Keep your mouth shut and your nose clean." Because when it came time for citizenship, you didn't want anyone speaking against you.

Still, I met most of my friends in the street. That's where I learned English. In the summer, the family that gave us the affidavit asked me to come up there, and I learned English from their small children. By the time I came back from that summer, I spoke fluently.

We also listened to the radio. There was nothing else. You could get lost in the show. I knew when the Lone Ranger or the Shadow came, there was nothing else. Jack Benny, for example, was a sacrosanct hour. Nobody budged at seven o'clock on Sundays. I was hysterical, although it passed over my father 100 percent. He just couldn't understand the humor.

The radio was very real to me. I probably thought there really was a Lone Ranger. I remember hearing when the little girl was stuck in the well. No one did anything but listen to the radio. Wherever you were, people asked each other, "Did you hear anything new?" That lasted for two or three days, until they found out she was dead.

The Boy Scouts also gave us a very good sense of belonging. It kept us off the street. We went to the camps, and we had a chance to build our egos because we did things to rise in the ranks, which was very important to us.

We moved to our apartment on 157th Street because it was a six-room apartment and we could rent out the extra rooms to newcomers. That's how we lived rent-free. I lived in the tiny servant's room. My parents had one room, and we rented out maybe three or four rooms. Only after we did better did we move into a smaller apartment and we lived by ourselves. That took about four or five years.

The first synagogue we went to was on 149th Street and Riverside Drive, but we did not feel at home there. I think we didn't feel welcome as refugees. Then we went to Hebrew Tabernacle, on 161st Street, which catered to the refugees. The style of the music was European. The rabbi knew how to deal with the refugees. The board of trustees was amenable to our being there, and so the whole attitude was a positive one.

I was bar mitzvahed there. We had a lunch at my home and that was it. There might have been fifteen people there. One family sent me a gift, and it contained a single dollar bill, and it was the most expensive thing I got that day.

ADINA BERNSTEIN: My family was Hungarian, and the German community over here separated themselves. The Germans had an interesting and offensive attitude. They were brought up that way. [*She speaks in an overly proper voice:*] "But we've always known this." "But we do this better."

It was a kind of arrogance. For some of them to come to the States and make a new life was very difficult. A woman said, "I never carried a package from the store in my life." It was a terrible comedown for them. Some of them couldn't deal with it. They went into terrible depressions. Part of it was due to their own self-image, and some of it was due to what was happening over there.

In 1939, Rabbi Breuer came to America. I was teaching one of his daughters. I heard there was a little bit of dissension because he had chosen me and I was not German. They didn't dare say it to me, but I said to one of them, "Why don't you find out where the rabbi was born?" He was Hungarian. They didn't believe me, but they went and asked, and there weren't any more problems.

RICHARD ARNSTEIN: There is some truth to that. The German Jews were usually highly educated, and the Jews who came from Poland were very much more involved with the Jewish religion and Jewish customs. They looked down on them, no doubt about it. I probably felt like most people did. I was pretty open-minded, but there are certain things that just were.

ROBERT LEHMAN: I don't think German Jews felt they were superior—not in my household. Yes, we were better educated in philosophy and what have you, but of course from a Jewish point of view the Eastern European Jew was far better educated than any German Jew ever hoped to be. Our people went to the universities of Berlin, Hamburg, Leipzig, and so on, but they knew nothing of Jewish lore, whereas the Eastern European went by way of Vilna and the like and knew everything. So it all depends on what's important to you.

We didn't know many Eastern European Jews, but that was because we came from a circle of German Jews and stayed with them until my generation married Eastern European girls. That became more and more frequent as young people met at social clubs and the like.

STANLEY MARX: Despite some of the terrible things going on, for the kids of my generation, it was a time of innocence. We were, in a sense, remnants of the Victorian Age. The people who were older in the '20s and '30s were breaking out in the Jazz Age. The kids had no knowledge of it. They were ruled by parents who were from the Victorian period. As a result, you had the kinds of mores among middle-class Jewish people that were pretty straitlaced.

The boys were interested in sex, but they had Victorian morals. When you were young, you believed if you gave a girl a soul kiss, you'd get her pregnant. Kids really didn't know how babies were made. One of the kids got this book, *Growing Up*, which told in a very gentle way how babies were made, but it really didn't come out and tell you.

We followed a code. We had kissing games, maybe a little bit of touching, but nothing serious. I remember necking in the back, in a rumble seat, while somebody else was driving the car, but it was harmless. The boys believed that girls were sort of sacred, that real sex was something you saved for marriage. I'm talking about up to the age of fifteen or sixteen. Later, it was different. But I was a virgin until my early twenties, and you expected the girl you married to be a virgin.

On a date, we'd go to the Dyckman Theater, then to the ice-cream parlor next door. I had a real embarrassing experience there one night. I had all the money figured out, but then my girlfriend said, "Gee, I have a real urge for a banana split."

Well, a banana split was a quarter. Normally, you'd have a soda, which was a dime. When the bill came, it was seventy-five cents. That's all I had. I didn't have any money for a dime tip. So I put down a dime so my girlfriend wouldn't think I was a cheapskate. Then, when she got up, I picked it up again.

ROBERT LEHMAN: There was almost a natural dividing line among our young people. There was a five-year difference between my generation and the next generation. Our generation, those under sixteen, was the one that was given an education. We didn't want to go in the Army, because we wanted to finish. In my case, I was able to finish high school, and the very next day I was inducted.

Those who were sixteen or older had no opportunity for school. They immediately went into full-time work. For them, the war was a godsend in some ways, because they could get out of the factory and go into the Army. From that point of view, they could expand and learn and become Americanized—no more behind the machine.

I know a number of people who said, "Had I had a chance to become educated, I may have been such and such." They became white-collar workers, as opposed to professionals. Some very bright people never had a chance.

RICHARD ARNSTEIN: Things were difficult up through the war, and then it became a bit easier. I still worked in the textile field. I still do. Some of my customers today I got in the '30s. Some are the third generation. We never joined a temple. We celebrated Christmas. We celebrate Hanukkah in a very small way. It sounds strange, but that's how it was.

The schools were first-rate. They were prepared for non-English-speaking children, and the teachers were outstanding. When our daughter came back from her first day in school, she said she didn't understand a word. Three weeks later, she already helped newcomers with the English. For our children, America was very good. Both went to City College. Our son got a master's degree at Columbia, and later he got a Ph.D. at Northwestern University in British history. He is very successful in his field. Our daughter was for many years a buyer for Ohrbach's. She has since retired and is now the vice president of the League of Women Voters.

We went back to Germany a number of times. We first returned in 1954. We were very nervous. We had some very faithful friends, and we wanted to see them. Half the city was still in ruins.

CHARLOTTE ARNSTEIN: They couldn't do enough for us. I had some friends who weren't Jewish. When I was about to leave, there was a new rule that one couldn't take along any silver. I had very beautiful cutlery, and I felt very bad about it. I didn't want to sell it. I told my friend about the silver. She said she would hold it for me. "One day, we will see each other again. I know that's for sure."

When we went back a second time, in 1957, I had completely forgotten about it. One day, I decided to look them up. I didn't even know if they were still alive, but they were, and she came right away. She said, "You know I still have your silver. You have no idea what we went through. Our house was searched by the

French and then by the Americans. They were all taking things. I always said, 'We have to preserve that. One day we will see her.' " They buried it in the garden to keep it safe.

ANGELA CORRADO: When the war started, I got a job on a switchboard with a Midtown liquor company. I loved the work. Then I worked for the Navy Yard's switchboard. After the war, I worked as a clerk for Naval Intelligence. I did that until I retired.

I never married. I never met the right guy. I was looking for something that didn't exist. I had boyfriends, but as soon as it came to sex, that was that. I'll tell you the kind of people I met. When I went to my mother's grave in 1950, I was there by myself, and I was sitting there praying. A man came up the aisle. He looked me over and said, "My wife—a—she died, about 19—a—47. I'm a lonesome man. Don't you wanna be married?" That was the kind of thing I got.

WILLIAM EXTON: We tried to keep Robert Moses from putting a road through Inwood Hill Park. I was a trustee and treasurer of the Municipal Arts Society, and I moved very strongly on the board to have them vote against Moses' plan. I remember that Electus D. Litchfield, a very prominent architect, with whom I was normally very friendly, more or less supported Moses' plan. We had quite a debate on the board, which was not a common thing. We usually were very unconfrontational. I can still remember Moses was saying the view from the road would be outstanding, and I said, "Yes, but the view *of* the road would not be."

Several of the trustees said, "Hear, hear."

Moses was a nasty person. He was also very able and very purposeful. He concentrated on what he wanted to do, and he was very effective in getting it done. I don't know whether I ought to say this, but the head of the Park Association at that time was Iphigenie Ochs Sulzburger, whose family owns the *New York Times*. She's a lovely person and admirable in every way. She was very much interested in parks and very active in the Park Association, but Moses was a pet of hers, and nobody could say anything bad about Moses to her. There were several instances where the *Times* would come out with an editorial condemning Moses in the very earliest edition, and it wouldn't appear in the other editions.

We presented Moses with an alternative plan for Inwood Hill
Park that everybody endorsed. But I think it was vindictiveness,
stubbornness, and all this sort of thing. When we finally got a
hearing, the trees were already cut down. That was the way he
operated. He faced you with a fait accompli.

Adina Bernstein: I met my husband at the Yeshiva. I was
married at the age of twenty. He became a rabbi in Birmingham,
Alabama, so we moved down there. He went into the service in the
end of '41, so I came home. He was a chaplain. At Hanukkah time
in '43, he was on his way to a post that hadn't seen a chaplain in
I don't know how long. It was in North Africa, and the pilot just
didn't see the mountain.

I got a telegram from Western Union: "We regret to inform
you . . ." I really didn't understand it at first. I was very angry. I
was twenty-three years old and a widow. He was twenty-seven years
old and was dead. It left a terrible void. He left no children, and
that was terrible. Your heart pours out, but he was one amongst
many.

After that, I was sitting down here near the water, and two
Irishwomen were sitting and talking, and they were complaining
that over in Europe Christian boys were fighting to save the Jews
in Germany. It went on and on and on and on, Christian blood
being spilled. Finally, I couldn't take it, and I said, "Did you lose
anybody in the service?"

"No."

"Well, I did. Do me a favor and just go away so that I don't
have to hear you or see you."

They got up, but she had the last word. "It's still a goddamn
Jewish war."

# Harlem

WHAT IT CAME DOWN TO was this: Philip Payton made the Harlem landlords an offer they couldn't refuse.

The year was 1900. The city had announced plans to build a subway line up Lenox Avenue. Immediately, property along the avenue was purchased at inflated prices. Buildings were hastily erected, and their owners braced themselves for the tide of newcomers that would soon flood this once-peaceful community in upper Manhattan.

But hardly anyone came. The apartments for the most part stayed empty, and the landlords quickly became desperate. Enter Philip A. Payton, Jr., a college man, who, like most blacks in Manhattan, could get work only as a menial laborer. Payton hit upon an idea that would help himself and a lot of blacks looking to find better housing in a market that was generally closed to them: he would represent the Harlem landlords and fill the vacant apartments with black families.

The arrangement met with spectacular results. Within three years, Payton had set up the Afro-American Realty Company and was a wealthy man. The landlords were pleased to fill their vacancies. Preying on the desperation of the black families, they were able to charge rents that were much higher than those paid by whites. As for the blacks, after years of living in some of the worst tenements in San Juan Hill and the Tenderloin, and despite the overcharging, they flocked to take advantage of the clean, modern space.

They created America's first black Mecca. In the coming years, Harlem would draw blacks from the South and the Caribbean islands with the promise of a home where they could live freely and where hard work would be rewarded with success. And although that was frequently far from true, Harlem became a remarkable community. For the first time, blacks were afforded decent housing and schooling. Black writers, artists, musicians, singers, dancers, comedians, and actors found opportunities in Harlem previously denied them, and they responded with a remarkable period of creativity, known as the Harlem Renaissance.

The neighborhood, bounded by 110th and 155th streets from Fifth Avenue west to the Hudson, was originally part of Nieuw Haarlem, which was established by Peter Stuyvesant in 1658. For nearly 200 years, the area was a small community of rich country estates owned by the likes of the Hamiltons and the Beekmans. But by the mid-1840s, the soil was exhausted, and most of the farms were sold. The once-lush estates were now occupied by poor Irish squatters, living in shanties of tin and wood. According to historian Gilbert Osofsky, so many hogs roamed portions of 125th and 126th streets that the area was known as Pig's Alley, and parts of Harlem Plains reeked so badly, it was said they could "knock the breath out of the mule."

Harlem's fortunes rebounded when it was annexed by New York City in 1873. Over the next few years, the city drained acres of Harlem's marshlands for new housing. Soon rows of new brownstones covered tree-lined streets. The most spectacular new homes were the row houses on 138th and 139th streets designed by Stanford White and known as Striver's Row (for the block's upper-middle-class residents), which are still some of the finest houses in New York.

Harlem had a large Irish and German population, but most of the newcomers were Jews who had succeeded in moving up from the Lower East Side. Turn-of-the-century Harlem was a solid middle-class community, which boasted one of the city's most beautiful synagogues, Temple Israel, and one of the city's leading cultural centers, the Harlem Opera House, built by Oscar Hammerstein in 1889.

In his social history of the city, *Incredible New York*, Lloyd Morris portrays Harlem of the 1890s as the quintessential American small town:

> It was a community of small, middle-class homes, impeccably respectable, conservative and prosperous. On pleasant summer evenings, you saw families sitting out on their stoops, and children playing in streets seldom disturbed by traffic. You surmised that the aroma of well-cooked meals saturated the low brownstone dwellings. You could be sure that every parlor displayed an aspidistra, a "suite" of mahogany-stained furniture upholstered in velveteen, an upright piano and gilt-framed chromos and engravings on the walls. Upstairs, the principal bedroom would have a gleaming knobby brass double bed, with cover and "pillow-shams" of crochet lace over a lining of pink or blue sateen. In these homes, pinochle was played and pyrography cultivated as a genteel art. As you walked past them you heard the strumming of mandolins and banjos, the tinkle of a piano and youthful voices singing "O, Promise Me," or "Only a Bird in a Gilded Cage."

Main Street was 125th Street. There, Harlemites could shop in some of the city's most exclusive stores. For entertainment, they could see Fanny Brice or Sophie Tucker at the Opera House, the latest vaudeville at Proctor's, or the show girls at Hurtig and Seamon's. For fine dining, there was Pabst's, where, according to *Harlem Magazine*, "Gentlemen and ladies can enjoy good music and a perfect cuisine amid surroundings which have been rendered as attractive to the eye and senses [as] good taste, combined with expenditure, could make them."

However, the years before World War I brought enormous changes to the neighborhood. Urban life noisily intruded on the quiet community. The subway rumbled below, bringing with it a new population. Though the newcomers brought in by Philip Payton and others paid higher rents, they were generally not as wealthy as the white Harlemites. The white community, and even some of the more established blacks, sought to stem the tide of immigrants. One woman even sued her next-door neighbor for renting to a black family. But when St. Philip's, the wealthiest black church in the city, purchased an entire block of fine homes on 135th Street in 1911 for its membership, the future of Harlem was decided.

Black businesses, many owned by West Indian immigrants, opened on the avenues. In 1913, the Lafayette Theater, long a segregated showcase on 132nd Street, opened its doors to blacks. Soon, some of the finest black talent in America began appearing on its stage, and, for the first time, talented actors like Charles Gilpin were cast as romantic leads instead of filling stereotypical roles, like handymen and butlers.

In the years before talkies, the Harlem movie theaters produced some of the best piano-playing talent in the city. At the Lincoln Theater, no one knew if the audience was there for the film or to tap its collective toes to the music of Harlem's hottest young pianist—Fats Waller. By all accounts, Fats was special. He was big as a barn, enormously talented, and full of life. He was also Harlem's own, having been raised on 134th Street. There is hardly an old-time Harlemite who doesn't remember seeing Fats behind the organ at the Lincoln, on the stage of the Apollo, or jamming at some Saturday-night rent party.

Fats turned many of his neighbors on to the new syncopated rhythms first called jass. Jazz was the logical development from ragtime music, and before World War I it was new and hot. Harlem took to it as if it was its own. The first and most popular of the dance-band leaders was James Reese Europe, the Duke Ellington of his time. His Clef Club Orchestra, an aggregation of more than a hundred local musicians, regularly sold out the Manhattan Casino on 155th Street.

The new music got a big boost from a white couple named Irene and Vernon Castle. The two were the most popular dance team in the country. Irene was slim and pretty. She bobbed her hair and didn't wear a corset. He was tall and gallant. Together they were arbiters of the new style and etiquette and the forerunners of the Jazz Age. They traveled across the country with James Europe's orchestra. Soon, it seemed nearly everyone was doing the Castle Walk, the Fox-Trot, the Texas Tommy, the Turkey Trot, the Black Bottom, or Ballin' the Jack.

In 1915, Europe gave up playing tea dances to form a band for the 15th Regiment, the black Army unit that served courageously in World War I. Whether or not blacks should serve in the war was a much debated topic in Harlem. One argument stated that until blacks received their due as citizens, they shouldn't participate in the war effort. A black regiment rescued Theodore Roosevelt's Rough Riders during the Spanish-American War, with no significant gains in civil rights in the years since. Others insisted blacks should demonstrate that under any circumstances they were patriotic Americans.

Many did sign up, but they found themselves unwelcome in the U.S. Army. When they were shipped overseas, the 15th, later known as the Harlem Hellfighters, was attached to the French Army. In the trenches for 191 straight days, the unit fought with extraordinary valor and played a crucial role in the Argonne offensive, which helped seal the final defeat of Germany.

The soldiers returned to a changed Harlem. During the war, thousands of blacks had migrated north to work in factories. When the armistice was declared, the jobs disappeared, and real poverty crept back into the neighborhood. Still, in many ways, the years after the war saw Harlem life hit its peak. There was no better time to see Harlem pride than on a Sunday afternoon when the Seventh Avenue churches let out and the fashion parade began. Longtime residents recall that if one stood at the corner of 136th Street and Seventh on a Sunday afternoon, within a half hour nearly every important Harlemite would pass by.

Parades, whether they were fashionable, funereal, or political, were a major part of Harlem culture. After the 1919 murder of James Europe by one of his musicians, Harlemites lined Seventh Avenue to watch the long cortege pass by. Europe's murder was only one of a string of crushing disappointments for Harlem. Civil-rights advancement was negligible—worse as the gains of Theodore Roosevelt's administration were largely rolled back by President Wilson. Race riots in several cities left scores of blacks dead. Lynchings, committed in epidemic proportions down south, left blacks more disillusioned than ever.

The man who most successfully tapped that anger was a stocky Jamaican named Marcus Garvey. Garvey had created the Universal Negro Improvement Association in 1917 to promote the return of blacks to their African homeland and, more important, to encourage blacks to show pride in their heritage. While many laughed, many more listened, and during the early '20s Garvey forged the largest mass black movement in American history.

After Garvey was jailed and deported on mail fraud charges,

Harlem embraced another charismatic leader. Father Divine didn't ask people to worship God, he said he *was* God, a claim that created quite a stir in the community.

Father Divine's fame had truly humble beginnings—in a jail cell where he was languishing on charges of disturbing the peace. His fortunes took a sudden turn when the judge who sentenced him died of a heart attack. When he was apprised of the news, Father Divine shook his head sadly and said, "I hated to do it."

Word of the incident spread quickly. In the next few years, he found himself hailed as the greatest black messiah since Garvey. With his reputation as Holy Man firmly established, Father Divine attracted thousands of believers, both black and white, largely by means of his food. He established centers around the city where his followers served excellent and abundant meals for as little as fifteen cents.

After 1919, abundance was the word in Harlem, especially when it came to bootleg liquor. The neighborhood rivaled Hell's Kitchen for the number of speakeasies and after-hours joints. Whites streamed uptown to swanky nightclubs, such as Smalls' Paradise, where the waiters danced the Charleston while serving dinner, and Connie's Inn, where revues written by Fats Waller and Andy Razaf premiered some of the finest songs of the Jazz Age, like "Ain't Misbehavin' " and "What Did I Do to Be So Black and Blue?"

Owney Madden's Cotton Club was billed as the "Aristocrat of Harlem." Undoubtedly, it was the hottest nightspot in the neighborhood, and maybe in all of New York. The Cotton Club had the best shows, the best music, and the best entertainers. The big bands of Duke Ellington, Cab Calloway, Jimmy Lunceford, and Fletcher Henderson all played there, fronted by Ethel Waters, Lena Horne, and the unofficial mayor of Harlem, Bill "Bojangles" Robinson. The Cotton Club revues, staged by Harold Arlen, Elida Webb, and others, were always spectacular, featuring wild, uninhibited dancing by light-skinned chorus girls.

Though the Cotton Club's entertainers and staff were black, blacks were not welcome as patrons. The sky-high prices were out of reach for most Harlemites anyway. Those who enjoyed good music and dancing had to go elsewhere. Probably the cheapest form of entertainment was the Saturday-night rent party, where for a quarter or fifty cents, the food was plentiful and the piano music jumped until all hours of the night.

When one of Harlem's best "professors," Art Tatum, James P. Johnson, Fats Waller, Willie "The Lion" Smith, or Luckey Roberts, showed up to play at a rent party—and they did often— the party was guaranteed to be a success. When more than one made an appearance, there was bound to be a cutting contest, in which the pianists took each other on in a showdown of musical skill.

In those years, Harlem was a second home to many of the top jazz musicians in the country. To them, Harlem was "the Apple," with the best clubs that paid the best wages to the best musicians. When the gigs were over at four in the morning, there were always the after-hours spots, where they could unwind after a show, jam, or just talk shop until the sun rose. Places like the Puspatuck, the Ranch, and others without names, just dark basements with a piano and some rickety chairs, were where some of the best music of all was heard.

If the blues weren't born in Harlem, they were raised there. For years, Perry Bradford played piano in bordellos and smoky clubs, trying to get patrons interested in his blues tunes with little success. Even blacks called the blues devil's music. They didn't want to be reminded of the bad times. Then, in 1920, backed by a five-piece band with Willie "The Lion" Smith on piano, Mamie Smith recorded Bradford's "Harlem Blues" on Okeh Records. The record sold some 75,000 copies in Harlem record stores. Mamie Smith went on to enjoy a wildly successful career, as did other blues artists, most notably Bessie Smith and Ethel Waters.

The postwar years also saw the emergence of a major literary movement. It was the first time black writers came together as a group and, according to Harlem historian Jervis Anderson, broke with the " 'genteel' tendencies that had been dominant in black writing . . . [to write] boldly and affectionately about the experience of the black urban masses." The young writers wrote imaginatively and fearlessly about racial pride and black independence, influenced no doubt by Garvey and other black radicals.

The movement had many stars. Claude McKay was already established in the literary world in 1922, but when his first collection of poetry, *Harlem Shadows*, was published that year, he became the most well-known black poet in America. In 1921, a seventeen-year-old high school student named Countee Cullen earned critical acclaim for a series of poems he wrote for his high school magazine. That same year, Langston Hughes, who would go on to be the greatest of the Harlem Renaissance writers, published his first poem, "The Negro Speaks of Rivers."

Many of the young black writers were published in *Opportunity*, the journal of the National Urban League, edited by Charles Johnson. Over the next few years, *Opportunity* published the works of Harlem's most outstanding talent, including Arna Bontemps, Rudolph Fischer, Nella Larsen, Zora Neale Hurston, and Wallace Thurman.

Johnson also orchestrated a series of literary dinners that provided invaluable entrée into the white literary world for the Renaissance writers. Of all the white writers, Carl Van Vechten took the most interest in Harlem life. His Upper West Side apartment was a popular literary salon during the '20s, where Harlem writers could meet white writers and, more importantly, white editors and publishers.

Although Van Vechten's efforts were appreciated in some quarters, other people were critical of his motives. Those who were leery of him found some justification in 1926, with the publication of his novel about Harlem, *Nigger Heaven*. Though the book took a sympathetic look at the neighborhood and featured contributions by Langston Hughes, the title angered many Harlemites, and for a while Van Vechten was banished from his favorite uptown haunts.

Another publication that caused some commotion was *Fire!!*, a literary magazine edited by Wallace Thurman, with contributions by most of the top young Harlem writers and artists. Among them were a short story by Thurman about a young Harlem girl who turns to prostitution and a stream-of-consciousness paean to homosexuality by Richard Bruce Nugent, which shocked the older guard of Harlem intellectuals. Though it was popular, *Fire!!* proved too expensive to produce and was snuffed out after only one issue in 1926.

Just as the Greenwich Village bohemians of an earlier generation had enjoyed the support of Mabel Dodge, Harlemites found a patron in A'Lelia Walker, the daughter of Madame C. J. Walker, who had made millions from her popular hair-straightening formula. Although she was no intellectual, A'Lelia played a major role in nurturing the Renaissance writers. When she died suddenly in 1931, Langston Hughes wrote that her passage ". . . was really the end of the gay times of the New Negro era in Harlem. That spring for me (and, I guess, all of us) was the end of the Harlem Renaissance. We were no longer in vogue anyway, we Negroes. Sophisticated New Yorkers turned to Noël Coward. Colored actors began to go hungry, publishers politely rejected new manuscripts, and patrons found other uses for their money. The generous 1920s were over."

When the boom flattened out, the economic impact on Harlem was devastating. Though Harlem had a large professional class, even in the best of times, most jobs for blacks were at the bottom of the economic scale. During the Depression, black academics with postgraduate degrees, who were forced to drive cabs when times were good, found they could no longer make a living doing even that.

In 1935, pent-up anger over the miserable economic conditions exploded in a riot that swept down Lenox Avenue. Almost immediately, Mayor La Guardia warned whites to stay away from the neighborhood. Nightclubs that catered to whites were finished by the violence. Within months, the Cotton Club moved downtown, where it lasted only another year before it closed up shop for good.

The Depression didn't shut down the Savoy. The "Home of Happy Feet" was perhaps the finest ballroom in the country. Blacks were welcomed at the Savoy, and they made the most of it. Its nimble-footed lindy hoppers drew wide-eyed visitors from around the world. The music wasn't bad either, with the likes of Benny Goodman, Chick Webb, Jimmy Lunceford, and others on its stages.

Harlem's toughest audience was the crowd at Frank Schiffman's Apollo Theater, which replaced the old Hurtig and Seamon on 125th Street. By then, through the efforts of two Harlem pastors, David Johnson and Adam Clayton Powell, 125th Street, the last bastion of white Harlem, had begun the process of integration. By the time the Apollo opened in 1934, 125th Street was about to become the Main Street of black Harlem.

The Apollo was soon the premier black showcase in New York. Comedians like Moms Mabley and Pig Meat Markham earned renown from their Apollo appearances. The Apollo stage also featured some of the most dazzling acrobatic dancing ever seen. The

Nicholas Brothers, the Berry Brothers, and a one-legged solo artist named Peg Leg Bates were huge favorites, as were two young black singers, Billie Holiday and Ella Fitzgerald. Holiday had enormous success as a singer, but her spectacular career was cut short by drugs, alcohol, and a series of overwhelming personal problems.

It was one of the tragedies of Harlem that so much of its talent died young. When the gentle, frail Chick Webb died prematurely in 1939, Harlemites felt a terrible loss. Webb, Fats Waller, James Europe, Billie Holiday, Bessie Smith, and many more died in middle age. The saddest of all may have been the death of Florence Mills in 1929 of complications from a burst appendix. When she took center stage in Lew Leslie's *Blackbirds* revue to warble her signature song, "I'm a Little Blackbird," whole audiences were reduced to tears. In a neighborhood that took pride in the size of its funeral processions, Mills' farewell was the largest of all.

The mid-1930s brought perhaps Harlem's greatest hero. Joe Louis was not a New Yorker, but he was adopted by Harlemites and worshiped as no one had been before. Louis symbolized the dreams of oppression- and Depression-racked Harlem. He was quiet, dignified, and afraid of no one. As he rose through the ranks of heavyweights, Harlemites rejoiced in his every victory. Then, in a stunning upset, he was knocked out by Germany's white hope, Max Schmeling.

That night, the neighborhood once again erupted in rage. Gangs of youths rioted in the streets, destroying thousands of dollars' worth of property. However, the young Louis quickly got back on track. He took the championship from James Braddock in 1937 and then set his sights on avenging his only defeat.

The rematch, on June 22, 1938, pitting the black American against a symbol of Germany's Aryan-supremacist policies, was heard around the world, but no one listened more carefully than the citizens of Harlem, clustered in edgy groups around radios in living rooms and in the streets. The bout was over in less than three minutes. Louis hit Schmeling so hard, the German screamed in pain as he lay draped over the ropes. Seconds later he was counted out. This time, Harlem erupted in ecstasy.

# The Witnesses

EDDIE BAREFIELD (1909–) is a saxophonist who has played for a number of big bands, including those led by Cab Calloway, Chick Webb, and Fletcher Henderson.

HELEN BROWN (1898–) is a pianist and concert singer. She has been a Harlem resident since 1923.

HAYWOOD BUTT (1897–) is a World War I veteran of the 369th Regiment, known as the Harlem Hellfighters. He is a retired clerk and lives in Queens.

EVELYN CUNNINGHAM (1919–) is a former newspaper reporter and editor. A Harlem resident for nearly fifty years, she now heads an activist group called 100 Black Women.

MARION MOORE DAY (1902–) is the daughter of Fred Moore, the former editor of the black newspaper the *Age* and, in his day, one of Harlem's most influential residents. She has lived in Harlem since 1919.

DR. HAROLD ELLIS (1893–) is a native of St. Vincent, in the West Indies. He is a 1920 graduate of McGill Medical School. A neuropsychiatrist, he still maintains a practice in Harlem.

ELTON FAX (1909–) is a graduate of Syracuse University. He is an artist and writer. His biography of Marcus Garvey was reprinted by Dodd, Mead in 1988.

CHARLES GREENWALD (1904–) is a retired business executive. He lived in Harlem until his family moved to Brooklyn in 1915.

HOWARD ''STRETCH'' JOHNSON (1915–) is a former Cotton Club dancer. He also taught black studies at New Paltz College and is now editor of the first black newspaper in Hawaii, the *Afro-Hawaii News.*

BARNEY JOSEPHSON (1902–88) was the former owner of Cafe Society, the city's first interracial nightclub. His story appears primarily in the Greenwich Village chapter.

NORA MAIR (1903–) emigrated from Jamaica in 1922 and settled in Harlem. She worked for many years in the garment industry. Her daughter is a cousin of the author.

ANNA MURPHY (1906–) was a longtime elementary-school teacher. In her retirement, she dances with a group called the 60+ Swingers.

RICHARD BRUCE NUGENT (1906–87) was a writer and artist and one of the last surviving members of the Harlem Renaissance movement.

ISABEL WASHINGTON POWELL (1908–) is a former actress and show girl. She was married for twelve years to former congressman Adam Clayton Powell, Jr. She works for the New York City school system.

FRANCIS ''DOLL'' THOMAS (1893–) is an electrician and jack-of-all-trades and has been an integral part of the Harlem theater scene since his arrival in New York in 1907.

DR. HERMAN WARNER (1897–1988) was a native of Jamaica. He was a World War I combat veteran and a graduate of Howard University Medical School. He later established a general practice in Harlem. His wife, MARION, a former professional entertainer, also participated in this interview.

NAOMI WALLER WASHINGTON (1902–) was born and raised in Harlem. She is the sister of Thomas "Fats" Waller.

ELTON FAX: When I was growing up in Baltimore in the '20s, Harlem epitomized a kind of freedom that we did not know: "Once I get to Harlem, I won't need to worry about anything. Nobody's gonna bother me in Harlem." We found out later, of course, that this was not as real as we imagined it to be. Harlem was more glamorous than the black neighborhoods of Baltimore, or of Norfolk, Virginia, or of Jackson, Mississippi, and it was known all over. Everybody wanted to see this tremendous community.

You also read Langston. You read Countee Cullen. We read Sterling Brown, and later Claude McKay and his book *Home to Harlem* and Van Vechten's *Nigger Heaven*. Countee Cullen came to Syracuse University when I was a junior as a convocation speaker, and he spoke about Harlem, and he spoke of his having been in Europe and being stopped by people who said to him, when they found out that he was an American, "Harlem, do you come from Harlem?"

I wanted to see Harlem, of course I did. I saw it first in the '30s, and it was fabulous. Let me tell you one of the things that meant so much to simple people. There was this big black giant of a policeman, Lacy, at 125th Street and Seventh Avenue, directing traffic, making white folks stop and go at his bidding. Where I came from, there was no black authority or authoritative figure who commanded respect. To see him pull over a car full of white people and *saunter*. He was quite dramatic, and he'd say, "As big and black as I am, you mean to tell me you can't see my hand in the air?" This symbolized, for us, something that we had not seen before, and while it was superficial, it was impressive.

EVELYN CUNNINGHAM: My mother, father, brother, and me, we came to New York from Elizabeth City, North Carolina, because of a very specific reason. As parents will do, my mother and father asked me, "Evelyn, what do you want to do when you grow up?"

I said I wanted to pick cotton, and I meant it, because if you have ever seen a cotton field, it's very beautiful. We had cotton fields and watermelon fields, all the clichés, right in town. Nothing is more beautiful than a cotton blossom. Nothing is more beautiful than a watermelon that's just been opened. You break it on the stone and all that red opens up. Who knows from "Ol' Man River" and what that meant? I had no concept of the sociological thing about cotton, but that was what I wanted to do: sit in the sun among all those blooms and blossoms, wear a big hat, and pick cotton.

So my father said to my mother, "Let us get out of this place." That was really the reason. They had planned to move out of the South, but this put them many years ahead of time, and they literally tossed a coin to see if they would come to New York or Chicago. They sold the house, sold the poolroom they owned, and moved to New York.

FRANCIS "DOLL" THOMAS: I grew up on my grandfather's farm in Maryland. It was around the size of Central Park. When I came here, money wasn't on my mind. The only thing on my mind was work. The farm was taken away from me after my grandfather died. I was fourteen then, in 1907. Those days were hard, especially for Negroes with no skill or anything else except the skill of farmwork, which isn't a damn bit of good in the city.

I didn't know anything about cities, but on 4th Street I had met several people at the carriage house there, so I knew if I got to New York, I would at least have a roof over my head, and I could make out with food by helpin' them take care of the horses.

There was nothin' in Harlem. The furthest most people lived uptown was the 50s. In those days, a fella would be gettin' to talkin' in the carriage house, and he'd say, "I'm goin' uptown." He'd be goin' to 14th Street.

Harlem was a place where the white folks lived. There was a lot of farmin' up there. It was even suggested that I go up there because some of the fellas in the stables drove some people that had farms up here. They wanted to take me up to talk to the people, so I could get a job workin' on a farm.

A few times on Sunday, a bunch would get together. Somebody would have the boss's horse and carriage, and we'd take a drive up here. It was mostly open land, a few buildings. There were workin' farms, especially to the west or on the east side.

The farmers were livin' in shacks. Of course, there wasn't much sightseein' that we could do, bein' colored. The Irish, who were predominant in New York in those years, they would see you and they'd start a chant.

*Nigger, Nigger never die.*
*Black face, shiny eyed.*

Somebody would come after us with a shotgun. We just had to keep on movin'. The only place we could stop to get a bite to eat and give the horse a breather would be in a stable, because most all the help in the stables was, naturally, colored.

After the war, colored folks thought this was where the streets were paved with gold. You just reached out and pulled the money off the trees. That was a fantasy which wasn't so. Lenox Avenue was the beginnin' of black neighborhoods. Before the war, they were confined to very few of the blocks below 136th Street. They ran from 136th to 140th. You couldn't stop in any place on 125th Street. They wouldn't serve you and they wouldn't sell you. If you went in and picked up a piece of merchandise, that was yours, whether it fit you or not. It was that way with the saloons and everything else. A lot of them had a lot of big Irishmen that would meet you at the door and let you know, "Nigger, you ain't welcome."

CHARLES GREENWALD: I was born on 115th Street between Seventh and Eighth Avenue in 1904. My father was a builder and contractor. He operated from a small shop in 112th Street and Fifth Avenue.

He was born in Russia. Our first apartment in New York was on 115th Street. Then he bought a brownstone on 120th Street between Lenox and Seventh for $8,000. They had nine children, and we lived in that house until about 1915.

There was a lot of open space around the neighborhood. There were a lot of those empty lots where these poor people would build shacks on the land and they sold chickens and milk from their farms. North of 130th Street there were a lot of individual, unattached homes. Land wasn't that expensive, and the further north you went, the more open space there was.

Our house was built only a few years before. The building was set back about fifteen feet from the sidewalk, and there was a big yard in the back. The only apartment houses were on the corners. There were also large spacious houses on the corners, with maybe eighteen rooms. Some of them further up had stables next door for their own carriages and land on either side. Those people were big merchants, real multimillionaires. They later moved down to Fifth Avenue and Park Avenue.

ANNA MURPHY: My brother couldn't go past Eighth Avenue to play, because he was black and that was Irish. Many times I would see my brother come in and get the broomstick in order to go out and fight. The Irish kids wouldn't let the black kids cross St. Nicholas to go into the park and sleigh-ride. But they didn't have guns or knives. I think they looked forward to those fights. One Saturday the Irish would run, and the next Saturday the blacks would run across that street. It was almost a ritual.

My parents were the equivalent today of college grads, although it was called Avery Normal School in Charleston, South Carolina. When they married, they immediately left Charleston for New York and never returned. My father was the head bellman of a large hotel, but he died when I was about six or seven. I was born in '06 in New York City, on 313 West 53rd Street. I was the seventh-born of ten.

Only four survived. I lost a brother at the age of nineteen. He was quite a musician. He had his own orchestra and everything. He had a history of asthma, and he succumbed to influenza during that epidemic in 1919. He was scheduled to play for a very fashionable wedding in Brooklyn. Because they were all black, and this was a white wedding, they told him to be there an hour ahead of time—the feeling that blacks were always late. He was such a stickler for time, he got there an hour earlier than the time they gave him. The church wasn't open. It was a snowy, bleak, terrible night. In one week he was gone.

NAOMI WALLER WASHINGTON: My mother's father was an Irishman, Thomas Dunn. My grandmother was a slave, and she had two children with him. My mother was second. She was very light. I don't think I ever saw my mother's brother. Fats met him in California once. He was living as a white man out there.

I was born in 1902 at 107 134th Street. My father said I was so small the midwife put me in the palm of her hand. My mother said when she saw this little rat, she turned her head to the wall and asked God to let me live. She promised God that if I would live, she would raise me for him. She wanted me to be a missionary, and she wanted my brother, Thomas [Fats], to be a minister. Needless to say, I believe in God, but I'm not missionary material. I liked my whiskey and my gambling.

She didn't want us out of her sight. I had a brother that drowned when he was nine years old. He was with my uncle in Jersey at the time. I think that's what made my mother cautious. I don't think she ever got over losing Alfred. She had twelve children. Only five survived, Edward, Robert, Thomas, Edith, and Naomi.

My father had his own trucking company for a while. He had a team of horses and an open truck. I don't know how he managed it when the weather was bad. It was a pleasure for us when he'd bring the horses by, and we'd be dressed up and we'd go to the stables and come back with him. It was fun because Fats or I never knew what it was to play in the street. We'd see children out having a ball, and our mother didn't allow that. They'd be dancing, having a good time. I knew all the dances only because my aunt Lucy told me them. The Turkey Trot, the Black Bottom, and the Grizzly Bear, Ballin' the Jack, and the Waltz, I learned all of them from her.

We weren't raggedy by a long shot, but we didn't have that much. My father managed. We didn't have an expensive home but we had a clean home. I had a Sunday dress, although all my life I wanted to have more than one.

We always had enough to eat. In the morning, we started off with cornflakes and milk. We had anywhere between three and four quarts of milk a day for the family. Mama'd send me to the Irish fellow, Pat, with the pail, and Mama would say, "Don't stir it so much." She liked the cream off the top. Milk was milk in those days. We'd also have grits, pancakes, sometimes biscuits, eggs, bacon. It was a meal.

We were plump, and my father was proud of his children because of our size. There was a man who was a deacon at Metropolitan Baptist Church. His daughter and my sister were as wide as this table. The two fathers would be walking and talking, and they'd be so proud of their children.

"Oh, mine is larger."

"No, mine is larger." Then they'd weigh 'em.

We were all fond of greens. We had pork stores where we bought fresh shoulders, chitlins, and hog maws, pig feet. That was the only part of the pig I liked. I loved pig feet. I didn't like meat, but Fats never got tired of it. He could eat two steaks, and then he could tell 'em when they brought those two, "Hold one in reserve."

ANNA MURPHY: We had rabbit. The wagons would come through the streets with the rabbits hanging all around the barrels, and they'd sell you those rabbits. My grandmother would skin 'im, and soak it overnight in brine and cook it. It tasted just like chicken. I hated to see it, but I loved to eat it.

DR. HAROLD ELLIS: I was born on the fourth of June 1894, on St. Vincent, in the West Indies. My father was a merchant, and he died when I was fifteen. I landed here when I was seventeen years and two months, on August 21, 1911.

I wanted to be a medical man as long as I can remember. I prevailed on my mother to let me come to America. You were never able to come out of the class in which you were born down there. In America, you could go in any damn place. There was prejudice here, but it was better than having no hope down in the West Indies.

When I came here, I was living with relatives on 23rd Street, and I was working as an indoor aviator—running an elevator up on 162nd Street. You'd come to work Saturday night at six o'clock and you don't get off until midday Sunday. It was cold at night, and the elevator man didn't have a room. If you had to sleep, you had to take a nap sitting up in the hall.

I quit and got a job with a ladies' tailor. Then I got a job at a raincoat factory. One day I came to work and the factory was closed, but the boss was there.

"What are you doing here?" he asked me.

"I'm coming to work."

"It's a holiday. Lincoln's Birthday."

"Who's Lincoln?"

He told me that Lincoln freed the slaves. But I said, "Lincoln didn't free me. My people were freed by royal decree of Queen Victoria."

Then I worked as a porter in the Flatiron Building. All a black person could get was a damn porter's job or a messenger. The New York *World* used to advertise these porter jobs, "West Indian preferred," because the West Indian was considered a foreigner, and he was more industrious than native-born blacks. He never had to borrow money before his payday. The native-born did not like it. There was bad blood between the two. The West Indian was getting along better. There were more colored lawyers who were West Indian, more West Indian colored doctors.

N O R A   M A I R : [*goes to a cupboard and pulls out what looks to be a silver stickpin with two initials, IP, on the end. But it is not an ornament. It is a branding iron her great-grandfather used to brand his slaves.*] That branding iron really strikes terror in you. They branded their slaves like they brand an animal, a piece of cattle. Isaac Philp was the owner of my people in Jamaica. The Philps were Scottish. I didn't know my father's parents. People don't talk about those things. They say it's a disgrace to talk about your descendants being slaves, but I didn't have control over it.

My mother's aunt was white. My grandmother was raised a slave. The boss man took a liking to this good-looking black wench and set her up in a home and had five children by her. My mother was one of them. She was the eldest, and she had four brothers.

I heard very little about New York before I came here. Harlem meant nothing to me, except a chance to get away from Jamaica. They sent me here to take nursing, which I really didn't like.

I had a terrible time when I arrived. My sister didn't meet me when I got off the boat. I neglected to tell her what time the boat was coming and what date. We had landed around eleven in the morning. When four o'clock came and there was no sister, they took me over to Ellis Island. They brought sandwiches and coffee that they poured from a kind of goblet that you used in Jamaica to wash your face. I didn't like that. I stood there with tears coming down my face. I wept all night. It was the first place I ever saw with a concrete toilet. You were locked up for the night. It was jail. I spent the night writing angry letters. I said, "If this is New York, I want to go home."

She came the next morning and took me uptown by elevated. The first thing I remember were the horse-drawn wagons, and these horses with their great big rumps and hooves. They looked much different from the elegant racehorses my brother trained. These were monsters. Another thing that killed me was when they were taking us from Immigration to Ellis Island, we passed by the Fulton Fish Market. The stench! When my sister picked me up, I asked her if all New York smelled like rotten fish. She told me it was the market.

"A market smells like that?"

The neighborhood seemed so cold and impersonal. My sister would leave me and go to work, and I would stare at the window and look out, and pray to God I would see someone I knew. It was like being in jail, because I was used to being in the country, free like a bird. I could go where I wanted to go.

NAOMI WASHINGTON: When I was about seven or eight years old, across the street there was a grocery store. One day, there was a man in the store who was dressed to kill—oh, a good-looking fellow. And this woman said to him, "Hello, pimp." He laughed.

When my father came in that night, I said, "Hello, pimp." Papa looked. Papa took his coat off and hung it up. He said, "Naomi, come here."

I went to him. He said, "Who did you hear say that?"

I told him that there was a man who came in the store, and he was dressed, and that's what this woman said to him. Papa said, "Now when I came in was I dressed like that?"

I said, "Well, you dress like that on Sundays."

"But this isn't Sunday. Today, I worked hard. I can't afford to go to work dressed like that, and I am not a pimp," he said. "I work every day to feed you, and I come home and bring my money to your mother. That man dresses up every day and takes his wife's money. He don't give her anything."

There were a lot of prostitutes, and it was nothing to see white men up and down the block, coming in. I was told they were bad women. They were all through Harlem.

My father was one of the many deacons of Abyssinia. Later, he became head deacon. He and my mother did what they call "testifying." They would preach on the corner. There were quite a few people doing that. If there was one on 135th Street and Lenox

Avenue, there might be another one on 134th and Seventh. They were called street meetings. They would sing, and many times Fats would be playing a small organ. Large crowds would come around and listen, and they would take up a collection.

I remember one time they had this meeting, and a white man handed a note to the leader. He was asking them to do the song "Where Is My Wandering Boy Tonight?" They played that and sang it, and he cried, and I said he must have been far away from home.

DOLL THOMAS: I got with a carnival. In my travels with them I realized how inefficient the lighting for theaters was. At that time, electricity was just startin'. I became one of the city's first licensed electricians, and with my brother had a very successful electrical contractin' business in New York. We did a lot of theaters, also whorehouses and bordellos. There were a lot of them.

I was constantly being reminded that I was a nigger doin' white man's work. "And don't try to act like a white man, and for God's sake don't try to speak to any of the white ladies." It was always a "white lady" and "colored woman."

I put the electricity up on 125th Street here for Con Edison for three dollars a day. I worked with Edison himself. He was just another man. He called me nigger like everybody else.

In 1913, I was with the group that opened the first theater in New York with entertainment where colored people would go without being segregated and could really feel at home and enjoy themselves—the Lafayette Theater on Seventh Avenue, between 131st and 132nd.

I had to go to the city and get the certificate of occupancy for the Lafayette. In New York, you had to belong to a political club and you paid through the club to get your theater license. Then it had to go through the Building Department, the Fire Department, the Health Department; about six or seven departments all had to give you the okay before you could open the theater. One group held ours up, the Fire Department, because bringin' niggers in a white neighborhood is not goin' to make anything but trouble.

Eventually I got the license. The Fire Department chief, Chief Croker, who had all the political pull, why he looked right at me and said, "Nigger, I'm telling you, if one of your people bothers one of my women, you are gonna be lynched." That was the re-action to integration.

The Lafayette gave the colored performers a chance to per-form in their own talent and not in the general white conception of the colored performer, which was that he was either a porter or a waiter, or the woman was a maid or something.

We weren't doin' coon shows either. We were doin' dramas. Then, hittin' the top of the scale, we even did light opera and then did complete opera. We did *Faust* with a complete colored cast. We went on the road with that about six or eight months.

Charles Gilpin's success in *Emperor Jones* came on Broadway, but he played it in the Lafayette when he was just comin' up. His biggest problem was he was an alcoholic. He had it hard. A man with his kind of talent, and the only work he could get was as an elevator operator.

NAOMI WASHINGTON: Until I was sixteen I didn't even know what a movie house looked like. My parents didn't allow me to go into a movie house because of their religion. They didn't know I used to go to the Lafayette Theater almost every day. The Lafa-yette had some wonderful dramas. They had people like Abby Mitchell and Andrew Bishop. But the first time my parents learned I had gone to the Lafayette Theater, you'd thought I had gone to a house of disrepute. I was punished. I couldn't go out for days.

My parents were strict, and—do you know?—I thank 'em. If I had the type of parents that would have let me do what I wanted to do, I guess I would be in Sing Sing somewhere. There were always temptations around. "Taste this. Taste that."

Fats was a con man even then. One day when we were up to no good, my mother said, "I've told you three times not to do that. Now, I'm going to whip you." So he goes to Mama, puts his arm around her neck. "Mama, the devil made me do that, but if you pray for me, I won't do that no more." She told my aunt, "Now you know I couldn't whip him after that."

I used to have to stand up for him around the neighborhood. They used to call me the Little Jack Johnson when I was around ten or twelve. When he passed away, he was around five feet ten and a half. He never made 300 pounds. I made 300. My brother wasn't timid, but he just wouldn't fight. He was very shy. He ate and slept piano. Naturally, they'd be calling him sissy, and then they'd see me a half a block away—"Here comes his sister"—and tear out, 'cause if I would catch one, I'd put a whuppin' on him. I'd be knocking him around. "Don't you bother my brother."

The name Fats started when he was a boy, 'cause he was chubby. They used to come to the house. "Is Fats home?"

Mama said, "Who is that? I don't have a child named Fats."

They'd whisper to one of them, "His name is Tom."

"Oh. Is Tom home?"

"Oh, Tom? Yes, he's home."

He didn't mind the nickname. I think he rather liked it. It kind of put him apart. Tom was really a gifted child. When we'd go to Abyssinia, he'd listen, and then afterward he would play on the organ. Adam Clayton Powell was the son of the minister of Abyssinia. They had the type of organ you'd have to pump, and Adam pumped while Fats played. Sometimes they'd climb through the church window, so Fats could play.

At home, he used to put two chairs together and say, "C'mon, let's sing," and he'd be pretending to be playing the piano. So one day my brother Robert said to Pop, "I think if Tom had a piano, he'd play."

Pop said he couldn't afford one, but Bob said, "I'll tell you what—you make the credit arrangements, and I'll pay for it." So Pop went and got a Horace Waters piano. That was a good piano at the time. My mother knew when it was coming, so that day she sent us to our aunt. When we came back, Mama said, "When you all get your things off, come in here."

Well, I naturally had mine off first, and my mother put her hand to her lips when I saw it. Fats took his time, but when he finally came into that room—I've often said I would give anything if I had a camera to catch the expression on his face. He said, "Mama, is that mine?"

Mama said, "Yes, that's yours." He sat down at that piano, and he had a ball just touching the different keys.

DOLL THOMAS: We were doin' vaudeville on Sunday 'cause it was against the law to do shows on Sunday, but we didn't call it vaudeville. We called it Sunday concerts, but it was vaudeville. We'd show a news or a two-reel comedy like Hal Roach or Mack Sennett's Bathin' Beauties.

That's what got us organized in the projectionist union. We had to go downtown to get the film before the theater started, bring it uptown, then after the showin' that night, you used to have to take the film back downtown. The average salary for a projectionist was about nine or ten dollars a week plus carfare. If you happened to have some kind of newsreel or Mary Pickford or something like that, that another theater wanted, when you went to get it you had to watch yourself, 'cause he'd have a gang down there to take the film from you, or they'd take it out of the can and start rollin' it down the street. Many times, if you came uptown without the film, you got fired. You were right in the middle of a fight between the theaters. We fought for years and years and finally got the union organized and got it strong. The first demand we made on exhibitors was that we were not goin' to take the film up and down to the film exchanges. It was too rough.

Now 125th Street didn't come into colored until much later. At the Loew's they'd tell you it was sold out even though it wasn't. Even the theaters that would admit you were segregated. At Hurtig and Seamon's, which later became the Apollo, you had to go 'round 126th Street and go up the back stairway. They tried to get fancy with it and call it the upper mezzanine, but everybody knew it as "nigger heaven," and it was built for that. If you look at the Apollo today, you'll see now they got a stairway, of course, but there's no connection. The only way you can get from the second balcony down to the theater, you have to jump down. The Alhambra was built the same way.

Before the Lafayette, the only other theaters open to colored were little dumps. There was one across 125th Street on the corner, a little frame shack that somebody turned into a little movie house. The Lincoln was a colored theater run by a white couple. That was a dump on 132nd Street. Then, Leo Brecher and some of his friends built a 3,000-seat house on 145th Street and Seventh Avenue. That was the Roosevelt. He built a 3,000-seat house, the Douglas, on 142nd Street and Lenox Avenue, where the Cotton Club was later built over the lobby.

HAYWOOD BUTT: Despite the problems, Harlem was a beautiful place in which to live before the war. I was born in Elizabeth City, North Carolina, in 1897. My father was an upholsterer and a cabinetmaker for the fabulous sum of nine dollars a week. His parents had been slaves. I didn't know any of them, except for my grandmother. Though they were slaves, they were from a moderate section of the country, and they didn't get the full pinch of slavery as some of the others did from further south. They were originally from Guinea, in Africa. I knew that because they used a term in regard to my grandfather, called "Guinea niggers," which is a term the colored people assumed from the whites.

We came up here in 1912 partly because they had segregation down there. They were supposed to be separate but equal, but there's no such animal. There were also a lot of lynchings down south. That wasn't a problem in North Carolina, but it was further down south, and it had an effect on all black people at the time.

In 1913, there was quite a bit of sentiment about the Negro participation in the country's defense. They were limited to four regiments, the 24th and 25th Infantry and the 9th and 10th Cavalry. They weren't invited and sometimes they were prohibited from joining the state national guards. A Negro boy couldn't even join the Boy Scouts. Actually, they had to start their own Boy Scouts, the United States Boy Scouts.

I thought there was a deficiency in the Negroes' participation in civic affairs and that they should go in and prove that they were really worthy citizens. That was my train of thought at the time, and it hasn't changed very much. We have participated in all of the wars of the country, even the Revolution. The first blood that was shed in the war for independence was that of a Negro—Crispus Attucks. Then we had Peter Salem, who fought in Salem, Mass. They were fighting for America, and America should recognize that, but they seem to ignore that part of history. One of the black regiments was really the saviors of Colonel Roosevelt's regiment in the Spanish-American War.

Our unit started in 1913. There wasn't much to it at first. Boys used to drill with broomsticks up on 63rd Street, at St. Cyprian's Church. We drilled once a week in front of Lafayette Hall or on Seventh Avenue. The Boy Scouts gave us some military training. They showed us various soldier's positions. We didn't get any heavy combat training until we shipped out of the city up to Peekskill and Camp Whitman upstate. I was in the First Battalion of the 15th New York. In August 1917, when we shipped out of the city, we became the 369th.

DOLL THOMAS: I was a damn young foolish American. About eight or ten of us enlisted, and that was unheard of. We embarrassed the white folks. They didn't know what the hell to do with us. The last incident was in Chillicothe, Ohio. They put me on guard duty out there, and there was one particular officer that I couldn't stand anyhow. He was the only person in the world that ever called me a nigger that really riled me, just the way he could say it, just like you were filth or dirt. "You don't have any business in this army, nigger. I hope I'm relievin' some fellas, and you're around 'cause, whether you're in the war or not, you're gonna get shot." All that shit all the time.

Anyway, they told us Army regulations—you stop a guy and tell him to halt three times to get the countersign. If he don't say anything, you shoot. I knew who it was, but I blasted him in the shoulder, and all hell broke loose. So they immediately put us on a ship and shipped us to Europe with the contingents of soldiers that were goin' over to make way for Pershing.

HAYWOOD BUTT: The camps were segregated. We objected to a certain extent, but we generally accepted it as our lot. The chefs were colored and they knew how to cook the kind of food we liked. There was a little resentment, but not very much toward the white officers. The fact is, the officers that really pushed us, we considered it our due.

In the camps, they had officers' clubs, but the ranks below major were excluded because we had very few Negro majors. We had quite a few captains, but no majors. This was all over.

We were discriminated against by the Red Cross. They would serve cocoa and doughnuts. A black man would get on the line, and the doughnuts and the cocoa would suddenly become exhausted. They couldn't replace it until the black man got out of the line.

The YMCAs were just about as bad. They were the chief offender at that time. They were supposed to supply us with cigarettes, but we couldn't go in there to get them. We resented it, but there was nothing we could do about it, so we accepted it. But then the Second and Third Battalions went down to Spartanburg, South Carolina, for training. One Sunday morning, Lieutenant Noble Sissle went into one of the hotels to buy some cigars and New York papers, and someone in there told him, "Take your hat off, nigger."

They kicked them out, and the boys took that quite seriously. They organized themselves to make a raid on Spartanburg, but somebody got to the colonel, and the colonel and several of the officers persuaded them to let them handle it.

NAOMI WASHINGTON: Our older brother was drafted. I remember we went down to see him off. They left from St. Philip's Church. He was kissing us good-bye, and my father cried. That was the time that Lawrence said, "Pop, don't send me away like this." He couldn't stand to see him cry.

It was very sad there. People were crying. War is one of those things, you're saying good-bye, and for many of those saying good-bye, it *was* good-bye.

DR. HERMAN WARNER: From the middle of 1916 to 1918 I was in the British West Indies Forces. I saw combat on the Western Front, in Belgium, for the most part, where some of the fiercest fighting was. The British West Indies sent eleven battalions. We had white officers. It wasn't the custom to give officer rank to black soldiers. You went as far as sergeant major.

In general, I didn't have any difficulty with the whites. What problems we had was when America got into the war and their white soldiers came in. Anytime they met us in the cafés there was trouble. They wanted to get us out, and there would be a fight. Then, a group of West Indian soldiers would decide "if we have any more trouble from the soldiers, we're gonna kill 'em." That's what they did. If another incident occurred, the soldiers would be marked, and they waylaid and butchered them.

HAYWOOD BUTT: Pershing wanted us to become laborers and to take our arms from us. That would have been sort of a disgrace, to disarm us. We went over to a New York regiment, and they didn't want us. None of the white units did, so we went around to the French. We fought side by side with the French. We were in five engagements. We fought in the Champagne. I was on the front lines for 191 straight days.

HERMAN WARNER: I saw hand-to-hand combat. You get scared. Anybody who tells you that he was not scared is a liar. There is a line of demarcation between fear and cowardice. When your buddy falls next to you, you regret it, but you're glad it wasn't you. You mourn for the person, but the French have an expression, *sauve qui peut*—"save yourself if you can."

I thought about the idea of killing another man. I came from a religious background, and at times you would feel, "What am I doing here?" Just the thought of killing a person. But you then get completely conditioned, not only to the environment but to that way of life. So many times, you were so taken up with escape, just trying to get away, that you didn't have enough time to look at the individuals you were fighting. And you didn't always kill. Sometimes you would maim, and then you go on about your business, depending on your situation. It's horrible, but it then shows you how complex a human being is. You know, I am the most peaceful man in the world.

HAYWOOD BUTT: I took the communiqué that apprised us of the armistice. I was relieved, because we were going over the top the next day. I daresay I wouldn't be here, because we were in Alsace, and all of that terrain was mined.

I didn't get back until February. We were taken to the Battery, and people were waiting for us there. Our band, with James Reese Europe as the conductor, led us. We were the first ones to pass through that victory arch at Washington Square, then up Fifth Avenue. People were five or ten deep on the sidewalk, and they were throwing money down at us.

NAOMI WASHINGTON: As God would have it, Lawrence did come back, and he wasn't injured. When they came back, they came up Lenox Avenue. People were watching from the roofs. The young kids were running with them and cheering. I never recognized my brother, but my mother recognized her child. "That's my son. That's my son." She was so glad, because there were a lot of boys who didn't come back.

HERMAN WARNER: When the war was over, I applied for a leave of absence to come to America for maybe six months or a year. The leave was granted. But after I was in New York for six months, I decided I'd stay here, because, frankly, I was fed up with colonialism, and I wanted to see what America was all about.

You cannot for a moment imagine what Harlem was like in those days. It was the most beautiful spot. The houses were some of the best houses in New York, and the people were of one class. Everybody seemed to know everybody else. It's hard to describe the feeling you got from belonging to that little space.

You know, Harlem then was a state of mind. It was more than just a physical place. There was something that it represented—a consciousness, if you will, a feeling that from there you could go anywhere. There were people who were middle-class and upper-middle-class who wouldn't live anywhere but Harlem. It just had so much to offer, sociologically and psychologically. It was the place to live. It represented the best. You would go into an apartment house, and the elevator man would have a doctorate. It was a common thing—a Ph.D. who couldn't get work.

HAROLD ELLIS: When I was working at a hotel on Central Park West, one of the residents was a graduate of McGill, and he convinced me to apply there. I graduated McGill with an M.D. in '20— five years. I worked through the influenza epidemic of 1918. It was so bad that four or five of my classmates came to class one day and then died the next. Aspirin hadn't come out yet. In twenty-four hours, you got it and you were gone. There wasn't anything you could do. They gave you poultices, maybe some mercury preparation, all that sort of primitive medicine.

Since I didn't have any money to start up, I went to work as a cook's assistant up in Massachusetts. In those days, you didn't come by a job in a hospital so easily. They weren't hiring black doctors. I came back to New York to the hotel on Central Park West, and I went back to work as an elevator operator. With a medical license!

> Anatole Longfellow, alias the Scarlet Creeper, strutted aimfully down the east side of Seventh Avenue. He wore a tight-fitting suit of shepherd's plaid which thoroughly revealed his lithe, sinewy figure to all who gazed upon him, and all gazed. A great diamond, or some less valuable stone which aped a diamond, glistened in his fuchsia cravat. The uppers of his highly polished tan boots were dove-coloured suede and the buttons were pale blue. His black hair was sleek under his straw hat,

set at a jaunty angle. When he saluted a friend—and
his acquaintanceship seemed to be wide—two rows of
pearly teeth gleamed from his seal-brown counte-
nance.

— Carl Van Vechten, *Nigger Heaven*

RICHARD BRUCE NUGENT: That sounds like me in my mon-
key suit, looking like all of those other dickty niggers. We all wore
those monkey-backed suits, bell-bottomed trousers, pinch-backed
suits. I had one made when I was in England. I shall never forget
that suit. It was blue-brown. It was *British*, and Seventh Avenue
was the Fifth Avenue of Harlem.

ELTON FAX: I first came up to Harlem on an Easter Sunday,
and that was something. I was out there in the parade. I'll never
forget it, because I was with Hamtree Harrington, Bojangles, and
all these people. Lofton Mitchell mentions this in black drama. He
said, "Man, we *strolled* in Harlem. This was our turf." That was
the feeling you got. There were people in the parade who were
quite seriously elegant, in top hat, tails, cutaway coat, spats, cane—
anything that mimicked white upper-class living, mimicry of that
which was opulent, that which was approved, that which white folks
aspired to be—J. P. Morgan.

NORA MAIR: Lofton Mitchell was right—we didn't walk, we
strolled. I loved it when my brother-in-law would take me strolling
on Seventh Avenue. You walked with your nose in the air, especially coming from Jamaica. Everybody was dressed to the teeth.
You would wear the finest you had, like chiffon dresses, white hats,
new shoes, and everything matched, from your pocketbook on down.
We had a friend who was an African. On Easter Sunday, he would
wear cutaway, striped pants, top hat, white spats, and cane, and he
strolled Fifth Avenue. He *had* to be there. Everybody was out there.
They would say if you stood at the corner of 135th Street and Lenox
Avenue, you would see every important person you ever knew.

ISABEL WASHINGTON POWELL: While Adam and I were
married, every Sunday morning after church, he would walk down

Seventh Avenue wearing tails and an ascot. He was immaculate. He was fantastic. I had my own milliner who did my hats. I had a lady that made my dresses. My whole deal was getting ready for church on Sunday and strutting down the aisle of Abyssinian Baptist Church, oh, sure. He would walk from 138th Street to 125th Street. The people would come around and greet him. This was before he ran for anything, but he was getting ready then. You know how there are people who are always standing back. He would break from me and walk over and throw his arms around them. "Hi, friend." Those were the people who put him in.

BRUCE NUGENT: I came to New York from Washington, D.C. In Washington, black society imitated white society with tragic fidelity. Of course, they didn't think it was tragic fidelity. They just thought, White folks take sabbaticals, I'll take sabbaticals. On the sabbatical, they looked it up to see what a sabbatical was.

You didn't trust yourself enough to innovate, and if you did, you got called outrageous. That's the name that's been applied to me all my life. I've always been sort of an exception to the rule. I have always said, "Well, I'm a Bruce. I can do whatever I please. I have the divine right of kings." It was always tongue-in-cheek, but I always meant it.

We came to New York after my father died. Mother came to get a job to take care of us. She had first worked for the National Geographic, but that didn't pan out, so she became a waitress. My brother was dancing at the time on Broadway. I worked at the Martha Washington Hotel. It was a women's hotel, and it was the A-number-one first-class hotel. I loved that hotel. There was a woman in the hotel who, around her bathtub, had quart bottles of perfumes, so whenever she took a bath, she put this perfume on. She always smelled so good. I used to go up with little bottles and steal the perfume, so I always smelled so good. She said, "You don't have to steal my perfume. I'll give it to you. Always take what you want. I like the way you smell if you smell like I smell."

Then I got a job as an assistant to an iceman. That was a thrill, because you stuck a pick in the ice, and it split so perfectly. It was like being a diamond cutter. I loved that.

When I first saw Harlem, I was scared to death. I had never seen so many black people in my life. It was the longest time before black was beautiful. I'm very much like a cat or dog. I go around a place before I settle down. After I got up there, I had to see the neighborhood, and I fell in love with 138th Street because of the trees—and Goat Hill.

Who could help but notice that great big rock? I had a predilection for Mediterranean people, so I got to know these Italians that lived on the hill. I was so sad when they blasted and blasted that rock to get the hill out of the way. These people had goats. They drank goat's milk and they ate goat. I learned a lot of Italian foods from them, but they never could get me to eat an eye of the goat.

ELTON FAX: When I think of the Renaissance, the Harlem Renaissance, I think of the basketball team of that name. The Rennies were a forerunner of the Globetrotters. They were a great advertisement for Harlem in those days.

HOWARD "STRETCH" JOHNSON: The Renaissance basketball team was owned by Bob Douglas, who was a very militant black entrepreneur. He owned the Renaissance Casino and the Renaissance Bar & Grill. When he took over the Renaissance Theater and Ballroom, he saw it as an entertainment center in line with the poetry and literary explosion, which was known as the Harlem Renaissance. The Renaissance Big Five basketball team was a part of that surge, which some called the advent of the New Negro.

My father was a very fine professional basketball player. He played with a group called the Puritans, which later became the Renaissance Big Five, with Fats Jenkins and Pappy Ricks. My father taught Pappy Ricks how to make his carom shot from the side.

Paul Robeson played with Alpha fraternity against my father when my father was playing with St. Christopher's, another semipro team that was popular in the '20s. Paul was a great figure. People used to swarm around him when he walked out on the street. He was the inspiration in every walk of life. Those blacks who went in for law had respect for his being a Phi Beta Kappa at Columbia University. Those who aspired to be successful in the athletic field had him as an exemplar with his record at Rutgers, where he got fifteen varsity letters—more varsity A's than any individual who ever went to Rutgers—in football, basketball, track, and baseball.

My father played baseball for some of the black barnstorming teams against all-star white teams which were composed of people like Babe Ruth and other top stars from the big leagues, and most often they would beat 'em.

Before World War I, he played on a team that was comprised of the redcaps at Grand Central, half of whom were Ph.D.s who couldn't get work in the white world, so they smashed baggage at Grand Central Station. They formed a very talented team called the Grand Central Redcaps.

He also played with the Lincoln Giants, who later became the New York Black Yankees. He would take me to Catholic Protectory Oval, which was over behind where Harlem Hospital is located now. That's where the Lincoln Giants used to play. I don't think the bleachers held more than 500 people. They played against the Wilmington Potomacs, the Pittsburgh Crawfords, the Baltimore Elite Giants, the Hillsdale Giants. There were some great teams at that time.

BRUCE NUGENT: There was a woman in Washington who was fantastic. She was a very good poet, Georgia Douglas Johnson, and she had salons. I met Langston at her home. We took to each other immediately. Someone wrote once that Langston and I were lovers. It is at least hinted that I had a crush on Langston. And the hint may have more truth to it than I used to think, because, as I look back on it, Langston had a physical appearance that was everything I liked at the time. He looked Latin, and he looked like me complexion-wise. Yes, I had quite a crush on Langston. Years later, I discovered Langston had a very strange kind of unnecessary envy of me, that I seemed to be so free and easy sexually, and apparently he wasn't. We kind of had a crush on each other.

We spent that whole night walking from his mother's house to my grandmother's house. They were only four blocks away, but we weren't anywhere near through talking, so we just walked each other back and forth all night long. That was the thing that was beautiful about Langston. There were always things to talk about. That's the night *Fire!!* was born. Hall Johnson, at whose house I was living, had written a spiritual called "Fire!":

*Fire, fire, Lawd fire burn my soul.*
*Fire, fire, Lawd fire burn my soul.*
*I ain't been good. I ain't been clean.*
*I been stinkin' low down mean*
*But fire, fire, Lawd fire burn my soul.*

Both Langston and I were very fond of that. As we were walking back and forth, I think it was Langston who said we—by *we* I mean blacks—should have a magazine of our own, in which they could have art, in which they could express themselves however they felt.

He was going to be coming to New York to receive a Krigwa Award—that was the award the *Crisis* used to give—and he invited me along. After the ceremony, Langston said the best food in New York was at the YWCA, so into the YWCA went we, and I must say that the smell of those biscuits and corn bread was wonderful. As we were walking along, Langston said, "Oh, there's Wallie Thurman." There were only two newspapers that I really cared for at that time, the St. Louis *Dispatch* and the *Christian Science Monitor*. Then I heard that the editor of the *Monitor* was black, and it was Wallie Thurman, but I was so disappointed when I saw him. I was brought up in Washington, where you can't be black and be any good. So my heart went down into my shoes. I was so disappointed. I said, "You mean that black boy with the sneering nose?"

I was awful, and I was so ashamed of myself afterwards, because I prided myself on having no prejudice. Later, I went to Wallie and apologized.

Anyway, there was a wonderful woman named Iolanthe Sydney who ran an unemployment office. She owned two houses, one on 136th Street and one on Lenox Avenue, and the one on 136th Street she, in essence, turned over to artists who were all indigent. She told me to go over there, at 267. "Because," she said, "you'll never be able to pay any rent."

I went there. Wallie was living there. It was bohemian—267 was a house that just felt free to be in, because she saw to it that you were free. She thought all artists needed to be indigent, so they didn't have to pay like other people did, and she elected herself to be one who did pay.

HELEN BROWN: When I first came to Harlem, Bruce was living down in the Village, which was a magnificent bohemian place. He said he was sleeping under the fountain at Washington Square. He was just living day to day. He was very much bohemian. I didn't find Harlem to be bohemian at all.

I was born February 4, 1898, in Quincy, Illinois. I went to Howard University, in Washington, where I majored in business administration. The other course I took was music.

In Harlem, I met people who had homes where we read poetry. The younger people who were doing things would meet and sit on the floor and have peanuts, and they'd read their plays and poems. You'd meet all types of people, and you'd see how knowledgeable they were. At Hall Johnson's, the door was always open, and people just dropped in. There was nothing special about it.

If you met anybody, Langston Hughes, let's say, "C'mon, we're going up to Countee's" or "We're going here." Everybody was there. Zora Neale Hurston was a classmate of mine, and she'd just say, "C'mon along."

They were hoping that they could constructively help each other. They had to push, push, and push to even get their works read by the publishers. They were fresh from school, and they were trying to sell their wares. They were hoping against hope.

BRUCE NUGENT: We talked so much, people used to say, "Don't you do anything but talk? Why don't you do something?"

"Like what?"

"Like use some of the stuff that you talk about."

"Use how?"

After a while, I didn't want to talk anymore, and I would go upstairs and lay down under Wallie's bed and go to sleep. It was one of the many places I dropped in. I got to know a lot of Wallie's secrets that way. You really get to know a person when you sleep under his bed.

HELEN BROWN: Among downtown people, blacks were in vogue if they had gone to school, like Walter White, James Weldon Johnson, or Jessie Fauset. [*She says in affected voice:*] "Ooh, how extraordinary, extraordinary."

People would always invite people like Langston and Countee to dinner. Don't you see? "This lovely colored poet."

And, "Oh, dear, that was magnificent. Just imagine, we have one Negro who is singing in our church choir. Do you know him? He is a singer, a baritone, you know."

Or, "Do you know Miss Anderson? She has a voice that is heard but every hundred years. Oh, she's mag*nee*ficent. Have you ever met her?"

Actually, her sister had a better voice. She sang with great soul, but she was like a water barrel. When Marian walked out on stage, she was elegant.

BRUCE NUGENT: There was nobody to be editor of *Fire!!* but Wallie Thurman. Langston and I spoke to him about it. We did most of the work on it at 267. We had done an unspeakable thing when we published. There were things in *Fire!!* that you didn't talk about, like the story about a prostitute or homosexuality. It was a scandalous magazine that didn't really have enough weight to be a scandal. So many people hated it. I remember soon after it appeared, Wallie and I went up to a restaurant in Sugar Hill, and there was Paul Robeson and his wife sitting there. She didn't like it at all, and Paul didn't want to say anything in front of her. He just turned his head toward us and gave us a wink.

I think everybody was upset who hadn't done it who thought they should have, like Du Bois. I remember Du Bois did ask, "Did you have to write about homosexuality? Couldn't you write about colored people? Who cares about homosexuality?" I said, "You'd be surprised how good homosexuality is. I love it." Poor Du Bois.

That kind of criticism bothered Wallie, but it didn't bother me. See, Wallie had a problem. He didn't like being black. He drank himself to death because he couldn't live with what he found life to be. It must have been very difficult for Wallie, because he had the dual problems of never being accepted in black society or white society, and it was tragic for him.

I've been asked how I was able to write so openly about homosexuality in 1926, and I've never been able to make anybody understand that Langston and I said there should be a magazine where we could say whatever we wanted to. Harlem was very much like the Village. People did what they wanted to do with whom they wanted to do it. You didn't get on the rooftops and shout, "I fucked my wife last night." So why would you get on the roof and say, "I loved prick." You didn't. You just did what you wanted to do. Nobody was in the closet. There wasn't any closet.

The '60s were like the '20s in many ways. I've thought seriously of writing something about the '60s called "The '20s Revisited." They were alike in every way.

N O R A  M A I R : My husband knew of the young writers Langston Hughes and the Jamaican poet Claude McKay.

*If we must die—let it not be like hogs*
  *Hunted and penned in an inglorious spot,*
*While round us bark the mad and hungry dogs,*
  *Making their mock at our accursed lot.*
*If we must die—oh, let us nobly die,*
  *So that our precious blood may not be shed*
*In vain; then even the monsters we defy*
  *Shall be constrained to honor us though dead!*

*Oh, kinsmen! We must meet the common foe;*
  *Though far outnumbered, let us still be brave,*
*And for their thousand blows deal one death-blow!*
  *What though before us lies the open grave?*
*Like men, we'll face the murderous, cowardly pack,*
  *Pressed to the wall, dying, but—fighting back!*

My husband quoted that poem of McKay's all the time. When we came here, so many terrible things were happening in the South. Even today, I hate to think of them. We would always say we must fight back.

My husband had been a bellhop in a hotel in Cuba. During Prohibition, Americans used to go down there to wallow in rum. This man got drunk. Ernest took him to his room and took his wallet and had it put in the hotel safe. The next morning, the man asked to see him, and told him if he ever wanted to come to America, he could have a job as an interpreter for Dunn Pen.

So he brought him here, and he worked there for a while as an interpreter. He went to the YMCA down there to apply for a room, and they said they were sorry, they don't handle colored people. He would have to go to Harlem. From that day on, he had absolutely nothing to do with the YMCA.

We were married in September 1925. At that point, he was working for Garvey's newspaper and he was also driving an elevator. I don't know how they met up with each other. I just know Garvey was preaching, and he was listening, because we all had to listen to what Garvey was saying in those days.

He was the paper's business manager, but lots of times he didn't get paid. He also wrote editorials and news stories for the paper. It was called the *Negro World*. [*She takes some yellowed issues from a drawer in the dining room and reads from one of her husband's editorials:*] "Now, Mr. Negro America, go ahead and fight the program of African Nationalism. You don't need any better protection than is afforded you by the high-minded and unprejudiced enforcers of U.S. laws. Maybe you don't, and maybe I'm a Chinaman."

NAOMI WASHINGTON: I thought Garvey was terrible. My aunt bought these bricks that he sold. A book was made up of bricks. And each brick was a dollar. I said to my aunt, "When are you going back to Africa?"

She said, "I don't know. It's one of those things that one day you'll do."

I said, "Oh, yeah, well you're sure going without me."

DOLL THOMAS: Marcus Garvey had a wonderful idea, but he didn't know what the devil to do with it. The United States government couldn't run a steamship line, so what gave him the idea that he could have a steamship line and then take all the Negroes back to where they come from? They didn't wanna go anyhow.

He made all his followers officers and dressed 'em up in pretty uniforms and let 'em parade up and down the damn place. That's what people liked. That's the secret of bein' successful with Negroes, especially those Negroes. They had come from the West Indies, and they see the way people live. Here comes a man who makes everybody a general, gives 'em a uniform and marches 'em up and down the street. You thought you were the biggest person in the world.

NORA MAIR: My husband never went along with the idea of returning to Africa, but when it came to stark prejudice, he was right there with him. Garvey was militant, like my husband, much more militant than, let's say, the NAACP. I had only seen Garvey once, even though my husband worked for him. Ernest took me to see him. I thought he was a little too loud. But it was the first place I ever saw a picture of a black Christ, because that was what he had on the wall.

His followers were all dressed outlandishly. He had on a hat with many colors. He was wearing a sash and gold braids. I think the uniform was supposed to be African. Right after that, Garvey started to go downhill. He was a good man. Garvey had his faults, but he had good ideas—the idea of having pride in our race. We should not be ashamed of our race, because there is so much our race has contributed to this world, and it's all there for us to find out. We don't because the white man is there to make sure we don't find it out. In that way, he was a positive influence for both Americans and West Indians.

DOLL THOMAS: There was another fella who did more than Garvey did for the people—Father Divine. He bought property up in New York State and out in Long Island and took all the Negroes and made 'em farmers. They raised their own food, and you could go in his place, and for fifteen or twenty cents you could buy a dinner with seconds and everything else. His food was very good. I wish for even five or ten dollars I could buy a meal like that anywhere up here.

ELTON FAX: Did I eat in Father Divine's? Let me tell you, I went into Father Divine's one day and I said, "Please, sister, I don't have any change. I haven't been paid. I wonder if you would trust me for a meal."

She said, "Father doesn't trust, but Father will permit me to give you a meal."

I said, "That's truly wonderful, sister. Bring it on."

It was good stuff.

NAOMI WASHINGTON: It angered me when people said he was God. They had to be nuts. I've seen the girls standing there fanning him. One woman said to me, "Just because he's black, you don't think he's God."

I said, "If Father Divine is God, here I come, hell." This woman had about $6,000 or $7,000. She was a West Indian woman. They were very good savers. She turned over every dime to him.

I asked her, "What makes you think he's God? Because he preaches? Because he gives you a free meal?"

That he did. Oh, my lord, he fed a lot of people. And when I tell you it was good food—I went. As much as you could eat. If you were hungry when you went in, when you came out, if you didn't eat for two days, you had enough.

•   •   •

MARION MOORE DAY: I was born in Brooklyn in 1902. We came up to Harlem after World War I. My father bought two houses, 228 and 230 on 135th Street. He made one into an office and the other we lived in. He was the editor and publisher of *New York Age*, which was a black newspaper. We were the only black paper with our own plant. We had our own press way down in the basement. Every Wednesday, the people used to stand outside looking at the paper rolling off there.

The *Age* was a respected paper. It went out through the mail around the country. My father was also greatly respected. The bums in the street used to tip their hats to him. "Good day, Mr. Moore." It was nice having a father like that. Then again, it was also a pain in the neck. There were a lot of things I would have liked to have gone and done, but I couldn't. Before we were married, I asked my husband if we could go to Smalls'. We got in, but I wasn't there very long before Mr. Smalls came. "Young lady, what are you doing here?"

I said, "I'm with my boyfriend."

"I see. Well, it's time for you to go home now. Good night." He was afraid of my father. My father went to those places like Smalls' and the Cotton Club. They were afraid of him. They were afraid of the paper. When my father died, he even got a great big floral piece from Owney Madden.

My parents had eighteen children, and I was the eighteenth. My mother was a tiny person. Once, I said to my father, "Do you ever let that woman out of bed?"

He always called me Miss Marion. He said, "Miss Marion, I don't want to hear you say that again, because I don't think that's very nice or in good taste."

That was a beautiful era. We had nice dances and parties. We also had to do work. My father was interested in the Katy Ferguson

Home for unmarried mothers on 130th Street. So all the girls that I went with would go and take them for walks.

I would say to my father, "Why do we have to take out those girls with their big stomachs?"

He said, "Because they need to walk and because they need someone to walk with them, and this I'm asking you to do."

I didn't want to do it but I did it, and then after that I got used to it. They were kids, sometimes twelve or thirteen years old.

NAOMI WASHINGTON: I can remember when I was fifteen, every other girl on the block was pregnant. My mother said to me, "Naomi, you're no different than those girls. But when you were born, I prayed, and I asked God to let you live and I would raise you with him. Now, please, don't disgrace me."

That stuck with me as long as I could remember. I had boys approach me, but I could hear my mother say, "Unh-unh." But girls were getting pregnant. Some of them were sent away. I'm sure some of the girls got abortions, but I was married a long time before I knew what an abortion was. Fats had two children when he was seventeen. Both of the women were fighting over him. He had to make up his mind, because he couldn't marry both of them, but he married Edith.

After a while, Fats had left home, and she had him in court. He promised the judge that he was going to give her so much, and he didn't. *[She laughs.]* And they put him over there on Rikers Island. I went over there to see him. Fats said, "All I do is drink liquor and play the piano. I'm havin' a good time."

My father died while he was in there. They wouldn't let him come to the funeral unless these detectives came with him, but he refused to go to his father's funeral in handcuffs.

Fats loved his women. He didn't know anything about birth controls. Girls didn't either. They just got pregnant. His valet said once, "Let me tell you about your brother. Every state, every city affords a new wife. He has a wife in every city."

MARION DAY: We didn't have any problems with the boys. None of us wanted to go to the Katy Ferguson Home. The boys were safe. Either they were afraid of our parents or they respected us. It was one or the other. I'm not sure which. *[She laughs.]*

There were very distinct class divisions in Harlem society. A'Lelia Walker had an adopted daughter, and she wanted friends for her, so she knew my father and she called him, saying she would like to start a group so that her daughter could meet the kind of people she would like for her to meet. She was very particular about the boys she invited over. I guess we were stuck-up. We felt we were something special.

We started what we called the Debutantes Group. We went to parties and dances. Sometimes we had parties up at Villa Lewaro, A'Lelia's mansion. We were always chaperoned. Mrs. A. Philip Randolph was one of our chaperones. She would take a drink though, and she didn't do much chaperoning. We didn't have to duck away from her, she'd duck away from us. We wore beautiful sequined dresses and fur coats to these dances. The people were beautiful, and we had lovely parties up at Madame Walker's.

We didn't bother with people who were outside our circle. There were very few dark people among our friends. Our group put a show on at the Lafayette, and there was one girl who was very, very dark, and when she was paired with me, they asked me, "Do you mind?" because she was so dark. She had dark skin and "bad" hair. Most people had their hair straightened. People were very conscious of hair and color. Except if you were somebody. Then they paid no attention to it.


ELTON FAX: Color wasn't the only problem. I remember a comedy routine that was popular at the Apollo as an outgrowth of the West Indian migration to Harlem. Two actors were onstage. Each was dressed as a woman, and each engaged in a heated exchange onstage about something minor. One would call the other "monkeychaser." The other would say, "Don't call me a nigger." All this sort of thing. It laid the audience out in the aisles, because they did it in dialect of the Caribbean and the dialect of the South.

It was funny, but it was really rather tragic, too, because in the final analysis—and this is what Garvey understood so well—that while blacks born on the mainland here were at swords' points with blacks from the Caribbean, and vice versa, neither had any right to do this, and neither had the edge over the other. It split the community in half.

In that period, light-skinned blacks were preferable in the employ of whites to black blacks, especially in their homes. I grew up in this atmosphere:

*If you're white you're white.*
*If you're yellow you're mellow.*
*If you're brown you stick around.*
*If you're black you head back.*

That was one of the things we said, and I realized how this can cripple a people. This was a rather strong thing in the black community when I came up—this business of light skin and good hair. In Harlem, for instance, there were no black women on the chorus line of the Cotton Club. They were all light gals. Jo Baker, who was in *Shuffle Along*—and Eubie Blake told me this himself—was such a show woman that she broke out of the mold. She was not black, but she was not white either. She was a high yaller.

STRETCH JOHNSON: Most of the girls at the Cotton Club were light or tan. Louis Armstrong's wife, Lucille, was one of the more chocolate-colored girls. That was at variance from the general pattern of tan to high yellow that was the desirable skin color. They had a number of songs which sort of stated the case for the public. Cab Calloway sang two of them—"Cotton Colored Gal of Mine" and "She's Tall, She's Tan and She's Terrific."

There were social clubs that catered exclusively to light blacks, like the Alphaphiles, a fraternity that was difficult for a very dark black to get into. There was a color hierarchy among the black fraternities during that time. Alpha, then Kappa, then Sigma, then Omega. The Omega fraternity were usually among the darkest of the college fellas. They were nicknamed "The Dog-assed Negroes." If tempers were frayed, people would call each other names— "black son of a bitch," "black bastard." The response would be "you half-white mother fucker" or whatever. That thinking reflected the penetration of racist thinking into the black community.

MARION WARNER: It goes way back to slave days. The people who lived in the house, they called them the house niggers. And the ones in the field, they called them the field niggers. And the house niggers didn't associate with the field niggers.

If you were dark, you were supposed to marry a lighter person. I had a grandmother who was very fair, and she felt that my father should have married a lighter person. My mother was part American Indian, so she was darker, and she had sort of straightish hair.

When my sisters went down to visit my grandmother in Raleigh, North Carolina, they were not allowed to play around the corner with the children that were not mixed.

ISABEL POWELL: I believe that one of the reasons that Adam has been forgotten is that he was fair. I walked picket lines with this man. I know what he has done, and I know he does not get the accolades he should get because of his fair skin.

Adam's mother was a German woman. She was a Schaefer. Adam used to say, "I'm neither fish nor fowl." He said when he grew up in Harlem the Irish boys would beat him because he wouldn't admit being white, and the blacks would beat him because he wasn't black enough to be black.

In those days, Old Man Powell used to preach that God made the most beautiful flower garden in the world when he made the colored race. He made 'em from alabaster white to ebony black and all the colors in between. His father was light. He was an American Indian. In church, he was a dramatic speaker. People told me that when the old man spoke on prayer-meeting night— and in those days they wore the celluloid collars and cuffs—he would get so wrapped up in the preaching that when he would throw his arms out, his cuffs would go flying out into the audience, and the women would grab them like a football.

DOLL THOMAS: Bein' light-complexioned, too, made it worse for me. Thank God none of that crap bothers me. To get down to actual facts, my people came from English and Indians. I was related to Lord Nelson of England through his son. Lord Nelson sent his son over here to look after his colony in America, and he got mixed up with a little Indian maiden, and along came the strain that I came from.

In show business, we even used to write shows about it. We

had one very successful show entitled *Yeller Gal.* Used to open up
with two comedians, Slim Evanson and John Mason, on the stage.
[*He recites from memory:*]

> Esau, what's the prettiest thing you ever saw in this real
> roun' world?
> Oh, man, a real high yeller gal.
> No, boy, I'm talkin' about pretty women. You must mean
> one of those sealskin browns.
> No, man, it's a yeller.
> Oh, man, they ain't no way in the worl' you can tell me that
> a yeller's all right. 'Cause when a yeller woman get thirty-five
> years old, she gonna grow up just like tripe.

And the patter would go on just like that. Coupla girls would
come on the stage with their backs turned. One of 'em turns around.
She was brown, and the other one was light. Then the two fellers
would come back on:

> See, I told you, boy.
> I don't care what you told me, man. A yeller put me out
> one time when snow was but two foot high.
> Just when I was about thawed out a brownskin happened
> by.
> And she took me to a house. I swear she had pork chops
> stacked that high.

So at that time, another girl walked on the stage with her back
to the audience.

> Man, I'm gonna betcha two dollars that that's a yeller.
> Man, I know that gal is yeller, 'cause she's dressed so neat.
> Oh, man, I can tell she's brown. Just look at them cute
> little feet.

Just about that time, the girl would turn around. She's made
up in cork. She says now:

I ain't yeller, and I ain't brown.
But there ain't no way that you can turn me down.
'Cause some of the raggedest, hungriest women that I seen here in this town
Are some of the same high yellers or sealskin brown.
And another thing. You take my tip.
What it takes to carry you is a dollar through this world, and Sweet Mama's got it on her hip.

And the house would go wild. All of that went out with high button shoes. Have you ever watched crabs in a basket? There'd be a whole basket of crabs. They're just as peaceful as anything in the world, but just let one try to climb out, and, goddamn, all hell will break loose. The whole goddamn basket would reach up and grab him and pull him back, and that's just the same way with the colored people. In other words, I was tryin' to be better than they were, by bein' an electrician. I should have been a waiter, a porter, or somethin' like that. To them, I was bein' uppity.

HELEN BROWN: Most of the people who were light-skinned were capable of going downtown and getting a job easier than others. Many people passed. McCreery's didn't hire black salespeople. I know this girl, when her mother went down there, she couldn't speak to her. She'd pass her a note.

There was another man, who worked in Macy's. Someone wanted a job, so he went to the man who was head of the department. The man said he didn't hire colored salesmen, but the man said, "Oh, but you do." He took him down to the shoe department and pointed out my friend who was passing. "There he is."

The manager almost died of hydrophobia. He took the salesman, and said, "Come, I want to talk to you. You didn't tell me you were colored."

He said, "You didn't ask me."

"Come and get your pay."

He left, and we don't know where he went to live.

ELTON FAX: This went on in Harlem society. If white folks approved of one and disapproved of the other, who wants to be among the disapproved? But in the final count, high yaller or not, we all knew that when the chips were down, white people put us all in one bag, and labeled the bag "Nigger." Garvey knew this, and that is why the Garvey movement was so popular among the masses.

DOLL THOMAS: Back in those days, the biggest joke that always got a big laugh at the theater was nappy hair:

> Man, you got mailman hair.
> Mailman hair? Yeah, wha do ya mean?
> Each knot's got its own route.

For some reason or other there were some colored people that came from foreign countries who were dark and had straight hair, so it just made them look better cosmetically to the other person. You used hair straightener or, with Madame Walker's thing, you used a hot comb, and that straightened the hair. With men, their compound was Vaseline mixed with lye. That was almost like bein' in an electric chair that was left on too long.

NAOMI WASHINGTON: I was a little girl when Madame Walker's product came out. Everybody had it done. My mother had a friend that took that course under her. She asked my mother to let her do my hair. Mama said yes. I was very tender-headed and afraid, because she had these hot combs. I was crying. She wasn't hurting me, but I was just afraid she would. When she was done, Papa said I looked like his grandmother, who was an Indian. I liked the way it looked, but I didn't like those hot combs.

DOLL THOMAS: The worst thing in the world was with the women. The back of their hair was what they called the kitchen. They could get the sides fixed and stuff like that, but they'd always leave that. That was a good joke for a long time:

> Child, your hair looks certainly good.
> Oh, yeah? Madame Walker just came over.
> Yeah, but she forgot to walk through your kitchen.

The house would just laugh. All of that stuff has been outlawed by people. They got more education.

BRUCE NUGENT: My God, to be like white people you had to do something with that hair. That's how Madame Walker made all that money.

A'Lelia Walker was like pigeon shit. She was everywhere. She was going to have a place where indigent artists could buy a meal cheaply. She had all these places, and she owned this house on 136th Street that she opened to indigent artists. Of course, when she opened, everything cost so much that nobody could go there to eat. It was called the Dark Tower, after Countee's column.

A'Lelia suffered from poor-little-rich-girl syndrome. She didn't know what it was like to not have money, and she didn't know what it was like to spend it in any way that was helpful to anybody, including herself. She didn't know how to spend her money, and we were only too pleased to teach her how to spend it, especially on ourselves.

MARION DAY: When A'Lelia's daughter got married, I was one of the bridesmaids. When we came down to Harlem the day of the wedding, the streets were lined with people, because they knew A'Lelia's daughter was getting married at St. Philip's. The church was packed, and people were waiting out in the street trying to get in, just because she was A'Lelia's daughter.

When I got married, it was really my father's wedding. There were so many people, when I got into the church, they were out on the stairways. They weren't invited, but they came anyhow. After the wedding, Casper Holstein [a numbers man and benefactor in Harlem] came to the house to see what gifts I had, and the next day I got this huge silver service from one of the very good stores downtown. Then Philip Payton came to see what I had, and he sent me a silver coffee set. All these people came to see what I had so they could outdo the other fellow. A'Lelia Walker gave me a banquet cloth that cost $500. I said, "What the hell am I going to do with a banquet cloth? I'm not going to entertain." I gave most of the things to my children so they could enjoy them.

◆ ◆ ◆

HAROLD ELLIS: Old Man Taylor was a doctor on 136th Street, and he started throwing some work to me. I learned more medicine from him than I learned in medical school. But doctors around here were having a hard time themselves. The black people who had money in those days were the schoolteachers and the garment workers, and they didn't believe in black doctors. They went down to Park Avenue to see their white doctors. They were brainwashed into thinking that a white doctor was a superior doctor.

In those days, a house call was five dollars. An office visit was three and sometimes two. On Thanksgiving morning in 1923, I had to go across the street to some people I knew to borrow a nickel to drive down to 99th Street to see a patient. The patient didn't have any money, so I had to walk back all the way up to 136th Street. Friends of mine were having a fine Thanksgiving party, but I didn't let them know I was broke or anything.

Little by little, things improved. I was finally able to cover my rent. My practice was mostly middle-class and native-born. I really grew up here, you know. I was more American. I also had white patients. They came from every damn place.

HERMAN WARNER: I started practicing in '29, but I had the groundwork of a practice by then. There were a lot of West Indians in Harlem, and I knew many of them quite well, so for me, there was never really any problem. There were times when my practice was pretty low, but I was never starved.

It was common in those days for a young physician to be attached to a pharmacy. The pharmacist would send you calls, and you would send him prescriptions. One day, I got a call from this pharmacist. He said a woman came in and she was frantic. Her husband had not urinated in two days. I had heard about this inability to urinate, so I went back to the office, and I sterilized a very, very slender—but not hollow—tube, and I packed it in my bag.

When I got there, there must have been about twenty people in the house, and they were praying in groups. They all came to share in her grief, because they were sure this man was going to die. I was pretty sure I knew what the problem was, so I just said to myself, "Boy, I'm going to make a grandstand play." *[He laughs.]*

I was very businesslike. The first thing we always holler for is hot water and towels, because that looks good. The man was lying on a couch with both feet and side extended to the wall. That gave him a little relief. Now if he had a locked kidney, I'd have to send him to the hospital, but I was praying it was a stricture, which I could fix with the tube. So I got the tube from my bag, and I passed it in, and it blocked, so I knew it was a stricture. Then I passed another one, and sure enough it opened. Oh, man, did it open! He urinated on me, on the wall, on the ground, and he started to be revived.

This old lady, she was one of the singing types, and she had been singing all along. When he urinated, she and her friends broke out into song, "Hallelujah, Hallelujah." Then she said, "Bless you, son, I never thought you had it in you." Mind you, the fee was three dollars. She gave me ten dollars. And after that, when I walked around the block, I was really a big shot. Man, she referred me to about 500 people.

HAROLD ELLIS: There were a few problems with the white doctors. In those days, at Bellevue and allied hospitals, graduates would spend their hospital year under supervision running the ambulances. Once, I had a patient who was ill with pneumonia. The intern, who was white, said, "Doctor, he hasn't got pneumonia."

I said, "You listen right there," and I showed him his mistake.

"Yes, he has pneumonia," he said. "That's very good for a black doctor."

I wanted to say, "You fucking son of a bitch." Now, I'd kick his ass. But I had to stand it. "Very good for a black doctor."

From 1920 to 1930—when they decided to open up Harlem Hospital for blacks—I worked in the clinic three afternoons a week for no money. It was the only way you could attain some standing. Then they took about six doctors to work in the clinic and gave them the first promotion upstairs. I had been working there while those fellows were in medical school, so I didn't think it was fair.

I complained and was referred to the secretary of the medical board—a *Hah*-vard man, the famous Louis Wright, the first colored police surgeon we had, a hell of a fella. So I went to see him. We talked over a bottle and so forth, and he said, "Harold, I'll tell you what I'm going to do. I'll see that you are promoted upstairs with the next batch. Does that satisfy you?"

I said it did.

Then he said, "Harold, there's an opening in neurology that I'd like you to take."

Out of spite, I said all right. Then he told me to study neuroanatomy under Oliver Strung, and I was still angry enough to say yes. I studied for fifteen years, and later I became chief of neuropsychology at Harlem Hospital. I have outdistanced all the fellows who went into general medicine. At one time, I was the only black neurologist on the Eastern Seaboard. It's down in the books that I am the sixth neuropsychiatrist in the United States that was black. If anybody told me in 1919, I'd have laughed, because I didn't want all those damn crazy people.

* * *

HELEN BROWN: I was with the Hall Johnson Choir, which was formed primarily to perpetuate Negro spirituals. Hall Johnson was a magnificent scholar. He was an excellent violinist and pianist. He was an elegant, elegant man, and he was also as simple as an old shoe.

The spirituals were looked down upon by blacks and whites. People didn't think there was any particular quality to them. They didn't know they were the soul of the black man. They claimed that their words and their language weren't "ultra-ultra." They were in very bad English. They didn't know they were better English because they had more meaning. My stepmother used to say, "What are you going to sing those things for?"

Because of the choir, more and more people started to sing them, until everybody was trying to sing them. We performed with the New York Philharmonic Orchestra with Toscanini three times. To see a group of Negro singers with the New York Philharmonic was a feat and a curiosity. It shouldn't have been. We were people with voices. We sang operas. People were surprised that we could sing other things besides spirituals.

I've heard blues all my life. My stepmother didn't like to hear blues. We had to be kind of careful at our house with the blues. I tried to play blues for Mr. Johnson, and he said, "You're trying to get in the groove. You got to swing, swing, swing. When you're blue, you're not singing fast, you're meditating." [*Slowly:*] "Man, I'm blue." Blues are really trouble. The minute they speak, they don't even have to say it, but you can tell. "He's feeling bad, real bad." That's blues.

DOLL THOMAS: We did dramas at the Lafayette because the white people hated you bad enough, but the colored people hated you worse if you sang blues. Blues was figured as the devil's music, and it was chastised by the church for years. About the only real place you could go where most of the real blues developed was in the bordellos or whorehouses. It's like everything else: just like colored performers got accepted, eventually the blues got accepted.

This was from 1913 into the '20s. The '20s was about the beginnin' of the blues. The queen of the blues was Bessie Smith. Bessie traveled with her own group of musicians. That gave her a leg up because all theaters where colored performers played were dumps, and they had what was jokingly referred to as a three-piece orchestra: a piano, stool, and drums. But with her, she had a cornet, trumpets, and a saxophone player, and she had a very popular musician leadin' the organization called Johnny Dunn, which of course helped her popularity.

She was illiterate, ignorant, and arrogant—the trouble we had to try to get her to the studio to make records. If it hadn't been for somebody like John Hammond, nobody in the world would have heard of Bessie Smith, 'cause nobody in the world would take that shit. She wouldn't come to the studio. She didn't want her voice recorded—broke up microphones, broke up equipment. And we had a hard time gettin' her to perform. It was just one of her moods. She didn't wanna go. She just wanted to rest. [*He lowers his voice:*] "Lemme rest!"

I was with John when he went through all that. He put $20,000 in a bank account for Bessie when times really got tough for her in the '30s. She was really on the balls of her ass then, but she was just beginnin' to come back when she got killed in an automobile accident. I lived with Bessie. I suffered with Bessie. She was really an artist.

I first heard the blues in the bordellos and the whorehouses. All the piano players in those joints, they didn't call 'em piano players, they called 'em professors, and being that the theater business was so segregated, there was practically no place else to go. I knew Scott Joplin very well. I saw Joplin in the whorehouses in St. Louis before he was so crippled by syphilis. There were plenty of piano players and plenty of musicians who could play as well as Joplin could, but the thing that made him different from all the rest, he was the only one that could write the notes on paper.

We opened up the Lafayette with a musical, *Darktown Follies*. It was received so damn well that we bought syncopation to the white music. We even had a number that was put in Ziegfeld's follies, "The Darktown Strutters' Ball." The syncopated music was ragtime music with an orchestra. They didn't call it ragtime, on account of the churches. That was the devil's music, so you gave it another name.

EDDIE BAREFIELD: My people always had music in the house. They had the blues and the jazz records of that period and ragtime. The first jazz band I really remember was Fletcher Henderson's. Jazz started to develop with his band—I mean our kind of jazz, swing jazz. Fletcher's music really inspired me. I listened to Coleman Hawkins, who was his saxophone player, and that's how I learned how to play. I listened to his records, and then I would practice his solos. He was the best up to the day he died, because he graduated along with the times.

I had a teacher who taught me the chromatic scale, but mostly I played by ear for about six years. Then I started playing with bands around there and Chicago, Minneapolis, Milwaukee, Kansas City, Cleveland, and Detroit, and I learned how to read. I would always get in the local house band playing, because I could read good and play lead saxophone. I liked to go from place to place, just get on a train or bus and go. I liked the different sounds of the different towns. Every place you'd go, you had plenty to do, but after a while you'd just get tired and leave and go someplace else.

NAOMI WASHINGTON: Fats didn't start playing jazz until he met Jimmy Johnson. James P. was the best, and Fats followed him foot by foot. Sometimes James P. would come over to Fats' house. Fats would be playing, and James would say, "No. Get up. I'll show you how to do it."

Just jabbing with one another. Naturally, James P. would sit down, and he'd play his version.

"Aha," Fats said. "Now you get up."

And they would carry on like that.

I loved Fats' playing. He used to relieve this woman at the Lincoln, and he'd play the music for the picture. Then they got this organ. Now Fats took over that organ. You play as many notes with your foot as you do with your hands, and he had it all down after six lessons.

When Mama was sick, Fats used to come in early and play, and Mama would think, "Well, he's in for the night." He'd go back out as soon as she fell asleep. He did that until the day she died.

My mother was a very good singer. We all more or less liked to sing, and we all liked to sing while he played. The neighbors liked to hear Fats play the piano. Instead of shouting, "Stop that music," they'd say, "Raise that window, let us hear." He didn't have to raise that window. They could hear when it was down, but they enjoyed it.

My mother had her first heart attack when she heard Fats was playing at the Lincoln. My brothers tried to explain to my mother to face it, that's all that he was going to do. He just wanted to be a musician. Fats was playing at the Lincoln Theater when my mother died. We always thought that contributed to my mother's death. She was just forty-nine.

People would go to the theater just to hear Fats play. There used to be a fellow who used to sit up in the balcony, and when Fats would play, this boy would whistle along, and when he did, you could hear a pin drop.

HERMAN WARNER: I used to see Fats at the Lincoln. He was really in a class by himself. I am a piano enthusiast. I think piano is my first love, even above medicine. I used to follow a lot of the piano men, especially the classical performers. Fats was great, you know. This is what he'd do. He would go off into a jazz number. He'd play something that unless you were paralyzed, you couldn't possibly sit still, and then he'd calm down and play Chopin. This man was a rare type.

◆ ◆ ◆

ISABEL POWELL: Adam and I met at Eastertime when I was on Broadway in a show called *Harlem*. Every time he came in from Colgate we saw each other. When he graduated, the old man sent him to Europe to get him away from me, because I was a show girl—a girl that danced and showed her legs.

When he came back, the old man took him before the deacon board and told him he couldn't be a minister, and Adam told him, "Well, Dad, I don't want the church if I can't have Isabel. We love each other." To a deacon, they stood up in deference to Adam, and the old man knew there was just no way now he was going to stop it.

When I met Adam, I knew to remain with him I had to be baptized, and I was. All the girls from the Cotton Club were up in the balcony. When the old man put me down in the water and held his hands over my face, I was worried he might drown me. Actually, he was very sweet.

We got married at high noon on March 5, 1933. You couldn't get a cab anywhere in Harlem that day. The cabdriver would say, "You going to the wedding? Can't take you." It was too crowded. They sold rental space in the windows across the street.

I was married by four ministers. The old man knew I had been married before. He was fixing it up so this one would last, so he had four of them tie it up. They all stood up there to have their say to seal it—so they thought. After the ceremony, I shook over 3,000 hands. My wrists swelled up like that. They loved me to death, 'cause after I was baptized, I was suddenly legitimate. The way the wind blows, that's the way people go.

There was no reception, but my mother and some of the ladies of the church made something like 500 pounds of fruitcake in little white boxes tied with a ribbon. Each lady, gent, or child that shook my hand got a little box of fruitcake.

MARION WARNER: When Adam would walk down the aisle, it was very dramatic. His robe would be billowing out. I said to him once, "When I saw you coming down the aisle, I could swear you had a little fan in there." The girls would be sitting in the front row. He was a handsome fellow, and he liked the girls, too.

ISABEL POWELL: The women used to sit there and watch Adam. I gave them all the room they wanted, but I had no problems. It was a good twelve years. I had a marvelous time. I gave up show business when we got married. When we were divorced, it was just one of those things. It was just a man seeking more power, and he figured this was a way to get it. Still, I was surprised. I went down to Cafe Society with him and heard this woman play. I didn't know who she was. But Hazel Scott was a star, and he left me for her. I was so bitter then, I didn't talk to anybody and I didn't go out for a year. When I was over it, I realized how stupid I was. He was a man, and he had power, and he wanted more. But I'll say this: If Adam had been with me, he wouldn't have died the way he did.

For him to have wound up in Bimini like that, it was really a sad ordeal.

ANNA MURPHY: I had a fire-escape romance. My future husband lived across the hall, and we would go out, and as soon as we hit the bottom stairs coming home, his mother and my mother would open the doors as we came up. "Did you have a nice time?"

So we told them we had a nice time, and we'd get inside. We'd give ourselves about an hour, and then we'd go to the front window and open it up and hold hands across the fire escape. That was as far as we went, and it was really romantic.

NAOMI WASHINGTON: I was twenty years old when I was married. I went to work in a dress company. When men earned eighteen or twenty-five dollars and thought they were making good money, I was making forty-five or fifty dollars, but I worked. This particular time, my husband told me, "I wear the pants in the family." Was he going to boss my money? Unh-unh. I left him. Then he went to my father, and my father called me and told me he didn't mean what he said and that I should go back. I went back that time. I did it three times, and the last time I called my father and I said, "This is it, and don't call me, 'cause I am not going back," and I didn't.

Fats was then living on 118th Street, and two or three o'clock in the morning, very often, we would be together. He liked his alcohol and so did I. We would get together, and he'd be playing and drinking. I never saw him drunk. He could drink the whiskey, not to the point where he couldn't carry on. At times, it seemed like he could do better when he had a few.

I was with him in his apartment the night he wrote "Jitterbug Waltz." Evidently, it was something that was in his head already. He was playing piano, and then he stopped and said, "Oh, that don't sound bad." And I said, "No, that sounds good."

He wrote those notes down. Then he'd play some more and write some more notes. I don't think, in all, it took him more than a day or two. I don't think he thought it would catch on like it really did. Just before that, he wrote this song "June Night." He sold it for seventy-five dollars, and it was a million-dollar hit.

"Ain't Misbehavin' " was my favorite song of his. He wrote the beginning of that when he was in jail. He also wrote a song called "Stop Kissing My Sister." I said, "Where did you get that idea?"

When he wrote "Your Feet's Too Big," I said, "You sure got a nerve. Your feet's too big? As big as your feet?" He wore size-thirteen pedal stompers.

BARNEY JOSEPHSON: I first started to go to Harlem to hear Duke Ellington at the Cotton Club. This was around 1924, long before I dreamed I would be in this business. I was in the retail shoe business. The shoe manufacturers liked to entertain the out-of-town buyers. I asked them to take me to the Cotton Club. They had Duke Ellington and Ethel Waters, a line of girls, all light-skinned—high yellow, as they said—and the customers were only white, though the waiters and the maitre d' were black.

The Berry Brothers performed there, too. God, they'd jump up to the ceiling and go down into splits. What they used to do was absolutely amazing. The Cotton Club had all the top black acts of the period. They were on, like, a circuit. If you wanted to play for Owney Madden, you had to play his theater in Chicago. The mob owned the circuit. They owned you.

The booze was all bootleg. In those days you could bring your bottle. You brought your own pint on your hip, and they would serve you a glass bucket of ice cubes and splits of ginger ale or soda water, just one little bottle, enough to make one highball, and they would charge you a good price on it. They made as much on that shit as they did on whiskey.

Most of the people who went up to Harlem were people who went to all the class places downtown—the jet set. And it's now four o'clock and it's curfew, and there's no place to go. For their kicks they went uptown. It was safe. I don't think they were particularly interested in jazz. It was a place to go.

STRETCH JOHNSON: You know, when they hit 110th Street in their limousines or cabs, they were immediately entering into a segregated community, so it was like taking a trip from their white world into another mysterious dark world.

The shows were very sophisticated, but they were cloaked in primitive and exotic garb. They were top-flight performances designed to appease the appetite for a certain type of black performance, the smiling black, the shuffling black, the black-faced black, the minstrel, coon-show atmosphere which existed. It was almost mandatory to have a jungle number with shake dancers with a lot of flesh exposed. And while it wasn't stated as such, certainly the light color of the flesh gave it a kind of exoticism and kind of forbidden-fruit quality being displayed that added to the excitement and exhilaration of the audience.

My sister was a very talented tap dancer. Elida Webb, who was a choreographer at the Cotton Club, heard of her through the grapevine. She told my mother and father that she'd like to use Winnie in the show *Flying Colors*, which was the first Broadway musical to have black and white chorus girls onstage at the same time. It was also Agnes De Mille's first Broadway show.

Elida liked her performance in *Flying Colors* so much, she asked the family if they would permit Winnie to work in the Cotton Club, which was night work. Winnie was only fifteen years old at the time, but Elida said Winnie could be escorted to the club by members of the family. So the family agreed to move to New York so we wouldn't have to make the long commute from New Jersey every night. The gangsters that owned the Cotton Club had no problem getting us an apartment in the building next door. We could hear Duke Ellington and Cab Calloway or whatever band was playing at the time through our bedroom walls, so Winnie was never late for a show.

DOLL THOMAS: I dealt with all of that crowd. I only had problems with some of Madden's men, like Jack "Legs" Diamond. You would bring a bill in there, and if Owney wasn't there or Frenchie, you'd see Jack Legs. If Jack knew you had a bill, the first thing he'd do was reach for a gun, sink it in your ribs—"Give me the bill."

So you'd give him the bill, and then he'd tear it up, throw it on the floor, and it stayed. Then I'd meet Frenchie or Herman Stark. He'd say, "I see you ran into Jack." He'd smile and come over and have his hand out. You'd take it, close your hand. You'd go and look, and you always had $200 or $300 in your hand. Never less than $200. They knew Diamond was a nut.

I went up to Hot Springs, Saratoga, with Madden. I put an alarm system on his cottage and some additional electrical. I worked for Dutch Schultz, too. He used to have an undertakin' parlor on

138th Street, and all the caskets were just filled with alcohol. He would take and move his alcohol in and out of his funeral parlor in the caskets. All of the gangsters were very friendly to me, and I was very necessary to them, buildin' all kinds of electrical equipment. They had their own private medical facilities with X-ray equipment. Somebody had to install it.

There was also a black gang in Harlem. These were the Five Percenters. At the Apollo, we had to give 'em $5,000 a week in order to stay open. If he wouldn't give it to 'em, they'd take stink bombs or get in the middle of the show and call up the police bomb squad. You just paid 'em. That got rid of 'em. There was no use fightin' 'em, didn't even try. Hell, they burned Frank's restaurant all the way down to the ground.

STRETCH JOHNSON: In 1934, management at the Cotton Club decided to put in chorus boys. I was nineteen at that time, and I didn't know anything about dancing, but I was coordinated. Winnie said, "Stretch, if you come down to the basement and practice with me, maybe you can pick up enough dance steps to take the audition." So we woodshedded in the basement for a week, and I took the audition. They liked my work even though it wasn't polished, and I became a chorus boy.

Adelaide Hall was the star of the show. It was called the *Ill Wind Show*. It was an effort on the part of Harold Arlen and Ted Kohler and the Cotton Club management to repeat the success of the previous year's *Stormy Weather* revue with Ethel Waters.

The opening number of *Ill Wind* was a soft shoe, "As Long as I Live." That was the number where Avon Long brought Lena Horne out of the chorus and had her sing the bridge, and from then on she went on to stardom and never looked back.

The caliber of the performers there was always top-notch, and a lot of white celebrities would come to see the shows. We would peek out the curtains when some of the top celebs would come in, like Cole Porter, Texas Guinan, or Paul Whiteman and his orchestra, Jimmy Durante. On Sunday night, they usually had celebrity night, where Dan Hilly, who was master of ceremonies, a well-known raconteur and dancer, would emcee the introduction of celebrities from the ringside. They would stand up, take a bow, and Dan would invite the more prominent onstage to take a turn.

I saw Maurice Chevalier sing from the Cotton Club stage. I saw George Raft do his Charleston, saw Ann Pennington and Gilda Grave do their shimmies. Harry Richman sang from the Cotton Club stage. Al Jolson sang there one night. It was like, wow, where else in the world can you get something like this?

I really had no feelings about performing in front of a restricted audience. I knew no other society but a segregated one, and I was not at all surprised that blacks were not permitted into the Cotton Club except members of the families and a few prominent blacks like Adam Clayton Powell or Stepin Fetchit. The level of political consciousness was pretty low around 1932, '33, '34. The left had entered Harlem around 1929, '30 and had begun to make some waves around issues like the Scottsboro boys and began to organize demonstrations for relief and jobs, but they represented a minority force in the community. It was not until '35 that the impact of the Depression began to be met with more militant activity.

Management treated us with a kind of surface respect as performers. They recognized us as, in their opinion, a more talented group of blacks, but generally they thought of us as niggers, like everybody else. They were a bunch of hoods, and they were using the club as a money-making operation, so the rapport between the performers and the club management was rather distant. They would befriend a few Uncle Tom individuals, and rub their heads in typical racist patronizing fashion.

Herman Stark was friendly with our family, because my father had done some time, and he had a kind of record they had appreciated. In a sense, he was one of the boys. He could talk their language. We saw Owney, but we didn't have too much conversation with them. Sometimes, some of them would come backstage to look the girls over, but generally they kept their distance and we kept ours.

EDDIE BAREFIELD: In 1930, I was in Baltimore with a band called McKinney's Cotton Pickers. Roy Eldridge and I were out one night jammin', and Cab come in and heard me and asked me to join his band. Everybody's ambition was to come to New York, play in the Savoy Ballroom, Smalls' Paradise, and all the rest of the places.

Cab was one of the greatest entertainers in the world. He was top, then. Cab Calloway was the Elvis Presley of the time. Don't let nobody kid you. He didn't have the greatest band, but he was top of everybody. Each of us had twelve or fifteen uniforms. We'd go in a theater for a week, change uniforms for every show and not wear the same thing twice. That was from shoes out—shoes, suit, coat, tie. For instance, we had a brown tail, brown patent-leather shoes to go with, ascot tie and handkerchiefs. We'd have yellow tails, white suits, English walkin' suits. All the bands had at least one uniform. Duke had a well-dressed band, but Cab had more.

STRETCH JOHNSON: Jimmy Lunceford was the band for *Ill Wind.* The Lunceford band had come into Harlem and played the Lafayette Theater and just blew everyone's minds.

I had always been a great admirer of Duke Ellington's. As a twelve-year-old kid, I used to listen to him on our radio when they first opened up the Cotton Club. Ted Husing and Norman Brokenshire used to introduce the band, and you'd hear Ellington's theme song come on—"East St. Louis Toodleoo."

I was sitting in the box reserved for members of the family when Ellington first played "Mood Indigo" and "Sophisticated Lady." Just to hear Ellington work with the band during rehearsals was an exhilarating, exciting experience that I haven't gotten over yet.

Ellington was a genius. Like most geniuses, he had a certain kind of sense of self, a charisma, and also he was a very kind person. He exuded warmth to the musicians in the band and to the other performers. He was almost like a big brother or father figure to most of us. We just idolized Duke. He was really a prince of a person, with what they called in those days, plenty of savoir faire, which later came to be called "cool" during the bop period. Cool was already a part of the black ethic in those days. It was a kind of laid-back quality, taking things with grace, not being flustered or uptight, a kind of attitude toward life that the right is going to win out.

The Ellington organization was the Harvard of bands. Ellington sidemen, by getting to work with the Ellington band, got the equivalent of the Ph.D. of the musical world. The Basie, the Calloway, and the Lunceford organizations, while they were all highly respected and highly regarded as topflight, they didn't quite have the class of the Ellington organization.

• • •

MARION WARNER: I went to dancing school on 132nd Street when I was a young girl, because I was always jumping and dancing anyhow. My mother was a Shakespearean actress way back then. She loved to go dancing. I think that's why she let me be in show business, she was living vicariously through me. She performed at the Lafayette, but that was short-lived because my father thought that for a mother it wasn't very nice to go gallivanting around the stage.

In 1929, a friend of mine told me there was a show on Broadway that was taking girls for the summer. I told my mother, "It's just for the summer, only for July and August. Then I'll go right back to school," which of course was baloney. I got the job with the show, Lew Leslie's *Blackbirds.*

Bill Robinson was in the show. So was Ada Ward—you know, "I Can't Give You Anything but Love." It was a big Broadway show, only they never had a book. It was like vaudeville, with the Hall Johnson Choir, dancing girls, comedians, and stars like Robinson and Ethel Waters.

Ethel Waters was tough. You had to be careful around her. "Hello, Miss Waters." Once, when she was onstage, she stopped in the middle of a song, and she looked up at the spotlight man and said, "You know, if you can't follow me, we can have you replaced." And she picked up the song right where she left off and went right on singing.

Bill Robinson also wasn't very easy to talk to. In the first place, a lot of people don't know that Bill Robinson was illiterate. His wife would read all of his write-ups two or three times to him so he could memorize them. Then he'd say, "Look what they said about me in this paper."

If he ever caught anybody doing any of his dance routines, he'd show them his gold pistol. He wouldn't teach a black person anything. But little Shirley, when he was working with little Shirley, he adored her. He even bought her one of those little cars that she rode around her estate. He was not the nicest person to be around. Bill Robinson was for Bill Robinson. He couldn't help it. He was ignorant. We called him Uncle Tom. Oh, but he could dance beautifully. He could stop a show. And whenever his name was on the marquee, you could be assured a full house.

DOLL THOMAS: Bill Robinson was the mayor of Harlem. If people were evicted, he would stop the eviction. If they were hungry, he'd see that they got fed. If they were sick, he'd see that they went to the hospital.

He was one of the greatest as a performer, but he was really a white person's performer. He was one of the perfectionists of tap-dancin,' but he could've never made the money in tap-dancing, dancing for colored people. As a matter of fact, he started off like all colored dancers. If you were a colored performer, you were known by two names. If you could sing and dance, you were a darkie. If you could only dance, you were a pickaninny. Pickaninny was shortened to Picks. Bojangles started off dancin' with three fellows, and they called themselves the Three Picks. He was a marvelous athlete, too. He set the record for the hundred-yard dash backward. He would take bets up here, and down there on Broadway they would build up a race, and he would put on an exhibition. Right in front of the Palace Theatre, they stopped all the traffic.

Up here, he preferred to gamble. If he was up here, nine times out of ten he would spend most of his time gamblin'. We had nothin' but gamblin' clubs up here. They weren't legitimate, but they were just places where people got together and gambled.

MARION WARNER: Florence Mills was somebody who really was special. She sang like a mockingbird, and she could dance. She was lovely to watch.

HERMAN WARNER: Her stage personality was such that you adored her just seeing her. People loved her. Royalty went for her. You must have met somebody at first meeting that you seem just to like. That was what she had over and above the average. She was just one of a kind, man, one of a kind.

MARION WARNER: When we were little girls, my father bought tickets to see her in *Blackbirds*. We were sitting in the orchestra, and when she sang "I'm a Little Blackbird" to I don't know how many encores, well, Paul Whiteman was sitting near us, and he got up and he begged her to just sing it one more time. That's what she did to people. She really sang that song. [*She sings sadly and slowly:*]

> *I'm a little blackbird looking for a bluebird, too.*
> *Every little blackbird needs a little lovin' that's true.*
> *I've been all over from east to west in search of someone to feather*
>     *my nest.*
> *Why can't I find one the same as you do?*
> *The answer must be that I am . . .*
> *I'm a little jazzbo looking for a poor bluebo, too,*
> *Building fairy castles same as all the white folks do, that's true.*
> *For love I'm dying. My heart is crying.*
> *A wise old owl said to keep on trying.*
> *I'm a little blackbird looking for a bluebird, too.*

It made you cry. People who knew her and worked with her said she was very sweet, a very kind person. When she became ill, she didn't know what the heck it was. They just said to put some ice packs on it and it would go away. That's what they did, and then they found out she had a ruptured appendix, and that's how she died. Lew Leslie never got over that. Instead of going to a hospital, she was out there working. He felt responsible.

DOLL THOMAS: The performers were a strong close lot, and they'd always look out after the others if you weren't workin'. They used to all congregate under a tree in front of the Lafayette. If you weren't workin', you could stop by and get a snack or a drink, and they'd carry you through.

One day, some white producer came up and saw all these colored performers were all out of work. He hired all of them for *Green Pastures*. Then, when George Gershwin wrote his opera *Sportin' Life*, his performers came from there. None of the performers that hung out there had any agent, so the producers would come up there and pick up performers.

Then all of the performers who didn't have any jobs and were doin' bad started hangin' out there and gettin' work and makin' money. So they named the tree the Tree of Hope. Then along came the law and they widened Seventh Avenue and cut down the tree. When they made a new center aisle, Bill Robinson put a plaque there that said, "Here's a memory to your Tree of Hope." It's still there.

MARION WARNER: People are surprised to know that back in the '30s you couldn't go into a hotel in New York. I was in a show in '34. They were taking pictures of the girls for the theater lobby. The photographer's studio was at the Ritz Hotel downtown, so a group of us had to go over there a certain time to take the pictures. We walked into the lobby, and somebody walked us right to the service elevator.

There was an exotic dancer named Jigsaw Jackson. He came in after we did, and when we were finished, he said, "Girls, we're not going down the service elevator." He raised hell. He warned them: "You don't want us to break up this hotel." He would not allow us to get into the elevator until we could get a regular elevator to take us down. Some people fought it, and some walked away.

You couldn't even try anything on in 125th Street. You could go in there to buy something, but you couldn't sit down. You couldn't go to the five-and-ten and sit down and have a soda. Adam Clayton Powell opened up that street. I saw it myself. He would go up and down 125th Street and talk to these people and tell them not to go in there if you can't sit at the counter or if you can't buy this or that. He raised hell, and they were losing money because people weren't going in there to buy, so they finally opened up. When he became congressman, he saw to it that it was on the books that they couldn't discriminate.

The Apollo was on 125th Street. I played there when I was with a group called the Lang Sisters. We weren't sisters, and none of us was named Lang. We just happened to pass a store called Lang's while we were trying to figure out a name for ourselves. Our first job was with Count Basie at the Apollo. We traveled with him and Louis Armstrong in the big shows. We really worked. We were jumping and flying on that stage. We did well at the Apollo, and they were a tough audience.

DOLL THOMAS: They weren't tough at all. They were very helpful to a performer—if you were good. If you weren't any good, they'd let you know in nothin' flat, and you wouldn't be back in show business. A lot of 'em learned from the audience exactly what they had to do. It isn't easy. That's the trouble today—you got a whole lotta directors, a whole lotta people that don't know any more about a theater than a pig does about Sunday or napkins.

All the performers wanted to come here. If you hadn't played the Apollo, you hadn't been anywhere. The Apollo happened to have one of those peculiar types of audiences that appreciated a performer's talent and ability.

Here, they heard colored performers sing. They saw colored people dancin'. They saw a line of colored girls that were beautiful and talented, so naturally they appreciated it, that's all. You appreciate what your people can do.

We were successful with the Apollo because we gave people what show business was supposed to be—that's entertainment. You could be down in the dumps, a little sick or not feelin' good, and I guarantee you, if you came to the Apollo and spent seventy-five or eighty minutes with our show, when you walked out, you were like a rejuvenated person.

STRETCH JOHNSON: Schiffman probably screwed every performer that played there. He had possession of the theater, so that his word was law as to whether or not you performed. He set his own prices, and you worked for that price, unless you were a big star and could get plenty of weeks elsewhere. Most of the performers didn't have many weeks strung together, so they were at Schiffman's mercy.

DOLL THOMAS: Billie Holiday was a wonderful person. She was afraid to go onstage. She used to play around town, but when I booked her at the Apollo, she just stood right there, so I just gave her a push and she went on. Her drug problem came when she met John Levy. He had a gin mill down on Eighth Avenue. When she was first comin' up, she was clean.

MARION WARNER: Louis Armstrong was lovely to work with, no trouble at all. So was Basie. Basie couldn't read a note of music, but he had a good ear. He was into pot. They all had to go in and light up, Billie Holiday and the whole bunch, but it didn't affect them at all—except Billie. She got into something heavy, and she had some bad love affairs, and she couldn't adjust.

BARNEY JOSEPHSON: I didn't allow the musicians to smoke [pot] at Cafe Society because I could have lost my cabaret's license. So when they smoked, they did it outside. Billie smoked a lot. There was a taxi stand around there because there were so many night-clubs on Sheridan Square. Billie made a deal with one of these guys. Between shows she would get in that guy's cab, and he would drive into Central Park, and he would go around, around, around the park, and she would be smoking one reefer after another and come back high.

DOLL THOMAS: Louis Armstrong got put out of Europe for dope. His wife had smuggled it in her eyeglasses case. Everybody smoked it. There was a saxophone player called Mezz Mezzrow, who introduced all of 'em to marijuana. It wasn't called mari-juana at that time. The musicians would do those long gigs, two or three of 'em without gettin' any rest, and some of the musi-cians in his band asked him one day, "Mezz, how do you keep goin'?"

And Mezz says, "Well, it's easy. I just get me a Mezzroll."

They didn't know what he was talkin' about till he passed a couple of 'em around. That was the start of it. I happened to be talkin' with some musicians, and they said, "We gotta get some of that stuff. Man, you gotta hear that guy play."

STRETCH JOHNSON: Mezz's were big fat ones about twice as big around as the ones we were normally accustomed to, which we called the panatela. The marijuana was good. A couple of drags and you'd feel a buzz very fast. We used to call it busting down, which meant lighting up.

In the Cotton Club, the performers would smoke outside, be-cause the management wouldn't tolerate it. We used to go to what we called tea pads. One of the favorite hangouts was right next door in Hoskins', who was the superintendent of 646 Lenox. He used to serve corn whiskey and peach brandy and reefers. We'd go down after the show and light up in Hoskins' or we'd go to Frank's at 140th and Lenox. He had an after-hours joint there next to the Britwood, or we'd light up at Kaiser's, at 212 West 133rd Street, down in the basement. They all sold reefers. The joints were al-ready rolled. Guys used to sell 'em ten for a dollar.

NAOMI WASHINGTON: I was about twenty when I heard about marijuana. Eddie Condon, Andy Razaf, Fats, and I were sitting around. Eddie had a cigarette holder. I said, "Eddie, give me a cigarette."

He said, "Why, sure." I didn't stop to ask what it was. I drew, and I thought, "Hmm." And I coughed.

Eddie said, "I got her." He figured I was hooked.

I didn't know what he was talking about. I drew on it again. It had a peculiar odor, but he didn't say anything. Fats was playing, and he said, "You know that was a reefer?"

I said, "No kiddin'. Did you ever smoke one?"

He said, "Sure."

Then I got kinda interested. I knew it was supposed to have an effect on you, that you were supposed to get high. Well, all it did to me was made me sleepy. It wasn't all that great. I wanted to know why they were so crazy about it, and I never found out, and it was costing a quarter for each one. I would buy about ten or fifteen at a time, and they did nothing.

I smoked them about a year, I guess. When I gambled, they'd come in with them. It was growing everywhere, and it was pure then. It wasn't the junk they have now.

I loved to play poker and blackjack. I've come home on many a morning at four or five o'clock, just in time to get a bath and go to work. There were gambling houses all over the neighborhood. You could always buy a drink at these places. Most of it was corn and rye whiskey. Then they came out with a thing called peach brandy. You could give me a gallon for a nickel, I wouldn't touch it. I got drunk off that once, and I was sick for days, and I promised God that would be the last of the peach brandy.

I wasn't too crazy about corn whiskey, either. I've been in and out of a few speakeasies. My husband used to tell me, "If you go to a house, never mind everybody's drinking. You want a drink? Take that bottle. Shake it up. If it don't hold a bead, pass it up. You don't need it."

That was called shake-up whiskey. If it had good bubbles after you shook it, it was good. Some of that stuff was dangerous. Do you know what they would do? Some of them would take that Sterno and add a soda called Whistle, shake that up and drink it. Sterno! Oh, lord!

MARION WARNER: Fats used to drink about a fifth of bourbon every day. When he came off the stage from his bow, and people would be applauding, he'd take a drink, then go back and take another bow. I worked with Fats in one of these traveling revues. He was lots of fun. I've never seen a man eat like that in my life. Oh, my God!

Once while we were on the train, he invited my partner and me to the dining room at breakfast time. He ordered a half a dozen eggs, a pitcher of orange juice, cereal, some bacon, "and throw in a few pancakes there and a pot of coffee." Once we saw him order a half a dozen pork chops, a platter of French fries, a thing of salad. Oh, my God! We didn't feel like eating. How could you when you saw it? It was unbelievable. He'd take the pork chop, hold it by the end, and just go arrrrum! And it was gone. Then there was the booze.

EDDIE BAREFIELD: Fats would keep a gallon of whiskey under the piano, and when that night was over, that gallon would be gone, and Fats wouldn't stagger a bit. I never saw Fats drunk. He just got louder and louder.

We were all young and havin' a good time. I used to stay up three or four days at a time, just hangin' out—get off from work and hang out all night, go back to the theater and nap between shows, go back out again the next night. I used to hang out all day downtown, come home and eat supper, and then hang out all night.

When the Cotton Club closed, we hung out in the bars and after-hours places. There was a place called Mike's. All the show people from the different shows went there. We just sat around. Sometimes we did some jammin'. The musicians I knew played for musicians. If the people like it, okay, but they're musicians' musicians. There was always competitions. That's why they had jam sessions. A guy would go out and hear somebody playin' some ideas, then he would go home and practice and come back.

BARNEY JOSEPHSON: After Cafe Society closed at four o'clock in the morning, which was curfew, Lena or Hazel Scott would say, "C'mon, let's go out." They were night people. When they finished at four o'clock, they didn't go to sleep, they had to go someplace and relax like any worker who gets through at five or six o'clock.

Usually, these places they took me to were in apartment houses in Harlem. You'd go down in the basement, and the super of the building ran a joint down there. He'd have an old upright piano, always be dark with a red light here or there, and they'd serve liquor. Guys would come in, musicians, and they sat in.

For example, Art Tatum was with me for a long time. Art would come out, and he would play his five tunes or seven tunes. No matter how much the audience banged, he did his show and off. He wouldn't do an encore for nobody. Then one night, Lena says, "Let's go uptown." We walk into a basement place somewhere, and there's Art at an upright piano, bottles of beer stacked up on top. He's playing and drinking, and you couldn't get him off that piano. He was playing for his own people and not for pay. That's where he wanted to be. You could cheer your ass off in Cafe Society. "I did my show for you, ofays, fuck you."

STRETCH JOHNSON: There were a couple of whorehouses— one of 'em was on 140th Street—where sometimes they put on a show for visitors and members of the Cotton Club show. It was called Hazel Valentine's. There was a Turf Club, which was owned by Casper Holstein. We used to go there after the show to eat corn-beef hash and grits. It had great grits and hash. The food was good in all these joints. Blacks like to eat well, so there was plenty of fried chicken, potato salad, chitlins, greens, candied yams, hot biscuits. A joint that didn't have good hot biscuits and corn bread didn't last too long.

We used to listen to the musician at uptown's Monroe House. There was also the Britwood. Frankie Newton used to play there with his Britwood Stompers. There used to be a lot of jamming at the Hot Cha, where Billie Holiday sang.

Then there was a fellow named Bill Willis, who lived at 393 Edgecombe. He set up his basement as sort of an insider's jazz club, where only the chosen few were allowed to come. He had a big grand piano and a tuba sitting in front of the living room and the basement. The tuba had a blue bulb in it facing this Steinway grand piano. The top piano talent came by there to play. One night Art Tatum was there with Nat King Cole, Billy Kiles, who later joined the John Kirby Quintet, and Calvin Jackson, who was then a student at Juilliard. He could play both classical piano and jazz. They kept rotating, just playing their own variations on similar tunes all night long. It was like being in heaven—the greatest music in the world.

There was another place, where they had a chorus of all homosexuals, who used to come out and dance in drag. That was the 101 Ranch, which is where they invented a dance called the Shim-Sham Shimmy, which became a kind of a national anthem for dancers. Practically every dancer in Harlem could do the Shim-Sham Shimmy.

HERMAN WARNER: On 142nd Street between Lenox and Fifth, there was a famous after-hours place, which featured Gladys Bentley, who was a les, and there was another player who called himself Gloria Swanson. Bentley dressed up as a man, and Gloria Swanson dressed up as a woman.

Gladys and Gloria were extremely popular. Gloria Swanson used to sing a song called "Hot Nuts." The song was "Hot nuts, get 'em from the peanut man." As soon as you would enter, he would make you sing the song: "Hot nuts, tell it to the peanut man. You see that man walking there in green? He has good nuts but he won't keep 'em clean."

MARION DAY: We went to the Rockland Palace to the faggots' ball. My sister and I always had short haircuts. We'd go in our sequin dresses, and you couldn't tell the men from the women. They were dancing and having a good time, and they would come up to us. We'd say, "We're women, no, no."

My mother went, too. She enjoyed it. We'd have a box and sit there and watch. It was amazing. When they'd come up and talk to us, and they didn't know whether we were the real thing or not.

NAOMI WASHINGTON: I went to rent parties. Oh, my dear, you're talking about having a good time. I can't tell you. On a Saturday night, Harlem really jumped. You'd be going through the street, and you'd hear the playing, and you'd say, "That sounds good. Let's go up there."

Sometimes, the people at the rent parties weren't respectful, saying anything, you know, cussing and swearing, so we would leave. Sometimes at these parties, there would be people with cards inviting you to another party:

*If your life is bound
by convention and your
conduct always
above
reproach
tear this paper into
as many pieces as
possible*
BUT—

*If you dare to be
Entirely Emancipated
for one evening, then
come to*
FRANK BYRD'S PARTY
*at the*
BRONZE STUDIO
*227 Lenox Ave.*
JUNE *10th
a Friday evening;
from ten o'clock until—*

Most of the music was rag. Naturally, there'd be two or three pianists together. One is getting paid, and he'd play, and then another would say, "Get up. Let me play."

Fats used to play at those. He and Johnson, now they'd team. You can't imagine the good time you'd have. They'd want a quarter at the door, and pig's feet, chitlins, fried chicken, greens, you'd get anything you wanted to eat.

•   •   •

EDDIE BAREFIELD: I first played the Savoy with Don Redmon's band. The Savoy was one of the finest ballrooms in the country. The Savoy was the "Home of Happy Feet." It was worth the money to just go and watch those people dance.

They always had two bands, about eight, nine bouncers, great big guys, and twelve or fourteen hostesses for you to dance with. Sometimes they would start a dance on a Friday night and go through Saturday and Sunday with about forty bands. You could get in for fifty cents and stay all three days.

STRETCH JOHNSON: The insiders used to call it the Track, be-cause that's where all of the fast-track people would hang out to make contact with each other, the stallions, the mares, and the fillies. Thursday night was Kitchen Mechanics' Night. Women were admitted free, so guys always knew that on Thursday night they could easily find a woman to dance with.

The dancing was outta sight. Everyone showed their best steps. The top dancers in the world were at the Savoy. When the music got hot, the lindy hoppers would get out in the middle of the floor and do some acrobatic flash stuff that was incredible.

Chick Webb, Benny Moten, Zack White, Count Basie, Fletcher Henderson, Duke Ellington, they all played the Savoy, Jimmy Lunceford, the Blue Rhythm Band, and the Savoy Sultans, which was the house band. Every once in a while, one of the big white bands would come up for a contest. Benny Goodman came up and had a band contest with Chick Webb, and he got blown away. Chick Webb took over. Charlie Barnet came up, and the same thing happened to him. It was spectacular.

EDDIE BAREFIELD: Harlem was runnin' twenty-four hours a day then. When downtown closed, all of the people came up to Harlem in busloads to the Cotton Club, Connie's Inn, Smalls' Paradise. They all had chorus girls and a big show. The Depres-sion only hurt the rich people, oil magnates and all. Poor people never had nothin' in the beginnin' so the Depression didn't mean nothin' to 'em, because everybody was makin' their little money bootleggin', and everybody was out havin' a good time.

STRETCH JOHNSON: Most of the show people lived rather in-sular lives. They weren't out in the daytime that much. They were in the nightclubs, partying late at night and usually sleeping dur-ing the day. That was the routine I went through at the Cotton Club, but I happened to be very curious—we having just moved to New York—so I was up day and night. I had a lot of energy at the time. I could stay up eighteen to twenty hours, so I saw a lot of what was going on in the daytime.

I'd see the domestic workers lined up or the longshoremen lined up before the straw bosses. They would come and pick out who they wanted. Maybe you'd get a crowd of fifty to a hundred people just standing and a guy would get up on the tailgate of a truck and say, "Okay, you, I want you." It was a sickening sight. I stood in some of those lines myself when I heard there was a good job like working on a loading operation where you might make a couple of bucks an hour, which was big money in those days.

I remember how my heart was in my mouth as he would point to this one and that one. He'd bypass you and pick some other lucky guy. He'd pick 'em off and you'd know they were going to make a day's pay.

In Harlem, you'd also see thousands of men and women in the streets all day long, playing the numbers or just standing because there was absolutely nothing to do. They just talked about the weather, about women, about poverty, about food and all the other subjects that poor people who are out of work talk about. Poverty is a bitch whether you are black, white, or yellow.

NORA MAIR: My husband worked in the day and went to school nights. He graduated from Mechanical Institute in 1928, and right after that the Depression came, and he couldn't get work in his profession. In the meantime he drove a cab. It was no living at all as a taxi driver. I've known him to work around the clock and only make a dollar and a half.

He would come in in the morning and eat his dinner for his breakfast and then go to bed. I've known him to be so cold, because in those days the cabs only had three doors, that he'd come in and all he would take off was his hat, his shoes, and his overcoat and then into the bed until he was warm. Those things I did resent, because he had more to offer. He met so many people on the cab line—people he knew from Jamaica. He met professors who were driving cabs and couldn't get a job. First it was color. Then it was color and Depression.

There was nothing my husband did not do to make a living. He did not want welfare, and he wanted to be independent. But he couldn't get work as a draftsman. Once, while he was driving a cab, he saw an ad in the paper for a draftsman. He went downtown to this office, and there was the receptionist. She didn't even look up. She waved him around the back, so he thought to himself, "She didn't ask what I wanted. She just motioned me to the back of the building. What kind of office could be back there?"

When he got back there, a white man with a pail and a mop said to him, "There is the pail and the mop."

"Pail and the mop for what?"

And said Mr. White Man, "Well, that's what you're here for, isn't it? A porter's job?"

Well, I won't tell you what my husband said when he came home, because he came home frothing at the mouth, and told me what he told him.

When the WPA came in, that was the first time he got to work in his profession. He worked on theaters, schools. They did everything, and it meant a lot that he was finally able to work in his field.

ELTON FAX: I was teaching down south when one day a letter came saying that there was a job for me in Harlem. The job was a WPA job. Augusta Savage had at that time established art classes under government sponsorship on 136th Street, and she had classes there in weaving, drawing, painting, and sculpture, which she conducted.

Later on, when there was more money appropriated for it, the Harlem Arts Center was established at Lenox Avenue and 125th Street, just over Liggett's. It came to be the best-equipped art center under the WPA projects in the city.

My salary for the WPA was $23.86 a week. Rent was $35 a month. Through being frugal, I was able to save money. Man, I was eatin' hard rolls for my supper. I was kind of tough. This is the thing I take a little pride in. I was able to make it without stepping on anybody—without being a bastard.

NAOMI WASHINGTON: I lost my job during the Depression, but I did okay playing numbers and with the gambling. One day, I looked in the paper, and this place wanted a houseworker. I hated housework, but I figured I'd try it. I answered the ad, and the house was nice and clean, and I said to her, "How much do you pay?"

She said, "Five dollars a week."

So I'm looking around the room, and she said to me, "What are you looking for?"

I said, "I'm looking for what I can steal. You must expect me to steal something if you're gonna give me five dollars a week."

NORA MAIR: I played the numbers at a candy store run by Jack Bernstein. We'd pay five cents or whatever we could afford. We never won anything. Never. We were hoping against hope, like everybody else.

Poor Jack. He used to be caught so much with the numbers that he would put the slips in his mouth and eat the paper, and he died from a terrible disease all over his skin. The doctors claimed that that was what it was from, those dirty papers.

We were poor. We didn't pretend. But our gas bill was always paid. Our rent bill was always paid. And we always knew where our next meal was coming from. We shopped on Eighth Avenue. We had everything there. We moved out of West Harlem to 100th Street and Madison Avenue in 1933 because the rent was less than half of what we were paying in West Harlem. We were paying thirty-two dollars a month for a five-room apartment. In Harlem, we would have paid sixty-five dollars, and we had a lovely landlord who painted our house every year. It was a lovely neighborhood— a potpourri of many nationalities.

They sold cheese and butter out of buckets. I used to bring home the bucket, put earth in it and grow potatoes out on the fire escape. After the horses did their business on the streets, my sister would go out with a broom and dustpan, sweep it up and put it on her plants. That's how we lived—simply, genteel, and very nice. The neighborhood was all working people. There were occasional robberies, but we felt safe.

We ate Jamaican food and American food. Jamaican food is lamb and beef, but also swordfish, codfish, and something called ackee and yams, rice, and peas, tubers, cocoa. We had breadfruit that grows on a big tree. You can have them broiled or roasted. In Jamaica it's roasted over coals.

For breakfast, you would grate fresh green bananas and make porridge. It makes a delicious cereal. We called it pop. Of course, we had the Blue Mountain coffee. We had West Indian bread, which is called hard-dough bread. It's not sliced. You have to slice it yourself, but it's very, very firm. You had to chew on it.

We'd buy the feet of the chicken, because they make delicious hors d'oeuvres. Oh, yes, you stick that in boiling water and take the skin off, delicious.

HERMAN WARNER: In Depression days, if I made twenty-five dollars a week I was happy. There were times when I would see thirty patients in a day, and I'd make four or five dollars. I never saw the rest. I never expected to. They didn't have it. They made enough money to feed themselves and to pay a little rent, and that was it.

NORA MAIR: Dr. Warner worked hard. He used to have his evening meals with us. Some days, he would come down, and he would play the piano. I would say, "Herman, what is wrong today?"

He would say, "Man, I had eighteen patients this morning, and two paid."

Sometimes, he'd say, "I am so tired. I walked up there today, and the woman had a flu. Even though it was so greasy, I was so tired, I felt like I could lie down in the bed beside her."

STRETCH JOHNSON: We saw people starving, people raggedy. We saw people being evicted for nonpayment of rent, put out on the street. We also saw groups like the Communists and other militants putting furniture back after the city marshal would evict people. The Unemployed Councils were very active. After I was unemployed, I got very active in these movements. When I looked around, the Communists were more active than any other group. It seemed to me they meant business when they put furniture back and led demonstrations around the relief bureaus and marched in support of the Scottsboro boys or in protest against the Italian invasion of Ethiopia. As far as I was concerned, it was the only game in town.

NORA MAIR: We had a club that would get together and discuss poetry, or we would have discussions about medicine or about Jamaica. We tried to enlighten ourselves as much as we could, by reading poetry, and having doctors and dentists talking to us, and having poets discussing this and that. When the whites would come uptown, we were heading downtown to the theater, because clubs didn't mean that much to us. We couldn't afford it.

I worked in a linen shop on Madison Avenue through the Depression. It was a store, but it was so exclusive, it was called a shop. She never advertised. When she had a sale, she would send out cards to her customers. Then she would see to it that you would have your sheets and your pillowcases and your towels monogrammed so you couldn't bring them back.

I worked there for nine long years. I took care of stock, and I would even bring things home, like sheets and pillowcases, and wash them in my house, iron them, and take them back. There were times when things were so bad that I had to take my wages, as poor as we were, in linens, because she couldn't pay me.

When we went to war, business picked up. About a month later, I went to work on a Monday morning, and there was a white woman doing my job. I asked her what was going on. They said this woman would be doing my job, and I could do the cleaning of the shop. [*She laughs.*]

The day went by. I never fussed. I didn't say a word. But at the end of the day, whatever I had there, I took home with me. The next day I didn't show up. They called me. They asked me if I was sick. I said I wasn't.

"Will you be in tomorrow?"

I said no.

"Well, what day will you be in?"

I said, "I'm not coming back."

And that was that. As poor as we were, nobody was going to insult me and take advantage of me.


DOLL THOMAS: In the late '30s, I went with Billie Holiday and John Hammond down to do a recordin' with part of Basie's band and two or three other musicians. Teddy Wilson was playin' the piano, and I noticed then from observation that she had a problem. That session lasted until zupteen o'clock in the morning, and I got a minute and I walked up to her. I said, "Bill, baby, you're slippin'."

She said, "Yeah, I know it, but I'm gonna get control."

So I said, "Please do, Billie. If anybody tells you about that stuff, that's Levy's business. He sells it, and he'll get you hooked. You'll be makin' money, and he'll get rich."

"Oh, no. I remember the good times we used to have."

Well, it was a long time after that. I had gone overseas in World War II and come back. At that time I was stayin' in the Grantham Hotel, down on St. Nicholas Avenue between 119th and 120th. I was comin' from a show one night, and I heard all this excitement. There she was with Levy and two or three other guys rushin' into the hotel to get a room. There was a rush as they went upstairs. It wasn't fifteen minutes after that before the feds came in and took her out.

ELTON FAX: I never will forget the day I was delivering detective-story illustrations to my publisher in lower Manhattan and I heard on the radio Fats had died on the train coming from the Midwest into New York. I remember telling the editor, "Man, Fats Waller's dead." He was shocked, too, because Fats Waller was everybody's favorite. I just heard it that morning before I left the house. Oh, yeah.

NAOMI WASHINGTON: Fats was only thirty-nine when he died. He was just beginning, I think, to take life seriously. It just so happened that he was in California making three pictures, *Stormy Weather*, *Cabin in the Sky*, and *King of Burlesque*. He had had this heavy cold. His manager, Ed Kirkeby, said the doctor told him not to travel, but it was getting to Christmastime, and he always was home for the holidays. So he was traveling home on the Santa Fe, and he got sick on the train. He was sleeping when he started breathing funny. His manager called him but got no answer, so he pulled the cord and asked for a doctor. When they examined him, he was dead already.

My sister-in-law came to the house at three o'clock in the morning, and I heard her say to Lil, "Is Naomi home?"

She said, "Sure, she just came out of the hospital."

I couldn't help but notice that she was crying. So I said, "For goodness sake, what's the matter?"

She said, "Naomi, you know your brother is dead?" Now she was married to my oldest brother. I had no idea she was talking about Fats. I said, "No kiddin', when did he die?"

She said, "We heard it on the radio." When she said that, I knew she wasn't talking about that brother. So I said, "Oh, you sure?" I turned my radio on, and a man came on, and he said, "Ladies and gentlemen, there was a body taken from the Santa Fe this morning, supposed to be the body of Fats Waller. That hasn't been confirmed."

I said, "That's not my brother." But I was anxious. That was around ten o'clock. At eleven o'clock, he came on and he said, "Ladies and gentlemen, the body taken from the Santa Fe this morning was the body of Thomas 'Fats' Waller."

Well, I liked to die. It hurts me now when I think of it. I just didn't want to believe it. I lost all of them, three brothers in five years, Bob in '40, Fats in '43, and Lawrence in '45. They brought him home. He wanted to be cremated, and he was. I used to tease him, "Won't you get to hell fast enough without being burned?"

An airplane flew the ashes. It came up Lenox Avenue and dropped them over Harlem. His favorite hymn, "Abide with Me," Isabel Powell played it at his funeral. One of his singers, Myra Johnson, came up to me, and she said she wanted to talk. She said, "Naomi, I need a drink."

I said, "So do I." We went to the Monarch Bar on 139th Street and Seventh Avenue. I don't remember how we got home. We had quite a few. We were crying. She told me how much she thought of him, and he thought a lot about her.

He wasn't conceited at all. He liked all good music. If you mentioned another piano player who was good, he'd say, "Oh, he's a great piano player. I'm tryin'." He liked it when people clapped, but it didn't change him any. What he did was for hisself. If you liked it, fine. He and Andy would be working together, and Andy would say, "Fats, that's great!"

"Yeah? Glad you like it." And he *was* glad you liked it. Hearing his music used to kind of get to me. Now, I take it fairly well, but I still miss him.


ELTON FAX: One thing I'll never forget is the night Joe Louis lost to Max Schmeling. Man, Harlem was a sad and sorry place. Not only was it a sad place, it was a dangerous place to be in. People were distraught and very, very edgy. You were subject to being really hurt if you crossed anybody in the wrong way. Man, Joe Louis was such an idol, and it was assumed he could not lose. Wrong assumption. Anybody can lose. There was all that talk about him being doped, but guys like his manager said, "He was doped. Schmeling doped him with his right hand."


NORA MAIR: I will never forget when he was knocked out by Schmeling. Dear God, we all went into mourning. These were all professional people, and he was a boxer, but every time Joe Louis fought we had a party with rum punch and sat and waited for the knockout. He was gentle. He wasn't unctuous. He was down-to-earth. He was a clean-living man, and he was black. That was the most important.

HERMAN WARNER: I went to the first Schmeling fight, when he lost, and the whites applauded. I said, "What the hell is wrong with these people?" They knew how Hitler felt about Schmeling. You knew what was happening. Of course, blacks were all the way down.

I was associated with a Dr. Armstrong at the time, and Bert and I went to the second fight. Going to our seats, all the dust was stirred up, and a little bit got into Bert's eye, and you know the knockout was so fast he never saw the fight? [He laughs.]

I've never seen anything like that second fight. You could see hate in that fight. You realized that this was tragedy. He could have killed this man. When he got Schmeling against the ropes, he hit him so hard, Schmeling screamed. I was glad when it was over. Tragedy was lurking there. It was hate, because Joe Louis had been ridiculed, and when he won, people celebrated all night.

NORA MAIR: Oh, but everybody was out, and everybody was hail fellow, well met. Everybody loved everybody else. There was pandemonium the night he knocked out Schmeling.

We proved he was not superior to Joe Louis—to a black man. That a black man could floor him at some time—and did. That's where our joy came in. That he could really beat this German. It was really wonderful. I was not a boxing fan before, and I'm not since. I'm just a Joe Louis fan.

# East
# Harlem

BY ALL ACCOUNTS, Mulberry Bend down in Little Italy was a miserable place in the 1870s. The journalist Jacob Riis would later describe it as the "foul core of New York's slums." *An American Metropolis,* a turn-of-the-century guidebook, described the Bend in its heyday as a place of "unequalled squalor and viciousness."

It's no wonder that when the opportunity for escape suddenly loomed, the Bend's denizens left in droves. That their ticket out was scab labor on the First Avenue trolley lines didn't matter. After all, the Italians had long felt they were unfairly shut out of good jobs, which went to the politically connected Irish workers. Northern Manhattan would mean clean air and open space, far removed from the grimy clutches of the ghetto. It was too good a deal to pass up.

However, for most of the immigrants, East Harlem never became the Promised Land. Instead, they found backbreaking, often dangerous work, when they could get it, low wages, long hours, and openly prejudiced bosses. Those who survived carved out decent lives for themselves, although certain attitudes, particularly a tolerance for the organized crime that operated freely in the area, seemed at variance with the family and religious values that were the core of Italian life in East Harlem until the community's dissipation following World War II.

According to historian Robert Anthony Orsi, the first Italians in northern Manhattan settled in a shantytown along the East River, at 106th Street. The area had been a popular picnic spot known as Jones' Woods. The small community grew rapidly and eventually included a fair number of Jews, Irish, Czechs, and, later, Puerto Ricans. At its peak, in the 1920s, Italian Harlem reached from 104th to 120th streets from Third Avenue to the river.

Many of those who arrived from overseas had no intention of staying in the United States. To them, America meant a chance to earn some badly needed money for the family farm back home and to provide relief from *la miseria*, the terrible suffering from rampant poverty and disease in Italy. That was the intention. In reality, many remained here and were eventually joined by their wives and families. East Harlem was further subdivided into little communities that mirrored the divisions in Italy: Sicilians, for instance, could be found on 104th Street, and Neapolitans on 106th.

The Sicilian Black Hand was the most notorious of the early organized-crime gangs. The group specialized in extorting money from local businesses by threatening to shatter storefront windows if protection wasn't paid. Threats were always accompanied by the gang's personal signature—the ominous black hand. These early criminal activities now seem rather quaint in comparison with such later Mafia enterprises as bootlegging, racketeering, and drug-trafficking, which became the specialties of the New York crime families.

Although organized-crime activity was directed by Mafia chieftains living in the neighborhood, most East Harlemites had little fear of them. Today, many old-timers maintain that the local toughs looked out for their neighbors, particularly the women, and that their violence was played out only among themselves.

Unfortunately, the Mafia's notoriety unfairly sullied the reputation of East Harlem's more upright citizens. Church attendance in the neighborhood was high, and most East Harlem residents seemed to take their religious vows seriously. Children, particularly young girls, were raised under a strict moral code. They were also taught the importance of *rispetto*, respect, especially for the rule of their parents and the sanctity of the family. If the family rules or the moral code was somehow broken, the offender might be cast out of the family—the worst of punishments in East Harlem. Even such a revered figure as the local priest could not encroach on family rule, and a gangster could command respect only if he showed respect for his own family.

If the family was first, the church ran a close second. The largest church in Italian Harlem was Our Lady of Mt. Carmel, on 115th Street. The church was built in 1884, largely with funds from the German and Irish community, and until 1919 Italians who wished to worship there were relegated to the basement. With the warmth a child feels for his favorite aunt, the parishioners adored their jewel-laden statue of the Madonna. During Italian Harlem's peak years, the July festival honoring the Madonna drew tens of thousands of pilgrims to the neighborhood. Highlighting the festival was the parade of the statue through the neighborhood streets. Thousands of sometimes barefoot worshipers followed in the Madonna's wake, carrying money or candles to honor her. The candles weighed as much as 200 pounds each and were shaped like hearts, arms, or legs, depending upon the grace sought from the Madonna.

During the 1920s, a visitor to East Harlem might have gotten the impression that every day was a festival. The streets were alive and vibrant, crackling with the sounds of life: voices from crowded outdoor cafes, the haggling in the pushcart markets, and the gentle chaos caused by thousands and thousands of kids, swarming over the streets and sidewalks.

Despite the hard times, East Harlem had its share of success stories. On 116th Street between First and Pleasant avenues was a row of private houses occupied by doctors and lawyers, many of whom had been raised in the neighborhood. East Harlem's most controversial citizen was its congressman, Vito Marcantonio. For nearly thirty years, until his death in 1951, Marcantonio was one of the most powerful men in New York. His political career was extraordinary. A political radical, with views far to the left of his constituents, he was nevertheless a true East Harlem hometown hero. He lived on the same block of 116th Street his entire life. As a young man, in 1920, he led the city's first successful rent strike. He went on to become a protégé of Fiorello La Guardia, and as district leader and congressman eclipsed the popularity of the "Little Flower," who had also lived in East Harlem.

Marcantonio's constituency changed dramatically when Italians began moving to the suburbs in the 1920s. They were largely replaced by Puerto Rican immigrants, who found the neighborhood's deteriorating apartment buildings a good source of cheap housing. The transition in the neighborhood was not always smooth. Puerto Ricans were denied decent housing on the nicer blocks and were frequent targets for verbal and physical abuse. Even a popular guidebook of the period, *New York Confidential,* openly disparaged the newcomers:

> Puerto Ricans were not born to be New Yorkers. They are mostly crude farmers subject to congenital tropical diseases, physically unfitted for the northern climate, unskilled, uneducated, non-English speaking, and almost impossible to assimilate and condition for healthful and useful existence in an active city of stone and steel.

The first Puerto Ricans to arrive were skilled workers and artisans, including the *tobaqueros,* cigar makers, who were mostly self-educated. In both Puerto Rico and New York, they learned on the job by means of *lectores,* men hired to read aloud from newspapers and books while the workers wrapped their cigars.

Others, less skilled, had more difficulty making the adjustment. For them, the enormous cultural barriers, as well as the native prejudices, were, and are, too difficult to overcome.

# The Witnesses

COLUMBIA ALTIERI (1922–) is a lifelong resident of East Harlem, where she ran a neighborhood bakery with her husband for years.

RAY ARCEL (1899–) is retired after nearly sixty years as a boxing trainer. During that time, he trained nineteen world champions, including Benny Leonard, Ezzard Charles, and Roberto Duran.

BERNARD BURGOS (1900–) was trained as a mechanic in his native Puerto Rico. After emigrating to the mainland, he worked at St. Luke's Hospital until his retirement.

LENNY DEL GENIO (1915–) is a former prizefighter. He was a top-rated contender for the world lightweight championship in the 1930s until a hand injury forced his retirement from the ring. He was an investigator for the Internal Revenue Service and, in the 1970s, became an actor. He has had small roles in nearly forty films, including *The Godfather*. His wife, DOROTHY, and his sister, ROSE SMREK, joined in the interview.

VINCENT FERRARA (1916–) was born and raised in East Harlem. He is a retired family-court judge. His wife, CLARA, for many years a statistician with the International Brotherhood of Teamsters, joined in the interview.

PETE PASCALE (1915–) is a lifelong East Harlem resident. He is director of La Guardia House on 116th Street.

FATHER PETER ROFRANO (1916–) was born and raised in East Harlem. He is the parish priest at Our Lady of Mt. Carmel Church.

ANNETTE RUBINSTEIN (1910–) is a retired school principal. She is the coeditor of *I Vote My Conscience,* a book of writings by Vito Marcantonio.

ALVIS SANCHEZ (1927–) runs a cigar-making shop in New York City.

JOSEPH VERDICCIO (1909–) is a retired lawyer. He was born in Italy and raised in East Harlem.

DOROTHY DEL GENIO: I'm Polish and I come from Pennsylvania. When I was introduced to Lenny's family, I thought it was so different from the way I was brought up. They lived in apartments. Everybody knew you there. On his way home, he'd stop by every apartment in the building before he got to his mother's. In every one they tried to feed him. You know, *"Mangia, mangia."*

And they did things differently. There was a guy, Pepe. One day, he was being chased by the cops. He went up the fire escape. Lenny's mother was home, cooking, and Pepe comes into the kitchen from the window. She knew. She never turned around from her cooking. A little later, he went down that way to avoid the police. When it was over, nobody ever mentioned it.

LENNY DEL GENIO: Because that was an everyday occurrence. He was called the Count—never worked a day in his life.

ROSE DEL GENIO SMREK: The name Del Genio had an unusual beginning. Great-grandma Rose was our father's grandmother. She was born in 1807. In Italy, she was hired on as a
helper in the home of a man named Leonard Muscarelli. Well,
there was a little hanky-panky goin' on with Leonard, and she produced seven illegitimate sons, one of which was my grandfather.

Somebody killed this Leonard, and she had to go to the court
to arrange for the sons. The judge gave the sons the name Del
Genio. It means "of the genius." Then she came to America with
her oldest son, and they went to Chicago, where they had a bar.
She was a tough old lady, like the original Kitty in *Gunsmoke*.

PETE PASCALE: When my father came here around 1900,
everybody was hangin' out on Mulberry and Sullivan Street in Little Italy. By the time my relatives got downtown, everything was
practically taken. Over the years, the Italians started to move toward
this area. I was born on 121st.

Then, Pleasant Avenue wasn't there. That was all dumps, broken cars, broken wagons. On 111th Street and the river was the
coalyard. On 104th, 105th, down to the river, they were all junk-
yards and broken bottles and rags. People who collected all this
garbage and junk would sell it all bundled up in newspaper. That
was the waterfront, from 96th up to 128th Street.

I was born here seventy-three years ago. My father and uncle
were blacksmiths. They built fire escapes, iron ornaments. They
would also make tools for the farms and knives for the houses.
They had a forge like the real blacksmiths. All the piano factories
were up on 133rd Street, and later on they worked there. My father
made the strings of the harp that was in the back of the piano, and
my brothers were piano makers for Steinway.

JOSEPH VERDICCIO: We lived on 115th Street before World
War I, right opposite the church. My dad had a shoe-repair shop.
There was an amazin' amount of people on that block—thousands
of them. For instance, the block at 112th Street between First and
Second avenues was lined with six-story buildings with families that
had twelve or thirteen children. You could imagine how many
people.

There were three shoe-repair shops on one block, from First
Avenue to Pleasant Avenue, three or four grocery stores, three bakery

shops. There were three or four barbers. Yet everybody made a livin', because there were so many people.

FATHER PETER ROFRANO: In East Harlem, people from certain towns lived on one block. On our block, 109th Street between First and Second avenues, lived the people from Sala Consilina. On 108th Street were Calabrese, from Calabria. One Hundred Seventh Street was definitely [he whispers] Sicilian. That's where we had the Mafia. On 104th and 105th were higher titles. They came from Piacenza, places like that. There were animosities between the blocks. Sometimes it flared up around the sports competitions. The 109th Street boys would play against 108th Street. There were tremendous games, with betting and everything—and fighting. One would accuse the other of stealing his girl, who came to watch the game—things like that.

Some kids did a lot of fighting, but not all the kids. Some were bad by nature. Once in a while you would get a bad kid, but we who thought we were elevating ourselves and were trying to advance ourselves with schooling, why, we wouldn't do such things. We were in the majority. There were 30,000 people in St. Ann's parish. In our church there were 60,000, so if you had 1,000 bad people, they were in the minority.

RAY ARCEL: We were living in Indiana when my mother got very, very ill. She was originally from Brooklyn and she wanted to go home to her folks, so my father closed his store, took whatever money he had, and came to New York and never went back. I was four years old. It must have been 1903. My mother died soon after that, and we were raised by my stepmother.

My father settled on the Lower East Side, on Broome Street. He tried to go into business, but he couldn't. It was so packed up and all. He tried to get a place to live where we'd have a little more room, so he came up to Harlem, 106th Street between Second and Third avenues.

The neighborhood was 100 percent Italian. We were the only Jews around there. My brother and I had it pretty rough, because it was Jew this and Jew that, sheeny this and kike that. We fought every night. The anti-Semitism was always amongst the Italians. It was awful. I can't explain to you how awful it was. You'd stand there and you'd argue over sports or about how good the Italian

Navy was, and the first thing you know somebody would say "Jew" this. One word led to another and you had a fight.

We fought with the guys that we hung out with, but we wouldn't fight on the block where we lived. We'd go over to Park Avenue under the tracks. Maybe four or five came along. If I got a bloody nose and he got a bloody nose, then they'd say, "That's enough."

Yet, with all the fights that we had, there was no deep hatred for the guys. I never felt that way, and I don't think they felt that way about me. The same guy I fought with the night before, if we'd see each other the next morning, we'd talk as if nothing happened. On Sunday, they'd invite us up for Italian dinner. I remember sitting at the house one time. I had a bit of a black eye, and the guy I fought with, he had a real shiner. So, the old man, he said to me, "Why you hitta my boy?"

I said, "I hitta your boy because he hitta me."

The father said to the boy, "Italiano?"

The boy said, "No, *matsa Christa.*" Christ killer.

LENNY DEL GENIO: Nobody liked Jews. It's hard to explain. They picked on them. Still, I was on the same team as a lot of those guys. We played ball together.

DOROTHY DEL GENIO: They used to call Benny Cohen a white Jew. So what was a white Jew? That was one they accepted.

LENNY DEL GENIO: I used to go to PS 29, which was on 125th Street. Comin' home, the wops suffered like the Jews suffered. One day, this Irish guy was chasin' me and I ran. I got tired and I stopped. First thing I know, I hit him and he went down. No more fight, and after that they let me walk home from school on that block.

PETE PASCALE: We hadda do a lotta fightin'. If ya didn't, they would pick on ya. If ya were somebody that they respected, then ya wouldn't have no trouble. But once ya backed down, ya were nothin'. If ya hadda fight one kid in another gang, ya didn't pick up a stick. Ya didn't pick up a gun. Ya'd fight wit' your hands. If ya pick up a stick, they bang your head in. Everybody jumps and smashes ya up—even your own friends. That was sort of a code. Ya would fight wit' the guy. The fights went on and on. By the time ya got through, ya was like both knocked out from the exhaustion. Half the time, ya couldn't even swing the punch.

We didn't have to worry about blacks in those days, because there weren't any. We worried about the Irish. On Third Avenue, there were all the furniture houses where the Irish were, too. In those days, the furniture came crated. When they took the furniture out of the crates, we would take 'em. We didn't chop the wood, because if ya chopped it, they would take it. Ya got it in your wagon and were on your way home, when the Irish would come and take it, so we used to fight with 'em. We took a lot of beatin's from them, but then we were the majority and we beat the shit outta them.

COLUMBIA ALTIERI: I'm in this neighborhood sixty-five years. I was born at 501 East 117th Street. My grandmother's name was Columbia. I'm the first female born after six males, and Columbia was my father's mother, so they named me after her.

My parents came from Salerno in 1910 just because my father was curious. They weren't poor. He just wanted to come to America. He was a custom tailor. He started workin' here, and he never wanted to go back. He loved this country. Anybody that would talk against it, he almost hit a man for that.

I had seven brothers and three sisters besides myself. We were eleven children. It didn't hurt my mother havin' so many kids. She was a beautiful woman. She died when she was eighty-two. There were families even bigger than ours, with fourteen or fifteen. Everybody had large families. A small family was considered four or five. Usually they were ten, eleven, or twelve. There were twenty-seven apartments in our building. That's a lot of kids. Our apartment was always so full of people, we called it Grand Central.

Everybody was born in the house. When the baby came, we were sent out to a neighbor upstairs. When we saw the midwife come with the satchel, we thought that the baby was in there. Nobody spoke about that. It was a hush-hush thing.

CLARA FERRARA: My mother had five children, but I never noticed her pregnant because she always wore loose dresses, and she was a big woman. I used to get so mad when the midwife came. "Son of a bitch, we're gonna have another kid in the house." Oh, I hated that lady.

When I was very young, one woman was upstairs giving birth. She was alone, and I had to help. I took one look and, oh, I turned away. It was terrible. Then they told me to get this and that. "Go get the blanket. Get the towels. Run to the drugstore." They made me wash the kitchen floor four times.

If a man came in, you knew there was trouble, because he was the doctor, but you didn't see much of that, and they always brought home a live chicken to make chicken soup.

JOSEPH VERDICCIO: Two of my brothers died the year of the flu epidemic. We had a casket maker on our block, and I would see him makin' those caskets so fast that it was just like a box, that's all—four pieces of wood put together, and they were piled up outside.

PETE PASCALE: Conte was the guy makin' caskets. He couldn't keep up. The influenza epidemic killed my sister. She was three. They were dyin' like flies. Nobody knew what the hell it was.

JOSEPH VERDICCIO: My parents were so scared that we might come down with influenza, my mother used to rub my chest with camphor oil. That was an awful smell.

In those days, you had to have music to get the body out of the house and to bring you to the cemetery. They had four or five musicians playin' outside your house, "Nearer, My God, to Thee," songs like that. You heard that every day, so that you knew them by heart.

VINCENT FERRARA: I was born in 1916 in our apartment at 107th Street and First Avenue. My father worked as a laborer, somewhere on Rikers Island. I know nothing about him. I would never see him. He would leave early in the morning, come home late at night, and Saturdays and Sundays they were working.

He was killed on the job in 1923. A crane grabbed him and cut off his leg. I understand he laid on the island about five hours until they got help and took him to Lincoln Hospital, where he died. They laid him out in the house. The funeral director brought in all the paraphernalia, the lace curtains, a scenic backdrop— everything—into the house. Then a horse and buggy came along with a band that played music. They carried him down, and we rode over to Calvary Cemetery.

My uncle Frank came to take the place of my father. He is only seven years older than I am, but he supported us for several years until he got married. He was a brilliant student, and the teachers begged us to allow him to go to high school, but he had to work, so he couldn't go. I owe a lot to him. He encouraged me to go to school.

My mother did homework. She worked on ribbons. I went out shining shoes in a barbershop with a shoeshine concession. I was seven when I started working, and I kept going until my mother remarried, when I was twelve. I got a quarter a week salary, but I made about seven dollars a week in tips. I also delivered caned chairs for a chair place for eight dollars a week during the summer. During the winter it was four dollars, because I only worked after school. If I wasn't working there, sometimes I took my shine box and went to Central Park and shined shoes until five.

Near the caning store was a junk shop. I would go in there and pick out clothes. I found an overcoat there once and a pair of shoes. The owner gave them to me. "What do you need? Take it."

We didn't have enough money to buy ice, so we used to wait for the snow to come out of the ice place at 108th Street. They couldn't use that. We would bring it home and use that in our refrigerators.

I remember writing letters to Santa Claus. I would say I had no father, and I would ask for food, or clothing. "We need help." And I'd get a reply. We'd get food tickets Christmas Eve to go to the armory on 28th Street, and they would give us a basket of food—chicken, turkey, ketchup, rice—dolls for the kids, a pair of skates. Sometimes, a basket would just arrive. We didn't know from where. Presents from my mother were out of the question. We never thought of it.

LENNY DEL GENIO: We always had a Christmas tree. I always got socks, long johns—clothing rather than toys. I was glad to get it. What the hell was I going to do with toys? I had a baseball glove. I don't know if I found it or I stole it. I wasn't much of a thief, but they used to play down in Jefferson Park. Usually, an outfielder leaves his glove on the side when the innin' is over, and that's when they did a job. Take it, throw it to your friend, and we didn't stop runnin' until 123rd, which was nine blocks away. By then, the innin' was over, and the guy couldn't find his glove. I don't think I ever bought a glove. Where was I gonna get the money?

PETE PASCALE: I played baseball in Jefferson Park. The field was cinder. Jesus, every time ya went for the ball, ya never knew when it was gonna hit ya in the face. Ya had a little glove that just about fit your hand. Oh, did it sting! We also played a lotta boxball and stickball. We used to have the teams go out and challenge the different blocks. Over here used to be the trolley cars, and we had a tough time playin' because of them. If the ball hit the tracks, tough luck, whatever happened happened. It was like hittin' the wall. If they catch it off the wall, you're out. Ya learned to play the track. Ya had to move over so that if it hit the crack of the track, it could jump by ya. If it hit the side, it would come straight at ya. We had the Second Avenue El. You hit it on top of the El, it was a home run, because by the time ya found the ball, the guy was gone.

PETER ROFRANO: I was not sports-minded, and I didn't go in with gangs. I went more toward the church, and I became an altar boy when I was seven years old. I was considered like a holy-holy, you know, untouchable. Later, I went to Immaculata High School, on 33rd Street. In those days, when you went to high school, you were the elite, the select. Very few people on the block went.

PETE PASCALE: We used to play the hook. We would hide in the park or we would go sit in one of the wagons in the dumps. We had a tough truant officer. Oh, jeez, he was a son of a bitch. His name was Flynn. I forget his first name. One day we played hooky. We were hitchin' on the trolley, and he was comin' down the next block, and he sees me and my friend Manure. We called 'im that because he worked in the stable. Anyway, he yelled out at us, and we went back to school.

I told Manure, "Let me do the talkin'. You just keep quiet." We got in the class. The teacher says, "Pascale, Mazale, Mr. Flynn would like to talk to ya."

We got up. He had a little office with a desk. So he says, "What were ya doin'?"

I says, "Let me explain, Mr. Flynn. I hadda get to Third Avenue. I hadda get to the drugstore to get some medicine for my mother."

He says, "You weren't goin' to school."

"Oh, I was. I jumped on the trolley car to get the medicine and take it home because my mother's sick." So this son-of-a-bitch friend of mine is laughin' like a bastard. He was laughin' so hard he was bent over, and we got into trouble.

We had tough teachers, too. He'd throw the chalk at ya. He'd throw the board eraser at ya. We had one guy, he had that big goddamn stick—the pointer. He'd hit ya over the head with it. But we were tough bastards, too, ya know. We couldn't hit the teacher. But the settlement house was right here, and there was a ledge where ya could walk out. We used to wait for the teachers to come out, and we would hit them with the fuckin' eggs, holy Jesus, and then we used to go and hide. They didn't know who the hell it was. Oh, Jesus, we were crazy kids.

Then you had the river. Over there you couldda touched the water with your hand. At 114th Street they had the sewer that went right out there when we went swimmin'. It was a big sewer—maybe six feet in diameter. We used to be on top, because it was encased in a concrete box. We would dive offa that. Every once in a while the sewer stuff would come out. Gheeegh! Everything came out. "Hey, it's comin', boys! Move out." It was riot. Ya got hit all over. Goddamn, we had to push that crap away when we went in there, otherwise ya caught it in the face. That stuff hit us left and right, but that was the only place we coulda swam, because in the other place there was a fence.

The other thing we hadda watch were the water rats. They were swimmin' round there. They were big son of a guns. We used to throw things at 'em, and they used to jump up and catch 'em.

On Election Day, we used to make a fire on the street. The question was who would have the best fire, because ya gotta go to school the next day. Then ya have another coupla fistfights. One guy would say, "We saw your fire. It was nothin'. Ours was bigger." They had another fight. Then it was all over, and next year it started all over again.

Everybody would go out and get wood, and for weeks we would store it here, store it there. Then we hadda watch. On the roofs, we used to line all the bottles, because they would come and steal the lumber. They would come in with the goddamn ashcans over their heads, and we would throw the goddamn bottles off the goddamn roof. Sometimes we'd go in the cellar. We would take the little wooden cubicles where they stored the coal and shove that wood on the fire. Then the landlord would get after ya.

We also took the empty wine barrels and used those. In October, they used to make the wine. They would buy boxes of grapes, and we would tell the guy, "Look, you gotta give us the boxes." We'd carry the grapes in, and then we'd get the boxes.

There was always action. You gotta remember there was no TV, and the radio you hadda put the damn phones on. The action was all out in the street—all the games. When it was cold, we'd make a fire on the square sewers, because they used to holler at us if we melted the tar. You never used ashcans. They had the number on them, and the guy would come after ya with a baseball bat. Ya'd be warmin' up, he'd warm your head up.

VINCENT FERRARA: There was a place in Jefferson Park known as the plots. During the summer, we would each be assigned a plot of land, and we would plant beets, endives, swiss chard, and corn. That would keep us busy for the summer.

DOROTHY DEL GENIO: In a big family, every week it was always somebody's birthday, or somebody was graduating or somebody was having a First Communion, if not in the family, then somebody in the neighborhood. New Year's there was a big party every year. The neighbors would all come in banging their pots and pans. You'd make a big parade, you'd go all over the six apartments, up and down the stairs. We'd all line up and go up '23rd Street with the pots and pans.

LENNY DEL GENIO: There was a little guy, Sammy Falgiano, who was about two years older than I. He played guitar so good. We used to sit there on Pleasant Avenue and sing "Red Hot Mama." It musta sounded good, because we kept doin' it all summer.

The Mills Brothers came around then, the original four. One of them played the guitar like a ukulele, and I couldn't get enough. There was a hockshop on Third Avenue and 124th Street. In the window there was a $1.50 ukulele. Where was I gonna get that? But my mother was good. She got the money and I got the uke.

Dorothy Del Genio: Now, my husband knows every song the Mills Brothers ever made.

[*He picks up a guitar that is sitting in the corner of the room. In a gruff voice and with dexterous fingers, he offers a fine version of the Mills Brothers' hit "Paper Doll."*]

Lenny Del Genio: We would sit out on the stoop and sing all summer. There would always be crowds. A warm night in Harlem, and everybody would be out. My sisters also sang good. Our family loved music.

My uncle played the violin for years. Everybody sang. Even Grandmother, who couldn't really speak the language, sang in broken English:

> *Daisy, daisy, give me your answer true.*
> *I'm a halfa crazy over the love for you.*
> *Da, da, da, da . . .*

She didn't know the rest of the words.

My uncle who played the violin, his name was Nick D'Amico, the same as my other uncles. They were all named after my grandfather. They were also musicians, and they played at nice hotels like the Plaza. One night, they were driving home with their violin cases in the car and the police stopped them for some infraction. Five of them were in there. The cop asked my uncle for his license.

The cop says, "Nick D'Amico, huh?"

And he looked at the other four gentlemen, and he says to one of them, "By the way, what's your name?"

"Nick D'Amico."

"What do you do for a livin'?"

"I'm a violinist."

And he went on to the other man. And the same thing happened. His name was Nick D'Amico and he was a violinist also. Now, the policeman is getting a little bit annoyed. He goes to number three, number four—all the same answer. When he got to the fifth guy, he says, "If you tell me that your name is Nick D'Amico and that you're a violinist, you're all goin' to jail."

He did, so he took them all down to the station. When they got there, the cop says, "I want to call your father and get to the bottom of this. What's his name?" It was another Nick D'Amico!

So the cop says, "All of ya get out of here!" They all laughed, and they took out their violins and played for them.

DOROTHY DEL GENIO: Lenny's family was so poor, the children didn't even have dressers to put their clothes in. Each kid had a little paper box, and in that paper box was his underpants and his socks so it wouldn't confuse their looking for 'em.

LENNY DEL GENIO: Seven kids, that was all they could afford. We were living on 123rd Street when I was born in 1915. My father worked for the Knickerbocker Ice Company. He made fifteen dollars a week, delivering ice to bars, but we always had enough to eat.

DOROTHY DEL GENIO: It was some neighborhood. It was like a small town. They really protected each other. Right across the hall from Lenny was this family that was just making it. They wanted their son who was fifteen to quit school to help. Lenny's mother says, "Don't make him quit school. Let him finish school."

She cried. "I don't have the carfare to send him, and I haven't got the lunch money to give him."

So Lenny's brother Joe took over the responsibility for the next two years. He made sure he got what he needed.

LENNY DEL GENIO: My mother was the greatest cook in the world. Everybody thought their mother was the best. I don't know why they think that, but my mother *was* the best. It was a fact. Her bread was the best-smelling bread in the whole world. When she made bread, the whole house smelled—three floors. Everybody knew that Antoinette was making bread.

My sister lived on the first floor of our building. My grandmother was on the second floor, and we were on the third. Years ago when I come home from church, my sister would make meatballs, and I would steal a couple. My grandmother would make meatballs, and I would take from her, and by the time I got to my mother's I was full. My mother made good meatballs, but my grandmother had something different in hers. I think it was more garlic. Anyway, it was good. You came into that house, and you got such a good aroma. It was a wonderful feeling.

There was a woman next door named Jenny. She was Neapolitan. Her meatballs were different. They were good, but they weren't as good as my mother's or my sister's or my grandmother's.

DOROTHY DEL GENIO: His mother used to say on the q.t., "Oh, Jenny can't cook like I can cook." But Jenny came from an area that ate a lot of fish, so she excelled in fish. And Jenny would say, "Oh, Antoinette is good, but she can't cook fish like I can."

PETE PASCALE: For breakfast, we had coffee and hard bread. What ya think, we had eggs? We never had no eggs. Everybody had oatmeal, every morning oatmeal, because the oatmeal spread, ya know? So we had the oatmeal, coffee, and the stale bread ya dunked. No butter. Butter was a luxury. After a while ya got used to everything. Milk was only eight cents a quart. Ya used the milk for the coffee and the cereal. We didn't get a glass of milk. Ya use up all the milk.

We used to get cod-liver oil. Drove us crazy. She didn't buy the five cents. She used to buy it in a gallon. That thing was so thick. It was oil—real oil. When she wasn't lookin', ya threw it in the sink. Ah, it was the worst stuff. Every morning ya got that big goddamn tablespoon. Every morning, "Open your mouth."

We came home for lunch. My mother would make milk with the rice, and we'd have a big dish of that, a slice of bread, and coffee. One thing about those days, we never said we were poor. We always had something to eat. We just didn't have steak and everything that they ate.

We used to go to the movie once a week. They used to come to the show and stay all day. Then, they had some shows where they'd give you half a chicken to pull you out, 'cause they had to get the other people in for the second show.

CLARA FERRARA: There was a Saturday matinee at the Liberty Theater. All the kids went in there with their lunches and never came home. It was a dirty place. If the boys had to go, they went right over the first balcony. It was run by a woman named Mrs.

Sutton. If your mother wanted you, she would run across the stage, "Joey, your mother's looking for you!'"

PETE PASCALE: On 128th Street and Second Avenue was Metro-Goldwyn-Mayer. We used to go there and watch 'em make the pictures, the guys on the horses with the wooden axes. We'd go, "Bullshit, that's made out of wood, the goddamn axes."

It was just a big lot, and they were hittin' each other with the axes. Marion Davies was there. We'd go see her. Harold Lloyd, Hoot Gibson, and there was Fatty Arbuckle. We used to go there the day before Christmas, and they used to give us gifts, little gifts. Marion Davies used to give 'em out because we were supposed to be poor kids.

•  •  •

COLUMBIA ALTIERI: All the merchants here were Jewish. They were hard-workin' people. They had a lot of pride. They were very kindhearted people. We had a grocer named Max Rottesman. He had a store right on the corner. He was the kindest man you'd ever wanna meet. I think he fed the whole neighborhood. You'd go in there, and he'd say to my mother, *"Shana madelich?* Take it. Don't vorry. When you got the money, you pay. Got no shekels? Don't vorry."

PETER ROFRANO: We were surrounded by Jewish people. They were all in business. My mother looked like a Jewish woman. She had reddish hair. She would go to the chicken market and they would speak Yiddish to her. She would go along Park Avenue to the outdoor market there. They were all Jewish, too.

PETE PASCALE: The market went along First Avenue from 115th Street to 111th Street. Every morning my mother would take the shoppin' bag from 116th Street and walk all the way down to 111th to see what the story is. After 111th, she comes back and starts buyin', because she might have figured that at 116th it was more expensive than 114 or 111. All the aristocrats would go at 115 and 116. My mother had to go at 113 and 114. Everything was cheaper there. Ya hadda know how to shop.

It was a show—the Jewish merchant and Italian, it's a riot. I went with my mother. I hadda buy a suit. Gotta get a green suit.

He says, "Nice. Try it on. Everything fit good, huh?" Yeah, very good, very good.

My mother says, "Nah, this don't look too good."

I said, "But, Ma . . ."

"Shut up." *[He slaps his palms.]* She says, "I don't know. I don't know about the colors." Then she says, "Well, how much?"

"Twenty-seven dollars."

"Four dollars."

I'm thinkin', Oh, Christ, there goes the suit.

And they argue back and forth. My mother got to nine dollars. Now he says eighteen.

"All right, I'll give you another dollar and that's it," my mother says.

"Wait, make it fourteen."

My mother says, "Tell ya what I'll do—eleven."

I walked out with the suit for eleven dollars—with two pairs of pants.

Some of the Jews, they never wanted to lose the first customer. They hadda *hox* on that. They would lose money, but if they lost the first customer, that day was gone. So everybody would go early to be the first customer. "Wait till he opens. No, me first."


VINCENT FERRARA: In public school, there were a lot of Jewish boys. They were the ones that inspired me, because when I went there, their father was a doctor. Another one's father was a lawyer. Another one's father was a prosperous businessman. They owned furniture stores along Third Avenue, big hardware stores. I looked up to those guys. They all had money. They had telephones in the home. They had showers in their homes. They had baths. Whoever heard of a bath? We had to stand up in the sink. The lavatory was out in the hall. It was freezing to get out there.

I was about the most studious of my group. I would go upstairs, get in a corner, and read a book I got from the library on 110th Street. On a cold winter night, I'd sit by the coal stove, put my feet in the oven, and read the book.


CLARA FERRARA: I met his sisters when I was in junior high. They started to work in neighborhood factories, and I swore I wouldn't. I started talking about going to college. My mother said,

"I'll break your legs." I was the oldest. They wanted me to get out and get to work and bring some money in. She used to throw the books after me, and I'd cry. I wanted to go to school. I couldn't go to the park either. My mother had four others. I had to watch them. They fell. They got hurt. I got hit. Then I got lucky. There was a neighbor upstairs who said she would help my mother with the kids, and I got to go to school.

COLUMBIA ALTIERI: A girl was kept very strict. They had little rowboats on the river, and we used to go rowboatin'—not that my mother knew or my father. That was a no-no for girls. And heaven forbid you went on a bike. That was forbidden. It was considered not ladylike.

Skatin'? That was a no-no, too. That wasn't ladylike. You were no good. We were supposed to be ladies. Come out of a school and go to the convent and learn how to embroider and sew. Then you come home from school and do your homework and houseclean.

Horseback ridin' you hadda sneak. But I did all those things. One day I said to my father, "Look, Dad, I'm goin' horseback ridin', and I want you to know I'm goin', so if anybody sees me and they tell you, you know it already."

He said, "But don't let your mother know."

My father was a little more lenient compared with my friends' fathers who were illiterate. My parents had an education, but some of the others had evil minds. They believed what anybody told them. "If she does that, then they're gonna talk about her." That's what they did in those days.

If they saw you talkin' to the same boy, right away they said something was goin' on. Once one person says something, then everybody else adds on even if it never was a true story.

PETER ROFRANO: A girl couldn't date more than three or four times with the same man, and if you dated five or six different men, you were no good. "She doesn't know how to stay with one man." It was much more difficult for a girl than a man. In the Italian mentality, a man could do anything.

If she got a bad name, my God, you moved out, went to Pennsylvania, Jersey, and finally married and got away. I've heard many stories about that. Your reputation was everything.

COLUMBIA ALTIERI: It happened to a friend of mine. She was goin' with this boy, and they probably musta saw her kissin' him or something, 'cause that was a no-no, you know. Before you know it, they started sayin' she was goin' to bed with him. The family, from the shame, they moved out. In those days a kiss in front of people in public, it wasn't kosher—let's put it that way. You had to go sneakin' around.

PETER ROFRANO: Unless they were ready to get married, they would never bring a girl home. If you were serious with that girl, after two or three dates the families would come in and talk. That was it.

CLARA FERRARA: If a girl got married in the building, the rest of the neighbors got together and they made sure the building shone. They scrubbed down the steps, and then we'd go upstairs and make sure she got everything she needed.

If she didn't learn what was expected of her from the street, then she found out from her husband. They knew, more or less, not from our mothers. You always had a married girlfriend who told you. Some girls learned from the street. You knew which girls to stay away from.

"Don't go with her. She's no good."

"How do you know, Ma?"

"Don't you dare."

She might have come home late at night once.

PETE PASCALE: Everybody wanted a clean-cut guy, a nice workin' man. If you were unemployed, you were a bum. Ya hadda work or "get the hell out of the house." The fathers used to come lookin' for ya. Some of them old men were son of a bitches. Oh, Jesus Christ, if ya fucked around, ya were in trouble. They'll knock the brains out of ya.

When I went out with my wife, she didn't tell the old man. She would come down with her sister and a girlfriend. They would go to the movies. We would meet. Then we would go home together. If ya went up the house, then ya hadda bring your parents up the house, and ya hadda have good intentions. Then ya go and your mother goes up there and they bring the proposal.

LENNY DEL GENIO: Kissin' was dangerous. Girls in our neighborhood, they were very strict. You, as the boy, especially respected Joe the Heat's sister, or Sammy the Bull's sister. You didn't mess with their sisters. Joe the Heat would break your leg. Now the Irish girls, they were always available. That's a nice way to put it. They were soft touches. Some of them were pretty fresh.

COLUMBIA ALTIERI: Heaven forbid a girl got pregnant. They threw her outta the house. And girls got pregnant. They either had to go with somebody else in the family, or sometimes a neighbor took them in, but that was the worst thing anybody ever did. It wasn't like they went around lookin' for anything. It just happened. A guy tells you "I love you" and this and that. They bulldoze 'em. They didn't know anything like birth control.

PETE PASCALE: We had a lotta midwives. They did abortions. They did a lot of them. Some of these mothers here did their own abortions with the needles. They didn't want nobody to know that they were pregnant.

Some of them would go to the midwives even if they were married. Jesus Christ, they already had six kids. They get through with one, two or three months later they get started again. "Oh, Cowboy Joe, here comes another one." A small family was considered four. If you had one or two kids, that was like nothin'. There was one guy with twenty-one kids.

The thing is, they couldn't even afford the abortions, and ya hadda watch where you went for the abortion because people watched. You go to the midwife, and they see ya, they say, "Jesus, she's goin' there. I guess she's goin' for an abortion."

There wasn't too much talk about birth control. The only control there was was a condom. Ya got 'em from the drugstore. The church didn't stop 'em, but they didn't have a sign on the window, if you know what I mean. You would go in there. You call the guy on the side. If there was a woman behind the counter, you'd say, "Where's the pharmacist?"

There was also these here stores that sell, like, shavin' cream, razor blades, and medicine, like a lotion store. They sold 'em. And there used to be the guys that went around with the suitcases. They sold razor blades and [*out of the side of his mouth*] condoms. They would go through all the motions of sellin' the other stuff. The big brand was Excello. They were the cheaper ones. Then they had fish skins. They were supposed to be very thin but strong. Ya paid a little bit more. For the Excello, you'd would get a dozen for a quarter. For fifty cents, you'd get the Trojans.

Lexington Avenue from 117th Street all the way to about 122nd Street was like a red-light district—hundreds of 'em. It was cheap—fifty cents. Most of 'em were not Italian—a lot from Pennsylvania. There were Polacks, and you had the gals from Finland and the Swedes up on 125th and 126th. Then ya had the dance-hall girls, like from the Rainbow Garden up on 125th.

There were some classy ones you couldn't get, what they would call today "the hundred-dollar broad." In those days they were in the ten-to-fifteen-dollar bracket. They were the more aristocratic ones.

Everybody had their own clientele, too. Some of the girls were in their thirties and some were in their teens. They used to stick up those places a lot. Ya hadda watch out when you're in there or they would take whatever ya had.

• • •

LENNY DEL GENIO: My brother Henny wasn't a fighter, but for some reason or other, he was a good puncher. Once I heard these men talking that once or twice he hit this guy and knocked 'em right out. He became known as "Champ." Because of his reputation, nobody picked on Lenny. In the meantime, I learned to take care of myself. I went to the boys' club at 126th Street and Lexington Avenue. The dues was ten cents a month. If you boxed—no dues. One time the boxing instructor had somebody in the ring. They were lookin' for a guy his size and he picked me. I said, "I can't fight."

"Come up here. We'll teach you."

Luckily, I threw a right hand, hit the kid on the chin, and knocked him down. The instructor said, "Where did you fight before?"

I said, "I never fought. Honest to God."

I was workin' in a blacksmith's shop in the neighborhood. It made my hands strong. I was seventeen when I went to the Golden Gloves. I scored seven knockouts in a row—one in seven seconds, which was the record. I wanted to go to the Olympics, but that was the Depression, and we needed the money.

Something nice did happen after I won the Gloves. We had a teacher in school, Miss Blankenstein. She was six foot two, all gray hair. She had a French class. I couldn't read French. I was lucky I could speak English. She really wanted me to learn. She put me in Italian. She thought I could do well, but my parents were born here, they never spoke Italian at home. In seventh grade she said in front of the class, "That bum, that quiet one, he's going to be the first one to beat his wife."

Anyway, after I won the Gloves, I went back to the school, and I went to see her. She couldn't believe that I was the Leonard Del Genio who got all that publicity. She said, "Vell, I am glad to hear you are good at something." She was proud and she was pleased.

VINCENT FERRARA: After my father died, my mother remarried. My stepfather purchased a pizza parlor. A week later came the Great Depression, and we were in bad straits again. He managed. He baked bread on the side, and he fed people. It was twenty-five cents for a dish of spaghetti, twenty-five cents for a dish of meatballs. Sometimes people didn't have money, and my father would say, "Okay, give him a dish."

CLARA FERRARA: During the Depression, my father worked wherever he could. "You got a chair to fix? I'll fix it." You didn't have to pay him if you didn't have the money. Then he went to work fixing office furniture for the WPA. One year he was without work. He didn't want to go on welfare. They came to your house and investigated. They would see if you had a radio. My father didn't want anybody in his home.

PETE PASCALE: I left school in '29. I went to help Pop. My brothers did too. In those days, when ya reached the sixth grade or the seventh grade, ya made it. When ya graduated, it was very big. You also wanted to go to work. You wanted to buy yourself things. I sold chewin' gum in the stations. You could sell maybe twenty packs a day—five cents a pack. But somebody would take a pack and drop a dime. I got a job in a newspaper stand on Sunday makin' three dollars. You kept a little, but most of the money went to the house.

VINCENT FERRARA: I didn't have the opportunity to date until I got involved with Clara. We had a pizzeria which was open seven days a week. If I wasn't there, I was in school or I was doing my homework. Saturday night was a busy night, so was Sunday. I saved my tip money, and I worked in the church hall for thirty-seven dollars a month, and all that put together enabled me to pay for my tuition at Fordham. I went during the day, and at night I was in the store. I did my homework on the rear table.

CLARA FERRARA: I wanted to go to college. [*She mimics a parental voice*] "The doctor's daughter goes to college, not the worker's daughter around the corner," but I went to Hunter, which was a free college. I worked for the NYA [National Youth Administration] in the school library. Then I came home and put bra straps through buckles with a book propped up in front of me. I don't think I ever slept.

PETER ROFRANO: I don't recall seeing much suffering. People who were thrown out on the street were considered outcasts because they didn't know how to control their own money. My father didn't get a pay cut. He was only making eight a week anyway. The rent was four dollars a month. Food was very cheap.

LENNY DEL GENIO: My father worked for the WPA as a foreman, but he wouldn't press anybody underneath him to work harder, so they fired him.

He was a nice guy. He tried to make whiskey in the house. The whole neighborhood would smell. He was always scared. Sure enough, somebody came up and knocked on the door and told him that the bulls were coming. They dumped everything into the toilet, and they broke down the still into pieces of metal. He was the only one who ever did it and got caught.

We had to go on relief until I started boxin' professionally. Relief then was a disgrace. I think there was one check that we got when I was seventeen or so. My mother cashed the check. My father wouldn't do it 'cause he was so humiliated.

I had won the Gloves, and there was no money. But when you won, they gave you these little gold gloves that were actually made out of gold. We took them to a pawnshop on Lexington Avenue and 124th Street. They gave us seventy-five dollars for them.

The first professional fight I had was on the Jack Sharkey–

Primo Carnera card. I boxed four rounds and got $150. I gave the money to my father and mother. I boxed maybe three times a month, and I got $150 to $300. I'd get the check, sign it, cash it, and give the money to my father. I saw some of it. There was a Howard's on 125th Street between Third and Lexington. Every time I had a fight, I went in and bought a suit for fifteen dollars. My mother used to complain, "Where are we gonna put the clothes?"

The mob guys never bothered me when I fought. My brother Joe was a bookmaker. He was connected with Joey Rao. With that knowledge, nobody ever bothered me.

DOROTHY DEL GENIO: And when times were tough, Joe made sure they ate.

LENNY DEL GENIO: Joe was a lot older than me. He studied to be a dental technician, but he found out he could make more money as a bookmaker. My parents had no problem with what Joe was doing. Nobody was getting hurt. If you wanted to make a bet, instead of going to the track, you went to Joe.

Numbers were big. It was all based on the prices at the track. At four or five o'clock, you would walk by the store, and he'd have a three up there, because three was the first number. Then after the races another number would appear—a two. The number was three two, and then the third number would appear, maybe a zero, and the number was 320.

My uncle Willie, he was a nice guy. Him and Johnny Hayes used to have a sheet up at my grandmother's with all the numbers that were played on it. They made a lot of money. He never had to work. Then he became a loaner—a loan shark. People always paid back. You see the bad stuff in the movies, not in life.

DOROTHY DEL GENIO: You would have to see Uncle William, he was so quiet. You could almost refer to him as a sissy kind— spotlessly clean, immaculately dressed. He never cursed, rarely even spoke, so he would never be a crude or rude person. That's why he only loaned to people who he knew.

LENNY DEL GENIO: He did no breakin' of legs. That's only an expression.

RAY ARCEL: When we lived in that neighborhood, the Black Hand predominated. The Black Hand was like the Mafia. You'd see the guy who supposedly was the boss of the whole thing. People would tip their hats to him. It was nothing to see a guy killed on the street. Every once in a while they would shake down the little storekeepers. If they didn't pay up, they broke the windows.

LENNY DEL GENIO: Pop Bullets was our boss. He was the Jimmy Hines of Harlem. Anything that went on there illegally, he had a piece of.

PETE PASCALE: Ciro Terranova lived across the street in 336. He was the Artichoke King. He got two cents for every artichoke that was sold practically all over the United States.

DOROTHY DEL GENIO: The thing was, nobody knew anything. You kept your mouth shut.

LENNY DEL GENIO: When you didn't have respect, you were in trouble.

DOROTHY DEL GENIO: That was fear.

LENNY DEL GENIO: Respect or fear, whatever it is you want to call it. They're very close. You could respect a guy out of fear.

PETER ROFRANO: A criminal can be deserving respect as a person if he's kind and decent—which sounds contradictory—and respects me. If he's a butcher, a baker, a candlestick maker, or a crook, that's his business. What do you want me to do about it?

The Black Hand would extort money from businesses, but very, very discreetly. They didn't have to ask for the money. The fellow would go in there and simply remove his hat. It was understood that if the businessman didn't hand it over, they would retaliate. That's wrong, but I admire the subtle art to the whole thing. I admire them. They know how to deal their business, like a Jewish person knows to deal in goods. By nature; it's in his blood.

They were still respectful of their families. I think today we are having so many troubles because we've lost respect for the family. If we would go back to that, I think it would solve some of our problems. He could be a criminal and demand respect for being a criminal. You had to respect him. I think that that's a great attitude. You respect me beyond all causes.

PETE PASCALE: That was one of the most peculiar things. People feel that well, this is their life, and that is what they decided. What's the difference? If they didn't do it, somebody else would do it. You get all this camouflaged talk. I don't think they care one way or another, as long as they're not involved, as long as it's not happenin' to them. The other thing is to keep your mouth shut and mind your own business. That was the classic of any neighborhood that was hard.

We knew them all. You gotta remember that these guys were my age. They used to hang on the corner. There was the Artichoke King, Rao, Joe Stutz, Joe Stretch. They were big. Joey Rao was tough. He was a hard man; so was Stutz. Oh, boy, they think nothin' of breakin' your legs. Of course they had a lotta gunmen who they would send out to knock somebody off.

They made a fast buck, handlin' stolen goods, sellin' things. They did shylockin'. I couldn't see that. I was always against these guys for that, and they knew it, so they went their way and I went my way. Most of them married the daughters of the other hoods. A lot of them intermarried in the hood families.

DOROTHY DEL GENIO: Lenny's sister went out with one of the big racketeers in Harlem, and she told him in no uncertain terms that she didn't like his business, because he wasn't legit.

ROSE SMREK: That was Tippi. She went out with Joe Morrone. He was [*she whispers*] no good. Papa was furious. I don't know how he put a stop to that, but when Tippi married Buff, she eloped, and Papa thought she went off to marry Joe Morrone. I remember my father actually cryin'. "My first daughter, if she went with that rackets guy, good-bye, that's the end of my daughter."

Then they got a telegram that she had married Buff. I remember our neighbor Mr. Mancuso came in before he got the telegram. He said, "Now, Francis, anything I can do—I know a lot of people." He was gonna break their legs. [*She laughs.*]

LENNY DEL GENIO: A lot of my friends ended up in the can, mostly holdups with a gun. Why they turned, I don't know. Money,

I guess. There's no easy money. I could never have money, because my mother and father would want to know where I got it. Boxing saved me, too. I always had to train.

PETE PASCALE: The real tough guys, they were all by themselves. They didn't walk up and down the block like Don Juans. They didn't hang out on the corners. They carried out their business secretly. They hung out at the Vesuvio Restaurant between Third and Lexington. There was a slaughter there. That was where some of the big mobsters got killed.

LENNY DEL GENIO: A guy like Joe the Heat handled dope. He sold it around the neighborhood to the older guys. One guy was called Joe the Coke. The reason he got that name was because he'd come home from work—shining shoes down at Grand Central Terminal—and he was tired. He'd be walking so slowly that he'd just about make his block. Then, two hours later, you'd see him all shaved and cleaned up scooting down the block, king of the hill. He already had some bahbah, as we called it. Joe the Heat was a nice guy. He didn't bother me. He had to make a livin'. This was how he made a livin'.

Joe Fats had a dozen guys who gave him the numbers, and he in turn went down to 116th Street, where these other people were involved. If he had too much on a number, he'd give it to Pop Bullets or whoever was up the ladder.

ROSE SMREK: Jimmy Fats was also a bookie. Him and Joe Stretch were all in the numbers; so were Joe and Rocky Morrone. Boy, all the names. There was Joe the Heat, Joe Fats, Jimmy Fats, the Dwarf, the Count, Charley Nigger, who was dark, and his brother Yella, who was light, and they had a brother Jimmy Hershey, because he was also dark.

There was another guy, Fat West. I was sittin' in the kitchen. We were on the top floor, and he was a big man, Fat West, and just like the Count, he dropped in from the roof. He said, "Toni, I gotta hide. The cops are after me."

"Go in the bedroom." She looked at me and told me to go next door. Then she went right on doin' what she was doin'. It was like nothin' to her.

CLARA FERRARA: Some friends of mine were married to some boys. We never asked what they did for a living. We didn't ask. We never knew what Joey Rao did. His wife was a lovely woman. When he died, I didn't know what to do. She was a member of our church group. I asked Father what I should do. He said, "We go, we come right out." I went wearing dark glasses. I said the rosary, and I left. What can you do?

Some girl I knew, her husband was a hit man. I never knew what he did. You didn't ask, especially if you knew he was a hood. She was a little ashamed, so you had to be careful. When her daughter got married, I was a little scared to go, but I went.

PETE PASCALE: Eventually, they all got it. One guy got it right in the building here. The only thing we were worried about was when we were on the block and ya never knew when they would start gunnin' for each other. We saw quite a bit of that. We were in front of the Cosmo Theater when they got Bill Dick and Joe Slattery. They shot 'em right outside the restaurant. We were duckin' under the goddamn signs that they had in front. They were machine-gunned just like ya saw it in the movies. They must have got hit by fifteen or twenty bullets.

I started to work in the settlement house when I was quite young. In 1931, I came on staff here. I've been here ever since. We hadda lotta good guys, too. Corsi, Marcantonio, and Mayor La Guardia came out of this house. Marcantonio was under the wing of Mayor La Guardia. Marcantonio was more to the left, but he was never for Communists, whatever they said. He had a lot of Communists backin' him, but these guys just came up, whether he asked 'em or not. They liked his ideas, and Marc was a guy who spoke his mind. He was the loneliest congressman in Congress. He had the big respect here, though. The old Italians knew him, and they knew he was an honest man.

COLUMBIA ALTIERI: Marcantonio was a half-assed politician. He actually brought all them Puerto Ricans up here for votes, all the low class.

ANNETTE RUBINSTEIN: He won the Puerto Ricans when they came, but it's ridiculous to say he brought them into the neighborhood for votes. Puerto Rico was in a desperate situation, and the people came in looking for jobs.

East Harlem was cheap. It was run-down, and once a certain group came, others followed. You sent for your cousin. You sent for your in-laws. They lived in tenements that had been occupied by Italians, who were moving out to Corona. The '20s were a prosperous time, comparatively, and a lot of the Italians very badly wanted to own property, so they put a down payment on a place and moved.

I first met Marc in 1934, in connection with the American Labor party. They asked me to be a candidate for their board, and naturally I met Marc, who was congressman from the ALP, and we became good friends.

People just loved him up in Harlem. He couldn't walk a block without being stopped thirty times. He took care of the community. In the neighborhood, they didn't think of it in terms of setting up legislation, they thought of more immediate problems. I was walking with him on 115th Street, and this woman came up to him and said, "Oh, Marc, the landlord wants to charge me five dollars a month for having an aerial on my roof, and that's not fair, is it?"

He said no. He took the name and address and walked on. About a quarter of a block later, he turned around and walked back to her, and he said, "You're only three doors from my house. Why don't you put your aerial on my roof until we get this straightened out?"

Inside his headquarters there would usually be 100 to 150 people sitting there with problems about the toilet, about the landlord, or an immigrant might be having some difficulties. Everybody whose number was called would come up and sit down at Marc's desk. In about two and a half minutes he would know what the problem was. Mostly it was routine.

He would say, "Now we have a lawyer who specializes in rent problems, and he'll take care of you." He would direct him to that desk, but everybody had been seen by Marc and taken care of by Marc. It was genius, politically, but you couldn't have done it unless you really liked people.

His work was political, as well. For example, he fought for the WPA, and he fought for jobs. Italian-Americans were barred from certain factory jobs because Italy was an enemy. He stopped that.

That was what he did more than most radicals: he kept the long-distance objectives and the individual needs in tandem.

B E R N A R D  B U R G O S : That's a very good, very good people, Marcantonio. He helped the Puerto Rican people—everybody. Everybody called him a Communist because he helped the people. I remember that time it was very hard to pay the rent. If the landlord wanted to get the rent, he put all your belongings in the street. That happened. They called Marcantonio. He come himself. "Put it back again." They put it back.

I was born in 1900 in Puerto Rico. My father worked on a farm. He picked bananas, yams, potatoes, rice. It wasn't his farm. I had two brothers and two sisters. We lived in a very small country house. They used the sugarcane to make a roof. They put it all together, tie it up, and make a roof from it. It was very tight, and it kept the water out. We got no toilet. We had to go outside in the ground under the tree.

There was no running water. We had to take it from the river. Sometimes we had to go through a plain from here [Madison Avenue] to Third Avenue with a big can—five gallons in a can. In the house we had a big barrel to keep the water.

When I was eleven, we moved because my father died, and my mother needed a job to support us. She worked as a houselady. I started to work when I was fifteen years old to help my mother. I learned a trade. I became a mechanic. Sometimes I had to work ten hours a day, sometimes eleven to make $1.50 a day.

I worked fixing machines in a shoe factory. When I was twenty, I told my mother I wanted to go to New York. I got two cousins over here in Brooklyn. They write me and they said, "If you want to come, come, because maybe you get a job over here."

My mother helped me to pay the fare. It cost fifty-five dollars. She had to work about five years to save the money. She had to borrow some of it. When I come over here, I paid it back. I left Puerto Rico in 1925. I came over here after five days. I didn't like it here. I tried to go back, but my cousin told me, "You'll get used to it. Don't worry."

I came to live in an Italian neighborhood in Brooklyn, and they treated me very nice. I got nothing to say against them. But I missed my mother. I missed my family. I read in the paper that

New York was very nice, but in the house where I came to live, we had nothing. There was no hot water, no place to take a shower. The toilet was in the yard. It was like Puerto Rico.

I had a letter of recommendation, and my cousins helped me to get a job in a factory. They gave me a machine to cut pipe for thirty-five cents an hour. It was a lot of money. Then I worked in a shoe factory. I worked on a machine that shined shoes. I wanted to be a mechanic, but my English was not good enough. The English I learned was on the job. Then I go to school from seven to nine, three times a week. I went to the school about two months, but I was very tired, so I didn't go anymore.

ALVIS SANCHEZ: In those times, the cigar makers were radical people. Samuel Gompers was a cigar maker. The first organization of labor was the cigar makers. While the cigar makers worked, the workers would pay maybe five or ten cents a week and they hired people to read to them. The reader would read any kind of newspaper, the union paper, every day, and any kind of books, like *Les Misérables*. Not everyone had an education, and many people didn't understand books like that. But when they finish, sometimes they would have a discussion about what they hear. The discussions were more open in America. The tobacco shops were the best place for talking, because the cigar makers were very radical, very partial in their politics. My father understood. He was an accountant, but he found that cigar makers made more money. An accountant made ten dollars a week. Sometimes a cigar maker makes ten dollars a day.

To make a cigar is an art. Some day the cigar maker come and make 200, and some day he cannot make one cigar. It depends how he feels. The artist says, "No, I can't work today. No feel nothing." It is the same with the cigar maker. He says, "I no go to work today." Most of the bosses understood this, because he puts his soul into making this cigar. Some people don't have the soul. They make anything like the machine.

There's also devotion—this is separate from the art. That is when the people want to make the best in quality. When your mother make the food, she put devotion to make the food the best for the family. For the laborer is the same thing. They make a beautiful cigar.

I was about nine years old when I started making cigars. My father was a *cigarrero*. I watched him. In the old times, when the kids come from the schools, they helped the father. When you come from the school, your mother give you lunch to take to your father. You go to the factory or the place where your father is working and you deliver the lunch to him. You watch. That's the old system.

BERNARD BURGOS: I came to Harlem in 1928. I got some friends over here, and they said they could get me an apartment here. I come to live on 102nd Street and Third Avenue. At that time, we got a mix over here of Jew, Italian, and Irish, not too many Puerto Ricans. Sometimes it was hard. I got a girlfriend, and I tried to get an apartment to live with her. I see a sign, "Apartment to Rent." I knocked on the door. When the lady she see my face, she said, "Ah, you Puerto Rican bastard. I got no apartment to rent."

I find an apartment from Italian people on 103rd Street and Third Avenue. I got along with the Italian people, but not the Irish. We got a lot of trouble with the Irish. We got a block over here, 111th Street. On one side was only Irish people. Any Puerto Ricans who walk on that side are looking for trouble. "Goddamn Puerto Ricans."

One day, I was walking and a bunch of Irishmen jumped on me, and I have to run. Somebody call to Brooklyn. The next day, about twenty-five people from Brooklyn come to the block with sticks, knives, everything. They had a big fight. The police came, and from that time it was better. I could walk on the block.

ALVIS SANCHEZ: I came to America when I was fifteen years old. I came because when you are living in America, you are living in a free country. You are free in Puerto Rico, but it's different over here. When I see the police coming here, I am happy. In other country, the people see the police, they get scared.

Over 50,000 were making cigars in New York in maybe 1,000 shops. There were factories and *chinchals*—small shops. The word comes from the Spanish slang for fleas. There were strippers, packers, choosers, who chose the colors. They were Italians, Jews, Germans.

At first I worked on 125th and Lexington. There were about twelve people in that shop. In *el barrio* you find on any corner a cigar shop. The Depression didn't hurt the cigar maker. But the artists disappeared over here. In Cuba, they believed they *made* the best cigars. Here, they wanted to *sell* the most cigars. They have cigars made by machine. Also cigars came from all over the Caribbean and from Europe. And the people who lead the union, they were becoming radical, like the politicians, and in some ways it was good and in some ways not. The farther consequences were bad, because the owners put in the machinery and they put the cigar makers out of work.

BERNARD BURGOS: In the Depression, I was working in the same place in Brooklyn. After that they closed the factory. That time you don't got compensation. I was about two months without job. Then I found another job in St. Luke's Hospital. I was working over there housekeeping. I got thirty-one cents an hour. That was good at that time. My mother and my sister was working. My mother worked in a laundry. It was a very hard job.

I broke off with my girlfriend, and I was living on Madison Avenue and 112th Street with my mother. She came in 1927. I didn't get married until I was fifty years old, because I like to *baile*, to dance, and I know if I get married when I am very young, I'm gonna have trouble with my wife.

When you live with a girl and you don't get married, people don't like that. But I don't care. The girl, she didn't want to get married. One time, the father and mother of the girl tried to fight with me, but I said, "She don't want to get married. What am I gonna do?" After that I meet the wife I have. I met her in 1948. She was a widow. She got three children. She got pregnant, and I married her. I am here many years now, but I don't want to go back to Puerto Rico. Better living here, but I don't think I am a New Yorker. I think I'm Puerto Rican.

ANNETTE RUBINSTEIN: Marc fought for the legislation that enabled people to take their literacy tests in Spanish. He got 10,000 letters a year from the neighborhood, and many of them were from Puerto Ricans. He used to boast about a civics exam in Puerto Rico, where the question was asked whether Puerto Rico has a congressman, and one young man wrote, "Yes, Marcantonio." He was very pleased with that.

PETE PASCALE: Marc was always broke. He never had a nickel. He'd give his last money to anybody that asked. If ya went up to him and said, "Marc, I need two dollars," if he had two dollars, he'd give ya his last two dollars. We had a barbershop right next to the center. He used to go there and get a haircut and a shave from Red. He'd go in there and we'd all be there, and he would say, "Red, give me a couple of bucks. I just gave a guy my money."

And Red would say, "Jeez, you're always givin' your money away. How much did the guy take?"

"C'mon, you got it."

And they would go back and forth like that. It was hot shit. We would laugh like hell. He was an honest man. We never had to worry about him.

ANNETTE RUBINSTEIN: He was always in that barbershop. For some reason, he didn't like to shave himself. People would come while he was in the chair. He really liked being in touch with the people that way. Marc and Miriam lived right in the area, on 116th Street. It was five or ten doors from where he was born. They lived in a tiny little apartment. They had an open house every New Year's. Hundreds of people would come and go all day.

He was extraordinarily learned in American history, and he had a real feeling of excitement about the opportunities of democracy in the United States. He said when he was going to high school that he had to hide his books before coming into the neighborhood, because none of the boys he went to school with were going. After his first victory, they had a big rally at 116th and Lexington. That became known as the "Lucky Corner." It became traditional after that that they would hold the final election rally on that corner. They would get thousands out there.

PETE PASCALE: The night before the election, from Lexington Avenue to Park Avenue was packed. I would say there would be maybe fifty to 70,000 people there. About 10:30 he would say, "All right, everybody go home and get a good rest. Get up bright and early, and don't forget to vote." That's the way it was. Every corner, there used to be a speech prior to the election. We knew more about politics than anyone. We knew so much that we could argue. When I was goin' to NYU later on, they used to talk about politics, and I'll never forget the class where they were talkin' about the captains who worked for the political group. I don't know where this stupid ass of a teacher lived. He said, "They were very prominent people. They were educated."

I started to laugh like hell. "What the hell are you givin' me? You wanna talk about the captains? I'll talk about the captains. They're stupid as hell. They're crooks. They're the opposite of what you're talkin' about. These guys are captains because they got a no-show job. These are the guys who go out and say, 'Look, do me a favor. Vote for him because I'll lose my job if he don't get elected.' "

Marc had his men, but his captains were a little different. His captains were more Republicans. He would get some money, and he would give it to the guys, who would pass it around to hand out these little postcards to vote for So-and-So.

ANNETTE RUBINSTEIN: He was bitterly anti-Mussolini from the beginning. They took his word for it. Still, they had been proud that Mussolini had put Italy on the map. It wasn't until the rise of Hitler and Fascism in general that people started having problems with him. The trains ran on time was the general idea. A good many of his older admirers had admired him as a Socialist. There was one old Italian who was convinced the real Mussolini was in a dungeon, that this was an impersonator, and the real Mussolini was still a Socialist.

CLARA FERRARA: Some people gave their gold rings to raise money for the war against Ethiopia. They used to have parades for that idiot. I didn't like him, and my parents opposed him. But there were a lot of people in those parades. We had to lock my father up when they had those parades. We didn't want him to talk. There were too many people for Mussolini. He would say, "I'm in America. I can call them names." He was right, but we were afraid.

•  •  •

LENNY DEL GENIO: After all my fights there would be a big celebration, win or lose. My grandmother would cook, and the whole neighborhood came up to the house. There was always enough food for everybody.

I was just twenty-three years old, but I was growin' broadwise and I couldn't make 145 pounds. I also couldn't get a title fight.

Tony Canzoneri was the champ and, in my mind, Tony was ready to go. I thought I would get a shot, but it didn't happen.

Tony would fight anybody, but his manager didn't want it. Lew Ambers was comin' up, but they wouldn't match me with him either. They thought, "Why put a guy who is in line for a title fight with a guy who is a good puncher? He could get hurt." My punchin' power was an advantage, but it also hurt me.

Then I hurt my hand. I hit this guy on the forehead and bang! I could feel it in my whole arm. It was broken in three different spots. Hands weren't made for bammin' people in the head. They said I hit too hard for my bones. I stayed off three or four months. I had it operated on. [*There is still a large bony mass protruding from the back of his hand.*] When you can't punch, it's like goin' to war with a gun with no bullets. I boxed with a bad hand a couple of fights — stupid. I won but I wasn't knockin' anybody out. Then I fought Al Netlow, and he licked me. I couldn't punch. The first punch I hit him, oh, God, I knew I was kiddin' myself, and that was it. I was twenty-three and a retired fighter. I had lost about nine fights out of seventy, not too bad, but I lost important fights.

PETER ROFRANO: I was about seven or eight years old when I decided I wanted to be a priest. It's the funniest thing. I used to go to church every Sunday, and in the church there was the orchestra and the balcony. For one reason or another I had to go up to the balcony, because I was late or it was crowded. I resented that I couldn't see so well from up there, and I kept saying, "I don't want to be up here, I want to be down there," and that was one of the reasons why I became a priest.

All during that time, we were indoctrinated that we would have to give up the idea of having a family. That never bothered me. After I graduated high school in 1933, I went to the seminary in Rome until 1939. It was like going to prison. For six years, I was not allowed to smoke or read a newspaper or listen to the radio. When my time was done, I came back.

As a child, I wasn't allowed to come on 116th Street, so I knew hardly anything about the feast of the Madonna. I just knew it existed, because it was customary for anybody who lived outside New York City to come and stay with the family for a few days before, eating, feasting. This I always remember.

The celebration really kept the people up here together. You'd see the statue pass by on 109th Street. People would follow with candles in their hands. I had an aunt who had a very bad birth, and she promised that as long as she lived she would carry this square with candles on it in the parade. She would parade without shoes. A lot of people did that. That was the sacrifice she made.

Others would order candles, sometimes nearly a hundred pounds, from the shops around here. They would bring it in, and the church would accept it. We loaded them in a chute that went downstairs. We used them during the year for services or gave them to the other churches. Sometimes, if they were badly melted, they would be sold as old candles.

CLARA FERRARA: I was in church night and day during the fiesta. There were so many people, I had to learn first aid, because they were collapsing on line. People came barefoot. People came on their knees to the altar. Some women would be licking the ground. Some would bring in wax candles of the hand or a foot. I got handed a pair of earrings that were worth a lot of money. She [the Madonna] wears them on centennials. To us, the Blessed Mother is alive. She's a person to us. We devote time to her. They had a brand-new dress made for one of the celebrations, and it was a great honor when the father asked me if I wanted to dress the infant for that occasion.

RAY ARCEL: They used to have all those banners. The poor people didn't have what to eat, but they used to pin that buck up there. I'll never forget the first time we saw the nuns with the crosses— we were scared to death. I ran upstairs, and I said to my father, "These women were walkin' around with swords!"

PETE PASCALE: We participated in the feast by buyin' a sausage frankfurter. In those days they had everything—a bottle of beer, soda, pizza. We liked the sausage. I don't know why it always tasted better there. No matter how your mother cooked 'em, that guy did it better. Even the frankfurter, no matter how you cook frankfurters at home, you can't beat the guy on the corner. Maybe because the water was in there for a month or something. If it didn't taste right, we used to say, "You usin' fresh water?"

Vincent Ferrara: I graduated from law school in 1940. No jobs were available. I didn't want to get involved with politics. To me it was a dirty word. I wrote to various departments for a job. I sent one letter to the district attorney's office. I went in for an interview. I told him where I was from, and I went to work there. Later, I became a judge in domestic-relations court.

Clara Ferrara: He was my girlfriend's brother, but his mother frowned on our talking to each other. He was to become a lawyer and marry a doctor's daughter or something. Anyway, we managed. We went out secretly for six years. I was twenty-one when we started. We went to the Music Hall downtown. Then we'd go out every Saturday morning, because he had to work on Saturday night making pizzas. Saturday mornings—I could never understand those dates. We had to come home at a different time, too. He would come visit me at my friend's house.

When I was at Columbia, I would tell my girlfriend, "He's going to pass to see if I'm going to school or not." She wanted him, so she wouldn't tell me he passed. His friend's father owned a coal truck. Sometimes, if he couldn't get one of the cars, he'd come in that. Finally, his parents found out. I think his uncle followed us, but it was the same as everybody else. They realized that they couldn't break us up, and we got married in 1945.

Dorothy Del Genio: I was a beautician. I came from Pennsylvania looking for work. I got a concession of my own in a barbershop on 125th Street, and I was the manicurist. Lenny's whole family came in for manicures. You got a shave, haircut, and a manicure for $1.50.

He would only come in for a haircut on occasion, but everybody bowed to him. He was the neighborhood hero. After he met me, he started coming in just to make a date. Right?

Lenny Del Genio: Oh, yeah. I needed a manicure like a hole in the head.

Dorothy Del Genio: He came in just to hold hands. I knew it.

You couldn't keep anything secret in that neighborhood. His uncle knew. Everybody knew he was hanging around the barbershop too much. Especially him, because he had some popularity. They used to say to me, "Don't you know who he is? That's Del Genio, the fighter."

But I never went to a fight. He had just stopped fighting when I met him. His family was very cordial to me. We were married in our little hometown, in my own church. They all came to the wedding.

LENNY DEL GENIO: After I quit fightin', I took up accountin' for two years and I went to work for the IRS. A few years ago, I was playin' guitar for this fella. He told me they were gonna make a picture called *The Godfather,* and they were lookin' for Italian-lookin' people in my age group. I went down there, and I knocked on the door. This guy said, "If you're not Italian, don't come in."

I said, "My name is Del Genio and I'm Italian." He asked me to say something. I took a screen test Monday. He called me Tuesday. Wednesday I was in *The Godfather.* In one scene I was pitchin' quarters while Jimmy Caan was makin' love to somebody upstairs. In another scene I knocked off Moe Green. It was something. I kept thinkin', "Here I am, from Harlem, where all this stuff was actually goin' on." It was wonderful. All I had to do was act natural.

I've been in forty pictures since then. I was in *Flamingo Kid.* They wanted someone to do the Peabody. That was right down my alley. I used to do it for hours at Roseland.

RAY ARCEL: One day, I said to my father, "You think it might be possible to move to a Jewish neighborhood?" I told him we were fighting all the time. "These fellows are supposed to be our friends, but we do nothing but fight with them."

I said I was getting tired of it. My father had a friend who lived on 118th Street between Fifth and Lenox. That was a Jewish neighborhood, so we got an apartment up on the fifth floor.

Living there, I met a fellow who was a boxer—Benny Valger. He was a Russian. He was about my age, and he was an excellent boxer. Through Valger, I eventually realized this was what I wanted to do, and I'd go to the gym all the time.

At that time, Benny Valger was managed by a man named Doc Bagley. Sometimes I worked in his corner. I used to swing the towel. The fights were in small club rooms. Everybody in there was smoking. From the back of the room, you couldn't see the fight because of the smoke, so you had to do something to get a little air, so you swung the towels.

Doc Bagley used to chew tobacco. When a fighter would get cut, he would take the chewing tobacco out of his mouth and squeeze it on him. That would stop the flow of blood. Now Bagley had a preliminary kid, and he booked him over in Jersey. This night he couldn't make it, so he called me at home and asked me if I would go over and handle the fighter. I was going to be Doc Bagley. The first thing I did was buy some chewin' tobacco for a nickel. I sat in the corner, and I was praying for the guy to get cut. *[He laughs.]* Then all of a sudden, there was an imaginary flow of blood. I took a bite of the tobacco, and I kept chewing it. The next thing I knew, I was out, underneath the ring. I didn't know what happened. They called the ambulance. I was white as a sheet. The doctor was examining me, and he says, "What did you do?"

I says, "I must have swallowed the chewin' tobacco."

There were a lot of kids who wanted to be fighters, and there were a lot of clubs up in Harlem. And you know, the same guys I used to fight with, they used to come and visit me at the gym. They were hungry, and there was no way you could make a dollar, but you could fight for three or five dollars. That was a lot of money. You could bring that money home to your family. My father knew what we were going through. I think deep down he felt that he was responsible for it. We did the best we could. You just went through life and hoped that tomorrow would be a better day.

ANNETTE RUBINSTEIN: Marc used to say when people asked him about local things, "Look, I'll have to talk it over with my grandmother." They thought it was a joke, but it wasn't. His mother was what was considered a stereotypical Italian hausfrau. She really knew nothing, but his grandmother was deeply interested in politics. Her father was one of Garibaldi's men, and she was very, very proud that, when she was a little girl of three or four, Garibaldi had kissed her.

Marc went to school with Thomas Luchese, and there were a lot of those guys in Harlem. It was his grandmother who said to him, "You'll grow up to be either a great man or a gangster, so plan to be a great man."

After he died, Cardinal Spellman refused to allow Marc to be buried in a Catholic cemetery, because he wasn't really a practicing Catholic. I sat with Miriam in the funeral parlor as the people came to view the body, and one after another the old ladies said, "If only the old lady were here, she would go to the cardinal with her stick. She would never allow this to happen." By the way, the funeral director named one of his sons Vito and the other Marc, after him.

Marc always voted his conscience. In 1950, the administration wanted a unanimous vote from Congress in support of the Korean War. They got it—except for Marc. He was the only one in both houses who stood against it. He was offered all kinds of things to change his vote, including the Democratic nomination for mayor, which would have been his life's ambition, because it was tantamount to his winning the election.

It was 400 and something against one, so there was no practical reason for his vote, except, he said, "There has to be some record for history that there are some Americans who vote their conscience."

PETE PASCALE: Nobody took that McCarthy bullshit serious. The problem was that the children of the fathers became the blowhards—the idiots, who understood everything, which is a lot of shit. The fathers knew a lot more than their stupid-ass sons. We had a lot of fights in the old neighborhood with these young guys about this Communism. Half of them didn't even know what the hell Communism was.

There was another batch who felt that he [Marcantonio] brought in all the Puerto Ricans to get elected. That was another bullshit. He didn't bring anybody in. We still hear it today. That's a lot of shit. I knew him, and I knew him well. He had some faults, like everybody else, but he was a helluva guy.

# The
# East
# Side

THE MOST IMPORTANT tea party of the American Revolution didn't take place in Boston, but in Manhattan—Murray Hill, to be exact.

It was September 15, 1776. From their moorings in Kip's Bay, the British landed on Manhattan Island behind a hail of grapeshot that sent the remainder of Washington's army fleeing north in terror. Then, just as he was about to ensnare the laggard rebels, General Howe made a disastrous—but typically British—move. He stopped for tea.

When the Redcoats appeared at the farmhouse belonging to the widow Mary Lindley Murray, she invited the general inside for refreshment, an offer sweetened by the sight of the widow's three pretty daughters. Murray, who knew what she was doing, made sure the little visit, at what is now 37th Street and Park Avenue, lasted a few hours. By then, the Americans had escaped the British trap, and Washington was able to regroup his forces for a counterattack the next day. Howe's tea was easily the most expensive refreshment in the history of the empire.

The neighborhoods of Manhattan's East Side from 14th Street to 50th Street took widely divergent paths in the years following the Revolution, ranging from the terror-filled streets of the Gashouse area to the cloistered elegance of Gramercy Park. They also included the upper-middle-class blocks of Stuyvesant Square, the aristocratic homes of Murray Hill, and the Old World tenements of Kip's Bay and Turtle Bay.

Much of the southern portion was owned at one time by Peter Stuyvesant. Dutch residents dominated the area until the last half of the nineteenth century, when an influx of German and Irish, as well as Jews and Slavs, occupied the brownstone homes. The families were largely middle- and upper-middle class, many of them doctors associated with nearby hospitals, which are still plentiful in the neighborhood.

St. George's, one of Manhattan's distinguished churches, was erected in 1847 on East 16th Street. J. P. Morgan was its most prominent parishioner, and he is still remembered fondly by St. George's elders. Morgan was a senior warden there and was buried from the church in 1913 following a service that drew thousands of curiosity seekers to the neighborhood.

Stuyvesant Square and Irving Place were also O. Henry's stomping grounds. The short-story writer found his inspiration everywhere around the neighborhood, from the tables at Healy's pub (now Pete's Tavern) for his short story "The Lost Blend" to the birds flocking in a park for "The Sparrows in Madison Square":

> "Birds," I said fiercely. "The brown-throated songsters carolling songs of hope and cheer to weary men toiling amid the city's dust and din. The little feathered couriers from the meadows and woods chirping sweetly to us of blue skies and flowering fields. The confounded little squinteyed nuisances yawping like a flock of steam pianos, and stuffing themselves like aldermen with grass seeds and bugs, while a man sits on a bench and goes without his breakfast. Yes, sir, birds! look at them!"

Sometimes, the source of a neighborhood's name is a matter for debate—Hell's Kitchen, for instance, where a number of popular legends are bandied about. There is no such question about the Gashouse area. Before World War II, anybody wandering around that neighborhood simply had to look up and breathe deeply if he was curious about its name.

The first of the four gashouses was built in 1842 at the foot of 21st Street. Although they were only a few stories tall, they were relative skyscrapers in their day, towering over the area like scarecrows in a bean field. They were also leaky affairs, so much so that only the most desperate tenement dwellers would live in the neighborhood.

As if the fumes weren't enough, the neighborhood also gave rise to some of the most notorious gangs in the city's history. The most famous was the Gashouse Gang, a conglomeration of thugs and burglars, who reigned for decades, until Police Captain Alexander S. "Clubber" Williams arrived on the scene in 1871. Williams had earned his nickname and did well by it in his new assignment. One night, he dramatically demonstrated the success of his persuasive powers for reporters. He hung his watch and chain from a lamppost at Third Avenue and 23rd Street and then strolled around the block. Before his tenure, such an act would have been akin to dangling a side of beef in front of a hungry lion, but when Williams returned, his jewelry was untouched.

Williams did not eliminate the gang, however. He simply drove it from his precinct. The gang soon found that the area from 11th to 18th streets provided spoils aplenty. According to Herbert Asbury, some 200 Gashousers committed nearly thirty holdups a night until 1914, when their leader, Tommy Lynch, was knocked off by a rival gang.

Due to the numerous gangs operating on the East Side, turf battles were frequent. Names that once struck fear into the hearts of neighborhood residents now seem wonderfully colorful and noticeably Irish, with monikers like the Terry Reillys, Corcoran's Roosters, and the Jimmy Curley Gang.

The Fourth Avenue Tunnel Gang operated just out of the Gashouse district. The group took the name from its hideout, a railroad tunnel under Fourth Avenue (now Park Avenue) that stretched from 32nd to 42nd Street. Their leader was one of the best fist fighters in the city. He eliminated his only rival by throwing him in front of a passing train. The chief was Richard Croker, later the boss of Tammany Hall and supreme ruler of New York until he was deposed by the reformer Seth Low in 1901.

Another fearsome ensemble was the Car Barn Gang, formed in 1911 by hoods who hung around the East Side docks. The Car Barn Gang was so powerful it posted notices in its district warning police to stay out. After several cops had been stabbed and beaten by the gang, the police would venture into the area only in groups of four and five. The Car Barners' leader was Big Bill Lingley, who enjoyed parading around with two revolvers, a blackjack, and a slingshot on his belt. Lingley's sidekick, Freddie "The Kid" Muehfeldt, supposedly came from a good family, went to Sunday school, and had aspirations to the clergy. The dreams of both men ended abruptly when they were convicted and subsequently executed for the murder of a wholesale liquor dealer.

To be sure, there was more going on in the area than murder and burglary. Even an East Side tough always had time for romance. So went the popular song of the 1890s, "The Belle of Avenoo A":

> I am de belle dey say ov Avenoo A,
> And if yer strollin' down dat way
> Yer pretty sure to see me on de street.
> 'Cos I'm somethin' of a walker,
> And de fact dat I'm a "Corker"
> Is de talk ov ev'ry copper on de beat.
> Billy McNeil he is me steady,
> And yer'll allus find him ready
> Fur a scrapp'n match or any sort of fight.
> He's de bouncer at Clary's,
> And he says of all de fairies
> I'm de only one he tinks is out o'sight.
>
> Git off de Earth, and don't attempt to stay
> 'Cos I'm a queen! De belle of Avenoo A.

"De Belle of Avenoo A" may have been a queen, but her realm did not extend very far. Just a few "avenoos" to the west was what must have seemed to some outsiders to be a real principality. The buildings surrounding Gramercy Park huddle together to protect their charge like the old Western stagecoaches circling together to repel rampaging Indians. That ring of protection extends to the park itself, which is surrounded by a high locked fence. The flowers and shady benches inside are only for local property owners and approved neighbors.

Actually, the park is less a park than a yard belonging to the houses that ring the square. That was the plan of Samuel B. Ruggles, who laid out Gramercy Park in 1831, knowing that the private lot would enhance surrounding property values.

The property was originally farmland owned by Peter Stuyvesant, who, according to Gramercy Park historian Stephen Garmey, bought it along with its "dwelling house, barns, woods, six cows, two horses, and two young Negroes." The Dutch originally called the area "Krom Moerasje" or "Little Crooked Swamp." It was later called Crommashie Hill. Still later, when James Duane later built his home on the land, he called it "Gramercy Seat."

Ruggles had no problem selling the homes that overlooked the park. The neighborhood's residents would soon include some of the city's most well-known names, like Mayors James Harper, Abram Hewitt, and Edward Cooper. Edward Cooper's father, Peter, built the "Tom Thumb" railroad engine (which lost a famous match race against a horse in 1831) and also founded Cooper Union in 1859, so that the city's young could get a higher education without charge.

Mrs. Stuyvesant Fish, pretender to *the* Mrs. Astor's society throne, was a Gramercy Park resident in the 1890s. According to Garmey, Mrs. Fish owned the first car to appear on the square, but she didn't know much about driving it. Supposedly, on her first time behind the wheel, she ran over the same gentleman three times before he fled in horror, never to be seen again.

Gramercy Park was also home to Cyrus Field, the man who laid the transatlantic cable; Samuel Tilden, who had the 1876 presidential election stolen from him; and Edwin Booth, one of this country's most celebrated actors. As illustrious a group as this was, most of it was lost on the young Henry Noble MacCracken, who later wrote a delightful memoir of his Gramercy Park childhood during the 1890s. To little Henry, Booth and Field were no more than a couple of curious old men who liked to play marbles.

Murray Hill was another popular roosting spot for members of New York's Four Hundred in those years. Because of covenants in the original leases, it was nearly as exclusive as Gramercy Park, barring, as it did, all commercial development in the area, until the ban was broken in 1915.

It hadn't always been so desirable. Just over a half-century before, Murray Hill had been wide-open farmland, so deserted that when one downtown merchant, Coventry Waddell, drove out to buy a piece of property in the area, his wife sat under a tree and cried because she was going to be living so far away from the city.

Eventually, the New York and Harlem Railroad united the area with the city, bringing with it the pain and pleasures of city life. The railroad dumped enough soot and steam on Park Avenue to make it all but unlivable for humans. In fact, many of its early inhabitants were of the animal genus, pigs and goats owned by Irish squatters.

In 1871, Commodore Vanderbilt built the Grand Central Depot, on 42nd Street and Fourth Avenue. While the rest of the area around the station was built up, the Commodore's son, William H. Vanderbilt, kept the ground to the west of the terminal beautifully green, as a pasture for Maud S., his trotter and the most famous racehorse of his day.

While the Fourth Avenue Tunnel Gang rivaled the Gashouse group to the south, Murray Hill belles had a song trumpeting their qualities. Written for one of the famed Rogers brothers revues, this one entitled *The Rogers Brothers in Wall Street* (1896), "The Belle of Murray Hill" was a bit more refined than her counterpart to the south:

> *Of a charming young belle*
> *whose first name was Nell*
> *I will sing.*
> *She dresses with taste*
> *in a lovely shirtwaist*
> *the real thing.*
> *In artistic ways*
> *the piano she plays*
> *to a standstill.*
> *And none can excel*
> *this beautiful belle*
> *of Murray Hill.*

To the east lay the neighborhoods of Turtle Bay and Kip's Bay, the latter named for a farmer and the former for the rocky indentation of the East River by 42nd Street, which resembled a turtle. The usually penniless Edgar Allan Poe, who apparently slept in more houses than George Washington, lived for a while at a nearby farmhouse. As he did on the West Side, Poe wandered the banks of the East River searching for inspiration. In an 1844 article for the *Columbia Spy*, he foresaw the eventual destruction of his arcadian retreat. "I could not look on the magnificent cliffs, and stately trees, which at every moment met my view, without a sigh for the inevitable doom—inevitable and swift," he wrote.

Poe's prophecies proved true. As the city's grid plan took effect, the hills were leveled and the wetlands drained. A few years hence, the Second and Third Avenue Els would insure further deterioration. Soon, 42nd Street near the river housed a series of meat-packing plants and slaughterhouses, which regularly dumped gallons of blood and entrails into Poe's beloved cove. In 1939, *The WPA Guide to New York City* described Turtle Bay as a faceless neighborhood of flimsy tenements. It was also—at least according to current card catalogues—without a belle to call its own.

# The Witnesses

ROMAN ALVAREZ (1922–) was a lightweight boxer before he served in World War II. After the war, he worked in construction and as a bus driver until his retirement in 1983.

TONY ARRIGO (1923–) is a World War II veteran. He worked for Railway Express until he retired in 1974. His friend ROCKY ALFREDO also participated in this interview.

JOHN SEAMAN BAINBRIDGE (1915–) was born and raised on Gramercy Park. He is a retired law-school dean. His sister, BARBARA BAINBRIDGE MCINTOSH, offered her recollections via a detailed letter recalling her youth.

DR. BEATRICE BISHOP BERLE (1902–) is a graduate of Vassar College and Columbia University medical school. After her graduation, she practiced community medicine for many years.

VINNIE CASLAN (1915–) is a World War II veteran. He worked as a steamfitter until he retired at the age of sixty-two.

HENRY CROOKHORN (1912–) served in the Signal Corps in World War II. He is a retired telephone-company employee. His wife, EVELYN, also participated in this interview.

HENRY FENNER (1901–) was in the real-estate business in New Jersey for many years. He now lives in New Hampshire.

DR. OLIVE HUBER (1904–) earned a Ph.D. in physiology from Hunter College and taught there until her retirement.

FLORENCE WILLISON (1902–) grew up in the Gashouse area and then escaped to Greenwich Village to live the bohemian life. She was married briefly to the painter Jack Tworkov. Her second husband, George F. Willison, was an editor of the WPA guidebook series. She now lives in upstate New York.

FLORENCE WILLISON: My grandmother grew up in Central Park. They had a farm there and were squatters, really. This was before the Civil War, when they had regular epidemics, and her parents died in one of them when she was just a child. When they died, the hired man took over the farm, and she had to work awfully hard. She remembered getting up early in the morning and taking their produce down to market. Apparently, she didn't have shoes, and she developed very bad rheumatism.

She never learned to read or write, although she knew what was going on. She was affianced to a young man who went off to the Civil War. He told his brother that if something ever happens to him, he wanted him to go back and tell her. Well, he was killed in the war. His brother went back, and she married him. He was a tinsmith. She had been working so hard, and when she got married, she worked even harder. They had eleven children. One of them was my mother.

They lived on East 19th Street. One day, at the age of forty-five, my grandfather came home and, having sired eleven kids, said, "I'm not going to work anymore. Now, I am the *herr* in the house." My mother had to go to work when she was fourteen. She became a very fine seamstress. She made all our clothes, and they were lovely clothes. She didn't like her own father, but she loved her father-in-law, who was also a wood-carver, like my father. She thought he was a prince among men.

HENRY CROOKHORN: My father was born in England in 1861, and my mother in 1871. He was the head butler for August Belmont and Ogden Mills Reid. My mother also worked for them. She was a governess. The head butler ran the whole household in those days. As my father got older, it got to be too much for him, and he left and became a doorman in an apartment house on Park Avenue. They liked his English accent.

My father, bein' English, had this autocratic way about him. He was always dressed carefully, even at home. He used to annoy us with his preciseness. On his dresser he kept a powder box which he used to powder his hair every morning.

In his later years, when he worked at 277 Park, he wore his plaid suits and a wing collar and maybe an ascot. He had fallen off a streetcar on Lexington Avenue—one of those summer cars— and when he recovered, he walked with a cane. He looked so proper, they used to call him the Mayor of Third Avenue.

He was a typical Englishman, very proud. He insisted my mother walk us up on Park Avenue. He wouldn't let her cross Third toward Second and First, and he insisted that we play on Lexington and Park Avenue. In those days the mothers wore those hats with a lot of feathers in 'em, and they had very narrow waistlines and long skirts. They'd be rollin' their carriages along Park Avenue and Lexington Avenue. I envied the wealthy people, and I would tell my mother that. She would say, "When you grow up and do right and get a good education, and keep your nose clean, you can be a wealthy man." It never turned out that way.

HENRY FENNER: Mother was born in '75 and she came here in '87 from Germany. This childless couple brought her over, and she was indentured to them. They lived on 68th Street between First and Second avenues. Across the street from them was a large hill with goats up there. Years later, when we visited them, I can remember climbing up there and still seeing the goats.

My father was seventeen when he came. He was born in '75, also. When I was two years old, in 1903, he opened his own store on the corner of 17th Street and Third Avenue. We had the whole building. We lived on the first floor and Dad rented the second floor. Ours was a cold-water flat with three bedrooms, kitchen, and parlor. There were four of us.

I bathed in the kitchen until I got too big. After that I took my baths in the barbershop. You went through the shop into a back door, and he had two or three separate rooms with the old-fashioned bathtubs on legs. You could have all the hot water you wanted plus soap and towel for twenty-five cents. In those days, every customer had his separate shaving mug with their names on them, and I can still see my father's mug on the shelf above where I took my bath.

I had several jobs around the house. The kitchen had a coal stove, and I had to sift through the coal ashes to make sure any that were only half used up were reused again. I also worked in the store every day, even on Sunday. Packaging wasn't a big thing in those days. So many things came in bulk. Sugar came in barrels and tea came in casks. After school, I had to weigh off different quantities in small bags and tie them off. I had to take out rolls and milk before I went to Sunday school and deliver it to different customers.

DR. OLIVE HUBER: Henry used to deliver to this house. We got our milk from him or Sheffield's or Borden's. It was fresh and delicious. The deliveries were left in the windows downstairs, outside the house. We got milk, cream, sour cream, butter, eggs. All that was left in the window around six in the morning. You would get up at seven or so and they were taken in.

FLORENCE WILLISON: Our milk was miserable. It wasn't until after I had grown up and had left that I really tasted good milk. You bought it at the corner grocery store in a tin bucket, and it was always sort of blue. It came in a great big can, and I'm sure they must have watered it. I never tasted real milk until I got it in bottles. I've heard the stories about the cream that would rise to the top. Well, there was never any cream on the top of our milk.

OLIVE HUBER: This house was built in 1850. My father bought it in 1890. The metal grates on the windows were installed on account of the draft riots in Union Square during the Civil War. The house was gaslit until the '20s. You had to light each lamp of the chandelier individually. The desk lamps had to be lit by running a line from the chandelier. Each fireplace still has a Franklin stove to heat the rooms, and each room upstairs is equipped with a register where the heat can be turned off and on through the chimney.

I was born in this house in 1904 and I've never lived any place else. My grandfather came from Germany in 1848. My mother's family goes back to 1700. Her last name was Bingham. My father graduated from medical school in 1877. He did everything. He was a surgeon, a gynecologist, an obstetrician, a pediatrician. He and Dr. Jacobi, for whom Jacobi Hospital is named, were the founders of the American Pediatric Society. From 1899 or so, the specialties began to arise, and the pediatric specialty was one of the first.

The change in medicine that has come about is gargantuan. He was on the staff of just about every major hospital, and there was no remuneration at all. My father never sent out a bill in his life. He took care of anybody who needed care. He said, "I don't need to make out a bill. What's the point? When they come, they pay three dollars. If they can pay, they pay."

There was no such thing as an appointment. He had office hours from 9:00 to 11:00 in the morning. Everybody knew that, and they'd come from 9:00 to 11:00. Then in the afternoon he did volunteer work at the hospitals.

He started practicing before a bacillus was discovered. You just took care of communicable diseases the best way you could. Most of it was hygiene. They didn't know what viruses were. If a kid had a fever, they put him right in a cold bath. It worked. There were few pills. They knew about creosote for coughs and things like that. They would remove congestion in an area by putting a poultice in another area to draw the congestion away. They used leeches for clots. They're getting back to that kind of thing now. There was a lot of physiotherapy, which meant he often prescribed rest and exercise.

My father was the first one to remove a nail from a trachea that a kid had swallowed. The samovar in my living room was given to him by the tsar. He was one of the foremost physicians in the country, so he was sent to Russia in 1910 to see what could be done about the hemophilia of Alexis. Doctors from all the countries examined him, and they all decided that there was nothing that could be done. They each were given a samovar and sent home.

He did obstetrics, so he never knew when he was going to be called, but he always went. He never complained. He had the most passive disposition I have ever seen. I don't remember him ever raising his voice. He carried his little black bag, which had the same things it does today, except he always carried a flashlight, because many of the places he went to didn't have good illumination.

He also had a gun. I don't know if he ever used it. My father stabled his horses in the Gashouse district, which was a rough area. You didn't go over there unless you had a car or somebody was with you. There were people who were killed there in the evening hours.

VINNIE CASLAN: It was a rough neighborhood. The Gashouse Gang was before my time, but we always had groups for protection and things like that. The Irish and the wops were always fightin' and the Jewish boy was the arbitrator.

They called it the Gashouse district 'cause there was a gashouse on 16th Street and one on 20th Street. They used to remark that the fumes from the gashouses kept ya healthy. I never noticed 'em, and I never heard any complaints.

My people were here over a hundred years. They came in the 1880s from Ireland. I was born in 1915 on 17th Street and Avenue C. I was the last of nine. My father worked for the city in sanitation. It was steady income. My mother was a janitor. We lived in a normal tenement house—a walk-up, no electric, no hot water, toilet in the hallway.

There were all big families in this neighborhood. They couldn't afford condoms, I guess. My religion was to have sex to have a child. People who couldn't afford one had two. That was a stupid thing in the religion, but people practice it, and I never heard of abortions in those days.

FLORENCE WILLISON: We lived at 340 East 19th Street, between First and Second, on the same block as my grandparents. I guess that was the Gashouse area, too. On our block, the houses were perfectly beautiful. There were areaways in front, and on the second floors of the houses were balconies with wrought-iron railings. It was quite beautiful.

The streets were paved with large square pieces, maybe slate. It was very beautiful after it rained, very subtle colors. It was so subdued you could barely see, but it was lovely. You could see through to New Jersey on a summer day, and as the people walked by on the street they had these long shadows behind them.

Out back, the wash line extended from the back window to the pole. I remember once the rope broke, and all the clean laundry fell into the backyard and had to be done all over again. Well, the person who fixed it was called the "Line-up man." Once in a while, he would come around and stand in front of the backyard and yell, "Line up, line up."

Our neighborhood was mostly Irish Catholics. We were the only German people, and there was one Italian family. We would play in the middle of the street, because there was hardly any traffic at all.

The man next door, Mr. Callahan, had a hansom cab, and then he had the first taxicab. It was the first car on the entire block. For a great treat, he would fill the cab up with kids and drive them around the block. It was pretty exciting.

OLIVE HUBER: When I was born, the subways were being built, so you could imagine what it meant for transportation. My father used a horse and carriage and in the wintertime a horse and sleigh. We didn't ride the sleigh. It was for my father, and that was it. It was not for the kids, and the horse had to be taken care of, and it had to be given a rest.

HENRY FENNER: We went to the market with our horses. We also used them to make deliveries. The horses were stabled behind the house at first. Inside, my sister or mother would turn the arm of the gaslight towards the window so the driver would get some light while he was going though the functions of putting up the horse. On one occasion, she got it too close to the curtains and up it went. The driver came up there with his coat and doused the flames. Shortly after that, the city drew up new ordinances, and the horses had to be sent to a regular livery stable a few blocks away on 13th Street, just east of Third Avenue.

FLORENCE WILLISON: In those days, the fire engines were pulled by horses, and they were really gorgeous creatures. My mother loved to follow fire engines and go to fires. It was really dramatic. I can see the manes all wild, and the smoke coming out of the brass-polished steam engines. We all went to the fires, but I was afraid. My father told me the story of the Triangle fire and he made it so vivid that I thought that people died at every fire. I hated it when my mother used to go, and I used to beg her not to.

HENRY FENNER: Our horses lasted until they were stolen. They used to insure the horses like they do automobiles today. Father lost two horses. They were stolen when the delivery was being made. These were all western horses that came branded. They were good horses, and it was almost impossible to recover them.

When I made deliveries, the apartments had blow tubes down at the foot of the cellars next to the dumbwaiters. You would blow in there, and that would "Woooo" in the apartment. They usually had maids, and she would open up the dumbwaiter door on her floor. Then I'd pull it up, and she would call down when to stop. She would unload the box, put it back down, and say "Okay," and I'd bring it down. My arms got very strong from pulling those dumbwaiters. I didn't get tips, except on Christmas, when I would get ties and handkerchiefs, which they would put in the box I took the groceries in.

OLIVE HUBER: We had four in-help. They lived on the top floor, where there were a lot of little rooms, but they became members of the family. When they got married, they got married right here. We had a cook, a governess, an upstairs girl, who was a duster, and another girl whose job it was to open the door for my father's patients. When we got older, we were given the job of opening the door on Saturdays.

BARBARA BAINBRIDGE MCINTOSH: In the front of our apartment at 34 Gramercy Park were usually two men, one at the door and one at the elevator. At night, the front door was locked, and one man operated the elevator and opened the door for late-returning revelers.

Down in the basement were the firemen. I think there were at least two, who worked shifts and kept the central heating going. They were cheerful and chatty. I think they were Irish, too. There were also laundry cubicles in the basement where our black laundress, Katy, did the washing. She brought it back upstairs in a great basket—sheets, pillowcases, towels, shirts, blouses—all impeccably white.

Katy visited our kitchen and went back to Harlem at night. She read Shakespeare and was always in the clouds, muttering to herself. My father, who was a surgeon, looked after her health and even took her appendix out, for nothing of course. While Katy was recovering, Anna, our cook, roasted a chicken and took it up to her in Harlem.

Anna had a little bedroom off the kitchen where she sat on her bed to play solitaire, which she called "solitary." Bessie slept upstairs in the maids' dormitory. She waited on tables, made the beds, answered the door, kept the apartment clean, washed and put away the dining utensils, and always looked impeccable in her uniform, with a little white cap and white apron on a black dress.

EVELYN CROOKHORN: My parents were in service. My father came to this country in 1918 from Sweden because his sister got in trouble, you know, and they brought the baby with her. He served in the Army here in World War I. Then, when he came out of the Army, he went into service, because that's all the jobs there were for people who were uneducated.

OLIVE HUBER: We got the help from Ellis Island. You'd go there and come home with a greenhorn. Our cook was a German woman named Margaretha Duenkelberg. She was in this family for fifty-seven years. She loved the kids. She would take all the Sunday funny papers, put them together with a piece of cloth between each one, and with a needle and thread she would make books out of them.

She was also very friendly with the iceman, who used to come every day. When she died, she left him a thousand dollars. He thought he had hit the jackpot. I never saw him deliver ice after that.

Our cook never had a night out. She didn't like to go out. They had an odd way of cooking back then. The vegetables were boiled and boiled. How we ever got a vitamin was beyond me. You cooked the beans forever. There weren't a lot of vegetables. For instance, broccoli is something new. We had string beans, peas, carrots, eggplant—that's about it. They were called string beans because their sides were full of string, and you had to peel the strings down before you ate them.

She was a wonderful cook. She made *daufleglazen* and sauer-braten, which is venison. Venison was hard to make because you had to soak it for a couple of days to get the animal out of it. I didn't like it. The meat is too tough. She used to make mince pies, which you have to start three months in advance to get right. It has a lot of things like suet, and it all has to homogenize and marinate.

EVELYN CROOKHORN: Both my parents worked for George F. Baker, who founded National City Bank. They traveled with these people to Newport and Deal, New Jersey, and Florida in his own private railroad car.

They stopped after I was born. The woman was so fond of my mother, she came to visit when I was a baby, and my mother told me she was ashamed because all the diapers were drying on the line in the kitchen. There was such a difference between the way the lady was living and my parents lived.

My mother was a good worker. I even have a recommendation that one lady wrote for her after she left [*She reads from a yellowed handwritten note:*]

> Alice Olive Rundblad has been chambermaid for me for six months. She is very capable, honest, sober, with a very good disposition. She is leaving of her own accord.
>
>                                          Mrs. H. A. Murray

That she was sober was important. A lot of them were sneaky drinkers. My aunt was. She was let go a couple of times because of that. But I remember seeing her brokenhearted when I was a young girl. She had been a nursemaid. The rich ladies hired these young girls to take care of their babies from the time they came home from the hospital. The nursemaid was with the child for two or three years. The lady would·see the child twice a day. She would come up to the nursery and say, "That's very nice." She would never change a diaper. Maybe she held it for a little while.

The nurse became the mother for the child and became very attached to it. Then, all of a sudden, when the lady felt the maid was too attached or they decided it was time to go on to a govern-ess or whatever, they just let them go. My aunt was crying her heart out, with my mother consoling her and all us little kids around the table there saying, "Don't cry, Auntie. Don't cry, Auntie."

Olive Huber: The governess took you everywhere when you were young. The day that the *Titanic* sank was the first day I was allowed to walk alone on the street. I was on Second Avenue, going to visit a friend of mine on 13th Street, when I saw a newsman shouting, "Ship sunk by iceberg!" on Second Avenue and 15th Street.

My mother taught me how to cook. She believed that children should learn how to do everything so they can assume independence if necessary. We got considerable care from my mother even though we had a lot of help. She thought it was important for children to get to know their parents. I don't think that was typical.

I must say I didn't see much of my father except in the morning and at dinner. We all ate dinner together. The cook rang the dinner bell at precisely six o'clock. If you weren't there, God help you, you better have a good excuse. We were served by the upstairs maid and the door opener, and they ate in the kitchen while we ate in the dining room.

Evelyn Crookhorn: They used to follow the society pages. They would see Mrs. Whitney and Mrs. Payson, and they knew all the dirt about them, like who had an abortion and who did this and that. When my mother and aunt and father got together, they would giggle and laugh about all the antics of these people. They really enjoyed all those days. You know, they were all young. They didn't look upon being servants as demeaning. They considered it an honor. To be in service, as they called it, was wonderful.

My father was tall and handsome. He was a footman. The madam of the house picked handsome men. He said the ladies used to make eyes at him all the time. In those days, there was a lot of hanky-panky going on.

Henry Crookhorn: My father was also a very handsome man, and he would get into trouble because the guests would come with their wives, and the women would be fascinated by him. He said he had to ward them off.

Evelyn Crookhorn: Their social life was in the evening, at dinner down at the servants' quarters. They were all thrown together. My father had an affair with my aunt before he met my mother. They were not promiscuous, but if they liked each other, they went for them. It was easy to go into each other's rooms. My mother said there was a lot of that going around.

HENRY CROOKHORN: They imitated the rich people they worked for. They said, "If you can fool around, we can fool around."

My father tried to bring us up as wealthy kids. He had us dress like the rich kids. We hadda wear straw hats, knickers, and short socks, like English kids. When I went to school with the kids from the east side of Third Avenue, they'd make fun of us and take the hats. I kept comin' home and cryin', and my mother would have to walk us to school.

He was also very tough on our mannerisms. We had to eat properly, and we had to set the table properly, just like the way it was in the mansions. There were proper dishes, and we had to say grace. We couldn't fool around. On Thanksgiving and Christmas, the wealthy families would send down their chauffeur with turkeys and Louis Sherry ice cream. He did the carvin' very high class and with precise slices. He would put plum puddin' on the table and pour whiskey over it. Then he would set it on fire.

My dad worked twelve hours a day. Then he'd go into his room and go to sleep. Once in a while he complained that his back ached, so he'd get out the liniment and you rubbed his back for him and he'd give you a five-dollar bill. He even tipped us like he got tips from the wealthy families.

EVELYN CROOKHORN: We always felt superior to our immigrant neighbors, because we felt we had some culture. We weren't allowed to scream or yell. We had to modulate our voices. We were really disciplined.

◆ ◆ ◆

OLIVE HUBER: Sex was a closed issue. I was given a book, and I learned what it was all about because I read the scandal sheet on Saturday night. That was part of the *Journal-American*. All the kids on the block used to get that and read it. It had all the doings of people in the eye of the public. It had to do with the Guggenheims and all the messes they got into. It was theatrical mostly, and it had a lot of the white slavery, Chinese, and all that.

I also learned from my father's medical journals. When I was eight, I read the jokes in them. They were all either about reproduction or excreta. I loved the journals. I also read all I wanted to read in the encyclopedia.

Kids talked about it on the street, but they had a lopsided idea of things because they didn't know anything. But I had my books to straighten them out.

HENRY FENNER: There was one chap who came around one day with these French pictures. For a while we thought it was pretty good, and then we decided that the guy was nuts.

After we got our first car, we attempted to go out of the neighborhood and see if we could spot a girl we could entice inside. We never found anybody. Of course we were scared to death that we would.

FLORENCE WILLISON: I had a lot of playmates, but no friends, until I was in high school. My sister loved all the little Irish-Catholic kids, but I was an atheist, even then, and I would have no truck with the Catholic church. My father was an agnostic, and it rubbed off early on me. It all came to a head when I was to be confirmed. My mother made me go through with it, which I held against her for years. I considered that a sin against the Holy Ghost, to force someone against their principles.

My father was also Socialist. He voted for Debs every time, and our house was the only one on the block that had a "Votes for Women" sign in the window.

My father and I used to do a nice thing on Sunday mornings. We'd get up very early. He'd put an apple or two in his pocket, and we'd take a walk around Gramercy Square and up to Madison Square and sit on a bench and eat our orange or apple. My father said he often saw Mark Twain sitting in Madison Square in his white suit and Panama hat. The square was elegant then. Madison Square Garden was a lovely building. It was exotic, with arcades like a Venetian palace, and the statue of Diana on top was just lovely. I was heartbroken when they took it down. And we loved to hear the chimes of the Metropolitan Life Tower. We also liked to go watch the Seventh Avenue subway being built. We'd go on Sunday afternoon to see how far they'd gotten.

OLIVE HUBER: Hubert's Flea Circus was on 23rd Street, and then it moved to 14th or 15th Street. I went to it once to see what it was, and it was adorable. They had little fleas carrying little carts. I don't know how they did it, but it was fantastic. The carriage was just a little bit of a thing. You really had to get down to look at it.

There was something on 23rd Street that also enchanted me: The Eden Musée was a wax museum, but it also had a person dressed up in heavy armor like the king in a deck of playing cards. He had a great big crown on top and heavy clothes, and he was playing chess. There was an empty chair opposite him, and you could sit in the chair and play chess or checkers with him.

He was supposed to be a robot. He moved very mechanically and deliberately, but you could see his eyes. When he won, he knocked the pieces off the board. I convinced my mother that I would like to play checkers with him, and of course he wiped me off the board in one minute flat, but I was only eight years old.

FLORENCE WILLISON: The cemetery was a place where poor New Yorkers went to, not for recreation, exactly, but to get a breath of fresh air and see greens and flowers. We used to enjoy it. It was like going to a park. The family would go on a Sunday afternoon. We went to the cemetery in Queens. One of the things we saw was a monument to the *General Slocum*. Of course, people loved to say, "I would have been on that excursion, except" something or other happened.

HENRY FENNER: Father would get his fruits and vegetables from the Gansevoort Market. He would leave at five in the morning, and he'd be home by seven o'clock at the latest. One morning, Father went to the Gansevoort Market for the usual pickup, and he was supposed to be in time so Sis and I and Mother could board a boat and go on this excursion, but he was delayed. Mother was furious to have missed that trip on the *Slocum*. The rest is history.

FLORENCE WILLISON: We'd play hooky from school and walk up Fifth Avenue and look in Lord & Taylor's and see the beautiful things, and the jewels at Cartier's and Tiffany's. We thought how unfair it was that these things should be on people who were old and ugly. I resented it that these old hags could buy such beautiful things, and they looked horrible in them. They should have been on us instead.

My memories of my childhood are mostly sensuous ones, of smells and feelings. There was a pork store that sold only pork and pork products, and they always smelled so good. Next to our school, PS 50, was a long row of stables. There was also a nice smell of horses, pungent but pleasant. On the other side of the school was a pickle factory, which also had a nice smell. The 23rd Street ferry pier was a nice place to go on a sunny hot day. The water always smelled like cucumbers to me.

•  •  •

OLIVE HUBER: I went in Gramercy Park a couple of times, but I didn't like it. It was too stuffy, so I didn't go up there too often. I had enough to do around here. Stuyvesant Park has always been an integrated neighborhood. That's the way I like it. There were no automobiles, so the streets were clear, and we used to play in the streets in summer and spring evenings. My mother would sit at the top of the stoop, and there were Catholic, Jewish, Protestant, Chinese, and Negro kids. We all played together, games like red rover and stoopball. The high stoop was great for stoopball. If you hit the rounded edge, it was good for a hundred.

DR. BEATRICE BISHOP BERLE: I first moved to Number 5 Gramercy in the mid-'20s. The heyday of the park was during the generation before. That was when Mayor Abram Hewitt's two daughters, Miss Sallie and Miss Sarah, lived there. They were really picturesque characters. They always wore Worth dresses made of gogra, a black, special kind of half-silk material, pinned in at the waist. They kept a horse and carriage long after people had cars.

I loved the park, but my children hated it. They weren't allowed to do anything there. It was a very good place to sit in, but it was not intended for play.

JOHN SEAMAN BAINBRIDGE: I was born at 34 Gramercy Park. It was my home until I came back from the service in 1946. My father was a surgeon, and he came to the park because it reminded him of Cavendish Square in London. Cavendish Square was filled with doctors, and he had very pleasant associations with the British surgeons and general practitioners.

My father's car and chauffeur were always right out front. Sometimes the chauffeur would watch us as we played in the park. Very often we would go in alone. Mother would unlock the gate, and we would go into the park and play there until she returned or the gate was opened by someone else.

BARBARA MCINTOSH: The park key hung on a string in our hall cupboard. Dad loved the area and was proud of it. He would walk me around the park, telling me who lived where—Cyrus Field, Stanford White.

JOHN BAINBRIDGE: The park was ruled by a man named Teck. Teck's real name was James A. Hannan, but he was called "Teck" as a contraction from detective. He was the custodian, and he did everything, from putting fertilizer on the flower beds to disciplining the children.

He was in charge from 1901 to 1951. We loved him. He was such a warm and friendly person that the alumni of Gramercy Park would always want to come back and see Teck. In disciplining, his sanctions varied, depending on the extent of the heinous offense. If you violated his rules, such as stepping on the flower bed or fighting, you might have to sit by yourself on the west side of the park, where it wasn't very active, for a half hour, or you might have to walk around the park on the inside, maybe two, three, or four times, whatever he thought would be appropriate.

Teck was seventy-nine when he retired in 1951. They asked him what he was going to do when he retired, and he said he was going to come back to check up on things, to make sure nothing untoward happened. He was a little bit uncertain about whether or not his successor would be able to take over the job, and he had been coaching his assistant for fourteen years.

HENRY FENNER: Once in a while when we played cat, the catty would go into a window and we'd all disappear. Usually, I got blamed for it. I'd get a good lickin.' They didn't spare the rod in those days, and it was a damn good thing they didn't.

Usually, I got it with a broomstick over my rump. Father would put me over his knee, or else I'd get put down in the cellar with the light turned out and stay there for an hour or so. You could hear the mice running around and maybe an occasional rat.

Barbara McIntosh: When we went roller-skating, we were not allowed to go anywhere except around Gramercy Park. I was aware of the tougher areas round about, but we never walked on Third Avenue.

One day, I was skating in front of 34 when some boys went by heading for Third Avenue. I must have been about ten, maybe less. I looked at the oldest boy and he looked at me. I tried to think of something really tough to say. "Aw, shut up," I told him. He never said a word, but it seems to me he looked positively benign, if not tender, and they went on their way.

Vinnie Caslan: If we were playin' stickball, the police made ya go out in the gutter, and ya couldn't ride or roller-skate on the sidewalk. If he told ya to get in the gutter with that bike, and ya were a wise guy, he stuck his nightstick in your spokes, and ya didn't do that no more. The cop was held in the height of respect, 'cause he knew your mother and father anyway. If ya did something wrong, he told your mother and she knocked the shit outta ya.

Henry Fenner: We got into all kinds of mischief. We'd go down the street, and if we saw one or two windows open, we'd have some nice juicy tomato that we could throw through that window.

If we really wanted to get away from a cop, I'd put myself in a dumbwaiter and haul myself up and then wait and see what the developments would be, hoping nobody would open up their door between floors.

We were more mischievous than anything else. We didn't believe in destroying things. One time I found my father's silver cache in his bedroom. I took out a batch of dimes, and when I got to school I put them in inkwells. A dime was a dime in those days, and it was great to see those kids go for them and get that ink all over their fingers and everything else. Father found out, of course, and I got another licking.

When there was snow on the ground, we'd try to take some passerby's hat off with a snowball. We were choirboys in St. George's Church, and after the service we would wait for the wealthy people with their high silk hats, and when they came out of the eleven o'clock service, we'd be laying for them.

There were a lot of wealthy people that went there. J. P. Morgan was a regular. I don't remember if we went after him with a snowball. He used to help take up the collection money. Once, when I was sitting in the front seat, he came up the aisle and tripped. Down went Morgan and down went the silver collection plate. He always had a large bulbous nose anyway, but, oh boy, did it flame up after that incident.

He was a big solid man, and he was bighearted. He did so much for us young folks with the boys' camp. We were asked to sing at the funeral. That day, they cordoned off 16th and 17th streets between Second and Third avenues so that only those attending the funeral were admitted. The church down below held a few thousand and it was filled. I don't remember much about it, except afterward we were given five dollars each.

We were paid a small stipend each month as choirboys. But if you committed any infractions, the director would fine us, and before you know it, you got very little at the end of the month. Sometimes, I wasn't paid at all. I can't blame him. We would put itching powder in the inside rim of the male choirboys' hats and then watch the fun. So, I guess I deserved it.

I gave a penny every week for the collection. Once, I swallowed the penny, and told Mom when I came back from Sunday school. She said, "That'll teach you a lesson, but you watch out for it, and you'll probably find it again." I did, and I donated it the next week, but it got plenty of washing first.

VINNIE CASLAN: I went to church every Sunday till I grew up. It was mandatory. I went to school at Immaculate Conception. I had Christian Brothers. I think before they came in they had to be in the Golden Gloves.

I got a workout one time with the brother 'cause I was fuckin' around doin' somethin' I shouldn't have been doin'. So I come home with a black face and this and that all scuffed up. I didn't tell my mother, but she really gave it to me. I just said, "Aah, one of them guineas started trouble up there."

Anyway, on Sunday, my mother hits me bing, bing, bing. She had been to church, and it turned out the brother who worked me over came from the same part of Ireland as she did. He meets her in church. "Oh, hello, Mrs. Caslan. [*In a brogue:*] Did yer son tell ye about th' wallees I gave 'im? Oh, brother, I gave 'im quite a few wallees." So I got another workout from my mother. There's no such thing that he couldda been wrong. So I got the doubleheader.

Ya had the confession on Saturday. Even if ya didn't do nothin', ya went. So you tell him ya cursed—what else could ya do? Ya used profanity, that's all. Ya hadda say two Hail Marys, three Our Fathers. When we had somethin' rough goin', we used to go to the Italian church on 11th Street. He didn't comprehend so good. Ya could tell him ya shot ten guys—it was all right with him. He didn't know what the hell ya were sayin' anyway.

HENRY FENNER: For two years, my father played the part of Santa Claus and fooled us. He had to go someplace, and while he was gone, Santa appeared. He was all dressed up, and we never got wise to him. He made us sing songs like "O, Tannenbaum" in German.

We'd hear the ring of the bells and Mother would say, "That must be Santa Claus." Boy, did we get scared. We hardly breathed waiting for Santa Claus to come in. He had a bag over his shoulder with presents. One year I got a lot of coal in my stocking, because I didn't do so well that year. We also got hard candy and fruit. We'd get gloves and scarves, maybe a shirt or a pair of trousers, whatever we were in need of. I might get a fire engine or a wooden wagon.

When Pop gave up bein' Santa Claus, then Santa came the night before, while we were asleep. The next morning we'd be callin', "Mom, can I get up? Has Santa Claus been here?" Then Sis would be callin' from the other room. We got dressed quickly, 'cause we didn't have much heat. We'd go down to the parlor and look under the tree. It was decorated with tinsel and candy sticks and popcorn and little pictures of a church or a white barn. We hung lit candles. I was warned once to stay away from the candles, but when the folks went into the kitchen, little Henny had to experiment, and, before you know, they heard me scream, and the tree went up in a blaze.

VINNIE CASLAN: I remember objectin' to gettin' clothes for Christmas, 'cause they're gonna have to buy it for ya anyway. What's the big deal for Christmas? I wanted a bike and stuff. Instead, I got a shot in the head.

•   •   •

FLORENCE WILLISON: My father knew I was afraid of thunder and lightning. We used to have big storms in the summer, and if we had a storm when he was home, he would stand in front of the French windows at the balcony, and to calm me down, he would say, "Jove, throw down your thunderbolts!" That made me think that we were in control, we didn't have to be afraid of thunderbolts, because we were telling him to do it.

• • •

OLIVE HUBER: We had birthday parties all the time. We played going to Jerusalem, where someone played music and there was one less chair, and we played spin the bottle. My mother supervised that. It was fine. In those days, we didn't regard a kiss as an item that was going to lead to sexual intercourse.

We'd stand around the piano and sing all the popular songs like "Pony Boy" in 1910 and "Smiles" in 1921. We knew all the songs because we bought the song sheets on 14th Street.

JOHN BAINBRIDGE: My parents averaged one dinner a week, and that would always be a black-tie affair. Everybody did that sort of thing. Those dinners were excellent, always raw oysters, a fish course—the whole rigmarole of a formal dinner.

BARBARA MCINTOSH: On arrival at those dinner parties, a gentleman was given a little white envelope, in which was a card with the name of the lady he was to escort to dinner. He would then make a point of finding out which of the guests she was. When dinner was announced, he would give her his arm for the ceremonial walk to the dining room. In our apartment was a long hall, some fifty-two feet from front to back. We children could hear them talking as they passed our bedroom door.

It was expected that the men would do most of the talking, and the conversation would be about world affairs and local politics. It was also expected that one of the guests would be lionized and have his tale to tell of recent adventures.

"Never have two lions at the same dinner party," my mother warned me. "They antagonize each other, and you don't get the best out of either."

JOHN BAINBRIDGE: People would always be very carefully se-lected from a very substantial listing. Willie K. Vanderbilt would always come. The singer Harry Burleigh would sometimes come in on Sunday and sing for everyone. Norman Vincent Peale was in and out. Dad had a lot to say about the effect of self-esteem. Peale mentions him in his book on positive thinking.

BEATRICE BERLE: We dressed for dinner, of course. Men wore black ties at our small dinner parties. I didn't like living like a bum. It's very pleasant to dress for dinner at the end of the day.

BARBARA MCINTOSH: Our apartment was kept fairly cool. Mother thought sixty-four degrees was a proper warmth, but she had a variety of pretty shawls ready for the ladies who arrived dé-colleté.

The dining room was candlelit, of course, the silver gleam-ing—normally, a lace cover ran the length of the refectory table, added to, either end, by extensions which hooked underneath. At each place was a place card, often bought abroad and colored in by our mother. I remember for one party she had Venetian ones with gondolas. There was also a little silver basket in front of each place, containing assorted nuts and, to the left, a glass finger bowl with a colored glass fish, blown in Venice, in the middle.

JOHN BAINBRIDGE: After dinner, the women would all adjourn to the living room. The men would go to the dining room. They would all be passed cigars and coffee, and that's it. My parents were teetotalers. Their guests knew it, so some of them got pretty laced up before they came.

BARBARA MCINTOSH: After the coffee cups were removed, iced water was brought in to cool the conversationalists. None of the drinks were alcoholic, but they were delicious and subtle, and sometimes there were those who thought they were drinking wine. Before dinner, there might be a chilled tomato juice flavored with a variety of fruit juices and spices or sauerkraut juice packed with crushed ice. At the table, there might be ginger ale spiked with fruit juices. Sherry might be used to flavor a dessert, but not enough to upset teetotalers.

FLORENCE WILLISON: The saloon on our corner had a ladies' entrance on 19th Street. My mother was always very fond of beer, and we had two Irish neighbors, Aunt Em and Aunt Mary, who were housebound. After supper, my mother would go to the corner with three pails, one for her, one for my grandmother, and one for Aunt Em and Aunt Mary. She always had a shawl, and, to be respectable, the cans were always covered with that shawl. There was a lot of drunkenness on the streets. There were a lot of women drunks. My mother used the phrase "lady bums," which was kind of sweet, I thought.

OLIVE HUBER: You didn't see many people who were poverty-stricken, because they were taken care of. There was a place downtown called Mrs. Zero's Tub. People in the neighborhood were all given these tickets, and if a man came to the door and begged, you'd give him the ticket, and he'd go down and eat.

You always had to be wary of the people who came to the door for food. If they wanted food, I'd give them food, but what happened was, you'd give them a sandwich and they'd dump it in the areaway, because they really wanted liquor.

VINNIE CASLAN: Then, all the wops made wine. They would get deliveries of grapes on the sidewalks. Ya'd wait for the wop to get his grapes. Whoosh! We'd grab 'em and run like bastards. The guinea would yell out, "You son of a bitch. You son of a bitch."

The guinea girls were chaperoned completely. If ya took her to the movies, one of her aunts went with ya. They were a very mistrustin' race.

Wops were also good dancers, and Irish girls liked to dance, so there they had the edge. The Irish guy would get jealous and that would lead to a lotta fights. Still, there was no deep animosity. My sister married a wop. The weddin' was like the North and South. The wops were here, and all the Irish were here. I remember my brother-in-law sayin' he expected the fireworks to start in church, never mind at the party, but these were higher-grade Italian people, and everybody got along great. They were all on guard, I guess. Everybody got instructed.

The Jewish girls liked to dance, too. And the wops had the edge there. I had a friend up the block who was a Jew. His sister was gonna marry a guinea. Her old man told me about it, but I told him he couldn't stop it. I went to the wop and told him her old man was gonna beat the shit out of him, but, don't ya think, they got married. The old man went into mournin'. He was sittin' there and *shiverin'* [sitting *shivah*]. She wasn't allowed to come to the house. She was dead as far as he was concerned.

There was none of that "Jew son of a bitch" around here. The Irish kids that learned that went to public school. It didn't happen among the kids who went to Catholic school. If I said to my mother about the "Jew bastard," I'd get killed. I heard a Jew bein' called a "Christ killer" on several occasions. We kidded about it. "Hey, Willie, why'd ya hang my friend, there." But we took it in a light vein.

FLORENCE WILLISON: I was always unhappy with my life at home. It was very conventional. I knew there was a different kind of life out there, because I read Ibsen and Shaw or whatever young people read, so I knew there were people who were not like my neighbors and not like my mother's relatives. Things were happening outside, and I didn't want to be crammed into this existence. I remember thinking, "If I am trapped with these people, I will go mad."

My sister and I continually competed for my mother's attention, and it seemed she always gave it to my sister. I felt my mother never understood me. I wanted to be understood. Now, I think, "Thank God she didn't understand me."

I loved high school because there I met the kind of people I knew were out there somewhere. These were girls who were Jewish and from the Lower East Side. They were people who read and went to museums and loved pictures, my kind of people. We all loved high school. I was with a group of girls who were sort of adopted by our English teacher. We did college English our last year of high school.

I just had to get away. Most of my Jewish friends felt the same way. They came from these very Orthodox families, and they could hardly wait to leave. My mother didn't like my Jewish friends. I hated her family. She had all these brothers and sisters who seemed to me were feuding and fighting all the time. Some of them were so vulgar. I don't think they ever read a book or went to a concert. I just felt they weren't related to me.

Around that time, I fell in love. Mrs. Haggerty across the street was the only one who had a telephone. When my friend wanted to speak to me, he called her, and she would send her son to get me, which I was very grateful for.

I fell in love with a young Jewish man, and we wanted to get married. My mother was against the relationship, not because she was anti-Semitic, but because he could not support a wife, which he couldn't. He was an art student. He couldn't tell his family he was getting married, because they were Orthodox and they would have said he was dead, but when I was nineteen I left home and we lived in the Village.

• • •

ROMAN ALVAREZ: I was born in 1922. I came here in '24 from Colorado. My father was a coal miner until the coal mines came down. My uncle lived here on 42nd and Second, so he came to New York City to work on the Second Avenue El.

Our house was a five-story walk-up. On the first floor you would smell "covelta" fish. Second floor you would smell spaghetti and meatballs. The third floor you would smell, maybe, goulash, and the fourth floor you would smell corned beef and cabbage. All the Irish lived on the top floors because they wanted to fly birds, I guess. That was our house, Jewish, Italian, Polacks, Greeks, and Irish. It was like the UN, except we all got along. My mother had tears in her eyes when the Burrow boy died, a Jewish kid. They were great people.

TONY ARRIGO: I was born in '23. My mother had thirteen kids. Five died. We lived in a walk-up on 29th and Second. My father worked past 59th Street. There was farms there, and he worked up there carryin' railroad ties. Then he worked on the WPA, makin' the 14th Street subway. Prior to that, I never saw him. He went out in the morning to go to work before I woke up, and I was in bed when he came home at night. Them guys worked sixteen, seventeen hours a day.

Bein' from a poor family, we never knew we were poor. I just knew I had macaroni ninety-nine different ways with broccoli, cauliflower, or lentils. The Irish people had potatoes in all different ways. Who knew that people ate steak? Who knew that people ate pheasant under glass? Hell, I never went hungry. Even if my mother gave me a lump of bread and hot milk, we ate.

My mother did give me the home-relief ticket to go down on 30th Street and First Avenue to get the coal from Knickerbocker Ice. We also had the book we used to bring to Sheffield's Grocery Store. Everything was on the book, because you didn't have the money.

VINNIE CASLAN: We used to get coal from the Democrats, but mostly we went down to Burns Brothers on the farm and stole it. My mother never knew that. She thought we helped the guy on the truck and he gave it to us.

When the Irish people got off the boat, we used to kid that they stamped 'em "Irish, Democrat." If ya needed a job, ya went over and saw some Irishman. My father was a cop for one day, and he didn't like it. Then he went down to Tammany Hall. He never got to Charlie Murphy—that was like going to the pope—but he saw his intermediary, and they put him in sanitation. That's where he worked till he died. He always voted straight Democrat. If there were ten Chinese against ten Irishmen, ya'd still vote for the Chinese if they were Democrats.

HENRY FENNER: Father used to say, "They know how you're voting. You can't fool them." He was a Republican at heart, but he had to vote Democratic in order that they didn't find out and make it difficult for him. They could spread the word around, and anybody who had real Tammany connections would refuse to do business with him.

TONY ARRIGO: I know that we lived in Depression times, but it was great in the summertime. We had the Johnny pump. We were down on the docks. We played stickball. We played off-the-wall. We played punchball, basketball, boxball, ring-a-levio, Johnny on the pony. There were so many games.

Every block had a gang. If a kid from another block came down our street, we questioned him. First of all, you wanted to know what was he doin' on 30th Street. Maybe he says he's datin' somebody's sister. We'd ask the guy, "Hey, Harry, is that Jewish kid goin' out with your sister? This kid, Izzy, says he's goin' out with your sister."

Everybody protected the block. We protected it from bein' robbed. Did we steal? Of course. When you went by a fruit stand, you always took an apple or a banana. When you went to Sheffield's and the guy turned around, you always put a cupcake in your pocket.

If you got caught, not only would the guy kick your ass, but he would tell your mother and father and they would kick your ass in. Me? I never got caught. I was fortunate.

ROMAN ALVAREZ: I was a good kid. I never went out stealin'. All my tribe was good, but they were tough kids. Huntz Hall came from the neighborhood. He was the Dead End Kid, except in real life he couldn't lick a lollipop.

I had pigeons on the roof. I had Homers. They were the race birds. I had Tiplets and Brights, Owls. Tiplets had the bigger beaks. The smaller ones were the Flights. Owls look like little owls. There were Tumblers—they fall over while they fly. Most people wanted Homers, race birds. You take them to Connecticut or Chicago, and they fly back. If you tried that with a Tiplet, they'd get lost.

I'd go up to 125th Street and buy 'em for a dime or a quarter apiece. You'd get a big pole up on the roof, and you'd fly 'em around. Sometimes, they go fifteen times around before they hit the roof again. A friend of mine had birds, and if one of his birds hit the roof, he didn't like that, because another one would hit the roof and then another, so when that first bird come back, he would twist its neck and get rid of it. He said that bird would ruin the other birds.

I said, "Why don't you give 'im to somebody else?"

He said, "He's liable to fly back here."

If your bird landed on somebody's roof, he'd give 'im back to ya for a quarter. They never had no trouble, in my neighborhood anyway. Maybe on the West Side they'd kill one another.

TONY ARRIGO: I didn't steal that much. I was always a hustler. I sold shoppin' bags, two cents a bag, on the corner. I always shined shoes. You got a nickel a shine. I had a box, with brown and black polish. You also had a spit shine. You spit on the shoes, and that made a good shine. A guy might want a cream shine. Cream was like fifteen cents a bottle. If you had it, then you charged an extra nickel, but if you couldn't afford to buy it, you might say, "I don't have the cream, but I'll give ya a spit shine." You "ptt" on that shoe, rub it up, and it would come out sparklin'.

ROCKY ALFREDO: But when you spit on the shoes, you didn't give 'im a lunger, because when you got up a lunger, that thing has acid in it. A guy used to spit on my friend's pants, and he would burn holes in them with those lungers.

TONY ARRIGO: We wore the knickers with the high socks, and Keds, which were the best. They were expensive, too, a buck and a quarter. American Flyers cost like forty-nine cents. They were good, but not as good as Keds.

ROCKY ALFREDO: The knickers were great, because you used to make a hole in the pocket and then shoplift.

TONY ARRIGO: Whatever you stole, you could drop it in your pocket, and it would go to the bottom of your knickers. That was where you kept whatever you took. Your mother always wondered why you had a hole in the pocket.

When you finished grammar school, then I knew I was gonna get my long pants. It was like a Jewish kid waitin' for his bar mitzvah. When I went down to get them, "Hey, I'm a man now."

She took you to Blinder's on Second Avenue. You got whipcord or corduroy. You always got 'em two sizes too big, so you grew into 'em.

HENRY CROOKHORN: I remember hangin' around B. Altman's at Madison Avenue and 35th Street. They had canopies outside the store, and on top of these canopies was a great big metal box, and it had numbers that flashed. The point was, when a chauffeur delivered his boss to the shop, they'd park on 35th Street, and when she came out, she told the doorman, "My number is 535," and he would flash those numbers in the box, tellin' the chauffeur to come and pick up his boss.

West of Third Avenue was all private families. They were business people, very, very few kids—at least you never saw 'em. They were sheltered indoors most of the time, while you were out in the street playin' stickball on 35th Street between Park and Lex.

The cops from the 15th Precinct would get complaints from these town houses, and they'd come up and grab our bats and balls and put 'em down the sewer. I often wonder if that's why the sewers are so jammed up now.

ROMAN ALVAREZ: We had a beautiful relationship with the cops. They would always hit us with the bat. We could play stickball on 42nd Street between Second and Third because there were never any cars. We would be just playin' stickball or we were standin' on the corner. He'd come up and say, "Whatta ya doin' on the corner?"

"I live here."

Boom! "Get off the corner."

Where am I supposed to hang out? And we had Johnny Broderick in our neighborhood, the toughest cop in New York. He beat up a lotta people, and not just young kids. But he wasn't alone. A lotta those cops were mean. One time, we were playin' association football on Second Avenue and 41st. So who comes but this big mean Irish cop. He hits a kid with a bat. Boom! The kid fell down. So we all picked 'im up and we went down to the 35th Street station house to tell 'em the complaint we had. The sergeant looked at us, and he called three cops on us. We went flyin' out, and we hit some woman. She fell right on her ass, and she says, "Boy, I seen many guys gettin' thrown into the police station, but I never seen any kids get thrown outta there."

TONY ARRIGO: There were four theaters in the neighborhood, the Arch, the Regent, the Superior, and the 34th Street. It was the cheapest, a penny. The Regent was three cents. The Superior was a nickel. The Arch was all benches and the guy played the piano.

The serials were great. We had *The Lone Ranger, Dick Tracy, Zorro,* and a lotta Westerns. They always left you hangin'. You better believe you wanted to come back next week. Like the guy was fallin' off the cliff. You knew he was goin' down. The next week you come back, and there was a branch comin' out of the mountain and he lands on it.

There was a race-car guy, *Burn 'em Up Bart.* Ralph Byrd was the guy. He'd be ridin', and he was gonna go right through the stands! You figured the thing blew up and all. Well, next week he went through it, and somethin' else blew up, but he didn't, and he come back out on the track again. Did we believe it? You bet we did. I went out, shined shoes and worked like hell to make a few pennies just so I could go the next week.

Back in them days, you listen to the radio in the living room, and on the *Inner Sanctum,* the door would open up [*high squeaking voice*], "eeeeeek." The funny thing about it, you really imagined it happenin'. It scared the shit outta you. When you listened to "The Shadow," you really thought those people were real. I thought there was a Jack Armstrong, the All-American Boy. I loved the "Green Hornet," "Inner Sanctum," "Gangbusters" on Friday night, Eddie Cantor, "Fibber McGee and Molly."

ROCKY ALFREDO: There was also Mr. Anthony, who was the divorce guy. He settled domestic problems, but they later found out he was divorced four times. What a phony.

ROMAN ALVAREZ: We hung out by the river seven days a week. There was a baseball field where the UN is now. The Dragons, the Maroons, they used to play there. The slaughterhouses were there, too. They used to kill sheep and cattle. They had a big sewer pipe goin' into the dock, and every now and then there would be a big gush of blood into the river while we were swimmin', and we'd get caught in it and be covered with blood.

I used to watch 'em kill the sheep. They got a ramp like a merry-go-round. They hung 'em up by the back legs. As they go by, the rabbi would give 'em that one slice in the throat, and all the blood would go down the hill into a pool. We felt sorry for the sheep, but what're ya goin' to do? I never seen them kill the cows, although I know they hit 'em with a sledgehammer.

TONY ARRIGO: Still, the best place in the world was the Madison Square Boys Club. All your friends were there. You learned how to box. They had Ping-Pong. You played everything. The only thing they didn't have there was a pool. You learned about winnin' and losin', and in the summer they sent us to camp. It was just great.

ROMAN ALVAREZ: I started fightin' at the Kip's Bay Boys' Club. My mother didn't like it. My father didn't give a damn what I did. He said, "Let 'im get beat up. He's gonna quit." Whenever I was fightin' and it was on the radio, she'd go to a movie to calm her nerves.

Durin' them days, I can remember my father sayin' grace, and I looked up on the table and all there was was scrambled eggs. I used to wonder what we were sayin' grace for, scrambled eggs and potatoes? Everyone went through that. Some kids didn't even eat, for chrissakes. For me, boxin' was great. Where would ya get twenty-five dollars for twelve minutes? That time, kids worked for six dollars a week and they had to work six days.

I started in the amateurs when I was sixteen. I won the Golden Gloves in 1939. In the amateurs, they'd give ya a watch. I'd sell 'em for fifteen dollars. Once, I got an eighty-five-dollar Bulova watch. That, my brother conned outta me for fifty dollars. Then he says, now give your mother the money to pay the rent. It was twenty-eight dollars a month for rent. So I ended up sellin' it to him for twenty-two dollars.

I left school when I was seventeen, and then I turned pro when I was eighteen. I had Pete Riley manage me. He had more champions than anybody in the world. He did know a lot of people. He introduced me to Damon Runyon, Milton Berle, Harry James. I had a big bungalow up in Kingston, New York. Funny thing though, that place took some gettin' used to. I slept under the El my whole life. The trains go right by, trolley cars, trucks with their horns. I go up to the country, and the little crickets'd keep me up. I went around with a flashlight tryin' to kill 'em.

My first professional fight was in St. Nick's in 1940. Then I fought in the Broadway Arena, Ridgewood Grove, the Garden, Chicago, Cincinnati, California, and Honolulu. I fought a lot of champions, but I never fought for a title.

◆ ◆ ◆

ROCKY ALFREDO: When my father died, he was laid out for three days and four nights in the house, everybody screamin' day and night. They put his favorite hat on the bottom of his casket. My grandfather died at the track. He had the winnin' ticket in his hand when he had the heart attack. They put the ticket in the casket wit 'im. My cousin was tryin' to get the friggin' ticket out. He says he got ninety days to cash it.

·   ·   ·

VINNIE CASLAN: I wasn't deprived, but I wasn't interested in goin' to college. I was workin' for Du Pont in Alabama when the war started. We came back here and enlisted in the Navy.

After we got back, some of the guys came home lookin' for their mothers, and they couldn't find 'em. It was all tore down. There was an editorial in the *Times:* "Do away with the ghetto." There was no ghetto. There was poor people, but they were all white-collar workers, blue-collar workers, no ghetto. There were synagogues, Catholic churches, Protestant churches. But who knows? If they didn't tear it down, you know what would be livin' there now—San Juan right on each corner.

FLORENCE WILLISON: The '20s were so exciting. It was a wonderful time to be alive. So much was going on in arts and writing. You could imagine—every day you woke up and wondered what wonderful thing is going to happen today. It was like that time in England when somebody wrote, "heaven to be young." Well, it was.

Jack and I slept together a couple of months before we got married. We couldn't sleep together at home, but we had lots of friends, so it wasn't a problem. Still, my mother threatened us, so we decided to get married. Early in the morning, we rushed down to the Municipal Building for the ceremony, which was as revolting as I thought it would be. The dentist's office where I worked was at 30th Street and Second Avenue. Before I went back to work, I tore the marriage certificate up and tossed it into a sewer grate on 30th and Third.

That day, I sent a note home telling my mother, and that night they came up to the apartment on Vandam Street and knocked on the door. I think she wanted to check and make sure we were really married. I hated her for that, I really did.

After Jack and I were finished, I met my second husband. We were together forty-four years but we were never married.

Years later, my mother fell and broke her hip. I had to take care of her, and she was so good and so patient, and so pleasant and so courageous, I couldn't believe that it was the same person that I had held this terrible resentment against for years and years.

When she was able to be moved, she came to my home, and I began to think maybe I was crazy, maybe I had made this all up. One night we were at the kitchen sink, and I finally confronted her, and I said, "What was on your mind the night Jack and I were married?"

The look on her face had been kind and sweet and pleasant, and as I asked the question, her entire expression changed, and she looked like the person I had hated for so long. If she had only said then, "I'm sorry, it was too bad," but she didn't. She looked like she had before, so I knew I wasn't crazy. She only said, "It's all water under the dam," and that was it.

# Greenwich Village

❧

HIPPOLYTE HAVEL was a part-time cook and waiter, full-time anarchist, and very much a Villager during the area's bohemian heyday before World War I. It was Havel who best described the Village scene when he said, "Greenwich Village has no boundaries. It is a state of mind."

Actually, Greenwich Village had loosely defined physical boundaries in Havel's time: 14th Street to the north, Canal Street to the south, the Hudson River to the west, and Lafayette Street to the east. For those who streamed into the area after the turn of the century, it meant more than winding streets and cheap rents. To them, the Village was the freedom to express themselves in the way they lived, dressed, read, and worked.

The newcomers were the latest in a long line of immigrants seeking a freer, more independent life-style within the Village's confines. In the years before the arrival of the Dutch in 1611, Indians called the land Sapokanikan, the tobacco plantation, because its fertile soil grew the finest crop on the island. Then, white settlers looking to escape the structured life of the burgeoning city to the south traipsed north through swampy marshland to find the wide-open territory, dominated by Minetta Brook and populated by nomadic Canarsie Indians, freshwater trout, black bears, and snakes.

Soon the area became known as the Green Village. With its narrow streets carved from twisted old Indian paths and huge farms run by prominent families like the Warrens, Bleeckers, and Brevoorts, the area became a favorite retreat for the colonial social set. New Yorkers fleeing a series of smallpox epidemics increased the Village's population dramatically in the early 1800s. But the city's own mushrooming growth easily outdistanced the Village's, and in 1825 New York officially swallowed it in one large gulp.

One of the city's first decisions regarding the Village was to create a parade ground out of its potter's field and public gallows, on the site later to become Washington Square Park. Although hangings were a popular spectator sport, after 1819 the square's sturdy elms no longer served that purpose. For the record, the last victim was a young Negro girl named Rose, who was charged with setting fire to a nearby house.

In the 1850s, the Village housed the city's first bohemian population. The group had its headquarters in the basement of Pfaff's Ale House on lower Broadway, where its members wrote passionate poetry, spoke openly of free love, and longed for the more sophisticated Parisian life. They also published a magazine, the *Saturday Press*, whose most lasting contribution was to introduce Mark Twain's writings to East Coast readers.

The Civil War dispersed the bohemians. The Village became the Ninth, or American, Ward, a stronghold of the Tammany machine. Its population consisted of old-line society, based mostly in the Washington Square area, and Irish families in the districts to the west and south. There was also a sizable black population, which suffered terribly as the target of antidraft rioting in 1863.

Within a few years, the Irish felt pressure from the Italian community, which began spreading north from the Canal Street area. Soon, nearly all of the Village's southern portion was Italian, pushing the Irish stronghold to the north and west. The black population also dwindled sharply, until only a few families remained in the Gay Street area west of Sixth Avenue.

The twentieth century brought another immigrant group hoping to establish an independent life-style in the Village. The newcomers were writers, journalists, and social reformers. Their headquarters was a three-story rooming house run by Madame Branchard, at 61 Washington Square South. At one time or another, her boarders included John Reed, Lincoln Steffens, Theodore Dreiser, Upton Sinclair, O. Henry, Willa Cather, and Stephen Crane. With such illustrious tenants, it is not surprising the building was called the "House of Genius."

Out of that group, a new bohemian era blossomed. Soon, writers, artists, and freethinkers descended on the Village en masse, attracted as much by the creative atmosphere and Old World charm as by the low rents. A small room on Christopher Street with a bathroom down the hall cost only a few dollars a week. The spacious garrets overlooking 10th Street were havens for starving artists who needed cheap but large studio space and were willing to tolerate the absence of heat in the wintertime.

The newcomers brought startling changes to the Village. They wore unconventional clothes, painted their apartments funny colors, and spoke freely in crowded tearooms and cafés about such previously hushed topics as sex and revolution. Many were in open rebellion against the period's Victorian sexual mores. Early feminists like Inez Mulholland quickly gained a large following for their ideas about equal rights and sexual freedom, which were practiced and preached with equal gusto. Many women cut their hair, and wore sacklike dresses and sandals without stockings. Some also smoked in public, and took much abuse for their revolutionary ways from the local Irish toughs, who were still very much a part of Village life.

Like the Irish remnants of the once-powerful Hudson Dusters street gang, the Italian community, for the most part, remained aloof from this new revolution. The Italians were now well established in the Village. A tourist wandering past the 8th Street cafés down to Houston and Sullivan streets found a different world, filled with the tempting odors of freshly baked bread and the laughter and shrieks of children playing in the streets.

Likewise, the bohemians were largely oblivious of their Old World neighbors. Many became active in progressive politics. Their voice was the Liberal Club, a gathering spot located in a brownstone on MacDougal Street. With Walter Lippmann, William English Walling, John Reed, Emma Goldman, and the radical suffragette Henrietta Rodman as members, the club became the center of the nation's most original political thinking.

The bohemians extended their energy and flair to artistic and literary life, as well. By 1910, the Washington Square area counted among its resident writers Sinclair Lewis, Theodore Dreiser, Edna

St. Vincent Millay, and many others. There were artists, such as John Sloan, Stuart Davis, Boardman Robinson, and Art Young. There were dancers, too—the renowned and controversial Isadora Duncan, wearing her trademark flowing scarves, was a common sight around the park. Like Hippolyte Havel's vision of the Village, the bohemians' influence had no boundaries.

Actually, Havel was one of the few who remained largely unappreciative of the newcomers' dedication and talent. As the sole cook and waiter at Polly Holladay's small cafe below the Liberal Club, he was known to glare at his patrons and refer to them as "bourgeois pigs."

Another popular rendezvous for the new bohemians was the Fifth Avenue residence of Mabel Dodge. Unlike Polly's, Mabel Dodge's Wednesday-night salons were by invitation only. Nevertheless, in 1912, her "evenings" became the leading meeting place of the city's intellectual elite.

Whether it was Mabel Dodge's living room or a crowded cafeteria on Eighth Street called Three Steps Down, a congenial milieu became an integral aspect of Village bohemian life. The hottest spots were the cafés of two hotels, the Brevoort, on Fifth Avenue and 9th Street, and the Lafayette, on University Place. The Albert Hotel also had a well-attended café.

"I hang at the Waldorf" was a familiar refrain. Only, the Waldorf in this case was not the elite hotel, but a cafeteria on Sixth Avenue and 3rd Street that was a haunt of many struggling writers and poets. Other favorites were the Mad Hatter, Luke O'Connor's Working Girls' Home (where John Masefield, later Great Britain's poet laureate, worked as a porter), and the Golden Swan, better known as the Hell Hole. The last was a favorite with the Hudson Dusters as well as playwright Eugene O'Neill and his drinking buddy Dorothy Day, who later founded the *Catholic Worker*.

At all these places, one could sit for hours over a single drink or cup of coffee or tea. This was a particularly important aspect of café life, since most of the newcomers were on their uppers, something that seemed to worry mostly the bill collectors. For the bohemians, financial security was something only the older generation worried about. They were too busy having fun. That attitude was delightfully committed to paper by none other than John Reed, a fine poet as well as reporter, in one of his lighter works, "42 Washington Square":

*In winter the water is frigid,*
*In summer the water is hot;*
*And we're forming a club for controlling the tub*
*For there's only one bath to the lot.*
*You shave in unlathering Croton,*
*If there's water at all, which is rare—*
*But the life isn't bad for a talented lad*
*At Forty-two Washington Square!*

*The dust it flies in at the window,*
*The smells they come in at the door,*
*Our trousers lie meek where we threw 'em last week*
*Bestrewing the maculate floor.*
*The gas isn't all that it should be,*
*It flickers—and yet I declare*
*There's pleasures or near it for young men of spirit*
*At Forty-two Washington Square!*

*But nobody questions your morals,*
*And nobody asks for the rent—*
*There's no one to pry if we're tight, you and I,*
*Or demand how our evenings are spent.*
*The furniture's ancient but plenty,*
*The linen is spotless and fair,*
*O life is a joy to a broth of a boy*
*At Forty-two Washington Square!*

Life was a joy for Reed, the bohemians' guiding spirit and a peerless organizer as well. In 1912, he filled Madison Square Garden for a massive rally on behalf of striking mill workers in Paterson, New Jersey, a remarkable achievement for someone who was then only twenty-five years old.

If Reed was the movement's spirit, its voice was *The Masses,* a handsomely illustrated monthly magazine published from 1912 until it was shut down by the government in 1917. *The Masses'* political opinions were radical, but decidedly independent. It was a magazine without loyalty to any group, not even its readers, as it boldly declared on page two of each issue. Under the leadership of Max Eastman and Floyd Dell, *The Masses* satirized many aspects of American life, including other magazines, like the *Metropolitan,* with its penchant for girlie covers. One famous cover by John Sloan showed two rather plain women. The caption read: "Gee, Mag, Think of Us Bein' on a Magazine Cover!" The depictions of plain-looking women didn't please everyone, however, as evidenced by one poetic complaint from the Village troubadour Bobby Edwards:

*They draw nude women for the Masses*
*Thick, fat ungainly lasses—*
*How does that help the working classes?*

*The Masses* was also a uniquely democratic paper. None of its contributors were ever paid for their work, and only Dell, as managing editor, drew a salary. Each month, the pieces that the editors could not agree upon were put to a vote at a meeting of the magazine's contributors. If a majority by a show of hands ruled in favor of an article or drawing, it went into the magazine.

Although *The Masses* sold well, its financial health was always poor. In typical Village fashion, its editors turned hard times to good times by hiring out Webster Hall on 11th Street and Third Avenue for a series of fund-raising masquerade balls. Though the balls never boosted the health of the magazine's ledger, they became a staple of bohemian social life.

A number of other Village magazines appeared and disappeared during the period: *Broom, Dial, Seven Arts,* the *Quill,* and *The Little Review.* All subsisted on shoestring budgets, but also featured a startling array of young, talented writers, including Malcolm Cowley, Matthew Josephson, and Margaret Anderson, whose *Little Review* was the first to publish excerpts from James Joyce's *Ulysses* after it was banned by the U.S. Postal Service.

Government actions against *The Masses* were more successful. The magazine campaigned strongly against President Wilson's war preparations. The Post Office responded by refusing to deliver it. Government officials also threatened news distributors who carried the magazine. Then, in 1918, several *Masses* editors were tried for interfering with enlistments. There were two trials. Both ended in hung juries, but the ordeal was more than the magazine's delicate financial condition could handle, and it folded. With it went much of the spirit of the new bohemians.

Washington Square began to change in the 1920s, much to the dismay of those bohemians who were suddenly looked upon as old-timers. The Village was now "Greenwich Thrillage," as Floyd

Dell called it, an attraction for uptowners and tourists, to see how these strange Villagers lived. Playing on their curiosity, entrepreneurs such as Guido Bruno opened up garrets and charged visitors a fee to see "real" bohemians in their homes.

The Provincetown Players, though, were creating genuine excitement. This group of Village writers and actors, who had organized some years before while vacationing on Cape Cod, now operated from a theater on MacDougal Street. The ensemble hit its peak in the early '20s with the introduction of several new works by Susan Glaspell and resident genius Eugene O'Neill. *The Emperor Jones* and *The Hairy Ape* received worldwide attention and injected new life into American theater.

The postwar period brought a third generation of bohemians. They were writers — e. e. cummings, John Dos Passos, and Thomas Wolfe among them — who, after returning from service in World War I, became disillusioned with Western civilization. Many of them went back to Europe, to write and generally carry on as their forerunners in the Village had just a few years before.

Though few years separated them, there was tension between the groups. Malcolm Cowley, who spanned both generations and was about to go off to Paris himself, noted it after spotting several of the "old-timers" while he was drinking in the Working Girls' Home with friends.

> Their ages ran from sixty down to twenty-three; at one end of the scale there was hardly any difference. But the Village had a pervading atmosphere of middle-agedness [*he wrote in* Exile's Return]. The Village in 1919 was like a conquered country. Its inhabitants were discouraged and drank joylessly. "We" came among them with an unexpended store of energy: we had left our youth at home, and for two years it had been accumulating at compounded interest. . . .

The period also saw the birth of the Greenwich Village "characters," who gained notoriety for their odd tendencies. There was the Baroness, who liked to shave her head and keep her smooth scalp nice and shiny with a coat of lacquer; and Max Bodenheim, a talented writer with startling good looks and an unmatched thirst for alcohol, who left equally long trails of empty bottles and broken hearts. A few years later came Joe Gould, an unkempt little man, known to many local residents as Professor Seagull. Gould was frequently seen scribbling furiously in a notebook, compiling what he claimed was his "Oral History of the World."

The '20s also brought Prohibition. Speakeasies opened all over the Village, along with a host of nightclubs that took advantage of the increased tourism and lax enforcement of the Volstead Act. Wine and liquor were more prevalent than ever. Nearly every Italian family was either making or knew somebody making wine. For the first time, Prohibition brought together some of the bohemian and Italian sections of the Village. As bohemians searched for connections to purchase alcohol, the Italians seemed more than willing to help out.

However, the stock-market crash of 1929 ground prosperity to a halt. Families who had put in backbreaking hours to save money had to work even harder just to keep alive. Artists and writers who struggled during the best of times found themselves panhandling on the streets to keep from starving. Some were lucky enough to live in buildings run by the beloved Albert "Papa" Strunsky, who allowed his poorer tenants to stay for months without paying any rent.

In 1935, many artists found help through the Works Progress Administration, a federal program that put them to work in their fields of expertise. In the worst of times, the WPA gave some artists the first steady jobs they ever had.

Through the Depression years, the Village continued to draw tourists and thrill-seekers stopping off to enjoy nightclubs like Cafe Society and Barney Gallant's Greenwich Village Inn before heading to their uptown homes for the night. Young artists and writers still came to stay. Though they mostly found hard times, they were also the next generation of Villagers. For many of them, that was good enough.

# The Witnesses

MARC BURNSZIC (1904–88) was a former merchant seaman and was a resident at the Village Nursing Home until his death.

TONY DAPOLITO (1920–) was born and raised in Greenwich Village. He owns and operates the Vesuvio Bakery on Prince Street and is also active in local politics.

HAROLD GATES (1906–88) worked at many jobs in his life. He was born in Greenwich Village and lived on a farm in New Jersey.

HUGO GELLERT (1892–1986) was the last surviving contributor to the radical magazine *The Masses* and was cofounder and a regular contributor to *The Liberator* and the *New Masses*. He also wrote and illustrated several books. His work regularly appeared in the *New York Morning World* and other newspapers and magazines.

MAX GORDON (1903–) owns the Village Vanguard, a popular jazz club on Seventh Avenue South in the Village.

HARRY GOTTLIEB (1893–) is an artist, specializing in silk-screening. He still works out of a studio in his apartment on Manhattan's West Side.

Barney Josephson (1902–88) operated BBQ, a popular Greenwich Village restaurant on University Place, until his death. His Cafe Society nightclubs were forced out of business during the McCarthy era.

Rube Kadish (1913–) lives in a former brothel on East 10th Street. He is a sculptor and a teacher at Cooper Union.

Olga Marx (1894–88) was a writer and translator. Her story appears primarily in the Upper West Side chapter.

Emily Strunsky Paley (1896–) is the daughter of Albert "Papa" Strunsky, the "Greenwich Village Saint." Her brother, English Strunsky, also participated in this interview.

Jacob Rachlis (1898–1986) and his wife, Freda, collaborated on two books of poetry and a historical novel. For many years, they owned and operated a luncheonette on Christopher Street and gave regular poetry readings around the Village.

Florence Willison (1902–) lived the bohemian life in Greenwich Village. Her full story appears in the East Side chapter.

Ruth Wittenberg (1898–) is a longtime Village activist and is widely credited with being the most important force behind the successful effort to grant the Village landmark status. She lives in a brownstone on West 10th Street and still wears her hair in the bobbed style that was so popular in the Village's bohemian heyday.

Florence Willison: The Village was a small town. I'll never forget the south side of Washington Square the first time I saw it. It was a row of houses with long yards. I had lots of friends. There was lots of singin' in those days. These people were so talented, and we were all so poor. I only made twenty-five dollars a week as a dental assistant. You'd get together in someone's apartment with some wine and you'd sing songs and tell lies.

Marriage was looked down upon in the Village. I despised the whole institution of marriage, because the marriages I had observed seemed so hypocritical. There was so little love. In my group, relationships were real. You didn't whore around, but you changed partners every six months or a year. We all just loved bein' in love. Those who were out of love looked for somebody else to be in love with.

RUTH WITTENBERG: To anybody who was inquisitive, the Village was a myth and a challenge. I don't have to tell you the kind of people who lived in the Village. People like Sherwood Anderson and Sinclair Lewis lived here on 10th Street. Dorothy Parker lived next door. In the row across the street are studios at the tops of the buildings where many of our better-known artists lived.

Before World War I, I was in Barnard College, and I started a Socialist club there. I asked Louise Bryant to come up and talk, and was called down by the dean, who said we didn't do things like that in Barnard. My answer was that I didn't stay there very long, even though I was on a Pulitzer scholarship. It just wasn't my cup of tea.

The ferment was just beginning. I wondered what I was doing there, taking these silly classes, being dictated to by a stately lady called Dean Gildersleeve. It was a time of great excitement, but those times are created by people who live them. You needed to be with others who felt the same thing. I didn't like going to sleep. There were too many things going on. There was no time for such frivolities.

The Village was full of so many different kinds of people. There was a real mobility of thinking and an impulse toward change there. There was a freedom. People were here for many reasons: artistic, low rents, free love, convenience. I thought the Village was where it was at.

TONY DAPOLITO: We didn't have any connection with the poets and writers. I don't think we were even aware of them until we got older. In this area below Washington Square Park, it was, like, ninety-nine percent Italian-American. That was it. If you walked in this building, every name was Italian-American. There was some

Irish in the West Village, where they continued for a number of years, and you still have some there along Hudson Street. I heard stories how they really gave it to the Italians, but I didn't have any problems, because we dominated. We were in our own world, except if I went to school. There you'd meet, like, different kids. I remember a Shapiro who lived on King Street and a Weissman. I think they were the only two Jewish kids in the class.

I was born on Houston Street in 1920, right here between Sullivan and MacDougal. My mother came from Italy in 1914. My father must have come about the same time. They met here.

My grandfather had a candy store on Sullivan Street, right opposite St. Anthony's Church. The left side of the store used to be a candy store and the right side was a bakery. Pop was learning how to be a baker, and my mother popped into the store, and I guess he made eyes at her. In 1919, on Columbus Day, they got married.

I had four brothers. I'm the oldest. When my father got married, he opened up his own bakery on West Broadway. He was there until 1933. Since then we've been in this store.

HAROLD GATES: Twenty-five years before the 1930 Depression, down around Grove Street it was all Irish. I lived on Bank Street, I lived on Gansevoort, I lived on 12th Street—all in that section. The old man was a tugboat engineer for a towin' company. It was tough. He worked steady, but it didn't pay outrageous wages. To make seven dollars a week was a miracle.

He was a union man. He wouldn't permit the Hearst papers in the house. You couldn't read that son of a bitch because he was antilabor. The old man was sympathetic to the Wobblies. He was a member of an early organization at that time, the Knights of Labor.

The old lady came from an Irish family. They came from up around New England and they migrated. Boston Irish. Some of the sisters left the family nest and came to New York. The old lady looked just like Whistler's Mother.

The old man's folks came from upstate New York. His father was in the Civil War. They hated the South. They didn't like blacks, either, but they hated the South more. The grandmother was at Lincoln's funeral when the body came through Albany. She said the place was so packed that she nearly lost her dress.

I was an only child. I guess my folks' marriage was late. I remember the first time I went on a boat with my old man. I thought the boat was sinkin'. It would rise up and down in the water. He told me don't go near the edge. I wasn't too happy with it, because I wasn't allowed to walk around or play or anything for fear of fallin' in.

I swam the Hudson from New York to New Jersey. We swam off Perry Street. That and Gansevoort and Christopher had open docks. They had the boats comin' in with a lot of sand. It was better than the beach. There was more goddamn oil on the beaches than there was on the harbor.

We used to go on the ships, like the *Berengaria*, and dive off. It was about five stories, so it was quite a dive. We didn't wear clothes at all. We just went balls naked, and the boats that would pass, the kids would all be runnin' up and down wavin' at the passengers, not a stitch on. What we called the big guys, the kids around seventeen or eighteen, they would wear something or they'd get locked up.

MARC BURNSZIC: I came to New York when I was seventeen, in 1921. I left Easton, Pennsylvania, because I couldn't get along with my father.

I knew about New York, but I didn't know where it was. I just knew it was in this direction, so I started walking, and I figured if I went far enough, I would hit New York. Soon, a guy came by driving a Ford. He hollered, "Where you going?" I said I was going to New York, and he told me to hop in.

I landed near Chatham Square in the Bowery, and I saw a line of old men, so I went over and stood on the line. I asked one man, "Why are we standing here?" He said it was a mission for people who had no home. Inside, a minister was conducting a service. I was sitting next to this guy, who told me, when the preacher says, "Come up, you sinners," go up, because there were two benches back there. "If you don't get one of the benches, you are going to sleep on the floor." I went up when he called, and the two of us had benches. That was my first night in the city.

HUGO GELLERT: My family emigrated from Hungary in 1906 when I was thirteen. When I was fifteen, I answered an ad in the *World* and went to work in a lithograph house on Horatio Street.

At the time, the movies were first coming in, and I made some of the first movie posters.

I went to night school to get some training, but in those days you couldn't be an artist unless you studied in Paris. I got cash prizes at the Academy in New York that were enough to pay for my ticket.

When I got to Paris, I decided to visit my relatives in Hungary. The newsies were shouting, "War!" when I got there. I didn't like what I was seeing. I remember visiting an uncle who had just gotten a letter from the War Department. The poor guy's hands were trembling when he opened it. Fortunately, it was only to inform him that his son was being transferred from the Serbian front to the Russian front.

I went down to the train station there. The soldiers were being transported in boxcars that weren't fit for cattle. There was a big crowd, and the railroad man was alternately shouting angry words and weeping. He'd lost five brothers on the Russian front. All that made a big impression on me. It turned me against the war.

When I got home, I was doing some monkeying around the house, and I picked up two of my black-and-white drawings, and I took them down to *The Masses*, because they were against the war, as I was. When the next issue appeared, it had my drawings, and I became a regular contributor.

JACOB RACHLIS: I came to the Village in 1920 from New Haven. I came because I was stupid. I didn't pass the Yale entrance exams. The next best thing was to go to New York University, where all you needed was a high-school diploma.

School cost me $120 a semester, and I lived on St. Marks Place, right next door to the public baths. We were five fellas in one room. We paid fifteen dollars a week for the room—three dollars apiece— and the heat from the baths used to knock us out.

Across the street were four or five family restaurants. You'd get an egg and a cup of coffee, all for about fifteen or twenty cents. There used to be baskets of rolls on the tables. We did a lot of basket hopping, and we'd finish off all the rolls on the tables. Sometimes, we'd really treat ourselves and go to Nedick's.

HARRY GOTTLIEB: I wanted to be an artist way back. I didn't know any artists or anybody who wanted to be an artist, but I used to copy the covers of the *Saturday Evening Post.* I was constantly confronted by my father when I told him I wanted to be an artist: "Can you make a living at it?"

I wasn't concerned whether I could make a living at it. I was concerned about making a life for me. I took a two-year course at a Minneapolis art school. After that I joined the Navy. A lot of kids from the Midwest joined—I guess for the romance of it. It turned out good for me, because I was living in Connecticut, and on Sundays I came to New York to go to museums and art exhibitions. After I left the Navy, a friend of mine told me there was an opening for an assistant at the Provincetown Playhouse for thirty-five dollars a week.

After I got the job, I told another friend that I was having trouble finding a decent place to live. She got me an apartment on Patchin Place, in the basement. There were three of us, three artists, living in this basement apartment.

RUBE KADISH: It was in 1921 that I first visited New York City. I loved it here. I saw those Courbets at the Metropolitan and practically got a hard-on for those nudes. It was that kind of thing that made me think that a life as an artist was a great way to live.

The next time I came here was in 1930, when I got out of high school in Los Angeles. I hitchhiked across the country and found a room on MacDougal. I paid seven dollars a month for the room, in the home of a longshoreman. It was all right—full of bedbugs though. You had to sleep with the light on. That would keep them under the wallpaper.

RUTH WITTENBERG: The Village then was a much simpler and much less organized world than we have now. People struggled then, but there were places they could struggle in. If you look out on 10th Street, the tops of those houses used to be for blacks. They were called garrets. The heat didn't go up there, so they were used for servants. Then the artists came, because they could rent those places cheap and people left them alone. Now, those places are precious and they command great rents.

Patchin Place and Milligan Place were full of actors and artists. They didn't live there because it was romantic. The buildings were pedestrian buildings. They didn't offer any great beauty. They offered space at a very low rate. Later, they became sort of romantic because the artists and writers were there.

HAROLD GATES: The rents were cheap, ten to twelve dollars a month. It was cheaper to move than pay rent. You'd get one month rent-free when you moved into a tenement house, and you paid a month, and then it took a month to put you out, and then you stuck it out and you got another month. Then you moved. That was it. People didn't talk about you, either. Nobody gave a shit. We were all in the same boat.

In our place we had a toilet in the hallway. That was progress. You shared it. In some places, the sinks were in the hallway, too. The kids would get into that water, and it would run down the stairs. Holy Jesus! You'd hear the parents yellin', "Get them goddamn kids out of the hallway. They're playin' with the water again!"

TONY DAPOLITO: The building I was born in is really not there now because they tore down buildings on Houston Street to make way for the Eighth Avenue subway.

Now, St. Anthony's is the corner. In those days it wasn't the corner. It was in the block. There were buildings that went out to where the mall is in the middle of Houston. Houston is now two ways. In the old days, the other side of the street was Houston Street. The south side of Houston Street was really buildings. Thousands and thousands of people lived there, and now it's all torn down. They tore down everything from there all the way down to the East Side.

My mother used to take us to school and back. After she took us home, we used to play in the backyards. The area that they tore down, they used to call that "forty yards," because that's what they had. All of those buildings along Sullivan Street, you could have gone in one building over here and come out in another building like a block away. That must have been great for criminals.

We used to hear stories, like the other guys used to play hooky. The truant officer would never catch them because they'd go in the back and they'd never find them no more. You could go into MacDougal Street and come out on Sullivan.

I didn't go into Houston Street. My mother wouldn't let me. Once, I got lost. I must have crossed the street and went around the corner, and I remember crying. I was lost, and to think of it, I wasn't a hundred feet from the damn front door.

Even after they tore down so many buildings, this was still one of the busiest areas in the city. It was even busier than Orchard Street. There were pushcarts on both sides of the street. There were people all over the place and bakeries like you see here. I bet you if I walked, like, ten blocks from here, I'd find fifteen bakeries like this.

RUTH WITTENBERG: A lot of the buildings from the old days are lost. The artist-studio building on 10th Street was one. It was built in the 1850s, and it took up the whole space of the apartment house that is there now. It was a long, small building, and, inside, construction was very unusual. There were partitions that could be moved aside so that you could have one large exhibition space instead of small studios. It was so old, I don't think it even had gas in it.

Every now and then they have water difficulties in the new building. The garden outside has had to be dug up a couple of times because they have the water rising up, and they couldn't find the source of it. The verdict was that it was part of the old Minetta Brook that runs through there and every so often rises. The brook also rises through a building on Washington Square. A pool of water back there keeps coming back. It's just the Minetta Brook raising its head. There's a story connected with the brook that Aaron Burr dumped a body in it near his home on Vandam Street. That's one of those legends that keep circulating around the Village. Another one is about the elm tree in Washington Square Park that is supposed to have been used for a gallows.

One thing that was not a great loss was the El. Underneath that station down on 3rd Street was the darkest, dreariest place you ever saw. We have a beautiful building, the Jefferson Library, here at the corner. You didn't even see the building at all, because it was obscured by the El. It was a different world under there. It's bad enough now, but you don't have the nooks and shadows that the Elevated gave it. It was a great day when that came down.

ENGLISH STRUNSKY: I earned my first money at the Jefferson Market Jail on 10th Street. There were bondsmen on 10th Street who were always playing cards. When the Black Maria would drive up to the women's night court and the prostitutes would get out, you'd stand there and say, "Lady, want a bondsman?"

If she said yes, you'd run across the street and get a bondsman, and he'd give you a quarter. He didn't want to give up his card game.

EMILY STRUNSKY PALEY: I remember watching Mrs. Whitney painting her museum on 8th Street. She liked a certain color pink. If it wasn't the right shade, she had it painted over and over again. We could see the garden in back and see her sculpture, the things she did. It was lovely. It was like living in an enchanted part of the city.

HAROLD GATES: In our neighborhood, men were longshoremen, and it was a terrible life. They had three or four kids. The wife was sick. The church was workin' with the goddamn boss. The women were goin' to the church and then fightin' with their husbands: "The Father said you should go back and do your work instead of fightin' and drinkin'."

They went on strike, and the goddamn bastards came and took their children away. They had this guy called Gerry—the Gerry Society. That son of a bitch, he'd go in and take those kids, 'cause the kids was hungry, so they justified it by sayin' they had an interest in the kids.

When the old man died and the wife couldn't take care of the kids, the church "kindly" took them over and put them in. They used to have Catholic homes then, and they had brothers and sisters that took care of them. They had Jewish homes, too, that were just as bad. They closed all of them. They were regular concentration camps—ruthless, no good. You would see kids around the neighborhood that got outta those places, and they'd tell you stories. They were terrible places.

RUTH WITTENBERG: There were two spots in the Village that everybody in our crowd knew, the Brevoort and the Lafayette, which were the centers of political and writing activities. I remember the Brevoort distinctly. It had a cellar with little white tables. You could sit there all day, and drinks were very inexpensive. That wasn't a problem for me. I was very young, and if I was having a claret lemonade, I was being very daring. None of us had very much anyway.

Max Eastman was very much lord of the manor there. If he walked in, all activity—even conversation—stopped. He was a very handsome man and very dominating, very important in literary and political circles in the Village, and so a hush always came over the room when Max walked in.

Both the Brevoort and the Lafayette have come down. That's what really changed the Village. The physical aspects of it have a real effect on the population. People weren't isolated in apartment houses where they didn't know what was going on next door. They collected in small cafés.

On Sixth Avenue was Mama Bertolotti's, a very popular Italian restaurant. If you were very wealthy, you got a bowl of oatmeal for seventy-five cents. Otherwise you went to Bleecker Street and got a dessert for a nickel and sat there for hours and hours.

Polly's was another gathering place. It was a restaurant right over the Provincetown theater, which was also a center. Polly's was a small café. If you didn't have the money to eat, you ate anyway, but not forever. She was part of that little world where people took care of each other, more or less; not always, not if you were in big trouble, but only if you were in a little trouble and were hungry.

There was also a restaurant called Strunsky's on Second Avenue below 13th Street. That was a great meeting place for political people, mostly Socialists from the Lower East Side. I think I got my first drink of vodka there. It burnt my throat. It was given to me by some smart aleck who was going to see this brash young girl inebriated.

Another important place was Three Steps Down, on 8th Street. That was owned by the other, more famous, Strunsky family. It was a great haunt for all kinds of people, chiefly because it was a meeting place that cost very little, less even than the places on Bleecker Street. I remember Emily Strunsky there. She was one of the most beautiful girls you ever saw.

HUGO GELLERT: I met Louise Bryant once or twice at Three Steps Down. I often went there because it was convenient to everything. It was good food, and I liked the girls, nice kids who used to wait behind the counter.

EMILY PALEY: I didn't know Louise Bryant, but I remember her as being very pretty. A lot of famous people came in, but we didn't pay too much attention. Later, when I found out who they were, I was surprised. Like, the man who came to eat Spanish rice all the time was Langston Hughes.

I was in college when my family came down to the Village around 1917. Three Steps Down was a cafeteria, and until only recently, if you went to 19 West 8th Street, you'd see there were three steps down.

The restaurant was wonderful. It had dark maroon tablecloths with candles on them. On the wall was a piece of yellow paper— you know, paper you use on typewriters—with the menu. There was a pot roast and potato pancakes for twenty-nine cents; Spanish rice for nineteen cents; bread and butter, three cents; or a marvelous lemon meringue pie for ten cents. The cooking was done by a terrific Dutch cook, and we helped behind the counter.

My mother ran the restaurant. It was very successful. All the sailors came in, but my mother, with four pretty girls, wasn't going to have the sailors come in at night, so we closed at nine o'clock, after dinner.

We had all the New York University boys and we had artists who didn't have much money. We never checked up on anybody, but we always knew who was cheating, although we didn't tell them. I think NYU cheated on bread and butter, and artists cheated on dessert, just three cents and ten cents, but the whole bill was not very much.

ENGLISH STRUNSKY: You said to the cashier, "I ate fifty-two cents' worth." Or you said, "I had bean soup, pot roast, two pieces of bread and butter, apple pie, and coffee," and they said, "Fifty-eight cents." Although one of my sisters had an eagle eye, and, for the hell of it, she would sometimes say, "And didn't you have apple pie?" There might be a little bit of embarrassment. "Oh, yeah, I forgot."

EMILY PALEY: Max Bodenheim used to come in. He and his wife ate there all the time. They never had any money, so my mother said, "Just keep a little book of what you owe us," never expecting them to pay it. There were a lot of people like that. There was a little old lady from the Bronx who came with her grandchild every day. They never paid. She would smile and walk out. My mother felt it was part of the expenses, but it was so inexpensive, and most people were honest.

MARC BURNSZIC: We also hung out at a coffee shop called the Waldorf on Sixth Avenue near 8th Street. Most of us were poor, so when we went to the cafeteria, we would order a full meal and sit there and wait for somebody to come in and bail us out by paying the check. That's what it was called, "bailing you out."

FREDA RACHLIS: But later, management discovered that they were making no money fast, so they had a new rule—the minimum check was ten cents. Pastry was a dime. So if you wanted a cup of coffee and a piece of pastry, you had to pay fifteen cents. After a certain length of time, the waiter would bustle around and remove the plates and generally give you the idea that you had to order something else if you wanted to stay.

TONY DAPOLITO: Before I went to school, my mother always made me breakfast: bread and butter and black coffee with milk in it. That was it. Bread and butter was a big deal. The loaves we have today are much smaller. You have a loaf of bread like this one-pounder and a guy says today that it's a large loaf. When I was a kid, everybody would buy three five-pound loaves. Like, for a family, one of these would be a joke. To eat one a day was nothing.

My mother used to come and get us for lunch. There would be a regular meal: pasta, pepper, and eggs. For dinner, oh, we ate—and Sunday you had to eat together. Nobody got up until we were through. No bullshit like "I'm goin' to the country."

I made a joke because the dishes we ate as poor kids are now delicacies. Now, rich people go, "linguini with clam sauce—twelve dollars."

We ate pasta, but we ate pasta with a vegetable, pasta with broccoli, pasta with lentils. Pasta was most of the nights, if you think about it. Now, if you go to a classy restaurant, that's a first dish, and they want eight and a half dollars for it.

HAROLD GATES: I went to school from Bank Street and Greenwich up to 13th Street and Seventh Avenue. That was quite a walk.

We played a bit of hooky, but you had to work it out so you didn't get caught. You always had a handy kid who could write a note, "Please excuse—. He was not well."

You played hooky not always for the worst reasons. You tried to make a few cents, maybe sixty or seventy cents, and go home and give it to the old lady.

Mondays, I didn't go to school because the ships come in on the Clyde Line, and I used to go down there when the ships come in and smash bags. "Smash ya baggage, smash ya baggage, smash ya baggage." For ten cents you carry it over to the elevator station at Desbrosses Street.

September, I worked loadin' on the Erie pier. The drivers would go in, and when they pick up the grapes in boxes, you'd go down there and you get to know a driver. Then, you'd go with him when he'd deliver the grapes. You'd sit up on the truck and throw the grapes off. I was eleven or twelve then. You'd get a quarter a week.

It was busy down there. There were stables off West Street. They also had the trolley car and freight trains, and the farmers would come into the Gansevoort Market and unload their vegetables. There was a chicken market and a city dump, and the barges used to come in with coal around there, too.

That area was teemin' with people, all down Washington Street to the Battery. Kids worked the pier to get coal. You'd hit the hatch on the truck and the coal would fall out, and whatever fell in the street, kids would get.

You got wood from Sills, a meat outfit that had boxes. There was a lot on Bethune, where they had barrels from the brewery. They had mountains of barrels. Kids used to go in there with their axes and break 'em up. You'd chop it and bring it home or sell it for a quarter a bag.

Brown sugar used to come in on the docks. There were bags of it. You'd go down there, and every kid would have a knife and cut the bag and take it home in a pillowcase. The guy that made me hip to that, he later became a priest with Father Zungul's on Staten Island.

I was about seventeen when I worked on the docks. I went on the shape. My first day was on Pier 61. I shaped with the mob. I got picked up by a guy by the name of Mickey Marr, and he put me in the service gang. I was runnin' the winch even though I had no experience.

I figured I might hurt somebody, so I wanted to shape with the dockworkers. The guy Mickey Marr got kinda teed off. He wanted me to stay with that gang. When you worked down at the dock, you had an in, and you had to stick with the gang.

TONY DAPOLITO: I always worked in my father's shop. When I was five years old, he used to wake me up at 5:30 in the morning, and I used to go in the horse and wagon with him. We'd deliver bread, and we also used to look for wood for the ovens. After school, I'd go and play ball. Then I would mix the dough. After dinner, I'd go and work in the bakery till one or two o'clock in the morning.

• • •

RUTH WITTENBERG: The fact that the Village had a reputation for obscenity was attractive to certain types of people. The promiscuous world of parts of the Village was not part of my psyche at all. It wasn't necessary for me to be. I was raised in a liberal household, and later I would have as much or as little of it as I wanted. In my group, it was more casual than some of what went on in the Village. Frequently, it was indulged in because there was a preconception that that was what the Village was about.

JACOB RACHLIS: Let's be realistic. The Village was an open whorehouse. The life-style was free then. We were looking for it, and we were right in it. Of course [*glancing at his wife*], this was before I was married.

FREDA RACHLIS: There were three old-fashioned houses on 10th Street. They were called Faith, Hope, and Charity. They were given those names because the women there had faith. They gave the men hope, and they freely gave charity.

OLGA MARX: When I was in Provincetown, I used to see a lot of Villagers who vacationed there. You'd see one of them on the street, and she'd be carrying a toothbrush, and she'd say, "I'm spending the night with Jim." Of course, that was perfectly okay.

When I was in Barnard around 1912, it was considered practically immoral to go around without a corset. But the girls who were rebellious would "park" their corsets, because it was more fun to dance with a boy when they were not so well armored.

MARC BURNSZIC: The Village was very freewheeling then. I laid a lot of women. The Village got a bad name for all the activity, but it was natural. If a woman liked a guy, she would approach him. I was asked many times, because I happened to be very good in bed. I remember sitting in the Waldorf and listening to a woman proposition this fellow. "Don't you see?" she was saying. "I want to go to bed with you."

I remember one waitress invited me up to her room. She asked me to marry her, but here she was laying everyone from the Village all the way up to Harlem, and she wanted to marry me.

I was working on a ship for Standard Oil at that time. There were no problems with food, clothing, or money. When I came in, I went out looking for whores. There were plenty of 'em. Third Avenue below 14th Street was the red-light district. You picked 'em up on the street, and you took 'em to your furnished room.

TONY DAPOLITO: When I turned eleven or twelve, the girls started to appeal to me. My mother didn't mind, we were men. They warned the girls, not the men.

You never cursed in front of the girls. There was respect. Sometimes you slipped and said "ass" or something, but a lot of times if you slipped, the girl would have nothing to do with you. If you were out in the street and someone said, "Fuck you," a guy would say, "Hey, there's a girl here." You could flirt with them of course. That hasn't changed. Men are men. We're a bunch of bastards.

We had fun then, and I don't mean going to bed. I mean you thought about how you were going to do it, but you respected her. You had to figure out how to maneuver. I think it was more fun that way.

If a guy and a girl went out for a year, of course they did it. I mean, they're not made of wood. If the guy's a bullshit artist, he's going to maneuver her. But then, a girl always talked like a virgin, even if she wasn't.

When you were on a date and you had a car, like I did, you went someplace like the Cloisters and parked, or we could go to Bleecker Street. There was an ice-cream parlor there where you could order a fifteen-cent soda, a double ice cream with whipped cream and a cherry. You could stay there all night and put nickels in the jukebox and listen to Artie Shaw play "Begin the Beguine." Everybody would be dancing, and you had a wonderful time.

You'd also go to Washington Square and hang around at night. The girls would come up. You would go with a couple of them, maybe three or four of the guys, and if you met the right girl, sometimes you'd take a walk to the docks. There you would get a couple of kisses, that kind of stuff. There was a lot of smooching.

RUTH WITTENBERG: In those days there were circles around characters. Max Eastman was editor of *The Masses*. He was a character. John Reed was another character. I met him through Louise Bryant. Louise was a girl who made the grade very quickly, and she was a very arrogant little lady. She was quite bright, but she wasn't a great thinker. She was popular, but she was used by the radical groups. She wanted to be used.

Reed was a dominating man, a tall big man. His physical presence alone was dominating. That, and the things he did were very exciting. In the early days, there was gossip about him and Mabel Dodge. She lived in an elegant building over here at the corner of Fifth Avenue. She had a salon. It was a social honor to get invited there, and people angled to get into the salon. I was lucky enough to get in at various times. There was always much food and liquor and big crowds. It was very exciting, especially for a young girl like me. You would see people there like Emma Goldman. She was a tough lady. She was blowsy, dumpy, loud, and exciting, and if you quote me I'll slit your throat.

There were a lot of little magazines then. Of course there was *The Masses*. There was also *Broom* and *Seven Arts*, which didn't come out for very long. *Broom* was an experiment that also didn't last. Lots of small magazines came and went. Someone had a little bit of money. They invested it for a while. Then the money ran out and the magazine died.

HUGO GELLERT: After you became a contributor to *The Masses*, you were invited to their monthly meetings. At the meetings, all the contributors would participate in discussions of those items about which the editors themselves disagreed. Everybody had a voice, and that's why they were able to make such an interesting magazine.

The meetings were run in *The Masses'* office, off Union Square, by Floyd Dell, who was a very capable managing editor. There was some arguing during the meetings, but not much.

Once, Floyd read a poem. It was voted on and accepted. Then an irate voice came from the back of the room.

"Phooey, bourgeois bunch, they vote on poetry." It was Hippolyte Havel, who was an anarchist. There was complete silence in the room until Floyd spoke.

"Mr. Havel, you are the editor of *Mother Earth,* an anarchist magazine. Don't you ever make any decisions?"

"Yes, yes," he said, "but we don't abide by them."

That was the first meeting I ever went to. I think it was in July 1916. After that, I went to meeting after meeting very religiously. I found later that when my first drawings came up, there was an argument over them, but Louis Untermeyer and his wife stuck up for them and they were accepted. When they were printed, everyone thought they were wonderful.

Jack Reed rarely went to the meetings, but once I saw him there talking with a couple of fellows. That was the first time I ever met Reed, and to my amazement he said he was looking for a job. He was the ace reporter of our time, but he had just come back from Europe, and he was taking a very determined stance against the war. His writings were more and more incompatible with the editors of many publications, and they began to close him out.

Jack was a very nice guy, very accessible. He was quite a practical joker. One day he came into the office and he pointed to this big office safe.

"What do you need a safe for?"

He picked it up all by himself and he put it out in the street. They had to get two men to put it back.

The day he came back from Russia in 1918, I was visiting a friend on 8th Street just opposite MacDougal Alley. When I opened the door to leave, I found myself face to face with Jack. Three weeks before, my brother, who had been a conscientious objector, was murdered while he was in the Army, and Jack didn't even say hello. He just wanted to know all about my brother.

He told me all about the Russian Revolution, but he was terribly upset because they had taken all his papers away when he had returned. His notes later became *Ten Days That Shook the World,* but then, he didn't know if he would ever see them again.

Jack didn't get along with Max Eastman at all. Nobody did. He was egocentric. He knew it all. Unless you flattered him you were out. Eastman married a woman called Ida Rauh, and they had a boy they called Dan. I still remember Boardman Robinson saying, "Sounds like Damn Rauh to me."

There was kind of a motto printed on the inside of *The Masses.* It read something like this: "It is an independent magazine. It has no respect for the respectable and doesn't want to please anybody, not even its readers." It was written by Jack. He was a real radical. He went out and helped organizers at the 1913 Paterson strike. He went to jail. He stood up against the cops.

But Max would get up and say at a meeting that he was not going to be a martyr. In other words, he didn't have the guts to back up his views. He was willing to play the game as long as he could without paying for it, that's all. He later became an associate of the worst reactionaries and degenerates. It wasn't a surprise. You knew something was stinking.

OLGA MARX: Ooh, I didn't like Max Eastman at all. He was affable enough, but he was terribly complacent and overconfident. He thought that nobody could resist his charm.

I remember what really set me against him. One day up in Martha's Vineyard, I was embroidering a shirt collar for my husband, and Max came up and said, "Well, in this arty place it's a comfort to find one little woman who is satisfied being domestic and embroidering her husband's shirt."

I was outraged. I was a scholar, having published several essays, and here was Max Eastman relegating me to being a comfortable person to have around because I was so domestic. You couldn't blame me for being so upset.

HUGO GELLERT: *The Masses* was always in trouble. We had a lot of problems with the Post Office. For instance, they refused to carry one issue in the mail because it had a nude figure that was drawn by George Bellows. So Floyd cut a skirt out of a fashion magazine and had it printed over the nude. Then it was mailable. They also used to threaten newsstand operators who carried us, things like that.

When we got into financial trouble, Max would go out and see some rich old lady and come back with a hatful of money. Mabel Dodge was a great friend of his. Whenever he got into trouble, he went over to her and she bailed him out.

They also used to have these parties at Webster Hall to raise money, but they were never able to raise much there, never. They were costume parties, and they were fun. I didn't wear a costume. My wife danced with a sheik once, but she said he had too much garlic and it wasn't too enjoyable.

RUTH WITTENBERG: I remember going to masquerade balls at Webster Hall. There were many of them, and they raised money for all kinds of things, *The Masses*, political prisoners, but largely they were social. I don't remember what I wore. There were a lot of men who were Roman senators, all dressed up in white sheets. It was the cheapest costume and the easiest one to get together. I can still see all those white sheets floating around.

The women were more imaginative than the men. A lot of them put on imitation dancers' costumes, the kind worn by the Duncan girls. They used scarves and drapery of one kind or another. Later on there was a lot of nakedness. The balls had a reputation for that. There were just a lot of people who wanted notoriety. People wanted recognition, something to distinguish them from the herds.

TONY DAPOLITO: We also had a lot of festivals in the neighborhood. Around here was Saint Cologero, and my father was involved with one, Saint Filumena. They all had saints from their old towns in Italy. A lot of them carried the tradition here, and they had these festivals to honor them. A lot of that was done to take care of themselves. When people were poor and somebody died they couldn't always afford to bury the person. If it was three or five dollars apiece, they would help out. Those societies were like an insurance policy.

There were a lot of teams and clubs. We always played ball—stickball or punchball. We had teams on every block. We had the Prince Street Boys, the Prince Arrows, the Dudleys around the corner, the Montvale All Stars on Mott Street, and the Washington Square Boys. All you had was guys playing.

We had club jackets also, nice ones. Then, as we got older, a lot of guys started hanging around a poolroom, and we would rent a store and pay dues, two dollars apiece, whatever, and you had a lot of those kinds of clubs in the neighborhood.

We'd have a little dance at night. You'd have a recorder and an amplifier, charge fifteen cents or something, because then you'd make a little money to pay the rent. "You patronize me and I'll patronize you." It used to run like that. You'd go to Broadway, the Eden Valley Boys would sponsor a dance and there'd be a thousand guys, or the Dudleys might have a hundred at their dance.

HAROLD GATES: The clubs also carried a little weight, which was good, so if one of the boys got in a little trouble, you'd go to the local politician, and he'd go up and talk and get him out.

The politicians used the gangs like the Hudson Dusters for elections. They'd use 'em in rallies. They'd get a horse and wagon and the kids would all get on it and throw circulars around the neighborhood—"Vote for the local crooks," you know. When it snowed they gave out jobs for five dollars a day. They went through all the local clubs. That's why it was important to have a club.

Politicians knew who had the poorest families. Around Thanksgiving they'd come around with a horse and wagon and they'd make up a Thanksgiving dinner. They'd give 'em a ton of coal or something. In the windup though, they'd rip 'em off in some other way. Like, for instance, Jimmy Walker, you know, he was a bastard, strikebreaker, every goddamn thing. Yet, at the same time, he was the most liked guy by them people.

TONY DAPOLITO: The clubs were also the safety of this neighborhood. There were men there. If something happens, there's an army. People used to say, "Who's hanging out there, Italians? It's all Mafia." Forget that. It's all bullshit. What would happen if your sister was walking down the street and started to scream? She was safe. We protected each other.

HAROLD GATES: There were gang wars, but it would be with another Irish gang, the Perrys and the Gansevoorts, over some dance or something. They used to call them rallies. They used to fight with rocks and everything, back and forth. Then they would settle it up.

Now Bank Street was only two blocks from Perry Street, but I went to a school that was in 13th Street, which was mostly kids from Horatio, Gansevoort, and them streets. The dividing line would be more or less Bethune Street. Anything north of Bethune would be connected with the Gansevoorts, and anything south of Bethune Street would be Bank Street. I was on that borderline, so I had to tread a very narrow path. I couldn't be seen throwing rocks at the Perrys, because I lived within reach of the Perrys, and I knew a whole lotta the other kids. I went to that church and everything, and I couldn't be on that side either. [*He laughs.*] It wasn't easy in those days.

ENGLISH STRUNSKY: Every once in a while, we were all told that if we wanted to go east, we had to go west first to 12th Street and Hudson Street and then come up Greenwich Avenue. I never understood quite why we had to take that route, but it was because the school principal or the teachers didn't want us to go straight up to Seventh Avenue on 13th Street, because there were still remnants of the old Hudson Dusters hanging out there.

There were a lot of tough kids in my school, and if you were Jewish, it didn't help. I didn't use my first name in public school. If I had used the name English, I would have gotten beaten up every day. When I graduated, my mother was there, and afterward she was crying. "You didn't graduate."

I said, "Sure I did. Didn't you hear William Strunsky?"

That was the name I used until I was halfway through high school, and she never knew it.

•   •   •

HUGO GELLERT: I think I drew the cover for *The Masses*' last issue, in November 1917. After that the editors went on trial. It lasted a long time. Art Young made a drawing of himself that said underneath, "Art Young on trial for his life." He was sitting there *zzzzzz*.

One of Josephine Bell's poems was an issue at the trial. After it was read, the judge said, "You call that a poem?"

I think it was our attorney, Morris Hillquit, who said, "So it says in the indictment."

And the judge dropped the charge against her.

*The Masses* was finished after the trial. *The Liberator* replaced it. We tried to make it the same kind of magazine as *The Masses*.

During this time, I got to know Lincoln Steffens very well. He was asked to look after Jack Reed by Reed's father, who was very leery about Jack's radical ideas. Of course, Steffens didn't see Jack very much. He couldn't control the whirlwind.

It was a great shock when Jack died in 1920. I had heard that he was in jail and had some kind of disease. He had some kind of trouble before, but it was negligible. We had a meeting after he died. Konrad Bercovici spoke, and then Max Eastman spoke. He said, "He didn't want to be a martyr. He didn't want to go to jail." That was a stupid thing to say when a man gives his life for something.

HAROLD GATES: My parents didn't have too much political consciousness. They didn't pay too much attention at all. During the war, they took sides. They took our side. They were American. I was made treasurer in the school. They used to raise funds — like I'd sell war saving stamps. The kids had a book. They'd get the stamps off me, and I would turn the money over.

Sometimes, I'd have four, five, six dollars, but there'd be an interval, like I'd have to turn it in the last of the month. There'd be five or six dollars in the house, and the old man'd dip into it for a dollar at a time and it would disappear.

RUTH WITTENBERG: After the war, there were many divisions among the radicals. There were bigger divisions than there were between the Republicans and the Democrats. You were either for one form of government or the other, and there were many makings and breakings of friendships over these arguments.

The suffrage movement was very big then. We marched many times in New York. I can still see Edna St. Vincent Millay marching behind Inez Mulholland, who was riding this big white horse down Fifth Avenue. It was very impressive. I was walking right behind the horse's tail.

A group of us, organized by Inez or Carrie Chapman Catt, went down to Washington and burnt Mr. Wilson in effigy for not giving us the suffrage. We were all arrested, but we were never booked. They herded us into the basement of some big building and kept us there overnight. We had a marvelous time. We sang songs. We played games. We never went to bed, there was no place to, and then we came back fully exhilarated with our great accomplishment.

This was an era when it was very important for a woman to use her name when she got married. It was very important for me to have my name alongside my husband's on the doorbell. It went along with suffrage. The mailman objected strenuously. A lot of people did.

I used my own name when I had my baby at the hospital, but they didn't object. They said, "You can do what you want. We know all about this kind of thing. Freda Kirchway was here." You see, it was Freda, who was editor of the *Nation*, who helped break down those barriers. I think we had the same doctor.

Getting married was also an issue. It came up in my own life whether or not I was going to submit. It wasn't a personal thing at all. It was an objection to the power of the state to determine your life. We finally went down to City Hall and got married without a ceremony of any kind, much to the distress of my parents and my husband's parents.

My own family had come from Russia and had been part of a nihilist group over there, but it didn't always include their own children. For instance, I cut my hair when it came into vogue, and my mother, who had done the same thing in her youth, wept bitter tears.

· · ·

OLGA MARX: Susan Glaspell was a forerunner of Eugene O'Neill. She wrote *Suppressed Desires* when Freud was just coming into his own. She wrote another play in which she had four people opposite each other. Each pair was dressed exactly alike. One of the pairs spoke, and the other pair said what he was really thinking. That was a forerunner of *Strange Interlude*. It was very new, and everyone loved it.

Susan was very avant-garde, but to look at, she was so Victorian-looking and so slender. I can still see her wading in the water up at Provincetown, picking up her skirt very delicately so it wouldn't get wet.

I saw *Strange Interlude* up in Provincetown. A lot of plays were performed there before they went on in New York, and I don't remember a single one that was not acclaimed. The Provincetown

Players sometimes would make up numbers themselves during their shows. I remember one song:

> *Just a little house by the sands,*
> *Just a little dress held up by safety pins,*
> *And just a cradle for the twins.*

O'Neill had two small children at the time, and they were living in a house on the beach. When we were picnicking and we ran out of water, it was always Eugene O'Neill who would come and give us what we needed and be very nice. We would go to his house, and he would say something like, "We have just made some scones. How about joining us?" He was very pleasant.

Once, when his daughter, Oona, was a teenager, she was visiting Boston and she missed the last train to Provincetown and had to stay overnight at the Y in Boston. When she came back, she told me, "Just think, here I was with no chaperone to inhibit me, and I was fool enough to go to the Y and spend the night there." She was very jolly and just lovely.

JACOB RACHLIS: I think I lived at the Provincetown Playhouse on MacDougal Street. When I saw O'Neill's *The Great God Brown*, I flipped. O'Neill changed play writing. There was noise, commotion, turmoil. It was drama, real drama.

HARRY GOTTLIEB: Working at the Provincetown theater meant that I did everything. I helped design the sets. I took care of the stage. I cleaned out the theater after a performance. I did everything.

I was there for two seasons, right when O'Neill had his big beginning with *The Emperor Jones* and *The Hairy Ape*. There were about eight or nine scenes, and most of them were not in the city, so it didn't require very much. We put up trees and suggested a road and maybe some rocks. It was very simple. The flats were two halves and they closed.

I thought O'Neill was a very sick man. He was morose. I stayed as far away from him as I could. There was a brownstone next door, where, after every play, the actors and directors used to get together. There was music you could dance to. This was my first experience with this kind of setting, and, anyway, there was O'Neill sitting up on the sofa with his wife. I decided to ask her to dance. I was a very proper person. We were dancing for not very long, and O'Neill comes and hauls her away very crudely. "Sit down!" It was so embarrassing they didn't talk at all for the rest of the evening.

His success, though, made it possible for a black actor, Charles Gilpin, to get a part like the one he had in *The Emperor Jones*. After a while, they took the play on the road, and it was very successful. Gilpin was such a creative guy that during the play, if he had a new idea about the role, he put it in, so when they came back, they had to have a week's rehearsal to put it back in its original form.

When they got an offer to take the play to London, O'Neill wanted to reduce Gilpin's salary. He said with the offer they had from London, they wouldn't make as much. Gilpin gave him what for. "I helped make this play a success. If anything, I should get a raise," he said. He didn't go and Paul Robeson later took over. Later I had a small part in *The Hairy Ape*, when the play went to Chicago.

When I came back, I had a long talk with George Cram Cook, who headed the theater. I told him how I felt the success of O'Neill changed the whole relationship of the people who worked in that theater. When I first came there, everybody did everything that had to be done. The actors did any job, clean out the theater, anything. But when success came, everything changed. "Let the slaves do it" was the attitude. I also said I wasn't getting anywhere with my art. The only time I had to myself was on Sundays, and I was so damn tired from the week's work that it was very difficult for me. I used to sit on a curbstone and do what I could, but it wasn't enough, so I left.

HUGO GELLERT: I used to see Dorothy Day around the Village. She later edited the *Catholic Worker*. She was a nice girl despite her religion. Dorothy brought O'Neill up to my studio. He was a nice guy, but sometimes he drank too much. They used to drink together at a rough bar called the Hell Hole. Dorothy talked about that place a lot, but I stayed away from there.

EMILY PALEY: We lived in a large apartment above Three Steps Down. There were many people living in the building. One was

Adele Kennedy, who was the first person I ever knew who wore barefoot sandals. Once, when she went to visit my father, he looked at her and said, "Young lady, never come into my office again without stockings. No lady walks around without stockings. Put stockings on and come visit me." You can imagine how long ago that was.

HAROLD GATES: I didn't know any artists or writers. The first time I found out about writers was one summer when I was older. We used to go down to Midland Beach in Staten Island. It was like country there.

At that time, automobiles were becoming the in thing. A couple of the guys were learnin' to drive. This time, they'd seen a car and they took it to Midland Beach and left it there. Anyway, the police found it on Midland Beach. Some fellow seen who was in the car, and they were the guys in the bungalow that we had. The car belonged to Edna St. Vincent Millay. But she wouldn't press charges. I didn't know who the hell she was from the man in the moon at that time. She was a different kind of person.

MARC BURNSZIC: Sometimes we used to go to the San Remo or the Minetta Tavern. Joe Gould used to hang out there. He was supposed to be a Harvard graduate. He had a favorite saying:

*In the winter I'm a Buddhist,*
*In the summer I'm a nudist.*

FREDA RACHLIS: Joe Gould used to carry around a stack of manuscripts. He was writing his history of the world. He used to hang out under the statue at Sheridan Square. I never saw him when he was clean. He was dirty, absolutely dirty. If you saw him, you wanted to give him a cube of soap and tell him to wash himself.

One time the police got ahold of him. They were giving some kind of exhibition on the Village, and they cleaned him up and they gave him a suit, and they paraded him around as one of the oldest Village characters.

The day after the exhibition, there was Joe Gould in his filthy old clothes, just the same as he always was. But for one day he was respectable and he had a clean shirt on. That's my memory of Joe Gould.

HAROLD GATES: Gene Tunney lived across the door from me. He had a brother Sap, who got killed in a social club, and a brother Tim, who was Gene's bodyguard when Walker was mayor. They were very Irish, big family, three or four brothers. He had a sister who was a nun. I think there were two sisters. He had one big sister, gee, she was as big as Gene, big, husky. She was like a man.

His brother Tim was a big man. He became a detective. Politicians and the church. Before Gene was champion, he used to work at night in a school on Greenwich Avenue. He'd play basketball. He was like a bouncer. Kids would get in fights, and he'd keep order. But by the time he was champ, he moved out, and no one ever seen him no more.

I didn't like Gene. I liked Dempsey. Gene's old man and me never got along. His old man . . . See, the icehouse was on Bank Street. Kids used to hang around there, because sometimes they'd shoot it out and if the guy didn't pull it away fast enough, a second one would come down and busted it. Well, the iceman didn't want those pieces because they were too small, so we used to go after them sections that broke off and bring them home.

Gene Tunney's old man would steal them from us. He'd take your piece and bring it home. The big fellas who used to hang out on the corner, they'd holler when he'd go by, "Freeloader." He didn't like them either.

RUTH WITTENBERG: Max Bodenheim was another Village character. He was drunk most of the time. I liked Max, but I couldn't abide him drunk. It was too bad, because he was a man of many capabilities.

RUBE KADISH: He was always drunk, but he wasn't alone. Max Bodenheim took a girl away from me one night. I was sitting in this bar with this girl who was a dancer with Martha Graham. He came over and started spouting poetry and telling her how much he loved her. The next thing I knew, he was walking out the door with her. And this was no fly-by-night girl I had just picked up.

MAX GORDON: Max Bodenheim used to come by my place, the Village Fair. He was a good poet. I remember him reading when I was in college in Oregon. He was a strange guy. He was full of anger, but I don't know what he was angry about. He was a womanizer, and he had a bad end. Most of those guys had a rotten end.

EMILY PALEY: After my husband and I were married, we used to have something called Saturday Nights. We were living at 16–18 West 8th Street. There was a basement in the house with a large table for fifteen or sixteen people. People would walk by the house and look in and think it was a restaurant.

Eddie [Edward G.] Robinson and George and Ira Gershwin used to come over. They were friends of ours, and Ira later married my sister Leonore. Oscar Levant came also. This went on from about 1920 to 1923. I was at Mabel Dodge's salon once. Our Saturday Nights were like a salon.

After dinner we would go one flight up to our apartment, where we had a piano. Underneath us was Howard Dietz. On Saturday nights he said his chandelier used to shake back and forth so much he was afraid it would fall.

One night, before he and his wife were going to the theater, the noise was so bad he came upstairs to ask us to quiet down. He came to the door when George was playing, so I motioned him inside. He sat down and forgot all about his wife. Then she came to the door and sat down inside. They never got to the theater.

ENGLISH STRUNSKY: In Farmingdale, New Jersey, I had a canning factory. I made tomato juice and ketchup and chili sauce. Shortly after I bought the canning factory, I was visiting Ira. He was always interested in knowing what people were doing and how they were doing it. He asked me how I got my tomatoes.

I explained it to him, and at one point he said, "Gee, English, you used to say 'to-mah-toes.' Why are you saying 'to-may-toes'?"

I said, "Look, Ira, if I said 'to-mah-toes' to my farmers, they wouldn't know what the hell I was talking about."

He said, "Ah, you're just like your sister. I say 'ee-ther,' but she has to say, 'eye-ther.' "

About six months later the song was written, and he always said that that's where he got the idea.

EMILY PALEY: My father came to the Saturday Nights also. He and my mother were separated, but it was a friendly separation. They just thought differently about life. My mother was efficient to the point. My father was always ready for any adventure. I remember once he was trying out colors on his hair. He came home and his hair was green. I don't know what he was doing. I don't think anybody knew.

### FRIEND OF ARTISTS IN THE VILLAGE DIES

#### Reluctant to Evict, He Housed Many Struggling for Fame Without Any Rent

WORKS DEDICATED TO HIM

#### But Money Usually Was—Never Available—Albert Strunsky, 75, Had Long Been Ill

*—The New York Times*, Jan. 1, 1942

'KINDLIEST LANDLORD'
LAID TO REST

Known generally as the Village's 'kindliest landlord,' one always lenient with those struggling in the creative arts, Albert Strunsky was laid to rest after simple services last Friday at the Riverside Memorial Chapel.

*—The Villager*, Jan. 8, 1942

MAX GORDON: Everybody in the Village knew Papa Strunsky. If you needed a place, you would go to him. He always had an empty room.

FLORENCE WILLISON: I lived in one of his buildings. I can still see him. He was a little runty man, not prepossessing in the least, but so kind and so loving, and so interested in his impoverished tenants.

EMILY PALEY: I think it was my husband who said, "Your father was like Christ." Anything he had belonged to anybody else.

The Lang Sisters: Peggy Walton, Ludie Jones, Marion Warner, ca. 1932

Ella Fitzgerald with her band, 1939; Eddie Barefield first row, third from right

New Year's Eve, 1942; Herman Warner and Nora Mair first row, center; Ernest Mair to Nora's left

Numbers 3 and 4 Gramercy Park West *(Photo by Berenice Abbott; Courtesy of the Museum of the City of New York)*

John Seaman Bainbridge at the Gramercy Park gate, ca. 1930

Lightweight contender Lenny Del Genio, ca. 1935

Hugo Gellert; self-portrait, ca. 1930

Emily Strunsky Paley; portrait by
George Gershwin, ca. 1936

Strunsky family hotel in Belmar, N.J., 1926; *in front:* George Gershwin; *first row:*
Marjorie Paley, Morris Strunsky, Elsie Payson, Howard Dietz, Cecilia Hayes,
Arthur Caesar, Emily Paley, Phil Charig, Leonore Gershwin, Ira Gershwin,
George Backer, Harold Goldman; *second row:* Cecilia Ager, Mrs. Bela Blau,
Mischa Levitzski, Henrietta Malkiel Poynter, Jim Englander, Anita Keen;
*third row:* Milton Ager, Lou Paley, Bela Blau, S.N. Behrman, Mrs. Arthur
Caesar, English Strunsky, Harold Keyserling, Barney Paley; *rear right:* Albert
"Papa" Strunsky

Jackson Pollock, Morris Kadish, unidentified friend, and Reuben Kadish on an 8th Street rooftop during World War II *(Photo by Lee Krasner)*

Bresci Thompson (standing in rear) with family on Chelsea rooftop, ca. 1914

Bresci and Mary Thompson, 1933

Alice Tibbetts, portrait by Frank
Mahan, 1929

Joe Stack, ca. 1945

Edgar Lee Masters, Alice Tibbetts, and Theodore Dreiser, ca. 1940

Hell's Kitchen street scene, ca. 1890 *(From the collection of the Library of Congress)*

Bill Bailey with his mother on a 10th
Avenue rooftop, ca. 1936

Louise Barlow and her husband Al in
their vaudeville days, ca. 1916

When my father was young, there used to be a big coffeehouse where the family went on Saturday and Sunday. He didn't go. He went to Ellis Island, and if an immigrant wasn't met by someone, he was taken in by my father. They would sleep in his home until they were set. That happened all the time.

I was married in our apartment over Three Steps Down in 1920. My father was late. Where was he? We waited and waited. Finally, he showed up, and we said, "Papa, where have you been? We've been waiting for you."

He said, "Eugene O'Neill needed some liquor. I went up to the Bronx to get it for him."

My aunt told me he was walking along the street one chilly day and he saw an older man with no coat. He said, "Don't you have a coat or jacket?"

The man said no.

He said, "Are you cold?" The man said he was freezing, so my father took his jacket and gave it to him. He himself did not have another jacket. Now, nobody would believe that.

Sholem Asch was a great friend, and years later I met him on 8th Street, and we were talking about my father. He said, "You know, I always wanted to write a book about Albert, but it's too big for me."

I said, "What do you mean too big? You wrote a book about the Bible."

He said Albert was too big. Nobody would believe it.

My father and his brother leased the buildings on a square block between Washington Square South and 3rd Street and MacDougal and Sullivan. The buildings were three and four flights up. They were leased from Columbia on a ninety-nine-year lease. My uncle was supposed to run them, but he was no businessman at all. He was a writer for the *Call*, a Socialist paper. He was the worst businessman in the world. My father was a little better, but not much.

My father was amazing. He had a secretary, and once when she went on vacation my father asked me to come and look over the books and help a little bit. So I looked over the books and found that nobody was paying any rent.

I wrote letters to the tenants, very nice letters, saying, "You haven't paid the rent in six months, don't you think it's time to pay?"

My father found out, and he went around to all of them and said, "My daughter is writing letters. Don't pay attention."

For a while, my father lived in the basement of one of the buildings. He had given up whatever apartment he had and moved into the basement. It was horrible, heartbreaking. So we finally got him out and moved him into a nice little apartment on the ground floor. I fixed it up for him, very pretty with bookcases and a desk, curtains, everything. I went back a week or two later, and half of it was gone. He had given the stuff to anybody who came in and said, "I don't have any curtains" or whatever. I wasn't happy about that, but that was the way he was.

My father did dispossess a few tenants for not paying the rent. Once he drove a tenant he had just dispossessed to his new apartment. The man got out of the car and showed my father the new place. He didn't like it and neither did my father, so they got back into the car, and my father gave him back his old apartment.

There was a woman who he brought to court. What could the judge do? She hadn't paid her rent in months, so he started to lecture her and she began to cry. My father took out a handkerchief and he wiped her face. Then he said, "Don't pay any attention to the judge, he's heartless," and then he took her home.

Others did pay the rent or he could not have gone on. A lot of them dedicated books to him. I have a lot of paintings here that were given to him by tenants who couldn't pay the rent. He had a basement full of them, and some of them are worth a lot of money now.

He was better than anybody would believe. The *New Yorker* wanted to do a profile of him, but he refused. "No, nothing about me. I have enough trouble as it is. If you write about me, I'll have every poor writer and artist coming after me."

They would have, too. He used to go to the park and just about hide so that people couldn't find him. He just couldn't say no. Eventually, he lost the buildings because he didn't collect enough of the rents, but he lived life the way he wanted. He didn't need a lot of things. That was just the way he was. There never was anyone like him, and there never will be again.

* * *

RUTH WITTENBERG: Prohibition came after the war. It was dreadful, really dreadful. First of all, it was this living surreptitiously, where you sneaked into places. But it wasn't only that. That was public. It was in your house where life became different, because it centered around liquor instead of ideas.

People went to places, and my house was one of them, where you could always find a drink. There were always places where you could buy liquor. People also came by the house and offered it to you. And it wasn't always bathtub gin. It was good liquor that somebody smuggled in somehow.

Practically every restaurant was a speakeasy. The good restaurants all had liquor, and police raids were infrequent. There was more liquor than there had been before Prohibition.

Actually, I remember one good thing that came out of it. The Downtown Gallery was an important gallery that operated out of a brownstone on 13th Street. Once during Prohibition, a man was wandering around there looking for a speakeasy. By accident, he went into the gallery. He was one of the Aldriches, and he was collecting art for the Rockefellers.

The gallery was run by Edith Halper, and he asked her for a drink. She had to convince him that it was a gallery and not a speakeasy, but it was through that meeting that a lot of the artists she represented were later taken up by the Rockefellers for their collections.

TONY DAPOLITO: There was always wine, even during Prohibition. My father made it. They all did, and the guys that were drinking it were lawyers and judges. When I was a kid, I remember a huge explosion. It didn't hurt anybody, but I was bawling. It wasn't a building. It was a still.

RUBE KADISH: After the '29 crash, there was a tremendous amount of unemployment in New York. There were a lot of people who were willing to do anything for a quarter. There were the usual apple sellers, and there were the guys shoveling snow for the twenty-five cents or whatever it was they could get as a handout. There were people working in restaurants for just the room and board.

Things were very cheap then, but if you weren't making anything, a quarter was a hell of a lot of dough. It's a funny thing, I really don't know how it is that so many people survived, but I do know if you were flush, and somewhere along the line you had two or three dollars in your pocket, you certainly shared it. You didn't say, "Well, I'm going to put this away for myself for a rainy day."

If there was any kind of little job or something that gave you six or eight bucks, you'd throw a party, invite a bunch of people over and have a big spread.

I got by through friends mostly, that and by occasional jobs. Every now and then you'd hear about somebody painting an apartment or working for somebody for a while or helping somebody move.

Many times I didn't even have one meal a day, or I might have just a loaf of bread. You'd go to the bakery and get day-old bread. I still do. There's nothing wrong with it.

HAROLD GATES: A guy got to be about twenty-one and he'd wanna make a buck. He'd get a hack license, so your club would get the local politician to give a push and get out a hack license. You could always get a cab to make a few bucks. At that time they made it easier to get a hack license, because there was unemployed, and the guys could get a cab, but there was no money in it. You could work all night and you would only get a dollar. People weren't ridin' in cabs. There was too many of 'em, and they were fightin' each other, too—tryin' to take calls away from each other.

I was workin' for Yellow Cab. When La Guardia first became mayor, we went on strike. That was a big strike. Boy, we had balls, but they broke it—the mayor and Yellow Cab.

We had riots in the street. They had the cops with the horses. Twenty-third and Seventh was a riot if there ever was one. We come out of a meetin', and we went up Broadway and the bastids that was scabbin', we pulled the doors off their cabs.

Then we would go through streets. Like they were just beginnin' the one-way street—well, we'd walk in the opposite direction. If the street was westbound, we'd walk east and wreck any cab on the block, and then they couldn't get through because of the traffic. Then they would throw bags of marbles under the horses and cut the tires of the police cars. It was something.

RUBE KADISH: A lot of artists were living in the Village then. Willem de Kooning was there, so was Jackson Pollock. We were all close. None of us were established in any way. De Kooning was a house painter, and Jackson was doing odd jobs and getting by. There was a man over here named Rosenthal who used to have a paint-supply place. He was supporting Jackson with paint but getting paid back each time. One of the things a lot of the merchants found was that sooner or later the artists paid back.

There was a lot of bartering going on. People bartered with doctors and dentists, but not Jackson. Jack had such a highly developed sense of professionalism that even then there wasn't any question of him going to Washington Square and hanging a painting over the railing. He'd never go to the market with a painting and trade it for a bowl of soup. Others would. They still do.

Tom Benton had a place on 8th Street. I used to go to a lot of parties at his place where he entertained with a harmonica and country music. And his wife was a marvelous cook. Benton was a terrific guy, and he was very helpful for young artists in that he would place them in jobs. He was a combination ward heeler, rough talker, and a little bit like a robber baron that came to town and scooped everything up. He gave you that impression with his wheelings and dealings.

He was tough, but there was a part of that machismo that everyone admired because he was a guy that put it on the line with these museum people or the gallery people when an artist was getting screwed. He was always telling stories about what he did to this one or said to that one, and you knew it was true—he wasn't bullshitting.

OLGA MARX: Tom Benton was one of the most darling, lovable people I ever met, just absolutely a dear. Don't let anybody tell you otherwise.

The Bentons were our closest neighbors in Provincetown, and they gave wonderful parties. It was always a mixed group. You had the summer people and the fishermen, too. Tom played the mouth organ, and people would get up and dance when he played. It was just great.

I always liked people who could make fun of themselves, and Tom did that charmingly. He said when he was just beginning to get known, some society women offered him a grant to travel through the States and paint. He said to them, "I'd like the money very much, but if it means that when I get back I have to lecture your group and tell how I did it, I don't want the money."

They wrote back, "We still want to give you the money because we have great faith in your gift, but your letter was so rude we don't even want you to come and speak to our group."

RUBE KADISH: I have a letter from Sandy McCoy, Jackson Pollock's brother. It was written in 1935. He told me that Benton had just been to Washington and talked to a bunch of politicians about this outlandish thing where artists are going to get paid for doing things for the government. He was talking about the beginning of the WPA. Listen. [*He reads:*]

> Benton told us the other night of a conference he was in with a group of artists, museum directors and government officials where it was disclosed that Washington was going to spend a large amount of money on murals in federal buildings throughout the country. It seems they already have the money appropriated and are only awaiting the completion of plans for allotting the jobs. The jobs will be in two divisions, five to fifteen thousand dollar jobs to be given to established men such as Boardman Robinson, Grant Wood and Benton. Two to five thousand dollar jobs to be given to the younger painters on a competitive basis. Those painters who have themselves represented in a museum will be given additional consideration. It is not quite clear exactly how it is to be handled as the plans are incomplete and have not been made public yet, but there is something in the air, and it might be well to get some paintings shown either here or in Los Angeles. . . .

I couldn't get on the arts project. The quota was filled and that was it. The quota was set for political reasons. With the theater project, there was a suspicion that it was filled with Communists. There was a fringe suspicion that the arts project was filled with Communists, and they very definitely knew that the writers project was full of Communists. As a result, there was a reactionary group that would have been very happy to get rid of the WPA or at least put a quota on it, so there were always too many artists, and not enough openings.

There were other projects, though. Some people were attached to prisons or hospitals. They were still artists, but they did fringe work. I worked for a publishing company that had been set up by the WPA. They did the work very cheaply and very professionally. They had a print shop. They bound the books. They did everything. There were writers from the writers project that wrote the stories and artists from the artists project that illustrated them. Then there were individuals like me who did the technical work.

HARRY GOTTLIEB: The WPA saved many artists. I think they paid us about twenty-four dollars a week, which was good money. I was on the arts project.

There were always problems. It might be a question of the length of time we were given to complete a work or other things. Management always had to have the last word. They were not artists. The artists had a different concept, and they had to fight for it.

Whenever they tried to get rid of the WPA we had picket lines set up. In 1936, a strike was organized by the artists, but I was told to stay in the office, since I was president of the local. That night, the artists sat in on the headquarters, and police beat them up— mercilessly. Cops were never art lovers, you know.

HAROLD GATES: I was just beginning to realize that the goddamn system was against the people. Fact is, you're conditioned to think of the system as good—American. But then you find out it wasn't like that. There were really riots for food and everything. You see families sleepin' in the subways, hundreds of 'em. And you see lines from one wall to the middle of the street to get a cup of coffee, and riots at the Home Relief office and no jobs. People were beginnin' to get reckless. You'd see the furniture out on the street, and the people would bring it back in.

The people in the neighborhood was beginnin' to get restless and nervous. You couldn't pay the rent. What could you do? You couldn't make it. You'd try. You'd go out to hustle and try to make a buck. And when you did make a buck, you had to pay the rent, and there was nothin' left. Boy, it was really rough.

RUBE KADISH: Artists and writers were very radical in that particular period. I, for instance, was doing things for the Communist Party even though I wasn't a member. I wasn't alone. The party at that particular time was very forceful in bringing together the efforts of union people and artists. If you went through those areas that suffered fantastically and saw the breadlines and saw the things that nobody else was doing anything about, you might have been sympathetic to the party, too. This aspect of the WPA contributed to the desire to get rid of it, because all it was goin' to be was a source of trouble, and eventually they succeeded.

HARRY GOTTLIEB: I don't think the meaning of the WPA has sunk in as much as it should. It opened up for the first time the government's concern and responsibility for culture. Despite its problems, the WPA was a great step forward, not only for the artists, but for the people of the United States. The artists also taught in the WPA, and the murals that they made were all over. There were art exhibitions. In other words, the WPA helped to broaden the knowledge in all the arts, whether it was music, literature, dancing, or art. It helped save the lives of a few artists, too.

RUBE KADISH: We were making a living while we worked for the WPA. Most of my friends were in it. That lasted for about six years. I guess you can say it was a period of prosperity for us. We got to go out a little more. We went to places like the Boccie Club on MacDougal where they actually played boccie in the back. I liked to go to Cafe Society Downtown on Sheridan Square. I saw the Mills Brothers there, Billie Holiday, and Lena Horne. It was worth dropping five dollars or so to see them.

> Manhattan has many a hotspot, many a white-tie joint, but few nightclubs in which a connoisseur of jazz would care to be found. Two years ago, a mild-mannered little Trenton, N.J. shoestore owner named Barney Josephson opened a subterranean nightclub in downtown Manhattan. He wanted the kind of place where people like himself would not be sneered at by waiters, cigaret and hatcheck girls, or bored by a commercial girl show. He called it Cafe Society. . . . . .
>
> —*Time*, October 21, 1940

> For a man who knew only how to sell shoes, Barney Josephson deserves lasting credit. He was a pioneer who remained true to his principles and, incidentally, prospered because he did.
>
> —From *John Hammond on Record* by John Hammond

BARNEY JOSEPHSON: I was selling shoes in Trenton, New Jersey, when I came to the Village in 1938 to open a cafe. I didn't know much about the Village except I knew it was an area where there were a lot of progressive-thinking people. I thought I'd have a friendlier audience for what I wanted to do, which was to set up the first truly integrated nightclub in this country.

The rents were also lower here, so I started walking around the Village looking for "For Rent" signs. This was in the depths of the Depression, so there were a lot of them. In the basement of 1 Sheridan Square had been a restaurant that was shuttered. I inquired about it, and I rented it on the spot for two hundred dollars a month, no security, no nothing.

I wanted an integrated place with jazz music and also entertainment in a political sense. I saw some of that in Europe, and they were very successful operations. There was nothing like it in this country, an interracial nightclub with black and white entertainers on the same bill before an integrated audience, but I was determined to do it and make it successful.

At the same time, there was an operation called TAC—the Theater Arts Committee. It was a committee for progressive theater people. They had a comic named Jack Gilford who was doing political stuff. He agreed to work with me, and he emceed my first show.

Then somebody told me about John Hammond. He was out to promote black musicians and artists, and when I told him what I wanted to do, he agreed to put together my first band.

He got Frankie Newton, a wonderful trumpet player. They called him Trumpet Tootin' Frankie Newton. He also introduced me to a boogie-woogie piano player named Albert Ammons. He sat down and played for me and I went crazy. I had never heard anything like that before. Then John said he had a singer for me. "She's great," he said. "Her name's Billie Holiday."

I opened with her. Nobody had ever heard of her before. Before we opened, we sent releases to the local press, to the national magazines, and to all the black papers, telling them all about the place and to urge their readers to come. They were welcome. That was it.

We were jam-packed opening night and there were no incidents. Oh, sometimes there were problems. People would come in and they could handle seeing Billie Holiday and Jack Gilford on the same program, but to see black people sitting at the next table or at ringside tables being served like everybody else, and then on the dance floor touching elbows with whites, a lot of them were not ready for that.

These people would come in and say, "What is this, a nigger joint? What are all those jigs doing here?" People like that were given their check and asked to leave immediately.

The café was also a new experience for performers. Lena Horne never worked in such an environment, and it was reflected in her performances, the others' too. Billie Holiday sang with Artie Shaw's band but in black clubs with black waiters and cooks, but all-white audiences. How do you think she felt seeing black people coming to the door and being turned away? How could she work her best?

Now, she works at Cafe Society. Black people come to the door. The headwaiter bows to them, escorts them in, seats them at a ringside table. Somebody says, "What are all these niggers doing here?" She sees them get put out. Well, she goes and sings her fucking guts out. That's why a lot of them became stars after performing here.

Jack Gilford stayed for fifty-six weeks. I also had Imogene Coca, Betty Comden and Adolph Green, and Judy Holliday. Then one day, a friend sent a comic named Sam Mostel over for an audition. He was a riot, but I told him because of anti-Semitism he should change his name. My press agent, Ivan Black, was sitting there, and he suggested the name Zero, "because he's starting from nothing."

Zero didn't mind at all. "Call me shit if you want," he said. "I just want to work."

Others bombed. I fired Carol Channing after two weeks. Do you remember Mr. Magoo? Jim Backus also bombed. Look what happened to both of them.

There were loads of clubs in the Village then. There was the Greenwich Village Inn, a club with a line of girls for the out-of-town buyers, the good-time Charlies. Around on Grove Street was El Chico, run by a Latin guy, Benito Collado, who brought a lot of good talent from South America. On Barrow Street was a place called the Nineteenth Hole, where Fats Waller was playing piano. Around the corner was a bar opened by a fellow named Jack Delaney with a good piano player. Next door was the Village Nut Club, a really crazy kind of place. In the basement of the Eighth

Street Playhouse was another club, with country music and square dances. Then on Grove, going west of Sheridan Square, were more clubs. On Seventh, Max Gordon had the Village Fair, where he is now. He felt the same way I did, but the Fair wasn't a jazz club yet. At first, none of them adopted my policies. A lot of the cafe guys, not necessarily from the Village, came down to see this big deal at Sheridan Square. I'd hear them say to the headwaiter, "What's this shoe jerk from New Jersey doing here? He's got all these niggers here, and the place is jammed. How does he do it?"

Well, I was a shoe salesman and I didn't know anything about the nightclub business, and at first I lost a lot of money, but I learned. When I opened up another place uptown, they both were making money until we were shut down during the anti-Communist business.

As blacks were welcomed to Cafe Society, a lot of them demanded to be allowed into other clubs. They weren't going to take this shit anymore. They began to push, and the other clubs started letting them in. At first, it was the worst tables in the back, but they were letting them in. You see, I was getting the publicity in all the magazines, more publicity than all of them put together, and it had an impact on everybody, on every goddamn restaurant in New York.

# Chelsea

" 'TWAS THE NIGHT before Christmas" may be the most famous opening line in American poetry. And 'twas penned in Chelsea by Dr. Clement Clarke Moore, a fact learned in childhood by proud residents of this neighborhood, which reaches from Fifth Avenue to the Hudson River between 14th and 34th streets.

It is ironic that a poem celebrating the gentlest of childhood memories came out of what may be the most brutal neighborhood in Manhattan. While America was making the world safe for democracy, Chelsea brought the Wild West back east. But on the Chelsea docks, justice didn't explode from the end of a gun. There was no justice, only a ruthless labor system lorded over by an iron-fisted union boss.

Joe Ryan used terror the way a politician spreads charm. His primary weapon was the shape-up, the archaic hiring system where dozens of longshoremen would gather around the clock boss (in this case a Ryan henchman) hoping to be one of those selected for a day's work. If a longshoreman didn't kick back a part of his wages, he didn't get hired. If he complained about the system, he found himself blacklisted or, worse, in the hospital or at the bottom of the river. That threat was persuasive enough to tame any potential dissident who was also a father of seven or eight and knew there was little work to be found elsewhere.

Ryan's stranglehold over the neighborhood was all the more remarkable because, through generations of hard work, the men of Chelsea were not timid by nature. Chelsea *was* a tough town. Long before Ryan's goons appeared on the scene, people there *did* settle their disputes with their hands. Education was prized, but it generally came from the streets and not the classroom. For decades, life in Chelsea was dominated by the demons of poverty, sickness, starvation, alcoholism and violence.

But, as in the old Westerns, there was a guy in a white hat, too. John Lovejoy Elliott appeared on the scene in 1895 to begin the Hudson Guild. He and his staff turned hundreds of lives around, particularly those of children. At times, Chelsea seemed like the stage of a morality play, where the forces of Ryan and Elliott battled for the souls of its natives.

The Chelsea of Elliott and Ryan would have been unrecognizable to the man who celebrated the arrival of St. Nick. Clement Clarke Moore's grandfather, Captain Thomas Clarke, might be called "the Father of Chelsea." In 1750, Clarke, a veteran of the French and Indian War, purchased what was first the hunting ground of the Manhattan Indians and later a farm belonging to one Jacob Tennis Somerendyke. He built his home on the side of a hill that sloped gently toward the North River. Though the house was situated near what is now 23rd Street, it was then a country home, some three miles north of the bustling city.

Clarke named the estate Chelsea, after an English home for invalid soldiers. During his fatal illness in 1776, his house burned down. It was rebuilt, however, by his widow, Mistress Molly Clarke, about 200 feet from what is now Ninth Avenue.

The widow Clarke lived there until her death in 1802. The house and a portion of the estate passed to her son-in-law, Bishop Benjamin Moore. The bishop, in turn, left it to his son, Clement, who donated his beloved apple orchard to the Episcopal Church on condition that they build a seminary on the site. The cornerstone of the east building of the General Theological Seminary was laid in 1825. Work began on the west building, which still stands, in 1835.

The Moore property on 20th and 21st streets between Ninth and Tenth avenues is now historic Chelsea Square, whose dignified, elegant brownstones date back to the 1830s. In 1845, Dr. Moore leased a large parcel of property along 23rd Street between Ninth and Tenth avenues which became known as Millionaires' Row, from the number of wealthy merchants, lawyers, and diplomats in residence. Most of the surrounding area was occupied by truck farms and single-family frame residences.

In a remarkably evocative series of letters written in the 1880s, a Chelsea native, Gene Schermerhorn, recalled the neighborhood of his youth, some forty years before. The letters were found in a thrift shop and published in 1982 under the title *Letters to Phil: Memories of a New York Boyhood.* In one letter, Schermerhorn wrote:

> I have told you about the little farm next door to our house: both sides of the street all the way to Ninth Avenue were very much the same in appearance. There were very few houses and only at or about the corners of the Avenues. The rest was all open lots and market-truck gardens. . . .

In another letter he wrote:

> At the corner of 23rd Street and Fifth Avenue was the country seat of the Mildenburger family: a beautiful rural picture with gardens and orchards extending along the street. I remember very well the apple trees drooping over the sidewalks, which were often covered with fallen blossoms. On the north side of the street were the grounds of a then, and for many years before this, famous road house known as Colonel Thompson's. This house faced Madison Square near where the main entrance of the Fifth Avenue Hotel now is. On the grounds in the rear were held the "cattle fairs" where prize cattle and fine horses were to be seen—the Horse Show of those days. I remember a convenient hole in the fence on the 24th Street side through which *some* boys entered "D.H."

Schermerhorn wrote those letters because the Chelsea of his youth was long gone. The process began in 1847 when the Hudson River Railroad lines were laid down on Ninth and Tenth avenues. The railroad brought several factories to Chelsea, along with an impoverished working class housed in hastily erected tenements. The newcomers were largely immigrants: weavers from Scotland, German cabinetmakers, and Irish farmers fleeing famine, who dominated the area for the next century.

Irish Catholics and Protestants fought a tragic battle in the streets of Chelsea in 1871. A Protestant parade commemorating William of Orange's victory at the Battle of the Boyne was met with sniper fire from the windows and rooftops at the intersection of 25th Street and Eighth Avenue. By the time order was restored, fifty-four people lay dead in the streets.

The opening of Pike's Opera House in 1868 on 23rd Street marked Chelsea's introduction to the gaudy wealth of the Flash Age. The following year, James Fisk and Jay Gould bought out Pike, renamed the theater the Grand Opera House, and installed themselves in plush top-floor offices, where they also ran the New York Central Railroad. The theater downstairs served as a vehicle for Fisk's paramour, the beautiful Josie Mansfield. Fisk also installed a secret tunnel under the stage, which led to Mansfield's home, a few doors away, making a convenient and well-trod path for offstage matinee performances.

Unfortunately, Miss Mansfield's temptations proved Fisk's undoing. In 1872, he was gunned down on the staircase of the Grand Central Hotel in the Village, by Edward Stokes, his rival for Josie's favors. Fisk did go out in true Flash Age style, though—his body was laid out in state in the opera house's rococo lobby.

The Grand Opera House, while splendid indeed, was not 23rd Street's only attraction. For several years, the famed Shakespearean actor Edwin Booth performed from his own stage at 23rd and Sixth Avenue. There was also Koster & Bial's Concert Hall on the opposite corner, which was for a time the top vaudeville house in the city.

Another attraction on 23rd was the Eden Musée, a wax museum of sorts fashioned after England's Madame Tussaud's. Perhaps the Eden Musée's biggest draw was Ajeeb, the chess- and checker-playing automaton. The public was invited to challenge this amazing machine, and many did so, with little success.

Actually, Ajeeb was a succession of very short chess geniuses, hired to perform in the heavy (and hot) robotlike garb. Legend has it that the short-story writer O. Henry, a nearby resident, was one of those in on the secret. O. Henry, who was known to take a drink, enjoyed challenging Ajeeb and would kindly, but discreetly, slip a bottle under the armor to his grateful opponent.

Farther west, between Sixth and Seventh avenues, was Proctor's, another music hall, which spotlighted the talents of Lillie

Langtry, "the Jersey Lily." The Weber & Fields stock company was also a fixture in the neighborhood. Their Broadway Music Hall was on Sixth between 29th and 30th, just around the corner from the old Haymarket, the most notorious of the Tenderloin dives. The Weber & Fields shows boasted the talents of Frankie Bailey, who was said to own the best set of legs in show business. For years her gams were so widely regarded that a girl with long sleek legs was said to have a great pair of Frankie Baileys.

In 1882, the Hotel Chelsea opened its doors as a co-op apartment house on 23rd Street. The building's tenants came from the most prestigious entertainment and literary circles. They included Lillian Russell, Sarah Bernhardt, O. Henry, Mark Twain, ashcan-school artist John Sloan, and, later, the poet Edgar Lee Masters, author of *Spoon River Anthology*.

Another resident was Thomas Wolfe, who in 1937 was shopping around for a new publisher and a new home when he stopped in at the Chelsea to seek Masters' advice and check out the hotel for himself. He soon took his cartons of manuscripts, settled into Room 831, and promptly created a storm around the hotel with his excessive drinking. His room had one particular feature that also generated some talk—a toilet that sat on a raised platform. For that small touch of royal charm, he referred to his bathroom as "The Throne Room."

It was in Chelsea that the movie business began to develop in the 1890s, beginning with Thomas Edison's demonstration of the Vitascope machine at Koster & Bial's Music Hall on 34th Street in 1896. During the showing of his film *Sea Waves*, members of the audience panicked at the sight of the towering waves that appeared to sweep toward the crowd from the screen. Soon, fledgling movie studios popped up all over Chelsea. There were the Biograph Studio on 14th Street, where D. W. Griffith made his name, and Famous Players on 26th, featuring Ina Claire, James O'Neill, Sarah Bernhardt, and Chelsea native Mary Pickford.

If a visitor to the neighborhood wasn't interested in the movies, theater, or chess with Ajeeb, there was always shopping on the Ladies' Mile. Several of the city's leading department stores were located within Chelsea's boundaries. R. H. Macy opened his first shop on 14th Street. Though the store long ago moved to 34th, the faint red lettering of Macy's can still be seen over the doorway at 56 West 14th. Other stores included A. T. Stewart, Hearn's, O'Neill, and, perhaps the best known, Siegel-Cooper, at Sixth Avenue and 18th Street. A turn-of-the-century shopper would advise her friend, "Meet me at the fountain," in Siegel-Cooper's atrium. The fountain served much the same function as the Biltmore clock did a generation later.

Most Chelsea residents saw little of the flash and the wealth, beyond a glance at a passing hansom cab or a peek through the window of one of the London Terrace homes on 23rd Street. Proctor's, Koster & Bial's, and even the Haymarket were for the upper crust, and there was nothing glamorous about the struggle of a family for survival. In her biography of Dr. Elliott, Tay Hohoff described the neighborhood that Elliott saw when he first wandered through Chelsea's streets:

> There were the waterfront bars, lumber yards, freight yards, hovels, docks, "Death Avenue," Ninth Avenue blackened by the elevated, side streets thick with gaunt and dirty tenements, lots empty of everything but rubbish sodden in the corners or blowing up in every wind, a sinister-looking loft building now and again, dingy saloons on every corner, a church or two. And life—fecund, hungry, violent, unpredictable, unconquerable. When the wind blew right, a whiff of ocean swept through the tousled streets. The deep-throated call of an ocean-going steamer was a sound as commonplace as the shriek and rattle of the elevated railroad or the scream of a woman out a window at her son in the street below. The old people had the brogue on their tongues and it spilled over, a little, to the shrill-voiced second generation. The girls often were pretty as the mavourneens for whom songs had been made. The boys roamed the streets which never slept, alert and vulnerable, dreadfully knowledgeable and wildly ignorant.

Dr. Elliott was a direct descendant of the fiery abolitionist Elijah Lovejoy. He was also a disciple of Felix Adler, who founded the Society for Ethical Culture. Ethical Culture's motto was "Deeds not creed." It was Adler's belief that through moral and ethical teaching, people's lives could be improved. The society was also allied with the burgeoning settlement movement, which had already founded successful neighborhood houses in some of the poorer areas of the city.

In 1895, Elliott decided that Chelsea would be the site of what he would call the Hudson Guild, perhaps the most successful neighborhood house of all. After Elliott had moved into a tenement apartment on 28th Street, he met a group of youngsters shooting craps on the sidewalk and asked them if they'd like to hang out indoors. When they agreed, he set them up in the basement of his building. Others soon asked to join. When a group of girls and then some parents joined, the Guild was suddenly too large for its headquarters.

Dr. Elliott knew that if the Guild was going to survive in Chelsea, its programs would have to reflect the needs of the neighborhood. He established a Clubs Council, which had real power in determining how the Guild was to be run. He'd created programs unique to the neighborhood. For instance, the Guild offered a scrubwoman's course, so that local women could get work cleaning houses. In 1911, he began a program to teach youngsters the rudiments of printing, one of the larger industries in the area. The program was so successful that it eventually became the New York School for Printing, one of the city's leading vocational high schools.

The Guild was instrumental in opening a public bathhouse for Chelsea. Dr. Elliott also lobbied successfully for public housing in the area. Most important, he made a personal difference in the lives of hundreds of area residents. If Dr. Elliott didn't reach them all individually, his staff of counselors, teachers, and social workers saved countless families on the brink of extinction. Not only did the Guild's staff provide food, clothing, books, health care, and rent money, but also, for the first time, they showed youngsters from broken homes that somebody cared and believed in their potential. Many old-timers who attended the Guild in Dr. Elliott's day still claim today that the Guild's staffers were the most important people in their lives.

Ironically, it may have been Chelsea's rich potential that was the largest contributing factor to the local poverty. Although there were jobs in the larger factories, such as National Biscuit and Stanley Soap, it was the docks that provided most of the employment opportunities. Through World War II, there was hardly a Chelsea resident who didn't have a connection to the waterfront in one way or another.

In the first half of the century, the port of New York was probably the busiest in the world. On any given day, the flags of many nations fluttered in the North River breeze, signaling the docking of large liners, including the *Ile-de-France,* the *Mauritania,* the *Normandie,* and the *United States.* For passengers and freight that had crossed the ocean, the West Side was the first stop in America.

The docks and the supporting industries employed thousands of men, but the population of Chelsea in 1900 exceeded 100,000, with more arriving daily and heading to the docks in a fruitless search for employment. Even when they could get work, it was low paying and dangerous, with the highest injury rate of any profession. For those few who got steady jobs, the best they could hope for were wages that would raise their standard of living to the poverty level.

Their fate rested largely on the whims of Joe Ryan, a longtime Chelsea resident. Ryan worked on the docks only briefly, in 1913, before he was injured and moved to a desk job for Chelsea's local union, Number 791. His ascension through union ranks was rapid, and in 1927 he was elected president (and later "president-for-life") of the entire union. Union democracy was not one of Ryan's strong points. During his tenure, local meetings were as rare as snowflakes in July. Elections, like the one that elevated him to president-for-life status, were won by questionable means embarrassing to even hardened machine politicians.

Through it all, Ryan put in regular appearances at Guardian Angel Church, known as Shrine Church of the Sea, then on 17th Street, and he insisted that stories of corruption on the docks were lies spread by dissidents who almost certainly were Communists. While he was admired by those who had steady jobs, it was fear that was his chief ally. One of his close associates, John "Cockeye" Dunn, was known to have been responsible for thirty-two murders. His last such effort, the killing of dissident Andy Heinz, earned him a 1947 walk to the electric chair, along with another Ryan henchman, Andrew Sheridan.

Ryan maintained his grip on the waterfront until after World War II. Then, spurred by newspaper investigations, several courageous dissidents, and the work of the waterfront priest Father John Corridon, of St. Francis Xavier Church, a waterfront crime commission was set up to air the lurid tales of life on the docks. The commission helped bring Ryan's lifetime term to a premature end in 1953, when it was found that he had used union funds earmarked to fight Communism to pay for a country-club membership and other perks. In 1955, Ryan was convicted of accepting a $2,000 bribe from a stevedore. His power broken, the man who had been a friend of mayors and governors was reduced to spending his final years playing cards with the last remnants of his old gang.

Longshoremen were not the only force on the waterfront. For years, merchant sailors came in and out of the neighborhood from Chelsea's piers. Their poverty and the crude conditions of their work nearly matched those of the longshoremen. Other than that, the two groups had little in common and rarely saw eye to eye. As the seamen moved to the political left and showed increasing strength, Ryan, fearing for his own position, sent the longshoremen to battle on management's side when the seamen engaged in two long and violent strikes in 1936–37.

Under the nominal leadership of Joe Curran, the seamen fought a veritable guerrilla war along the West Side waterfront. Though the union lost both strikes, they won recognition in 1937, and the National Maritime Union headquarters is now firmly anchored on the other side of the Hudson in New Jersey.

The Chelsea that witnessed the birth of the NMU was a far cry from the Chelsea of Josie Mansfield and Millionaires' Row. By 1937, the Grand Opera House had ceased to be grand, and was just another dusky movie theater with a fancy lobby. Koster & Bial's, the Eden Musée, and Ajeeb were long gone, and Proctor's was reduced to seven letters on a 23rd Street sidewalk. The original London Terrace was gone, having been replaced by massive apartment buildings of the same name. The elegant Chelsea Cottages had also disappeared, and Millionaires' Row became a series of rooming houses, providing a home for destitute seamen at six dollars a week.

Thugs killed each other on the street, or in more exotic locations, like the phone booth at London Chemists on 23rd and Eighth, where Vincent "Mad Dog" Coll breathed his last amid a hail of machine-gun bullets. But the Hudson Guild was still there, providing hope for anybody who reached out for it. The patrician Dr. Elliott, his walrus mustache now polar-bear white, continued to toil in the neighborhood until his death in 1942. Only at the Hotel Chelsea did it seem that life continued as it had. The proper ladies enjoyed their afternoon teas, while the literary crowd burned their candles at both ends.

# The Witnesses

BILL BAILEY (1910–) is a former longshoreman and seaman. His story appears primarily in the Hell's Kitchen chapter.

EDDIE BURNS (1909–) is a Chelsea native and a retired longshoreman.

FATHER PHILIP CAREY (1906–) is a Jesuit priest at St. Francis Xavier Church, on 16th Street, and a longtime labor activist.

DAN CARPENTER (1909–) was formerly head of the Hudson Guild, which he first joined as a social worker in 1931. He now works for the National Association on Drug Abuse Problems, which finds jobs for rehabilitated addicts.

JOHN CORCORAN (1914–) is a third-generation Chelsea native. He is a former fireman and Off-Track Betting official.

PEGGY DOLAN (1923?–85) is a pseudonym. She was born and raised in Chelsea.

JOHN DWYER (1915–) is a retired longshoreman and one of the leaders in the battle against the forces of union boss Joe Ryan. He lives in Florida.

HAROLD GATES (1906–88) was a former longshoreman. His full story appears in the Greenwich Village chapter.

SAM MADELL (1906–) is a former longshoreman and organizer for the Communist Party.

ROY SAUNDERS (1909–87) was a North Carolina native. He worked on the docks for many years, until health problems forced his retirement.

GEORGE SCHWARTZ (1909–) is a retired seaman. He was formerly an official with the National Maritime Union.

JOE STACK (1916–) was one of the key figures in strikes by merchant seamen in 1936 and 1937 that led to the founding of the National Maritime Union. After being purged from the union in the McCarthy period, he went into the construction business. Now retired, he is an avid marathon runner.

BRESCI THOMPSON (1908–) has lived on the West Side his entire life. He was a display manager for the A&S department store in Brooklyn. In his retirement he paints and also appears as an extra in feature films. His wife, MARY, who also participated in this interview, was a teacher and social worker. She died in August 1986.

ALICE TIBBETTS (1901–88) lived in the Chelsea Hotel from 1933 until her death. She was formerly a secretary and public relations copywriter.

JIMMY GARVIN, BEATRICE GHENT, ADELE MAC-FARLAND, and HANNAH VANCE all grew up in Chelsea. They were interviewed together one afternoon at the Hudson Guild farm in New Jersey.

JOHN CORCORAN: There was nothing gracious about life back then. It was hard, hard living. You had manual workers who were used to working with their hands, and they were used to settling disputes with their hands.

On 26th between Ninth and Tenth was predominantly Irish; 26th between Eighth and Ninth was predominantly Italian. There were fights between the blocks. They would come in and take the banister posts and use them as clubs against one another.

Those guys were able to kill each other with impunity. I never knew people who were interested in the community. I knew people who were on the take. "What's in it for me?" I saw a guy named Bill Cavanaugh, who people referred to as "the Leader," because he was the Democratic leader in the district. I saw the exalted position he held in the community. I saw him and his wife and daughter sit in a certain pew in the church, which was a position of distinction. He was a deputy commissioner in the Department of Water Supply. My guess was that he knew about as much about the Department of Water Supply as I knew about the forthcoming atomic age. He was there because he had a political position. He didn't work. He did whatever he had to do to maintain a front. The other place people worked was the docks. In those days, the docks were Chelsea. Then, everybody had some connection to the docks.

DAN CARPENTER: The docks dominated the neighborhood. So many of the industries supported the work on the docks. There was always concern about corruption, but I don't remember a meeting at the Guild where that was the central thing. We were functioning in a neighborhood where many of the families depended on the docks. There was more of an interest in trying to do things for health and getting better housing and recreation and better schools than fighting the corruption on the docks.

JOE STACK: After the seamen struck, we took scabs on the West Side near the railroad—take his legs and put 'em on the goddamn railroad track and [stamps foot] jump on 'em, bust his legs. We know he wasn't gonna sail for a couple months. There was no such thing as Queensberry Rules. For instance, one time there were about four, five guys beatin' up a scab and some woman comes down the street hollerin', "Hey, hey, leave that man alone!"

Some guy hollers back, "Madam, that ain't no man, that's a scab!"

We had to do that. If we hadn't done those kind of tactics we wouldn't have had a union. We were in the same position as a lot of these people they call terrorists today. To the guys, it was perfectly normal and natural. We were fightin' for our very lives. We'd get off these ships to build a union, and so they'd put these guys on the ships. They're on the ships workin', right? They're takin' our money. That was our psychology. If we didn't use these tactics we'd have never won.

• • •

BRESCI THOMPSON: Mostly, I remember that Chelsea was a series of smells. You had Runkle Brothers on 30th Street between Ninth and Tenth, which made chocolates. And the smells from there were beautiful sweet smells. On the corner of 31st and Tenth, there was Consolidated Chocolate, another great smell. You had smells brought in from National Biscuit on 14th, 15th, and 16th that were just tantalizing.

Then there were the horrible smells of the slaughterhouse on 41st and Eleventh Avenue as the wind from Jersey came in. Then you had the smell in each hall and yard of cats' pee. Everybody had a cat to get rid of the rats. And of course there were body smells, because there weren't many facilities for bathing.

The Grand Opera House had vaudeville and a movie. It looked immense to me as a child. The seats were plush velvet. It had rococo kind of sides with columns. There were angels and cherubs. But there was no air conditioning in those days, so there were smells in the theater of sweat and lack of air and urine. You'd go in there with a bunch of kids. These families were large, and instead of taking them to the bathroom they'd just squat down and do it. It was so stifling in there a man would come along with a spray gun and he'd spray perfume.

My father jumped ship in New York to escape military servitude in Argentina. He had been raised in a Catholic family in a Catholic school, hating the corporal punishment that the priests would hand out to the children. He hated the stories about the fear of the devil and hell that were put in the minds of young children, whose lives, he felt, should have been sweet and beautiful and full of happiness and wonderment. So he turned against religion, especially the Catholic religion—so much so that he never named any of his children by saints' names.

He was quite poetical. There was my sister Liberta. Then there was Alba, which is Spanish for daybreak. There's Savia, which is the sweetest part of the flowers that all the insects seek, and Senda. La Senda in Spanish is the road to Utopia which we all seek.

In 1895, my father was working in a silk mill in Paterson, New Jersey, with a man named Gaetano Bresci, an Italian who was an anarchist. He and my father became very friendly because they shared the same ideas. Well, Gaetano Bresci was saving money each week to send for his sister, who was a silk worker in Italy. But they had a strike there, and the king sent out the soldiers to disperse the strikers, and in that melee his sister was killed.

Gaetano then said to my father, "Giuseppe, this money has a purpose. I'm going to Italy to kill the king." He left, and he went to outside of Milan, and he approached the carriage of Humbert the First, Umberto Primo, and he shot and killed him. That was in 1900. He was imprisoned for life, and it was ruled that the name Bresci, which was a surname, should not exist anymore.

My father was saddened, because this man was like a brother to him, and he said, "If I ever have a child, I'm going to name him Bresci," and that's how I got my name.

I was born in 1908 on 49th and Tenth Avenue in Hell's Kitchen. Then my family moved down and settled on 27th Street between Ninth and Tenth, not far from the Hudson Guild. My father tried to get work on the docks, but it was rough. Those who had a toothpick behind their ear on the shape-up were selected. At the end of the day, you'd go to a saloon and the hiring boss would come by for his money, but my father said, "I wanna get paid for what I worked for. I don't wanna pay back somebody who hasn't worked."

He was beaten up. He tried to get the Italian people to do something together about the system. He'd say, "I've got four children. Those guys over there, you pick them every week." They said, "Just keep your mouth shut and do your job." He went to a Spanish bar on 26th Street between Tenth and Eleventh, and from there they went down to 14th Street to the hiring local to complain. One night while walking home a few days later, he was jumped and beaten up. He came home with black eyes. He couldn't really get work after that, so he had to leave the docks.

My father had the will to work, but the docks were the meal ticket for most of the Chelsea residents. He had a tough time when he couldn't work there anymore. My father played the guitar. He liked to sing Argentine songs and folklore. That was great, but when he didn't have a job, the guitar was in the pawnshop, so we knew that was bad times. But once we heard the guitar playing again, good times came to the house because my father had a job again.

JOHN CORCORAN: My grandfather had a dairy farm on 28th Street west of Eleventh Avenue. Later on, the street bordering on the river from 23rd Street north was known as the Farm. There was a lot of space—enough that they were able to play baseball there. When we'd go by there, my father would say, "This is where your mother's father used to water the milk."

I was born at 26th and Ninth. My mother was born on 28th Street between Tenth and Eleventh. My father was born on 26th just west of Tenth Avenue. She was born in '82. He was born in '84. My father's father was obviously an alcoholic by today's terms. In those days he would have been a bum. He didn't work, so my father had to go to work when he was eleven. He was carrying baggage at the Erie Ferry at 23rd Street and the river. There was no childhood that he talked about. His childhood was work.

I had to be home by ten at night until I was eighteen years old. I still remember one memorable night in which I had four aces in the same hand. Another guy had had four tens. I forgot about the time. When I realized it was after ten, I ran down Ninth Avenue. When I got up the stairs I saw the light under the door and I knew he was home. He had a great capacity for reasoning, my father. He reasoned with me by grabbing me and trying to lift me up by my shirt. He was not a mean man. He was not a hard man, but he had had a hard life.

FATHER PHILIP CAREY: My father worked as a conductor on the 23rd Street trolley line. See, if you were literate, they made you conductor. Otherwise, they put you on the front end of the car. He was off two days a year. We used to see him Sunday afternoon, when he let us ride on the front of the trolley.

There must have been about six or eight ferries that came in on 23rd Street. The starter would ring up, say, a hundred fares. They had a little board on the side of the car, and that's where my father would have to go, because the people were hanging from the sides. If he didn't collect the fares, they came out of his pocket.

There was a trolley strike in 1916. During the strike, he came down to the waterfront to get some work. He worked the barbed wire and the cement, because no one would handle that. The breathing was awful. The barbed wire just tore all his clothes. There was a wonderful priest at that time at Guardian Angel, Father McGrath, who told my father after two days, "You're not the man for this kind of work. Get back. Don't stay around here."

Soon, we were down to having tea and toast. Every week the superintendent would come around and beg my father to come to work. Then they brought in all these scabs from the Bowery. They didn't know anything about the operation of trolley cars. But we knew it was over when they brought in all the fellows from out of state. They were all put up in the yard with Red Cross supplies. When the strike was over, my father went back to work, but he always wore his union button inside his hat.

The brutality of the job was incredible. Like on the Fourth of July once, he was an extra man, and he was over in the West Farms barn trying to get another car. He was over in the back, and there was an open inspection pit. He fell down a whole flight and hit his head against a snowplow. He was pounding at the door for the longest while before they found him. They put him on the front of a trolley car and took him down to the hospital, and he was out about a month. But the guy who was in charge of compensation had skipped off with all the funds, so he didn't get a nickel.

He was a man with an enormous sense of justice. God would love him. A normal man would have been bitter at the treatment he was getting. He wasn't that way. He would say, "I am thankful to God that I will not have to face my Judgment Day with that on my soul. They will have to do it. I won't." He was always that way. When he was makin' enough money to pay his first income tax, he said, "Heretofore, I've been a freeloader. Now, I'm beginning to pay my own way."

PEGGY DOLAN: My mother was born in Canada, and my father was born in Cardiff, Wales. When he married my mother, he was fifteen, she was fourteen. They had eight children by the time they were thirty. It could have gone on forever, lord have mercy on them Irish parents.

BRESCI THOMPSON: If you were going to have a baby, you'd go to Paddy's Market on Ninth Avenue, and you'd see signs for a levitrice—midwife. The kids were all shooed into a neighbor's house, and you'd hear the screams of labor pains. The kids would be frightened, and they'd start crying.

Chelsea was a Catholic community, so the families were large. You'd always see the mothers out on the street breast-feeding their babies. They would take out these voluminous breasts with the nipples as large as pancakes. It was a little less common with the Irish mothers, but that corner of 31st Street or 30th with the Italian group, there the mothers didn't care. They'd have a big breast hanging out, and they'd be talking as they did it.

Yet there was such hypocrisy. There was lots of drinking and no control on sex, so you had more and more kids. You just couldn't talk about sex. I don't think they even ever heard of the rhythm method.

BEATRICE GHENT: They knew what it was, but if you were a Catholic you ignored that. They always had rhythm, but it didn't always work.

HANNAH VANCE: In our buildin' on 28th Street we had the Wolfs with eight kids. We had the Lynches with twelve kids. My mother had three. The Applegates had about fourteen. One day, there was all of us comin' out of the house, and this man came by, and he thought it was a school.

MARY THOMPSON: Down at PS 11 one morning, one of the boys came late, and they were very strict about attendance and punctuality in those days. I said, "William, what happened?"

He said, "I couldn't find my books."

"William, did you put them away at home?"

"Gee," he said, "you wouldn't be able to find your books either if you had nine kids in your family."

So I said, "Well, William, I guess you're right."

And then another little boy raised his hand. He said, "You think nine kids is a lot? That's not much. We have seventeen." So, shortly after that, this child was absent from school, and I went over to visit the family. Sure enough, there were seventeen, and almost every chair had a mattress rolled up on it.

I said to the mother, "How do you keep track of them?"

She said, "Well, every night the old man buys seventeen buns, and if there's one left over, we know someone's out."

BRESCI THOMPSON: Actually, Paddy's Market was responsible for my first sex experience. I was about nine or ten, and on 31st Street we were sharing a railroad apartment with another family. This woman and my mother would go together to Paddy's Market. They had a daughter who was fifteen, sixteen. The daughter was scrubbing the floor. She had a very low-cut dress. She said, "What are you looking at?"

I said, "Nothin'."

"Yes you are."

"No I'm not."

She opened up the rest. She came over and she kissed me, and she wanted to feel my body. It scared me, but I liked it.

Later on, you took girls home after dances, but the mother was always looking out the window. If she'd see you coming up the block and you tried to fool around in the hall, she'd have a bell that she'd ring. Sometimes I'd sneak up to the roof. That was a great spot. In those days the girls had a garment called "teddies." There were two buttons in the crotch. That was a great source of conversation. "Did you two button? Did you two button?"

"Sure."

"Ah, get outta here. You're lyin'."

If you got past that two button, you were almost home. I did, plenty of times.

•  •  •

JOHN CORCORAN: We had toilets in the yard when we were growing up. My brother and I helped to dismantle those sheds. This was an event. Jimmy Walker is credited with the comment that the greatest invention in the world was the one by the guy who put the toilets in the house. Boy, was he right. It was remarkable.

When you went down in the yard, you sat down on the toilet. When you sat, the water began to circulate in that bowl. Those houses had the small-gauge lead pipes. When the water supply came into the toilet bowl, and anybody upstairs wanted to get a drink of water, they would come to the window and say, "Let up the water, please." So you would get off your seat, and when you got off, the water stopped circulating in the bowl, and they could get a drink of water. If they wanted to fill a kettle of water, you had to have extreme patience off the seat.

MARY THOMPSON: There was great neighborliness in the old houses. And there was so much trouble that everybody shared everybody else's troubles and everybody else's joys.

BRESCI THOMPSON: So much of the misery was caused by the drinking. I never drank because of the things happening around me. There was a lot of wife abuse. You'd see lovely, lovely mothers with black eyes and their kids crying. On Sunday, you'd see Mrs. Normyle. She couldn't afford powder, so she'd put flour on to cover up the black eye.

And yet the people were caring for each other. There was always a neighbor on your floor or downstairs who would share food or take care of somebody who was sick. There was great concern for a family when somebody died. Believe you me, the Irish children were beautiful children, pink cheeked and blue eyed, freckled, and in spite of the misery there was lots of laughter and good humor. I've loved the Irish people all my life. They were very good to me and my family, and we were considered foreigners.

BEATRICE GHENT: At times, it was very, very hard. I remember our neighbor Mrs. Downs. She had reached the point where she had used up everything, and she was ashamed to take anything more from the people in the house because they weren't much better off than she was. She went off very early one morning to home relief, and she came into the hallway with a cardboard box. She said to my mother, "Alice, look what they gave me." They gave her a little thing of flour, a little thing of raisins, some kind of fat, and something else. How could you survive on that? And they were ashamed to take anything.

HANNAH VANCE: We had a Jewish man who sold linens, table-cloths, and you paid him five cents a week, ten cents a week, and he would come and he would knock on the door, and my mother would say [*whispers*], "Tell him I'm not here, lovely girl."

I'd say, "My mother isn't here. She said to tell you 'Come back next week.'"

He said, "Next week, it's going to cost you fifty cents."

My mother would scrounge around tryin' to get that fifty cents, but we had to have a white tablecloth on the table and napkins. But he was a sweet man, and he would go up and down those five flights of stairs tryin' to collect those nickels and dimes every day of the week.

Everybody was poor, but I remember every time the insurance man would come—it was a nickel policy—my mother would have him sit down, and she'd give him a cup of tea. If one of the older men came in and we were havin' soup, it was always, "Sit down and have a bowl of soup." And we had nothin'. Whoever came into the house, if it was a bum who knocked on the door to beg for bread, she would think nothin' of makin' him a sandwich.

PEGGY DOLAN: We lived in an old tenement on 17th Street. There was a lady that lived in the back. She loved her beer and she was old, and they wouldn't give her no beer, the family. So when we were havin' a party, like on Friday, when you had a couple of extra dollars, I used to tie a can of beer and throw it over to her. There wasn't much room in the shaftway, and she could catch it.

Come Friday nights, the men would come home and get drunk. The Haggertys, the Finnegans, and the Flynns, they all got drunk. And the women would say, "That bum, that bum, here he comes again. Friday night, here's the racket startin'."

But, Jesus, if *you* said he was a bum, well, his family would kill you. The wife would say, "How dare you talk to my husband like that. This is a man that works. He works all day."

Upstairs was an Irish girl and an Italian man who were married. She never wanted him drinkin'. It came payday, and he had a few bucks, she'd be sayin', "Goddamn you, were you drinkin' again?"

"No, I didn't have a drink." But meanwhile he had tied his wine bottle out the window on a cord. And when she wasn't lookin' at him, he'd take a slug, swipe a bit and hang it back.

When he got drunk, she would always give him fish, and he hated fish. Out would go the goddamn fish. Then the dishes that were in the kitchen would go out, and she would leave him. The next day they was back together again.

MARY THOMPSON: The low-rise buildings meant that everybody had access to the street, so that most of the children were watched not only by their own parents, but by everyone else's parents. As a matter of fact, when some of the old-timers get together, they often say, "Every time I did something wrong, I was beaten by three mothers." There was a lot of hanging out in the streets.

BRESCI THOMPSON: The great thing was to have your father make a soapbox wagon. The soapboxes were Curtin Soap and Octagon Soap, and there were many, many wheels of old baby carriages around because there were lots of children.

We'd use the wagons to go around picking up wood or we'd get food from the yards. At Eleventh Avenue and 30th Street, Borden's had a great big terminal with refrigerator cars coming in with milk and cream cheese and ice cream. They also had refrigerator cars for fruits and vegetables. There, the hucksters would pull in their wagons, which were horse-drawn, and they would empty out these refrigerator cars. Some of the produce would be tainted and would be thrown out, and the kids would pick through the food. There was a constant battle between the kids and the Polish women, who had these huge aprons and gunnysacks. My mother would wash everything and cut away the rotten fruit, and I'd have fruit salad.

My father used to say you shouldn't steal, but we needed that coal and the ice. Sometimes, when the longshoremen unloaded bananas, they'd give us some. They'd be green, and my mother would hang them real high so they'd turn yellow. If she didn't hang them up so high, we would have eaten them.

Some of the big boys would open up the doors of the refrigerator cars, and then they would knock the tops off those big milk cans. It looked like ice cream inside but it wasn't. It was sort of cottage cheese or cream cheese. We all wore these peak caps. We unsnapped them, put it in the peak cap, and ran like hell. When I got home, I emptied it out, and it was great. But I paid for it. That cap always had a sour smell.

The yard detective was called a dinny. The call for any warnings was "Footso the dinny." That meant the guard was coming. If you were caught, he'd give you a kick in the ass or a smack across the rump with that club he had.

PEGGY DOLAN: There was a guy there who probably left the doors open 'cause he knew there was a load of kids sittin' there waitin'. There was also a policeman ridin' behind the train on his horse. He knew us kids were takin' the stuff. After a while, he would slow down a bit. At 42nd Street the horse would stop for water, so we would be brave and get in and out with whatever we could.

BRESCI THOMPSON: The Police Department was aware of the poverty in the neighborhood. When we were living on 31st Street, a policeman came around and asked whose family didn't have a working parent. And there were many. He came to my family and asked my mother, "What does your husband need?"

She said, "Well, he needs an overcoat and pants and a few other things."

So they took the information down and they sent a postcard from the 30th Street police station: "Mrs. Thompson, please bring a baby carriage or a soapbox wagon because there will be a bundle."

We came back and it was a bonanza. We opened up this bundle on the round table in our kitchen and there was a coat for my father. Now the owner of the coat must have been an admiral or a doorman. It had brass buttons and all kinds of epaulets. Really, it looked elegant.

Well, my mother, who was a genius at survival, set out to fix it. She took all the braiding and the buttons off so my father could wear the coat without being saluted. Then she came to the white flannel tennis pants. If my father wore them down to the docks, they would have thrown him in the water. So my mother gave me some money to buy dye. There was a dye called "Never say dye, say Rit." Navy blue. I bought it.

The biggest pot we had was a cooking pot. There she put the white flannel pants, the dye, and the stick. Now flannel shrinks, but not to worry. We had wooden floors, no rugs. She took out those navy blue pants and she nailed, stretched, and nailed. We had to walk around this thing that looked like a big stiff codfish. Then, when it came to cooking the spaghetti in that big pot, it came out purple. So she washed off the purple and it became lavender. But as she washed it more and more, it congealed into a solid. Not to worry. She poured the Italian tomato sauce over it and cut it into slices.

That reminds me of another story. It was Thanksgiving time, and my father wasn't working. The Hudson Guild would give you a basket and a turkey, but they only had so many. My little sisters were cutting out pumpkins and turkeys and pasting them on the windowpanes. They wanted a turkey.

My mother said to me, "I have a secret. We'll have a turkey."

She bought chopped meat, and she got, I don't know from where, two tongue depressors, and she sculpted a turkey, which was beautiful. The two tongue depressors were the legs. She basted that, and she surrounded it with potatoes and parsley. And there we had this turkey with my mother, father, and I winking at each other. The kids were happy, but it was hard. It was really hard.

I knew we were poor. I didn't care much for me, but those little kids . . . I remember passing a toy store in the winter and seeing them stare at the window. It was heartbreaking. Sometimes, I would see those fancy homes on 24th Street. That was a different world. They had small lawns, and the houses were set back. I wanted to live in a house like that. And a house with an upstairs. That was a real dream.

Anything that had the country or trees or flowers, I loved. One source of wonder to me was a window box, even if it had just weeds. I have some weeds in my potted flowers now, and I hate to pull them out, because I just love them. Just to see this wonder, this beauty coming out of the soil, was a joy.

Despite the poverty, there were a lot of joys around Chelsea. On the corner of 30th and Tenth there was a bridge that spanned diagonally across Tenth Avenue. It was there because the Sheffield Farms and Borden's Milk trains crossed the avenue, and sometimes they would stall there so you couldn't cross. That was a great place. It was about two stories high, and we would lean over the railing as kids. As the locomotive came through, it spewed white smoke and we were in the clouds like angels. If it wasn't spewing smoke, we'd lean over and spit down the funnel. That was a great joy.

HANNAH VANCE: With all that steam, you thought you were in heaven.

BEATRICE GHENT: My friend was going to make his first Holy Communion, and he had his white suit on and white shoes. That's where he went—to the bridge. As soon as the train went right underneath and the smoke poured out he looked terrible. Of course his mother nearly murdered him.

BRESCI THOMPSON: Messmore and Damon made papier-mâché figures for motion pictures on 27th and Ninth. They had huge rooms below, and you looked through the grating into this room where they had these huge monsters. But my favorite place was Reilly's Stable on 31st between Ninth and Tenth. They housed the proscenium parts of stages along with the big drops and scenic backgrounds. They also housed the animals that were in some of the acts.

　　Well, sad to say, there was a tragic fire, and about six or seven horses and some of the animals died. But because of that fire they threw out all the costumes. The next morning the kids all had brightly colored ribbons. You'd see the girls with bright brilliant bows and sashes, and the boys all had spears and helmets. For years after that I kept a paste jewel. As I looked at it the facets would turn, and I'd see different worlds. That was a treasure.

JIMMY GARVIN: Off 30th Street was where we did our swimming. They had two or three barges filled with sand. That was our beach. We'd go up there, swim out and dive off, and if you wanted to go down a couple of blocks, you went out to the current and swam down.

BRESCI THOMPSON: The big kids were the brave ones. You had the barges with the freight cars on them. They'd dive off the tops of these things. Then United Fruit would come along. We'd hail them, and they'd throw big bunches of bananas and coconuts over the side. The coconuts were floating all over the place. The ingenious big guys would tie a couple of shirts together, and they made sort of a net so they could corral the coconuts. But I didn't like swimming in the river. The sewage emptied right into it, and it had an awful odor.

BEATRICE GHENT: They always said they knew who swam off the docks because they always used to do the breaststroke.

JIMMY GARVIN: Yeah, to push the garbage away. It was filthy.

BRESCI THOMPSON: I remember watching one day when they fished some guy out. He was all swollen up. They put a tarpaulin over him, and there was an eel that came swimming, slithering out from underneath. That scared us. Then there was a kid who dove in and got his head caught in the milk can. His shoulders were wedged in and he died. I wasn't there for that.

JIMMY GARVIN: Oh, we heard that one. That story always made the rounds. I don't think it ever happened though. It was one of those things that the mothers would say to you to scare you.

PEGGY DOLAN: We could all swim like rats. We'd lay on our backs, and we'd float up to 42nd Street with the tide. Then we'd stay up there on the pier till nine or ten o'clock, when the tide turned and we'd float back down. There were gangs of kids floatin' on the river. It was part of livin' and it was a great life. We loved the dirty greasy water. It kept us up, I suppose. All we did was float all the way down, then float up.

HANNAH VANCE: Oh, she was a bad girl. Only the boys swam in the river. We were never allowed past Tenth Avenue. We went to the pool.

MARY THOMPSON: Actually, it was the public baths. They got it through the pressure of the people in the neighborhood, who paraded up and down, saying, "We need a bath."

DAN CARPENTER: That's true. In 1911, the mothers' clubs of the Hudson Guild made a survey of the neighborhood. In the four blocks right around the Guild, there was only one bathtub. In other places around the city they had these baths, so they invited down the president of the Board of Aldermen and had a big meeting on the top floor of the Guild. When this man came in, they chanted, "We want a bath. We want a bath," and they got a bath. It came in 1912 on 28th Street.

MARY THOMPSON: It became a ritual. Every Saturday morning you'd see all the kids from all over Chelsea running to the baths with their underwear and a towel under their arms.

BRESCI THOMPSON: I had three sisters at the time, and there was no privacy when you had to have your bath, so my mother would send me on Tuesday and Saturday mornings to the 28th Street baths. It was compulsory to take a shower before you entered the pool, but we'd just put a little water on. Then, if they spotted us with a little black on our feet, whack! The same guy who used to patrol the pool would squeegee the water along the aisle into the trough. Once, this fellow got even with him by taking a big crap right into the aisle.

When I was younger we swam naked. But if you began to get a little manly and had hair follicles around your privates, you were not permitted to swim naked. There was a candy store at the corner of 28th and Ninth where you could rent a little loincloth, a small towel, and a small piece of soap for two cents. After you did your swimming, you'd come back with the loincloth and towel, and they would repay you a penny.

Now two cents in those days was a fortune. Maybe some of the kids could get one penny. So the enterprising storekeeper would say, "Okay, I'll take the penny, but you have to leave one shoe as a deposit." So you'd leave the shoe and go along with your loincloth, and you'd hop, hop along to the pool. You'd always have one dirty foot.

Now my first recollection of the Hudson Guild was when I was four. My father had no job. We were living in a basement apartment. Those days you had gaslight that was controlled by a little box near the ceiling called the quarter meter. You would feed that and the gas would come up. But we had no quarters. We had no coal, and we had no food, and we were going to be dispossessed.

Mrs. Delaney, who was the janitress, said, "Mrs. Thompson, go to the Guild. They'll help you." It was a desperate situation, because in those days the babies were breast-fed. My mother had no milk because she had no food, but the Hudson Guild gave us coal, and they gave us food. My introduction to the Hudson Guild was one of the biggest things in my life. Through that I went to kindergarten. I had the warmth of a heated building. There was electric light. There was a library, where we were exposed to beautiful paintings that were changed every month, and there were books that you could borrow.

But, more so, there was a concern by the people there. There was a love and an ambience that was a fairyland. As you went into the library there for various occasions, they had a wood-burning fireplace that you'd read about in books. You had access to arts and crafts. You had a gymnasium. You had a park that social workers took you to.

The Guild was *the* thing, but my first day there was traumatic because I didn't speak any English. I spoke Spanish. I was left there with all these people, and I was an outcast. Then Miss Bergen brought over this man with black hair and a black mustache. He spoke to me in Spanish. That opened up my world to me, and from then on I was in love with the place. That man was Dr. Elliott.

DAN CARPENTER: When I first came [to the Guild] in 1931, I was hired to work in the after-school program, and I went into the street like Dr. Elliott. I found kids playing stickball or stoopball or just hanging around, and I said, "Would you like to come over and join the Guild?" And by and large it worked, just like it worked for Dr. Elliott.

Dr. Elliott, more than any other, always felt that people should have a good deal to say about what went on in the settlement, so in the early years, they started the Hudson Guild Clubs Council, which had quite a good deal of power and status in the organization. This gave it a distinctive quality which many of the settlements didn't have. These personalities like Dr. Elliott and Mary Simkovitch and Lillian Wald, who started these settlements, were very strong-minded people as leaders. Some of them weren't as democratic in their attitude as Dr. Elliott was, and so while their programs were valuable to the neighborhood, they weren't developed out of the neighborhood.

Dr. Elliott always thought of the dignity of the people. No matter what your economic status was, there was dignity there. At the Hudson Guild, we never talked about working in the slums. We never talked about the poor. I think he was smart enough to know that, for social workers, just good will wasn't going to make the difference. You had to harness up the resources of the neighborhood, and that was the people. Some families had stability. They knew where they were going and had aspirations for the kids. So you set a standard for the neighborhood, and gradually, if you are strong enough, it impacts in a broad way.

At the same time, Dr. Elliott had to be careful. Somehow, Dr. Elliott, in this Catholic culture and in the eye of the ministry of the church, was an irreligious son of a bitch. Many of the priests from the altar told their parishioners to stay away from the Guild. "It's a Communist place."

That was a constant thing. Ethical Culture made a lot of people mad. I remember arguing with Father Dunleavey, of St. Columba, really getting into a lot of unhappy kinds of situations. One time, a member of our staff apparently had fondled a little boy, and his mother went to the priest about it.

"Well," he said, "what do you think would happen in that godless place?"

I was always very conscious of the families being torn. They were Catholics through and through. They went regularly to Mass. The kids went to parochial school and went through all the rituals. Yet at the same time they were active at the Guild. So they had to be torn. There were two loyalties. When Dr. Elliott died, they said he was a saint, which was quite different from the attitudes the priests like Father Dunleavey and the others had. That was part of the conflict.

ADELE MACFARLAND: The church always thought the Guild was Communist. My father always said that about the Guild and the Guild farm. I came home one day, and I said, "Daddy, do you know that at the farm they are so proper that the husbands and wives don't even sleep with each other? They're in separate houses."

He said, "Of course they are. They're sleeping with other people's wives."

DAN CARPENTER: They had quite a group of youngsters that belonged to the Guild. Tony Zullo and Lefty Phillips used to go across the street and mug people. This kind of crime was a part of growing up for those kids, just like fighting. They just loved to fight. If they didn't have a fight, they didn't think it was a very good day.

We frowned upon the kids bringing in and selling stuff when a crate broke open on the docks. They tried, though. They'd steal things out of the department stores. I remember stopping in one club as they were dividing the loot they had stolen from Macy's or Gimbel's. There was a group at the Guild called the El Rey club. One of their members, Willie Larraghty, was quite an expert. He was also a natural athlete. He walked out of Macy's with a canoe, and then he went back to get the paddles.

JIMMY GARVIN: Yes, and he got caught walking out with them. Actually, Lala didn't steal a canoe from Macy's. That story got embellished over the years. He stole a bicycle.

Willie was a sleight-of-hand artist. I remember when Flip Rodriguez got a watch from his father for his birthday. It wasn't working properly, so he, Willie, and I went down to Fulton Street or wherever the watch places were. When we got there, the man said, "Oh, yeah, I remember your father. This wasn't a good watch, so I won't repair it. I'll give you another."

So he put twelve watches down on the pad. Flip picked one, and the man went to the back room. When he came back he saw that another one was missing. We looked at each other. Nobody was near that tray of watches. So he called the cops. The cops came in and questioned us and searched us, but they didn't find anything and they let us go.

Outside, Flip said, "I never was so embarrassed in my life."

But Lala said, "Don't worry about it. I got the other watch here."

We asked him how the hell he secreted the watch.

He said, "Well, while they were searchin' Flip, I put it in your pocket. While they were searchin' you, I put it in Flip's pocket." It was fantastic.

Once, Lou Fleming, who was also a member of the El Reys, was going over to Macy's to buy reelies. That was a shooter in marbles. All of a sudden a little boy walked by, and Mrs. Fleming said, "Let's ask that little blond-haired boy to come with us." She didn't know Willie Larraghty.

So, off they went. Inside the store, Lou was fingering the reelie to get the feel of it, and he was about to say to his mother, "I'll take these," when Willie said, "Put them back, Lou. I already have four."

He never got caught. Others did, though. I was playing baseball with the Edison Company and this day the game was at Sing Sing. I had a Hudson Guild jacket on. I'm up taking my swings in batting practice, and half the place stood up and said, "Hey, Hudson Guild." The guy from the Edison Company asked me who those fellows were.

I said, "All the guys from home who got caught."

HANNAH VANCE: My mother used to clean Dr. Elliott's house. She would come in the morning, and she knew how many suits he had hangin' in the closet. He'd say, "Margie, have these drycleaned," or whatever. And my mother comes in one day, and there's no suits in the closet. Now she knows he couldn't have worn all the suits in one day. So she leaves him a note, "Dr. Elliott, there are no suits in your closet. Did you bring 'em to the cleaners?" And he comes home and says, "No, they've robbed me again, Marge. I'll go down to the pawnshop."

See, he would always leave his door open. So the fellas in the neighborhood who needed a few dollars would go in and take his suits, bring 'em up to the hockshop and get a coupla bucks. Then Dr. Elliott, or my mother, would have to go there and get them back. He never caused a fuss. He never said a word.

BEATRICE GHENT: All the fellas on 28th Street would wait until he went in for the night, and they'd take his car. Most of them learned how to drive by taking his car at night and just parking it in the same spot when they were done.

MARY THOMPSON: Sometimes a kid would come into class and say to his friend, "Psst, cucumbers are comin' in." He would say he saw them on such-and-such piers. Then they would go down there on their lunch hours and break open a crate, or the longshoremen would do it for them. But there was no feeling that it was a crime or it was stealing. They felt it was food coming into New York City, and they were hungry.

Still, when I came here, the children were so beautiful. I was sunk immediately. I knew this was my life. I got a job as a teacher in Astoria after I graduated, but I still came to the Guild every day as a volunteer. One day, I said to the girls' head worker, "I think I better change my career. I want to be a social worker." I thought they were doing a better job of education than the schools, and she said, "I'll give you a job right now." That changed my whole life.

BRESCI THOMPSON: The Hudson Guild always had a spare closet. "Let's look in the closet. Maybe there's something that will fit you, Bresci." They'd find something. Mostly I wore sneakers that were very cheap. When I needed shoes, my mother went to the Salvation Army. Once, she brought home a pair that were high and pointy with eyelets and hooks. My father cut the tops off and also cut the bottom and blackened them. I wore the shoes to school and it was all right, but I knew they were little girl's shoes.

HANNAH VANCE: Annie Bromley was special. When the thrift shop was there, she'd wait till the women who ran it left, and she'd say, "Margie, send the children down around five o'clock," and my mother would send us down. Then we'd be given shoes, dresses, anything to wear, without charging. All of us got clothing and things from them. Without the Guild we never would've survived.

Annie's husband was a vegetarian, but Annie loved meat. So my mother used to say, "Lovely girl, bring this over to Annie. Mr. Bromley is out of the house," and I'd bring it over, and she'd shovel it in.

BRESCI THOMPSON: The library at the Hudson Guild had the *National Geographic*. The magazines opened automatically to the bare-bosomed natives. We loved that magazine.

"Hey, hey, it's great this month."

The Guild also sponsored the outdoor movies at Chelsea Park, which were just great. It seemed like thousands were there. The park was filled. They hung two big sheets on the backstop. That was the screen.

PEGGY DOLAN: You just took your newspaper. Your brothers and sisters and all the Finnegans, about fifty kids you got stuck with to go to Chelsea Park on Friday night, 'cause that gave the mothers and fathers a break.

All the parents chipped in. A box of Oysterettes was five cents and a dill pickle was five cents. So we used to get about three pickles and four boxes of Oysterettes and divide it between all of us. Oysterettes are those things you'd put in soup, you know? We'd take this load of kids down and sit in Chelsea Park. We all knew each other.

"Heyeeeey. Yaeeeeey. Here comes that stinkin' Finnegans with that Dolans."

"Aaaah shut up." That's what we used to say: "Aaah shut up." 'Cause they wouldn't dare fight us 'cause we was too strong.

So we would sit and sit. The reel was always going wrong, and we'd scream anything we'd want to scream. "Ya bum. Boooo!" That's how we got all our energy out. Then there was the sing-along, and we was all whistlin' between our front teeth. We was all enjoyin' ourselves.

DAN CARPENTER: Dr. Elliott loved those movies. He would shout at the kids, "I want you to yell 'We want housing' so loud that Mayor La Guardia will hear you in City Hall." They'd yell, and he'd shout, "Louder! I don't think he heard you." That was always quite a lot of fun.

Still, putting on those movies was a horrible job. They usually came with a jellied apple and a bottle of pop, and they'd throw it at the screen or they'd throw stones. After they were gone, we'd have a committee and they'd clean up the park. For a while we could burn everything—have a hell of a big bonfire. That was always pretty exciting.

•  •  •

BRESCI THOMPSON: Death was around us a lot in those early years. The worst came in with the Spanish influenza epidemic of 1918. It was all around you. My sister Liberta was eleven months old and very sick.

I remember going down to a drugstore and calling the doctor, "Please come. Please come." But he just couldn't handle the cases, and he couldn't come. I came back up and I heard the screams, and the baby died in my mother's arms.

Then came the hassle. We had no insurance, so there was no money for a burial. He went around to collect from friends, but they were strapped, too. Finally, my father got so mad he said, "I'm gonna get a macaroni box, and I'll bury her in the backyard." But some of our Italian neighbors knew an undertaker, and they buried her free of charge.

So many people died that summer. In those days you had the wakes in the houses. You'd see those funeral crepes all over the neighborhood. Also, the families wore black armbands. The one fear was to receive a black-bordered letter in the mail—that meant death. You saw a lot of those also. There was a lot of crying, a lot of sadness.

That was also around the time of the war. In the classroom of PS 33 we had two receptacles—one was to collect peach pits, the other was to collect tinfoil. These were for the war effort. The peach pits were ground into something that went into gas masks. We also had thrift stamps. They were little books, and you came in with your nickel or so, and the teacher would paste these stamps into your book. But my father was a pacifist, and I had a very difficult time because he would not let me collect peach pits or tinfoil, and I did not have any thrift stamps.

We had an angel of a man whose name was Herman. He had a grocery store on 31st Street and Ninth. He would trust most of the neighbors. He had a little mahogany-colored book, and he would put down all the things he would trust you with, expecting to be paid either Friday night or Saturday morning. And he overlooked many of the debts because of the hardships.

He'd always give you a piece of baloney or something as you went. And I enjoyed looking in his window because he had corn-flakes boxes in a pyramid, and a cat he had would go in and out of these boxes without knocking them down. But all of a sudden the boxes were removed from the window, and he had a huge American flag put up. The family lived in back of the store, and they had a nice blond boy. Then somebody had broken the window, and the store was all boarded up. I never found out what happened to Herman, and it was so sad. My father made the big point, "Look what happens. There was a nice man. He trusted us. He trusted everybody, but he was forced out by the rah-rah-rah of the war."

Around that time, my father finally got work as a fireman for the National Biscuit Company. That means they had to warm up the ovens for the bakers to come in. He had to stoke those fires. Then, because I showed some talent as an artist, through Dr. Elliott I got a scholarship to the Ethical Culture school. The kids there were quite wealthy, and I would tell my father of the deliveries by limousines and chauffeured cars and of the kids with their tennis racquets and their horseback riding in the park. He asked me if they treated me well. I said, "Yes, but I am ashamed because I haven't got the clothing or the tennis racquets."

He said, "You should never be ashamed of poverty, never. It's because of people like that that you haven't got what they have." [*He laughs.*] He was a real anarchist. He used to read *Les Misérables* to us as kids. He would tell us that we didn't have toys and sweets at Christmastime because of the capitalistic system.

Right after that first year he died of a heart attack at National Biscuit. He was forty-five. Because the scholarship only meant tuition and not carfare, clothing, or books, my mother said I couldn't carry on. But Dr. Elliott said, "Don't worry, Mrs. Thompson, we'll see what we can do." So he scouted around, and he got a family on Park Avenue to take care of my lunches, my carfare, and my books. Then Dr. Elliott gave me another address. That was Pauline Stern. She had lost her husband and her son in the period of a year. There was great sorrow. He thought it would be nice to have someone like myself be a chauffeur, maid, everything, so she provided for my clothing and my dental bills.

I must have been a bother to Dr. Elliott, but he looked after my welfare. I was a very lucky guy. He even put me up in his apartment on 28th Street. Dr. Elliott was something else. Here was the kind of a man who made you think of the poem "If." "If you could walk with kings and not lose the common touch." He knew Roosevelt and all the city leaders. Then you'd see him walking down the block, and he'd pick up a snot-nosed kid in his arms. He didn't mind dirtying his hands to have a job done.

At Christmastime he was in Chelsea Park, and he'd ask the people on the ground floors of the buildings around there to put a candle in the window, and that would be a station where the choral group would sing Christmas carols. He would join them on those cold nights.

The man never locked his door, and the smell and aura about Dr. Elliott was Old Gold Tobacco. He was a handsome man. Later on, he got portly, and he had gray hair, a gray mustache, and a booming voice. I don't know how he escaped all those rich women who were after him.

. . .

JOHN CORCORAN: My father went to the fourth grade. My mother may have gone on to the sixth. I was the first one in my family to go to college. I went as an adult. There is a great desire for equality in certain societies. The one which I came from also had the great desire for equality. Everybody should be equally lousy. God forbid anybody should try to rise above the pack. You were then a subject for scorn and ridicule. If you tried to become better, this meant you were debasing those who were left behind.

When I was in high school I can remember one of my favorite uncles saying with scorn, "What the hell do you want to be, a banker?" These people never had any association with learning— none at all. They assumed I'd do what they did—work in the factory, on the docks, or for the city. In Chelsea, you became a cop or a fireman or you went to jail.

DAN CARPENTER: I think Corcoran put his finger on something. That was one of the things the Guild and Dr. Elliott tried to overcome. He tried to reach people like Frank Rosemondo. They got him to go to Cornell and he became a doctor. That part really was always a struggle. It was the work ethic. You worked with your hands, not necessarily with your mind, in the docks, the trucks, and the factories. Printing was all right, too. Only later on, when I first came to the Guild, you might find a half-dozen kids that were going to college or were planning to go to college. Gradually that all changed. Before, I think they were afraid. If you went to school, you would leave the neighborhood.

BRESCI THOMPSON: A lot of girls would fake their ages to get jobs at places like National Biscuit. Some of them were fourteen or fifteen. Some of them were less than that. However, National Biscuit knew they were young, and they'd say, "Whoops, you'd better hide in these barrels, because the inspectors are coming."

One of the great stories was that if the children were acting up, the supervisor would say, "If you don't behave, I'll send you down to Fig Newtons."

MARY THOMPSON: Which they hated because of the sticky mash.

BRESCI THOMPSON: The mash and the sticky floor. That was Siberia, Fig Newtons.

MARY THOMPSON: Up at the Guild farm in New Jersey, Bresci was known as the Sheik of the Neighborhood. All of the girls were swooning over him. As the girls' social worker, I had several girls who were adolescent. I'd say, "Take it easy. Dance with him, but don't take him seriously, because you're gonna get hurt." And one of them went back and told him.

BRESCI THOMPSON: I said, "Listen here, Mary Fox, you mind your own damned business." This was during Prohibition, and at the farm they would have dances on Saturday nights. But the young folks would leave the dances to go to speakeasies around Lake Hopatcong. At 10:30, the band would be playing for four people. And Mary's a wonderful dancer, and even though we didn't like each other much, we started dancing. When we finally got married, they said, "Foxy Mary Fox, she wanted him for herself."

Things were rough at that time. The poverty of the Depression was different from the poverty I knew growing up, because here I could see there were few jobs for anybody. The spirit was broken because so many adults were out of work. In my father's time there might have been hundreds out of work. Now, there were thousands. I was married. I was working for the Temporary Emergency Relief Agency as an elevator operator. Even though it was for $1,250 a year, I was blessed. Thank God for Mary—she had a civil-service job.

There were no jobs for artists, although Dr. Elliott did a wonderful thing. He had a bunch of artists and craftsmen who had no place to go, and he sent them to the farm, so they got their food and they got their lodging. It was like a small WPA. I didn't go join that, but finally I did get a job as an artist. I sort of prostituted my talents and became display manager at A&S in Brooklyn for thirty-three years. But I loved it.

PEGGY DOLAN: Depression days it was very, very hard. Nobody had nothin' to eat. If a kid had an apple, we'd be lookin' at 'im, thinkin', Gee, I hope he throws it away. The core of the apple. We used to love the core of the apple. I hate apples today. Then, we used to wait for the kid. "You gonna eat the core of the apple?"

"Naah, I don't want that." Sometimes they was generous and left a little bit on it.

We was all skinny. The school gave you Tastee Eez. It used to come in a little pack. It was a wafer. It had somethin' in it that kept you alive.

We lived in cold-water flats, no heat. There was nothin' but a black stove in the kitchen. That's how we all stayed warm, in the kitchen. Then you run like hell to get into the bed. We never had sheets. We had Indian blankets underneath us and Indian blankets above us. Sheets used to make the beds cold. You were lucky you had a mattress to sleep on. Otherwise, you slept on the floor.

Then, there was a lot of colds and stuff because there was no heat. I think we were the first ones to take penicillin. We used to have an icebox that didn't keep the stuff cold. There was nothin' to put in it anyway, let's face it. My momma used to take the grease from the bacon; she kept a can of it in the icebox. On top there was somethin' like four inches of green mold. When we had a bad croup or somethin', my father said, "These kids are sick."

Then he'd say, "Line up." He'd take that tablespoon and stick it into that grease. Goose grease, that's what it was. Then he'd pour honey on top of that so you wouldn't taste it.

They gave free shoes to poor kids. But the poor kids wasn't gettin' the shoes. Kids was sayin' that kids that's fathers had the jobs were gettin' the shoes. So I wrote a letter to La Guardia, and I told him how from this day forward we are not going to school. There are eight of us. Because we have no shoes and we're tired of walkin' with our feet on the ground.

Do you know that he sent me a beautiful letter back, and he told me that each one of us kids was to get two pairs of shoes each. They had the shoes in the school, but this one woman was in there. Excuse me, she was a bitch. She said, "You ain't gettin' nothin'."

"Mayor La Guardia gave me somethin', honey. Get up a pair of shoes for him. What kind of shoes do you like, Frank? What do you like, Laura? Pick out the nicest ones—you know, the good heavy-sole ones."

She was sick. We got sixteen pairs of shoes. We were goin' home with shoes in our hands, like we were wealthy. And no more paper in our shoes. God help us, warm feet.

ALICE TIBBETTS: I am just one year younger than the century. I was born in 1901. In 1933, I was doing advertising for a very good bank in St. Louis, and a man from New York came out there and persuaded me to come to New York to be in his advertising agency. I always wanted to come to New York, so I did that. When I first came here with Ben Sweetland, rent was twelve dollars a week. But then I had some of my own furniture, and so, without my asking, the owners said, "You have your own furniture, we'll reduce it to nine dollars." Wasn't that nice of them?

This man I was supposed to get married to lived in London Terrace. It amuses me to think now how poor we both were, yet he got a room for me here at the Chelsea Hotel 'cause it would be near where he lived. No thought, never any thought, of me moving in with him.

Anyway, Benny Sweetland's agency went bankrupt. It was direct mail. He couldn't keep it afloat. So here I was, and I didn't have any job. I went around to the banks, and they just said, "We've let everybody go that was married, and we wish we could lose another hundred." There was nothing.

I was reading in my diary last night that then, if I could make a dollar typing something I was pleased. I met somebody who lived over here on Eighth Avenue. She said, "We need a baby-sitter some nights a week. Would you come over to stay with our baby, fifty cents an hour?" And I did it.

Many a time I see notations, "I made a dollar" or "made two dollars" typing for Fred Caswell, a short-story writer who lived upstairs. I'd pick up a dollar working for him, but we could go over to Cavanaugh's and get a fine steak dinner for a dollar ninety. The other little restaurants around here you could eat for as low as thirty-five cents.

In some ways it was a good time. Everybody had lots of time. That was another thing, there wasn't tension about getting a job like there is now, because nobody had jobs, and there was lots of time to sit around and talk. Day after, I read, this one came to my room, and that one came, and we sat around and talked. Somebody would bring some cheap wine, or else we made coffee. Oh, I drank too much coffee in those days.

I had good clothes in St. Louis, so I kept fixing those over if I needed to. I always got compliments on my clothes, even in the darkest Depression because Edgar Lee Masters used to take me to cocktail parties, and, God, I remember I met John Dewey, and Edgar used to say, "I don't know how you do it. I know you don't have any money."

I had one beau who was a millionaire out in Milwaukee. He just loved to dance. When he came in, he would invite me to the St. Regis and places like that, but this man had a wife back home. If he saw anybody in the restaurant he might know or knew him, he'd want to get out of there in a hurry. I explained after to Edgar Lee, and he made up a name for him—Old Man Afraid of His Horse.

Fred MacIsaac, who lived upstairs with his wife, wrote a story about me, called "The Girl on the Floor Below." I used to go up there, and they'd be sitting around drinking, drinking, drinking. I'd be so hungry. They'd invited me to go out to dinner with them, so I sat there through all this drinking just so I could get something to eat. Finally, somebody said, "Where we gonna go? Where we gonna eat? Then everybody had a different idea. Until they finally settled on a place, I was so hungry, I was about keeling over.

Still, I never went without gloves, and men never went without collars and ties. I think back then the men were so poor, but Edgar would always leave his tie on except in the real hot summer weather. To see anybody go out with just an undershirt or T-shirt, yuck. And they had a reason: they were poor, but they somehow managed to look nice.

PEGGY DOLAN: Mrs. Finnegan was on home relief, and she used to work, anything to feed the kids, any kind of a job. But one day this welfare lady comes and she says to Mrs. Finnegan, "Ooh, I see you got new sheets on the beds. Well, you're off relief today."

"Oh," she says, "bejeezus, is that right?"

"Yes, that's right."

"Well, by God, you're gonna be off for quite a few weeks."

And, bingo! She knocked her down a whole flight of steps. And she was out of action for quite a while, for three or four months after that.

DAN CARPENTER: In the wintertime during the height of the Depression, it was terribly cold and we put papers down on the gym floor and had people come in to sleep there. On the docks, people would get the crates and cardboards and sleep in them. The safety net at that time was the big families. Even though you were unemployed, there was always somebody working, and the families somehow managed to hold together. The people who were really the elite were the firemen, the policemen, the teachers. They had salaries, civil-service jobs.

Those that were working on the docks were doing pretty well, comparatively. But it was a rough life until you were a checker or were in with a boss who would pick you out of the shape. I recall a lot of anger around the bars. But the discipline of the union was terribly strong. So if the leader said, "Get out here. We're having a meeting" and raised his finger, they'd all stand up and shout. There was control.

JOHN CORCORAN: Even when I was young, I couldn't stand political corruption. I was old enough to read the newspapers and to know that there was something wrong with the democratic system and the Democratic Party on the West Side of Manhattan. I used to ask my father, "Why do you vote for the Democratic Party?" The answer I got was, "Three meals a day." I never realized what that meant until I got older. He obviously meant that his job depended on the Democratic Party. Civil service was relatively new. He and his generation didn't know about the relative security of civil service like me and my generation.

Though my father was a detective, his brother ran beer during Prohibition. I used to ask how this happened to be. There was also a fellow named Doc Pisicano who was a bookie, yet he was a respected citizen. I wondered if this was against the law or not. If it's against the law, why isn't something done about it? What it was, was the system. I have problems today with the goddamn system.

My uncle owned a couple of speakeasies. I remember graduating from school and going over to Uncle Johnny's speakeasy, and making my confirmation and then going over to Uncle Johnny's speakeasy. Here was a religious experience. It was confusing to me as a kid.

Owney Madden's Flanagan and Nay Brewery was on 26th Street

near Tenth Avenue. As a kid hanging out in the firehouse there, I used to see these trucks going in and out of the brewery. Eventually, revenue agents were in the firehouse, and they were checking this out. The best that I could ever make out that the revenue agents were doing was counting how many trucks there were, and later they went to some place and made a collection for themselves of so much per truck.

My brother worked on the docks, and my father's brother and brother-in-law, who were running beer, both worked on the docks. Later on, when I got involved in trade unionism during the Depression, I asked my brother why he didn't attend ILA union meetings. He said, "What makes you think they had union meetings?"

I said, "They have to have union meetings."

He said, "They do?"

"They're supposed to post notices."

"They do. They post them on the end of the dock."

I got to understand that if you were militant and were going to assert your rights, you might be found dead. They actually killed people. I found that shocking. I subsequently found out when I began to study labor history that it was not so shocking. It was part of life.

JOHN DWYER: I was born in 1915 on 12th Street between Greenwich and Washington down in the Village. My father was a longshoreman. He worked in the hold all his life. He told me to stay away from the waterfront, but he never said why. And he never said a word about the unions. The term "deaf and dumb," I guess it would fit in with 98 percent of the longshoremen. The less you say and the less you hear, the better off you are.

I don't believe that stuff about the payoffs on the West Side. I never saw it. I never paid a nickel for any job I got. I became hiring boss and nobody ever paid me a nickel. It might have happened in other parts of the city. I'm positive it never happened on the West Side. That's all fantasy as far as I'm concerned.

PHILIP CAREY: John knows the bosses were paid off, but a lot of them don't want to let outsiders know. Everybody knew it. The hiring boss got his payoffs. Then there was the numbers guy and loan shark. All those guys had to pay off for those jobs. Then they had to shake down everybody in sight. Goodness gracious.

I came to Xavier in 1939 to replace Father Joe Fitzpatrick. Joe was all over the question whether the utility workers at that time were a company union. Joe made a decision, but Cardinal Spellman's assistant, McIntyre, didn't like it, and he started to raise trouble. That bastard McIntyre, they said his stupidity was exceeded only by his piety, and he was a very pious man.

EDDIE BURNS [*he wears a watchman's cap on his head and has a cigar stub between his teeth; his voice is from a gravel pit and escapes from the side of his mouth*]: I went to the shape-up and got hired, that's all. I'm from 26th and Ninth. The boss was from the neighborhood. Ya knew the boss. He knew you, and ya got hired.

The toothpicks behind your ears, that was mostly with the foreigners. The pay was ninety-five cents an hour. I never gave back nothin'.

*On the Waterfront* was a lot of bullshit. Bullshit. It was a farce as far as longshorin' was concerned. When do you see a priest and a girl go down in the ship? That Father Corridan, he was in Xavier and that's all. He never was on the dock. Just always givin' out information. He did nothin' for nobody, Corridan. Kickbacks and the mob. Things like that happened, but they exaggerate it. It was silly stuff.

SAM MADELL: At the shape, there'd be about 300 or so standing around, and maybe a quarter of them got picked. Once in a while I was one of them.

The shape-up system is based on the principle of a tremendous oversupply of labor, so you had to be extremely lucky to get a job. Every dock would have a surplus. They had their regular gangs, and the only time that an outsider had any chance at all was if they were extremely rushed to get the ship out, so they might hire extra gangs.

It took something like three or four weeks, after shaping three times a day, before I finally got hired. If you got hired that way, chances are you would get the lousiest jobs, like carrying 220-pound bags of coffee, stuff like that. Those that worked in the hold of the ship, even if they worked steady, were like beasts of burden.

The hold work was the worst by far. There were blacks in the hold, a lot of Yugoslavs, the old-country Irish and Italians. There was no system of promotion. If you complained to the stevedore, you'd probably wind up out in the street.

ROY SAUNDERS: In 1943, a boy named Curley-haired Smitty, who lived next door to me on West 131st Street, said to me, "Why don't ya go with me down there on the waterfront this mornin'?"

I said, "Man, the day is Sunday, and I already got a job."

He said, "There's plenty of work down there."

When we got there, they called out the gangs, and when they called out the gang Smitty belonged to, I think he said to the boss, "I brought a friend of mine." The guy looked at me and said, "Hey, you wanna work?"

I didn't say "yes." I said, "Yessir." And the man put me in that gang.

The war was on. The ships were comin' from Europe with ballastses, which was sand to hold it down in the water to keep it from rockin'. I went down in that hold, and I had never been inside a ship before. It had these big vats filled with sand. We had to unload it. We would shovel all that sand out. When you get down to the bottom that's when you come into the big rats—dirty, filthy, and a foot long.

You only see gray rats in America. South American rats are black rats, and boy are they poison. You gotta kill 'em because they run right at you. There's no place for 'em to go. You've seen ships tied up. Well, they got that big round thing on the ropes so the rats can't get over that. These rats were so big that they could jump over that thing. They killed 'em with hooks or these three-by-five boards we called dunnage. You hit 'em with that. I see a boy there we called Felix. I see him take his knife and take the balls out of 'em. I said, "Boy, you got some nerve."

"I got my gloves on."

If the war wasn't on, I wouldn't have got hired, because they got a clique on the waterfront. The man has been in Sing Sing or has dirty shoes, he gets hired first. You go down there lookin' like you look now, I go down there lookin' like I look now, and you don't get hired, because they figure you gonna rat. You know what a rat is: Whatever's goin' on, you gonna tell somebody.

JOHN DWYER: I had every job on the waterfront. I carried bananas. I carried coffee. Cocoa bags were the worst, because they were the heaviest. A hundred pounds each. Now the bananas come in boxes, but you carried them on your shoulder for eight hours, and they had all kinds of bugs in them. A guy'd tell you you had a tarantula on your back, and you'd drop them and run.

ROY SAUNDERS: We loaded barbed wire. You got big heavy gloves on—and at that time you paid two dollars for a pair of gloves— and the barbed wire ripped them up along with your overalls. Then you put dunnage over the top of 'em, make it level, and start all over again. We did the same thing with railroad tracks. You'd get that old black stuff on you, creosote, that stinks. We would ship railroad tracks down to Cuba. You put 'em down and tie 'em over and marry 'em and work all the way up. They were so heavy that when the ship would go outta there, it was so low to the water the sailors didn't want to be on it.

Coffee was a 150-pound bag. Flour was heavy, too. At the end of the day, you barely had the strength to get up the ladder and climb out of that hold. The lightest work you had was when you put that hook on your shoulder and walked off that ship and down the gangplank. Oh, you'd be exhausted. You didn't get no break. We had one extra man we called the water boy. That's why we had twenty-one-man gangs. We had that extra boy who would go for water or for coffee. We had an hour for lunch, but by the time you got off that ship from down in the hold and walked way down the end of the pier to the timekeeper, you got fifteen minutes gone.

You've heard of iron ore. That stuff came from Barbados. Well, anyway, you get that stuff, you pick it up or you shovelin' it. Man, that stuff will go through you. Every guy that worked on that five or six days I know is dead now because that stuff got in their lungs. They gave that work to the black workers. They got the biggest, blackest man they could find, and they made him boss, and he loved it. They'd work 'em all day, day and night, the worst work.

SAM MADELL: It was vanadium ore, a powdery metal. They had no masks, nothing. After a while, this friend of mine, who was one of the most powerful men physically—he was huge, six six of bone and muscle—but he wound up getting silicosis from breathing in that dust. It was just pitiful. He died within several months. We raised it any number of times in the local, but the best we could get was one day when Joe Ryan was at the meeting, and he reported that he was going to try to get two or three cents more per hour for handling the vanadium ore. That was his solution. I wrote to several government agencies about it, but I was told I had to go through the local. But there were absolutely no health, no safety regulations. A man hurt his back, and when he went to the pier doctor, he complained that he could hardly breathe. He was told to breathe lightly.

JOHN DWYER: If somebody got hurt, they had a box every payday. The guys were good about throwing a buck or two in the box. If you got hurt, you got whatever was in the box. For about a year, one of the delegates used to take the box. We knew there should have been a couple of hundred or 300 in the box, but the guy would get fifty or sixty dollars. So then we got a little group together and said, "We're gonna take the collection." So we had one guy who was the safety man on the pier who was as honest as the day is long. We said, "You take the box. Give it to whoever got hurt, his wife or kids, whatever." It went up $200 or $300.

SAM MADELL: I'd say half of the longshoremen were in debt to the loan sharks, who, of course, were working with the stevedores and the union officials. You could borrow twenty dollars and wind up in a couple of months' time owing $100, with the way they charged you interest rates. If they gave you a job to enable you to pay them back, when you got paid they made sure they were there. The work was so irregular, you were almost in a position where you had to borrow. You were almost constantly in debt.

ROY SAUNDERS: Once, the hirin' boss at United Fruit started hirin' these Irishmen and Italians from this other local. Now we black boys, he would leave us out. He wouldn't hire us.

I said, "This mornin', they're goin' to throw me in the river" because I went to United Fruit. I asked for the headman, and we got down there, and I told them about this hirin' boss. Well, he went out and told the hirin' boss, "If this ever happens again, you're not only goin' to lose your license to hire, you ain't never goin' to work for United Fruit no more."

That surprised me, but it did happen. Now the hirin' boss comes to me, and he said, "Roy, why did you rat on me?"

I said, "I didn't rat on you. I told the truth. We fellas got families there. They got to eat."

He told me that them guys were so deep with the loan sharks that the loan sharks told him to hire their men first. He had to hire them. It wasn't his choice. He told me the man had a gun and was gonna shoot him if he didn't hire them.

SAM MADELL: There was a lot of stealing going on around the docks. It was pretty widely known among the longshoremen that the maritime police were involved with the stealing. It became particularly prevalent when a whiskey ship came in, and it seemed like everybody on the waterfront would descend on the ship. Talk about stealing! On the German lines, the stevedore himself was caught red-handed coming down the gangplank of the ship with a big bundle of cocaine. Think anything ever happened? Not a damn thing.

JOHN DWYER: I know one day a case of shoes disappeared. They sent another case and that disappeared too. That's when they started sending lefts in one case and rights in another case. That way, if you stole a case of shoes, it didn't do you any good.

ROY SAUNDERS: The whiskey business was bad, guys takin' cases and stashin' it. He'd tie it on a line and get it down in the water, so when he get there early in the mornin', somebody look around, they don't see nobody, and they'd pull it up and take out a couple bottles. And rum. When that rum was comin' in there in sixty-gallon barrels, 161 proof, the guys used to go down there and drill a hole in the barrel, make a peg first, so when he fill up his pail, he stick that peg in there to stop it from runnin'.

Well, he'd go out and buy a nickel's worth of ice from the hot-dog man, and he'd put four or five Pepsi-Colas in it, and come around like a water boy. He'd walk right by the boss with that thing. One half a pail would make twenty-one men drunk. That was the whole gang.

Liquor was about the only thing they could take, drink and get rid of. We got this guy there we called him Uncle Joe. He had to take somethin' all the time. What he liked was the bakala. That was that dried codfish. In the wintertime, he tied this stuff around above his shoes and walk right out the pier. And the cat was sayin' "Meow, meow" from behind him. The next day, this watchman said to me, "I don't know why the hell every time this man come out, the cat follow him." When he said that, I almost gave it away. I fell over. I almost busted.

Durin' the war, when the peoples had to get in line to get meat, that's when they wore them big coats. The meat come in. You're workin' on that meat. The meat was so hard and cold if you had a pork chop and it drops on your toe, it's broken. That meat was solid hard, you couldn't cut it with a knife. Billy the Kid, he brought him a hacksaw, and the rest of them got the idea from him. They'd be down there sawin' away and stuffin' the meat in their big coats. I don't know why they didn't get pneumonia gettin' that stuff outta there.

• • •

SAM MADELL: I knew of a guy by the name of Applegate up in 824, the Pistol Local, who had a record this long. He took the morning off, went out and shot somebody, and came back in the afternoon. Everybody on the waterfront knew it, and nothing ever happened to him. You couldn't blame the longshoremen for being reluctant to do anything.

ROY SAUNDERS: They hired tough men. Every man hired a tough man because he wanted protection for himself. That's why they hired men from up the river—Sing Sing. The mob—that's a word you can't use, because them guys would blow me away right now as quick as they would then. But when you see them come around, three or four in them big long Cadillacs, brother, you knew somethin' was up. That mean somebody is gonna get blowed away or somethin' is gonna get straightened out.

JOHN DWYER: I don't think they were afraid of getting beat up or thrown in the river or something. It was of not working. They need a buck. If somebody would say, "Let's go over and beef about this," the other guy would say, "What's the sense of beefin'? Then we won't work at all."

PHILIP CAREY: Basically, the fear was economic. If you didn't work, you starved, so you better keep your nose clean. The longshoreman's job always depended on the good will of the hiring boss or whoever told the hiring boss to hire him.

Sometimes there was fear for their lives. Joey Cuervo had been in the Navy. He once told me, "I knew what it was like to be under shellfire. I knew the fear that you had." But when Joey Rao shot out his window one night, he said, "When I took my little boy into bed with me, and I felt his body shivering all night, then I really knew what fear was."

EDDIE BURNS: I knew Joe Ryan good. Joe was the best. He took care of the men and everythin'. I don't say people weren't scared of him. Joe was a tough man. He was a good union leader. He had tough people on the piers that would do anythin' he said, but that goes with the business. He got a good contract, as good as he could every time. Ya'd see him in the street and ya'd talk to him. If ya needed money, he'd give it to ya.

JOHN DWYER: I never saw him give a nickel to anybody. Look at how much money he made on the ILA dinner each year. He must have made a fortune. He was lifetime president. Nobody ever beat him because nobody would ever run against him. He was picked because he was a big bully.

Ryan was a big bruiser. He had a good easy life. Here's something about Joe Ryan. He used to wear Sulka shorts next to his skin. They cost probably thirty dollars thirty years ago.

JOHN CORCORAN: Joe Ryan and my father grew up together. They had a relationship that was close. Ryan was a product of his time. When I began as a trade unionist, I was talking to my father about it. He told me he had been a steward in the Teamsters. I asked him how he got to be a steward, and he said he was able to kick the shit out of anybody else in that stable.

The guy who had gotten to be president of the Central Labor Council prior to Harry van Arsdale was Marty Lacey. Marty Lacey's claim to fame was scars on his body from fights in order to have an organization. They used their brawn to get to the top. And there was a respect for rank. There was a respect for authority that doesn't exist today. The respect came from fear and just for the fact that they had a ranking position. It didn't matter how they achieved that. It was the same kind of hero worship for the underworld. They were the top dogs. The best were the worst criminals.

JOHN DWYER: Joe Ryan put all the mobsters on the payroll and they defended him. The guys around him, they didn't look like goons. You never saw guys like Andy Sheridan or Cockeye Dunn with him. Once, I was workin' on Pier 25 as a loader. I saw myself workin' to seven or eight o'clock at night, and after the first paycheck, I was paid only till five o'clock, so I complained to the boss. I told him, "I'm not workin' past five o'clock unless you pay me overtime."

So he called Johnny Dunn, and a couple of his boys come down lookin' for me. They said, "You keep your mouth shut or you'll wind up in the river."

I said, "Don't worry about me. I'm not windin' up in the river." But next week I quit when I found out who he was. I would have wound up in the river.

PHILIP CAREY: Ryan used to go to Guardian Angel, the Shrine Church of the Sea, every morning, where you had that bum Monsignor O'Donnell. He was a nitwit, and Ryan used him to a fare thee well. You couldn't believe how he could operate. When they shot into Joey Cuervo's room, I said, "Joe, I know you have troubles." I gave him $500. I didn't have that money, but whatever I had was his. The next day he went to Mass, and O'Donnell turned his back on him and walked out. He was a horse's ass.

Guardian Angel was a very small parish. It should never have existed. In those times they were very loath to close up parishes. O'Donnell was very much disliked by the priests of the diocese. It was intended to serve the seamen, but it never did. O'Donnell didn't like seamen, and he didn't like longshoremen either. He was with the stevedores. That's what it became—a church for them. Spellman let him get away with it because he was good on raising money, which is a hell of a thing. Once a year, the ILA would raise a fund for the support of Guardian Angel, but he would get most of his money from the insurance companies down around Wall Street. Ryan didn't have that kind of money. The Rhinelander Church was equally important to Ryan, and the Tough Club was the most important thing.

HAROLD GATES: The cardinal and all them bastards were all lockin' barrels with each other. Of course, Tammany Hall was Catholic, too. And that bastard at Guardian Angel Church, he was like a storm trooper. Just a vicious bastard. All he needed was a gun on his hip.

PHILIP CAREY: No, O'Donnell wasn't a storm trooper. I wouldn't want to insult the storm troopers. God has a hell of a sense of humor. Here was this guy, and I don't know how the hell he ever got there.

Back then, people would ask me how the hell was it possible that this guy Ryan would go to church and down six Canadian Clubs before breakfast and then issue the order for 200 men to be not hired. "How the hell can you say the man is a good Catholic?"

I said there has to be a few things to understand. The guy has to know what's he's doing when he tells a lie. He has to do it with complete freedom of the will. That's why a guy on liquor or dope can't commit a serious sin, because he doesn't have freedom of the will. And he has to know what he's doing when he's doing it. People like Ryan don't know. They're caught in the web.

The difference between an immoral man and an amoral man is that an immoral man knows stealing and murder is wrong but he does it. An amoral man doesn't even know it is wrong, and they are probably the more dangerous. What Ryan was, I don't know. Ryan was just dumb. I think he was just so caught in the web that he couldn't see. I've met a whole lot of guys like that.

We were trying to get the whole problem out into the open. We wanted to end decasualization—to get the men regular work. We wanted to get some kind of seniority system so that you didn't have to shape every day. That you didn't have to be beholden to some damn politician for the bread that you put on your table. That's what all this was about.

The problem was the politicians. This was an enormous machine in which the longshoremen lived. All these things were organized. All the hiring was organized. The loan-sharking was organized. The numbers games were organized, and they were a tremendous source of income to the politicians. Frequently, the men couldn't work if they didn't want to play.

Among the politicians it was power, power, power. The shipping associations had it; so did the politicians and the political clubs.

A guy like Ryan was simply told what to do. Remember, the political clubs wanted to keep the men coming to them for their jobs. They were the ones who voted. But civil service had cut into their patronage, so the party had to look outside the government for the jobs, so they looked to the mob. This was the end of the Tammany machine, which had gone on so long.

SAM MADELL: In the beginning, it was a very, very rare thing to have a union meeting. Maybe you'd have two or three during the whole year. Even when they were held, they in no way resembled a union meeting. Some of the clique would gather, maybe ten or twelve, and in the summer months the discussion would be about baseball. If it was during the fall, it would be about football. In no sense was it a union meeting. If anybody tried to inject some working-conditions issue, they'd be hooted down. They'd be questioned. "Who are you?" "Are you a member of this local?" "Where is your book?" "Is your dues paid up?" If you were too persistent, they'd knock you down the steps. There were a number of cases like that.

ROY SAUNDERS: I went to a couple of union meetin's. There weren't too many of 'em. They didn't have any local meetin's until maybe once every four years. If they had 'em, sometimes we didn't know about 'em. Once, they were votin' on a shop steward. This guy stands up and says, "I second the motion." I said, "Excuse me, Mr. Chairman, who is this guy who seconds the motion? He don't work with us." I guess I didn't have enough sense to be afraid.

All the black boys were sayin' [*he whispers*], "Shut up, Roy, shut up, shut up." They was afraid. I said, "Man, this is your union. This is not one man's particular union. This is an ILA union." I says, "You pay your dues. If you don't pay 'em, they take 'em out anyway."

After we left, goin' home, I said, "Hey, I can't do nothin' by myself. If we stand together and let 'em know we workin' together, it'll be better for us."

And Little Willie, who talked like a woman, he said [*in a high-pitched voice*], "You right, Roy, you right," but they never did nothin'. What you gonna do? Oh, those elections were rigged. Joe Ryan, Five-Cent Ryan, that's what we called him. That's all the raise he asked for. He would have these meetin's down the West Side at the Catholic church. That's where we went to vote at. They would put the votin' machines on the truck and take 'em to Brooklyn, and they had a guy out there on the truck pullin' down the handle all the way to Brooklyn. [*He laughs.*]

BILL BAILEY: Joe Ryan would say that anybody who talks to you about improvin' the union had to be a Commie, because they were the only ones doin' all that bullshitting. "Anybody that attacks me is a Commie."

Then, if you're a longshoreman and you wanna get in good with anybody, why you belt these son of a bitches. If there is a soapbox on West Street, you go over and kick it off, bang it. That may put you in for a good job, once the word got around with the hoods. That's why they beat up all the poor teachers who came down to help get things goin'.

JOHN DWYER: There were Commies in the early days. They were always giving out leaflets on the waterfront, but they used to beat 'em up. Then they started sending girls down, and they beat them up too.

The West Coast was a Commie union. They turned that over to Harry Bridges. He got a better program for his men, but I wouldn't want them anyway. I just don't like the Commies, whether they get a better contract or not. Just because they're Commies. Where were they getting all their money to hand out pamphlets, when they weren't working? I know I was a rebel, but they're Commie rebels. That's the difference.

PEGGY DOLAN: We were taught about Communists. We were taught that you didn't go near those Communists. They're bad. Then would come May Day. Us kids used to save garbage on the roofs. Up here on Eighth Avenue, there was more garbage on the roofs than there was on the street.

Every corner wanted to outbeat the other corners to see that those Communists didn't make it to Union Square—that's where they used to go. When those Communists came, we used to dump the garbage on them. They were splattered with everything.

BILL BAILEY: I didn't wanna be a longshoreman. I preferred goin' to sea. The three meals a day were guaranteed for you. When that ship pulled away from the dock, the food may have been lousy, but it was there. Your stomach dictated what the hell you were gonna do. Longshorin' men had the responsibility. They had to face problems at home, get up in the mornin', and the possibility of gettin' in trouble. On the ship, you didn't have that trouble.

JOE STACK: I had two brothers that were merchant seamen at the time, my brother Walter and my brother Louis. And I just came to New York to get away from the orphanage I was in. I was fifteen, and I come to see my brother, and through my brother I got the contact, and I got papers to start goin' to sea.

There was thousands and thousands of seamen waitin' for a job then, because that was the height of the Depression in 1931. My brother came in on a ship. He knew a port engineer that was a homosexual. What he did do or didn't do he didn't tell me, but the port engineer gave him a big letter. I assume the guy gobbled his goose. That's the way things were done. It's as simple as that. For my brother, it was that or leave me on the bum in New York.

GEORGE SCHWARTZ: When I became a seaman, I moved to a roomin' house in Chelsea on 23rd Street. Everybody lived in those houses because they were adjacent to all the big shippin' companies around the waterfront.

I stayed in one with a shipmate of mine. We shared the room for six dollars a week, with maid service and towels and things like that. Very cheap. We left our gear there, and when he went out I was there. We kept the room goin'. It was run by an old Dutch couple—the Dutchman's at 458 West 23rd Street. When a ship come in, if I could recommend a couple of people to the Dutchman's house, he was very happy. I wasn't rough or rowdy, and I never brought any real prostitutes in—the ones who charged maybe two dollars.

I had a couple girlfriends who I lived with before I got married. Nobody minded. Most of the landladies in that area, if they were young enough, they shacked up with the seamen.

JOE STACK: I ended up stayin' in every roomin' house from Eleventh Avenue to Eighth Avenue on 23rd Street. See, in the early days, I used to go to bars, drink beer, and so forth. Consequently, you'd get evicted and thrown out of these different places. As a matter of fact, I was barred from all of these here places until after the union was formed. Then, we got a little more respectable and I started behavin' and I got reinstated.

I met my wife on 23rd Street. Her mother was the landlady. I had gone to this place on 23rd Street and Ninth Avenue, and I seen this place. It had a new fancy door. I said, "That's one place I haven't lived in." It's the only place didn't know me, and they rented me a room. Consequently, I met her.

I went with her a long time. I didn't get fresh. If I would of thought that she was loose, you can be sure I would have operated right away. Most seamen were like that. They wouldn't fool around with decent women unless they fell in love with some gal.

Usually, the reason why you shipped out of Chelsea was most of the shippin' was done through the U.S. Line. Twenty-third Street was a convenient area to check on jobs. All you would do was you would come off of a ship and you'd pay maybe four or five weeks' room rent in advance, hopin' to maybe ship out in that particular time. And then you would go down to these different shippin' offices and inquire for a job. And when you wasn't out lookin' for a job, you'd be in the bar drinkin'. Seamen spend 90 percent of their time in a bar. At least the seamen in my days. The union was organized in the bars. Without the gin mills nothin' would have been accomplished. Everythin' was done in the bar.

BILL BAILEY: I never had any money to hang out in the bars. The one bar we used to hang out in, we called the Bucket of Blood. That was way over on the East Side, on Third Avenue. A few radicals hung out there. They also had the counters loaded with salami, baloney. So we'd have a nickel beer and eat up everything we could get. If it was cold in the wintertime, we went to the party headquarters at 13th Street and Broadway, order some tea or hot water, stuff it full with ketchup and make tomato soup out of it, sit around and bullshit and plot and plan what we do the next day.

JOE STACK: Some of the bars were pretty wild. We had the Foghorn on Ninth Avenue. That was a combination of truck drivers, longshoremen, and seamen, so there used to be a lot of fights in there. It was also called Bucket of Blood. That was the most notorious. In the other places only normal fights would take place. A guy is on the ship for two or three months with a guy he hated.

Then he'd start drinkin' in the bar. He'd spot 'im and the next thing you know there'd be a fight. They wouldn't fight with knives, just with the fists.

The average guy, after two days on the beach he was broke. They spent all the money. They went in the bar and had a good time. Many seamen come in that they knew. Everybody was entitled. It was like the guy had won a lottery. The money went fast. They worked on the basis that they'd know they ate on the ship. They had a bed on the ship. So if worst came to worst they didn't need a penny. They didn't even have to go to shore. They'd just stay on the ship and go to bed every night. So consequently they blew their money.

Seamen were more or less a loose group. They just existed, that's all. They didn't make plans to put money in the bank. Only after the union was formed did seamen start savin' and lookin' forward to goin' ashore and stayin' ashore.

When you was out at sea, you might say, "Well, I'm goin' to go visit somebody when I get in." This time, you were goin' to save your drinkin' till you come back. I had a shipmate of mine. His name was Francis Kennedy. He had rotten teeth, but he was a-scared of the dentist, and every trip he says he's gonna go to this guy he heard about in San Francisco, Painless Parker. He could pull your teeth so they don't hurt you. Every trip he was goin' to Painless Parker. When you'd see 'im, you'd say, "Hey, Kennedy, did you go to the West Coast?"

He'd be back on the ship two days later, broke, not a dime. Spent all his money. This went on long as I knew him. Eight years. Finally, he died out at sea. He got an infection in his gums and that was that. When he was sober on the ship, you'd swear he was gonna go. His teeth are botherin' him. "The next trip I'm goin'. I ain't gonna stop and have one beer. I'm gonna catch that Greyhound and I'm goin' to California." He never did it, and that's the way most seamen were. They didn't get past the bar.

Of course, durin' the mid-'30s, all the seamen ever did in these bars was talk unionism. That was the main agitation, the main talk. That was why they went to these bars for. The first trip that I came in, my brother took me up to the Marine Workers Industrial Union and signed me into the union. The MWIU was in competition with the old International Seamen's Union, which was in with the shipowners.

Certain ships had certain little job actions over the food, officers havin' a better system of eatin' than the crew. The mates and
engineers would eat on regular plates, and the crew would eat on
enamel plates like in a jailhouse. The food was inferior. So they
were fightin' for better conditions, better food, better variety and
all that stuff. Fightin' for proper silverware, fightin' to eliminate
the straw mattresses. But the main agitatin' point was the wages,
'cause the wages went down in '31. The wages went down in some
companies as low as thirty dollars for an AB, and some companies
like the Munson Line was payin' scrip.

We had union meetin's on some issues that had to do with
better conditions, and we had guys get dumped in the meetin's.
We had guys get dumped before the meetin's by other seamen.
The seamen were a downbeaten scared bunch of rabbits. It was
only a few agitators in the MWIU, the Wobblies and a few more,
that would agitate on these ships, but a person had to be very careful. He had to be sure you know when to talk, when not to talk,
and how much you could talk about it, 'cause your life was in
danger. A guy gets thrown over the side and you never hear from
him no more.

I was active from the day I joined. In the spring of 1936, we
tied up the *California* for three days. Then Madame Perkins of the
Labor Department called up and said that if we sailed the ship
back up the East Coast, she'd see that there was no discrimination
taken against the crew. So we sailed the ship, and one day out at
sea, the yeoman comes down with log slips two for one, day's pay
taken away from every man that tied up the ship.

They claimed we had mutinied. When we got back to New
York, the word of what they said got out and everybody on the
waterfront that had ever agitated—Wobblies, Communists, Socialists, Trotskyites—they're all down there waitin' to back us up. Joe
Curran said, "If they're Communists, we won't have nothin' to do
with 'em. But if they're regular guys, we will."

Well, I wasn't a Communist at that particular time, and I went
out there and I seen Kennedy—he was a Wobbly—and three or
four Communists that I knew. I went back aboard ship and told
Curran, "I met all these guys, not a Communist amongst them—
good people."

With all the problems that seamen had, they looked upon it
like it was the Fourth of July. Here was an opportunity. So what

we did, we called a meetin' and got together and we declared a strike.

GEORGE SCHWARTZ: Joe Curran lived in my roomin' house for a while until he got a few bucks. He was picked as the nominal head of us when we went out on strike. He was about six foot four. He looked like a bosun on a ship. He looked good. He had his dues paid up in the old ISU. Politically, he was clean. You couldn't label him as a Communist, though he did carry the *Daily Worker* in his back pocket all the time.

He was a rough guy. Actually, the guy couldn't read and write. He came out of orphanages, a runaway, like Joe Stack. Curran was a pretty good guy when we started, but the money and the fame got him. He wore his dungarees until he was gettin' money and started buyin' suits.

JOE STACK: Curran was a big opportunist. He just went along with the left wing of the union. The day the *California* came in the harbor, the press came aboard, hundreds of 'em, like flies. Well, Curran was a con man in many ways. He went over to the number-one hatch and he started posin' like a movie actor. He knew they liked that, and he had on a salty watch cap and sea boots like a pirate.

All the agitators were all branded as Wobblies and Communists, but Curran had a clean record. He wasn't in the MWIU. He wasn't active in the waterfront, but bein' a deck delegate on the *California*, that gave him enough credentials to be a leader. The government later used Curran to eliminate the leftists from the union, but he knew that without their support we would never have won the revolt.

Durin' that first strike, the ISU used Joe Ryan. Ryan and his goons did everything. Our guys used to get dumped on the picket lines from these here goons at nighttime. They'd pull up in a car, and five or six goons with baseball bats would lump up a couple guys, terrorize them. We had a lot of that.

GEORGE SCHWARTZ: Some of them were pretty big, as big as the line on the Chicago Bears. And they had clubs. I got beat up a couple of times. But I was lucky. I never got anything broke.

Joe Stack: Durin' the strike, I was on the Educational Committee. The Educational Committee was for dumpin' finks. That was our method of educatin'. Say the Parmalee Taxi Company was haulin' a lot of scabs to the docks, guys who would come down from the lakes. Of course we had people in Detroit who would tip us off that finks were comin' in. They come in the station. We knew what train they were on. We'd follow 'em till they got in the cab. One of our guys would get in the cab too and tell 'em he wanted to get off a little earlier. He'd give 'em a certain street, and when he got there, we'd be there. We get the finks out of the car, dump 'em, give a dime to the cab driver and send 'im back. We had at least fifteen or twenty guys that wound up in jail for years. Of course anybody that wound up in jail got stamped on their cards Honorably Arrested for Union Duty, and we provided them with cigarette money and stuff like that.

We went into bars. We went into restaurants. We dumped guys in Madison Square Garden, Grand Central, Pennsylvania Railroad. We had a lot of shoreside people who tipped us off.

Sometimes the scabs would get real brazen, you know. They come on a few trips, they get by, nobody's botherin' 'em. Maybe a guy come out with a white coat on, a waiter on a ship. He'd go to a local bar and have a beer. We'd get ahold of 'im, tell 'im we're goin' to take 'im to strike headquarters, talk to 'im, see if it was a possibility of talkin' him out of bein' a scab. We could tell if he wasn't gonna conform. Then we'd take his seaman's papers away from him, tear 'em up, because it takes 'em a month to get another set of papers. That way there would be one less man to clear the ship.

There was only one guy I felt sorry for. He come out off the Panama Pacific ship with a white coat on. Either this guy is stupid or there's somethin' wrong with 'im. So we got ahold of 'im. They started tampin' up on 'im a little bit. But in the course of tampin' up on 'im, the guy you could see he didn't know nothin' about what it's all about. I got ahold of 'im, and we had a talk with 'im, and said, "It's not necessary to beat this guy up anymore."

We took 'im down to a soup kitchen. We told 'im, "The only way you can prove you're with the rank and file is you're gonna work in the soup kitchen. He worked in the soup kitchen all durin' the spring strike, and in the 1936, 1937 strike he got offa the ship and he was in the soup kitchen on that. He volunteered. In that case, it was just a helpless guy, you could see, and it was only fortunate that we didn't do a full educational job on 'im.

Durin' the organizin' period, if you told all the truth about what all the members did, you'd think we were nuts. You had to be nuts. We had two guys that wound up in Sing Sing for ten years. They got this fink and they dumped 'im. Well, they weren't satisfied that they dumped 'im. They got a pipe and they put it up his butt. So that shows you how mental everybody was. We had about eight guys killed of our own durin' the strike. But we had without a doubt built one of the strongest unions in the country. You had to fight fire with fire. If you tried to bullshit 'em with leaflets or talk, forget about it. Once we built the union, then we became legitimate. We couldn't carry on those activities anymore.

See, you gotta be against scabs. You really got to feel it. This guy's to you like some guy that's molestin' children. That's the mentality you have, and there's nothin' you won't do to stop the son of a bitch.

Guy's been on the picket lines maybe forty or fifty days. He's starved out. He ain't got no more money. He's goin' back on the ship. He says he gotta sail. We're only interested in one thing: that's winnin' the strike, winnin' the conditions. The hungrier you get and the longer the struggle goes, the more haywire you become. We had a guy named Broken Nose Burns, an ex-pug, who was on our picket line. He was walkin' around with three ears. He used to carry 'em around in his pocket. In other words, he was gonna identify these finks when he ever seen 'em by cuttin' their ears off. We finally got 'im off the picket line and sent him inland someplace when the strike was over, because it became a scandal.

We did this for about eighty-five days, and the guys started driftin' off. What was happenin' was we weren't able to tie up any more ships. They were sailin'. A lot of our guys were starvin' to death. There was no strike fund or nothin' like that. We didn't have no machinery or nothin'. That's where we got our money to feed these guys on strike—dumpin' these finks, takin' their money, and puttin' it into the soup kitchens. Otherwise we couldn't exist at all. In the beginnin' we tied up a lot of ships, but they were able to recruit scabs, and not only that, they were sailin' shorthanded, and they were waivin' the rules. They forgot about safety at sea, because the shipowners and the government worked together.

Anyhow we had that there strike and we lost it. But the strike committee, see, we suspicioned that there was gonna be a strike in the fall by the West Coast. So we had passed a word if there is a strike in the fall, we're goin' out. We came back by October, the West Coast went out on strike, and we went on strike again against the wishes of the international. So we had that strike for about eighty-eight days, and we lost that one. Second one in a row. But we were much better. We got more help from the shore, but the same thing happened—the guys started peterin' out. See, if we would have had the international machinery, we woulda won without any problem. We were fightin' everybody. We were fightin' Joe Ryan and the longshoremen. We were fightin' the newspapers. We had very bad press.

Then we had a scheme. We figured once we got on a ship, we could organize 'em because conditions were so bad. So we went back aboard the ship. Then after about two or three months we get the word: "Take the ships in any foreign port you're in. If you can agitate the crew, tie the ship up." So we did. We took the ships and tied 'em up all over the world. The shipowners were goin' crazy because they couldn't recruit finks, and the ships were tied up.

So the shipowners seen that they were playin' a losin' hand with the old union. They went into court themselves with the rank-and-file committee and they signed for an injunction against the old union because the old union didn't have no control over the membership. They threw the contract out with the old international, and they recognized us.

◆　◆　◆

   . . . Then who will know
About its ancient grandeur, marble stairs,
Its paintings, onyx mantels, courts, the heirs
Of a time now long ago?

Who will remember that Mark Twain used to stroll
In the gorgeous dining room, that Princesses
Poets and celebrated actresses
Lived here and made its soul. . . .

           —Edgar Lee Masters

ALICE TIBBETTS: There was nothing special about the neighborhood. In those days, it was just a kind of nothing neighborhood. It wasn't fashionable or anything. We were kind of close to the Village and the creative people there. We didn't have to bother about the rest of the neighborhood. The Chelsea [Hotel] was our neighborhood.

The Chelsea was the Chelsea, that's all. I don't think it was that noted as a bohemian place, not quite as much as it has since become. No, it still had some of the lingering tinge of the old times. There were a lot of older women. I guess that they lived on trusts, and they would have tea in the lobby in the afternoons.

They had a few writers. There were more artists, because the upper floor had studio space. John Sloan was up there. He had a duplex. He illustrated one of Edgar Lee's books, and I remember when he was ill—poor Dolly, she was drunk a good bit of the time—I remember an etching she gave me. It was his anniversary card. It showed the two of them clinging to a rock, and the caption said, "Still on the rocks."

I guess they had a hard time. She was noted for having been one of the leaders or participants in a strike in Philadelphia, one of the very first shirtwaist strikes. She was quite a radical.

Edgar Lee was known. He was about sixty-five when I moved in. He was in 214, and I was in 1010. His little granddaughter asked me, "Did you live with my grandfather?" Very stern. That was never permitted, and besides, we never thought of it.

There were lots of men living alone here. I got used to being with married men. I didn't think anything of that either. Edgar Lee was married, but I never thought anything about that because his wife and child were out in Kansas City. He said that's where they wanted to be, and he wanted the child to go to school there. The child was crazy about the grandparents, and Edgar Lee didn't want somebody camping on his trail. He said that when she was here, she was just waiting for him to finish writing, and he couldn't stand that because the writing came first. When he was writing, he wanted to be free to write.

He had a regular routine if he was writing a book. When he wasn't writing a book, he often just sat down and wrote poems. I'd have a poem in my box about every day. Some of them were very funny. They were poems just for me. He called them typewriter poems. He would sit down and type out a first draft, and that was it. I think poems went through his mind while he was sleeping.

Edgar didn't have much money. Whatever he did have, Macmillan was, and probably still is, collecting on *Spoon River Anthology*. He would occasionally sell something. He wasn't forgotten.

We had long reading evenings. We read Homer and poems and things like that. That's what we did together—we stayed home. He would read his own works or works of others. We'd go to dinner, and he would smoke a pipe in his room, and then he would come up and we would read. We had time to do that. Nobody had to get up and go to work the next day. We had those long evenings, Evenings with Edgar. I wrote a journal of about 500 pages about evenings we spent together. One time he said, "You know how many words we've said?"

Let's see. [*She reads:*] "In three years, 51,130,000." He arrived at some kind of system at estimating the amount of words. We just talked, talked, talked. He liked to talk. He talked to everybody. He said that everything is grist that comes to a poet. He liked to talk to the Irish maid. When she'd come in to dust his room, he'd tell her to sit down, and they'd talk, and he'd get her to talk about the fights her mother and father would have, and these Irish goings-on amused him.

He was a charming person. Of course a lot of people came here to quiz him. Then he'd be on the defensive. Then they saw him as bitter. They loved to call him bitter. People would call up Edgar Lee.

"I would like to come down and talk to you."

"All right."

So he sits there.

"All right, talk to me."

And what was he supposed to do? He just sat there, and they came along with their lumbering questions and nothing happens, but put him in a drawing room with other people and he just lights up.

I once asked him, "Are you bitter?" He said, "No. I'm skeptical." He could be very amusing. He loved to make jokes. He'd make up names for himself. Like he'd call himself Lute Puckett and write silly poems and sign them that way. He liked to do that. *Spoon River* was all made-up names. When he and Mencken wrote each other, which was almost every day, they'd say these funny little things to each other.

He was bitter about *Spoon River* only in that all people thought about was *Spoon River*. That hurt, because what would happen would be he'd bring out a book, and a reviewer knew nothing about him but *Spoon River*, so the writer would write a whole long column about *Spoon River*, and the last paragraph was about this book. This happened all the time. He says the critics were disappointed poets. They were just showing off what they knew, and in the end they'd say, "Oh, well, this isn't *Spoon River*."

Well, naturally, he wasn't going to rewrite *Spoon River* all the time. He wanted to write different things. He said he had written more types of poetry than anybody else in America. In other words, he wasn't just a one-book author. He kind of sneered at that. Anybody could produce one little slender book of verse, but he just kept on producing.

He spoke about other authors who experienced the same thing. You write one book that catches on early in your career, and by gosh no matter how hard you try, you cannot, no matter what you produce, it's not another whatever.

Tom Wolfe was over in one of those corner rooms on another floor. He wanted me to come and type for him, but Edgar Lee wouldn't let me, because Wolfe had already developed a reputation. He just had so much energy, but he'd get drunk, and then he'd be very abusive, even to his beloved sister. He loved his sister more than anybody in the world. She said he would go out and get drunk, and he would be *so* sorry because he was so abusive. Edgar knew that, so he said no.

Thomas Wolfe had so much energy. He came through that door, and he had to bend his head to get through, he was so tall. He was powerful, and I guess it all came out in his drinking. When his secretary left at five o'clock, there was nothing for him to do but go down and they'd start in drinking, and it would go on continuously.

His sister came over after he died, and she said, "Oh, it was so sad." He loved her dearly, but he would go out and get drunk every night and just be awful. She understood, and she forgave him, but not everybody did. Not everybody could take that.

By that time I was friends with the MacIsaacs, who lived in 1014. He was a story writer. It bothered Fred MacIsaac that Wolfe wrote for the "slicks" and he didn't. His wife, Vi, well, she was something else. She once said to me, "I'm gonna find out what makes Tom Wolfe tick," and so she just hung around him a lot. When he was ready to go down to the bar, they go down the three of them, and poor Fred MacIsaac would pass out very quickly. He was older, so they'd put Fred to bed and start out and keep going.

Of course, they never thought of eating. Nobody ever thought about eating until three or four or something like that. So Vi and Tom would start out and she'd come into my room sometime afterward, at two or three o'clock in the morning. She was elated, but poor Fred, he was hurt. He committed suicide later.

I remember going down to Wolfe's apartment with Vi Mac-Isaac. He already had that cold that was to presage his death. He wasn't doing anything about it. I guess he thought he was so strong that he could dominate anything. There were big cartons filled with manuscripts all around his room, which was almost bare. He overwrote. They used to say he'd take his manuscripts to Maxwell Perkins. He'd tell him to take out words. He'd take 'em out and put in some more.

He went west, and he never came back. He used to say that his next book was going to be about the Chelsea. Wolfe didn't endear himself to anybody living here, so nobody wept for him. The drunkenness kept me away from him. Otherwise he was kind of an easygoing, slow-talking kind of person. But that man could just pour out words.

I first met Edgar one night in the lobby. This man I was with said, "This is Edgar Lee Masters." I knew about the anthology, because it was originally published in a St. Louis newspaper. I think my aunt and my uncle took it, but they never read it. It was like "Ooh. It isn't nice." So I didn't really read it then. We didn't think it was for nice people.

But I told him I was from St. Louis. That was all that it took. He was kind of lonesome, as it turned out, and I think he had just put his wife and son on the train to go back to Kansas City. He said, "Oh, St. Louis." He pricked up his ears right away, so I think they both came up for a little while, and he sat here and talked until three-thirty in the morning. Of course, he loved to talk. And to find somebody who knew about *Spoon River* and the old days, he just talked and talked.

He called me in the morning and asked if I would like to go up to the Palisades in New Jersey. So we took a subway and we took a ferryboat over, and we walked around over there. I thought he was nice and interesting, kind of a brooding sort of person. I didn't think much about it. After a while he gave me one of his books. I sat on the fire escape and read it on a hot Sunday afternoon. I hadn't read poetry for so long, and then he came up. I told him how much I enjoyed the book. That pleased him. It was true. I was fascinated. He gave me more of his books. That was that. That lasted seven years. Seven years.

He liked being alone. For him this was a good bachelor place. He always said his work came first. He didn't want anybody to interfere with his work. He did Whitman here, and the Vachel Lindsay book. *Invisible Landscapes* had just come out when I knew him. Both of them were just coming out, and he was getting reviews on them, getting pretty good reviews. We did the Whitman book together. I went with him down to the Whitman House in Camden and slept in Whitman's bed. We went down there to interview the woman and her husband who were the caretakers of the place.

Contrary to those articles you read, he wasn't found starving to death. He had money in the bank. He did get sick. I called the doctor, and he said, "I don't need to come down. You just go and get such-and-such and give it to him." But he wasn't used to being sick, so he called up his friend, who called his wife, and [*in a singsong voice*] she got back what she had been waiting for. She'd been waiting all that time.

I loved him dearly. He was a very dear man, a wonderful man. I adored him. You couldn't help it. A poet, a real poet. I met so many, and there are real ones and the other kind, but the real ones, they're so gentle, so understanding. We were in love. I adored him. I guess he must of felt that same way. He used to write "I love you" on little pieces of paper and leave them at the desk. That was the way he was. He was a loving person, and that's what poetry is really. He had a big heart for many people.

I got married after he died. My husband is dead now. All my friends live in so much better places, I think, "My gosh, what am I doing in this hole?" Well, it's home now after so many years. It always had been. If it wasn't for the Chelsea, I wouldn't have met

Edgar Lee Masters, Thomas Wolfe, and John Sloan. There was a time here that I didn't know anybody who wasn't in *Who's Who*. It was kind of a special place. But I just took it in stride. I was just so used to it.

•  •  •

GEORGE SCHWARTZ: After the strike, I started to sail in the steward's department permanently. I had a good job and I made money. I got married and supported a family.

After the war, they started callin' us all Commies. A good many of us were Communists, but there was no law against it.

At the Coast Guard hearings on subversives, they asked me to identify the people in the organization I knew who were Communists. I said, "Curran . . ." They looked at me, and that was that.

JOE STACK: I got expelled [from the union] in '46. It was a railroad job. They just went ahead and did it. I think there were maybe two guys who weren't afraid to stand up for me. After that I couldn't get on the ships no more. I spent a couple of years puttin' out leaflets in front of the hall. Then I got a job in a corrugated factory. I'm still workin'. I'm in the buildin' trade with my family. I'm a waterproofer. I run every day. In a week I'll run my ninth marathon.

PEGGY DOLAN: My father was forty-two during World War II. He was drafted. With eight children, that's true, and he had four sons in the service.

We had a wonderful boy livin' with us. Boy? At that time he was forty-five years old. They took him in World War II. He was on Iwo Jima ten days, and he got it. They put his body on a horse and wagon. They drove it up Eighth Avenue. His name was Manny. He was nice. But what the hell? Could he run? He couldn't.

SAM MADELL: I was a Communist. I was really being paid by the Communist Party. I can assure you I wasn't getting very rich at it. I was always having a hard time with the party, trying to get them to understand the waterfront.

There was a strike in 1945. It was initiated by a group in Local 791 over wages and the size of the sling loads, and it rapidly spread all over the port. The whole port was tied up.

I was trying to get somebody to step forward as a leader of the strike. I couldn't do it because I was a known Communist, so the CP became impatient, and they decided if I wasn't going to do it, they would get somebody. So they went and found two longshoremen, who turned out to be stool pigeons. After that I got less involved, and I was out altogether by the 1950s.

Roy Saunders: I worked in the hatch for ten years before I got outta there. I had to fight for the deck. I went to the boss and we had it out, and I never went back in the hold no more. That was the dogs. That was the worst. Cold in the wintertime, hot in the summer. They thought the men in the hold was the lowest. We had the Italians and the blacks. I saw two Chinese, and Moby Dick was a Jew.

The white workers got the deck jobs and the high-low drivers—that was the forklift. It was easy work, just sit there and drive on it. United Fruit was one of the most discriminatin' companies in the world. You [*to the author*] can come there tomorrow and drive the forklift if you can. I'm there twenty years. I don't drive one of them machines unless they need me.

Since I retired, I learned I had an enlarged heart. The union doctors, they never told me that before. So now I gotta be real careful. But I was watchin' TV, and they said school is for everyone, and I thought, I'll be damned, that is right. Why can't I go? I've worked all my life. I never had a chance to go to school, night school or day school. Now they've taken me in. I learn reading, writing, and arithmetic. Not only that—history. It's a great thing to learn history. [*Roy Saunders died of a heart attack a few weeks after this interview.*]

Bresci Thompson: I was already married and working at A&S when I was called up for the draft. I told them I was a conscientious objector. Then I was called before the Selective Service. They said they couldn't substantiate my claim. I said my father was antiwar. He was a pacifist. They asked me my religion. I said I was no religion. I wasn't baptized.

I had a hearing down at Foley Square. I told the judge, "All my life I've been surrounded by Irish Catholics. 'Thou shalt not kill.' They're killing." Well, they went back and forth, and finally they just dropped the investigation.

One of the things I'll never forget was when Mr. Michellini, who was head of the local board, saw my name and he said to me, "This is ironical. You're a pacifist, and you have the name of an assassin."

DAN CARPENTER: Dr. Elliott was a pacifist in World War I. During World War II he came around to the feeling that we had to fight. Well, many of the Catholics in leadership in the neighborhood were opposed to our getting in there. They weren't unsympathetic to the Nazis. At that time the Guild took a real beating. It was anti-Semitism, sure. The Guild was supported, by and large, by Jewish money.

Dr. Elliott has been gone since 1942, but every year we still get together in his name. There seems to be an ever-growing interest and respect among people for his contributions. You talk to people who grew up in this neighborhood. He symbolized something. He made you feel like you had something worthwhile in you which you should try to develop.

The library and the staff and the people around him reached out to people the same way. They really meant a difference to somebody's life. Most important, I think somehow he gave you a feeling that you should believe in yourself. When Dr. Elliott put his hand on your shoulder or shook your hand, it had something. It carried a message that he cared about you. I think if the Hudson Guild had anything, it was this sense of caring. Each individual was precious.

# Hell's
# Kitchen

IT MAY BE of some surprise that the name Hell's Kitchen has an origin as Anglo-Saxon as Hancock or Adams. The truth is that historians seeking the source of the neighborhood's designation have apparently found it across the Atlantic, in a rough-and-tumble section of London also known as Hell's Kitchen.

Too bad, because it casts doubt on an oft-repeated legend— that nonetheless bears repeating here. According to the story, the neighborhood was christened in a conversation between two battle-weary cops during a riot at 39th Street and Tenth Avenue, not an unusual occurrence in the period before the Civil War—or afterward, for that matter.

"This place is hell itself," the younger man supposedly told his partner.

"Hell's a mild climate," his mate replied. "This is hell's *kitchen*."

Even if the conversation never did take place, it accurately portrays a neighborhood whose history is probably best recorded in police blotters. In its criminal heyday during the mid-1800s, Hell's Kitchen was the scene of heartbreaking squalor and home to the most notorious criminals in the city—men and women with color-fully descriptive nicknames like One Lung Curran, Spitting William, and Battling Annie. They made the neighborhood, as Herbert

Asbury wrote, "the most dangerous area on the American continent."

The name Hell's Kitchen was first assigned to a particularly notorious tenement at the corner of 39th Street and Tenth Avenue. Soon, the name applied to the entire block of 39th Street between Ninth and Tenth avenues, and then to the surrounding streets. Just how far the neighborhood extends is the subject of another dispute. While most agree that its east-west limits reach from Eighth Avenue to the Hudson River, there is little agreement as to its perimeters on the north and south.

The area covered here will be from 34th to 59th streets. One can't be too rigid, though: the infamous Tenderloin district (from 24th to 47th streets between Sixth and Eighth avenues) and the northern reaches of Chelsea have historic ties with Hell's Kitchen that have often left these borders blurred.

When the Dutch first arrived in New York, they found mid-Manhattan's western side to be a pleasant pastoral region of grassy meadows and freshwater streams. They called it Bloemendael (later Bloomingdale), or Vale of Flowers. The land reaching up to 110th Street and beyond was broken into small farm tracts and remained largely rural until 1851, when the Hudson River Railroad set up a station on what is now 30th Street and Tenth Avenue.

The railroad yard brought major changes to the area. Recent immigrants flooded the neighborhood to work in industries that mushroomed beside the tracks. They worked in breweries, warehouses, and brickyards, and on the docks. They lived in tenements amid the stench of the slaughterhouses that abounded around 39th Street, which was soon nicknamed Abattoir Place.

By the start of the Civil War, the neighborhood's population had soared to more than 350,000. Most were Irish and German immigrants. Nearly all suffered from the desperate poverty that would lead to the darkest episode in the city's history—the draft riots of 1863.

The violence erupted in protest against the Conscription Act of that year. The law decreed that no person could claim an exemption from service on the basis of his being the sole support of his family. However, exemptions would be granted to persons who could hire substitutes or who paid a fee of $300. Naturally, the bill caused great resentment among the poor, who were being targeted for the draft. Violence broke out in several of the poorest ghettos, the worst on July 13. By the time the fighting ceased three days later, 2,000 people were dead and 8,000 wounded. Property damage was estimated at five million dollars.

The years following the war saw poverty and despair increase as the neighborhood became even more populated. Thousands of homeless children roamed the streets and formed the nucleus of the first street gangs, which dominated Hell's Kitchen into the next century. The first to gain notoriety was the Nineteenth Street Gang, "a particularly vicious collection of young thugs with whom even the police did not care to battle," according to Asbury. The gang was led by a thief named Dutch Heinrich, who was reputed to have "the stickiest fingers in New York."

The neighborhood's living conditions shocked even the most hardened newspaper reporters of the day. While writing his own history of Hell's Kitchen, author Richard O'Connor uncovered several vivid newspaper accounts of neighborhood life.

At the Barracks, a wretched tenement at 38th Street and Eleventh Avenue, a reporter describing the quarters of one occupant said: "No carpet save one of filth covered the floor. . . . Furniture, fit to be called by that name, there was none. A bundle of rags and straw in a corner sufficed for a bed."

At the original Hell's Kitchen tenement, another reporter met a woman whose husband, according to O'Connor, "was in the comparatively orderly and healthful surroundings of Sing Sing." The woman, the reporter said, was

> . . . filthy beyond description, with bleared eyes, bloated face, and a breath that rivaled the odor of the soap factories. She poured forth a volley of blasphemous and obscene epithets. Maudlin in speech, swaggering in action, there were left no traces of womanhood in her. A torn and dirty garment was all that covered her nakedness, and without shame she staggered about in her limited quarters. . . .

Other buildings that earned citations for depravity included the House of Blazes, whose occupants enjoyed luring vagrants inside and setting them on fire, and Battle Row, a series of five-story structures on West 38th Street even more dangerous than the House of Blazes. Battle Row's preeminent resident was "Battle" Annie Walsh, the Queen of Hell's Kitchen and the most feared female brick hurler of her time.

If Battle Annie was the neighborhood's queen, its king was a red-bearded Orangeman named Bully Morrison, who, says O'Connor, was known to pluck lampposts from the ground and wield them as shillelaghs against the skulls of his enemies. Another feared character was "One Lung" Curran, who unintentionally started a Hell's Kitchen fashion trend one day when he offered a policeman's overcoat to his girl. The fact that the officer wasn't entirely willing to give up his frock coat meant little to the chivalrous Curran. Soon, many of the neighborhood molls were wearing them, making for a cold and abashed local constabulary.

A more curious character was "Spitting" William, who earned his nickname when he realized that his salivary glands and not his fists were his best defense. Not a great pugilist, he found instead that a well-aimed squirt of tobacco juice in the eye extricated him from several scrapes. Spitting William's luck ran out, though, after an ill-fated attempt to win the heart of "Euchre Kate" Burns. In that battle, his chaw proved no match for a gun-toting jealous husband, who brought William's life to an abrupt end.

By the turn of the century, the Gophers, under the leadership of Curran and, later, Newburgh Gallagher, "Stumpy" Malarky, and "Happy" Jack Mullraney, took over from the Hell's Kitchen gang as the dominant group in the area. But in 1910, the Gophers' own greed brought about their downfall. Tired of the Gophers' constant raids on their yards, the New York Central Railroad ordered its private police to retaliate with force. Gang members were clubbed and beaten indiscriminately, sending them into retreat and ending the stranglehold that gangs had held on the neighborhood for nearly fifty years.

The new century found the neighborhood still desperately poor, although the squalid living conditions were somewhat less severe. Crime was still a concern, and fighting and thievery a way of life for many, even without gang rule. While the Irish still dominated the neighborhood, Italians had begun to make their presence felt, and a small black population thrived from 59th to 65th streets.

For Hell's Kitchen children, life meant leaving school at an early age to work on the docks, the railroads, or in one of the local factories. The streets and the yards were their playgrounds, and dangerous ones at that. The railroad tracks that ran along Tenth and Eleventh avenues proved fatally irresistible to adventurous children, who fell from or were run over by passing trains. The number of fatalities was so alarmingly high that Eleventh Avenue was commonly called Death Avenue.

However, the trains did provide youngsters with one genuine rural thrill. The Tenth Avenue Cowboys, or dummy boys, were the legendary figures who rode their horses on the avenues to warn pedestrians of coming trains. Children's faces glowed with excitement as the young men rode by. Most of them longed to be in the stirrups themselves one day, and some of them succeeded.

Many of Hell's Kitchen's young men joined the 165th Infantry and went overseas in World War I. Popularly known as the Fighting 69th, the regiment, composed of many of the city's toughest characters, went on to become one of the most celebrated units in the country's history. For once, Hell's Kitchen had real heroes. Probably the biggest of all was the Fighting 69th's scholarly chaplain, Father Francis P. Duffy, who became pastor of Holy Cross Church in 1920 and was a familiar and beloved figure in the neighborhood until his death in 1932.

Prohibition followed on the heels of the armistice. Nowhere was the Volstead Act, prohibiting the sale of liquor, more defied than in the Irish-dominated Middle West Side.

"There are more speakeasies than kids in Hell's Kitchen, and there are easy 200 kids to a block," one resident told a *New York Telegram* reporter.

Prohibition also nourished a new generation of gangsters. They were the bootleggers, who operated speakeasies and nightclubs while dabbling in hijacking and an occasional murder. Chief among the new breed was Owney Victor Madden, who, by the age of seventeen, with five murders to his credit, earned the sobriquet Owney the Killer.

Unfortunately for Madden, his next killing earned him an eight-year stretch in Sing Sing. But upon his release in 1923, he quickly made up for his lost opportunities in the bootlegging business by monopolizing the beer trade. Unlike some of his cohorts, he learned to use violence with some discretion. The British-born Madden was not without charm or a clever sense of public relations, and he was a hero of sorts to the neighborhood. The admiration lasted long after he retired from the business and left town in 1935.

Madden did well during Prohibition, as did a host of others, who were involved in the more "legitimate" fringes of the bootlegging industry. Truck drivers delivering beer earned as much as fifty dollars a week. Speakeasies and clubs paid good wages to hundreds of entertainers, who played clubs like the Silver Slipper and El Fay. They sang and danced for frequently well-heeled customers, who drank liquor of varying quality, ranging from fine Scotch and whiskey smuggled in by rumrunners to poisonous home brews.

Although Prohibition continued to offer employment opportunities for some until 1933, the Depression meant increased hard times for most of the neighborhood's residents. The docks virtually shut down. Construction and railroad jobs disappeared. Relief, if one could get it, provided little real help, and neither unemployment insurance nor social security had as yet been invented. Helpless and facing disaster, most turned to the Democratic Party, which did what it could to provide work and relief for its supporters. Despite these efforts, many families lost their homes, and the sight of household furnishings set out on sidewalks was an all-too-familiar one around the neighborhood.

The '30s also brought major physical changes to the area, signaling the end of Hell's Kitchen's Wild West days. The expansion of the Port Authority of New York and New Jersey and the opening of the Lincoln Tunnel cut huge swaths through the old stomping grounds of Bully Morrison and Battle Annie. Gone, too, was Paddy's Market, the sprawling pushcart market under the Ninth Avenue El. And, although the removal of the ground-level tracks meant the end of Death Avenue, more than one youthful dream was dashed the day the last Tenth Avenue Cowboy took his final ride into the sunset.

# The Witnesses


BILL BAILEY (1910–) has been a longshoreman, merchant seaman, a Loyalist soldier in the Spanish Civil War, and most recently an actor. After appearances in two documentaries, *Seeing Red* and *The Good Fight*, he landed a lead role in *On the Edge*, a 1986 feature film starring Bruce Dern.


LOUISE BARLOW (1896–1986) performed in vaudeville and theatrical shows across the country. After her retirement, she was a dresser at the Latin Quarter for many years.


JAMES ''BUD'' BURNS (1911–) is a retired union official of the Brotherhood of Railroad Trainmen. He lives on Long Island.


MARIE CUTAIA (1915–) has lived nearly her whole life in Hell's Kitchen. She is retired after forty years with the New York Telephone Company.


HARRY FREEMAN (1905–) became a commercial photographer after his forced retirement from the bootlegging business. He runs a photocopy shop on the East Side.

TOM GERAGHTY (1905–85) was known as the Mayor of Hell's Kitchen, largely for his work on behalf of the neighborhood's children. He owned an auto-repair shop, situated just two doors from his father's blacksmith shop and stable.

JERRY IMPERATO (1915–) was born in Italy. He came to this country when he was six. For several years, he sold bananas from a pushcart at Paddy's Market on Ninth Avenue.

ED MCGEE (1907–) is a lifelong Hell's Kitchen resident. He was a bricklayer and today is a volunteer at Sacred Heart Church, on West 51st Street.

OWEN MCGIVERN (1912–) was formerly presiding justice in the New York State Supreme Court. He is now a counsel to the law firm of Donovan, Leisure Newton & Irvine.

JIM MINOGUE (1898–) is a World War I veteran and one of the last survivors of the famed Fighting 69th Regiment. He lives in Paramus, New Jersey.

JOHN MORAHAN (1914?–) is a former speakeasy proprietor, and later owned Morahan's Irish House, a bar on Eighth Avenue and 51st Street.

ALBERT SCHWEIZER (1906–) is a semiretired butcher. He immigrated from Bremen, Germany, in 1923.

OWEN MCGIVERN: I was born at 435 West 43rd Street, between Ninth and Tenth. A lot of operators worked out of there, and we used to say if a cat still had a tail on it, we knew it was a tourist.

My father had a racket. He was a wholesale ice dealer. In those days, there was no refrigeration, and the ice industry was one of the biggest in America. They cut the ice out of the Hudson and floated it down the river. Then they'd sell it to the peddlers on the docks. My father's dock was at 39th Street and Eleventh. He was lucky. Just before refrigeration came in the '20s, he sold his business to the Knickerbocker Ice Company. A lot of people were wiped out when refrigeration came in.

It was a rough neighborhood, but the people were safe. My father carried the day's proceeds home wrapped up in a newspaper or he put the money in a safe in a saloon on 39th Street. He was never mugged. Holdups like that were unknown.

Hell's Kitchen was wall-to-wall Irish, Italian, and German, with a smattering of a Jewish population around the local mom-and-pop stores. Basically, the employment rose out of the docks, the railroads, the restaurants, and the theaters. It was a real local operation. Very few people rode to work. They walked to work. They lived there, worked there, and died there.

The neighborhood derived its character for toughness from the gangs, but the gangs were really economic warfare. They fought for control of the docks and the rights to the shape-up. But the longshoremen were mostly family men. Very few of them participated in the rackets. Most of them worked very hard just to keep their families together. They had hard times, those fellows.

The number of deaths from heart attacks or pneumonia in the winter was heartbreaking, especially for those poor longshoremen. I walked by few windows that didn't have the black mourning crepes. The white crepes for children weren't unusual either.

Louise Barlow: My father had an acrobatic act that was famous in Europe. He came here to play in a theater on 23rd Street, Koster & Bial, and he ended up staying. My mother was from show business, too. I remember her talking about being in *Trial by Jury*. That was Gilbert and Sullivan. She played the National Theater in Washington, and later I played the same theater. Isn't that funny?

I was born on 28th Street between Broadway and Sixth Avenue. We didn't have much money, so we moved a lot, but we were always around show people. At one time, we lived on 37th Street. Dinty Moore was in the same building with his children. When we were on 38th Street, the Kliegl Brothers, who had the Klieg lights, lived there. We were also on 35th Street where Macy's is. My sister was born there, and we had to move because Macy's was moving uptown from 14th Street. She always used to say she was born in the doll department. My uncle used to tell her, "No, Carrie, you were born in their horse stable."

When we lived on 34th Street, the Indians who played the Hippodrome stayed in rooming houses across the street. They would come home from the matinees with their feathers and war paint and everything. I was scared to death. When I had to take my brother and sister out, I'd walk around the block to avoid them, but they never hurt anybody.

Because we didn't have much money, my parents had rooming houses. I had to help with the work. A dancer lived at one of them, and he was going to take me to England with him, so I used to practice, but it never worked out. What I really wanted to be was a housewife, which I never got to be. I wanted to marry a bricklayer like my boyfriend's father, because they bring home a regular salary. With my father, it was feast or famine. My boyfriend's father got a paycheck and sent it home. I thought that was wonderful.

My boyfriend's mother had six kids. They had four little rooms and they were poor, but they were lovely. I wanted six kids also, but I only had two.

Ed McGee: My father was a bricklayer. He worked when there was work to be done. I was a bricklayer, too, for over fifty years. I was born at 49th and Ninth in 1907. We moved to three or four different places around the neighborhood until we settled at 52nd and Tenth. It was called Hell's Kitchen, but there were a hell of a lot of nice people around the neighborhood. We had our share of bishops and all.

James "Bud" Burns: I was born in 510 West 29th Street. My father was a longshoreman. Then he went to World War I. He came out a disabled veteran, and he never worked no more. I had to go to a home until a Polish family took me in. I was raised by them.

In those days, there were three things that men worked, either as longshoremen, on the railroad, or truck drivin'. You had to be eighteen to work on the railroad. But when I was fourteen, I asked a politician to fill out my baptismal papers to say I was eighteen.

I had an uncle who worked there called Jack Fisher, so I went there under the name James Fisher, because bein' that you had a relation there it looked good. They asked me if I had any experience. I told them my uncle had a farm, so I went on the extra list to ride the horse as a dummy boy.

The dummy boys hung out on Tenth Avenue and 30th Street in what we called the Pebble Yard. You hung out until the whistle blew. If it was your train, off you went. When you were done you took the horse to the stables, at Geraghty's on 37th Street.

TOM GERAGHTY: I came down to Hell's Kitchen when I was four years old. My father was a hardworking horseshoer. He had a shop on West 37th Street. We lived up around 86th and Third. Pop used to get snowbound trying to get from the east side of town to the west. It was either move the shop uptown or move down there. My mother, being a headstrong dame, had us move in one night—the whole household—down to 37th Street.

Daddy and Mother used to have pretty frequent battles. You would find yourself ducking under the tables because the dishes were flying. Then your mother had the nerve to bring you to a clinic to see if you were normal. "Aren't you just a little bit too nervous?"

The bug doctor says, "Son, what causes ya to be so nervous?"

I'd say, as my mother would say, the sudden ringing of the bell and the postman's here; you're always wondering when last night's battle is going to begin again. I always had the feeling that they were going to kill each other. They'd bring out old sores like, "Who was your boyfriend when I first met you?" That jazz.

My father drank his share of horse sugar. My mother never drank. She was the domineering one. She was always throwing him out. Once, the police were called, and I had to go to court. My mother told a bunch of lies, and my father told a bunch of lies, and the judge said, "I don't ever want to see you before this bench again," and they went home.

MARIE CUTAIA: Mom was born in 430 West 46th Street. I was born in 434 in 1915. Mom moved here to 47th Street when they tore the buildin' down to put up a playground. When I got married, I lived underneath her. I moved to the East Side for one year. I couldn't wait to come back, and I lived underneath for thirty-five years.

We were five, three boys and two girls. We *were* six, but we lost a little girl when she was about eighteen months old. She had diphtheria. Everybody seemed to lose one. My mother's sister was eighteen years old when she died of influenza. There was nothin' for that.

BILL BAILEY: My father was one of those Irish Catholics who thought every time you take your pants off you have a baby. My mother didn't know what the hell to do. She ended up with thirteen kids. Fortunately for the other six, seven of 'em died in infancy. With the little amount of money that the father was takin' home, and the problems that go with havin' a big family, after work he'd just go to the gin mills with his friends. It ended up with his whole goddamn paycheck goin'.

The problem was, no matter how drunk he got, he couldn't eradicate the problem. The kids were there waitin' for him to come home with the ham or somethin' else to eat, and he wasn't bringin' home anythin'.

There were some scenes that took place more than once. You had to defend yourself someways. In order to shut her up, he'd throw a punch at her. She took a few of those until a bad one split her lip. While he was layin' there drunk, she said, "Okay, everybody, let's pack."

We all chipped in and took all the pots and pans and stuff that we could carry. We walked out the door and five or six miles to Hoboken, another rat-infested place. But there were no job opportunities there. Also, one of the other brothers was gettin' into fights down at the waterfront, and I got into one of those petty-larceny deals, stealin' copper offa rooftops, and I got arrested. She wanted to get out of that environment, plus she felt there were more job opportunities in New York, so we came to Hell's Kitchen.

The street we lived on was 38th Street between Ninth and Tenth avenues. That street was all Irish. Anybody who lived on that street and wasn't Irish didn't last long. Thirty-seventh Street was all Greek, and 39th Street was all Italian. That was the way it was.

JOHN MORAHAN: I had an uncle—actually he was really a cousin. His name was Charlie, but his nickname was Bullets Morahan. He got shot behind the bar over here at 49th. He was fooling around with some Frenchman's wife, and the guy come in and boom boom. He lived for seventeen years with the two bullets in 'im.

Somewhere around Ninth Avenue, he also had a piece of an undertaker parlor. My father used to be a railroad man. He'd come down, and all the Irishmen, all the cousins, would get together at the speakeasy. My old man got drunk one night down there. They took 'im to the undertaker's parlor. When he woke up in the morning, where do you think they had 'im? In the coffin.

They would sometimes take a guy right out of the coffin. One guy on one arm, one guy on the other right under the elbows and bring him down to the corner saloon. They'd put him right up there on the stool and have a drink. They were the funniest bastards, I'm telling ya.

BILL BAILEY: I went to the Schermerhorn School, on 38th Street. I was a good student there. I liked it and the teachers liked me. I think they saw more potential in me than I saw in myself. They knew I was goin' to school four days a week without any food in my stomach, and they were always givin' me a bag of jelly beans or an overcoat in the wintertime.

I would clean the erasers by bangin' 'em together out the window. One mornin', one of the erasers dropped out of my hand and fell into the street. When I went downstairs to get it, I guess it was about ten in the mornin', a doughnut wagon went by. This guy was pickin' up the stale stuff and bringin' it down to the stores. He saw me lookin' at 'im and he said, "You should be in school."

I told him I was, that I came down to pick up the eraser.

He said, "You had no breakfast?"

I said, "No, we don't have no breakfast, no breakfast in my family."

He gave me four doughnuts. I brought 'em upstairs, ate one, and gave the other three to the other kids. The next day, he's down in same place, and he did this five days a week. I got in the habit of goin' down every day, and I was bringin' back as many as fifteen or twenty-five doughnuts. Everybody in the class enjoyed 'em. Anybody would, and the teacher recognized this. She knew that we were primarily half-starved kids.

At one point, they started the thing where you got milk. Then, later on, every kid got a cookie or somethin'. That was tremendous. We just gorged it down. Generally, the other kids I checked with at least had a bowl of oatmeal in the mornin'. There wasn't a hell of a lot of food at our home. The mother was out scrubbin' floors until eight o'clock in the mornin', if she got the job. One of the sisters would get me up. I'd throw the clothes on and get to school.

We lived in a regular flat with a yard in the back. I think we had three rooms. We slept on the floor. We had old coats which we used to lay down first. The only one who had a mattress was the mother. She was the janitor. She'd clean out the place. With that you'd get a cheaper rent.

All the cans were put in the back, but you know the way the people were. Instead of bringin' the garbage down, at two o'clock in the mornin' they'd open the window and throw it out. Plop, plop, plop—you'd hear it all night long.

OWEN McGIVERN: We called it the midnight mail. You had to walk in the middle of the street. Otherwise you got hit by the midnight mail.

MARIE CUTAIA: We had the ten o'clock mail. There was a Mrs. Walsh who lived in 437. She never came down with her garbage. Boom! Walshie threw it down every night. Ten o'clock mail with Walshie.

Mom was the super in our buildin'. The cousins used to hang with us, and Mom used to get them to sweep down the stairs and wash them once a week. The barrels were never left out. When the garbageman came, they would take the barrels and put them in the back of the hall or out in the yard, because the barrels belonged there. Then in the mornin', they were put out.

Mom did a laundry practically every day. She would wash with the washboard. On the coal stove we had a great big, big tub where she boiled the clothes. After they were washed, they were boiled, wrung out and blued and then swung out on a big line. Blue—that was a liquid blue for the white clothes. We always blued them. Later, we got a washin' machine with the rollers. That was somethin'.

In Mom's room, she had a mattress made of cotton, the kind where you put your hand in to shake it up. When she washed it, maybe every six months, she'd get a big sheet and take the mattress off the bed. Then she'd empty the cotton on the sheet and wash the ticking, dry it, put the cotton back in and sew the hole back up.

You also had to clean for bedbugs with a hammer and a basin of water. You'd bang the springs with the hammer and the bugs would fall into the pan.

BILL BAILEY: We had a coal stove to heat the place. Mostly, we used wood. We never had any trouble gettin' that. We'd just take it from wherever we could.

"Always bring home a box," Mother said. "Bring home somethin'." We'd steal the coal if we could. We'd go down to the tracks or to the barges on 23rd Street. We'd take an hour or two to size up the place, make sure nobody was there, or somebody'd be brave and go up immediately and throw off a big rock of coal. As soon as it hit, it would break off into a dozen pieces and we would race for it.

For haircuts, either the sister would give me one or I'd get it at the barber college. Sometimes, the school would take the whole class over to the barber college. In the summertime, everybody'd insult the barbers by sayin', "We want a baldy." It was the last thing they wanted to give, because any jackass can give a baldy, so they'd protest like hell.

BUD BURNS: On 29th Street, there was a stable run by the Goodwins, Pete Goodwin, a big hairy Irishman. He had a son who was a lieutenant of detectives, Eddie Goodwin. These guys used to drink. We were all poor kids, and in the summer he would take us and use the shears they used on the horses to give us a baldy. Sometimes, they'd just run it up the middle for fun and you'd cry and holler. When they were done, they had this big round trough, and they'd stick your head in there and wash it off.

BILL BAILEY: In our buildin', everybody knew what everybody else was doin'. It was the very nature of the way we lived. We knew when Mrs. Kelly was bein' stomped on. We'd hear him goin' up the stairs, and we knew right away there was goin' to be trouble. Sure enough, ten minutes later, "He's beatin' me! He's beatin' me!"

It was tough for everybody, but mostly people looked after each other. Everybody was poor. If somebody got sick, we all cried.

Everybody looked in on each other and made gestures somehow. "C'mon and eat" or "Share this with us," things like that.

MARIE CUTAIA: We never visited a doctor. If we sprained our wrists from skatin', we always went to Grandma. She'd take a piece of twine and pull it apart. Then, she'd dip it in the white of an egg. When she set it on our wrists with a bandage, it got as hard as a cast, and it got better.

She was like a chiropractor from the other side. Grandma was a real Italian grandmother. She always wore black. She wore layers of petticoats and always a black shawl. Everything she had of value— her bankbooks and her jewelry—was on her. She had these big pockets under her petticoats, and that's where everything went.

I used to ask, "Momma, why does Grandma dress like that?" She just said that was how Grandma dressed. It was tradition. She had no big social life outside of her family. She never went on vacation. She was the janitor of 430. She'd just take care of her buildin' and sit and look out the window. She loved doin' that.

If we felt sick, we'd go to Grandma and say, "Grandma, my head doesn't feel good. I have a headache."

"Let me pass your head." She would say the prayers and make the sign and say, "Filame, my child, you are overlooked," and we were fine.

She also had certain oils she used to massage us. For temperature, she used to rub all the muscles in our hands and then pull a finger. For throat, she'd rub our glands and pull a piece of our hair. It worked.

TOM GERAGHTY: They had an epidemic of polio when we were kids. Your typical Irish mother would chop up some garlic and say, "Here, why don't you eat some?" Or they would put it in a bag and tie it around your neck to keep away disease, supposedly. So did the mothers of Benny and Morris Cohen. None of us were actually saved by these remedies.

I went to school at Sacred Heart, on 51st and Tenth. You could imagine the classroom smell with all these kids. Between the smell of olive oil on the greasy hair, the steamy radiators, and the garlic, it was far from a wholesome odor.

◆   ◆   ◆

MARIE CUTAIA: Mom and Dad got married by Father Duffy at Holy Cross Church. I made my Communion at St. Albert's, which was a small church around the corner. The pastor was a handsome Belgian named Father Rosen. He was a beautiful person. I always remember him with his hands. He was a big tall man with beautiful hands. His fingers, they were like a piano player's.

Another tradition was on Sunday night when we used to go to my pop's family on the East Side for dinner. Dad would take us by car and we all looked forward to it. All the oldest girls were named after my grandmother on that side. That was a tradition, too. I was known as Marie Westside. I had a cousin on Thompson Street, Uncle George's Marie—she was Marie Downtown. Then we had Aunt Lizzie's daughter Marie, who lived in Woodside. That was Marie Long Island. We had Aunt Mamie's daughter Marie, who lived upstate. That was Marie Syracuse.

Dad was an excellent cook. He used to make the skirt steaks and the homemade sausage. He would buy grapes and make wine in the cellar. There were three Italians. The other two had the presser and the barrels, and they would share. They'd make a fifty-gallon barrel of wine, but it was only for them. They wouldn't sell it.

BILL BAILEY: Dinner was whatever—whatever anybody would drag in. Between 38th Street and 42nd Street on Ninth Avenue was where they had all the pushcarts. That was called Paddy's Market. My job was to go up there and go underneath the pushcarts. If you could get in back of the pushcarts, you could steal anybody blind. There were always potatoes fallin' off the back and gettin' pushed out into the street. I'd go along with a little bag and pick up all this stuff. Of course, you always ran the risk of gettin' caught. I got whacked in the keester a few times, but sometimes you also picked up a nickel or penny that may have dropped.

After the markets had shut down, you could help take all the pushcarts back. Many of the guys would be exhausted from standin' there all day sellin'. They'd say, "Here, take my pushcart back. Here's a penny." So I'd race like a son of a bitch down to the warehouse and run back like an idiot to look for another one.

Sometimes, if there was somethin' left on the pushcart, he'd say you could take that home, too. There might be a head of cabbage, a tomato, some potatoes or rotten oranges. Whatever, it all helped. It was unbelievable, but that's what kept the family goin'.

There was also a fish shop in the neighborhood that I worked in. He used to sell crabs in big bathtubs, no water, just plain crabs. Somebody come in and say, "Gimme a dozen crabs."

You'd take the first dozen crabs you got to and throw them in a paper bag. You'd get a lot of dead ones that had suffocated or were stepped on, broken up or somethin'. People would say, "I don't want those. Make sure he moves. If he don't, I don't want 'im."

Well, you gave 'im a little push, and if he don't move, you don't give it to 'im. At the end of the day, the fish man says, "Get 'em outta here. Take 'em witchya." You might end up with ten or fifteen crabs, and they were perfectly good to eat.

MARIE CUTAIA: The apartment was always hot in the summertime. As soon as supper was over, all the parents would go down and sit on the stoop. It was mostly the women. The fathers would come down and stroll off to the corner and b.s. The kids would be playin', and they would spend maybe two or three hours just talkin' about the weather, what they cooked, recipes, things like that.

Every once in a while, one of the younger fellas would holler, "Let it go!" Before you knew it, a bag of water came poom! right down from one of the windows above. One or two of them were mischief-makers, and the mothers would get up and say, "I know it was you, Red. That was you up there. You're at it again," and then you'd see Red come out of another buildin'. "What am I gettin' blamed for?"

None of us caused them a great deal of problems, although once I rode a motorcycle with my husband before we got married. My father threatened me with a fryin' pan for that.

They kept us even stricter when we got older. We had to account for everythin', like if we went out, you always went out in groups. Every Saturday night we had dances at Hartley House with a Victrola. We'd get up in our dresses and dance with all the young boys. As far as doin' things with the boys, we used to call it "hall-way duty." I used to say to my cousins, "I saw youse doin' hallway duty last night." We'd go to a movie balcony and "swap spits." I think all girls were bad, but everythin' was hush-hush. They did the same thing they're doin' now but not as open. Like livin' together, we'd never do that.

We used to have ath-a-letic in school, and there's where all the girls got their education. And then I had older cousins that educated us. My mother more or less knew it, because I used to say, "Oh, what Cousin Marion told me, is that true?" Then, when they told us we were goin' to get our periods and things like that, I couldn't believe it. But when it came, we accepted it, because the oldest would watch out for the next one.

We really were like family on this block. My husband's family lived on the third floor. He was a friend of my brother. My cousin Sonny Tassiello, who had a bar here on 47th and Ninth, married Joe Famularo's sister Mary. She lived across the street, and we went to school together. My husband's sister married Tony Perrato from the neighborhood.

Most all of us married in the block. But the college boys were different. With them, there was a lot of intermarriage. All our college boys never married Italian women. We used to be so mad, us girls. "There goes another Italian." All of them used to be with the Irish girls because they were so easy. They would get 'em drunk and have a good time.

Still, we were proud of them from the Hell's Kitchen neighborhood. Owen McGivern became a judge; so did Joe Famularo. The boy upstairs became a priest, and he taught in Washington, D.C. And we all loved George Raft. I think that's why we all wanted to become dancers, on account of George Raft.

BILL BAILEY: If you did anythin' with girls, you went to the theaters. The best was to go to some show where they'd have tall, long balconies and mess around there. There were always hallways, too. Where the hell else could you do it? Nobody owned cars or nothin'. Maybe you'd go to the park late at night. There was an old sayin' about a conscience and a stiff dick. These things were happenin' all over.

TOM GERAGHTY: The best-looking girls used to work at 36th and Tenth Avenue in the McGraw-Hill building. I was in love with one of them. Her name was Babby Dee. Jesus, I thought she was the greatest thing that ever happened, but the more I tried to make progress, the less she liked me. I used to buy two tickets to a

Broadway play and ask Babby if she wanted to go with me. No, she always had something else to do. On the night of the show, I would wait near her house, but she never would come out.

Later, I find out that she gets married to this guy and stabs him a few times in the back. Jesus. After that, she goes to upper Manhattan and puts a gun in her mouth and blows her brains out. Man, if I had known, I could have saved a lot of grief.

ED MCGEE: We dated girls in the neighborhood. You could pick any show on Broadway and go. They were cheap. We'd go down to the American Roof, on 42nd Street, on Sunday. There was burlesque on Wednesday or maybe you would take in the six-day bike races at the Garden.

We all knew each other since we were kids. But when we were young, we hated each other. One day, I was walking on the docks under the gangplanks of a ship, and the gangplank fell down. I got a double fracture of my leg. When I got out of the hospital, my father had to carry me up the stairs. There was this little girl across the street, and she kept throwing stuff at us as we were going inside.

I yelled at her. "You son of a gun, when I finish here, I'll get you." I always used to say I got her in the wrong way. I married her.

We spent quite a bit of time on the docks then. Our swimming hole was down the Hudson River. The Department of Sanitation had a dump over on 54th Street near Twelfth. We used to go down the pier and swim off there because the water was cleaner. Every once in a while a toad or something would pass you by, but it never bothered us. Sometimes I swam from New York to Jersey and come back on the ferry. You swam with the tide, but you were real tired when you got there.

BILL BAILEY: We did quite a bit of swimmin' in the Hudson. That was the only place we could go. We'd find an open pier where you could walk straight out and dive off. There was always fifteen or twenty-five kids jumpin' off the piers. You jumped off one and swam like a bastard to the next one, jumped on there and went around half-assed naked, but it was a lot of fun.

When I think about it now, the sweat goes runnin' down my neck. We swam among the condoms, the garbage, and the filth, everything the Hudson was noted for. As a matter of fact, the first intestines I ever seen came floatin' down there once.

People would throw milk cans in. One of them once went right to the bottom, and a kid dove off the pier and went right into it, head first. He couldn't get out. That stopped everybody from swimming for a couple of weeks, but then everybody went back.

ED MCGEE: We played marbles, Johnny on the pony, and cat and stick. That was where you had a stick and a small piece of wood. You hit the end of the wood with the stick, and when it went up in the air you hit it. You'd break a window, then run like a son of a gun.

They used horses for everything then. When the horse died, they'd put him out in the street for a day or two. We liked to run and jump on the dead horses. Once, the bladder broke on 'im— oh boy, the smell. Quite a few of the kids used to make rings from the horses' tails. You would go back there and pluck the hair yourself, or, if you asked the driver, he'd do it for you.

BILL BAILEY: You'd see a lot of dead ones in the summer. It would fall over, and the guy would be workin' over him, puttin' water up his keester and everything. Then the horse would get up and fall right down again. It got so bad in the summer that the SPCA put out these water tins for the horses all over the city.

OWEN MCGIVERN: As bad as it was for them in the summer, I think it was worse in the winter. The horses were always slipping and falling on the icy roads. Then somebody would get an ashcan out and put the ashes under the horse and try to get friction for the horse to get up again. They were sad sights, seeing the poor horses struggling to get up off the ice. Frequently, they didn't make it, and you'd see a lot of dead horses out on the streets.

I was coming home from school one day. A horse had fallen and broken its leg at 43rd and Ninth Avenue under the El. The policeman on duty held a gun to the temple of the horse and fired. Imagine that. I guess the policemen in those days were raised in that business.

TOM GERAGHTY: I used to help my father at work in the stable. I delivered the horses, and he had me helping to shoe them. Some of his customers used top brewery horses, and those things can weigh up to 3,000 pounds. They had a way of leaning on you. The horse may look stupid, but they know when they have a slob. It would just go to one side and let you have enough pressure to make things hurt for a while.

We took care of mustangs, and the mustang is a different breed than the usual horse. They were so tricky that they learned to pull the bolt out of the feedbox and let all the oats pour out so the other horses could eat. My father almost would have a heart attack when he came in on Monday morning, seeing all the horses having a picnic. They looked like they were in pregnancy.

We took care of quite a few breweries in those days. The story was if you had something to do with the horses, you could get away with stuff that the average guy couldn't. One of the breweries had a big copper tank filled with ice-cold beer. It was just running out and you were free to take all the damn beer you wanted. I used to have a few friends who were real glad to help me bring the horses from the breweries to the stables. In fact, some of the kids didn't come back for three days.

•   •   •

MARIE CUTAIA: Halloween was really nothin'. Our boys went out. They'd reverse their jackets and go out with a stockin' and flour. That's Halloween. They didn't dress.

On Thanksgivin', they all dressed and sang. I always wore a boy's outfit. On restaurant row, being as I was a boy, we used to open the cab doors and make money. Maybe I'd get a nickel or a dime. They all went in the backyards to sing. I'll never forget my brothers—they used to heat the dime and throw it out, and when the kids went for it they burned their hands. [*She laughs.*]

Every Fourth of July we also built a bonfire. You had to bring a stick or a piece of board. It was called "bringin' your license." By the end of the night, there was a big dent, burnt asphalt in the street.

ED MCGEE: The slaughterhouses were down on 42nd Street. In the summertime, when the wind was coming this way, ooh, you got an awful odor.

A couple times a week you'd get to see the lambs walking down Eleventh Avenue from the 60th Street yards. You had a Judas that always led them. As soon as they got to the slaughterhouse, the Judas went one way, and the others went in and got slaughtered.

BILL BAILEY: We loved to go down by the docks and watch the sheep come in. They'd block off the street up to the slaughterhouse before they let them out. I remember this Judas. We used to spit at him half the time. He had great big marble eyes. In fact, we used to talk about his eyes—what great marbles they'd make. We called them aggies.

He had a beautiful set of horns and a great big bell around his neck. They'd put the gangway down on these boats, and the sheep wouldn't move. We used to say, "Here's Judas!" They'd bring him out and he'd "baaaaa," and son of a bitches, they'd come right down that gangway. He'd turn around and walk right into that goddamn slaughterhouse. All them sheep, waggin' their tails right behind 'em, would go right in after him and that was it.

One day he disappeared. The old adage was that his collar fell off, he got mixed in with the others, and they knocked him off.

JERRY IMPERATO: Once, a bull got loose and ran through Ninth Avenue. There were cops all over it, but the animal wouldn't go down. Finally, they cornered him in one of the buildings around 36th Street, and one of the cops put a gun right to his head and got him. He must have had about a hundred bullets in him before he went down.

BILL BAILEY: The sisters worked at the slaughterhouse. They always came home with somethin'. That was one of the perquisites. They would steal all they could. But they also gave you a lot of stuff like liver and other stuff they threw away. I think the sister got caught once with a ham. They stopped her: "How long you been pregnant?" They pulled it out and she got fired. That was all right. The other sister went to work there a week later, and they started all over again.

Most of the young girls worked in the slaughterhouse or the battery factory. The battery factory's worse because you're breathin' all that acid. The sister picked up all sorts of lung problems there. At the slaughterhouse, the smell was bad but you got used to it, and the work was easy.

Marie Cutaia: We didn't get our meat from there. We got it from Tony the Butcher. The Washington Meat Market was a few blocks down. Sometimes we got our meat from there and sometimes we got it from Schweizer's at 46th and Tenth.

Albert Schweizer: Willi Schweizer always handled a good piece of meat. He would buy choice, where the other butchers would not. My uncle came to this country in 1887. Five years later, he opened the store on Tenth Avenue. The shop is now under the third generation. I came here in 1923 from Bremen, Germany, and worked with my brother there for nine years. From 14th Street to 63rd Street on Tenth Avenue was forty butcher shops. Today, Billy Schweizer is the only one. The railing that is in there and the equipment is still old-fashioned.

My training was only what I got in New York, but I come from a farm, and I knew about livestock. There isn't a bone in one of these cattles that I wouldn't know where it is situated, where to cut it. I know every bone in every cattle.

When Willi Schweizer bought a dozen hindquarters a week, he only sold a small amount of it here. The good stuff, like filet mignon, shell steaks, porterhouse steak, and prime ribs, he sold to butchers on Park Avenue and Broadway. In the West Side, they didn't want that. Here, we sold pot roast, roast beef, ground, salad meat, and this marble stuff where the fat is between the meat. When they wanted a good piece of meat, they'd say, "I'm going to Willi Schweizer."

We got our meat from 39th Street. On the West Side, the slaughterhouses were between 35th and 42nd streets. They killed approximately 3,000 to 8,000 hogs a day. In the New York Butchers Slaughterhouse that still stands, they killed between 1,500 and 3,000 cattle daily.

The animals all came in on the Grand Central Railroad from Jersey. They came from nearly every state in the union. The best meat came from Nebraska and Iowa. Texas had a good reputation for grazing cattle but not for meat.

Depending on the day of the week, the slaughtering started at eleven o'clock at night. By two o'clock in the afternoon, the slaughtering was finished. One house slaughtered nothing but calves. Another only slaughtered cattle. In the surrounding blocks were the wholesale houses. We ordered our meat from there.

The slaughterhouses tried to keep the places clean. They were well equipped and they were sanitary. They wanted to stay. It was only the Jews that drove the slaughterhouses out of town, and they didn't care how many thousands of them lost their jobs. They didn't care.

There was a smell, but it was never that bad. You get used to it. The people wouldn't die from that, not like gasoline. The smell of gasoline was much more dangerous. These fellows that worked in the slaughterhouses, they got old. These fellows that do these paint jobs where they don't wear masks, it takes no time to kill them. But the slaughterhouses disappeared because the Jewish people don't like the odor, and they forced the city to give them no more leases. They chased them one after another until, like today, there are none left.

It didn't bother me to slaughter an animal. I used to run a pork store. I had a friend next door who was an undertaker. He had a wife. She was German. She was born in this country, but she was just as German as you will ever want to see. On Saturday, when the embalmers didn't work, she was the one that done the embalming. She used to say, "Today the embalmers are not working, and I got seven bodies in."

I asked her, "Katy, don't it ever give you the creeps?"

She said, "I think of it as much as you cut me off six pork chops."

So, that's a trade, just like a butcher is.

◆ ◆ ◆

ED MCGEE: We all liked to go down to Eleventh Avenue and jump on the sides of the trains and climb on top. Quite a few kids got killed or lost their limbs. That's why they called it Death Avenue.

In front of the trains, they had the fellows riding the horses. I knew one who was a mute. That's why they got the name dummy boys.

TOM GERAGHTY: Those guys were called dummy boys because it seemed the horses they rode had only encountered boxcars before in the railroad yards, and when they saw those big black locomotives with the big eye, they panicked. So the city fathers decided to put a phony boxcar around the locomotives so as not to scare the horses.

My father had a contract with the New York Central to take care of the horses. I got to know some of those fellows pretty well. It seemed that, at the time, the women had an affinity for the horsemen—the Tenth Avenue Cowboys, they called them then. They call it macho now, but whatever the hell it was, the local girls would be hanging around 30th Street where all the cowboys were. I used to say that the girls used to follow these boys around with mattresses on their backs. There were a lot of military marriages then, especially if the girl had a few tough-minded brothers or cousins.

BILL BAILEY: Oh, the horses that used to run up and down Tenth Avenue. I tried to get on them for years, but I couldn't do it. We used to idolize those guys. They were great. They'd ride in front of the trains with a lantern at night or with a flag during the day. That was a big deal. Everybody wanted to ride one of those horses, but few were chosen.

Larry Angeluzzi spurred his jet black horse proudly through a canyon formed by two great walls of tenements, and at the foot of each wall, marooned on their separate blue sidewalks, little children stopped their games to watch him with silent admiration. He swung his red lantern in a great arc; sparks flew from the iron hoofs of his horse as they rang on railroad tracks, set flush in the stones of Tenth Avenue, and slowly following horse, rider and lantern came the long freight train, inching its way north from St. John's Park terminal on Hudson Street.

In 1928, the New York Central Railroad used the streets of the city to shuttle trains north and south, sending scouts on horseback to warn traffic. In a few more years this would end, an overhead pass built. But Larry Angeluzzi, not knowing he was the last of the "dummy boys," that he would soon be a tiny scrap of urban history, rode as straight and arrogantly as any urban cowboy. . . .

—Mario Puzo, *The Fortunate Pilgrim*

BUD BURNS: The canyons and everything, that was book talk. I think Puzo was writin' about his brother, who was a dummy boy. It was just like any other job, although the girls did look up to you. But they never came after me with mattresses.

I just met a woman at a teamsters' affair. It turned out she was from Greenwich Village. When I told her I used to ride the horses, she said her father forbid her to see dummy boys, because they had such a bad reputation. Anything that was missin' or stolen, they used to blame it on the dummy boys. Maybe one or two were involved, but not as a general rule.

Lookin' back, I guess there was something special about it, but then it was a day's work. You had eight to four and that was it. I looked at it as a pay job, not a glamour job. Some kids wanted to go on for the glamour, but not me. It's true though, the kids loved us, but the parents sure didn't.

In those days, the trains came in the 60th Street yards down Eleventh Avenue to the 30th Street yards. After it switched to a smaller engine, it went down Tenth to St. John's Park, stoppin' at different places to unload. When it got to Canal Street, it made a sharp curve and turned around and started back uptown.

Stealin' was a problem down there. In the summer, the kids would climb on top and take the ice from the refrigerator cars for the iceboxes. In the winter, they would steal the Christmas trees that were being carried in.

On 32nd Street was the turntable. The carloads of silk that came into there used to disappear. The saying was that it was Owney Madden and his gang. Those train yards were a little rough because of the gangs. Over the years, they cut down on the number of guards and they never replaced them, so as a rule they weren't around. I couldn't tell you whether they were bein' paid to leave. Your guess is as good as mine. [*He laughs.*] You can form your own conclusion.

A lot of people got hurt on the tracks. That's why they called it Death Avenue. The kids climbin' on trains was a big problem. Many of them got killed fallin' off the sides. On summer nights when I was real young, I got on the trains and rode down to the park and back. Of course it was dangerous. One of the kids that played with me, Danny Driscoll, got cut up and killed on 23rd Street. There were loads of them. Ditch Conklin, one of the dummy boys, his mother was killed right near 26th Street. She walked underneath the train while it was stopped. In the meantime, the engineer got the steam goin' and he cut her up.

There was a ferry at 42nd Street. People were goin' to work and comin' back. When the train stopped there, they tried to go under it or cross through it. All of a sudden the train would start and a lot of them got hurt. It was dangerous for the railroad people, too. Sometimes you'd stop and people would run into the back of the train. As far as insurance was concerned, the only people who paid more were bartenders. I guess a lot of them were gettin' beat up and shot.

There was one engineer named Joe Weber who had a lot of accidents. He was very darin'. He'd go too fast. He hit a trolley car at 14th Street. He hit a peddler on his wagon and killed him. He hit a couple of people steppin' off the curb at Canal Street. He was the one who ran over Ditch Conklin's mother. It wasn't always his fault. He was just accident-prone.

Every corner along the tracks had a man in the little shed. That was the flagman. The fellow would have a stop sign for when the train went by. A lot of them also had a little side racket. Say you were goin' out and had a little baby. You put it there by the shanty and he watches him, maybe gives him a bottle. He got maybe twenty-five cents or fifty cents.

They also might hold a package for somebody who stole something. Another guy maybe sold coal from the trains. He had a bucket. From every train that went up and down he got more coal.

The most tearful thing was when they took the trains off the avenue. All those old-timers that worked there years and years got fired. They just put a notice on the bulletin board: Effective Monday, you're out. No pensions, no jobs, no nothin'. Their wives came cryin' with their children. Those flagmen were just old men, and they just threw them out.

TOM GERAGHTY: The biggest ambition in your life was to have money for the movies all the time. The movies were on Ninth Avenue and 38th, 39th streets. We called it the Nickel Dump. On Saturdays, you didn't require a chaperone. You'd see Pearl White and the Iron Claw, scary stuff. The most prevalent odor in the theater was garlic.

Nearby on 38th Street was the soap factory. There was a family where four of the girls used to work there. All you had to do was go to one of the Saturday-night dances, and if you didn't see them, you could smell them. We used to say, "Hoo, boy, the soap factory's here."

BILL BAILEY: That was the soap factory across the street. I think it was the Palmolive Soap Company. I never worked there. All I ever tried to do was steal soap from there. You always hoped a worker would stick his head out of the window. "Hey, how about a couple of bars of soap?" If nobody was around, you'd find some way to do it.

When things were grim, I also opened taxi doors. We'd go to the Astor Hotel on a rainy day. All those people would be standin' around and not a cab in sight. Well, you'd run around the block and practically throw yourself at a cab. Then you jumped on the runnin' board and directed him back to the hotel just to get two bits from the guy when he got in.

There was also some Jewish fellows who I made a few dollars from. I'd be standin' around on one of the holidays and the Jewish man would say, "Come up and light my fire. I'll give you a nickel." So, great, I'd go up the stairs, but I never could understand the whole concept of the Jewish holidays where somebody would stand right next to you and you would light it for them, but who was gonna question them? A nickel here and a dime there—that was big money.

Everything you wanted you had to steal. It was no accident that when a shop advertised a coat, they practically tied the god-damn coat to the bulkhead so you couldn't pull it off and run down the street. If you found a store that had some clothes hangin' on the outside, that was all you needed. You could always find some-one to buy 'em off you, but you would never punch anyone out for it or steal a woman's pocketbook.

ED McGEE: I hung out with nice fellas and I hung out with bad guys. The only thing was, with the bad guys, I never went for their stuff. I didn't steal much of anything. I didn't have the nerve, to be truthful with you.

I used to hang out with a fellow and his father, and we started making these radios. I had to go out and get an oatmeal box and so much copper wire to wrap around it. Then you had to get a piece of crystal and a cat's whisker, which was a piece of wire. That picked up the stations. Of course, there weren't too many of them then. You listened through a pair of earphones.

I had it finished and all ready the night of the Dempsey-Firpo fight. But my father and his friend each took one of the earphones and heard the fight. That's what I wanted to hear.

BILL BAILEY: The brother got beat up by cops. He beat up a cop himself, and the cops waited for him and nearly beat him to death. The cops in them days were mean bastards. The brothers was also mean, and one day there was a battle. The brother beat the shit out of the cop, and they got their revenge. When we called the ambulance up, the guy asked, "What's the problem?"

"Well, this man's layin' there bloody."

"Yeah? How'd it happen?"

"Well, he got in a fight with a cop."

"Oh, he did, huh?" Well, the son of a bitches never did come.

TOM GERAGHTY: I remember one honest cop had a brogue you could cut with a knife. He could throw his club at you and knock you down at fifty paces. His name was Scatter McMahon. "Scatter, me boys or I'll scatter ye bones."

These poor unfortunates they arrested for fighting with their wives or stealing watermelons were taken down to the 37th Street station house. We used to climb up the iron rail outside the building to see what was happening inside. "Oh, he just belted him again. Oh, he's up. Oh, he's down."

JOHN MORAHAN: The toughest cop in New York, Johnny Broderick, walked this beat. He used to walk around with a newspaper, and he would hit all these guys on Broadway, pow! Hell's Kitchen kids—pow! He used to beat everybody up.

Years later, I let him use my American Legion office when he was running for office. He lost. Those kids on the West Side and their fathers before them all hated him. I told him that before. "How many of those guys did you beat up?" Of course he lost.

BILL BAILEY: We had a bunch of tough kids, no doubt about it. There was one kid in particular, a redheaded Irish kid named Sheean. He dominated the whole neighborhood. He was the son of a blacksmith and was pretty tough. Sheean would box your ears in no time flat. He'd also air it out before he did anything. He'd say, "I think I'll go beat Bailey today," and he'd have six or seven kids trailin' him. When you saw them comin' toward you, you knew you were in trouble. *[He laughs.]* "What'd you say about me?" The next thing you know, bang, bang, bang, and the other kids were sayin', "Give 'im some more."

As young kids, we didn't fear the Italians. Only when they got older was there trouble. If you were just a young kid walkin' down the street, you had no beef with anybody. But if they saw you stealin' something from the cars, it was their thing to steal. "Who the hell are you to give the neighborhood a bad name?" Not only that, but you weren't goin' to share the profit with them.

MARIE CUTAIA: We used to fight the Irish kids. They used to call us guineas all the time, or wops or meatballs. They used to say they were better Americans than us. But we were born here, too. We called them "Irish micks—fifty cents a half-pint." Their mothers were always drunk. It's traditional.

The Tenths and Elevenths [avenues] would come down to fight. When they started, we'd try to get our brothers or our mothers and fathers. Our parents fought for their children. I remember Grandma goin' after them once. She saw them grab one of my cousins and she whacked them. Mostly, though, there were a lot of names called.

BILL BAILEY: These were kids. The older guys, the real toughies, carried guns. We never messed with 'em, but we used to idolize 'em. They always had money, and none of 'em ever looked like they were workin.' They'd wear suits with colored shirts, patent-leather shoes, and they were always full of that Jimmy Cagney stuff.

TOM GERAGHTY: The Gophers were around then, but we were too young to realize their importance to the neighborhood. You'd see certain guys on the corner. This one was in jail. That one was a real bad egg. I knew Newburgh Gallagher. He was a new boy born in the family, so they called him Newboy. Later on, they changed it to Newburgh [probably pronounced Newboigh]. He was always a gentleman to me. He actually sat up one night with me, helping to write an essay on how to keep the city's streets clean. I won a gold star for that. He had already been in jail three or four times.

BILL BAILEY: With us kids, if there was a way of makin' a nickel or a buck without anybody gettin' hurt, you'd do it. You were nobody unless you had a nickel or a dime. You certainly had the incentive to steal. As soon as you got into the house, "Did you get a job today? How come you didn't get a job? The kid down the street got a job. The kid down the street takes care of his mother. The kid down the street loves his mother. He got a job and made fifty cents. You ain't got nothin'."

You had this type of pressure on you all the goddamn time, so you have to have somethin' so that when you came home it was a great reward to give her twenty-five cents and hear, "Oh, you're such a good boy," and all that bullshit.

•　•　•

MARIE CUTAIA: I was just a little girl then, but I remember there was a big celebration after the war when Nick Gelati came home. He came back wearin' his leggins and his hat at an angle. He was with the Fighting 69th, Father Duffy's regiment.

He lived on the top floor, and he came from a large Italian family, so there was a lot of partyin' goin' on, a lot of excitement. My mother explained that he had just come back from the war and that we had peace. I was astonished. What was this thing, a war? As kids, even though we didn't really understand it, we were so proud we beat "the Krauts." If we didn't like somebody, they were "the Kaiser." They were bad.

TOM GERAGHTY: Some of the fellows who worked for my father as horseshoers were in the 69th. They gave me their souvenirs. I got a gas mask. I even got one of those Kaiser hats with the points on them. Most of the veterans felt they got a lousy deal. During the Depression, they didn't get the bonuses they were supposed to get, so they marched on Washington and got the hoses turned on them.

I knew Father Duffy when I was an altar boy. He was a publicity hound. His big thing was attending dinners and telling how he won the war, or helped win it or something. Of course, there were stories how he tended to the dying hordes in their last moments, but I didn't like him much.

JIM MINOGUE: Hell's Kitchen was a tough neighborhood, but I came from Irishtown in Brooklyn. We never took any horseshit from the West Siders, the East Siders, or anyone else. We New Yorkers always felt we were in a class by ourselves, but once you became a member of a company, you didn't practice your toughness on anybody. You got your orders and did what you were supposed to do. What they did before didn't make a difference once you got into the regiment. Nobody tried to impress himself that he was any tougher than the others, because somebody was likely to come along and kick the shit out of you.

Father Duffy was a real New Yorker. He came from a district where the actors were, and he was equally at home with the Jewish people as he was with the other ethnic groups who made up New York City. He was in an outfit that had a name for fighting, and he had to set an example. You can only die once. They say a coward dies a thousand times.

He wasn't reckless or anything, but he was right up there when he was needed. He wasn't on the front lines. It would be ridiculous for him to be there. As the casualties were brought to the rear, where the medical was, he would tend to the wounded in the dressing stations.

Father Duffy wasn't any better than the others—he was just better advertised. All your media was up there in that particular section of New York. You had the *Times* and the others, so he got more publicity than any other chaplain. But he did what he had to do, and he was a regular fellow. We liked him.

OWEN MCGIVERN: I went to the Holy Cross parochial school on 43rd Street between Eighth and Ninth avenues. The school was run by the Christian Brothers, and they ran it with a rod, no nonsense. If you didn't behave, they sent you to public school, so you behaved.

In 1920, Father Duffy became pastor of the church. I think he took an interest in me when I graduated from grammar school with some kind of medal. I got a scholarship to St. Regis High, and at that juncture, he became the biggest influence in my life. I saw a great deal of him then. He was a real scholar, and he had a vast library. We didn't have books around the house, so he would load up my arms with them. I was reading Thackeray, Sir Walter Scott, and Shakespeare when I was thirteen, fourteen years old.

He was a very dominant figure, very tall, with a commanding presence. The public side of life didn't mean anything to him. He was well liked by the theatrical people, but that was because Broadway and the theaters dominated the area. Naturally, he knew all the actors and actresses. Spencer Tracy, Barrymore, Walter Hampton—they were all friends of his. Many of them lived in the neighborhood.

He was the last guy in the world you would think to be a chaplain of a tough regiment, but he was deeply admired by his men. He was very understanding of human weaknesses. That's also why he was popular in the theatrical world. Coupled with his wide scholarly interests in politics, history, and literature, he was a very unusual man. Remember, many of the priests in those days were certainly not scholars. They were the sons of firemen and policemen whose mothers wanted to have a priest in the family. They went to a seminary, picked up Latin and learned how to perform the rituals of the Mass, but very few of them became great thinkers or theologians. Yet, on Friday nights, you'd see him, Bernard Gimbel, and Gene Tunney walking up 42nd and up Eighth to go to Madison Square Garden to see the fights. He was a great fight fan.

He was the pastor of a large and poor parish. There was nothing high-hat about him. He'd walk up and down Tenth Avenue a great deal, and everybody knew him. He was always trying to get jobs for his kids at the ticket offices, and I think he spent most of his time trying to shake down his wealthy friends for the church.

He was in many ways a great man. How many great men do you meet in life with unusual dominant personalities? I've met very few. You rarely meet the man with leadership, who has that magical "x" quality. He had that elusive quality.

•   •   •

LOUISE BARLOW: My father knew Florenz Ziegfeld. When he took me to see the *Follies of 1908*, he introduced me to him. That was very exciting. It was a gorgeous production with Nora Bayes and Jack Norwith and Lillian Lorraine. They were big stars then. The show was at the New York Roof on Broadway between 44th and 45th. It was a big production house that had a roof garden.

The first *Follies* were performed there before they went to the New Amsterdam.

When I was eighteen, a girlfriend of mine invited me to watch her rehearse for a show. The director saw me there and asked me to join the show. It was a musical called *Bunny in Bunnyland*, starring Jack Bunny. He was a fat man who starred in movie comedies. I was in the chorus. It was supposed to be a kids' chorus, except some of us weren't kids. They were pretty big, my goodness.

We were on the road for seven months. When I came back, my friend and I read in the papers that a "tab show" was rehearsing at 47th and Ninth. It was called tab for tabloid, because it was small. It was like burlesque, except we also had a dramatic sketch. Ours had a minstrel act, a straight man, a dramatic sketch, an Irish comedian, a soubrette, and Jack Lyle, the original Happy Hooligan. I played Millie the Maid in the sketch. I met my husband in that show. He was the choreographer.

We traveled all over the South. We did two, three shows a day. In Atlanta once, we did five. When I got back, I worked a lot of vaudeville acts, mostly girl acts. In vaudeville, there were regulations about what you could and could not say. Your act couldn't be risqué. You had to be careful about double entendres.

I remember one show down at Wallach's. The last scene was a doorman sitting outside the theater. He was looking around for the cat. Every theater had a cat in back, and he said, "Where the hell is that cat?" Well, there was such a terrible controversy over that one word. You weren't supposed to say things like that. You couldn't say hardly anything. They even had signs posted saying what you couldn't say.

I was also with a minstrel act with seventeen girls called the American Serenaders. I worked with blackface comedians like Paul Armstrong and Honey Boy Evans. They were very popular. When I was a child, I saw a blackface comedian, but he didn't black his face—he *was* black. His name was Ernest Hogan, and they called him the Unbleached American. He isn't well known now, but he was almost as popular as Bert Williams back then.

I also worked with a few animal acts. There was Madame Nola's Dogs, somebody's mules and another called Swayne's Rats and Cats. They did all kinds of tricks. He had them running around the stage, and the rats were in little costumes. The dogs, I remember, did the opposite of what they were commanded. When they were told to lay down, they stood up. When they were supposed to play dead, they jumped around. There were a lot of unusual acts. One was called Singer's Midgets, but the animal acts were so popular that nobody wanted to follow them. I remember Jumbo the Elephant played the Hippodrome. Nobody wanted to follow that one.

When I worked a speakeasy on 41st Street, we had a cat called Muggsy. The act next door at the New Amsterdam used to borrow her all the time. The act was called Williams and Wolfers. While Williams played piano, a piece would break off, then another and another. At the finish, the whole thing fell apart and the cat ran out of the piano. That was some act.

It was easy to get roles. There were agents all over the neighborhood—in the Gaiety Theatre, the Astor Theatre, the Paramount or the Roseland building. Sometimes you'd meet them out in the street. They'd tell you to go see So-and-So because he was putting on something.

There were a lot of shows going on, and there were a lot of actors around. They stayed at places like the Court Hotel on 48th and Eighth. Then, the show-business people would write in and say, "Save a room for me in the summer," because the show-business people didn't work in the summer.

The one on 50th Street—Mansfield Hall—many stars lived there, too. They would hang out in front of the Strand Theatre on Broadway and 47th Street. In front of the Palace on 42nd Street, the actors would get together all the time to tell stories, bragging how they sold out this place and that one. They used to lie, mostly. [*She laughs.*] Everyone knew it.

My husband and I never had a real home, because we were on the road most of the time. We played in all kinds of theaters. The worst one was up in the Bronx. It was called the Elsmeer. It was so cold, the water didn't run in the faucets, and the piano player had to take matches to warm his fingers before he played.

I never played the Palace. I never cared to, either. It just didn't mean that much to me. I only wanted a home and children and everything together. We had a nice soft-shoe act, but I was used to being with a whole lot of people, so we gave up the act and joined a tab show. Eventually, though, I had to choose between staying with my husband or going home to my children in New York. Al wouldn't stay home. All he wanted to do was stay in show business.

He never could work a regular job. I decided to come home to my children, and it broke up our marriage.

BILL BAILEY: I went to reform school for knockin' off junk in George M. Cohan's warehouse on Eleventh Avenue and 26th Street. I forget the year. It was loaded with theatrical stuff, a lot of copper and brass. We went up there with a hammer and chisel, choppin' up all the chandeliers, strippin' the brass off. God knows the amount of damage we were doin' to get fifty cents or a dollar's worth of brass. This went on for a week until we got careless and were caught.

They gave me ten months. I remember my sister goin' up and pleadin' with George M. Cohan, tryin' to explain, "Well, he's only a boy, no job, and they're goin' to send him away to jail."

He said, "I'll tell you what I'll do. I'll send a letter to the judge, and I'll tell the judge that I'll put him to work, and he can pay off all the damages."

I remember the judge gettin' the letter in court and readin' it off. He's a nice bastard. "I want it to be known, let this guy George M. Cohan, whoever he is, do his hoofin' and dancin' on Broadway. Let him take care of that, and I'll take care of correctional matters. As far as you're concerned, you're goin' off to reform school."

It was awful there. We had a riot in the place. There were beatin's and clubbin's. It was a very bad experience. I was never in fear of the guards. The people that make hell for you are the inmates. They were the bastards. I decided they'll never get me in a place like that again, and I never was.

My brother also went to reform school. Somebody had to take his place to earn money, and that was me. There was a guy named Flynn in our buildin' who was a big man on the waterfront. When he came home from work, the mother would wait for him as he was climbin' the stairs. "How about puttin' my boy to work?"

"No, I ain't puttin' anybody to work."

"What kind of Irishman are you?"

She bothered him so much that finally he told me to go down there for the shape. I didn't want to work. I was standin' there tryin' to look as small as possible, but of course he recognized me. I drove a hand truck for $23.72 a week.

I got political because of the job. This guy would come around and say, "It's the boss's daughter's birthday next week, gimme twenty-five cents to buy her somethin'." I didn't even know the boss's daughter. I didn't know it was her birthday, and what the hell did I care? Nobody comes around and gives me twenty-five cents.

Okay, so you find yourself sayin' all right, just for the sake of givin' it. Then the next day, the same guy comes around again. It's the boss's mother in Ireland. It was her sixtieth birthday and we gotta send her somethin'. This goes on, fifty cents here, ten cents there, and finally you can't sleep at night because you're so pissed off at this. That's rebellion settin' in. You're beginnin' to think about gettin' even. You're all ears when someone says, "You and I will tell 'em to shove it. We're not gonna do it." That's the beginnin'.

A couple of guys showed it to me. Every time they saw the guy comin' over to me, they'd say, "Keep away from that bastard. Here he comes again." Well, the next time he came around, we made him so miserable, like by dumpin' cargo near his feet or rollin' a barrel near him or tryin' to run him over with a truck. You made it known that you didn't want to be bothered, and you weren't goin' to kick in no more.

I risked my job, and I lost it, but not because of that. He found out I was underage, and I got fired. My mother told the insurance guy when he came out. I remember she said, "I wish you could get my boy here a job."

He said, "Why doesn't he get himself on a cattle ship or somethin'?" He said they needed people. That sort of motivated me. I wanted to get a job on a cattle ship. There were no such jobs, but the idea stuck in my head. I walked all over New York City until I got a job on Pier 1 on a ship goin' south to Texas.

•  •  •

TOM GERAGHTY: It seems our family was a bit involved in bootlegging. In fact, I think that about twenty minutes after Prohibition started, my father made a deal with the tinsmith to make him a still.

I was in school at the time, and I was always hanging around after class, helping the chemistry teacher, cleaning out the sinks, trying to get information. I finally found out how to put a pressure gauge on a copper still. We used it later on. I think my mother was the force behind all this, but my father didn't mind a bit. He used to sit watching the still, and it would come out drip-drip-drip. Every time he'd get an ounce, he'd take a belt and say, "Ahhh, that's great stuff."

JOHN MORAHAN: My uncle had a joint right near the Garden. He had a candy store, but when you went in, there was no candy. The windows were all painted green. There was a door off a big room with a little peephole. The guy opened the door with a chain. If he didn't know you, you didn't get in.

We had four speakeasies, one by the *Daily Mirror*, one by the *Daily News*, one on 36th Street, and another on 28th. In one place, we had two apartments, all green shades in the joint, and we had the cops. The cop would be sitting inside in a room like this bar smoking a cigar. We called it the living room. He sat there by the side door so that when the place got raided, he'd send the customers next door. We gave him five dollars a day.

We got raided many times. They'd break the goddamn door down with axes. We had a slide behind the bar where we kept the whiskey. You pushed the bottle down and it would drop down the cellar and break. No evidence.

There were guys going around selling beer, and you had to buy it. You just couldn't switch outfits. They may blow you away. Owney Madden's beer would come and the guy would say, "You take this beer," and you didn't have much choice.

BUD BURNS: The big shots like Owney Madden, Frenchie de Mange, and Legs Diamond hung out at Gaffney's on 34th Street. During Prohibition, Madden owned the Phoenix Beverage Company on the West Side. It was a brewery. I worked there in the summer as a driver. I got the job when I was standin' on the corner one day, and this fellow said to me, "You got a license, ain't you?"

I said, "Yeah."

"Okay, you can go to work for us."

I worked there as a driver with another guy. We took the place of two fellows, Red Martin and Red Carr, around '29 or '30. They had to go for "vacation" in Jersey until things calmed down.

The name on my truck was "F. W. Irish 'Follow the Green Line' Electrical Supply." That was a phony. We worked out of the Colonial Garage on 52nd Street. They got the beer from big trucks that came from the brewery. Then we went out in little trucks that held maybe thirty barrels. I worked from 3:30 in the morning to 5:00, maybe 6:00. We made deliveries, let's say "house calls," to about four or five places, all on the West Side.

I usually made about fifty dollars a week. The trucks weren't armed. If somebody had a gun and wanted the beer, you just got off and gave it to him. We didn't lean on the speakeasies. If he gave you a check and it bounced, or if he didn't pay, you had to send out for the collector. Madden's collector was Jimmy O'Neill. O'Neill was the dapper one. He was a nice short guy. He would speak to him. If that didn't work, well, Madden wasn't in business for nothin'. Madden didn't do it, though. Bill Dwyer took care of it. Like everybody else, they had strong-arm men and smart men.

BILL BAILEY: When my brother got out of reform school, he got in with Madden's gang. He got caught runnin' booze down to Philadelphia. I think he was in jail for about ten minutes. He made a telephone call and they got him right out. They paid him good, like about ten dollars a day.

> Th' saloon desthroyed th' home, but th' home has turned like a rattle snake an' desthroyed th' saloon—th' home an' th' home brew. Where are all th' cheerful saloons ye used to know? Cobwebs hang on th' wall, th' cash register chimes no more. Where arte all me old customers most iv th' time? At home, be dad. Th' fam'ly don't see much iv thim. They're down in th' cellar stewin' hops.
>
> —Mr. Dooley

HARRY FREEMAN: We were a family operation. Word got around that we had a good rye and a good Scotch, but we were small and we wanted to remain small. We only dealt with the big-timers. We didn't want to be dealing with no Johnny-come-lately overnight bunch.

We made the booze in a cutting plant on the Lower East Side. Our clients were all around here and the Times Square area. We never went east of Fifth Avenue. We worked by word of mouth, and we didn't know anybody on the East Side.

My four brothers and my father worked at the plant. I did the deliveries at night. We made up about twenty-five cases a day. It cost us about twenty dollars a case. We got about sixty dollars. That was a lot of money, and we were happy with it. There could have been a lot of trouble if we wanted to get big. Guys like Owney Madden or Legs Diamond never bothered us. Once, though, we made a delivery in Rockaway, and we found out later it wasn't a good practice, so we cut it out. It wasn't good to cut in. There's a way of operatin' and there's a way of operatin'. Those who stepped on somebody else's toes got hurt.

There was room for all of us. There were speakeasies on every corner in this neighborhood. There were speakeasies in every hole-in-the-wall. Every street had their famous speak. Texas Guinan had her place. El Fay, Larry Fay, had one. I wouldn't go in there. All the tough guys from the mob went there, like Vincent Coll. He got shot in a phone booth. The machine-gun bullets cut 'im in half.

There was another place that wanted us to serve them—the Silver Slipper, where the Latin Quarter is now. They knew we had a good-quality product, but we told them that we would have to cut out the people that we know. We had to be careful with our own customers, too. We didn't own the city. You never know when somebody is going to ring the bell on you.

We started just after Prohibition began. My father had a friend who lived in the Gashouse district. This fellow told my father about a bonded warehouse in the neighborhood that had thousands of cases of American Pride whiskey. The only way to get it was through the drugstores by prescription—"for medicinal purposes," they called it. What he had to do was get a doctor's prescription and then get a druggist to fill it. He had to get enough prescriptions to put him in business. After they found a doctor, I think it cost two dollars a prescription. Who do you think we sold the American Pride whiskey to? Bellevue Hospital. All the doctors there would pay ninety dollars a case for it, and they would send an ambulance there to pick the stuff up.

In our neighborhood, there was a distillery across the street called Kraus's. Before Prohibition, the odor from there was so strong, we used to get drunk just going to school. Pop learned all the rudiments of bootlegging from Kraus. They showed him how to blend and mix the stuff and where to buy the bottles and the labels.

Pop set up the plant on Third Avenue and Avenue C. Rent was nineteen dollars a month. It took up the whole first floor of an apartment house. The place was filled with bottles and boxes of tissues. There was a corking machine with all kinds of corks for the different-shaped bottles, and there was a big vat we used to mix the stuff.

It was perfect. We had easy access to get all the supplies up. We didn't even have to disguise it. The landlord didn't care. He had a saloon downstairs. Now, he got all the liquor he wanted. The only bad thing about it was the odor. People in the building knew what was going on, but they minded their own business.

The police knew what was going on too, but Pop took care of them. The cop would come around underneath an umbrella, rain or shine, so no one would see his face. We knew everybody in the precinct. They knew what was going on, but they turned their heads away. It was an unpopular law. You were happy, they were happy, and nobody squawked.

JOHN MORAHAN: Every cop was on the take. Owney Madden's beer would come, and the cop would get a dollar a barrel. Now if he didn't see you get a delivery, you didn't give 'im none.

He'd come by and say, "Did you get a delivery today?"

"No, we didn't get nothin' today." You kept a sawbuck. You know what ten dollars was like in them days? Like a hundred.

In one raid, the agents took about sixty cases of booze. The cops put it on a big moving van. I called the connection, one of the lieutenants, and went down to see him at the police station. I gave him a hundred bucks and brought the truckload back—put it all back in the joint. They only needed a couple of bottles for evidence.

BUD BURNS: When we left the Colonial Garage with the beer, they gave us twenty-five dollars for the police. Once that was gone, you were out of luck if you met up with another cop. If there was anything left, that was yours. When we delivered to the Mayfair Club on 44th Street, the cop across the street would put a stick across the cellar door. When you opened the door to make the delivery, the stick dropped to the ground. The first time, I never thought of puttin' it back. A couple of days later, he was waitin' for us.

"You delivered Tuesday."

"No, officer. I wasn't here."

"Don't tell me. I had the stick there."

From then on, I paid him, if I had the money. But every time I knocked that stick off, I'd look around—then put it back.

They used to bring the liquor in from boats on 35th Street. There was a fireboat there, and the firemen would work for them. I was workin' for the railroad. We used to get five dollars to block the crossin' with the train so nobody could see.

When the boat pulled in, the firemen would be ready to unload it onto the trucks. We pulled the cars up, sat in the shanty and had our lunch. This way, when they were unloadin', you would go by Twelfth Avenue and not see them. You'd see the train. Then the guy would come around to tell us they were finished, and we'd open it up. We all got five dollars and the flagman got a bottle.

HARRY FREEMAN: We still bought the whiskey by prescription from the drugstore. We'd get a case of Old Overholt, a bonded whiskey, for sixty dollars and make three cases out of one. Pop would use the finest rye, a caramel coloring, a fine-grain alcohol, and mix it up.

Scotch was a different thing entirely. We'd buy the coloring, the fine-grain alcohol, then add malt and hops. The malt and hops came in fifty-gallon barrels, which ran about $2,500. After we got it in there, we ran it down to a lab to have it analyzed. Pop was careful about that. We didn't trust our suppliers. We trusted the laboratory to make sure they gave us the right ingredients. Before we cut the stuff up, we'd have their report.

We paid top prices for everything, but everybody wanted us because we put out a product that was as good as the original. There was a lot of what they called "third rail" going around. People would die from that. There were more deaths from wood alcohol than influenza.

BILL BAILEY: I remember the Flanagan and Nay Beer that Madden sold. You'd hold it up to the sky, and half the bottle would be ether that had settled to the bottom.

TOM GERAGHTY: It could be said that the people who drank Geraghty's rye never died from it. We had a conscience, whereas some of the other bastards were putting some deadly stuff together. They didn't worry whether you got blind or not.

HARRY FREEMAN: After the stuff came from the still, Pop would take a glass of it, put it on the windowsill, and let it settle there. He knew how to examine it, how to make sure it was the right shade. He was sort of a connoisseur. Then he would match it with the genuine. There were people who drank the genuine and what he made and thought ours was better. He used better ingredients, and he was very minute about everything. If he wasn't satisfied with the color, he'd throw the whole thing down the drain.

We'd also buy the finest bottles, like Johnny Walker. The labels were forgeries, of course. The guy who sold us the bottles got ahold of the printer. We made a drink called King's Ransom. It had a ribbon on it and a special label. All that was done by hand. He even made sure the wax was on the bottle straight.

I made about ten deliveries a night. I wore a big overcoat with two big pockets for the money. My father was in the taxi business before, so we had a big Packard, which I drove. It was a club coach with the big trunk, but it was always empty. That was a decoy. The back seat had a false bottom. The Scotch went inside the car. We always made sure before we made the delivery that there was a mounted policeman nearby so that nobody would bother us. He was well paid. He didn't walk in with me. He would just make sure the car was okay.

One place I delivered to was right here on 52nd Street, called Frances Lewin and Ollie Fitzgerald. To find it, you'd walk through this cab company and go downstairs. A lot of judges would be in there.

When I walked in there, I was treated like a big celebrity. Ollie Fitzgerald loved me, because every time I walked in, she knew there were profits for her. She told me she tried other suppliers, but the customers asked her, "What happened all of a sudden?"

I'd also go to 46th Street between Eighth and Broadway. There was a guy named Maitland who had the Burlesque Club. It was also subterranean. He had been a trapeze performer in the circus. Then he opened up this speak. Another place was called Joe Young, another garage, this one on 49th off Sixth. Every celebrity in New York used to go there.

There were a lot of beautiful show girls in these places. They knew I had money, and they were attracted to me. In those days, things were easy. They'd push themselves on me, but I'd tell them to get lost. They were beautiful women, too, but you never know who you're dealing with. Keep your nose clean, know what I mean?

If I wanted anything, I knew where to go. Like, I'd go to Riverside or to a house on Madison Avenue. That was fashionable. There was Polly Adler, Sadie the Chink, or the House of All Nations. I'd go up there, and they knew me. The fee was five dollars, and I tell you those Southern gals were beautiful, and they were professionals. You'd go into the living room and you'd have your choice of fifteen girls, redheads, brunettes, blondes. In those days, we didn't know what was good or what was bad. If you liked the looks of 'em, you went to bed with 'em. If you gave 'em a two-dollar tip, oh boy, they'd put your coat on, treat you real nice.

JOHN MORAHAN: When I was working for my uncle, I delivered booze to Jimmy Walker. Betty Compton, his girlfriend, used to open the door sometimes. Wasn't she some good-looking broad. I was sixteen, seventeen years old, and once she opens the door wearing a negligee and lace and nothing down there. I just stood there stuttering, "I-I-I-I-I-I." The first time I ever saw a woman's pussy.

Once, she gives me a hundred dollars. I say I got no change. She says, "You always say you got no change. That's okay, keep it." Boy, she was a gorgeous broad.

•   •   •

LOUISE BARLOW: After I came back in 1920, and I decided I would not go out on the road anymore, I went to an agent in the Astor building to see him about an opening in a show called *Pretty Baby*. There were no openings, so he sent me to another agent.

He said, "While you're waiting for something, I am booking clubs, and I have a little place called the Cloverleaf." He told me to bring an evening gown and four or five songs.

The club was down on 32nd Street. It had a little bit of a dance floor and an orchestra called Harry Ford and the Indiana Five. This was Prohibition. Our customers, of course, were all the gangsters. They owned the Cloverleaf. Frankie Yale had a piece of it. One of our customers was Al Capone, who was Al Brown at the time. The gangsters never caused any trouble. In fact, they protected you if somebody got a little bit out of order. They'd throw the tips out on the floor. If they were going to give you a dollar, they'd change it to quarters so it made a lot of noise.

At the Cloverleaf, each one of us sang a little verse to introduce the show. I still remember mine:

> *Hello, everybody, hello, hello, hello,*
> *We're here to introduce you to the Cloverleaf's new show.*
> *Each one of us can sing a song and dance with a lot of pep,*
> *And when it comes to jazz and boys you gotta watch your step.*
> *Jazz time, we all love jazz time.*
> *If you're feeling sad we'll chase your blues away.*
> *If you're lonesome it's a pity,*
> *We'll just sing our little ditty,*
> *And we hope you're gonna like our cabaret.*

At first I was show business, dancing my head off, but that didn't go over so good. Later, I got wise to the kind of songs they liked, the torchy songs like "Melancholy Baby" or "I Wonder Where My Old Boy Is Tonight." All of those sad songs. I got good at that. Frankie Marlow liked "Melancholy Baby" so much I got ten dollars every time I sang it.

Waxy Gordon came in, too. He was terrible. We were afraid of him. But once, he spilled a drink on a friend of mine's dress and he gave her a hundred dollars, so that was okay. Owney Madden came in. He was tough, also. But he was a different kind of a tough. He was known as a good guy. That time, you knew who the tough guys were. Now, you don't even know. It's everybody.

B ud  B urns : Around the neighborhood, Madden was like the Democratic Party. If you needed a favor, you went to him. If you're a kid and you broke a window or got into a little petty larceny, your mother or father went to a political club like McManus or Madden. They would either straighten with the cops or whoever was after you.

Madden was worshiped around the neighborhood. He done a lot of favors for the poor. A neighborhood guy died, he buried him. People around 34th Street that needed money for rent, he paid it. On Sunday, when the guys in the bars played stickball for a barrel of beer, well, Madden paid for that. They didn't get anything in return. What could you do for him? These guys were a fact of life in the neighborhood. They went after the guys they wanted, they didn't bother the people in the neighborhood.

TOM GERAGHTY: Owney Madden's brother Marty made money bookmaking, but he was a guy that shared the wealth. You'd find him every morning on the corner of 35th Street and Tenth Avenue. He was always good for a touch.

Then it seemed that a couple of busybodies decided they had to get rid of this immigrant. Madden came here when he was two years old from England, and now that he was a fully grown man they decided to get rid of him. I went to a minister and got him to write me a letter that this guy was okay to have in the neighborhood, regardless of his brother's reputation. I went to a rabbi and talked him into writing a nice letter, too.

There was no trouble with the Catholics, because Madden was very good to the church. I had to laugh myself. It was one of my early lessons on how the church itself could be swayed with a monetary reward. Not that I was against it.

Marty loved the idea that we backed him up. I liked him because he was a good guy. I guess I liked anybody who was kind to his fellow man.

The one guy who came out of Hell's Kitchen that we never had too much use for was George Raft. He told stories which seemed to indicate what a vicious guy he was. We never saw hide nor face of the guy. Here's how he got into the pictures: it seemed that Timmy 'Mara and Jimmy O'Neill were all told that they should go out to the West Coast to get in on some of the big union dough out there. Georgie Raft was their gopher—go for cigarettes, go for that. They took him on one of their trips to the coast, and he got into films.

He told a story in the *Saturday Evening Post* how he carried around a baseball bat. Once, a guy cut him off in traffic and he threw the bat like a javelin and left him unconscious in the gutter. That was a lot of malarkey. If he was always so tough and vicious, how come it never showed up in the police blotter? He was never arrested for anything.

HARRY FREEMAN: I never counted the money I picked up, just threw it on the table when I got home. We never kept no books or anything. Pop used to bank it at a small German-American bank called Lederer's. He'd just bring it in and say to the teller, "I got no time to count it. You take care of it. Just make sure that everything is accounted for and make out the deposit slip." The guy must have peeled off a few, but Pop didn't care. He'd just go back to his Packard and drive away with his gloves on. There was nothing kosher about my father. He was a real playboy, but when he wore his spats and tails on a Sunday, you would think he was a minister the way he walked around.

The only one who wasn't happy was my mother. She didn't even know I was driving the car. She knew I was going to City College during the day, but when I came home at night, she'd look at me very suspicious. She didn't like it, but to keep peace in the family, she kept mum. When somebody knocked at the door, she'd shake. She kept calling it dirty money. "Get out of the house with that filthy money."

I only got into trouble a couple of times. Once, I was making a delivery to a fellow in a brownstone on 54th Street near Fifth. I get up there with six cases and I see the mounted cop. He was waiting for me to get out, and I didn't like the looks of him, so I took one case and brought it up the steps. He followed me right up there, horse and all.

"What do you have in there?" he asked.

"Glassware," I said.

Just then, the Japanese butler opened the door. He grabbed the case and down I went. Then one of the people from the house went around the corner and straightened with the cops. It cost $500 and we had to make it good, but we were glad enough to give it to 'em.

Another time, there was a big political affair at the Pennsylvania Hotel. My father contributed all the champagne. It wasn't the best, but he made it look good with the wrappers around, nice bottles and everything else.

I was watching the stuff in a room upstairs when a couple of Prohibition agents walk in and show their shields. The windup was I called my father, who was downstairs in the ballroom. He came up with a couple of guys from the U.S. attorney's office. Once they saw them, the agents left.

It was an Eleventh Ward Association dinner. All the bigwigs were there. I think Izzy Einstein and Moe Smith were at that dinner, too. Izzy and Moe were the famous Prohibition agents. Before the Volstead Act, Moe was a boxing referee, and Izzy was very tight with the leader of the Eleventh Ward, John F. Ahearn. He appointed Izzy as a Prohibition agent.

Izzy had a thick accent, and he looked like a foreigner. Nobody would ever take him for an agent. They always masqueraded in different costumes, and they were very successful in breaking up a lot of places. He and my father would hang out at a restaurant on the Lower East Side called Berger's. Izzy was there every day; so was my father. You know one reason why the bigger guys never bothered us? Because we knew Izzy Einstein and Moe Smith. They knew if they interfered, one way or another they were in big trouble. Of course Izzy and Moe knew what we were doing. I hope I'm not talking out of school.

LOUISE BARLOW: We were raided several times. I lost lots of salary that way. In one raid, they took my boss, who was a little bit of a guy like me, and they threw him across the room. I lost a week's pay from that place, about thirty dollars.

When they sent you to a place, you never knew where you were going. There were so many around, and they were in all kinds of buildings, but most of them were nice inside, with a grand piano and a little dance floor.

The quality of the drinks varied. There might be what we called twelve-mile-limit Scotch or champagne that was good or bad. Sometimes, there might be a dead fly in it. Oh, God. One boss that hated everybody, Louis Millay, "French Louis," gave me vinegar one night, thinking it would make me sick. I love vinegar, so it didn't mean a thing. He thought he was doing something smart.

Sometimes when we were drinking with the customers, they gave us "downs," which were ginger ale or something like that. Then you had to pretend it was real. That was awful. You could get in real trouble with the people. Once, a man wanted his money back because he realized the drinks were really ginger ale. They beat him up so badly, they had to close the place.

Sometimes, they'd serve me ginger ale, but the customers got real drinks. Every place was different. You had to drink with the customers if they asked you to. You'd get them to order more. After the show, if they wanted you, you sat down with them.

The customers at the Cloverleaf liked big, heavyset blondes. Once, the boss brought me over to a table and introduced me, and the man said, "I wanted a blonde." Others didn't want that. The college kids, they wanted a certain type, not like me at all. The elderly men didn't like me either. They wanted a very young girl, but the doctors and lawyers, those kind of people, that's the kind they used to sit me with.

The waiters would bring you over and introduce you. It wasn't a big deal. You only had trouble if the cabdriver that brought them told them that you would go home with them. You see, the cab-drivers would pick up the men and bring them in. They got a third of what the customer spent. Many times the customers expected the girl to go home with them. There were women that would do that, but if you refused, that was where the trouble would start.

Once, the girl who this fellow was sitting with was the boss's girlfriend. The customer had been promised a good time by the taxi driver, and he had spent about thirty dollars. There was a big fight then. Everybody was running out in the street. You couldn't blame them for getting angry when you refused. It was always very hard to get out of it without offending the person. Some of them left. Some of them argued. Some of them didn't do a darned thing, they just stayed and enjoyed it.

Then you had the out-of-towners who would ask you out the next day for a show and dinner. That paid off very good, and they didn't want to take you home. They'd just give you a ten-dollar or twenty-dollar tip so they wouldn't be alone. I didn't object. If you objected, you couldn't work.

HARRY FREEMAN: We worked hard, but we had a good life. I was only a kid when I was doing it, and I never saw so much money. I used to go down to these fancy places in the Village and people wanted to know, "Gee, who is this kid?"

I'd go to the six-day bike races or to the racetrack. I'd spend the whole month of August up in Saratoga. Even with those tough guys around the neighborhood, like the Herberts, Waxy Gordon, Lepke, and Gurrah, I figured I was the toughest guy down there. I was running around in a Packard car, and I wasn't even old enough to drive.

Even the crash didn't bother us that much. My father must have had about a million dollars' worth of stock. It was bought on margin. After the crash, it was worth nothing. We bought property down in Florida—vanished. We bought property that was under water. We never cried about it. We made $400,000 in one year, and we thought we had something going on forever. But when Prohibition ended, that was the end of the empire. We had to go to work and find a way to make a living.

BILL BAILEY: There was a lot of hunger during the Depression. It's difficult to deal with anytime. Hunger is hunger. Your guts is gonna growl, except that as a younger person you can move faster. You pick up a rumor: "They just opened a soup line at 14th Street and Seventh." Bang, right over to 14th and Seventh. You knew exactly where the good soup lines were and where the bum ones were. You knew how you could go from one soup line to the next one and have one for lunch at 42nd Street and then go down to 23rd and Sixth and be there in time for supper. You learned all these tricks. Otherwise, you became dazed or befuddled.

They opened up all these depots and made up food boxes. You'd line up for that. We learned how to be cooks and what you could do with a box of noodles and a can of evaporated milk.

OWEN MCGIVERN: In the '30s, I worked for John J. Dooling, who was the district leader. Then, everyone gravitated to the club. It had its tentacles throughout the neighborhood. Every block had a district captain, who was a big figure. Tammany Hall took the place of social security, old-age pensions, and home relief. You had none of those institutions. Those Tammany clubhouses did their best to take care of the destitute. Sometimes they were all that held those neighborhoods together.

They helped a lot of people who were about to be thrown out on the sidewalk. They hired people to shovel snow. During every snowstorm, there'd be thousands of these guys out on the street day and night. They were tough times. A fellow lost his job and had no money, there was real anguish. Those people really suffered a lot, and they bore their sufferings with great valor. The only saving grace was they didn't know any different. They sort of accepted that as a way of life.

BILL BAILEY: I joined the Communist Party in 1932. I had been in the Marine Workers Industrial Union. Those guys were all radicals and left-wingers, but I joined mostly because of what I was seein' around me.

Just to eat, I'd shovel snow for the city for fifty cents an hour. Boy, we'd hope there'd be a blizzard. But it became a racket because the politicians took care of their friends first. One day, we lined up 500 guys outside the clubhouse. If they were goin' to open it up at five, we were there at three, stompin' our feet, freezin' in the cold outside this goddamn little clubhouse with all these politicians inside.

Meanwhile, people were walkin' in and out with letters and handshakin'. The more people goin' in shakin' hands with letters meant less jobs for us, and the line was gettin' bigger and bigger. Then a guy came out, and instead of hiring 500, he made the stupid announcement that they were only hirin' twenty-five. Well, everybody got so pissed off that they smashed in all the windows. Of course, the cops surrounded the place, and they were bangin' and clubbin' and pushin'. The guys fought back, beat the shit out of the cops. There was no shovelin' that night because it was so bad.

You'd see furniture bein' moved out on every block. That's how we started off the Unemployed Councils. They'd say, "They're chasin' Mrs. Gallagher. They're gonna put her furniture out."

"Oh, we better do somethin'."

"How much rent she payin'?"

"Eighteen dollars."

The sheriff would come with a couple of cops. They'd move the furniture out and put a lock on the door. As soon as they'd leave, we'd go up and chop the lock off and move all the furniture back in again. Sometimes, we'd collect some nickels and dimes, and that would satisfy the landlord for a while.

The councils were offshoots of the CP. We had the neighborhoods organized. We knew everybody in every goddamn house. We knew who was out of work, who was workin'. We knew when there was a strike, and we knew how to support the strike. By knowin' all the people that were out of work, that gave us the first shot at tellin' everybody that So-and-So Iron Works is goin' out, and all you people that's unemployed don't fink. That's how many of these strikes were won, although in other strikes there'd be a little brutality. I remember a fur workers' strike where the gangsters came down and busted everybody up.

There was tremendous despair. People who were much older, with tremendous know-how—engineers, musicians—just said the hell with it and went on drinkin' sprees. They'd get gassed up and become winos. You'd be walkin' down the street and somebody would say, "See that guy there? He used to be with the New York Symphony. See that other guy there? He used to be a stockbroker." They'd just be sittin' there dejected, with a wine bottle in their hands.

I hung out with a guy who once worked in the stock exchange. He said once, "Let's walk down to Wall Street. I want to see if I can pick up a few bucks." He was a handsome guy who somehow made a lot of money and then somethin' went wrong. He ended up bein' a sailor. He was a boozer, but he straightened out now and then. We walked down to the New York Stock Exchange. I remember him brushin' his filthy suit off and tryin' to look respectable. He went in and tried to put the bum on some people. It was very difficult. He came out lookin' really dejected.

"I gave those people hundreds of dollars. I can't even get a dollar now." That was a helluva long walk, too.

I even sold apples when the apple fad came out. I did all right for a while, but then everybody was sellin' apples and things got tough. Then a friend got an idea that we could stow away on a ship to St. Petersburg. There was supposed to be a lot of work there for seamen. We did and got caught. I went on a chain gang for thirty days. I helped dig up Jacksonville, Florida. If you ever go to Jacksonville airport, you can say you know somebody who helped make that son of a bitch.

HARRY FREEMAN: I used to meet a lot of those tough guys down at Berger's. We'd sit down. I'd pick up their check. They'd pick up my check. I was working hard, and I was going to school, and those guys thought I was the biggest damned fool. They'd have all these cars lined up, and talk about the women! But we were careful, and none of us got hurt. My father died of a natural death. My brothers died of a natural death. They called me a chump, but how many of those guys are here today?

ED McGEE: In the Depression, there were so many guys out of work in the union, they had a list. As your name came up, you got work. Then I got wise, and I got good and friendly with the union delegate, and I began working steady again.

My wife and I had a little girl. When she was eight years of age, she had leukemia. Talk about this neighborhood! Word got around that she needed so much blood. In two days, the doctor called me up and said, "Mr. McGee, I want you to know that 200 pints of blood came in." That was without asking. People just called up. I didn't even know them.

LOUISE BARLOW: I didn't lead a glamorous life. If I had to do it over, I wouldn't do it—show business, yes, but forget the clubs. It was too hard. You had to sleep all day and work all night. "Lullaby of Broadway" was exactly right [*sings*]:

*When a Broadway baby says goodnight,*
*It's early in the morning.*
*Manhattan babies don't sleep tight until the dawning.*
*Goodnight babies, sleep tight, milkman's on his way.*
*Goodnight baby, sleep tight, let's call it a day.*
*Listen to the lullaby of old Broadway.*

# A
# Partial
# Bibliography

NONFICTION

Abbott, Berenice, and Henry W. Lanier. *Greenwich Village, Today & Yesterday*. New York: Harper and Brothers, 1949.

Anderson, Jervis. *Harlem: The Great Black Way, 1900–1950*. London: Orbis, 1982.

Asbury, Herbert. *The Gangs of New York: An Informal History of the Underworld*. Garden City: Knopf, 1927, 1928.

Baral, Robert. *Turn West on 23rd: A Toast to New York's Old Chelsea*. New York: Fleet Publishing, 1965.

Birmingham, Stephen. *Our Crowd: The Great Jewish Families of New York*. New York: Harper & Row, 1967.

———. *Life at the Dakota: New York's Most Unusual Address*. New York: Random House, 1979.

Bolton, Reginald Pelham. *Washington Heights Manhattan Its Eventful Past*. New York: Bolton, 1924.

Botkin, B. A. *New York City Folklore, Legends, Tall Tales, Anecdotes, Stories, Sagas, Heroes and Characters, Customs, Traditions and Sayings.* New York: Random House, 1956.

Caro, Robert. *The Power Broker: Robert Moses and the Fall of New York.* New York: Random House, 1974.

Chapin, Anna Alice. *Greenwich Village.* New York: Dodd, Mead, 1917.

Churchill, Allen. *The Improper Bohemians: A Re-creation of Greenwich Village in Its Heyday.* New York: Dutton, 1959.

Coffey, Thomas M. *The Long Thirst: Prohibition in America, 1920–1933.* New York: Norton, 1975.

Colon, Jesus. *A Puerto Rican in New York.* New York: International Publishers, 1961.

Delaney, Edmund T. *New York's Greenwich Village.* Barre, VT: Barre Publishers, 1967.

Delaney, Edmund T., and Charles Lockwood, with George Roos. *Greenwich Village: A Photographic Guide.* New York: Dover, 1976.

Edmiston, Susan, and Linda D. Cirino. *Literary New York: A History and Guide.* Boston: Houghton Mifflin, 1976.

Federal Writers Project, *New York Panorama.* New York: [1938] Pantheon, 1984.

———. *The WPA Guide to New York City.* [1939] New York: Pantheon, 1982.

Fox, Ted. *Showtime at the Apollo: 50 Years of Great Entertainment from Harlem's Famous Theatre.* New York: Holt, Rinehart & Winston, 1983.

Garmey, Stephen. *Gramercy Park: An Illustrated History of a New York Neighborhood.* New York: Rutledge Books, 1984.

Gurock, Jeffrey. *When Harlem Was Jewish, 1870–1930.* New York: Columbia University Press, 1979.

Howe, Irving. *World of Our Fathers.* New York: Harcourt Brace Jovanovich, 1976.

Iglesias, Cesar Andreu, ed. *Memoirs of Bernardo Vega.* New York: Monthly Review Press, 1977.

Irving, Washington. *A History of New York by Diedrich Knickerbocker.* New York: Putnam, 1864.

Irwin, Will. *Highlights of Manhattan.* New York: Century, 1926, 1927.

Joselit, Jenna Weissman. *Our Gang: Jewish Crime and the New York Jewish Community, 1900–1940.* Bloomington: Indiana University Press, 1983.

Keller, Allan. *Scandalous Lady: The Life and Times of Madame Restell, New York's Most Notorious Abortionist.* New York: Atheneum, 1981.

Kouwenhoven, John A. *The Columbia Historical Portrait of New York: An Essay in Graphic History.* New York: Harper & Row, 1953.

Lewis, David Levering. *When Harlem Was in Vogue.* New York: Knopf, 1981.

MacCracken, Henry Noble. *The Family on Gramercy Park: A New York Boyhood at the Turn of the Century.* New York: Scribner's, 1949.

McConnon, Tom. *Angels in Hell's Kitchen.* Garden City, NY: Doubleday, 1959.

Metzker, Irving, ed. *A Bintel Brief: Sixty Years of Letters from the Lower East Side to the Jewish Daily Forward.* New York: Behrman House, 1971.

Morris, Lloyd. *Incredible New York: High Life and Low Life of the Last Hundred Years.* New York: Random House, 1951.

Moscow, Warren. *The Last of the Big-Time Bosses: The Life and Times of Carmine DeSapio and the Decline and Fall of Tammany Hall.* New York: Stein & Day, 1971.

Moss, Frank. *The American Metropolis.* New York: Peter Fenelon Collier, 1897.

Northrop, H. D. *New York's Awful Steamboat Horror*. Beaver Springs, PA: American Publishing, 1904.

O'Connor, Richard. *Hell's Kitchen: The Roaring Days of New York's Wild West Side*. Philadelphia: Lippincott, 1958.

Orsi, Robert Anthony. *The Madonna of 115th Street: Faith and Community in Italian Harlem, 1880–1950*. New Haven: Yale University Press, 1985.

Osofsky, Gilbert. *Harlem: The Making of a Ghetto, Negro New York, 1890–1930*. New York: Harper & Row, 1963.

Parry, Albert. *Garrets and Pretenders: A History of Bohemianism in America*. New York: Covici-Friede, 1933.

Riis, Jacob A. *How the Other Half Lives*. New York: Scribner's, 1901.

Scheiner, Seth M. *Negro Mecca: A History of the Negro in New York City, 1865–1920*. New York: New York University Press, 1965.

Schermerhorn, Gene. *Letters to Phil: Memories of a New York Boyhood, 1848–1856*. New York: New York Bound, 1982.

Stein, Leon. *The Triangle Fire*. Philadelphia: Lippincott, 1962.

Walker, Stanley. *Mrs. Astor's Horse*. New York: Stokes, 1935.

———. *The Night Club Era*. New York: Stokes, 1933.

## FICTION

Dunbar, Paul Laurence. *The Sport of the Gods*. New York: Dodd, Mead, 1901.

Gold, Michael. *Jews Without Money*. New York: Horace Liveright, 1930.

Henry, O. *The Four Million*. Garden City, NY: Doubleday, 1905.

Ornitz, Samuel. *Allrightniks Row, "Haunch Paunch and Jowl": The Making of a Professional Jew*. New York: Boni & Liveright, 1923.

Puzo, Mario. *The Fortunate Pilgrim*. New York: Atheneum, 1964.

Van Vechten, Carl. *Nigger Heaven*. London: Knopf, 1926.

There are a number of writers whose reporting on Old New York City was superb. Among a growing list of my favorites are Red Smith, A. J. Liebling, John McNulty, McCandlish Phillips, Joe Madden, Meyer Berger, E. B. White and, particularly, Joseph Mitchell. I am sure none of the above ever put on his pants one leg at a time.

# Acknowledgments

Gene Rachlis, who had a long and distinguished career in journal-
ism and publishing, acted as agent, editor, and friend to someone
with whom others in his position wouldn't have bothered. Gene
was reading the Chelsea chapter of this book when he died all too
soon in November 1986. He was the most decent man I've ever
met, and this book would never have been written without him.

Several people pushed my proposal along when it was stalled.
For that I'd like to thank Victor and Joanne Rabinowitz, Aaron
Asher, Claire Reich Wachtel, and Mary Ryan.

Since my agent, Susan Bergholz, stepped into the picture, she
has read every word of this manuscript several times, offered wise
counsel and helpful encouragement and always, always done for
me what was far above the call of duty.

Daphne Merkin at HBJ took a chance on me. Her assistant,
Elizabeth Harper, has always been pleasant and helpful.

My father, Samuel Kisseloff, offered many excellent editing
suggestions (including the Yiddish transliterations in the first chapter), came up with needed financial support, and also turned out
to be a great interview.

Laura Mitgang did a lot of wonderful editing in the early stages
of this book's preparation. Barbara Cohen of the New York Bound

Bookshop kept me fed literally and literaturally. Edith Tiger's generosity was also crucial to keeping this book going.

Joe Doyle not only gave me several terrific leads, but also lent me the tape of his interview with Peggy Dolan, which appears in this book. William Littmann and Jean Crichton did the first interviews with Tom Geraghty and Bresci Thompson, respectively. Bresci is a man of incredible grace. He and his wife, Mary, consented to see me while she was in the final stages of cancer, which wouldn't surprise anyone who knew or worked with them the last sixty years at the Hudson Guild.

Those whom I interviewed know how grateful I am to them. However, I would like to mention Olga Marx, my special friend, whom I interviewed many times over a period of years. The cycle was broken when Olga broke her hip and a subsequent operation caused her to lose much of her memory. Sitting with her during her long recovery and watching her determined struggle to reclaim the lost recollections of her youth was both a wonder and a thrill. Up until her death at ninety-four, she was still working on her poetry and looking at the world with all the wonder and romance of a teenager in love.

This book really wouldn't have been possible without an extensive network of helpers, who put me in touch with many of the people who appear in the text. Some sat down for interviews that, alas, could not be included. Others made editing comments or arranged introductions, while still more came up with solid leads or just useful suggestions. I've listed as many as I can remember. I apologize to any I've missed, and I'm afraid there are many, but here goes:

Betty Gubert, Arthur Geller, Nora Sayre, Bill Dyer, Arlene and Roger Preisick, Kit Rachlis, Jim McManus, Bernie Kinzer, Ruth Strunsky, Nancy Sameisky, Tony Hiss, Alger Hiss, Susan Chin, Patricia Berman, Tom Spicuzza, Lori Perkins, Jack Blumstein, Terry Ptaczek, Lil Resnick (T.G.), Joe Breed, Paula Grey, Joseph Mitchell, Bess Fleischer, Peggy Kisseloff, Eric Schultz, Jose Guzman, Katy Flanagan, David Weiss, Ira Miller, Scott Greenhouse, Livia Gellert, Art Shields, William Reuben, Victor and Macy Navasky, Steven Hirsch, Bill Barol, Jim Revson, Bob Trentlyon, George Teaney, Mr. and Mrs. Ralph Taylor, Minnie Hoffman, David Goldstein, August Goertz, Howard A. Rodman, Red Jackman, Alberta White, Barbara Kross, Jared Lee, Pauline Battschinger, Ruth Rossini, Stanley Michels, Libby DiTrapani, Ruth Abrams, Anita Jacobson, Milt Machlin, Lisa Rubin-Woods, Rena Benmayor, Susan Anderson, Cindy Hatcher, Mary Banbury, Marie Ryan, Karen Brain, Gail Schwartz, Theresa McGinty, Josephine Coccaro, Holly Jacobs, John Hammond, Joe Fuchs, Mike Cosenza, Allen Taub, Helen Gilson, Leo Latz, Jean Pitter, Sam Friedman, Milton Newman, Ellen Hay, Berdie Ballenberg, Eileen Weiss, Andy Kirk, Guichard Parris, Sara Hyland, Nate Wright, Duke Duhart, Minerva Rios, Sadie Berger Powell, Peggy Carnegie, Alan Kisseloff, Phil Gilston, Dolly Gallo, Harry Arouh, Anna Quindlen, Jennie Glazer, Lilian Fable, Wendy Kisseloff, Iggy Carrozza, Monica Burke, Robert Amon, Joe Marlino, Marvin Gelfand, Mallory Thomas, Barney August, Harold Krinsky, Louis J. Lefkowitz, Mr. Surma, Michael Sascino, Ethan Carr, Kate Kristen, Mary Ann Giordano, Roger Rosenblatt, Hamilton Fish, Bill Price, Gayle Brewer, Mickey Rachlis, Ethel Sheffer, Sally Goodgold, Leonard Farbman, Bob Isaac, Corliss Lamont, Bill Miles, Thomas Wirth, Leon Stein, Pauline Newman, Elizabeth Burger, Helen Buttenweiser, Judy Gorenson, Ira Wolfman, Alan Scheinman, Douglas Donald, Jane Walburn, Connie Gibson, Peter Ryan, Fritzie Kort, Jimmy Dell'orto, Ann Gazner, Michael Pope, Frederick Pierce, Doris Rosenblum, Bill Goidell, Eliot Asinof, Herbert and Shirley Mitgang, Steven Smrek, Doris Diether, Lucy Strunsky, Grace Mok, Douglas Watkins, Phil Jasper, and Roberta Leighton.

A portion of the comments by Olga Marx and Frances Loeb came from previously written sources.

This book is also for Emily, Caroline, and my mother.

# Index

**Library of Congress Cataloging-in-Publication Data**

Kisseloff, Jeff.
    You must remember this : an oral history of Manhattan from the 1890s to World War II /
Jeff Kisseloff.—Johns Hopkins paperbacks ed.
      p.    cm.
    Originally published : San Diego : Harcourt Brace Jovanovich, c1989.
    Includes bibliographical references and index.
    ISBN 0-8018-6306-6 (alk. paper)
    1. Manhattan (New York, N.Y.)—History Anecdotes.   2. Manhattan (New York, N.Y.)—
Social life and customs. Anecdotes.   3. New York (N.Y.)—History—1898–1951 Anecdotes.
4. New York (N.Y.)—Social life and customs Anecdotes.   5. Manhattan (New York, N.Y.)
Biography Anecdotes.   6. New York (N.Y.) Biography Anecdotes.   7. Oral history.   I. Title.
F128.5.K55   1999
974.7´1—dc21                                99-38714